EDITION

5

Theories of Personality

EDITION

5

Theories of Personality

Duane Schultz

University of South Florida

Sydney Ellen Schultz

Brooks/Cole Publishing Company
Pacific Grove, California

I(T)P ™ The trademark ITP is used under license.

Consulting Editor: *Lawrence S. Wrightsman*

Brooks/Cole Publishing Company
A Division of Wadsworth, Inc.

© 1994, 1990, 1986, 1981, 1976 by Wadsworth, Inc., Belmont, California 94002.

Printed in the United States of America
10   9   8   7   6   5   4   3   2   1

Library of Congress Cataloging-in-Publication Data

Schultz, Duane P.
    Theories of personality / Duane Schultz. — 5th ed.
       p.   cm.
    Includes bibliographical references and index.
    ISBN 0-534-16650-4
    1. Personality.   I. Schultz, Sydney Ellen.   II. Title.
BF698.S36   1993
155.2—dc20   93-6486
                                       CIP

Sponsoring Editor: *Marianne Taflinger*
Editorial Assistant: *Virge Perelli-Minetti*
Production Editor: *Penelope Sky*
Manuscript Editor: *Laurie Vaughn*
Permissions Editor: *May Clark*
Interior and Cover Design: *E. Kelly Shoemaker*
Cover Illustration: *James Endicott, Stockworks*
Art Coordinator: *Susan Haberkorn*
Interior Illustration: *Reed Sanger; Ron Grauer; L M Graphics*
Photo Editor: *Larry Molmud*
Photo Researcher: *Robin Sterling*
Typesetting: *Weimer Graphics*
Cover Printing: *Phoenix Color Corporation*
Printing and Binding: *Arcata Graphics/Fairfield*

To Don and Helen G.,
who shoved us into the computer age.

CONTENTS

PART I *Introduction*   *1*

O N E   *The Study of Personality:*
         Assessment, Research, and Theory   *3*

The Study of Personality   4
The Place of Personality in the History of Psychology   6
Definitions of Personality   8
Assessment in the Study of Personality   10
Research in the Study of Personality   18
Theory in the Study of Personality   24
Images of Human Nature: Issues in Personality Theory   27
Summary   30
Critical Thinking Review   31
Suggested Reading   32

PART II   *The Psychoanalytic Approach*   *33*

TWO   *Sigmund Freud*   *35*

The Life of Freud (1856–1939)   36
Instincts: The Propelling Forces of the Personality   41
Id, Ego, and Superego: The Structure of Personality   43
Anxiety: A Threat to the Ego   46
Defenses Against Anxiety   47
Psychosexual Stages of Personality Development   50
Freud's Image of Human Nature   56
Assessment in Freud's Theory   58
Research in Freud's Theory   60
A Final Commentary   66
Summary   68
Critical Thinking Review   69
Suggested Reading   70

PART III   *The Neopsychoanalytic Approach*   *73*

THREE   *Carl Jung*   *75*

The Life of Jung (1875–1961)   77
Psychic Energy   79
The Systems of Personality   81
The Development of the Personality   88
Jung's Image of Human Nature   92
Assessment in Jung's Theory   93
Research in Jung's Theory   96
A Final Commentary   99
Summary   100
Critical Thinking Review   101
Suggested Reading   102

FOUR   *Alfred Adler*   *104*

The Life of Adler (1870–1937)   105
Inferiority Feelings: The Source of Human Striving   107
Striving for Superiority or Perfection   110

Style of Life   111
Social Interest   113
Birth Order   114
Adler's Image of Human Nature   117
Assessment in Adler's Theory   118
Research in Adler's Theory   122
A Final Commentary   125
Summary   127
Critical Thinking Review   128
Suggested Reading   129

FIVE   *Karen Horney*   *130*

The Life of Horney (1885–1952)   132
The Childhood Need for Safety   134
Basic Anxiety: The Foundation of Neurosis   136
Neurotic Needs   137
Neurotic Trends   138
The Idealized Self-Image   141
Feminine Psychology: The Flight from Womanhood   142
Horney's Image of Human Nature   145
Assessment in Horney's Theory   145
Research in Horney's Theory   147
A Final Commentary   148
Summary   150
Critical Thinking Review   151
Suggested Reading   151

SIX   *Erich Fromm*   *152*

The Life of Fromm (1900–1980)   154
Freedom Versus Security: The Basic Human Dilemma   155
Personality Development in Childhood   158
Psychological Needs   160
Character Types   162
Fromm's Image of Human Nature   164
Assessment in Fromm's Theory   166
Research in Fromm's Theory   166
A Final Commentary   168
Summary   169
Critical Thinking Review   170
Suggested Reading   171

SEVEN   *Henry Murray*   *172*

The Life of Murray (1893–1988)   174
The Principles of Personology   177
Id, Superego, and Ego: The Divisions of Personality   177
Needs: The Motivation of Behavior   179
Personality Development in Childhood   182
Murray's Image of Human Nature   184
Assessment in Murray's Theory   184
Research in Murray's Theory   188
A Final Commentary   190
Summary   191
Critical Thinking Review   192
Suggested Reading   193

PART IV   *The Trait Approach: The Genetics of Personality*   *195*

EIGHT   *Gordon Allport*   *197*

The Life of Allport (1897–1967)   199
A Definition of Personality   201
Personality Traits   202
Personality and Motivation   204
Personality Development in Childhood: The Unique Self   206
The Adult Personality   209
Allport's Image of Human Nature   210
Assessment in Allport's Theory   212
Research in Allport's Theory   213
A Final Commentary   215
Summary   216
Critical Thinking Review   217
Suggested Reading   218

NINE   *Raymond Cattell and Other Trait Theorists*   *219*

The Life of Cattell (1905–)   221
Cattell's Approach to Personality Traits   222
Source Traits: The Basic Factors of Personality   223
Dynamic Traits: The Motivating Forces   224
The Influences of Heredity and Environment   225

Personality Development   227
Cattell's Image of Human Nature   229
Assessment in Cattell's Theory   230
Research in Cattell's Theory   232
A Final Commentary   234
Other Trait Approaches   235
Hans Eysenck: Extraversion, Neuroticism, and Psychoticism   235
Robert McCrae and Paul Costa: The Five-Factor Model   237
Arnold Buss and Robert Plomin: The Temperament Theory   239
Summary   243
Critical Thinking Review   244
Suggested Reading   245

PART V   *The Life-Span Approach*   **247**

TEN   *Erik Erikson*   *249*

The Life of Erikson (1902–)   251
Psychosocial Stages of Development: Coping with Conflicts   252
Basic Strengths   259
Basic Weaknesses   260
Erikson's Image of Human Nature   261
Assessment in Erikson's Theory   262
Research in Erikson's Theory   263
A Final Commentary   268
Summary   270
Critical Thinking Review   271
Suggested Reading   271

PART VI   *The Humanistic Approach*   **273**

ELEVEN   *Abraham Maslow*   *275*

The Life of Maslow (1908–1970)   277
Motivation and Personality: The Hierarchy of Needs   279
Characteristics of Self-Actualizers   285
Maslow's Image of Human Nature   290
Assessment in Maslow's Theory   292

Research in Maslow's Theory   294
A Final Commentary   296
Summary   297
Critical Thinking Review   298
Suggested Reading   299

TWELVE   *Carl Rogers*   *300*

The Life of Rogers (1902–1987)   302
The Importance of the Self   304
Actualization: The Basic Human Tendency   305
The Experiential World   306
The Development of the Self in Childhood   306
Characteristics of Fully Functioning Persons   309
Rogers's Image of Human Nature   311
Assessment in Rogers's Theory   313
Research in Rogers's Theory   315
A Final Commentary   319
Summary   320
Critical Thinking Review   321
Suggested Reading   322

PART VII   *The Cognitive Approach*   *323*

THIRTEEN   *George Kelly*   *325*

The Cognitive Revolution in Psychology   327
The Life of Kelly (1905–1967)   328
Personal Construct Theory   330
Anticipating Life Events   331
Kelly's Image of Human Nature   337
Assessment in Kelly's Theory   338
Research in Kelly's Theory   342
A Final Commentary   344
Summary   345
Critical Thinking Review   346
Suggested Reading   347

PART VIII   *The Behavioral Approach*   **349**

FOURTEEN   *B. F. Skinner*   *351*

The Life of Skinner (1904–1990)   354
Reinforcement: The Basis of Behavior   357
Schedules of Reinforcement   361
Successive Approximation: The Shaping of Behavior   363
Superstitious Behavior   364
The Self-Control of Behavior   365
Applications of Operant Conditioning   366
Skinner's Image of Human Nature   368
Assessment in Skinner's Theory   370
Research in Skinner's Theory   372
A Final Commentary   373
Summary   375
Critical Thinking Review   376
Suggested Reading   377

PART IX   *The Social-Learning Approach*   **379**

FIFTEEN   *Albert Bandura*   *381*

The Life of Bandura (1925–)   383
Modeling: The Basis of Observational Learning   384
Processes of Observational Learning   388
The Self   390
Developmental Stages of Modeling and Self-Efficacy   392
Behavior Modification   394
Bandura's Image of Human Nature   398
Assessment in Bandura's Theory   400
Research in Bandura's Theory   401
A Final Commentary   403
Summary   404
Critical Thinking Review   405
Suggested Reading   406

SIXTEEN   *Julian Rotter*   407

The Life of Rotter (1916–)   409
Social-Learning Theory   410
Psychological Needs   415
Locus of Control   416
Interpersonal Trust   417
Rotter's Image of Human Nature   417
Assessment in Rotter's Theory   419
Research in Rotter's Theory   420
A Final Commentary   423
Summary   423
Critical Thinking Review   425
Suggested Reading   425

PART X   *The Limited-Domain Approach*   427

SEVENTEEN   *Limited-Domain Theories of Personality*   429

David McClelland: The Need for Achievement   430
Marvin Zuckerman: Sensation Seeking   440
Martin E. P. Seligman: Learned Helplessness   446
Summary   455
Critical Thinking Review   457
Suggested Reading   458

References   459
Index   481

PREFACE

A textbook must be as vital, dynamic, and responsive to change as the field of study it covers. It must grow with each edition if it is to reflect the development of the field and remain an effective teaching instrument. It should be more than a mirror of other texts, challenging its readers by suggesting, organizing, and presenting topics not yet widely offered.

The Fifth Edition

A major change in this edition is expanded coverage of human behavioral genetics, bringing together the work of Cattell and Eysenck with the Buss and Plomin temperament theory and McCrae and Costa's five-factor model. Recent theory and research supports the reemergence of traits as central to understanding the human personality.

Seligman's concept of learned helplessness has been added to the chapter on limited-domain theories of personality, joining McClelland's achievement motivation theory and Zuckerman's sensation-seeking theory. Thus, the limited-domain chapter now represents three of the major approaches to personality: the social-learning, neopsychoanalytic, and trait positions.

Other topics receiving fuller treatment are psychological types, neurotic trends, self-efficacy, locus of control, and achievement motivation in women.

Biographical material and research findings have been added, as well as more than 300 new references.

Organization

Theories of Personality retains its orientation toward undergraduate students with little previous exposure to personality theories. Our purpose is to objectively inform beginning students and ease their task of learning about diverse personality theories. We have chosen theorists who represent psychoanalytic, neopsychoanalytic, trait, life-span, humanistic, cognitive, behavioral, and social-learning approaches, as well as clinical and experimental work. The chapter on limited-domain theories deals with conceptions that focus on a single personality construct rather than the total personality.

Where biographical data warrant, we suggest how the development of a theory was influenced by events in a theorist's personal and professional life. This shows students that the development of science through theory construction is not always objective but can begin with intuition and personal experiences that are later refined and extended by more rational processes.

Each theory is discussed as a unit. Although we recognize the value of an issues or problems approach that compares several theories on specific points, we believe that the issues-oriented book does not always allow beginning students to synthesize all facets of a theory and understand its essence. We present each theory in a way that most clearly conveys its ideas, assumptions, definitions, and methods. We discuss each theorist's image of human nature, methods of assessment, and empirical research, and offer an evaluative comment. The recurring section, ''Image of Human Nature,'' deals with six fundamental issues: free will or determinism, nature or nurture, the importance of childhood experiences, uniqueness or universality, goals, and optimism or pessimism.

Except for placing Freud first, in recognition of his chronological priority, we have not arranged the theories in order of perceived importance. They are presented in nine parts, placing each theory in the perspective of competing viewpoints. Each part is introduced by a brief description of its major themes.

Features

Pedagogical aids include chapter outlines, summaries, critical thinking review questions, annotated reading lists, a running glossary, key terms in boldface type, illustrations, and a reference list. The test item file for instructors is available in print and computerized formats.

Acknowledgments

We would like to thank the many colleagues and students who have written to us about the book and have offered suggestions for this edition. We are especially grateful to the following reviewers: James Aiken, California Polytechnic State University; Mahlon Dalley, University of Northern Colorado; Bruce Haslam, Weber State University; Gary King, Rose State College; Jan Williams, Clemson University; and Matt Zaitchik, University of Massachusetts Medical Center.

We are grateful for the assistance and enthusiasm of the entire Brooks/Cole team, especially sponsoring editor Marianne Taflinger, production editor Penelope Sky, and manuscript editor Laurie Vaughn. Kelly Shoemaker produced a splendid book design and cover, and Larry Molmud developed a unique portfolio of photographs. Their professionalism and attention to detail show on every page. It has been a joy working with them.

Duane Schultz
Sydney Ellen Schultz

I

Introduction

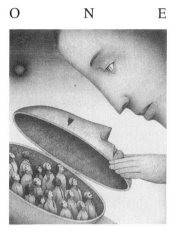

The Study of Personality: Assessment, Research, and Theory

The Study of Personality
The Place of Personality in the History of Psychology
Definitions of Personality
Assessment in the Study of Personality
    Standardization, Reliability, and Validity
    Self-Report Inventories
    Projective Techniques
    Clinical Interviews
    Behavioral Assessment
    Thought Sampling
Research in the Study of Personality
    The Clinical Method
    The Experimental Method
    The Correlational Method

Theory in the Study of Personality
    Formal Theories and Personal Theories
Images of Human Nature: Issues in Personality Theory
    Free Will or Determinism?
    Nature or Nurture?
    Past or Present?
    Uniqueness or Universality?
    Equilibrium or Growth?
    Optimism or Pessimism?
Summary
Critical Thinking Review
Suggested Reading

Personality theories are maps of the mind.

—Harvey Mindess

The Study of Personality

If you are like most students, you began your first course in psychology eager to learn about personality, your own or someone else's. The attempt to explain human behavior may be one of life's most exciting and challenging searches. We want to know why we act, think, and feel the way we do. We want to understand ourselves.

Why do you respond to a good grade in one way and your friend in a different way? Why is one person aggressive and another inhibited, one courageous and another fearful, one sociable and another shy? What makes us the way we are, and a brother or sister, reared in the same household, so different? Why do some people appear successful in relationships and careers, whereas others, perhaps with equal potential, stumble from one failure to another?

You probably thought you would find answers to these questions in your first psychology course, but as soon as you examined the syllabus and the textbook you discovered that personality is only one small part of psychology. In the standard 600-page introductory psychology textbook, perhaps 3 or 4 chapters out of 20 are devoted to the topic that may have sparked your interest in the field. To your surprise, you found yourself reading about the nervous system, drives, perception, learning, thinking, and statistics. Some students feel cheated, as though they had signed up for one course and were given another course instead.

Here you may find answers to some of those questions. The textbook and the course you are now beginning are devoted to a study of theories that have been proposed to explain the nature of the human personality. We discuss nearly two dozen theories or explanations, differing views of what personality is all about. The array may seem bewildering at first, but in studying these theories you will find common themes and similarities. We have grouped the theories into categories, each with its own assumptions, definitions, and methods. Although there are differences among the theories in each category, they share enough characteristics to distinguish them from the theories in the other groups.

The categories of personality theories we have chosen are psychoanalytic, neopsychoanalytic, trait, life-span, humanistic, cognitive, behavioral, social-learning, and limited-domain. You are probably familiar with most of these terms from other psychology courses. Some of these approaches represent major forces influential throughout psychology, not just in the area of personality.

Each personality theory we present offers tantalizing insights into human nature—insights based, for the most part, on years of probing, questioning, and listening to what people have to say in a clinical setting or observing their behavior in a laboratory. These theories are the work of intelligent and perceptive individuals, each of whom has looked closely at humankind through the uniquely ground lens of his or her theoretical viewpoint.

All the theorists have something important, impressive, and provocative to say about what we are like as human beings. If they do not always agree, we must look to three factors to explain the dissension:

1. The complexity of the subject matter;
2. the differing historical and personal contexts within which each theory was formulated; and
3. the fact that psychology is a relatively young discipline, a recent entry in the catalog of sciences. The study of personality is even more recent, having begun in the 1930s.

Its complexity and newness make the study of personality a fascinating one. It is not a closed or finished subject for which we can memorize rules and definitions and then move on. The study of personality is evolving, and for those who like the challenge and excitement of exploring areas not yet fully mapped, there could be no more appropriate or useful field of psychology than personality.

As reflected in the professional literature, interest in personality theories is strong in contemporary psychology. Virtually every college psychology department offers courses in personality, and most of these courses follow a theories approach. Personality theory remains a fundamental part of psychology's continuing effort to understand human nature.

The Place of Personality in the History of Psychology

Because of the importance of the study of personality and its role in under-standing behavior, you might assume that it has always occupied a central position in psychology. For more than half of psychology's history as a science, however, psychologists paid relatively little attention to personality.

Psychology emerged as an independent and primarily experimental science from an amalgam of ideas from philosophy and physiology. The birth of the discipline took place more than a century ago in Germany and was largely the work of Wilhelm Wundt, who established psychology's first laboratory in 1879 at the University of Leipzig.

The new science of psychology focused on the analysis of conscious experience into elements, and the methodology was modeled on the approach taken by the natural sciences. Physics and chemistry appeared to be unlocking the secrets of the physical universe by reducing all matter to its basic elements and analyzing them. If the physical world could be understood by breaking it down into elements, why couldn't the mind or the mental world be studied in the same way?

Physicists and chemists pursued their work by using the experimental method. So convinced was Wundt of the efficacy of this approach that he studied only those psychological processes that could be investigated by the experimental method. He chose, for example, to study reaction time, the time taken for various conscious processes to occur.

Wundt and other psychologists of his day who were concerned with studying human nature were greatly influenced by the natural science approach, and they proceeded to apply it to the study of the mind. Because these researchers limited themselves to the experimental method, they studied only those mental processes that might be affected by some external stimulus that could be manipulated and controlled by the experimenter. In practice, that restricted them to studying sensory and perceptual processes and other experience of narrow dimensions. There was no room in this experimental psychology for such a complex, multidimensional topic as personality. It was not compatible with either the subject matter or the methods of the new psychology.

behaviorism The school of psychology, founded by John B. Watson, that focused on psychology as the study of overt behavior rather than of mental processes.

In the early decades of the 20th century, the American psychologist John B. Watson, at Johns Hopkins University in Baltimore, Maryland, sparked a revolution against the work of Wilhelm Wundt. Watson's movement, called **behaviorism**, opposed Wundt's focus on conscious experience. More devoted than Wundt to a natural science approach, Watson argued that if psychology was to be a science, it had to focus only on the tangible aspects of human nature—that which could be seen, heard, recorded, and measured. Only overt behavior could be the legitimate topic of psychology.

Watson's approach was highly successful, and his definition of psychology as the "science of behavior" became the standard for many decades. (At about the same time, the Gestalt psychology movement arose in Germany to protest Wundt's approach. Our focus, however, is on behaviorism and the uniquely American form of psychology it shaped.)

Consciousness, Watson said, cannot be seen or experimented upon. Therefore, like the philosophers' concept of the soul, consciousness is meaningless for science. Psychologists must deal only with what they can see, manipulate, and measure—external stimuli and the subject's behavioral responses to them. According to Watson, whatever happens inside the person after the stimulus is presented and before the response is made cannot be seen. Because we can only speculate about it, it is of no interest or value to science.

Behaviorism presents a mechanistic picture of human beings as well-ordered machines that respond automatically to external stimuli. It has been said that behaviorists see people as a kind of vending machine. Stimuli are put in, and appropriate responses, learned from past experience, spill out. In this view, personality is nothing more than the accumulation of learned responses or habit systems, a definition later offered by B. F. Skinner (see Chapter 14). Thus, behaviorists reduced personality to what could be seen and observed objectively, and there was no place in their conception for consciousness or for unconscious forces. However, the social-learning theorists (Chapters 15 and 16), who offer explanations derived from Watson's behaviorism, have restored to personality some measure of consciousness.

If Watson and the early behavioral psychologists dismissed all those notions, feelings, and complexities that come to mind when we use the word *personality*, then where were they? What happened to the consciousness you know you experience every moment you are awake? Where were those unconscious forces that sometimes seem to compel us to act in ways over which we feel we have no control?

Those aspects of human nature were dealt with by a third line of inquiry, one that arose independently of Wundt and Watson. They were investigated by Sigmund Freud, beginning in the 1890s. Freud, a physician in Vienna, Austria, called his system **psychoanalysis**. Psychoanalysis and psychology are not synonymous or interchangeable terms. Freud was not by training a psychologist but was a physician in private clinical practice, working with persons who suffered from emotional disturbances. Although trained as a scientist, Freud did not use the experimental method. Rather, he developed his theory of personality based on clinical observation of his patients. Through a lengthy series of psychoanalytic sessions, Freud applied his creative interpretation to what patients told him about their feelings and past experiences, both actual and fantasized. His approach was thus quite different from the rigorous experimental laboratory investigation of the elements of conscious experience or of behavior.

Inspired by Freud's psychoanalytic approach, a group of personality theorists developed unique conceptions of human nature outside the mainstream of experimental psychology. These theorists, the neopsychoanalysts (Chapters 3 through 7), focused on the whole person as he or she functions in the real world, not on elements of behavior or stimulus-response units as studied in the psychology laboratory. The neopsychoanalysts accepted the existence of conscious and unconscious forces, whereas the behaviorists accepted the existence only of that which they could see. As a result, the

psychoanalysis
Sigmund Freud's theory of personality and system of therapy for treating mental disorders.

early personality theorists were speculative in their work, relying more on inferences based on observations of their patients' behavior than on the quantitative analysis of laboratory data.

We see, then, that experimental psychology and the formal study of personality began in two separate traditions, using different methods and pursuing different aims. We should note that experimental psychology in its formative years did not ignore personality—some limited aspects of personality were studied—but there did not exist within psychology a distinct specialty area known as "personality" as there was child psychology or social psychology.

It was not until the late 1930s that the study of personality became formalized and systematized in American psychology, primarily through the work of Henry Murray and Gordon Allport at Harvard University (see Chapters 7 and 8). Following their initial efforts, professional books appeared, journals were founded, universities offered courses, and research was undertaken. These activities signaled a growing recognition that some areas of concern to the psychoanalysts and neopsychoanalysts could be incorporated into psychology. Academic psychologists came to believe that it was possible to develop a scientific study of personality.

Today, experimental psychologists are making increasing use of concepts from Freudian theory and its derivatives, and followers of the psychoanalytic tradition are seeing the benefits of the experimental approach. However, a merging of the two camps has not occurred. They began separately and so, for the most part, they remain. Each offers advantages and disadvantages, and we shall see examples of both in the chapters to follow.

Definitions of Personality

Personality is a word we use frequently when describing ourselves and others, and we all believe we know what it means. Perhaps we do. One psychologist suggested that we can get a good idea of its meaning if we examine what we intend when we use the word *I* (Adams, 1954). When you say *I*, you are, in effect, summing up everything about yourself—your likes and dislikes, fears and virtues, strengths and weaknesses. The word *I* is what defines you as an individual, as a person separate from all others.

In our effort to define the word more precisely, we can look to its source. *Personality* derives from the Latin word *persona,* which refers to a mask used by actors in a play. It is easy to see how *persona* came to refer to outward appearance, the public face we display to the people around us.

Based on its derivation, then, we might conclude that personality refers to our external and visible characteristics, those aspects of us that other people can see. Our personality would then be defined in terms of the impression we make on others; that is, what we appear to be. One definition of *personality* in a standard college dictionary agrees with this reasoning. It states that personality is the visible aspect of one's character as it impresses others.

Is that all we mean when we use the word *personality?* Are we talking only

Our personality may be the mask we wear when we face the outside world.

about what we can see or how another person appears to us? Does personality refer solely to the mask, the role we play? Surely, when we speak of personality, we refer to more than that. We mean to include many attributes of an individual—a totality or collection of various characteristics that goes beyond superficial physical qualities. The word encompasses a host of subjective social and emotional qualities as well, ones that we may not be able to see directly, that a person may try to hide from us, or that we may try to hide from others.

We may also, in our use of the word *personality,* refer to enduring characteristics. We assume that personality is relatively stable and predictable. Although we recognize, for example, that a friend may be calm much of the time, we know that he or she can become excitable, nervous, or panicky at other times. Personality is not rigid and unchanging but can vary with the situation.

In the 1960s, promoted by the psychologist Walter Mischel, a debate erupted within psychology about the relative impact on behavior of personal variables (such as traits and needs) and variables relating to the situation (Mischel, 1968, 1973). The controversy continued in the professional literature for 20 years and ended in the late 1980s. Most personality psychologists resolved the issue by accepting an interactionist approach, agreeing that personal traits, aspects of the situation, and the interaction between them must all be considered in order to provide a full explanation for human nature (Carson, 1989; Magnusson, 1990).

Our definition of personality may include the idea of human uniqueness. We see similarities among people, yet we sense that each of us possesses

personality The unique, relatively enduring internal and external aspects of a person's character that influence behavior in different situations.

special properties that distinguish us from all others. Thus, we may suggest that **personality** is an enduring and unique cluster of characteristics that may change in response to different situations.

Even this, however, is not a definition with which all psychologists agree. To achieve more precision, we must examine what each theorist means by the term. Each offers a unique version, a personal vision, of the nature of personality, and that viewpoint has become his or her definition. And that is what this book is all about: reaching an understanding of the different versions of the concept of personality and examining the various ways of defining the word *I*.

Psychologists interested in personality have done more than formulate theories in their attempts to define its nature. They have devoted considerable time and effort to measuring or assessing personality and to conducting research on its various aspects. Although the primary focus of this book is theories, we will also describe relevant assessment techniques and research findings.

Assessment in the Study of Personality

To assess something means to evaluate it. The assessment of personality is a major area of application of psychology to real-world concerns. Let us consider a few examples.

Clinical psychologists try to understand the symptoms of their patients or clients by attempting to assess their personalities, by differentiating between normal and abnormal behaviors and feelings. Only by evaluating personality in this way can clinicians diagnose disorders and determine the best course of therapy.

School psychologists evaluate the personalities of the students referred to them for treatment in an attempt to uncover the causes of adjustment or learning problems. Industrial/organizational psychologists assess personality to select the best candidate for a particular job. Counseling psychologists measure personality to find the best job for a particular applicant, matching the requirements of the position with the person's interests and needs. Research psychologists assess the personalities of their laboratory subjects in an attempt to account for their behavior in an experiment or to correlate their personality traits with other measurements.

It is likely that you will have your personality assessed in some way, whether formally, through personality tests and interviews used by counselors and employers, or informally, by your acquaintances, family, and friends.

Standardization, Reliability, and Validity

Some assessment techniques are more objective than others. Some are wholly subjective and open to personal bias. The results of subjective techniques may be distorted by the personality characteristics of the person who is making the assessment. The best techniques of personality assessment meet three requirements: standardization, reliability, and validity.

standardization
The consistency or uniformity of conditions and procedures for administering an assessment device.

Standardization involves the consistency or uniformity of conditions and procedures for administering a test or other assessment device. If we want to compare the performance of different people on the same test, then they must all take that test under identical conditions. Everyone taking the test must be exposed to the same instructions, be allowed the same amount of time in which to respond, and be situated in an identical or highly similar environment.

Any variation in the established testing procedure can affect the test-takers' performance, and so lead to an inaccurate assessment. Suppose, for example, that the air-conditioning system in the university counseling center failed on an unusually hot day. The people taking tests that day would be operating under a disadvantage. In their haste to escape the heat, they might answer the questions less carefully than people who took the test the day before, when the room temperature was more comfortable. If an inexperienced tester failed to read the complete test instructions to a group of people, those test-takers would not be taking the test under the same condition as people tested by a more conscientious test administrator. Appropriate standardized testing procedures can be designed into a test by the psychologists who develop it, but if those procedures are not followed precisely, an otherwise excellent test can be rendered useless.

reliability The consistency of response to a psychological assessment device. Reliability can be determined by the **test-retest, equivalent-forms,** and **split-halves** methods.

Reliability involves the consistency of response to an assessment device. If you took the same test on two different days and received two widely different scores, the test could not be considered reliable because its results were so inconsistent. Researchers could not depend on that test for an adequate assessment of your personality. It is common to find some slight variation in scores when a test is retaken, but if the variation is large, then it is likely that something is wrong with the test or with the method of scoring it. Research has shown that test-takers' personal characteristics, such as age and degree of normality of the personality, can affect the reliability of personality tests.

The reliability of a test must be determined before it is used for assessment or research. Several procedures can be used to determine reliability:

1. the test-retest method
2. the equivalent-forms method
3. the split-halves method

The **test-retest method** involves giving the test twice to the same people and statistically comparing the two sets of scores by calculating the correlation coefficient. The closer the two sets of scores are to each other (the higher the correlation coefficient), the greater the test's reliability.

In the **equivalent-forms method,** instead of taking the test a second time, the subjects take two equivalent forms of the test. The higher the correlation between the two sets of scores, the greater the test's reliability. This approach is more expensive and time-consuming than the test-retest method because it requires that psychologists develop two equal forms of the test.

A third way to measure reliability is the **split-halves method.** The test is administered once, and the scores of half the test-takers are compared with the scores of the other half. This is the fastest approach because the test is given only one time. Also, there is no opportunity for learning or memory to influence performance.

validity The extent to which an assessment device measures what it is intended to measure. Types of validity include **predictive, content,** and **construct.**

Validity refers to whether an assessment device measures what it is intended to measure. Does an intelligence test truly measure intelligence? Does a test of anxiety actually evaluate anxiety? If a test does not measure what it claims to, then it is not valid and its results cannot be used to predict behavior. For example, your score on an invalid intelligence test, no matter how high, will be useless for predicting how well you will do in college or in any other situation that requires a high level of intelligence. A personality test that is not valid may provide a misleading portrait of your emotional strengths and weaknesses.

As with reliability, validity must be determined precisely before a test is applied. There are several kinds of validity, including predictive validity, content validity, and construct validity.

From a practical standpoint, the most important kind of validity is **predictive validity**—how well a test score predicts future behavior. Suppose you apply for flight training to become an astronaut. As part of the selection process, you are given a lengthy paper-and-pencil test to complete. If the majority of the applicants over the last several years who scored above 80% on the test became successful astronauts, and the majority of those who scored below 80% failed as astronauts, then the test can be considered a valid predictor of performance in that situation. In establishing predictive validity, we must determine the correlation between a test score and some objective measure of behavior, such as job performance. The higher the correspondence between the two, the greater the test's predictive validity.

Content validity refers to the test's individual items or questions. To determine content validity, psychologists evaluate each item to see if it relates to what the test is supposed to measure. For example, the Sensation Seeking Scale is a test designed to measure the need for stimulation and excitement. One of the test items is the statement "I would like to try parachute jumping." A content analysis would ascertain how well this statement (and all other statements) distinguishes between people high in sensation-seeking behavior and those low in sensation-seeking behavior.

Construct validity relates to a test's ability to measure a construct—a hypothetical or theoretical component of behavior, such as a trait or motive. Anxiety is one example of a construct. How can we tell if a new test that promises to measure anxiety really does so? A standard way to determine this is to correlate the scores on the new test with other, established and validated measures of anxiety, such as other psychological tests or some behavioral measure. If the correlation is high, then we can assume that the new test truly measures anxiety.

The personality theorists discussed in this book have devised unique methods for assessing personality, ways that suit their theories. It is from applying these assessment devices that they derived the data on which they based their theories. Their techniques vary in objectivity, reliability, and validity, and they range from dream interpretation and childhood memories to paper-and-pencil tests. In the practice of psychology today, the major approaches to assessing personality are:

1. self-report or objective inventories
2. projective techniques
3. clinical interviews
4. behavioral assessment procedures
5. thought-sampling assessment procedures

Self-Report Inventories

self-report inventory
A personality assessment technique in which subjects answer questions about their behaviors and feelings.

The **self-report inventory** approach involves asking people to report on themselves by answering questions about their behavior and feelings in various situations. These paper-and-pencil tests include items dealing with symptoms, attitudes, interests, fears, and values. Test-takers indicate how closely each statement describes their characteristics or how much they agree with each item.

Two popular self-report inventories are the Minnesota Multiphasic Personality Inventory (MMPI) and the California Psychological Inventory (CPI). In surveys of mental health clinics, counseling centers, and psychiatric hospitals, it was found that the MMPI was administered to adolescents and adults more frequently than any other device and may be considered the world's most widely used psychological test (Archer, Maruish, Imhof, & Piotrowski, 1991; Buie, 1989; Lubin, Larsen, Matarazzo, & Seever, 1985).

First published in 1943, the MMPI was revised in 1989 to make the language more contemporary and nonsexist. Items were also rewritten to eliminate those words (such as *queer*) that over the years had acquired alternative meanings or interpretations (Ben-Porath & Butcher, 1989).

The 1989 revision, or MMPI-2, consists of 567 statements to which one responds "true," "false," or "cannot say." These items cover physical and psychological health; political and social attitudes; educational, occupational, family, and marital factors; and neurotic and psychotic behavior tendencies. Statements similar to those on the MMPI-2 are shown in Table 1.1. The test's clinical scales measure such personality traits as gender role, defensiveness, depression, hysteria, paranoia, hypochondriasis, and schizophrenia. Some items can be scored to determine if the test-taker was faking, was careless, or misunderstood the instructions. The MMPI-2 is used in research on personality, as a diagnostic tool to assess personality problems, and for vocational and personal counseling.

However, the test does have its shortcomings, one of which is its length. It takes considerable time to respond diligently to 567 items. Many people

Table 1.1   *Simulated items from the Minnesota Multiphasic Personality Inventory (MMPI). Answer "true," "false," or "cannot say."*

At times I get strong cramps in my intestines.
I am often very tense on the job.
Sometimes there is a feeling like something is pressing in on my head.
I wish I could do over some of the things I have done.
I used to like to do the dances in gym class.
It distresses me that people have the wrong ideas about me.
The things that run through my head sometimes are horrible.
There are those out there who want to get me.
Sometimes I think so fast I can't keep up.
I give up too easily when discussing things with others.

lose interest and motivation long before they finish. Also, some of the items on this and other self-report personality tests deal with highly personal characteristics, and some people consider the questions an invasion of privacy, particularly when someone is required to take the test to get a job. Nevertheless, despite the length and privacy issues, the MMPI-2 is a valid test that discriminates between neurotics and psychotics and between emotionally healthy and emotionally disturbed persons. Thus, it remains a highly valuable diagnostic tool.

The California Psychological Inventory, developed in 1957 and revised in 1987 (Gough, 1987), is designed for use with normal people age 13 and older. It consists of 462 items that call for a "true" or "false" response. The CPI has three scales to measure test-taking attitudes and provides scores on 17 personality dimensions, including sociability, dominance, self-control, self-acceptance, and responsibility. The CPI has been successful in profiling potential delinquents and high school dropouts and in predicting success in various occupations, such as medicine, dentistry, nursing, and teaching.

Other self-report inventories measure personality traits or focus on larger dimensions, such as sociability, introversion-extraversion, and emotional maturity. Some personality theorists have devised tests to assess the characteristics relevant to their theories, and some theories have inspired other psychologists to develop additional tests.

Self-report inventories are scored objectively. Virtually anyone with the proper answer key can score these tests accurately. The test results do not depend on the scorer's personal or theoretical biases. This objectivity in scoring, combined with the widespread use of computers, has led to automated personality assessment programs for the MMPI-2, the CPI, and dozens of other tests. Computerized scoring provides a complete diagnostic profile of the test-taker's responses.

Projective Techniques

Projective tests of personality were developed primarily by clinical psychologists for their work with emotionally disturbed persons. Inspired by Sigmund

projective technique
A personality assessment method in which subjects are presumed to project personal needs, fears, and values onto their interpretation or description of an ambiguous stimulus.

Freud's emphasis on the importance of the unconscious, projective tests attempt to probe that invisible portion of our personality. The theory underlying **projective techniques** is that when we are presented with an ambiguous stimulus, such as an inkblot or a picture that can be understood or interpreted in more than one way, we will project our needs, fears, and values onto the stimulus when asked to describe it.

Because the interpretation of the results of projective tests is so subjective, these tests are not high in reliability or validity. It is not unusual for different test administrators to form different impressions of the same person, based on the results of a projective test. Nevertheless, such tests are widely used for assessment and diagnostic purposes. Two popular projective tests are the Rorschach inkblot test and the Thematic Apperception Test (TAT).

The Rorschach was developed in 1921 by the Swiss psychiatrist Hermann Rorschach, who had been fascinated by inkblots since childhood. As a youngster, he had played a popular game in which ink was spilled on a piece of paper, which was then folded symmetrically to produce a variety of shapes. As an adult, Rorschach made his inkblots the same way, by dropping blobs of ink on blank paper and folding the paper in half. After trying numerous patterns, he settled on ten blots because he could not afford to have more than ten printed. Figure 1.1 shows an inkblot similar to those used in the Rorschach test.

The inkblot cards are shown one at a time, and test-takers are asked to describe what they see. Then the cards are shown a second time, and the psychologist asks specific questions about the earlier answers. The examiner also observes behavior during the testing session, noting test-takers' gestures, reactions to particular inkblots, and general attitude.

Responses can be interpreted in several ways, depending on whether the subject or patient reports seeing movement, human or animal figures, animate or inanimate objects, and partial or whole figures. Attempts have been made to standardize the administration, scoring, and interpretation of the Rorschach. The most successful of these, the Comprehensive System, claims, on the basis of considerable research, to lead to improved reliability and validity (Exner, 1986). Although the Rorschach is primarily an instrument for clinical applications, it is increasingly being used for personality research as well.

Psychologist Wayne Holtzman developed the Holtzman Inkblot Technique (HIT), a test consisting of 45 inkblots (Holtzman, 1988). It has a standardized scoring system that yields high reliability for well-trained scorers. The test procedures are simpler than those for the Rorschach, so it can be given to a large number of subjects at the same time. It is widely used in research on assessing personality characteristics.

The Thematic Apperception Test was developed by Henry Murray and Christiana Morgan (Morgan & Murray, 1935). The test consists of 19 ambiguous pictures, showing one or more persons, and 1 blank card. The pictures are vague about the events depicted and can be interpreted in several ways. A

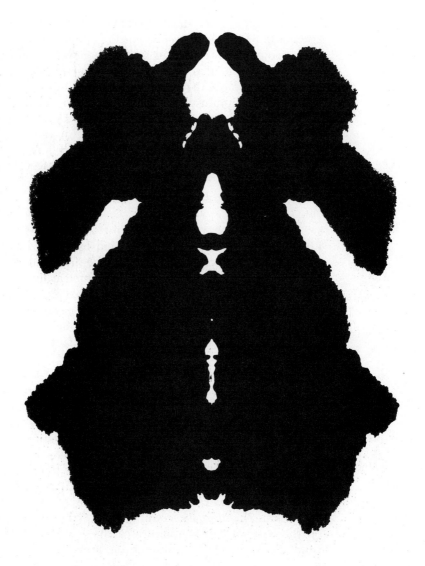

Figure 1.1

An inkblot similar to a Rorschach inkblot.

sample TAT picture and a possible interpretation are shown on page 188. Persons taking the test are asked to construct a story about the people in the picture, describing what led up to the situation shown, what emotions the people are feeling, and what the outcome is likely to be.

In clinical work, psychologists consider several factors in interpreting these stories, including the kinds of personal relationships involved, the motivations of the characters, and the degree of contact with reality shown by the characters.

There are no objective scoring systems for the TAT, and its reliability and validity are low when used for diagnostic purposes. However, the TAT has proven highly valid for research; for that purpose, scoring systems have been devised to measure specific aspects of personality, such as the needs for achievement, affiliation, and power.

Word association and sentence completion are additional projective techniques that psychologists use to assess personality. In the word-association test, a list of words is read to the subject, and he or she is asked to respond with the first word that comes to mind. Response words are analyzed for their commonplace or unusual nature, for their possible indication of emotional tension, and for their relationship to sexual conflicts. Speed of response is considered important. The sentence-completion test also requires verbal responses. Subjects are asked to finish such sentences as "My ambition is . . . ." or "What worries me . . . ." Interpretation of the responses with both of these approaches is, of course, highly subjective.

Clinical Interviews

In addition to the specific psychological tests used to measure an individual's personality, the assessment procedure usually includes at least one clinical interview. After all, it is reasonable to assume that valuable information can be obtained by talking to the person being evaluated and asking relevant questions about past and present life experiences, social and family relationships, and the problems that led the person to seek psychological help. A wide range of behaviors, feelings, and thoughts can be investigated in the interview, including general appearance, demeanor, and attitude; facial expressions, posture, and gestures; preoccupations; degree of self-insight; and level of contact with reality.

Armed with the results of the psychological tests, which are usually administered before or during a series of interview sessions, the psychologist can focus on problems indicated by the test results and explore those areas in detail. Interpretation of interview material is subjective and can be affected by the interviewer's theoretical orientation and personality. Nevertheless, clinical interviews remain a widely used technique for personality assessment and a useful tool when supplemented by more objective procedures.

Behavioral Assessment

In the behavioral assessment approach, an observer evaluates a person's behavior in a given situation. For example, psychologists Arnold Buss and Robert Plomin developed a questionnaire to assess the degree of various temperaments present in twins of the same sex (Buss & Plomin, 1984). The mothers of the twins were asked, on the basis of their observations of their children, to check those items on the questionnaire that best described their children's behavior. Sample items from the questionnaire are listed in

Table 1.2	*Sample items from the Buss and Plomin EASI Temperament Survey.*

Child tends to cry easily.
Child has a quick temper.
Child cannot sit still long.
Child makes friends easily.
Child tends to be shy.
Child goes from toy to toy quickly.

Table 1.2. As you can see, the kinds of behaviors the mothers reported on were specific and easy to observe.

In a psychiatric ward for adults, hospital staff members were trained to observe their patients' behavior and were asked to watch the patients systematically for two seconds of every hour (Mariotto & Paul, 1974). In this way, the staff developed daily records of patient activities so that behavioral trends could be identified. Some of the specific behaviors observed and recorded included mumbling, pacing, and talking to oneself.

As we noted in the section on clinical interviews, counselors routinely observe their clients' behavior—considering facial expressions, nervous gestures, and general appearance—and use that information in formulating their diagnoses. Such observations are less systematic than formal behavioral assessment procedures, but the results can provide valuable insights.

Thought Sampling

In the behavioral approach to personality assessment described in the preceding paragraphs, behavior in the form of specific actions is monitored by trained observers. In the thought-sampling approach to assessment, a person's thoughts are observed systematically to provide a sample over a period of time. Because thoughts are private experiences and cannot be seen, the only person who can make this type of observation is the individual whose thoughts are being studied. In this procedure, then, the observer and the person being observed are the same.

In one study, over several weeks, adolescent subjects were given electronic beepers that sounded whenever it was time for them to record their thoughts, moods, and fantasies. In this way, the psychologists were able to evaluate how various activities, situations, and life events affected the subjects.

The thought-sampling assessment procedure is typically used with groups, but it has also been applied to individuals to aid in diagnosis and treatment. A client can be asked to record thoughts and moods on paper or on a tape recorder for later analysis by the psychologist.

Research in the Study of Personality

One criterion for a useful personality theory is that it must stimulate research. In other words, a theory must be testable. Psychologists must be able to conduct research on its propositions to determine which to accept and which to reject. Ideally, a theory will be shaped, modified, and elaborated on—or discarded—on the basis of the research it generates.

Research psychologists study personality in different ways. The method used depends on the aspect of personality under investigation. Some psychologists are interested only in overt behavior—what we do and say in response to certain stimuli. Other psychologists are concerned with our feelings and conscious experiences as measured by tests and questionnaires, the most frequently used research techniques. Still other investigators try to understand the unconscious forces that may motivate us. A method that allows the researcher to examine one type of subject matter may be inappropriate for another type. As we discuss the various theories, you will see examples of all these expressions of personality—behavior, conscious processes, and unconscious processes—and the different techniques used to study them.

The three major methods used in personality research are the clinical method, the experimental method, and the correlational method. Although different in their specifics, these methods rely on the fundamental defining characteristic of scientific research in any discipline: objective observation. Researchers must base their conclusions only on objective evidence and must consider that evidence dispassionately, without any preconceived ideas or personal biases.

The Clinical Method

case study A detailed history of an individual that contains data from a variety of sources.

The primary clinical method is the **case study** or case history, in which psychologists search their patients' past and present for clues that might point to the source of the patients' emotional problems. Undertaking a case study is similar to writing a mini-biography of a person's emotional life from the early years to the present day, including feelings, fears, and experiences.

Sigmund Freud used case studies extensively in developing his theory of psychoanalysis. He probed into his patients' childhood years, seeking those events and conflicts that may have caused their present neuroses. One such patient was Katharina, an 18-year-old woman suffering from anxiety attacks and shortness of breath. In reconstructing what he considered to be the relevant experiences in her childhood, Freud traced Katharina's symptoms to several early sexual experiences, including a seduction attempt by her father when she was 14. With another patient, Lucy, Freud linked her reported hallucinations to events in her past that related to her love for her employer, a love that had been rebuffed.

It was through a number of such case studies that Freud developed his theory of personality, with its focus on sexual conflicts or traumas as causal factors in neurotic behavior. Freud and later theorists who used the case study method searched for consistencies in their patients' lives. On the basis of what they perceived as similarities among the reports of large numbers of patients, these theorists generalized their findings to everyone.

To investigate personality, psychologists use a variety of clinical methods in addition to case studies. These methods include tests, interviews, and dream analysis, techniques that can also be used for assessment. We can distinguish between assessment and research based on whether the data are used to treat a patient (assessment) or to test a theory (research). Some theorists use the same methods for both purposes.

Although the clinical method attempts to be scientific, it does not offer the precision and control of the experimental and correlational methods. The data obtained by the clinical method are more subjective, relating to mental and largely unconscious events and early life experiences. Such data are open to an interpretation that may reflect the therapist's personal biases, more so than data obtained by other methods. Further, memories of childhood events may be distorted by time, and their accuracy cannot easily be verified. However, the clinical method provides a window through which to view the depths of the personality, and we shall see many examples of its use, especially by the psychoanalytic and neopsychoanalytic theorists.

The Experimental Method

As stated earlier, the fundamental defining characteristic of research in any scientific discipline is objective observation. The clinical method does not meet that requirement very well. Two other requirements of scientific research are even more difficult to fulfill by using the clinical method but are satisfied by the experimental method.

One of these requirements is that observations be well controlled and systematic. Such control is not possible when dealing with a person's past life events or unconscious phenomena. The other requirement involves duplication and verification. With careful control of experimental conditions, a researcher working at another time and in another place can duplicate the conditions under which the earlier research was conducted. Events in a person's life cannot be repeated or duplicated.

An experiment is a technique for determining the effect of one or more variables or events on behavior. We are constantly exposed to stimuli in our everyday world—lights, sounds, sights, odors, instructions, demands, or trivial conversations. If a psychologist wants to determine the effect of just one stimulus variable, he or she can arrange an experimental situation in which only that variable is allowed to operate. All the other variables must be eliminated or held constant during the experiment. Then, if the subjects' behavior changes while only the stimulus variable is in operation, we can be certain that it alone is responsible for any change in behavior. The change could not have been caused by another variable because no other variable was allowed to influence the subjects during the experiment.

Scientists distinguish two kinds of variables in an experiment. One is the **independent** or **stimulus variable**, which is manipulated by the experimenter. The other is the **dependent variable**, which is the subjects' behavior or response to that manipulation. To be sure that no variable other than the independent variable can affect the results, researchers must study two

independent variable
In an experiment, the stimulus variable or condition the experimenter manipulates to learn its effect on the dependent variable.

dependent variable
In an experiment, the variable the experimenter desires to measure, typically the subjects' behavior or response to manipulation of the independent variable.

groups of subjects: the experimental group and the control group. Both groups are chosen at random from the same population of subjects.

experimental group
In an experiment, the group that is exposed to the experimental treatment.

control group In an experiment, the group that does not receive the experimental treatment, thus serving as a basis for comparison with the experimental group.

The **experimental group** includes those subjects to whom the experimental treatment is given. This is the group exposed to the stimulus or independent variable. The **control group** is not exposed to the independent variable. Measures of the behavior being studied are taken from both groups before and after the experiment. In this way, researchers can determine if any additional variables have influenced the subjects' behavior. If some other variable was operating, then both groups would show the same changes in behavior. But if no other variable was in operation—if the independent variable alone influenced the subjects—then only the behavior of the experimental group would change. The behavior of the control group would remain the same.

Let us demonstrate the experimental method in action, using data from psychologist Albert Bandura's social-learning theory of personality. Bandura wanted to determine whether children would imitate the aggressive behavior they observed in adults. What was the best way to study this problem? Bandura could have observed children on neighborhood streets or at a playground, hoping to catch their reactions if they happened to witness a violent incident. He could then have watched and waited to see if the children imitated the aggressive behavior they had seen.

This approach is unsystematic and uncontrolled, and it does not allow for duplication and verifiability; it is unlikely that the same conditions would recur. Also, observing children who happened to be present on a street corner would not necessarily provide an appropriate sample of subjects. Some of these children might already possess the tendency to behave aggressively, regardless of the adult behavior they observed. It would be impossible to decide whether their behavior resulted from witnessing a violent act or from some factor that had long been part of their personality.

Further, observing children at random would not allow the researcher to control the type of aggressive act to which the subjects might be exposed. Children see many kinds of violence—television actors in a gun battle, teenagers in a fistfight, parents slapping each other, drive-by shootings. Each form of aggression would have to be studied individually before its effects on behavior could be determined reliably. For Bandura to study the phenomenon, then, it was necessary that all the children he observed be exposed to the same instance of aggressive behavior.

Bandura approached the problem systematically by designing an experiment in which children whose preexperiment levels of aggression had been measured were exposed to the same display of adult aggression. Children in the control group witnessed nonaggressive adults in the same setting. Both groups of children were watched by trained observers to see how they would behave.

Children who watched the aggressive adult behaved aggressively; children in the control group exhibited no change in aggressiveness. Bandura concluded that aggressiveness can be learned by imitating the aggressive behavior of others. (We discuss this study and Bandura's subsequent research, which led to the formulation of his personality theory, in Chapter 15.)

The experimental method is the most precise method of psychological research, but it has several limitations. There are situations to which it cannot be applied; some aspects of behavior and personality cannot be studied under rigorously controlled laboratory conditions because of safety and ethical considerations. For example, psychologists might be better able to treat emotional disturbances if they had data from controlled experiments on child-rearing techniques, to determine what early experiences might lead to problems in adulthood. Obviously, however, we cannot take groups of children from their parents at birth and expose them to various child-rearing manipulations to see what happens.

Another difficulty with the experimental method is that the subjects' behavior may change not because of the experimental treatment (the manipulation of the independent variable), but because the subjects are aware that they are being observed. They might behave differently if they thought no one was watching. When people know they are participating in an experiment, they sometimes try to guess the purpose and behave accordingly, either to please or to frustrate the experimenter. This kind of response defeats the purpose of the experiment because the resulting behavior (the dependent variable) has been influenced by the subjects' attitudes. This is quite a different response from what the researcher intended to study.

Objective experimental research has its limitations, but when it is well controlled and systematic, it provides excellent data. We offer examples throughout the book of how the experimental method applies to understanding aspects of personality.

The Correlational Method

correlation
A statistical technique that measures the degree of the relationship between two variables, expressed by the **correlation coefficient.**

In the **correlational method**, researchers investigate the relationships that exist among variables. Rather than manipulating an independent variable, the experimenters deal with the variable's existing attributes. For example, instead of experimentally creating a level of stress in subjects in the psychology laboratory and observing the effects, researchers study people who already function in stress-producing situations, such as police officers on the job, race-car drivers at the track, or college students who score high on a test that measures anxiety.

Another way the correlational method differs from the experimental method is that in the correlational approach subjects are not assigned to experimental and control groups. Instead, subjects who differ on an independent variable—such as age, gender, order of birth, level of aggressiveness, or degree of neuroticism—are compared with their performance on some dependent variable, such as personality test responses or job performance measures.

Researchers applying the correlational method are interested in the relationship between the variables—in how behavior on one variable changes or differs as a function of the other variable. For example, is birth order related to aggressiveness? Do girls score higher than boys on a test of assertiveness? Do people who score high on an IQ test make better computer programmers than people who score low? The answers to such questions are useful not only in research but also in applied situations where predictions must be made about a person's chances of success. The college entrance examinations you took are based on correlational studies that show the relationship between the variables of standardized test scores and classroom success.

A great deal of correlational research has been conducted on various facets of the human personality. Consider the need for achievement, a concept formulated by Henry Murray and subsequently studied by David McClelland. Much of the research on that topic compared the measured level of the achievement need with performance on a number of other variables.

For example, researchers wanted to determine whether people high in the need for achievement earned higher grades in college than people low in the need for achievement. The psychologists could have chosen to use the experimental method and designed an experiment in which children would be reared by adults who had been trained in techniques known to increase the achievement need. Years later, when the children attended college, the grades of those high in the achievement need could be compared with the grades of those low in the achievement need. You can see, of course, that such an experiment is ridiculous to contemplate.

Using the correlational method, the researchers measured the achievement-need levels of college students and compared them with the students' grades. The independent variable (the different levels of the need for achievement, from high to low) was not manipulated or changed. The researchers worked with the existing data and found that students high in the need for achievement earned higher grades than students low in the need for achievement (Atkinson, Lens, & O'Malley, 1976).

We present examples of the correlational method in personality research throughout the book, especially in discussions of the development and application of assessment techniques. The reliability and validity of assessment devices are typically determined through the correlational method. In addition, many facets of personality have been studied by correlating them with other variables.

The primary statistical measure of correlation is the **correlation coefficient**, which provides precise information about the direction and strength of the relationship between two variables. The direction of the relationship can be positive or negative. If high scores on one variable are accompanied by high scores on the other variable, the direction is positive. If high scores on one variable are accompanied by low scores on the other variable, the direction is negative.

Correlation coefficients range from +1.00 (a perfect positive correlation) to −1.00 (a perfect negative correlation). The closer the correlation coefficient is to +1.00 or −1.00, the stronger the relationship and the more confidently we can make predictions about one variable from the other.

The primary limitation of the correlational method relates to cause and effect. Correlation does not imply causation. Just because two variables show a high correlation, it does not necessarily follow that one has caused the other. There may be such a relationship, but researchers cannot automatically conclude that one exists, as they can with a well-controlled, systematic experiment.

Suppose a psychologist applied the correlational method and found a strong negative relationship between two personality variables: shyness and self-esteem. The higher the level of shyness, the lower the level of self-esteem. Conversely, the lower the level of shyness, the higher the level of self-esteem. The relationship is clear: people who are shy tend to score low on measures of self-esteem. We cannot conclude with certainty, however, that being shy causes people to have low self-esteem. It could be true that low self-esteem causes people to be shy. Or some other variable—physical appearance or parental rejection—could cause both shyness and low self-esteem.

This restriction on drawing conclusions from correlational research presents difficulties for researchers, whose goal is to identify specific causes. However, for practitioners, whose goal is to predict behavior in the real world, the correlational method is more satisfactory. To be able to predict success in college on the basis of the need for achievement, for example, we need only establish that the two variables have a high positive correlation. If a college applicant scores high on a test of the need for achievement, we can predict that he or she will earn good grades in college. In this case, we are not concerned with determining whether the level of the achievement need causes good academic performance, but with whether the two variables are related and whether one can be predicted from the other.

Theory in the Study of Personality

Although all scientists use them, theories are sometimes referred to in contemptuous or derogatory terms—"After all, it's only a theory!" Many people think that a theory is vague, abstract, and speculative—really no more than a hunch or a guess and quite the opposite of a fact.

It is true that a theory without research evidence to support it is speculation. However, a mass of research data can be meaningless unless it is organized in some sort of explanatory framework or context. A theory provides the framework for simplifying and describing empirical data in a meaningful way. A theory can be considered a kind of map that represents the data in their interrelationships. It attempts to bring order to the data, to fit them into a pattern.

Theories are hypotheses or sets of principles used to explain a particular class of phenomena (in our case, the behaviors and experiences relating to personality). If personality theories are to be useful, they must be testable, capable of stimulating research on their various propositions. Researchers must be able to conduct experiments to determine whether aspects of the theory should be accepted or rejected. Personality theories must be able to clarify and explain the data of personality by organizing those data into a coherent framework. Theories should also help us understand and predict behavior. Those theories that can be tested and can explain, understand, and predict behavior may then be applied to help people change their behaviors, feelings, and emotions from harmful to helpful, from undesirable to desirable.

Formal Theories and Personal Theories

Scientists are not the only people who use theories; nor are all theories formal proposals containing numerous postulates and corollaries. We all use implicit personal theories in our everyday interactions with other people. We have some idea of the concept of personality, and we make suppositions about the personalities of those with whom we interact. Many of us speculate about human nature in general. For example, we may believe that all people are basically good or that people care only about themselves.

These suppositions are theories. They are frameworks within which we place the data of our observations of others. We usually base our personal theories on data we collect from our perceptions of the behavior of those around us. In that respect—that our theories derive from our observations—personal theories are similar to formal theories.

Formal theories in psychology, as well as in other sciences, have certain characteristics that set them apart from our personal theories. Formal theories are based on data from observations of large numbers of people of diverse natures. Personal theories are derived from our observations of a limited number of persons, usually our small circle of relatives, friends, and acquaintances, as well as ourselves. Because formal theories are supported by a broader range of data, they are more comprehensive. We can generalize more effectively from formal theories to explain and predict the behavior of more kinds of people.

A second difference is that formal theories are likely to be more objective because scientists' observations are, ideally, unbiased by their needs, fears, desires, and values. Our personal theories are based as much on observations of ourselves as of others. We tend to interpret the actions of other people in terms of our thoughts and feelings, evaluating their reactions to a situation on the basis of what we would do or how we would feel. We view others in personal and subjective terms, whereas scientists try to observe more objectively and dispassionately.

Another difference is that formal theories are tested repeatedly against reality, often by a scientist other than the one who proposed the theory. A formal theory may be put to many objective, experimental tests and, as a consequence, be supported, modified, or rejected in light of the results. Personal theories are not so tested by ourselves or by a neutral party. Once we develop a personal theory about people in general or about one person in particular, we tend to cling to it, perceiving only those behaviors that confirm our theory and failing to attend to those that contradict it.

In principle, scientists can recognize and evaluate data that do not support their theories. Unfortunately, in reality, this is not always true. Many examples exist in both the history of science and the history of psychology of scientists who were so prejudiced by their theory, so emotionally committed to it, that their objectivity was compromised. However, the ideal of objectivity remains the goal toward which scientists strive.

The intent of formal theories is greater objectivity; personal theories tend to be more subjective. We might assume that personality theories, because they belong to a discipline that calls itself a science, are of the formal and objective variety. That conclusion would be incorrect. Psychologists recognize that some personality theories have a subjective component and may reflect the theorist's life events as a sort of disguised autobiography. The theorist may draw on these events as a source of data to support the theory. No matter how hard scientists try to be impartial and objective, their personal viewpoint is likely to influence their perception to some degree. This should not surprise us. Personality theorists are human beings and, like most of us, may find it difficult to accept ideas that diverge from their experience.

Thus, the distinction between formal and personal theories may not be so notable in the area of personality as in other branches of psychology. This does not mean that all personality theories are personal theories. Personality theories have the characteristics of formal theories. Some are based on the observation of a large number and variety of persons. Some are tested against reality either by the theorist who proposed it or by others. These scientists attempt to be objective in making their observations and in analyzing their data, which may or may not support the theory. Ultimately, the theories are as objective as their subject matter—the complex human personality—permits, but their propositions may owe much to the personalities and life experiences of their originators.

The first stage in constructing a theory may be based primarily on intuition, but in later stages these intuitively based ideas may be modified and refined by the theorist's rational and empirical knowledge. Thus, through the application of reason and data analysis, what began as a personal theory assumes the characteristics of a formal theory. Whatever level of objectivity is found in personality theories (and some are more objective than others), there is no denying that they are also partly subjective, reflecting the experiences and needs of the theorist.

If we want to understand a theory fully, we should learn about the person who proposed it. It is important to consider how the development of a theory may have been influenced by specific events in a theorist's life. Where sufficient biographical information is available, we can suggest how a theory reflects those events. At least initially, the theorist may have been describing himself or herself. Later, the theorist may have sought appropriate data from other sources to support the generalization of that personal view to others.

We must introduce a note of caution into this intriguing relationship between a personality theory and the theorist's life experiences. Perhaps it is not the life experiences that influence the development of the theory, but the theory that influences what the theorists remember about their lives (see Pervin, 1984; Steele, 1982). Most of our information about a theorist's life comes from autobiographical recollections. These accounts are usually written late in life, after the person has proposed, strengthened, and defended his or her personality theory. The years spent developing the theory and affirming a commitment to it may distort the theorist's memory of early life experiences. Does the person recall only those events that support the theory? Are events that do not fit the theory conveniently forgotten? Are experiences invented to enhance the theory's credibility? We cannot know the answers to these questions, but it is important to keep them in mind while we explore the notion that personality theory may be partly autobiographical.

Images of Human Nature: Issues in Personality Theory

An important aspect of any personality theory is the image of human nature expressed by the theorist. Each theorist has a conception of human nature that addresses a number of fundamental questions, issues that focus on the core of what it means to be human (see Table 1.3). For centuries, poets, philosophers, and artists have phrased and rephrased these questions, and we see their attempts to answer them in our great books and paintings. Personality theorists, too, have addressed these troubling questions and have reached no greater consensus than have artists or writers.

Table 1.3	*Images of human nature.*

1. *Free Will/Determinism*
   Do we consciously direct our own actions, or are they governed by other forces?
2. *Nature/Nurture*
   Are we influenced more by heredity (nature) or by our environment (nurture)?
3. *Past/Present*
   Is our personality fixed by early events in our lives, or can it be affected by experiences in adulthood?
4. *Uniqueness/Universality*
   Is the personality of each human being unique, or are there broad personality patterns that fit large numbers of persons?
5. *Equilibrium/Growth*
   Are we motivated simply to maintain a physiological balance or state of equilibrium, or does the urge to grow and develop shape our behavior?
6. *Optimism/Pessimism*
   Are we basically good or evil?

The various images of human nature offered by the theorists allow for a meaningful comparison of their views. These conceptions are not unlike personal theories; they are frameworks within which the theorists perceive themselves and other people and within which they construct their theories. The issues that define a theorist's image of human nature are described below. As we discuss each theory, we will consider how the theorist deals with these questions.

Free Will or Determinism?

A basic issue that defines an image of human nature concerns the age-old controversy between free will and determinism. Theorists on both sides have asked the following questions: Do we consciously direct the course of our actions? Can we spontaneously choose the direction of our thoughts and behavior, rationally selecting among alternatives? Do we have a conscious awareness and a measure of self-control? Are we masters of our fate or victims of past experience, biological factors, unconscious forces, or external stimuli, forces over which we have no conscious control? Have external events so shaped our personality that we are incapable of changing our behavior?

Some personality theorists take extreme positions on this issue. Others express more moderate views, arguing that some behaviors are determined by past events and some can be spontaneous and under our control.

Nature or Nurture?

A second issue has to do with the nature-nurture controversy. Which is the more important influence on behavior: inherited attributes (our nature or genetic endowment) or features of our environment (the nurturing influences of our upbringing, education, and training)? Is our personality determined by the abilities, temperaments, and predispositions we inherit, or are we shaped more strongly by the conditions under which we live. Personality is not the only topic affected by this issue. Controversy also exists about the question of intelligence: Is intelligence affected more by genetic endowment (nature) or by the stimulation provided by home and school settings (nurture)?

As with the free will-determinism issue, the alternatives are not limited to extreme positions. Many theorists assume that personality is shaped by both sets of forces. To some, inheritance is the predominant influence and environment of minor importance; others hold the opposite view.

Past or Present?

A third issue involves the relative importance of past events, our early childhood experiences, compared with events that occur later in life. Which is the more powerful shaper of personality? If we assume, as some theorists do, that what happens to us in infancy and childhood is critical to personality formation, we must consequently believe that our later development is little more than an elaboration of the basic themes laid down in the early years of life. Our personality (so this line of thought goes) is mostly fixed by the age of 5 or so and is subject to little change over the rest of our life. The adult personality is determined by the nature of these early experiences.

The opposite position considers personality to be more independent of the past, capable of being influenced by events and experiences in the present and by aspirations and goals for the future. An intermediate position has also been proposed. We might assume that early experiences shape personality but not rigidly or permanently. Later experiences may act to reinforce or modify early personality patterns.

Uniqueness or Universality?

Is human nature unique or universal? This is another issue that divides personality theorists. Personality may be viewed as so individual that each person's action, each utterance, has no counterpart or equivalent in any other person. This obviously makes the comparison of one person with another meaningless. Other positions allow for uniqueness but interpret this within overall patterns of behavior accepted as universal, at least within a given culture.

Equilibrium or Growth?

A fifth issue involves what we might call our ultimate and necessary life goals. Theorists differ on what constitutes our major motivation in life. Are we simply a sort of self-regulating mechanism, content as long as some internal equilibrium or balance is maintained? Do we function to satisfy physical needs, to obtain pleasure and avoid pain? Is our happiness dependent on keeping stress to a minimum?

Some theorists believe that people are tension-reducing pleasure-seeking animals. Others consider us to be motivated primarily by the need to grow, to realize our full potential, and to reach for ever-higher levels of self-expression and development.

Optimism or Pessimism?

One additional issue reflects a theorist's outlook on life. We may call it optimism versus pessimism. Are human beings basically good or evil, kind or cruel, compassionate or merciless? Here we are dealing with a question of morality, a value judgment, which supposedly has no place in the objective and dispassionate world of science. However, the question has been dealt with, at least implicitly, by several theorists. Some theorists' views of the human personality are more positive and hopeful than others, depicting us as humanitarian, altruistic, and socially conscious. Other theorists find few of these qualities in human beings, either individually or collectively.

The point to remember about these issues is that there are diverse ways of looking at the development and growth of the human personality. Perhaps one or more of these theories, or parts of all of them, will be congenial to you, or perhaps they will clash with your views and your image of human nature. Few of us can approach this study without preconceptions—it is, after all, the study of ourselves.

Summary

This book contains examples of several approaches to personality theory: psychoanalytic, neopsychoanalytic, trait, life-span, humanistic, cognitive, behavioral, social-learning, and limited-domain. Differences among personality theories can be attributed to the complexity of the subject matter, the historical and personal context in which each theory was developed, and the relative newness of psychology as a science.

Psychology was formally founded in 1879 by Wilhelm Wundt, who used the methods of the natural sciences to analyze conscious experience. Early in the 20th century, John B. Watson developed the behavioral approach to psychology as a protest against Wundt's focus on conscious experience. Watson argued that psychologists must study only overt behavior. Psychoanalysis, developed by Sigmund Freud, used clinical observation to probe the unconscious. The study of personality began in American psychology in the 1930s.

Personality can be defined as an enduring, unique cluster of characteristics that may change in different situations. Techniques for assessing or measuring personality must meet three requirements: standardization (consistency of conditions and procedures for administering a test), reliability (consistency of responses on a test), and validity (the degree to which the test measures what it is intended to measure).

Self-report inventories, in which people report on their own behavior and feelings in various situations, are objective in that scores are not influenced by personal or theoretical biases. Projective techniques attempt to probe the unconscious by having people project their needs, fears, and values into their interpretation of ambiguous figures or situations. Projective techniques are subjective, low in reliability and validity, and usually poorly standardized.

Clinical interviews are used to assess personality, but the interpretation of interview results is subjective. In the behavioral assessment approach, an observer evaluates a subject's responses in specific situations. In thought sampling, people observe and record their thoughts over a period of time.

Psychological research methods include the clinical, experimental, and correlational approaches. Such research requires objective observation, controlled and systematic conditions, and duplication and verifiability. The clinical method relies on case studies, in which psychologists reconstruct patients' backgrounds and lives to find clues to their present emotional problems. Other clinical methods are tests, interviews, and dream analyses. The clinical approach does not satisfy the requirements of psychological research as well as the experimental and correlational methods.

The experimental method is the most precise method of psychological research. Using this method, psychologists can determine the effect of a single variable or stimulus event on the subjects' behavior. The variable being studied (that is, the stimulus to which the subjects are exposed) is the independent variable; the subjects' responses or behavior is the dependent variable.

In the correlational method, psychologists study the relationship between two variables to determine how behavior on one variable changes as a function of the other. The correlation coefficient, the primary statistical measure of correlation, indicates the direction and intensity of the relationship.

A theory provides a framework for simplifying and describing data in a meaningful way. Personality theories must be testable, must clarify and explain the data of personality, and must be useful in understanding and predicting behavior. Formal theories are based on data from observation of large numbers and diverse kinds of people. These theories are objective and are repeatedly tested against reality. Some personality theories may be partially autobiographical, reflecting a theorist's life experiences. The first stage in theory construction may be intuitive; later, ideas based on intuition are modified by rational and empirical knowledge (the results of research and scientific study).

Personality theorists differ on basic questions about human nature: free will versus determinism, nature versus nurture, the importance of the past versus the present, uniqueness versus universality, equilibrium versus growth, and optimism versus pessimism.

Critical Thinking Review

1. List three factors that may explain the diversity and disagreement among personality theorists.

2. What was the fundamental point of difference between the approaches of Wilhelm Wundt and John B. Watson?

3. Give examples of some everyday situations that involve personality assessment.

4. How can we determine the reliability of a psychological test?

5. What is the difference between predictive validity and content validity?

6. Distinguish between self-report techniques and projective techniques for assessing personality.

7. Describe the behavioral and the thought-sampling procedures for assessing personality.

8. What are the advantages and disadvantages of the case study approach?

9. What three requirements of scientific research are met by the experimental method?

10. Give an example of personality research using the correlational method.

11. Describe the relationship between data and theory.

12. Describe the differences between formal theories and personal theories.

13. Six questions are posed in our discussion of images of human nature (pages 27–29). Write down your own thoughts on these issues now. At the end of the book you will be asked to consider these issues again to see how your views might have changed.

Suggested Reading

Atwood, G. E., & Tomkins, S. S. (1976). On the subjectivity of personality theory. *Journal of the History of the Behavioral Sciences, 12,* 166–177. Describes how personality theorists are influenced by personal and subjective factors in developing their perspectives on human nature. Notes, in particular, the work of Jung, Allport, and Rogers.

Buss, D. M. (1991). Evolutionary personality psychology. *Annual Review of Psychology, 42,* 459–491. Describes a field of study that seeks to identify the behaviors and psychological mechanisms that have evolved to help the human species adapt to its environment. Seeks to ally this field with personality psychology, which studies the various manifestations of human nature.

Enns, C. Z. (1989). Toward teaching inclusive personality theories. *Teaching of Psychology, 16*(3), 111–117. Reviews limitations and biases in current personality theories and recommends inclusion of viewpoints that recognize the diversity of cultural experiences, feminism, reformulations of traditional theories, and cognitive perspectives.

Mindess, H. (1988). *Makers of psychology: The personal factor.* New York: Human Sciences Press. Shows how the development of psychology can be related to the personal needs, biases, and personalities of its leaders, including Freud, Jung, Rogers, and Skinner.

Pervin, L. A. (1990). A brief history of modern personality theory. In L. A. Pervin (Ed.), *Handbook of personality: Theory and research* (pp. 3–18). New York: Guilford Press. Offers an overview of the study of personality from its beginnings in the late 1930s, and shows the impact of movements within psychology as well as the influence of World Wars I and II. Discusses images of human nature and the relationship of personality theory to other areas of psychology.

Ross, M. (1989). Relation of implicit theories to the construction of personal histories. *Psychological Review, 96,* 341–357. Suggests that people develop personal theories to provide a framework for understanding their own personality and that they use these theories as a basis for selecting and organizing their memories of past events, recalling incidents that are consistent with the theory and sometimes inventing material to fill in gaps.

Styles, I. (1991). Clinical assessment and computerized testing. *International Journal of Man-Machine Studies, 35*(2), 133–150. Reviews advances in computerized assessment and diagnosis. Documents the influence of subjective factors and shows the continuing need for trained psychologists in order to maintain acceptable levels of validity for various assessment tests.

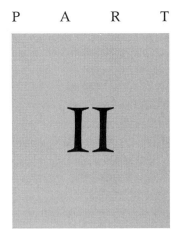

II

The Psychoanalytic Approach

The first approach to the study of personality was psychoanalysis, the creation of Sigmund Freud, who began his work in the closing years of the 19th century. So important and far-reaching were Freud's formulations that much of his theory of personality and his unique approach to psychotherapy remain influential today. Nearly every personality theory developed in the years since Freud's work owes a debt to his position, resulting either from building on it or opposing it.

Psychoanalysis reflects Freud's deterministic, pessimistic image of human nature. It emphasizes unconscious forces, the biologically based urges of sex and aggression, and conflicts in early childhood as the rulers and shapers of personality.

Freud's views had an impact not only on psychology but also on the general culture. He revolutionized our way of thinking about ourselves and our definition of the human personality.

T W O

Sigmund Freud

The Life of Freud (1856–1939)
Instincts: The Propelling Forces of the
    Personality
Id, Ego, and Superego: The Structure of
    Personality
Anxiety: A Threat to the Ego
Defenses Against Anxiety
Psychosexual Stages of Personality
    Development
    The Oral Stage
    The Anal Stage
    The Phallic Stage: Resolving the Oedipus
        Complex

    The Latency Period
    The Genital Stage
Freud's Image of Human Nature
Assessment in Freud's Theory
    Free Association
    Dream Analysis
Research in Freud's Theory
    Scientific Validation of Freudian Concepts
A Final Commentary
Summary
Critical Thinking Review
Suggested Reading

Turn your eyes inward, look into your own depths,
learn to first know yourself.

—Sigmund Freud

psychoanalysis
Sigmund Freud's
theory of personality
and system of therapy
for treating mental
disorders.

Contemporary personality theory has been influenced more by Sigmund Freud than by any other individual. His system of **psychoanalysis** was the first formal theory of personality and to this day remains the best known. Not only did Freud's work affect thinking about personality in psychology and psychiatry, but it also made a tremendous impact on our view of ourselves and our world. Few ideas in the history of civilization have had such a broad and profound influence.

Many of the personality theories proposed after Freud are, as we shall see, derivatives of or elaborations on his basic work. Others owe their impetus and direction in part to their opposition to Freud's psychoanalysis. It would be difficult to comprehend and assess the development of the field of personality without first understanding Freud's system.

An awareness of Freud's work is essential not only for historical reasons but also because of his continuing influence. Although followers offered revisions of certain ideas and concepts after Freud's death, psychoanalysis remains the basis for a contemporary study of personality. It would be difficult to justify any other starting point for our discussion of personality theories.

The Life of Freud (1856–1939)

Freud was born on May 6, 1856, in Freiberg, Moravia (now Pribor, Czech Republic); in 1990 the town changed the name of its Stalin Square to Freud

Square. Freud's father was a relatively unsuccessful wool merchant. When his business failed in Moravia, the family moved to Leipzig, Germany, and later, when Freud was 4 years old, to Vienna, Austria. Freud remained in Vienna for nearly 80 years.

When Freud was born, his father was 40 years old, and Freud's mother (the elder Freud's third wife) was only 20. The father was strict and authoritarian. As an adult, Freud recalled his childhood hostility, hatred, and rage toward his father. He wrote that he felt superior to his father as early as the age of 2. Freud's mother was slender and attractive, protective and loving. Freud felt a passionate, sexual attachment to her. This situation set the stage for his development of the concept of the Oedipus complex, an important part of Freud's system and an integral part of his childhood. As we shall see, Freud's theory reflects many of his childhood experiences.

Freud's mother took pride in her first-born, convinced that he would become a great man. Among Freud's lifelong personality characteristics were a high degree of self-confidence, an intense ambition to succeed, and dreams of glory and fame. Reflecting the impact of his early experiences, namely, his mother's continuing attention and support, Freud wrote: "A man who has been the indisputable favorite of his mother keeps for life the feeling of a conqueror, that confidence of success that often induces real success" (quoted in Jones, 1953, p. 5).

There were eight children in the Freud family, two of them Freud's adult half-brothers with children of their own. Freud's closest companion in childhood was his nephew, who was a year older than he. Freud later described his nephew as the source of his friendships and hatreds. Freud resented all the children in the family and felt jealous and angry when competitors for his mother's affection were born.

From an early age, Freud exhibited a high level of intelligence, which his parents helped to foster. For example, his sisters were not allowed to practice the piano lest the noise disturb Freud's studies. He was given a room of his own, where he spent most of his time; he even took his meals there so as not to lose time from his studies. The room was the only one in the apartment to contain a prized oil lamp—the rest of the family used candles.

Freud entered high school a year earlier than was usual and was frequently at the head of his class. Fluent in German and Hebrew, he mastered Latin, Greek, French, and English in school and taught himself Italian and Spanish. From the age of 8, he enjoyed reading Shakespeare in English.

Freud had many interests, including military history, but when it came time to choose a career from among the few professions open to a Jew in Vienna, he settled on medicine. It was not that he wished to be a physician, but rather that he believed that medical studies would lead to a career in scientific research, which might bring the fame he desired. While completing work for his medical degree at the University of Vienna, Freud conducted physiological research on the spinal cord of fish and the testes of the eel, making respectable contributions to the field.

He also began to experiment with cocaine. He used the drug himself and insisted that his fiancée, sisters, and friends try it. He became enthusiastic about the substance, calling it a miracle drug and a magical substance that would cure many ills. He earned much notoriety as a result of his endorsement of cocaine in articles and lectures, but he later regretted it when scientists recognized that cocaine could be addictive. For many years historians believed that by 1887 Freud had stopped using cocaine, but actually he had used the drug at least ten years longer, well into middle age.

A professor discouraged Freud from pursuing his intended career in scientific research, pointing out that it would be many years before Freud could obtain a professorship and support himself financially in the university system of the day. Because Freud lacked an independent income, he decided to enter private practice. A further impetus toward private practice was his engagement to Martha Bernays, which lasted four years before they could afford to marry. Freud established practice as a clinical neurologist in 1881 and began to explore the personalities of those suffering from emotional disturbances.

He studied for several months in Paris with the psychiatrist Jean Martin Charcot, a pioneer in the use of hypnosis. Charcot also alerted Freud to the possible sexual basis of neurosis. Another significant influence on Freud was Josef Breuer, a Viennese physician who had achieved success with mentally disturbed patients by encouraging them to talk about their symptoms. Freud, who grew dissatisfied with hypnosis (he was not a good hypnotist), turned to Breuer's talking-cure method and found it effective. It was to form the basis of free association, Freud's chief method for inquiring into the unconscious mind. Later, Breuer's impact on the development of psychoanalysis diminished when he disagreed with Freud about the central role of sex in emotional disturbance.

By 1896 Freud was convinced that sexual conflicts were the primary cause of all neurosis. He had found that the majority of his women patients reported traumatic sexual experiences in childhood. These events resembled seduction, with the seducer usually being an older male relative, typically the father. Today we call such experiences child abuse, and they often involve rape or incest. Freud believed that it was these early sexual traumas that caused neurotic behavior in adulthood.

About a year after he published this theory, Freud concluded that in most cases the childhood sexual abuse his patients had reported had never really occurred. They had been telling him their fantasies, Freud claimed, not what had actually taken place. At first this was a stunning blow, for it seemed that the foundation of his theory of neurosis had been undermined. How could childhood sexual traumas be the cause of neurotic behavior if the experiences never happened?

On further reflection, Freud came to believe that the fantasies his patients described were quite real to them. They believed that the sexual events had indeed occurred. Freud concluded that because the fantasies focused on sex, sex remained the cause of adult neurosis.

In 1984, nearly a century later, a psychoanalyst who briefly headed the

Freud Archives charged that Freud had lied, that his patients had truly been victims of childhood sexual abuse. Jeffrey Masson claimed that Freud called these experiences fantasies to make his ideas more palatable and acceptable to the public. Otherwise, who would believe that so many fathers and uncles were sexually abusing little girls? In other words, Masson said, Freud covered up the truth to advance his theory of neurosis (Masson, 1984).

The charges received much international publicity and were denounced by Freud scholars on the grounds that Masson offered little persuasive evidence (see Gay, 1988; Krüll, 1986; Malcolm, 1984). Freud never claimed that all the childhood sexual abuses his patients reported were fantasies; what he did deny was that his patients' reports were always true. "Such widespread perversions against children are not very probable," he wrote (Freud, 1985, p. 264).

Recent findings indicate that childhood sexual abuse is far more common than had been thought, leading contemporary scholars to suggest that Freud's original interpretation of these seduction experiences is correct. We do not know whether Freud deliberately suppressed the truth, as Masson claims, or genuinely believed that his patients were reporting fantasies. It may well be that "more of Freud's patients were telling the truth about their childhood experiences than he was ultimately prepared to believe" (Crewsdon, 1988, p. 41).

A similar conclusion was reached by one of Freud's disciples in the 1930s, and Freud tried to suppress the publication of his ideas. It has also been suggested that Freud changed his position on the seduction theory because he realized that if sexual abuse was so widespread, then many fathers, including perhaps his own, would be considered suspect of perverse acts against their children (Krüll, 1986).

It is an interesting paradox that Freud, who emphasized the importance of sex in emotional life, experienced personal sexual conflicts. His attitude toward sex was negative. He wrote about the dangers of sex, even for those who were not neurotic, and urged people to rise above what he called the common animal need for sex. The sex act was degrading, he wrote, because it contaminated mind and body. He apparently abandoned his own sex life at the age of 41, writing to a friend that "sexual excitation is of no more use to a person like me" (Freud, 1954, p. 227). He occasionally had been impotent during his marriage and had sometimes chosen to abstain from sex because he disliked condoms and coitus interruptus, the standard birth control methods of the day (Krüll, 1986).

Freud's problems with sex surfaced in the form of neuroses, the same way he believed sexual difficulties affected his patients. In his forties he experienced a severe neurotic episode, which he described as involving "odd states of mind not intelligible to consciousness—cloudy thoughts and vague doubts, with barely here and there a ray of light." A month later he wrote, "I still do not know what has been happening to me." He was troubled by a variety of physical symptoms, including migraine headaches, urinary problems, and spastic colon. He worried about dying, feared for his heart, and became anxious about travel and open spaces (Freud, 1954, pp. 210–212).

Freud diagnosed his condition as anxiety neurosis and neurasthenia (a neurotic condition characterized by weakness, worry, and disturbances of digestion and circulation) and traced both disturbances to an accumulation of sexual tension. In his writings he had proposed that neurasthenia in men resulted from masturbation, and anxiety neurosis arose from abnormal sexual practices such as coitus interruptus and abstinence. By so labeling his symptoms, "his personal life was thus deeply involved in this particular theory, since with its help he was trying to interpret and solve his own problems. . . . Freud's theory of actual neurosis is thus a theory of his own neurotic symptoms" (Krüll, 1986, pp. 14, 20).

For three years Freud psychoanalyzed himself through the study of his dreams. It was during this period that he performed his most creative work in developing his theory of personality. Through the exploration of his dreams he realized, for the first time, how much hostility he felt toward his father. He recalled his childhood sexual longings for his mother and dreamed of a sex wish toward his eldest daughter.

Thus, Freud's theory was formulated initially on an intuitive basis, drawn from his experiences and memories. He then constructed it along more rational and empirical lines through his work with patients, examining their childhood experiences and memories through case studies and dream analysis. From this material he fashioned a coherent picture of the development of the individual personality and its processes and functions.

As his work became known through published articles and books and through papers presented at scientific meetings, Freud attracted a group of disciples who met with him weekly to learn about his new system. Some of them later broke with Freud to develop their own theories. In 1909 Freud received formal recognition from the psychological community in the United States. He was invited to give a series of lectures at Clark University in Worcester, Massachusetts, where he was awarded an honorary doctoral degree. Although he was grateful for the honor, Freud did not like the United States, complaining of its informality, bad cooking, and the scarcity of bathrooms.

During the 1920s and 1930s, Freud reached the pinnacle of his success, but at the same time his health began to decline. From 1923 until his death 16 years later, he underwent 33 operations for cancer of the mouth (he smoked 20 cigars daily). Portions of his palate and upper jaw were removed, and he experienced almost constant pain, for which he refused medication. He also received X-ray and radium treatments and had a vasectomy, which some physicians thought would halt the growth of the cancer.

When the Nazis came to power in Germany in 1933, they expressed their feelings about Freud by publicly burning his books, along with those of other so-called enemies of the state, such as the physicist Albert Einstein and the writer Ernest Hemingway. "What progress we are making," Freud commented. "In the Middle Ages they would have burnt me; nowadays they are content with burning my books" (quoted in Jones, 1957, p. 182).

In 1938 the Nazis occupied Austria, but despite the urgings of his friends,

Freud refused to leave Vienna. Several times his home was invaded by gangs of Nazis. After his daughter Anna was arrested, Freud agreed to leave for London. Four of his sisters died in Nazi concentration camps.

Freud's health deteriorated dramatically, but he remained mentally alert and continued to work almost to the last day of his life. By late September 1939, he told his physician, Max Schur, "Now it's nothing but torture and makes no sense any more" (Schur, 1972, p. 529). The doctor had promised that he would not let Freud suffer needlessly. He administered three injections of morphine over the next 24 hours, each dose greater than necessary for sedation, and brought Freud's long years of pain to an end.

Instincts: The Propelling Forces of the Personality

instincts Mental representations of internal stimuli, such as hunger, that drive a person to take certain actions.

Freud defined an instinct as the mental representation of a stimulus that originates within the body. **Instincts** are the basic elements of the personality, the motivating forces that drive behavior and determine its direction. Freud's German term for this concept is *Trieb,* which is best translated as a driving force or impulse (Bettelheim, 1984). Instincts are a form of energy—transformed physiological energy—that connects the body's needs with the mind's wishes.

The stimuli (hunger or thirst, for example) for instincts are internal. When a need such as hunger is aroused in the body, it generates a condition of physiological excitation or energy. The mind transforms this bodily energy into a wish. This wish—the mental representation of the physiological need—is the instinct or driving force that motivates the person to behave in a way that satisfies the need. A hungry person, for example, will act to satisfy his or her need by looking for food. The instinct is not the bodily state; rather, it is the bodily need transformed into a mental state, a wish.

When the body is in a state of need, the person experiences a feeling of tension or pressure. The aim of an instinct is to satisfy the need and thereby reduce the tension. Freud's theory can be called a homeostatic approach insofar as it suggests that we are motivated to restore and maintain a condition of physiological equilibrium, or balance, to keep the body free of tension.

Freud believed that we always experience a certain amount of instinctual tension and that we must continually act to reduce it. It is not possible to escape the pressure of our physiological needs as we might escape some annoying stimulus in our external environment. This means that instincts are always influencing our behavior, in a cycle of need leading to reduction of need.

People may take different paths to satisfy their needs. For example, the sex drive may be satisfied by heterosexual behavior, homosexual behavior, or autosexual behavior—or the need may be channeled into some other form of activity. Freud thought that psychic energy could be displaced to substitute objects, and this displacement was of primary importance in determining an individual's personality. Although the instincts are the exclusive source of energy for human behavior, the resulting energy can be invested in a variety of activities. This helps explain the diversity we see in human behavior. All the interests, preferences, and attitudes we display as adults were believed by Freud to be displacements of energy from the original objects that satisfied the instinctual needs.

Freud grouped the instincts into two categories: life instincts and death instincts. The **life instincts** serve the purpose of survival of the individual and the species by seeking to satisfy the needs for food, water, air, and sex. The life instincts are oriented toward growth and development. The psychic energy manifested by the life instincts is the **libido**. The libido can be attached to or invested in objects, a concept Freud called **cathexis**. If you like your roommate, for example, Freud would say that your libido is cathected to him or her.

The life instinct Freud considered most important for the personality is sex, which he defined in broad terms. He did not refer solely to the erotic but included almost all pleasurable behaviors and thoughts. He described his view as enlarging or extending the accepted concept of sexuality.

> That extension is of a twofold kind. In the first place, sexuality is divorced from its too close connection with the genitals and is regarded as a more comprehensive bodily function, having pleasure as its goal and only secondarily coming to serve the ends of reproduction. In the second place, the sexual impulses are regarded as including all of those merely affectionate and friendly impulses to which usage applies the exceedingly ambiguous word "love." [Freud, 1925, p. 38]

Freud regarded sex as our primary motivation. Erotic wishes arise from the body's erogenous zones: the mouth, anus, and sex organs. He suggested that people are predominantly pleasure-seeking beings, and much of his personality theory revolves around the necessity of inhibiting or suppressing our sexual longings.

In opposition to the life instincts Freud postulated the destructive or **death instincts**. Drawing from biology, he stated the obvious fact that all living things decay and die, returning to their original inanimate state, and he proposed that people have an unconscious wish to die. One component of the death instincts is the **aggressive drive**, the wish to die turned against objects other than the self. The aggressive drive compels us to destroy, conquer, and kill. Freud came to consider aggression as compelling a part of human nature as sex.

Freud did not develop the notion of the death instincts until late in life, when his interest became personal. The physiological and psychological debilitations of age and his cancer worsened, he witnessed the carnage of World War I, and one of his daughters died at the age of 26, leaving two young children. All these events affected him, and perhaps as a result, death and aggression became major themes in his theory. In his later years Freud dreaded his death and exhibited hostility, hatred, and aggressiveness toward colleagues and disciples who disputed his views and left his psychoanalytic circle.

life instincts The drive for ensuring survival of the individual and the species by satisfying the needs for food, water, air, and sex.

libido The form of psychic energy, manifested by the life instincts, that drives a person toward pleasurable behaviors and thoughts.

cathexis An investment of psychic energy in an object or person.

death instincts The unconscious drive toward decay, destruction, and aggression.

aggressive drive The compulsion to destroy, conquer, and kill.

The concept of the death instincts achieved only limited acceptance, even among Freud's most dedicated followers. One psychoanalyst wrote that the idea could "securely be relegated to the dustbin of history" (Sulloway, 1979, p. 394). Another suggested that if Freud was a genius, then the positing of the death instincts was an example of a genius having a bad day (Eissler, 1971).

Let us reiterate the important point about instincts: All the psychic energy the personality needs is derived directly from the instincts. They provide energy, motivation, and direction for all facets of the personality.

Id, Ego, and Superego: The Structure of Personality

Freud's original conception divided personality into three levels: the conscious, the preconscious, and the unconscious. The conscious, as Freud defined the term, corresponds to its ordinary everyday meaning. It includes all the sensations and experiences of which we are aware at any given moment. As you read these words, for example, you may be conscious of the feel of your pen, the sight of the page, the idea you are trying to grasp, and a dog barking in the distance.

Freud considered the conscious a limited aspect of personality because only a small portion of our thoughts, sensations, and memories exists in conscious awareness at any time. He likened the mind to an iceberg. The conscious is the portion above the surface of the water—merely the tip of the iceberg.

More important, according to Freud, is the unconscious, that larger, invisible portion below the surface. This is the focus of psychoanalytic theory. Its vast, dark depths are the home of the instincts, wishes, and desires that direct our behavior. The unconscious contains the major driving power behind all behavior and is the repository of forces we cannot see or control.

Between these two levels is the preconscious (sometimes called the foreconscious). This is the storehouse of memories, perceptions, and thoughts of which we are not consciously aware at the moment but that we can easily summon into consciousness. For example, if your mind strays from this page and you begin to think about a friend or about what you did last night, you would be summoning up material from your preconscious into your conscious. We often find our attention shifting back and forth from experiences of the moment to events and memories in the preconscious.

In later work Freud revised this notion and introduced three basic structures in the anatomy of the personality: the id, the ego, and the superego. The **id** corresponds to Freud's earlier notion of the unconscious (although the ego and superego have unconscious aspects as well). The id is the reservoir for the instincts and libido—the psychic energy manifested by the instincts. The id is a powerful structure of the personality because it supplies all the energy for the other two components.

Because the id is the reservoir of the instincts, it is vitally and directly related to the satisfaction of bodily needs. As we noted earlier, tension is

id The aspect of personality allied with the instincts. The source of psychic energy, the id operates according to the pleasure principle.

pleasure principle
The principle by which
the id functions to
avoid pain and
maximize pleasure.

**primary-process
thought** Childlike
thinking by which the
id attempts to satisfy
the instinctual drives.

**secondary-process
thought** Mature
thought processes
needed to deal
rationally with the
external world.

ego The rational
aspect of the
personality, responsible
for directing and
controlling the instincts
according to the reality
principle.

reality principle The
principle by which the
ego functions to
provide appropriate
constraints on the
expression of the id
instincts.

produced when the body is in a state of need, and the person acts to reduce this tension by satisfying the need. The id operates in accordance with what Freud called the **pleasure principle**; through its concern with tension reduction, the id functions to increase pleasure and avoid pain. The id strives for immediate satisfaction of its needs and does not tolerate delay or postponement of satisfaction for any reason. It knows only instant gratification; it drives us to want what we want when we want it, without regard for what anyone else wants. The id is a selfish, pleasure-seeking structure, primitive, amoral, insistent, and rash.

The id has no awareness of reality. To offer a simplified example, we might compare the id to a newborn baby who cries and waves its fists when its needs are not met but who has no knowledge of how to bring about satisfaction. The hungry infant cannot find food on its own. The only ways the id can attempt to satisfy its needs are through reflex action and wish-fulfilling hallucinatory or fantasy experience, what Freud called **primary-process thought**. Left on its own, the newborn would die because it knows nothing of the external world. As it grows, it learns what objects in the environment can satisfy its needs, where these objects are, and which behaviors are appropriate to obtain them.

Most children learn that they cannot take food from other people unless they are willing to face the consequences, that they must postpone the pleasure obtained from relieving anal tensions until they get to a bathroom, and that they cannot indiscriminately give vent to sexual and aggressive longings. The growing child is taught to deal intelligently and rationally with the outside world and to develop the powers of perception, recognition, judgment, and memory, the powers adults use to satisfy their needs. Freud called these abilities **secondary-process thought**.

We can sum up these characteristics as reason or rationality, and they are contained in Freud's second structure of personality, the **ego**. The ego possesses an awareness of reality. It is capable of perceiving and manipulating the environment in a practical manner and operates in accordance with the **reality principle**.

The ego is the rational master of the personality. Its purpose is not to thwart the impulses of the id but to help the id obtain the tension reduction it craves. Because it is aware of reality, the ego decides when and how the id instincts can best be satisfied. It determines appropriate and socially acceptable times, places, and objects that will satisfy the id impulses. The ego does not prevent id satisfaction. Rather, it tries to postpone, delay, or redirect it in terms of the demands of reality. In this way it exerts control over the id impulses. Freud compared the relationship of the ego and the id to that of a rider on a horse. The raw, brute power of the horse must be guided, checked, and reined in by the rider; otherwise the horse could bolt and run, throwing the rider to the ground.

The ego serves two masters—the id and reality—and is constantly mediating and striking compromises between their often conflicting demands. Also, in a sense, the ego is never independent of the id. It is always responsive to the id's demands and derives its power and energy from the id.

It is the ego, the rational master, that keeps you working at a job you may dislike, if the alternative is the inability to provide food and shelter for your family. It is the ego that forces you to tolerate people you dislike because reality demands such behavior from you as an appropriate way of satisfying id demands. The controlling and postponing function of the ego must be exercised constantly, or the id impulses might come to dominate and overthrow the rational ego. Freud suggested that we must protect ourselves from being controlled by the id and proposed various unconscious mechanisms with which to defend the ego (see pp. 47–50).

So far we have a picture of the personality in battle, trying to restrain the id while at the same time serving it, perceiving and manipulating reality to relieve the tensions of the id impulses. Driven by instinctual biological forces, which we continually try to guide, the personality walks a tightrope between the demands of the id and the demands of reality, both of which require constant vigilance.

But this is not Freud's complete picture of human nature. There is a third set of forces—a powerful and largely unconscious set of dictates or beliefs—that we acquire in childhood: our ideas of right and wrong. In everyday language we call this internal morality a "conscience." Freud called it the **superego**. This moral side of the personality is usually learned by the age of 5 or 6 and consists initially of the rules of conduct set down by our parents. Through praise, punishment, and example, children learn which behaviors their parents consider good or bad. Those behaviors for which children are punished form the **conscience**, one part of the superego. The second part of the superego is the **ego-ideal**, which consists of good or correct behaviors for which children have been praised.

In this way children learn a set of rules that earn acceptance or rejection from their parents. In time children internalize these teachings, and the rewards and punishments become self-administered. Parental control is replaced by self-control. We come to behave at least in partial conformity with these now largely unconscious moral guidelines. As a result of this internalization, we experience guilt or shame whenever we perform, or even think of performing, some action contrary to this moral code.

As the arbiter of morality, the superego is relentless, even cruel, in its quest for moral perfection. In terms of intensity, irrationality, and insistence on obedience, it is not unlike the id. Its purpose is not to postpone the pleasure-seeking demands of the id but to inhibit them, particularly, in Western society, those demands concerned with sex and aggression. The superego strives neither for pleasure (as does the id) nor for attainment of realistic goals (as does the ego). It strives solely for moral perfection. The id presses for satisfaction, the ego tries to delay it, and the superego urges morality above all. Like the id, the superego admits no compromise with its demands.

The ego is caught in the middle, pressured by these insistent and opposing forces. Thus, the ego has a third master, the superego. To paraphrase

superego The moral aspect of personality; the internalization of parental and societal values and standards.

conscience A component of the superego that contains behaviors for which the child has been punished.

ego-ideal A component of the superego that contains the moral or ideal behaviors for which a person should strive.

Freud, the poor ego has a hard time of it, pressured on three sides, threatened by three dangers: the id, reality, and the superego. The inevitable result of this friction, when the ego is too severely strained, is the development of anxiety.

Anxiety: A Threat to the Ego

anxiety To Freud, a feeling of fear and dread without an obvious cause. **Reality** or **objective anxiety** is a fear of tangible dangers. **Neurotic anxiety** involves a conflict between id and ego. **Moral anxiety** involves a conflict between id and superego.

We have a general idea of what the word *anxiety* means and how we feel when we say we are anxious. We can agree to some extent on the internal experiences associated with such feelings. We know that anxiety is not unlike fear, although we may not know what we are frightened of. Freud described **anxiety** as an objectless fear; often, we cannot point to its source, to a specific object that induced it.

Freud made anxiety an important part of his personality theory, asserting that it is fundamental to the development of neurotic and psychotic behavior. He suggested that the prototype of all anxiety is the birth trauma, a notion elaborated on by a disciple, Otto Rank.

The fetus in its mother's womb is in the most stable and secure of worlds, where every need is satisfied without delay. But at birth the organism is thrust into a hostile environment. Suddenly it is required to begin adapting to reality because its instinctual demands may not always be immediately met. The newborn's nervous system, immature and ill prepared, is bombarded with diverse sensory stimuli. Consequently, the infant engages in massive motor movements, heightened breathing, and increased heart rate. This birth trauma, with its tension and fear that the id instincts won't be satisfied, is our first experience with anxiety. From it is created the pattern of reactions and feelings that will occur whenever we are exposed to some threat in the future.

When we cannot cope with anxiety, when we are in danger of being overwhelmed by it, the anxiety is said to be traumatic. What Freud meant by this is that the person, regardless of age, is reduced to a state of helplessness like that experienced in infancy. In adult life, infantile helplessness is reenacted to some degree whenever the ego is threatened.

Freud distinguished three types of anxiety, which vary as a function of the situation that produces them. They also differ in their potential for harm to the individual. The first type of anxiety, the one from which the others are derived, is **reality** or **objective anxiety.** This involves a fear of tangible dangers in the real world. Most of us justifiably fear fires, hurricanes, earthquakes, and similar disasters. We run from a wild animal, get out of the way of a speeding car, flee a burning building. Reality anxiety serves the positive purpose of guiding our behavior to escape or protect ourselves from actual dangers. Our fear subsides when the threat is no longer present.

These reality-based fears can be carried to extremes. The person who won't leave home for fear of being hit by a car or who won't light a match for fear of fire is carrying reality-based fears beyond the point of normality.

The other kinds of anxiety—neurotic anxiety and moral anxiety—are more consistently troublesome to our mental health. **Neurotic anxiety** has its basis in childhood, in a conflict between instinctual gratification and reality. Children are often punished for overtly expressing sexual or aggressive impulses. Therefore, the wish to gratify certain id impulses generates anxiety. At first the anxiety is conscious, but later it is transformed into an unconscious threat, a province of the ego. The neurotic anxiety that emerges is a fear of being punished for impulsively displaying id-dominated behavior. Note that the fear is not of the instincts, but of what may happen as a result of gratifying the instincts. The conflict becomes one between the id and the ego, and its origin has some basis in reality.

Moral anxiety results from a conflict between the id and the superego. In essence, it is a fear of one's conscience. When you are motivated to express an instinctual impulse that is contrary to your moral code, your superego retaliates by causing you to feel shame or guilt. In everyday terms, you might describe yourself as "conscience stricken."

Moral anxiety is a function of how well developed the superego is. A person with a strong inhibiting conscience will experience greater conflict than someone with a less stringent set of moral guidelines. Like neurotic anxiety, moral anxiety has some basis in reality. Children are punished for violating their parents' moral codes, and adults are punished for violating society's moral code. The shame and guilt feelings in moral anxiety arise from within; it is our conscience that causes the fear and the anxiety. Freud believed that the superego exacts a terrible retribution for violation of its tenets.

Anxiety serves as a warning signal to the person that all is not as it should be within the personality. Anxiety induces tension in the organism and thus becomes a drive, much like hunger or thirst, that the individual is motivated to satisfy. The tension must be reduced.

Anxiety alerts the individual that the ego is being threatened and that unless action is taken, the ego might be overthrown. How can the ego protect or defend itself? There are a number of options: running away from the threatening situation, inhibiting the impulsive need that is the source of the danger, or obeying the dictates of the conscience. If none of these rational techniques works, the person may resort to defense mechanisms, nonrational mechanisms designed to defend the ego.

Defenses Against Anxiety

Anxiety is a signal that impending danger, a threat to the ego, must be counteracted or avoided. The ego must reduce the conflict between the demands of the id and the strictures of society or the superego. According to Freud, this conflict is ever present because the instincts are always pressing for satisfaction and the taboos of society tend to limit such satisfaction. Freud believed that the defenses must, to some extent, always be in operation. Just as all behavior is motivated by instincts, so all behavior is defensive in the sense of defending against anxiety. The intensity of the battle within the personality may fluctuate, but it never ceases.

Freud postulated several **defense mechanisms** and noted that we rarely use just one; we typically defend ourselves against anxiety by using several at the same time. Also, some overlap exists among the mechanisms. Although defense mechanisms vary in their specifics, they share two characteristics: (1) they are denials or distortions of reality—necessary ones, but distortions nonetheless; and (2) they operate unconsciously. We are unaware of them, which means that on the conscious level we hold distorted or unreal images of ourselves and our environment.

Repression is a word used frequently in everyday conversation. When we say "I've repressed that," we usually mean we have put it out of conscious awareness, deliberately suppressing something we no longer want to think about. This is not how Freud used the term. As he explained it, **repression** is an involuntary removal of something from consciousness. It is an unconscious denial of the existence of something that brings us discomfort or pain and is the most fundamental and frequently used defense mechanism.

Repression can operate on memories of situations or people, on our perception of the present (so that we may fail to see some obviously disturbing event), and even on the body's physiological functioning. For example, a man can so strongly repress the sex drive that he becomes impotent.

Once a repression is operating, it is difficult to eliminate. Because we use it to protect ourselves from danger, we would have to know that the idea or memory is no longer dangerous in order to remove the repression. But how can we find out that the danger no longer exists unless we release the repression? The concept of repression is basic to much of Freud's personality theory and is involved in all neurotic behavior.

The defense mechanism of **denial** is related to repression and involves denying the existence of some external threat or traumatic event that has occurred. For example, a person with a terminal illness may deny the imminence of death. Parents of a child who has died may continue to deny the loss by keeping the child's room unchanged.

One defense against a disturbing impulse is to actively express the opposite impulse. This is called **reaction formation**. A person who is strongly driven by threatening sexual impulses may repress those impulses and replace them with more socially acceptable behaviors. For example, a person threatened by sexual longings may reverse them and become a rabid crusader against pornography. Another person, disturbed by extreme aggressive impulses, may become overly solicitous and friendly. Thus, lust becomes virtue and hatred becomes love.

Another way of defending against disturbing impulses is to attribute them to someone else. This defense mechanism is called **projection**. Lustful, aggressive, or other unacceptable impulses are seen as being possessed by other people, not by oneself. The person says, in effect, "I don't hate him. He hates me." Or a middle-aged mother may ascribe her sex drive to her adolescent daughter. The impulse is still manifested, but in a way that is more acceptable to the individual.

---

defense mechanisms Strategies the ego uses to defend itself against the anxiety provoked by conflicts of everyday life. Defense mechanisms involve denials or distortions of reality.

repression A defense mechanism that involves unconscious denial of the existence of something that causes anxiety.

denial A defense mechanism that involves denying the existence of an external threat or traumatic event.

reaction formation A defense mechanism that involves expressing an id impulse that is the opposite of the one that is truly driving the person.

projection A defense mechanism that involves attributing a disturbing impulse to someone else.

regression A defense mechanism that involves retreating to an earlier, less frustrating period of life and displaying the usually childish behaviors characteristic of that more secure time.

rationalization A defense mechanism that involves reinterpreting our behavior to make it more acceptable and less threatening to us.

displacement A defense mechanism that involves shifting id impulses from a threatening object or from one that is unavailable to an object that is available. For example, replacing hostility toward one's boss with hostility toward one's child.

sublimation A defense mechanism that involves altering or displacing id impulses by diverting instinctual energy into socially acceptable behaviors.

In **regression**, another mode of defense, the person retreats or regresses to an earlier period of life that was more pleasant and free of frustration and anxiety. Regression usually involves a return to one of the psychosexual stages of childhood development (see pp. 50–56). The individual returns to this more secure time of life by manifesting behaviors displayed at that time, such as childish and dependent behaviors.

Rationalization is a defense mechanism that involves reinterpreting our behavior to make it seem more rational and acceptable to us. We excuse or justify a threatening thought or action by persuading ourselves there is a rational explanation for it. The person who is fired from a job may rationalize by saying that the job wasn't a good one anyway. The loved one who turns you down now appears to have many faults. If you miss a ball in tennis, you may glare at the racket or throw it to the ground. Something is wrong with the racket, you are saying, not with your playing.

It is less threatening to blame someone or something else for our failures than to blame ourselves. This is a point to remember when you blame your instructor because you failed an examination.

If an object that satisfies an id impulse is not available, the person may shift the impulse to another object. This is known as **displacement**. For example, children who hate a parent, or adults who hate their boss, but are afraid to express their hostility for fear of being punished, may displace the aggression onto someone else. The child may hit a younger brother or sister, or the adult may shout at the dog. In these examples, the original object of the aggressive impulse has been replaced by one that is not a threat. However, the substitute object will not reduce the tension as satisfactorily as the original object. If you are involved in a number of displacements, a reservoir of undischarged tension accumulates, and you will be driven to find new ways of reducing that tension.

Whereas displacement involves finding a substitute object to satisfy id impulses, **sublimation** involves altering the id impulses. The instinctual energy is diverted into other channels of expression, ones that society considers acceptable and admirable. Sexual energy, for example, can be diverted or sublimated into artistically creative behaviors. Freud believed that a variety of human activities, particularly those of an artistic nature, are manifestations of id impulses that have been redirected into socially acceptable outlets. As with displacement, of which sublimation is a form, sublimation is a compromise. As such, it does not bring total satisfaction but leads to a buildup of undischarged tension.

As we noted, Freud suggested that defense mechanisms are unconscious denials or distortions of reality. We are, in a sense, lying to ourselves when we use these defenses, but we are not aware of doing so. If we knew we were lying to ourselves, the defenses would not be so effective. If the defenses are working well, they keep threatening or disturbing material out of our conscious awareness. As a result, we do not know the truth about ourselves. We have a distorted picture of our needs, fears, and desires.

It follows that rational cognitive processes, such as problem solving, decision making, and logical thinking, are based on an inaccurate self-image. To Freud, we are driven and controlled by internal and external forces of which we are unaware and over which we can exercise little rational control.

There are situations in which the truth about ourselves emerges, when the defenses break down and fail to protect us. This occurs in times of unusual stress or when undergoing psychoanalysis. When the defenses fail, we are stricken with overwhelming anxiety. We feel dismal, worthless, and depressed. Unless the defenses are restored or new ones formed to take their place, we are likely to develop neurotic or psychotic symptoms. Thus, defenses are necessary to our mental health. We could not survive long without them.

Psychosexual Stages of Personality Development

Freud believed that all behavior is defensive but that not everyone uses the same defenses in the same way. We are driven by the same id impulses, but there is not the same universality in the nature of the ego and superego. Although these structures of the personality perform the same functions for everyone, their content varies from one person to another. They differ because they are formed through experience, and no two people have had precisely the same experiences, not even siblings reared in the same house. Thus, part of our personality is formed on the basis of the unique relationships we have as children with various people and objects. We develop a personal set of character attributes, a consistent pattern of behavior that defines each of us as an individual.

A person's unique character type develops in childhood largely from parent-child interactions. The child tries to maximize pleasure by satisfying the id demands, while parents, as representatives of society, try to impose the demands of reality and morality. So important did Freud consider childhood experiences that he said the adult personality was shaped and crystallized by the fifth year of life. What persuaded him that these early years are crucial were his childhood memories and the memories revealed by his adult patients. Invariably, as his patients lay on his psychoanalytic couch, they reached far back into childhood. Increasingly, Freud perceived that the adult neurosis had been formed in the early years of life.

psychosexual stages of development The **oral, anal, phallic,** and **genital** stages through which all children pass. In these stages, gratification of the id instincts depends on the stimulation of corresponding areas of the body.

Freud sensed strong sexual conflicts in the infant and young child, conflicts that seemed to revolve around specific regions of the body. He noted that each body region assumed a greater importance as the center of conflict at a different age. From these observations he derived the theory of the **psychosexual stages of development**, each stage defined by an erogenous zone of the body. In each developmental stage a conflict exists that must be resolved before the infant or child can progress to the next stage.

Sometimes a person is reluctant or unable to move from one stage to the next because the conflict has not been resolved or because the needs have been so supremely satisfied by an indulgent parent that the child doesn't

In the oral stage of psychosexual development, pleasure is derived from sucking, biting, and swallowing.

fixation A condition in which a portion of libido remains invested in one of the psychosexual stages because of excessive frustration or gratification.

want to move on. In either case, the individual is said to be fixated at this stage of development. In **fixation**, a portion of libido or psychic energy remains invested in that developmental stage, leaving less energy for the following stages.

Central to the psychosexual theory is the infant's sex drive. Freud shocked his colleagues and the general public when he argued that babies are motivated by sexual impulses. Recall, however, that Freud did not define sex in a narrow way. He believed that the infant is driven to obtain a diffuse form of bodily pleasure deriving from the mouth, anus, and genitals, the erogenous zones that define the stages of development during the first five years of life.

The Oral Stage

The **oral stage,** the first stage of psychosexual development, lasts from birth to some time during the second year of life. During this period the infant's principal source of pleasure is the mouth. The infant derives pleasure from sucking, biting, and swallowing, with the attendant sensations of the lips, tongue, and cheeks. The mouth is used for survival—for ingestion of food and water—but Freud placed a greater emphasis on the erotic satisfactions derived from oral activities.

The infant is in a state of dependence on the mother or caregiver, who becomes the primary object of the child's libido. In more familiar terms, we might say the infant is learning, in a primitive way, to love the mother. How the mother responds to the infant's demands, which are solely id demands at this time, determines the nature of the baby's small world. The infant learns from the mother to perceive the world as good or bad, satisfying or frustrating, safe or perilous.

There are two ways of behaving during this stage: oral incorporative behavior (taking in) and oral aggressive or oral sadistic behavior (biting or spitting out). The oral incorporative mode occurs first and involves the pleasurable stimulation of the mouth by other people and by food. Adults fixated at the oral incorporative stage are excessively concerned with oral activities, such as eating, drinking, smoking, and kissing. If, as infants, they were excessively gratified, their adult oral personality will be predisposed to unusual optimism and dependency. Because they were overindulged in infancy, they continue to depend on others to gratify their needs. As a consequence, they are overly gullible, will "swallow" anything they are told, and trust other people inordinately. Such people are labeled oral passive personality types.

The second oral phase, oral aggressive or oral sadistic, occurs during the painful, frustrating eruption of teeth. As a result of this experience, infants come to view the mother with hatred as well as love. Persons fixated at this level are prone to excessive pessimism, hostility, and aggressiveness. They are likely to be argumentative and sarcastic, making "biting" remarks and displaying cruelty toward others. They tend to be envious of other people and try to exploit and manipulate them in an effort to dominate.

The oral stage concludes at the time of weaning, although some libido remains if fixation has occurred. Then the infant's focus shifts to the other end.

The Anal Stage

Society, in the form of parents, tends to defer to the infant's needs during the first year of life, adjusting to its demands and expecting relatively little adjustment in return. This situation changes around the age of 18 months, when a new demand—toilet training—is made of the child. Freud believed that the experience of toilet training during the **anal stages** had a significant effect on personality development. Defecation produces pleasure for the child, but with the onset of toilet training, the child must learn to postpone or delay this pleasure. For the first time, gratification of an instinctual impulse is interfered with as parents attempt to regulate the time and place for defecation.

As any parent can attest, this is a time of conflict for all concerned. The child learns that he or she has (or is) a weapon that can be used against the parents. The child has control over something and can choose to comply or not with the parents' demands. If the toilet training is not going well—if the child has difficulty learning or the parents are excessively demanding—the child reacts in one of two ways. One way is to defecate when and where the parents disapprove, thus defying their attempts at regulation. If the child finds this a satisfactory technique for reducing frustration and uses it frequently, he or she may develop an anal aggressive personality. To Freud, this was the basis for many forms of hostile and sadistic behavior in adult life, including cruelty, destructiveness, and temper tantrums. Such a person is likely to be disorderly and to view other people as objects to be possessed.

A second way the child may react to the frustration of toilet training is to hold back or retain the feces. This produces a feeling of pleasure (derived from a full lower intestine) and can be another successful technique for manipulating the parents. They may become concerned if the child goes several days without a bowel movement. Thus, the child discovers a new method for securing parental attention and affection. This behavior is the basis for the development of an anal retentive personality. Stubborn and stingy, such a person hoards or retains things because feelings of security depend on what is saved and possessed and on the order in which possessions and other aspects of life are maintained. The person is likely to be rigid, compulsively neat, obstinate, and overly conscientious.

The Phallic Stage: Resolving the Oedipus Complex

A new set of problems arises around the fourth to fifth year, when the focus of pleasure shifts from the anus to the genitals. Again the child faces a battle between an id impulse and the demands of society, as reflected in parental expectations.

Children at the **phallic stage** display considerable interest in exploring and manipulating the genitals—their own and those of their playmates. Pleasure is derived from the genital region not only through behaviors such as masturbation, but also through fantasies. The child becomes curious about birth and about why boys have penises and girls do not. The child may talk about wanting to marry the parent of the opposite sex.

The phallic stage is the last of the pregenital or childhood stages, and phallic conflicts are the most complex ones to resolve. They are difficult for many people to accept because they involve the notion of incest, a taboo in Western and other cultures. Between incestuous desires and masturbation we can see the seeds of shock, anger, and suppression being sown in the parents of the typical 4-year-old. Reality and morality come to grips with the evil id once again.

The basic conflict of the phallic stage centers around the unconscious desire of the child for the parent of the opposite sex. Accompanying this is the unconscious desire to replace or destroy the parent of the same sex. Out of Freud's identification of this conflict came one of his best-known concepts: the **Oedipus complex**. Its name comes from the Greek myth described in the play *Oedipus Rex,* written by Sophocles in the fifth century B.C. In this story, young Oedipus kills his father and marries his mother, not knowing at the time who they are.

The Oedipus complex operates differently for boys and girls; Freud developed the male part of the complex more fully. In the Oedipus complex, the mother becomes a love object for the young boy. Through fantasy and overt behavior, he displays his sexual longings for her. However, the boy sees an obstacle in his path—the father—whom he regards as a rival and a threat. He

Oedipus complex During the phallic stage (ages 4 to 5), the unconscious desire of a boy for his mother, accompanied by a desire to replace or destroy his father.

perceives that the father has a special relationship with the mother in which he, the boy, is not allowed to participate. As a result, he becomes jealous of and hostile toward the father. Freud drew his formulation of the Oedipus complex from his childhood experiences. He wrote, "I have found love of the mother and jealousy of the father in my own case, too" (Freud, 1954, p. 223).

With the boy's desire to replace his father is the fear that the father will retaliate and harm him. At the same time, the mother may be reacting to the boy's sexual interest with punishment and threats to withhold her affection. Worse, the boy develops a specific fear about his penis. He interprets his fear of his father in genital terms, afraid that his father will cut off the offending organ, which is the source of the boy's pleasure and sexual longings. And so **castration anxiety**, as Freud called it, comes to play a role, as it may have done in Freud's childhood. "There are a number of indications that [Freud's father] enjoined little Sigmund not to play with his genitals, and even threatened him with castration if he did" (Krüll, 1986, p. 110). Additional evidence to support this contention comes from Freud's later writings on masturbation, in which he sees such threats from fathers as common. Freud also reported that his adult dreams contained material relating to the fear of castration by his father.

Two other childhood events may have reinforced Freud's fear of castration. At around the age of 3, he and his nephew engaged in some rough sex play with his niece and discovered she did not have a penis. For a 3-year-old boy, this may have been sufficient evidence that penises can be cut off. In the opinion of biographer Marianne Krüll, "the threat of castration is particularly realistic to a Jewish boy, since it is easy to establish a connection between ritual circumcision and castration" (Krüll, 1986, p. 110). Freud confirmed this in his later writings.

So strong is the boy's fear of castration that he is forced to repress his sexual desire for his mother. To Freud, this was a way of resolving the Oedipal conflict. The boy replaces the sexual longing for the mother with a more acceptable affection and develops a strong identification with the father. By identifying with the father, the boy experiences a degree of vicarious sexual satisfaction. To enhance the identification, he attempts to become more like his father by adopting his mannerisms, behaviors, attitudes, and superego standards.

Freud was less clear about the **Electra complex**, the female phallic conflict. In Greek mythology, Electra cajoled her brother into killing their mother and the mother's lover, who had earlier killed Electra's father (another warm and happy mythical family). Like the boy's, the girl's first object of love is the mother, because she is the primary source of food, affection, and security in infancy. During the phallic stage, the father becomes the girl's new love object. Why does this shift from mother to father take place? Freud said it was the girl's reaction to her discovery that boys have a penis and girls do not. The girl blames her mother for her supposedly inferior condition and consequently comes to love her mother less. She may even hate the mother for what she imagines the mother did to her. She comes to envy her father and transfers her love to him because he possesses the highly

castration anxiety
A boy's fear during the Oedipal period that his penis will be cut off.

Electra complex
During the phallic stage (ages 4 to 5), the unconscious desire of a girl for her father, accompanied by a desire to replace or destroy her mother.

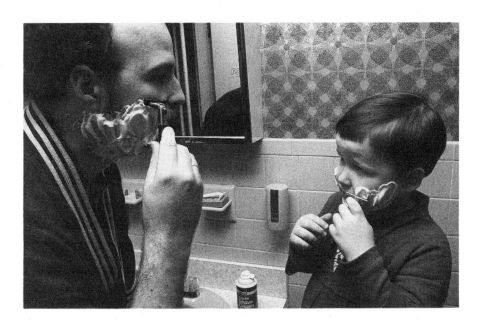

The boy comes to resolve the Oedipus complex by identifying with his father.

penis envy The envy the female feels toward the male because the male possesses a penis; this is accompanied by a sense of loss because the female does not have a penis.

valued sex organ. Thus, a girl develops what Freud called **penis envy**, a counterpart to a boy's castration anxiety. She believes she has lost her penis; he fears he will lose his.

The Electra complex, Freud suggested, can never be totally resolved, a situation that leads to poorly developed superegos in women. Freud wrote that an adult woman's love for a man is always tinged with penis envy, for which she can partially compensate by having a male child. The girl comes to identify with the mother and repress her love for her father, but Freud was not specific about how this occurs.

Phallic conflicts and their degree of resolution are of major importance in determining adult relations with and attitudes toward the opposite sex. Poorly resolved conflicts can cause lingering forms of castration anxiety and penis envy. The so-called phallic character or personality type evidences strong narcissism. Although continually acting to attract the opposite sex, these persons have difficulty establishing mature heterosexual relationships. They need continual recognition and appreciation of their attractive and unique qualities. As long as they receive such support they function well, but when it is lacking they feel inadequate and inferior.

Freud described the male phallic personality as brash, vain, and self-assured. Men with this personality try to assert or express their masculinity through activities such as repeated sexual conquests. The female phallic personality, motivated by penis envy, exaggerates her femininity and uses her talents and charms to overwhelm and conquer men.

The tense drama of the phallic stage is repressed in all of us. Its effects motivate us as adults at the unconscious level, and we recall little, if anything, of the conflict.

The Latency Period

The storms and stresses of the oral, anal, and phallic stages of psychosexual development are the amalgam out of which most of the adult personality is shaped. The three major structures of the personality—the id, ego, and superego—have been formed by approximately the age of 5, and the relationships among them are being solidified.

Fortunately—because the child and parents certainly could use some rest—the next five or six years are quiet. The latency period is not a psychosexual stage of development. The sex instinct is dormant, temporarily sublimated in school activities, hobbies, and sports and in developing friendships with members of the same sex.

Freud has been criticized for his apparent lack of interest in the latency period. Other personality theorists consider these years to present significant problems and challenges that involve getting along with peers and learning to adjust to an ever-widening world.

The Genital Stage

The **genital stage,** the final psychosexual stage of development, begins at puberty. The body is becoming physiologically mature, and if no major fixations have occurred at an earlier stage of development, the individual may be able to lead a normal life. The conflict during this period is less intense than in the other stages. Societal sanctions and taboos exist concerning sexual expression to which the adolescent must conform, but conflict is minimized through sublimation. The sexual energy pressing for expression in the teenage years can be at least partially satisfied through the pursuit of socially acceptable substitutes and, later, through a committed adult relationship with a person of the opposite sex. The genital personality type is able to find satisfaction in love and work, the latter being an acceptable outlet for sublimation of the id impulses.

Freud emphasized the importance of the early childhood years in determining the adult personality. According to Freud, the first five years are the crucial ones. His personality theory pays less attention to later childhood and adolescence, and he was little concerned with personality development in adulthood. To Freud, what we are as adults—how we behave, think, and feel—is determined by the conflicts to which we are exposed and with which we must cope before many of us have even learned to read.

Freud's Image of Human Nature

Freud's position is clear on those issues in personality that define an image of human nature. Freud did not present us with a flattering or optimistic picture. Quite the opposite—he suggested that each person is a dark cellar in which a battle continually rages. Human beings are depicted in pessimistic

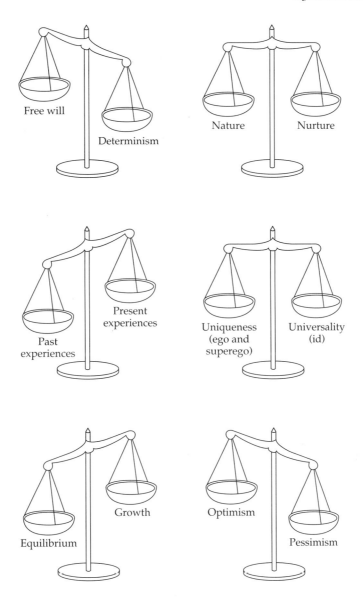

Freud

Image of Human Nature.

terms, condemned to a struggle with our inner forces, a struggle we are almost always destined to lose. Doomed to anxiety, to the thwarting of at least some of our driving impulses, we experience tension and conflict. We are endlessly defending ourselves against the forces of the id, which stand ever alert to topple us.

In Freud's system there is only one ultimate and necessary goal in life: to reduce tension. On the nature-nurture issue, Freud adopted a middle ground.

The id, the most powerful part of the personality, is an inherited, physiologically based structure, as are the stages of psychosexual development. However, part of our personality is learned in early childhood, from parent-child interactions.

Although Freud recognized a universality in human nature, in that we all pass through the stages of psychosexual development and are motivated by the same id forces, he asserted that part of the personality is unique to each person. The ego and superego perform the same functions for everyone, but their content varies from one person to another because they are formed through personal experience. Also, different character types can develop during the psychosexual stages.

On the issue of free will versus determinism, Freud held a deterministic view: Virtually everything we do, think, and dream is predetermined by the life and death instincts, the inaccessible and invisible forces within us. Our adult personality is determined by interactions that occurred before we were 5, at a time when we had limited control. These experiences forever hold us in their grip.

Freud's picture of human nature, painted in these bleak hues, reflects his personal view of humanity, which darkened with his age and declining health. Toward some people—unless they disagreed with his viewpoint—he expressed benevolence and optimism, but of people in general his judgment was harsh. "I have found little that is 'good' about human beings on the whole," he wrote. "In my experience, most of them are trash" (Freud, 1963, pp. 61–62). We can see this stern judgment in his personality theory.

Assessment in Freud's Theory

Freud considered the unconscious to be the major motivating force in life; our childhood conflicts are repressed out of conscious awareness. The goal of Freud's system of psychoanalysis was to bring these repressed memories, fears, and thoughts back to the level of consciousness. How can the psychoanalyst evaluate or assess this invisible portion of the mind, this dark arena that is otherwise inaccessible to us? Over the course of his work with patients, Freud developed two methods of assessment: free association and dream analysis.

Free Association

free association
A technique in which the patient says whatever comes to mind; a kind of "daydreaming out loud."

Freud developed **free association** over a number of years of seeing patients. Its origin owes much to Josef Breuer, the Viennese physician who befriended Freud during Freud's early years in private practice. In treating a young woman who showed symptoms of hysteria, Breuer found that hypnotizing her enabled her to remember repressed events. Recalling the events—in a sense, reliving the experiences—brought relief of the disturbing symptoms.

catharsis The expression of emotions that is expected to lead to the reduction of disturbing symptoms.

Freud used the technique with some success and called the process **catharsis**, from the Greek word for purification. After a while, however, Freud abandoned hypnosis, partly because he had difficulty hypnotizing some of his patients. Also, some patients revealed disturbing events during hypnosis but were unable to recall those events when questioned later.

Seeking a new technique for helping a patient recall repressed material, Freud asked the person to lie on a couch while he sat behind it, out of sight. (Freud may have chosen this arrangement because he disliked being stared at.) He encouraged the patient to relax and to concentrate on events in the past. The patient was to engage in a kind of daydreaming out loud, saying whatever came to mind. He or she was instructed to express spontaneously every idea and image exactly as it occurred, no matter how trivial, embarrassing, or painful the thought or memory might seem. The memories were not to be omitted, rearranged, or restructured.

Freud believed that there was nothing random about the information uncovered during free association and that it was not subject to a patient's conscious choice. The material revealed by patients in free association was predetermined, forced on them by the nature of their conflict.

resistance In free association, a blockage or refusal to disclose painful memories.

He also found that sometimes the technique did not operate freely. Some experiences or memories were evidently too painful to talk about, and the patient would be reluctant to disclose them. Freud called these moments **resistances**. He believed they were significant because they indicate proximity to the source of the patient's problems. Resistance is a sign that the treatment is proceeding in the right direction and that the analyst should continue to probe in that area. Part of the psychoanalyst's task is to break down or overcome resistances so the patient can confront the repressed experience.

Dream Analysis

dream analysis A technique involving the interpretation of dreams to uncover unconscious conflicts. Dreams have a **manifest content** (the actual events in the dream) and a **latent content** (the symbolic meaning of the dream events).

The other basic technique Freud developed for assessing personality is **dream analysis**. Freud believed that dreams represent, in symbolic form, repressed desires, fears, and conflicts. So strongly have these feelings been repressed that they can surface only in disguised fashion during sleep.

Freud distinguished two aspects of dreams: the actual events in the dream (the dream's **manifest content**) and the hidden symbolic meaning of those events (the **latent content**). Over the years, Freud found consistent symbols in his patients' dreams, events that signified the same thing for nearly everyone. Steps, ladders, and staircases in a dream represented sexual intercourse. Candles, snakes, and tree trunks indicated the penis, and boxes, balconies, and doors signified the female body. (Additional Freudian dream symbols are listed in Table 2.1.) Freud warned that despite this apparent universality of symbols, dreams must be interpreted within the context of the patient's conflict. Many symbols are specific to the person undergoing analysis and could have a different meaning for someone else.

Dreams reveal conflicts in a condensed, intensified form. Dream events

Table 2.1   *Dream symbols or events and their latent psychoanalytic meaning.*

Symbol	Interpretation
Smooth-fronted house	Male body
House with ledges, balconies	Female body
King and queen	Parents
Small animals	Children
Children	Genital organs
Playing with children	Masturbation
Baldness, tooth extraction	Castration
Elongated objects (e.g., tree trunks, umbrellas, neckties, snakes, candles)	Male genitals
Enclosed spaces (e.g., boxes, ovens, closets, caves, pockets)	Female genitals
Climbing stairs or ladders; driving cars; riding horses; crossing bridges	Sexual intercourse
Bathing	Birth
Beginning a journey	Dying
Being naked in a crowd	Desiring to be noticed
Flying	Desiring to be admired
Falling	Desiring to return to a state (such as childhood) where one is satisfied and protected

rarely result from a single cause; any event in a dream can have many sources. Dreams may also have mundane origins. Physical stimuli, such as the temperature of the bedroom or contact with one's partner, can induce a dream, and dreams can also be triggered by internal stimuli, such as a fever or an upset stomach.

Both Freudian assessment techniques—free association and dream analysis—reveal to the psychoanalyst a great deal of repressed material, but all of it is in disguised or symbolic form. The therapist then must interpret or translate the material for the patient. Freud compared this procedure with the task of an archeologist reconstructing a community that has been destroyed and buried under the accumulation of centuries. Just as the archeologist attempts to reconstruct a building from broken fragments, so a psychoanalyst reconstructs an experience from buried, fragmented memories. Thus, the evaluation or assessment of a patient's personality—his or her unconscious conflicts—depends on the skill, training, and experience of the analyst.

Research in Freud's Theory

Freud's major research method was the case study, which has several limitations: The case study does not rely on objective observation, the data are not gathered in controlled and systematic fashion, and the situation (the psychoanalytic session) is not amenable to duplication and verification. We cannot systematically vary the conditions of childhood in which patients are reared, nor can we duplicate in the laboratory a person's home environment. In general, then, clinical observations cannot be repeated in controlled psychological experiments.

A fundamental criticism of Freud's case studies involves the nature of his data. He did not keep verbatim records of the therapy sessions and he warned analysts against taking notes during the sessions, believing it would distract their attention from their patients' words. Freud made notes several hours after seeing each patient, which means that his data may have been incomplete, consisting only of what he remembered. It is possible that his recollection was selective, that he recorded only the experiences that would support his theory. On the other hand, it is possible that Freud's notes were highly accurate, but we cannot be certain. We are unable to compare his case reports with what his patients said.

Even if Freud had kept a complete record of the therapy sessions, we cannot determine the validity of the patients' comments. Freud made few attempts to verify the accuracy of his patients' stories, which he might have done by questioning patients' friends and relatives about the events described. Therefore, we must characterize the first step in Freud's research, the collection of data, as incomplete and inaccurate.

Another criticism of Freud's research is that it is based on a small and unrepresentative sample of people, restricted to himself and to those who sought psychoanalysis with him. Only a dozen or so cases have been detailed in Freud's writings, and most of these were of young, unmarried, upper-class women of good education. It is difficult to generalize from this limited sample to the population at large.

Freud's analysis of his data, the process of drawing generalizations and inferences, was subjective and hence potentially unreliable. He never explained his procedures, and because the data cannot be quantified, their statistical significance cannot be determined.

In addition, there may be discrepancies between Freud's notes on his therapy sessions and the case histories he published, which supposedly were based on these notes. One investigation compared Freud's notes with the published case study of one of his most famous patients. It revealed a number of differences, such as a lengthening of the period of analysis, an incorrect sequence of events disclosed by the patient, and unsubstantiated claims that the analysis resulted in a cure (Eagle, 1988; Mahoney, 1986). Thus, the published version of the case did not agree with the notes Freud made after his sessions with the patient. It is not possible to determine whether Freud deliberately made these changes to bolster his theory (or his ego) or whether they were the product of his unconscious. Nor do we know if such distortions characterize other Freudian case studies. It will remain a mystery because Freud destroyed most of his patient files not long after he compiled them.

The criticisms levelled against Freud also apply to most of the later personality theorists who chose a neopsychoanalytic approach. They, too, used the case study as their primary research method and based their theories on their patients' reports. This does not mean that their work is devoid of merit;

Freud and other analysts have offered a wealth of material about the human personality. If we accept their views as valid, however, we must do so on some basis other than experimental verification.

Although Freud was familiar with the experimental method, he had little confidence in it. An American psychologist once sent him information about experiments he had conducted to validate Freudian concepts. Freud "threw the reprints across the table in a gesture of impatient rejection" and wrote to the psychologist that he did not "put much value on such confirmation" (Rosenzweig, 1985, pp. 171, 173).

Freud believed that his work was scientific and that he had amassed ample proof for his conclusions. He asserted that only psychoanalysts who used his techniques were qualified to judge the scientific worth of his work. Freud wrote that psychoanalysis was based on "an incalculable number of observations and experiences, and only someone who has repeated those observations on himself and on others is in a position to arrive at a judgment of his own upon it" (Freud, 1940, p. 144).

Difficulty arises because Freud's observations cannot be repeated. We do not know exactly what he did in collecting his data and in translating his observations into hypotheses and generalizations.

Scientific Validation of Freudian Concepts

In the years since Freud's death in 1939, many of his ideas have been submitted to experimental testing. In an exhaustive analysis of some 2,000 studies in psychology, psychiatry, anthropology, and related disciplines, Seymour Fisher and Roger Greenberg evaluated the scientific credibility of some of Freud's ideas. In this evaluation, case histories were not considered. Every effort was made to restrict the investigation to data thought to have a high degree of objectivity (Fisher & Greenberg, 1977).

The researchers found that some Freudian concepts resisted efforts at scientific validation. Fisher and Greenberg reached no conclusions about the id, ego, superego, death wish, libido, and anxiety. Concepts found amenable to scientific validation, and which the evidence appeared to support, included aspects of the oral and anal personality types; the idea that dreams are an outlet for tension; and, in the male Oedipus complex, rivalry with the father, sexual fantasies about the mother, and castration anxiety.

Concepts not supported by research evidence include those of dreams as disguised expressions of repressed wishes; resolution of the male Oedipus complex by identification with the father and acceptance of the father's superego standards out of fear; and the idea that women have inadequately developed superegos and inferior body images because of penis envy.

Since Fisher and Greenberg's analysis, additional research has been carried out on Freudian ideas—especially on the unconscious. The notion that unconscious forces can influence conscious thought and behavior has been well established (Brody, 1987; Westen, 1990). Psychologists also recognize that a great deal of the information processing involved in cognitive activities is unconscious (Meichenbaum & Gilmore, 1984; Messer, 1986; Moraglia, 1991).

subliminal perception Perception below the threshold of conscious awareness.

Much of the research on the unconscious involves **subliminal perception** (also called subliminal psychodynamic activation), in which stimuli are presented to subjects below their level of conscious awareness. Despite their inability to perceive the stimuli, the subjects' conscious processes and behavior are activated by the stimuli. In other words, people can be influenced by stimuli of which they are not consciously aware.

When depressed subjects were exposed to subliminally presented verbal and pictorial stimuli representing aggressive behaviors, they became more depressed, as measured by self-ratings, than when they were exposed to neutral stimuli (Silverman, 1976). This supports Freud's contention that depression is caused by unconscious aggressive feelings toward others, which are then turned inward and directed against the self. The results of this research also indicate that the subjects were influenced by stimuli they could not consciously perceive.

In another representative study, subjects were shown a series of words and pictures for such a brief time that they could not consciously perceive them (Shevrin, 1977). Then they were asked to free-associate. What the subjects talked about reflected the stimuli they had been shown but had not actually been able to see. For example, when the stimulus was a picture of a bee, the associations included the words *sting* and *honey.* The subjects' thought processes were affected by the stimuli, even though they were unaware of having seen them.

Many such studies using subliminal perception support the idea that cognitive activity is influenced by the unconscious. Although some psychologists dispute this conclusion (see, for example, Balay & Shevrin, 1988; Holener, 1986), others are convinced that not only are we affected by the unconscious, but that its influence may be greater than Freud proposed (Jacoby & Kelley, 1987; Kline, 1987).

Experimental investigations of the Freudian defense mechanism of repression—the involuntary removal of some threatening idea or memory from conscious awareness—have provided supportive results, although some psychologists question whether the work relates to repression precisely as Freud proposed it (Holmes & McCaul, 1989).

In one study, subjects memorized two lists of words that were flashed on a screen (Glucksberg & King, 1967). Some words on the lists were conceptually similar; for example, *cats* and *dogs* are both animals. The subjects were given an electric shock with some words on the first list. No shocks were administered with the words on the second list. Then the subjects were tested on how well they remembered the words. The subjects forgot the words accompanied by the shock but recalled those not accompanied by the shock. They also repressed words on the second list that were conceptually similar to the words on the first list that had been accompanied by a shock. The researchers concluded that the threatening words had been pushed out of conscious awareness.

Research conducted in Australia identified subjects as "repressors" and "nonrepressors" based on personality test scores that showed repressors to be low in anxiety and high in defensiveness (Davis, 1987). Repressors were able to recall fewer emotional experiences from childhood—particularly those involving fear and self-consciousness—than were nonrepressors.

In related research, repressors and nonrepressors were compared on several experimental tasks. When shown pictures of neutral, nonthreatening stimuli and pictures of embarrassing, threatening stimuli, repressors avoided looking at the latter. When repressors were asked to free-associate to phrases with sexual or aggressive content (presumably threatening material), physiological measurements showed them to be highly emotionally aroused, yet their verbal responses gave no hint of anger or sexual arousal because they had repressed their emotional reactions. Nonrepressors did not inhibit their emotional reactions, and this was evident in their verbal responses.

A different kind of research investigated the complexity of the Freudian defense mechanisms to determine whether they form a hierarchy (Brody, Rozek, & Muten, 1985; Cramer, 1987, 1990). Perhaps, it was postulated, the simplest mechanisms are used early in life, and the more complex ones emerge at a later age. Studies showed that denial (thought to be a simple, low-level defense mechanism) is used mostly by young children and less by adolescents. Identification, a more complex defense, is used considerably more by adolescents than by younger children. The use of projection, another complex defense mechanism, increases with age and is found infrequently among children. Men were found more likely than women to use projection (Cramer, 1991).

Much research has been conducted on dreams, confirming Freud's idea that dreams, in disguised or symbolic form, reflect our emotional concerns. In general, however, research does not show that dreams represent a fulfillment of wishes or desires, as Freud proposed (Breger, Hunter, & Lane, 1971; Dement & Wolpert, 1958). Studies have demonstrated that the higher the subjects' level of anxiety, the more likely their dreams are to contain sexual symbols (Robbins, Tanck, & Houshi, 1985).

Dreams analyzed in research on the Oedipus complex support Freud's theory in that significantly more men reported dreams reflecting castration anxiety and significantly more women reported dreams reflecting castration wishes or penis envy (Hall & Van de Castle, 1965). Other research, however, has failed to support the Oedipus complex. For children to experience castration anxiety or penis envy, they would have to be aware of the physical differences between boys and girls. Studies asking 4- to 6-year-old children to assemble anatomically correct dolls (for example, matching a lower torso with female genitals to an upper torso with prominent breasts) showed that the majority could not assemble the dolls properly (Katcher, 1955; McGonaghy, 1979).

Freud proposed that the male Oedipus complex, with its hostile relationship with a threatening father, can be resolved by having boys identify with their fathers. However, research suggests that 4- to 6-year-old boys form a stronger identification with warm, nurturing fathers than with threatening, punitive fathers (Hetherington & Frankie, 1967).

An investigation of the oral personality type showed a strong relationship between the oral orientation, as identified by the Rorschach, and obesity (Masling, Rabie, & Blondheim, 1967). This supports Freud's contention that oral types are preoccupied with eating and drinking. Another study found oral personality types to be more conforming to the suggestions of an authority figure than anal personality types (Tribich & Messer, 1974). According to Freud, oral personalities are dependent and submissive and should be more conforming than anal personalities; anal types tend to be hostile and can be expected to resist conformity. Freud also contended that women were more orally dependent than men, but later research found no such difference between the sexes (O'Neill & Bornstein, 1990). In general, research support is greater for the anal personality than for the oral personality. There is little empirical evidence for the phallic personality type (Kline, 1972).

Another aspect of Freudian theory put to experimental test is the idea that aggression is instinctive and universal. Freud was not alone in taking this position. Some ethologists, who observe animals in natural surroundings, also posit an aggressive instinct in humans and in lower animals (Ardrey, 1966; Lorenz, 1966), but data from anthropology and psychology have challenged this view. Anthropologists have observed that people in some so-called primitive cultures do not exhibit aggressive behavior (Gorer, 1968). Psychologists who argue against an aggressive instinct suggest that aggressive behavior is caused by frustration (Dollard, Doob, Miller, Mowrer, & Sears, 1939).

Considerable research has demonstrated that although frustration can trigger aggression, it does not always do so. Aggressive responses to frustration can be modified by training, an idea that supports the role of learning in aggression. The psychologist Albert Bandura has shown that we learn aggressive behavior the same way we learn many social behaviors, primarily by observing aggression in others (family members and peers) and imitating what we have seen. Thus, Freud's position on aggression is a minority view in psychology today.

Freud proposed that personality was formed by about the age of 5 and was subject to little change thereafter. Studies of personality development over time indicate that the personality characteristics of preschool children changed dramatically, as shown by follow-up studies conducted over six to seven years (Kagan, Kearsley, & Zelazo, 1978). Other studies suggest that the middle childhood years (ages 7 to 12) may be more important in establishing adult personality patterns than the early childhood years (Olweus, 1979). Although our first five years of life clearly affect our personality, it is apparent that personality continues to develop well beyond that time.

Finally, in our overview of research on Freudian concepts, we come to the well-known "Freudian slip." According to Freud, what appears to be ordinary forgetting or a casual lapse in speech is actually a reflection of unconscious motives or anxieties (Freud, 1901).

In research to test this phenomenon, two groups of male subjects were shown the same pairs of words flashed on a computer screen (Motley, 1987). When a buzzer sounded, they were asked to say the words aloud. One group of subjects had electrodes attached and were told that during the experiment they would receive a painful electric shock. This situation was an experimental way of engendering anxiety. In the second group of subjects, the experimenter was an attractive, sexily dressed woman. This group was given a test of sexual anxiety.

Subjects anxious about the electric shock made verbal slips such as "damn shock" when the words on the screen were "sham dock." Subjects in the sexual anxiety condition revealed that anxiety in verbal slips such as "nude breasts" for "brood nests." Those who scored high on the sexual anxiety test made the highest number of sex-related Freudian slips. Men in a control group, exposed to the same words but to neither anxiety-arousing condition, did not make verbal slips. Not all lapses in speech are Freudian slips, of course, but research indicates that at least some may be what Freud said they were—hidden anxieties revealing themselves in embarrassing ways.

A Final Commentary

Freud's system has had a phenomenal impact on theory and practice in psychology and psychiatry, on our image of human nature, and on our understanding of personality. His influence has been felt in popular culture as well. *Newsweek* magazine wrote that Freud's ideas are "so pervasive that it would be difficult to imagine 20th-century thought without him" (November 30, 1981).

Psychoanalysis contributed to the growing interest of American psychologists in the study of personality, beginning in the 1930s. In the 1940s and 1950s, the ideas of psychoanalysis influenced the emerging study of motivation in psychology. Contemporary psychology has since absorbed many Freudian concepts, including the role of the unconscious, the importance of childhood experiences in shaping adult behavior, and the operation of the defense mechanisms. These and other ideas have generated a great deal of research.

We see further evidence of Freud's importance in the following chapters, when we discuss the personality theorists who built on Freud's system or used it as a source of opposition for their ideas. Great ideas inspire not only by being considered valid, but also by being perceived as incorrect. Thus they stimulate the development of other viewpoints.

Freud's theory of personality remains more influential than his system of psychoanalytic therapy. Although research on Freud's ideas and experimental tests of his concepts continue to be plentiful, psychoanalysis as a therapeutic technique has declined in importance. Growing numbers of people are seeking therapy for behavioral and emotional problems, but fewer are choosing the expensive, long-term approach Freud developed. Briefer courses of therapy—including some derived from psychoanalysis—have assumed importance, along with the use of psychotherapeutic drugs.

Before we leave Sigmund Freud, we must place his work within the context of legitimate criticism. We have already noted the flaws in the case study approach, Freud's primary method of research. In addition to those issues, raised mainly by experimental psychologists, there are questions asked by other personality theorists.

Some argue that Freud placed too great an emphasis on instinctual biological forces as determinants of personality. Others challenge Freud's focus on sex and aggression as major motivating forces and believe we are shaped more by social experiences than by sexual ones. Theorists disagree with Freud's deterministic picture of human nature, suggesting that we have more free will than Freud acknowledged and that we can choose to act and grow spontaneously, in at least partial control of our fate.

Another criticism focuses on Freud's emphasis on past behavior to the exclusion of our goals and aspirations. These theorists argue that we are also influenced by the future, by our hopes and plans, as much as or more than by our experiences before age 5. Still other personality theorists think Freud paid too much attention to the neurotic and psychotic—the emotionally disturbed—to the exclusion of the psychologically healthy and emotionally mature. If we wish to develop a theory of human personality, why not study the best and the healthiest, the positive human qualities as well as the negative ones? Theorists also take exception to Freud's views on women, specifically to the concepts of penis envy, women's poorly developed superegos, and women's inferiority feelings about their bodies.

Ambiguous definitions of certain Freudian concepts have been questioned. Critics point to confusion and contradiction in such terms as *id, ego,* and *superego.* Are they distinct physical structures in the brain? Are they fluid processes? In his later writings Freud addressed the difficulties of defining some of his concepts precisely, but the questions remain.

We will see in the following chapters how these and other criticisms inspired the development of personality theories to counteract these perceived weaknesses and errors in Freud's formulations.

Other theorists have remained largely faithful to the basic assumptions and viewpoint of Freudian psychoanalysis, although these theorists, too, have challenged certain premises. A major change introduced by these loyalists is an expanded emphasis on the ego, making it more independent of the id. Another change is a decreased emphasis on biological forces in favor of social and psychological forces. One leader of this neo-Freudian movement was Freud's daughter Anna (1895–1982). She developed an approach to psychoanalysis with children and established a clinic and psychoanalytic training center in London. Among her contributions in elaborating on the orthodox Freudian position was her description of the defense mechanisms, a description now considered the standard (A. Freud, 1936).

Some of Freud's formulations may not be as appropriate in the closing years of the 20th century as they were when the century began. As times change, psychologists seek new and better ways of describing the human personality. This book is a history of modern insights into personality. In our personal and social growth we are never free of our past, nor should we want to be. The past offers the foundation on which to build, as later personality theorists have built on Freud's work. If psychoanalysis has served no other purpose than to inspire others and provide a framework within which to develop new insights, then Freud's importance to the world of ideas is secure. Every structure depends on the soundness and integrity of its foundation. Sigmund Freud gave personality theorists a solid, challenging base on which to build.

Summary

Much of Sigmund Freud's theory may be autobiographical, reflecting his childhood experiences and conflicts. In Freud's theory, instincts are mental representations of stimuli that originate within the body. Instincts give rise to needs, which generate physiological energy that is transformed in the mind into wishes. Needs induce tension that must be reduced. Life instincts serve the purpose of survival and are manifested in a form of psychic energy called libido. Death instincts are an unconscious drive toward decay, destruction, and aggression.

The three structures of the personality are the id, ego, and superego. The id, the biological component of personality, is the storehouse of instincts and libido. It operates in accordance with the pleasure principle. The ego, the rational component of personality, includes the powers of perception, judgment, and memory. It operates in accordance with the reality principle. The superego, the moral side of personality, consists of the conscience (behaviors for which the child is punished) and the ego-ideal (behaviors for which the child is praised). The ego mediates among the demands of the id, the pressures of reality, and the dictates of the superego.

Anxiety develops when the ego is pressured too greatly. Reality anxiety is a fear of dangers in the real world. Neurotic anxiety is a conflict between instinctual gratification and reality. Moral anxiety is a conflict between the id and the superego.

Defense mechanisms operate unconsciously. They are distortions of reality that protect the ego from the threat of anxiety. Defense mechanisms include repression (involuntarily removing disturbing ideas from conscious awareness), reaction formation (expressing an impulse opposite to the disturbing one), projection (attributing disturbing impulses to someone else), regression (retreating to an earlier and more pleasant stage), rationalization (reinterpreting behavior to make it seem more rational and acceptable), displacement (displacing an impulse to an object other than the one intended to satisfy it), and sublimation (altering the troublesome id impulse).

Children pass through psychosexual stages of development, each defined by an erogenous zone of the body. The oral stage involves two modes of behavior: oral incorporative and oral aggressive. The anal stage involves the first interference with the gratification of an instinctual impulse.

The phallic stage involves the child's unconscious sexual longings for the parent of the opposite sex and feelings of rivalry and fear toward the parent of the same sex. In males, this is the Oedipus complex; in females, the Electra complex. Boys develop castration anxiety; girls develop penis envy. Boys resolve the Oedipus complex by identifying with their father, adopting their father's superego standards, and repressing their sexual longing for their mother. Girls are less successful in resolving the Electra complex, which leaves them with poorly developed superegos.

During the latency period the sex instinct is sublimated in school activities, sports, and friendships with persons of the same sex. The genital stage, at puberty, marks the beginning of heterosexual relationships.

Freud's image of human nature is pessimistic. We are doomed to anxiety, to the thwarting of impulses, and to tension and conflict. The goal of life is to reduce tension. Much of human nature is inherited, but part is learned through parent-child interactions.

Two methods of personality assessment are free association and dream analysis. In free association, resistances develop in which a patient resists talking about disturbing memories or experiences. Dreams have both a manifest content (the actual dream events) and a latent content (the symbolic meaning of those events).

Freud's research method was the case study, which does not rely on objective observation. It is not controlled and systematic, nor is it amenable to duplication and verification. Freud's data are not quantifiable, may be incomplete and inaccurate, and were based on a small and unrepresentative sample. His analysis of the data was subjective.

Some Freudian concepts have been supported by empirical research: the unconscious, repression, verbal slips, characteristics of the oral and anal personality types, dreams as an outlet for tension, and aspects of the Oedipus complex. Major portions of Freud's theory (the id, ego, superego, death wish, libido, and anxiety) have not been scientifically validated.

Personality theorists criticize Freud for placing too much emphasis on biological forces, sex, aggression, emotional disturbances, and childhood events. They also criticize his deterministic image of human nature, his negative views of women, and the ambiguous definitions of some of his concepts.

Critical Thinking Review

1. In what ways can it be suggested that Sigmund Freud's theory reflects his childhood experiences?

2. Describe the life instincts and the death instincts. How do they motivate behavior?

3. Describe the id, the ego, and the superego. How are they related?

4. Describe three types of anxiety. According to Freud, what is the purpose of anxiety? How do we defend ourselves against anxiety?

5. Describe the oral and anal stages of psychosexual development. What activities characterize the adult who is fixated at the oral incorporative phase? At the anal retentive phase?

6. How do boys and girls resolve the conflicts of the phallic stage of psychosexual development?

7. What are Freud's views on the relative influences of heredity and environment? What is Freud's position on the issue of free will versus determinism?

8. What type of information can be revealed by free association? What are resistances?

9. Describe the two aspects of dreams proposed by Freud. Discuss the recent research to test Freud's ideas about the content of dreams. Which of Freud's ideas have received empirical support?

10. What criticisms can be made of the case study method?

11. Describe research on the "Freudian slip."

12. How does research on subliminal perception support Freud's views on the unconscious?

13. What is the position of psychoanalysis within psychology today?

Suggested Reading

Ellenberger, H. F. (1970). *The discovery of the unconscious: The history and evolution of dynamic psychiatry.* New York: Basic Books. Traces the study of the unconscious from primitive times to Freudian psychoanalysis and its derivatives.

Freud, S. (1953–1974). *Standard edition of the complete psychological works of Sigmund Freud.* London: Hogarth Press and The Institute of Psycho-Analysis. Cumulates Freud's writings in 24 volumes edited by James Strachey. These are available in most college libraries.

Gay, P. (1988). *Freud: A life for our time.* New York: Norton. An insightful work on Freud's life and career that draws on much previously unpublished material.

Hornstein, G. A. (1992). The return of the repressed: Psychology's problematic relations with psychoanalysis, 1909–1960. *American Psychologist, 47,* 254–263. Surveys the impact of Freudian psychoanalysis on American psychology from an initial skepticism, through experimental testing, to eventual absorption of some concepts into mainstream psychology.

Krüll, M. (1986). *Freud and his father.* New York: Norton. Examines the lives of Sigmund Freud and his father and analyzes the influences of Freud's experiences as a son on the development of his system of psychoanalysis.

Lerman, H. (1986). *A mote in Freud's eye: From psychoanalysis to the psychology of women.* New York: Springer-Verlag. Describes how Freud's negative bias toward women developed from his personal experiences and permeated his theory of psychoanalysis. Shows how Freud's proposed stages of psychosexual development, as they apply to females, have been largely disproved today and offers criteria for a woman-based personality theory.

Roazen, P. (1975). *Freud and his followers.* New York: Knopf. A lively, well-written account of Freud's life and of the men and women who became his disciples, some of whom later broke away to form their own schools of thought.

Sulloway, F. J. (1979). *Freud, biologist of the mind: Beyond the psychoanalytic legend.* New York: Basic Books. A biography that places Freud's work in the context of its times and disputes the legend that Freud was a "lonely hero" working in isolation.

Young-Bruehl, E. (1988). *Anna Freud: A biography.* New York: Summit Books. An account of the life and work of Freud's youngest daughter, who developed a system of child analysis and served as her father's colleague and confidante.

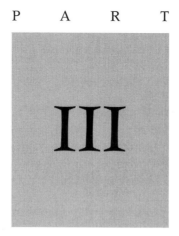

The Neopsychoanalytic Approach

Several personality theorists, who initially were loyal to Freud and committed to his system of psychoanalysis, broke away because of growing opposition to certain aspects of his approach. This is the case with the theorists we discuss in this section. Carl Jung and Alfred Adler were associates of Freud's before they rebelled and offered their own views of personality. Karen Horney and Erich Fromm did not have a personal relationship with Freud but were orthodox Freudians before seeking different paths. Henry Murray, the first American theorist we discuss, developed a view of personality that provides a unique interpretation of formal psychoanalytic concepts. (The work of Erik Erikson, presented in Chapter 10, is also derived from Freudian psychoanalysis.)

The neopsychoanalytic theorists differ from one another on a number of points but are grouped here because of their shared opposition to Freud's emphasis on instincts as the primary motivators of human behavior and to his deterministic view of personality. The neopsychoanalytic theorists stress social influences and present a more optimistic and flattering picture of human nature. They express the view that personality is more a product of environmental forces than of inherited physiological forces, a notion compatible with culture and thought in the United States at the time they were formulating their theories. The work of the neopsychoanalysts shows how quickly the field of personality began to diversify within a decade after it formally began.

Carl Jung

The Life of Jung (1875–1961)
Psychic Energy
The Systems of Personality
    The Ego
    Psychological Types
    The Personal Unconscious
    The Collective Unconscious
    Archetypes
The Development of the Personality
    Childhood to Young Adulthood
    Middle Age to Old Age
Jung's Image of Human Nature

Assessment in Jung's Theory
    Word Association
    Symptom Analysis
    Dream Analysis
    The Myers-Briggs Type Indicator
Research in Jung's Theory
    Studies of Psychological Type
A Final Commentary
Summary
Critical Thinking Review
Suggested Reading

My life is a story of the self-realization of the unconscious. Everything in the unconscious seeks outward manifestation, and the personality too desires to evolve out of its unconscious conditions.

—Carl Jung

analytical psychology
Jung's theory of personality.

Sigmund Freud once designated Carl Jung as his spiritual heir, but Jung went on to develop a theory of personality that differed dramatically from orthodox psychoanalysis. Jung fashioned a new and elaborate explanation of human nature quite unlike any other. To this day, his **analytical psychology** stands apart from other approaches to personality in its complexity and unique emphases.

The first point on which Jung came to disagree with Freud was the role of sexuality. Jung broadened Freud's definition of libido by redefining it as a more generalized dynamic force of personality, a psychic energy that includes sex but is not restricted to it.

The second major area of disagreement concerns the direction of the forces that influence personality. Whereas Freud viewed human beings as prisoners or victims of past events, Jung argued that we are shaped by our future as well as our past. We are affected not only by what happened to us as children, but also by what we aspire to do in the future.

The third significant point of difference revolves around the unconscious. Rather than minimizing the role of the unconscious, as did the other dissenters discussed, Jung placed a greater emphasis on it. He probed more deeply into the unconscious and added a new dimension: the inherited experiences of human and prehuman species. Although Freud had recognized this phylogenetic aspect of personality (the influence of inherited primal experiences), Jung made it the core of his system of personality. He combined ideas from history, mythology, anthropology, and religion to form his image of human nature.

The Life of Jung (1875–1961)

Black-frocked clergymen, deaths and funerals, neurotic parents in a failing marriage, religious doubts and conflicts, strange dreams and visions, and a wooden doll for a companion—all these marked Jung's childhood years. Born in Switzerland into a family that included nine clergymen (eight uncles and his father), Jung was introduced at an early age to religion and the classics. He was close to his father but considered him weak and powerless. Although kind and tolerant, Jung's father experienced periods of moodiness and irritability and failed to be the strong authority figure his son needed.

Jung's mother was the more powerful parent, but she had a number of emotional disorders that led her to behave erratically. As a result, Jung came to distrust women, a suspicion that took many years to dispel. In his autobiography he described his mother as fat and unattractive, which may explain why he rejected Freud's notion that every boy has a sexual longing for his mother. To avoid his parents and their continuing marital problems, Jung spent many hours alone in the attic of his home, carving a doll out of wood, a figure in whom he could confide. He had one sibling, a sister, who was born when he was 9 years old and who had little influence on his development; her arrival did nothing to ease his loneliness.

Distrustful of his mother and disappointed in his father, Jung felt cut off from the external world, the world of conscious reality. As an escape he turned inward to his unconscious—the world of dreams, visions, and fantasies—in which he felt more secure. This choice would guide Jung for the rest of his life. Whenever he was faced with a problem he would seek a solution through his dreams and visions.

The essence of his personality theory was shaped in a similar way. When Jung was 3 years old, he dreamed he was in a cavern. In a later dream, he saw himself digging beneath the earth's surface, unearthing the bones of prehistoric animals. To Jung, such dreams represented the direction of his approach to the human personality. They prompted him to explore the unconscious mind, which lies beneath the surface of behavior. So strongly was he guided by these manifestations of his unconscious that he entitled his autobiography *Memories, Dreams, Reflections* (1961), and he believed his approach to personality resembled a subjective, personal confession (Stevens, 1990).

As a child, Jung deliberately avoided other children. One of his few acquaintances from that time remembered Jung as an ''asocial monster'' (Wehr, 1987, p. 29). In describing his solitary childhood, Jung wrote: ''The pattern of my relationship to the world was already prefigured; today as then I am a solitary'' (Jung, 1961, pp. 41–42). Jung's loneliness is also reflected in his theory, which focuses on the inner growth of the individual rather than on relationships with other people. In contrast, Freud's theory is concerned more with interpersonal relationships; however, Freud, unlike Jung, did not have an isolated and introverted childhood.

Jung disliked school and resented the time he had to devote to formal studies rather than to ideas that interested him. He preferred to read on his own, particularly about religious and philosophical issues. To his delight, he was forced to miss six months of school because he had suffered a series of fainting spells. However, when Jung overheard his father say, "What will become of the boy if he cannot earn his living?" his illness suddenly disappeared, and he returned to school to work more diligently than before (Jung, 1961, p. 31). Jung later wrote that the experience taught him about neurotic behavior. He recognized that he had arranged the situation to suit himself, to keep him out of school, and that realization made him feel angry and ashamed.

Jung chose to study medicine at the University of Basel and decided, to the disappointment of his professors, to specialize in psychiatry, a field then held in low repute. He believed that psychiatry would give him the opportunity to pursue his interests in dreams, the supernatural, and the occult.

Beginning in 1900, Jung worked at a mental hospital in Zurich, under the direction of Eugen Bleuler, the psychiatrist who coined the term *schizophrenia*. In the years that followed, Jung lectured at the University of Zurich, developed an independent clinical practice, and conducted research using his word-association test to investigate the emotional reactions of his patients.

When he became associated with Sigmund Freud in 1907, Jung was a professional with an established reputation. Freud and Jung began their relationship through correspondence. When they met for the first time, they were so congenial and had so much to share that they talked for 13 hours. Their friendship became a close one. "I formally adopted you as an eldest son," Freud wrote to Jung, "and anointed you as my successor and crown prince" (Freud & Jung, 1974, p. 218). Jung considered Freud a father figure. "Let me enjoy your friendship not as one between equals," he wrote to Freud, "but as that of father and son" (Freud & Jung, 1974, p. 122). It has been suggested that their relationship contained many of the elements of the Oedipus complex (Alexander, 1991).

Jung remained in Zurich, but he met with Freud periodically, continued a voluminous correspondence, and journeyed with Freud to the United States in 1909 to lecture at Clark University. Freud was grooming Jung to take over the presidency of the International Psychoanalytic Association. Concerned that psychoanalysis would be labeled a Jewish science (as it came to be called during the Nazi era), Freud wanted a non-Jew to assume titular leadership of the movement.

Contrary to Freud's hopes, Jung was not an uncritical disciple. Jung had his own ideas and unique view of the human personality, and when he began to express these notions, it became inevitable that they would part. They severed their relationship in 1913.

That same year, when Jung was 38 years old, he underwent a severe neurotic episode that lasted for three years. He believed he was in danger of losing contact with reality and was so distressed that he resigned his lectureship at the University of Zurich. Although he felt unable to continue with his scientific work, he persisted in treating his patients. Freud had suffered a neurotic episode at approximately the same age and resolved it by analyzing his dreams, which formed a basis for his personality theory. Jung's situation offers a remarkable parallel. Jung overcame his disturbance by confronting his unconscious through the exploration of his dreams and fantasies. Although Jung's self-analysis was less systematic than Freud's, his approach was similar.

Out of Jung's confrontation with his unconscious he fashioned his approach to personality. "The years when I was pursuing my inner images," he wrote, "were the most important in my life—in them everything essential was decided" (Jung, 1961, p. 199). He concluded that the most crucial stage in personality development was not childhood, as Freud believed, but middle age—the time of Jung's own crisis.

Like Freud, Jung established his theory on an intuitive base, which derived from his personal experiences and dreams. It was refined along more rational and empirical lines by data provided by his patients, nearly two-thirds of whom were middle-aged and suffering from the same difficulties Jung faced.

The rest of Jung's long life was personally and professionally fruitful, and he remained productive in research and writing for most of his 86 years. His books became popular, and his analytical psychology attracted increasing numbers of followers. To broaden his understanding of human nature, he explored diverse cultures in the United States, Africa, and India. The University of Basel established a professorship for him, and a group of students organized a Jungian training institute in Zurich.

Psychic Energy

One of the first points on which Jung took issue with Freud concerned the nature of libido. Jung did not agree that libido was exclusively a sexual energy; he argued instead that libido was a broad, undifferentiated life energy. Interestingly, Jung, who minimized the importance of sex in his personality theory, maintained an active and anxiety-free sex life and enjoyed extramarital affairs with women patients and disciples. One of these affairs endured—with his wife's knowledge—for many years. Contrast this with Freud's troubled attitude toward sex and his cessation of sexual relations at the time he was fashioning a theory that focused on sex as the cause of neurotic behavior. "To Jung, who freely and frequently satisfied his sexual needs, sex played a minimal role in human motivation. To Freud, beset by frustrations and anxious about his thwarted desires, sex played the central role" (Schultz, 1990, p. 148).

libido A generalized form of psychic energy; a broader definition than Freud's concept of libido as sexual energy.

psyche Jung's term for personality.

Jung used the term **libido** in two ways: first, as a diffuse and general life energy, and second, from a perspective similar to Freud's, as a narrower psychic energy that fuels the work of the personality, which he called the **psyche**. It is through psychic energy that psychological activities such as perceiving, thinking, feeling, and wishing are carried out.

When a person invests a great deal of psychic energy in a particular idea or feeling, that idea or feeling can strongly influence the person's life. For example, if you are highly motivated to attain power, then you will devote most of your psychic energy to seeking power. The amount of energy so devoted or concentrated is called a value.

Jung drew on ideas from physics to explain the functioning of psychic energy, which provides the dynamic mechanisms and power for the operation of the personality. He proposed three basic principles: opposites, equivalence, and entropy (Jung, 1928).

principle of opposites The idea that conflict between opposing processes or tendencies is necessary to generate psychic energy.

The **principle of opposites** can be seen throughout Jung's system. "I see in all that happens the play of opposites," he wrote. He noted the existence of opposites or polarities in physical energy, such as heat versus cold, height versus depth, creation versus decay. So it is with psychic energy: every wish or feeling has its opposite. This opposition or antithesis, this conflict between polarities, is the primary motivator of all behavior and the generator of all energy. Indeed, the sharper the conflict between polarities, the greater the energy produced.

principle of equivalence The continuing redistribution of energy within the personality.

For his **principle of equivalence**, Jung applied to psychic events the physical principle of the conservation of energy. He stated that energy expended in bringing about some condition is not lost but rather is shifted to another part of the personality. Thus, if the psychic value in a particular area weakens or disappears, that energy is transferred elsewhere in the psyche. For example, if we lose interest in a person, a hobby, or a field of study, the psychic energy formerly invested in that area is shifted to a new one. The psychic energy used for conscious activities while we are awake is shifted to dreams when we are asleep.

The word *equivalence* implies that the new area to which energy has shifted must have an equal psychic value; that is, it should be equally desirable, compelling, or fascinating. Otherwise, the excess energy will flow into the unconscious. In whatever direction and manner energy flows, the principle of equivalence suggests that energy is continually redistributed within the personality.

principle of entropy A tendency toward balance or equilibrium within the personality; the ideal is an equal distribution of psychic energy over all structures of the personality.

In physics, the **principle of entropy** refers to the equalization of energy differences. For example, if a hot object and a cold object are placed in direct contact, heat will flow from the hotter object to the colder object until they are in equilibrium at the same temperature. In effect, an exchange of energy occurs, resulting in a kind of homeostatic balance between the objects. Jung applied this law to psychic energy and proposed that there is a tendency toward a balance or equilibrium in the personality. If two desires or beliefs differ greatly in intensity or psychic value, energy will flow from the more strongly held to the weaker. Ideally, the personality has an equal distribution of psychic energy over all its aspects, but this ideal state is never achieved. If perfect balance or equilibrium were attained, then the personality would have no psychic energy because, as we noted earlier, the opposition principle requires conflict for psychic energy to be produced.

The Systems of Personality

In Jung's view, the total personality, or psyche, is composed of several distinct systems or structures that can influence one another. The major systems are the ego, the personal unconscious, and the collective unconscious.

The Ego

ego The conscious aspect of personality.

The **ego** is the conscious mind, the part of the psyche concerned with perceiving, thinking, feeling, and remembering. It is our awareness of ourselves and is responsible for carrying out the normal activities of waking life. The ego acts in a selective way, admitting into conscious awareness only a portion of the stimuli to which we are exposed. It provides continuity, coherence, and identity—a stability in the way we perceive ourselves and our world.

extraversion An attitude of the psyche characterized by an orientation toward the external world and other people.

introversion An attitude of the psyche characterized by an orientation toward one's own thoughts and feelings.

Much of our conscious perception of and reaction to our environment is determined by the opposing mental attitudes of **extraversion** and **introversion**. Jung believed that psychic energy can be channeled externally, toward the outside world, or internally, toward the self. These attitudes of extraversion and introversion may be the parts of Jung's system most familiar to you. The terms and concepts have come into everyday usage and have generated considerable psychological research. We all have a good idea of what the words mean. When we say people are introverted, we mean they are withdrawn and often shy, and they tend to focus on themselves. Extraverts are more open, sociable, and socially assertive.

According to Jung, everyone has the capacity for both attitudes, but only one becomes dominant in the personality. The dominant attitude then tends to direct the person's behavior and consciousness. The nondominant attitude remains influential, however, and becomes part of the personal unconscious, where it can affect behavior. For example, in certain situations an introverted person may display characteristics of extraversion, wish to be more outgoing, or be attracted to an extravert.

From his work with patients, Jung came to realize that there were different kinds of introverts and extraverts. He developed additional distinctions among people based on what he called the psychological functions. These functions refer to different and opposing ways of perceiving or apprehending the external real world and our inner subjective world. Jung posited four functions of the psyche: thinking, feeling, sensing, and intuiting (Jung, 1927).

Thinking and feeling are grouped as rational functions that involve making judgments and evaluations about our experiences. Although feeling and

Extraverts channel the libido externally, toward the outside world.

thinking are opposites, both are concerned with organizing and categorizing experiences. The kind of evaluation made by the feeling function is expressed in terms of like or dislike, pleasantness or unpleasantness, stimulation or dullness. The thinking function involves a conscious judgment of whether an experience is true or false.

The second pair of opposing functions, sensing and intuiting, are non-rational functions; they do not use the processes of reason. These functions accept experiences and do not evaluate them. Sensing reproduces an experience through the senses the way a photograph copies an object. Intuiting does not arise directly from an external stimulus; for example, if we believe someone else is with us in a darkened room, our belief may be based on our intuition or a hunch rather than on actual sensory experience.

Just as our psyche contains some of both extraversion and introversion, so we have the capacity for all four psychological functions. And just as one attitude is dominant, so only one function is dominant. The others are submerged in the personal unconscious. Further, only one pair of functions is dominant—either the rational or the irrational—and within each pair only one function is dominant. A person cannot be ruled by both thinking and feeling, or by both sensing and intuiting, because they are opposing functions.

psychological types
Eight personality types based on interactions of the attitudes (introversion and extraversion) and the functions (thinking, feeling, sensing, and intuiting).

Psychological Types

Jung proposed eight **psychological types**, based on the interactions of the two attitudes and four functions:

1. the extraverted thinking type
2. the extraverted feeling type

3. the extraverted sensing type
4. the extraverted intuiting type
5. the introverted thinking type
6. the introverted feeling type
7. the introverted sensing type
8. the introverted intuiting type

The extraverted thinking type lives strictly in accordance with society's rules. These people tend to repress feelings and emotions, to be objective in all aspects of life, and to be dogmatic in thoughts and opinions. They may be perceived as rigid and cold. They tend to make good scientists because their focus is on learning about the external world and using logical rules to describe and understand it.

The extraverted feeling type tends to repress the thinking mode and to be highly emotional. These people cling and conform to the traditional values and moral codes they have been taught. They are unusually sensitive to the opinions and expectations of others. They are emotionally responsive and make friends easily, and they tend to be sociable and effervescent. Jung believed this type was found more often among women than men.

The extraverted sensing type focuses on pleasure and happiness and on seeking new experiences. These people are strongly oriented toward the real world and are adaptable to different kinds of people and changing situations. Not given to introspection, they tend to be outgoing, with a high capacity for enjoying life.

The extraverted intuiting type finds success in business and politics because of a keen ability to exploit opportunities. These people are attracted by new ideas and tend to be creative. They are able to inspire others to accomplish and achieve. They also tend to be changeable, moving from one idea or venture to another, and to make decisions based more on hunches than on reflection. Their decisions, however, are likely to be correct.

The introverted thinking type does not get along well with others and has difficulty communicating ideas. These people focus on thought rather than on feelings and have poor practical judgment. Intensely concerned with privacy, they prefer to deal with abstractions and theories, and they focus on understanding themselves rather than other people. Others see them as stubborn, aloof, arrogant, and inconsiderate.

The introverted feeling type represses rational thought. These people are capable of deep emotion but avoid any outward expression of it. They seem mysterious and inaccessible and tend to be quiet, modest, and childish. They have little consideration for others' feelings and thoughts and appear withdrawn, cold, and self-assured.

The introverted sensing type appears passive, calm, and detached from the everyday world. These people look on most human activities with benevolence and amusement. They are aesthetically sensitive, expressing themselves in art or music, and tend to repress their intuition.

The introverted intuiting type focuses so intently on intuition that people of this type have little contact with reality. These people are visionaries and daydreamers—aloof, unconcerned with practical matters, and poorly understood by others. Considered odd and eccentric, they have difficulty coping with everyday life and planning for the future.

The ego, the conscious level of personality, which consists of these attitudes, functions, and psychological types, is of obvious importance in the description of the human personality. However, consciousness forms only the uppermost level of the psyche's structure. Like the lower levels of a building, the two unconscious levels provide support for the upper level. Jung agreed with Freud on the relatively greater role played by the unconscious, but they differed sharply in their views of its nature.

The Personal Unconscious

personal unconscious
The reservoir of material that was once conscious but has been forgotten or suppressed.

In Jung's system, the two levels of the unconscious are the personal unconscious and the collective unconscious. The personal unconscious is the higher, more superficial level; the collective unconscious is the deeper, more profoundly influential level. The **personal unconscious** is similar to Freud's conception of the preconscious. It is a reservoir of material that was once conscious but has been forgotten or suppressed because it was trivial or disturbing.

There is considerable two-way traffic between the ego and the personal unconscious. For example, our attention can wander readily from this printed page to a memory of something we did yesterday. All kinds of experiences are stored in a sort of filing cabinet of our personal unconscious, and little mental effort is required to take something out, examine it for a while, and put it back, where it will remain until the next time we want it or are reminded of it.

complex A core or pattern of emotions, memories, perceptions, and wishes in the personal unconscious organized around a common theme, such as power or status.

As we file more and more experiences in our personal unconscious, we begin to group them into what Jung called complexes. A **complex** is a core or pattern of emotions, memories, perceptions, and wishes organized around a common theme. For example, we might say that a person has a complex about power or status, meaning that he or she is preoccupied with that theme to the point where it influences behavior. The person may try to become powerful by running for elective office, or to identify or affiliate with power by driving a motorcycle or a fast car. By directing thoughts and behavior in various ways, the complex determines how the person perceives the world. Jung wrote: "A person does not have a complex; the complex has him."

Once a complex is formed, it is no longer under conscious control but can intrude on and interfere with consciousness. The person with a complex is not aware of its influence, although other people may easily observe its effects. The majority of complexes Jung detected in his patients were harmful and at least partly responsible for their neurotic condition. However, he noted that complexes can also be useful. For example, a perfection or achievement complex may lead a person to work hard at developing particular talents or skills.

Jung believed that complexes originate not only from our childhood and adult experiences, but also from our ancestral experiences, the heritage of the species contained in the collective unconscious.

The Collective Unconscious

collective unconscious
The deepest level of the psyche containing the accumulation of inherited experiences of human and prehuman species; also called the **transpersonal unconscious.**

The deepest and least accessible level of the psyche, the **collective unconscious**, is the most unusual and controversial aspect of Jung's system; to critics, it is the most bizarre. Jung believed that just as each of us accumulates and files all personal experiences in the personal unconscious, so does humankind collectively, as a species, store the experiences of the human and prehuman species in the collective unconscious. This heritage is passed to each new generation. The collective unconscious contains a wealth of experience, the entire evolutionary catalog. It is somehow transmitted to each of us, repeated in the brain of every human being (Jung, 1919).

Whatever experiences are universal—those that are repeated relatively unchanged by each generation—become part of our personality. Our primitive past becomes the basis of the human psyche, directing and influencing present behavior. To Jung, the collective unconscious was the "all-controlling deposit of ancestral experiences." Jung linked each person's personality with the past, not only with childhood but also with the history of the species.

We do not inherit these collective experiences directly; For example, we do not inherit a fear of snakes. Rather, we inherit the potential to fear snakes. We are predisposed to behave and feel the same ways people have always behaved and felt. Whether the predisposition becomes reality depends on the specific experiences each of us encounters in life.

Jung believed that certain basic experiences have characterized every generation throughout human history. People have always had a mother figure, for example, and have experienced birth and death. They have faced unknown terrors in the dark, worshipped power or some sort of godlike figure, and feared an evil being. The universality of these experiences over countless evolving generations leaves an imprint on each of us at birth and determines how we perceive and react to our world. Jung wrote: "The form of the world into which [a person] is born is already inborn in him, as a virtual image" (Jung, 1953, p. 188).

A baby is born predisposed to perceive the mother in a certain manner. Assuming the mother behaves the way we generally think mothers should behave, the baby's predisposition will correspond with its reality. The inborn form of the infant's world determines how it comprehends and reacts to that world.

Because the collective unconscious is such an unusual concept, it is important for us to explore the reason Jung proposed it and the kind of evidence he gathered to support it. In his reading about ancient cultures, both mythical and real, Jung discovered common themes and symbols that appeared in diverse parts of the world. As far as he could determine, these ideas had not been transmitted or communicated orally or in writing from one culture to another.

In addition, Jung's patients, in their dreams and fantasies, recalled and described for him the same kinds of symbols he had discovered in ancient cultures. He could find no other explanation for these shared symbols and themes over such vast geographical and temporal distances than that they were transmitted by and carried in each person's unconscious mind.

Archetypes

archetypes Images of universal experiences contained in the collective unconscious.

The ancient experiences contained in the collective unconscious are manifested by images that Jung called **archetypes** (Jung, 1947). There are many such images of universal experiences—as many as there are common human experiences. By being repeated in the lives of succeeding generations, archetypes have become imprinted on our psyche.

Archetypes are not fully developed memories. We cannot see an archetype as we can clearly see a picture of some past event or person in our own life. Rather, an archetype is a predisposition that awaits an actual life event before its content becomes clear. Archetypes are expressed in our dreams and fantasies. Some of the archetypes Jung proposed are expressed in conceptions of the hero, the mother, the child, God, death, power, and the wise old man. A few of these are developed more fully than others and influence the psyche more consistently. These major archetypes include the persona, the anima and animus, the shadow, and the self.

persona The public face or role a person presents to others.

The word *persona* refers to a mask that an actor wears to display various roles or faces to the audience. Jung used the term with basically the same meaning. The **persona** archetype is a mask, a public face we wear to present ourselves as someone different from who we really are. The persona is necessary, Jung believed, because we are forced to play many roles in life in order to succeed in school and on the job and to get along with a variety of people.

Although the persona can be helpful, it can also be harmful. We may come to believe that the persona reflects our true nature. By playing a role, we may become that role. As a result, other aspects of our personality will be compromised and will not be allowed to develop. Jung described the process this way: The ego may come to identify with the persona rather than with the person's true nature, resulting in a condition known as inflation of the persona. Whether the person plays a role or comes to believe that role, he or she is resorting to deception. In the first instance, the person is deceiving others; in the second instance, the person is deceiving himself or herself.

anima/animus archetypes Feminine aspects of the male psyche/masculine aspects of the female psyche.

The **anima** and **animus** refer to Jung's recognition that humans are essentially bisexual. On the biological level, each sex secretes the hormones of the other sex as well as those of its own sex. On the psychological level, each sex manifests characteristics, temperaments, and attitudes of the other sex by virtue of centuries of living together. The psyche of the woman contains masculine aspects (the animus archetype), and the psyche of the man contains feminine aspects (the anima archetype).

These opposite sex characteristics aid in the adjustment and survival of the species because they enable a person of one sex to understand the nature

In the fully developed personality, a person will express behaviors considered characteristic of the opposite sex.

of the other sex. The archetypes predispose us to like certain characteristics of the opposite sex; these characteristics guide our behavior with reference to the opposite sex.

Jung insisted that both the anima and the animus be expressed. A man must exhibit his feminine as well as his masculine characteristics, and a woman must express her masculine characteristics along with her feminine ones. Otherwise, these vital aspects will remain dormant and undeveloped, leading to a one-sidedness of the personality. A person in this condition cannot be well-adjusted because one aspect of personality has been suppressed.

The most powerful archetype Jung proposed has the sinister and mysterious name of the **shadow**. When he wrote of the collective unconscious as the repository of past experiences, he included our prehuman or animal ancestry. The shadow contains the basic, primitive animal instincts and therefore has the deepest roots of all the archetypes. Behaviors that society considers evil and immoral reside in the shadow, and this dark side of human nature must be tamed if people are to live in harmony. We must restrain, overcome, and defend against these primitive impulses. If we do not, society will likely punish us.

But we face a dilemma. Not only is the shadow the source of evil, it is also the source of vitality, spontaneity, creativity, and emotion. Therefore, if the shadow is totally suppressed, the psyche will be dull and lifeless. It is the ego's function to direct the shadow's forces, to repress the animal instincts

shadow The dark side of personality; the archetype that contains primitive animal instincts.

enough so that we are considered civilized while allowing sufficient expression of the instincts to provide creativity and vigor.

If the shadow is fully suppressed, not only does the personality become flat, but the person also faces the possibility that the shadow will revolt. The animal instincts do not disappear when they are suppressed. Rather, they lie dormant, awaiting a crisis or a weakness in the ego so they can gain control. When that happens, the person becomes dominated by the unconscious.

self To Jung, the archetype that represents the unity, integration, and harmony of the total personality.

The archetype of the **self** represents the unity, integration, and harmony of the total personality. To Jung, the striving toward that wholeness is the ultimate goal of life. The self archetype involves bringing together and balancing all parts of the personality. We have already noted Jung's principle of opposites and the importance of polarities to the psyche. In the self archetype, conscious and unconscious processes become assimilated so that the self—the center of the personality—shifts from the ego to a point of equilibrium midway between the opposing forces of the conscious and the unconscious. As a result, material from the unconscious comes to have a greater influence on the personality.

The full realization of the self lies in the future. It is a goal, something to strive for but rarely achieved. The self serves as a motivating force, pulling us from ahead rather than (as in our past experiences) pushing us from behind.

The self archetype cannot begin to emerge until the other systems of the psyche have developed. This occurs around middle age, which, in Jung's theory, is a crucial period of transition, as it was in his own life. The actualization of the self involves goals and plans for the future and an accurate perception of one's abilities. Because development of the self is impossible without self-knowledge, it is the most difficult process we face in life and requires persistence, perceptiveness, and wisdom.

The Development of the Personality

Jung's personality theory looks toward the future; achieving self-realization involves plans and goals. Therefore, Jung believed that our personality is determined by what we hope to be as well as by what we have been. Jung criticized Freud for emphasizing only past events as shapers of personality. Jung believed that, individually and as a species, we develop and grow regardless of age, always moving toward a more complete level of fulfillment.

Jung took a longer view of personality than Freud, who concentrated on the early years of life and foresaw little development after the age of 5. Jung did not posit sequential stages of growth in as much detail as Freud, but he wrote of specific periods in the overall developmental process (Jung, 1930).

Childhood to Young Adulthood

Jung had relatively little to say about the childhood years and believed they were not very decisive in establishing a fixed personality pattern. Initially infants are governed primarily by physical instincts and have no psychological problems because their conscious ego has not yet formed. The baby is concerned with little more than food, emptying bladder and bowels, and sleep.

The ego begins to develop in early childhood, at first in a primitive way because the child has not yet formed a unique identity. What might be called the child's personality is little more than a reflection of the personalities of its parents. Obviously, then, parents exert a great influence on the formation of the child's personality. They can enhance or impede personality development by the way they behave toward the child.

Parents might try to force their personalities on the child, desiring him or her to be an extension of themselves. Or they might expect their child to develop a personality different from their own as a way of seeking vicarious compensation for their deficiencies. The ego begins to form substantively only when children become able to distinguish between themselves and other people or objects in their world. In other words, consciousness forms when the child is able to say "I."

It is not until puberty that the psyche assumes a definite form and content. This period, which Jung called our psychic birth, is marked by difficulties and the need to adapt. Childhood fantasies must end as the adolescent confronts the demands of reality. From the teenage years through young adulthood, we are concerned with preparatory activities such as completing our education, beginning a career, getting married, and starting a family. Our focus during these years is external, our conscious is dominant, and, in general, our primary conscious attitude is that of extraversion. The aim of life is to achieve our goals and establish a secure, successful place for ourselves in the world. Thus, young adulthood should be an exciting and challenging time, filled with new horizons and accomplishments.

Middle Age to Old Age

Major personality changes begin to occur between the ages of 35 and 40. This period of middle age was a time of crisis for Jung and many of his patients. The adaptational problems of young adulthood had been resolved. The typical 40-year-old was established in a career, a marriage, and a community. Why, Jung asked, when success has been achieved, are so many people gripped by feelings of despair and worthlessness? His patients all told him essentially the same thing: They felt empty. Adventure, excitement, and zest had disappeared. Life had lost its meaning.

The more Jung analyzed this period, the more strongly he believed that such drastic personality changes were inevitable and universal. Middle age was a natural time of transition in which the personality was supposed to undergo necessary and beneficial changes. Ironically, the changes occurred because middle-aged persons had been so successful in meeting life's demands. These people had invested a great deal of energy in the preparatory activities of the first half of life, but by age 40 that preparation was finished and those challenges had been met. Although they still possessed considerable energy, the energy now had nowhere to go; it had to be rechanneled into different activities and interests.

Jung noted that in the first half of life we focus on the objective world of reality—education, career, and family. The second half of life must be devoted to the inner, subjective world that heretofore had been neglected. The attitude of the personality must shift from extraversion to introversion. The focus on consciousness must be tempered by an awareness of the unconscious. Our interests must shift from the physical and material to the spiritual, philosophical, and intuitive. The one-sidedness of the personality (that is, the focus on consciousness) must be remedied, replaced by a balance among all facets of the personality. Thus, at middle age we naturally begin the process of realizing or actualizing the self. If we are successful in integrating the unconscious with the conscious, we are in a position to attain a new level of positive psychological health, a condition Jung called individuation.

individuation
A condition of psychological health resulting from the integration of all conscious and unconscious facets of the personality.

Simply stated, **individuation** involves becoming an individual—fulfilling one's capacities and developing one's self. The tendency toward individuation is innate and inevitable, but it will be helped or hindered by environmental forces, such as one's educational opportunities and the nature of the parent-child relationship.

To strive for individuation, middle-aged persons must abandon the behaviors and values that guided the first half of life and confront their unconscious, bringing it into conscious awareness and accepting what it tells them to do. They must listen to their dreams and follow their fantasies, exercising creative imagination through writing, painting, or some other form of expression. They must let themselves be guided, not by the rational thinking that drove them before, but by the spontaneous flow of the unconscious. Only in that way can the true self be revealed.

Jung cautioned that admitting unconscious forces into conscious awareness does not mean being dominated by them. The unconscious forces must be assimilated and balanced with the conscious. At this time of life, no single aspect of personality should dominate. An emotionally healthy middle-aged person is no longer ruled by consciousness or unconsciousness, by a specific attitude or function, or by any of the archetypes. All are brought into harmonious balance when individuation is achieved.

Of particular importance in the midlife process of individuation is the shift in the nature of the archetypes. The first change involves dethroning the persona. Although we continue to play various social roles to function in the real world and get along with different kinds of people, we must recognize that our public personality may not represent our true nature. Further, we must come to accept the genuine self the persona has been covering.

Next, we become aware of the destructive forces of the shadow and acknowledge the dark side of our nature with its primitive impulses, such as selfishness. We do not submit to them or allow them to dominate us but simply accept their existence. In the first half of life, we use the persona to shield this dark side from ourselves, wanting people to see only our good

Middle age is a time of transition, when one's focus and interests change.

qualities. But in concealing the forces of the shadow from others, we conceal them from ourselves. This must change as part of the process of learning to know ourselves. A greater awareness of both the destructive and the constructive aspects of the shadow gives the personality a deeper and fuller dimension, because the shadow's tendencies bring zest, spontaneity, and vitality to life.

Once again we see this central theme in Jung's individuation process—that we must bring each aspect of the personality into harmony with all other aspects. Awareness of only the good side of our nature produces a one-sided development of the personality. As with other opposing components of personality, both sides of this dimension must be expressed before we can achieve individuation.

We must also come to terms with our psychological bisexuality. A man must be able to express his anima archetype or such traditionally feminine traits as tenderness, and a woman must come to express her animus or such traditionally masculine traits as assertiveness. Jung believed that this recognition of the characteristics of the other sex was the most difficult step in the individuation process because it represents the greatest change in our self-image. Accepting the emotional qualities of both sexes opens new sources of creativity and serves as the final release from parental influences.

Once the psyche's structures are individuated and acknowledged, the next developmental stage can occur. Jung referred to this as transcendence, an innate tendency toward unity or wholeness in the personality, uniting all the opposing aspects within the psyche. Environmental factors, such as an unsatisfactory marriage or frustrating work, can inhibit the process of transcendence and prevent the full achievement of the self.

The final stage in personality development is old age. Jung wrote little about this period, but he noted a similarity between the last years of life and the first. In childhood and old age, the unconscious dominates the personality. Elderly persons should not look backward; instead, they need goals to orient themselves toward the future. Jung suggested that the decline in religious values was harmful to society because fewer people believed in the promise or goal of life after death. He thought that the inevitability of death should be viewed as a goal because our psychological well-being depends on having something for which to strive.

Jung's Image of Human Nature

Jung's image of human nature is quite different from Freud's. Jung did not hold such a deterministic view, but he did agree that personality may be partly determined by childhood experiences and by the archetypes. However, there is room in Jung's system for free will and spontaneity, the latter arising from the shadow archetype.

On the nature-nurture issue, Jung took a moderate position. The drive toward individuation and transcendence is innate, but it can be aided or thwarted by learning and experience. The ultimate and necessary goal of life is the realization of the self. Although it is rarely achieved, we are continually motivated to strive for it.

Jung disagreed with Freud on the importance of childhood experiences. Jung thought they were influential but did not completely shape our personality by age 5. We are affected more by our experiences in middle age and by our hopes and expectations for the future.

Each individual is unique, but only during the first half of life. When some progress toward individuation is made in middle age, we develop what Jung designated as a universal kind of personality in which no single aspect is dominant. Thus, uniqueness disappears, and we can no longer be described as one or another particular psychological type.

Jung presented a more positive, hopeful image of human nature than Freud did, and his optimism is apparent in his view of personality development. We are motivated to grow and develop, to improve and develop ourselves. Progress does not stop in childhood, as Freud had assumed, but continues throughout life; we always have the hope of becoming better. Jung argued that the human species also continues to improve. Present generations represent a significant advance over our primitive ancestors.

Despite his basic optimism, Jung expressed concern about a danger facing Western culture. He referred to this danger as a sickness of dissociation. By placing too great an emphasis on materialism, reason, and empirical science, we are in danger of failing to appreciate the forces of the unconscious.

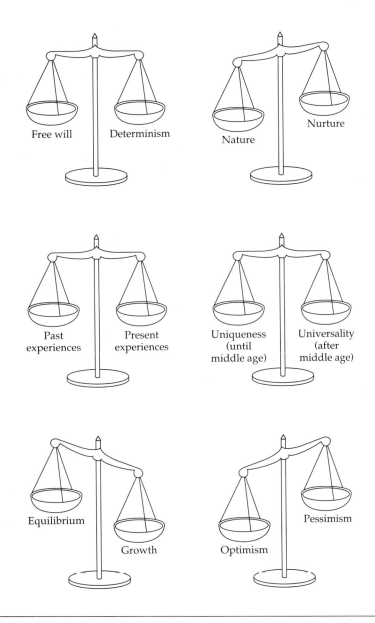

Image of Human Nature.

We must not abandon our trust in the archetypes that form our heritage. Thus, Jung's hopefulness about human nature was a watchful, warning kind.

Assessment in Jung's Theory

Jung's techniques for assessing the functioning of the psyche drew on both science and the supernatural, resulting in an objective and a mystical approach. He investigated a variety of cultures and eras and recorded their symbols, myths, religions, and rituals. He formed his personality theory through his patients' fantasies and dreams and his explorations of ancient languages, alchemy, and astrology. Yet the work that brought Jung to the attention of psychologists in the United States involved empirical and physiological assessments. His techniques were an unorthodox blend of opposites— not surprising for a theory based on the principle of opposition.

His sessions with patients were unusual, even chaotic. His patients did not lie on a couch—"I don't want to put the patient to bed," he remarked (quoted in Brome, 1981, p. 177). Usually Jung and the patient sat in comfortable chairs facing each other, although sometimes Jung faced a window so he could look out at the lake near his house. Occasionally he took patients aboard his sailboat. And sometimes he could be rude. When one patient appeared at the appointed time, he said, "Oh no. I can't stand the sight of another one. Just go home and cure yourself today" (quoted in Brome, 1981, p. 185).

The three basic techniques Jung used to evaluate personality are the word-association test, symptom analysis, and dream analysis. A widely used self-report personality test, the Myers-Briggs Type Indicator, was developed to assess the psychological types Jung proposed.

Word Association

word-association test
A projective technique in which a person responds to a stimulus word with whatever word comes to mind.

The **word-association test**, in which a subject responds to a stimulus word with whatever word comes immediately to mind, has become a standard laboratory and clinical tool in psychology. In the early 1900s, Jung used the technique with a list of 100 words he believed were capable of eliciting emotions. Jung measured the time it took for a patient to respond to each word. He also measured physiological reactions to determine the emotional effects of the stimulus words. Some of the response words he considered normal and neurotic are shown in Table 3.1.

Jung used word association to uncover complexes in his patients. A variety of factors indicated the presence of a complex; these factors include physiological responses, delays in responding, making the same response to different words, slips of the tongue, stammering, responding with more than one word, making up words, or failing to respond.

Symptom Analysis

Symptom analysis focuses on the symptoms reported by the patient and is based on the person's free associations to those symptoms. It is similar to Freud's cathartic method. Between the patient's associations to the symptoms and the analyst's interpretation of them, the symptoms will often be relieved or disappear.

Dream Analysis

Jung agreed with Freud that dreams are the "royal road" into the unconscious. Jung's approach to dream analysis differed from Freud's in that Jung

Table 3.1   *Normal and neurotic responses to Jung's word-association test.*

Stimulus word	Normal response	Neurotic response
Blue	Pretty	Color
Tree	Green	Nature
Bread	Good	To eat
Lamp	Bright	To burn
Rich	Beautiful	Money—I don't know
To sin	Much	This idea is totally alien to me; I do not acknowledge it
Needle	To prick	To sew
To swim	Healthy	Water

SOURCE: C. G. Jung, "The Association Method," 1909. In *The Collected Works of C. G. Jung,* Volume 2 (Princeton, NJ: Princeton University Press, 1973), pp. 442–444.

was concerned with more than the causes of dreams, and he believed that dreams were more than unconscious wishes. First, dreams are prospective; that is, they help us prepare for experiences and events we anticipate will occur. Second, dreams are compensatory; they help bring about a balance between opposites in the psyche by compensating for the overdevelopment of any one psychic structure.

Instead of interpreting each dream separately, as Freud did, Jung worked with a series of dreams reported by a patient over a period of time. In that way Jung believed he could discover recurring themes, issues, and problems, material that persisted in the patient's unconscious.

Jung also used amplification to analyze dreams. In Freudian free association, the patient begins with one element in a dream and develops a chain of associations from it by reporting related memories and events. Jung focused on the original dream element and asked the patient to make repeated associations and responses to it until he detected a theme. He did not try to distinguish between manifest and latent dream content.

The Myers-Briggs Type Indicator

An assessment instrument related to Jung's personality theory is the Myers-Briggs Type Indicator (MBTI), developed in the 1920s by Katharine Cook Briggs and Isabel Briggs Myers (Briggs & Myers, 1943, 1976). Katharine Briggs was interested in the similarities and differences among personalities and pursued an independent study of the topic. In 1923 she read Jung's book *Psychological Types* and found that her view of personality was similar to Jung's. Without research grant support, university affiliation, or graduate students to assist her, she and her daughter Isabel developed a self-report inventory that is still widely used for research and applied purposes, especially for employee selection and counseling (McCaulley, 1990; Saunders, 1991). Sample items from the MBTI are shown in Table 3.2.

The Myers-Briggs Type Indicator has become the primary method for conducting research on Jung's eight psychological types and the attitudes of introversion and extraversion. It has also spurred the development of a com-

Table 3.2   ***Sample items from the Myers-Briggs Type Indicator.***

Which answer comes closer to telling how you usually feel or act?
1. When you go somewhere for the day, would you rather
   (a) plan what you will do and when, or
   (b) just go?
2. Do you tend to have
   (a) deep friendships with a very few people, or
   (b) broad friendships with many different people?
3. When you have a special job to do, do you like to
   (a) organize it carefully before you start, or
   (b) find out what is necessary as you go along?
4. When something new starts to be the fashion, are you usually
   (a) one of the first to try it, or
   (b) not much interested?
5. When the truth would not be polite, are you more likely to tell
   (a) a polite lie, or
   (b) the impolite truth?

SOURCE: Consulting Psychologists Press. Copyright ©1976, 1977 by Isabel Briggs Myers. Copyright 1943, 1944, 1957 by Katharine C. Briggs and Isabel Briggs Myers.

puter software program, Negotiator Pro, that is used for training people in the skills needed to conduct successful negotiations. The program is based on MBTI profiles of the psychological types of persons involved in negotiations (Lewis, 1991).

In 1975, Isabel Briggs Myers and Mary McCaulley established the Center for Applications of Psychological Type for MBTI training and research. In 1979, the Association for Psychological Type was founded. Two journals publish research reports on applications of the test. The MBTI has become the most visible practical outgrowth of Jung's work on the human personality.

Two other personality tests, the Maudsley Personality Inventory and the Eysenck Personality Inventory, were developed by psychologist Hans Eysenck (see Chapter 9) to measure Jung's attitudes of introversion and extraversion (Eysenck, 1947; Eysenck & Eysenck, 1963).

Research in Jung's Theory

life-history reconstruction Jung's type of case study that involves examining a person's past experiences to identify developmental patterns that may explain present neuroses.

Jung, like Freud, used the case study method, which Jung called **life-history reconstruction**. It involved an extensive recollection of a person's past experiences in which Jung sought to identify the developmental patterns that he believed led to the present neurotic condition. The criticisms in Chapter 2 of Freud's data and research methods also apply to Jung's work. His data did not rely on objective observation and were not gathered in a controlled and systematic fashion. Further, the situations in which they were obtained—the clinical interviews—were not amenable to duplication, verification, or quantification.

Like Freud, Jung did not keep verbatim records of his patients' comments, nor did he attempt to verify the accuracy of their reports. Jung's case studies involved (as did Freud's) a small and unrepresentative sample of people, making it difficult to generalize to the population at large.

Jung's analysis of the data was subjective and unreliable. We do not know how he analyzed his data because he never explained his procedures. It is obvious that the data were subjected to some of the most unusual interpretations of any personality theory. We noted earlier that Jung studied a variety of cultures and disciplines. It was on this basis, and that of his own dreams and fantasies, that he interpreted the information gathered from his patients.

He reported similarities between his patients' dreams and the archetypes, those ancient and universal symbols and themes he said were contained in the psyches of all past and present generations. He suggested that the ritualistic and mythological history of the species was acted out in every person's life. Thus, an inquiry into the psyche of one of us is an inquiry into the psyche of all. The problem is that many of Jung's observations cannot be submitted to experimental test. Jung himself was indifferent to this criticism and commented that anyone who ''wishes to know about the human mind will learn nothing, or almost nothing, from experimental psychology'' (quoted in Ellenberger, 1970, p. 694).

Studies of Psychological Type

Despite Jung's view of experimental psychology, researchers have been able to submit aspects of Jungian theory to experimental test, with results that uphold some of Jung's propositions. Most of the supportive research uses the MBTI and focuses on the attitudes of introversion and extraversion. However, not all research supports the delineation of the psychological types (Cowan, 1989; DeVito, 1985; McCrae & Costa, 1989).

A study of college students found that their job interests were closely related to Jungian attitudes and psychological types (Stricker & Ross, 1962). Introverts showed strong interests in occupations that did not involve personal interaction, such as technical and scientific work. Extraverts were more interested in jobs that offered high levels of social interaction, such as sales and public relations.

Another study using the MBTI revealed that different psychological types are drawn to different professions (Hanewitz, 1978). The test was administered to a large sample of police officers, schoolteachers, and social work and dental school students. The teachers and social work students showed high levels of intuiting and feeling. Police officers and dental school students, who deal with people in a different way from teachers and social workers, scored high in extraversion and in sensing and thinking.

Jungian personality types appear to differ in cognitive or mental functioning. Researchers concluded that persons categorized as introverted thinking types have better memories for neutral or impersonal stimuli, such as numbers. Persons labeled extraverted feeling types have better memories for human stimuli with emotional overtones, such as facial expressions (Carlson & Levy, 1973).

Also, introverted thinking and extraverted feeling types differ in their ability to recall significant personal experiences (Carlson, 1980). When subjects were asked to recall their most vivid experiences involving such emotions as joy, anger, and shame, extraverted feeling types most often reported memories involving other people. Introverted thinking types more frequently recalled events that occurred when they were alone. In addition, extraverted feeling types recalled highly emotional details, whereas introverted thinking types remembered more emotionally neutral and factual experiences.

Persons classified as introverts and extraverts on the MBTI were compared on the quality of their classroom discussion in undergraduate psychology courses (Carskadon, 1978). Extraverts contributed little to the discussion, but introverts made frequent, thoughtful contributions. Students high in intuiting on the MBTI made the best classroom contributions, whereas those high in sensing made the poorest contributions.

Research using the Maudsley Personality Inventory and the Eysenck Personality Inventory also provides support for the psychological types. Persons high in extraversion were found to be more popular than those high in introversion (Brown & Hendrick, 1971). Introverts were more sensitive to pain and to stimulation, more easily bored, and more careful in their work than extraverts. Introverts also learned more quickly and forgot more slowly (Wilson, 1978). In other research, extraverts were shown to be more suggestible, more sexually active, more likely to earn lower grades in school, and more strongly predisposed to jobs that would bring contact with other people (Pervin, 1984).

The Sixteen Personality Factor (16 PF) Questionnaire, developed by Raymond Cattell (see Chapter 9), also measures introversion and extraversion. Research using this test suggests that occupational differences can be predicted from Jung's descriptions of the psychological types. For example, introversion was found to be high among researchers and artists; extraversion was high among engineers and fire fighters (Cattell, 1957).

Research on the origins of introversion and extraversion point to both genetic and environmental influences. Studies of twins provide evidence of an inherited component to the two attitudes (Wilson, 1977). Significant differences have been found among the parents of introverts and extraverts. Parents of introverts were described as rejecting and cold; parents of extraverts were more accepting and loving (Siegelman, 1988).

In research on dreams to study the occurrence of the archetypes, subjects were asked to recall their most recent dream, their most vivid dream, and their earliest dream (Cann & Donderi, 1986). For approximately three weeks, they were asked to record the dreams of the previous night as soon as they awakened each morning. Subjects were also given the MBTI and the Eysenck Personality Inventory. The results showed that introverts were more likely than extraverts to recall everyday dreams, those that bore no relation to archetypes. Intuiting types recalled more archetypal dreams than did sensing types. Persons who scored high in neuroticism recalled fewer archetypal dreams than those who scored low in neuroticism. The researchers concluded that these findings agreed with predictions made on the basis of Jung's personality theory.

A Final Commentary

Jung's complex and unusual approach to the human personality has had a considerable impact on such disciplines as psychiatry, cultural history, sociology, economics, political science, philosophy, and religion. Recognized by the intellectual community at large, Jung received honorary degrees from Harvard and Oxford universities and has been acknowledged as a powerful influence on the work of many scholars.

Within psychology, Jung made several important and lasting contributions. The word-association test is a standard projective technique and inspired the development of the Rorschach inkblot test and so-called lie-detection techniques. The concepts of psychological complexes and of introverted versus extraverted personalities are well accepted in psychology today, and the personality scales that measure introversion and extraversion are widely used as diagnostic and selection devices.

We will see Jung's influence on the work of several theorists discussed in later chapters. Jung's notion of individuation, or self-actualization, anticipated the work of Abraham Maslow and other personality theorists. Jung was the first to emphasize the role of the future in determining behavior, an idea adopted by Alfred Adler. Portions of Henry Murray's theory can also be traced to Jung's ideas. Jung's suggestion that middle age is a time of crucial personality change was embraced by Maslow, Erik Erikson, and Raymond Cattell. The idea of a midlife crisis is now seen by many as a necessary stage of personality development and has been supported by considerable research.

Despite the significance of these formulations, the bulk of Jung's theory was not received enthusiastically by psychologists. One reason concerns the difficulty of understanding Jungian concepts. Sigmund Freud, Alfred Adler, Erich Fromm, and others wrote with a clarity of style that allows their books to be easily read and understood. Jung did not write for the general public. Reading his work can be frustrating, so beset are his books by inconsistencies and contradictions. Jung once said, "I can formulate my thoughts only as they break out of me. It is like a geyser. Those who come after me will have to put them in order" (quoted in Jaffé, 1971, p. 8).

In addition, the lack of systematization in Jung's theory makes it difficult to evaluate. Jung opposed the notion of presenting a finished and consistent system and was distrustful of establishing an orthodoxy, an approved path to the truth. "Thank God," he wrote, "I am Jung and not a Jungian."

Jung's embrace of the occult and the supernatural is probably the source of most of the criticism directed at his theory. Evidence from mythology and religion is not in favor in an era when reason and science are considered the only legitimate approaches to knowledge and understanding. Critics charge that Jung accepted as scientific evidence the mythical and mystical occurrences his patients reported. However, the mystical and religious content of Jung's theory may be responsible for the burst of growth, vitality, and acceptance enjoyed by Jungian psychology in the 1960s and 1970s. Several books about Jung and his analytical psychology were published during that time, and many people, particularly college students, found his ideas congenial with their interests in Eastern religions and existentialism and with a growing disaffection with materialism.

Formal training in Jungian analysis is available in New York, San Francisco, Los Angeles, and several other American cities. There are also Jungian training institutes in a number of European countries. The Society of Analytical Psychology publishes the Jungian *Journal of Analytical Psychology.* Thus, interest in Jung's ideas remains strong.

Summary

Carl Jung broadened Freud's definition of libido, redefining it as a more generalized dynamic force. Jung argued that personality is shaped by the future as well as the past, and he placed greater emphasis on the unconscious. Jung used the term *libido* in two ways: a diffuse, generalized life energy and a narrower energy that fuels the psyche. The amount of energy invested in an idea or feeling is called a value. Psychic energy operates in accordance with the principles of opposites, equivalence, and entropy. The principle of opposites states that every aspect of the psyche has its opposite and that this opposition generates psychic energy. The principle of equivalence states that energy is never lost to the personality but is shifted from one part to another. The principle of entropy states that there is a tendency toward equilibrium in the personality.

The ego or conscious mind is concerned with perceiving, thinking, feeling, and remembering. Part of our conscious perception is determined by the attitudes of introversion and extraversion, in which libido is channeled internally or externally. The psychological functions include thinking, feeling, sensing, and intuiting. Thinking and feeling are rational functions: sensing and intuiting are irrational. Only one attitude and function can be dominant. The psychological types are formed by combinations of the attitudes and functions.

The personal unconscious is a reservoir of material that was once conscious but has been forgotten or suppressed. Complexes, which are part of the personal unconscious, are patterns of emotions, memories, perceptions, and wishes centering on common themes. The collective unconscious is a storehouse of the experiences of humankind transmitted to each individual. Archetypes are images that express these experiences. The most powerful archetypes are the persona (the role each person plays in public), anima (the feminine aspects of a man's psyche), animus (the masculine aspects of a woman's psyche), shadow (the repository of primitive animal instincts and of spontaneity and creativity), and self (the unity, wholeness, and integration of the personality).

The ego forms when the infant can distinguish between self and other objects. Psychic birth occurs at puberty, when the psyche assumes definite form and content. Preparatory activities mark the time from adolescence through young adulthood. In middle age, when success has been achieved, the personality changes. Psychic energy must be rechanneled into the inner world of the unconscious, and the attitude must shift from extraversion to introversion. Individuation (the realization of one's capabilities) can occur only in middle age, when people must confront the unconscious and abandon the behaviors and values that guided the first half of life. Transcendence involves the unification of the personality. In old age, as in childhood, the unconscious is dominant.

Jung's image of human nature was more optimistic and less deterministic than Freud's. Jung believed that part of personality is innate, and part is learned. The ultimate life goal is individuation. Childhood experiences are important, but personality is more affected by midlife experiences and hopes for the future. Personality is unique in the first half of life but not in the second.

Jung's methods of assessment include the investigation of symbols, myths, and rituals in ancient cultures; the word-association test, used to uncover complexes; symptom analysis, in which patients free-associate to their symptoms; and dream analysis. Assessment instruments deriving from Jung's approach are the Myers-Briggs Type Indicator, the Maudsley Personality Inventory, and the Eysenck Personality Inventory.

Jung's case study method, called life-history reconstruction, did not rely on objective observation, was not systematic and controlled, and was not amenable to duplication and verification.

Research has supported Jung's ideas on attitudes and functions, but broader aspects of his theory have resisted attempts at scientific validation. His work has had considerable influence in several fields. Widely accepted Jungian ideas include the word-association test, complexes, introversion-extraversion, self-actualization, and the midlife crisis.

Critical Thinking Review

1. Discuss three major points of difference between Carl Jung's theory of analytical psychology and Sigmund Freud's theory of psychoanalysis.

2. Describe the principles of opposites, equivalence, and entropy. How do they relate to the concept of psychic energy?

3. How does the principle of opposites apply to the attitudes and functions?

Explain how the eight psychological types derive from the attitudes and functions.

4. What is the relationship between the ego and the personal unconscious? How does the personal unconscious differ from the collective unconscious?

5. What is a complex? According to Jung, how can a complex be helpful to a person?

6. Distinguish between the persona archetype and the self archetype.

7. What are the similarities between Jung's concept of the shadow archetype and Freud's concept of the id?

8. Discuss Jung's ideas on the development of personality throughout the life span, especially the periods of adolescence and middle age.

9. What is individuation? How must our archetypes change for us to achieve individuation?

10. How does Jung's image of human nature differ from Freud's?

11. What is the purpose of the word-association test? What are the purposes of dreams?

12. Describe recent research on the introverted and extraverted personality types.

Suggested Reading

Ellenberger, H. F. (1970). *The discovery of the unconscious: The history and evolution of dynamic psychiatry*. New York: Basic Books. Traces the study of the unconscious from primitive times to Freudian psychoanalysis and its derivatives. See Chapter 9, "Carl Gustav Jung and Analytical Psychology."

Freud/Jung letters. (1974). Princeton, NJ: Princeton University Press. Contains some 360 letters, dating from 1906 to 1913, that show the development and dissolution of the friendship between Sigmund Freud and Carl Jung. Edited by William McGuire.

Hannah, B. (1976). *Jung: His life and work*. New York: Putnam. A biographical memoir by a Jungian analyst who was a friend of Jung's for more than 30 years.

Jung, C. G. (1961). *Memories, dreams, reflections*. New York: Vintage Books. Jung's recollections of his life, written at the age of 81.

Jung, C. G. (1967–1976). *Collected works of C. G. Jung*. Princeton, NJ: Princeton University Press (Bollingen Series). Collects Jung's writings in 19 volumes edited by Herbert Read, Michael Ford-

ham, and Gerhard Adler. These are available in most college libraries.

Roazen, P. (1975). *Freud and his followers*. New York: Knopf. A lively, well-written account of Freud's life and of the men and women who became his disciples, some of whom later broke away to form their own schools of thought. See Part 6, "The 'Crown Prince': Carl Gustav Jung."

Schultz, D. (1990). *Intimate friends, dangerous rivals: The turbulent relationship between Freud and Jung*. Los Angeles: Tarcher. Describes the personal and professional collaboration between Freud and Jung and describes parallels and differences in their childhoods, midlife crises, and relationships with women.

Stern, P. J. (1976). *C. G. Jung: The haunted prophet*. New York: Braziller. A provocative biography depicting Jung's life as a war against "inner demons."

Tilander, A. (1991). Why did C. G. Jung write his autobiography? *Journal of Analytical Psychology, 36*(1), 111–124. Uses Allport's personal-document technique (see pp. 212–213 of this book) to evaluate Jung's autobiography (*Memories, Dreams, Reflections*). Suggests that Jung chose to present those personal experiences that appeared to support his personality theory.

Whitmont, E. C., & Perera, S. B. (1989). *Dreams: A portal to the source.* London: Routledge & Kegan Paul. Provides a guide to the Jungian approach to understanding and interpreting dreams, which are seen as crucial to personality development.

Alfred Adler

The Life of Adler (1870–1937)
*Inferiority Feelings: The Source of Human
    Striving*
Striving for Superiority or Perfection
Style of Life
Social Interest
Birth Order
    The First-Born Child
    The Second-Born Child
    The Youngest Child
    The Only Child

Adler's Image of Human Nature
Assessment in Adler's Theory
    Early Recollections
    Dream Analysis
    Measures of Social Interest
Research in Adler's Theory
A Final Commentary
Summary
Critical Thinking Review
Suggested Reading

The goal of the human soul is conquest, perfection, security, superiority. Every child is faced with so many obstacles in life that no child ever grows up without striving for some form of significance.

—Alfred Adler

individual psychology Adler's theory of personality.

Alfred Adler fashioned an understanding of human nature that did not depict people as victimized by instincts and conflict and doomed by biological forces and childhood experiences. He called his approach **individual psychology** because it focused on the uniqueness of each person and denied the universality of biological motives and goals ascribed to us by Sigmund Freud.

In Adler's opinion, each individual is primarily a social being. Our personalities are shaped by our unique social environments and interactions, not by our efforts to satisfy biological needs. Sex, of primary importance to Freud as a determining factor in personality, was minimized by Adler in his system. Rather than being driven by forces we cannot see and control, we are actively involved in creating our selves and directing our future. Thus, to Adler, the conscious, not the unconscious, is at the core of personality.

We have with Adler and Freud two vastly different theories created by two men brought up in the same city in the same era and educated as physicians at the same university. There was only a 14-year difference in their ages. We will see that, as with Freud, aspects of Adler's childhood may have presaged his way of looking at human nature.

The Life of Adler (1870–1937)

Adler's early childhood was marked by illness, an awareness of death, and jealousy of his older brother. He suffered from rickets (a vitamin D deficiency characterized by softening of the bones), which kept him from playing with other children. At the age of 3 he saw his younger brother die in bed. At 4, Adler himself was close to death from pneumonia. He heard the doctor tell his father, "Your boy is lost." He later said that was when he decided to become a doctor himself (Orgler, 1963, p. 16).

Pampered by his mother because of his sickness, the young Adler was dethroned at the age of 2 by the arrival of another baby. Biographers have suggested that Adler's mother may then have rejected him, but he was clearly his father's favorite. Therefore, his childhood relations with his parents were different from Freud's. (Freud was closer to his mother than to his father.) As an adult, Adler discarded the Freudian concept of the Oedipus complex because it was so foreign to his childhood experiences.

Adler was jealous of his older brother, who was vigorous and healthy and could engage in the physical activities and sports in which Alfred could not take part. "I remember sitting on a bench," he wrote, "bandaged up on account of rickets, with my healthy elder brother sitting opposite me. He could run, jump, and move about quite effortlessly, while for me, movement of any sort was a strain and an effort" (quoted in Bottome, 1939, pp. 30–31).

Adler felt inferior to this brother and to other neighborhood children, who all seemed healthier and more athletic. As a result, he resolved to work hard to overcome his feelings of inferiority and to compensate for his physical limitations. Despite his small stature, clumsiness, and unattractiveness—legacies of his illness—he forced himself to join in games. Gradually he won his victory and achieved a sense of self-esteem and social acceptance. He developed a fondness for the company of other people and retained this sociability all his life. In his personality theory, Adler emphasized the importance of the peer group and suggested that childhood relationships with siblings and with children outside the family were much more significant than Freud believed.

In school Adler was initially unhappy and was only a mediocre student. Believing that the boy was unfit for anything else, a teacher advised his father to apprentice him to a shoemaker. Adler was particularly bad in mathematics, but he persisted and eventually rose from being a failing student to the top of his class.

In many ways, the story of Adler's childhood reads like a tragedy, but it is also a textbook example of his personality theory, of overcoming childhood weaknesses and inferiorities to shape his destiny. The theorist who would give the world the notion of inferiority feelings spoke from the depths of his own childhood. "Those who are familiar with my life work," he said, "will clearly see the accord existing between the facts of my childhood and the views I expressed" (quoted in Bottome, 1939, p. 9). One of Adler's biographers gave her book the subtitle "triumph over the inferiority complex" (Orgler, 1963).

Fulfilling his childhood ambition, Adler studied medicine at the University of Vienna. He entered private practice as an ophthalmologist but soon shifted to general medicine. He was interested in incurable diseases but became so distressed at his helplessness to prevent death, particularly in younger patients, that he chose to specialize in neurology and psychiatry.

Adler's nine-year association with Freud began in 1902, when Freud invited Adler and three others to meet once a week at Freud's home to discuss psychoanalysis. Their relationship never became close; Freud said that Adler bored him. Adler was never a student or disciple of Freud's and was not psychoanalyzed by him. One of Freud's colleagues charged that Adler did not have the ability to probe the unconscious mind and psychoanalyze people. It is interesting to speculate on whether this supposed lack led Adler to base his personality theory on consciousness and to minimize the role of the unconscious.

By 1910, although Adler was president of the Vienna Psychoanalytical Society and co-editor of its journal, he was also an increasingly vocal critic of Freudian theory. A year later he severed all connections with psychoanalysis and went on to develop individual psychology, his own approach to personality. Freud reacted to Adler's defection with bitterness and hostility. In his anger, he belittled Adler's height (Adler was five inches shorter than Freud), saying, "I have made a pygmy great" (quoted in Wittels, 1924, p. 225). He wrote to Carl Jung:

> Adler is a very decent and highly intelligent man, but he is paranoid. . . . he puts so much stress on his almost unintelligible theories that the readers must be utterly confused. He is always claiming priority, putting new names on everything, complaining that he is disappearing under my shadow, and forcing me into the unwelcome role of the aging despot who prevents young men from getting ahead. [Freud & Jung, 1974, p. 373]

Adler evidenced equal bitterness toward Freud and denounced psychoanalysis as "filth" (quoted in Roazen, 1975, p. 210).

In 1912, Adler founded the Society for Individual Psychology. He served in the Austrian army during World War I (1914–1918) and afterward organized government-sponsored child counseling clinics in Vienna. In his clinics, Adler introduced group training and guidance procedures, forerunners of modern group therapy techniques. In 1926, he made the first of several visits to the United States, where he taught and gave popular lecture tours. On a strenuous 56-lecture tour in Scotland in 1937, he suffered a heart attack and died.

Inferiority Feelings: The Source of Human Striving

inferiority feelings
The normal condition of all people; the source of all human striving.

Inferiority feelings is one of many terms from psychology that have come into everyday use in the English language. It derives from Adler's approach to personality. Adler believed that a general feeling of inferiority is always present and is a motivating force in behavior. "To be a human being," Adler wrote, "means to feel oneself inferior" (Adler, 1933/1939, p. 96). Because this condition is common to all people, it is not a sign of weakness or abnormality.

compensation A motivation to overcome inferiority, to strive for higher levels of development.

Adler proposed that inferiority feelings are the source of all human striving and the force that determines our behavior. Individual progress, growth, and development result from our attempts to **compensate** for our inferiorities, whether real or imagined. Throughout our lives, we are driven by the need to overcome this sense of inferiority and to strive for increasingly higher levels of development.

The process begins in infancy. Infants are small and helpless and are totally dependent on adults. Adler believed that the infant is aware of its parents' greater power and strength and of the hopelessness of trying to resist or challenge that power. As a result, the infant develops feelings of inferiority relative to the larger, stronger people around it.

Although this initial experience of inferiority applies to everyone in infancy, it is not genetically determined. Rather, it is a function of the environment, which is the same for all infants—helplessness and dependency on adults. Thus, inferiority feelings are inescapable, but more important, they are necessary because they provide the motivation to strive and grow.

Suppose a child does not grow and develop. What happens when the child is unable to compensate for his or her feelings of inferiority? An inability to overcome inferiority feelings intensifies them, leading to the development of an **inferiority complex**. People with an inferiority complex have a poor opinion of themselves and feel helpless and unable to cope with the demands of life. Adler defined this condition as an "inability to solve life's problems," and he found such a complex in the childhoods of many adults who came to him for treatment.

inferiority complex A condition that develops when a person is unable to compensate for normal inferiority feelings.

An inferiority complex can originate in three ways in childhood: through organic inferiority, through spoiling, or through neglect.

The investigation of organic inferiority, Adler's first major research effort, was carried out while he was still associated with Sigmund Freud, who approved of the notion. Adler concluded that defective parts or organs of the body shape personality through the person's efforts to compensate for the defect or weakness, just as Adler had compensated for rickets, the physical inferiority of his childhood years. For instance, a child who is physically weak might focus on that weakness and work to develop superior athletic ability. History records many examples of such compensation: In ancient times the Greek statesman Demosthenes overcame a stutter to become a great orator. The sickly Theodore Roosevelt, 26th president of the United States, became a model of physical fitness as an adult. Efforts to overcome organic inferiority can result in striking artistic, athletic, and social accomplishments, but if these efforts fail, they can lead to an inferiority complex.

Adler's work is another example of a conception of personality developed along intuitive lines, drawn from the theorist's personal experience, and later confirmed by data from patients. Adler's office in Vienna was near an amusement park, and his patients included entertainers and performers, such as gymnasts. They possessed extraordinary physical skills that, in many cases, were developed as a result of hard work to overcome childhood disabilities.

Many people with physical disabilities strive to compensate for their weaknesses.

Spoiling or pampering a child can also bring about an inferiority complex. Spoiled children are the center of attention in the home. Their every need or whim is satisfied, and little is denied them. Under the circumstances, these children naturally develop the idea that they are the most important persons in any situation and that others should defer to them. The first experience at school—where these children are no longer the focus of attention—comes as a shock for which they are unprepared. Spoiled children have little social feeling and are impatient with others. They have never learned to wait for what they want, nor have they learned to overcome difficulties or adjust to others' needs. When confronted with obstacles on the path to gratification, spoiled children come to believe that they must have some personal deficiency that is thwarting them; hence, an inferiority complex develops.

It is easy to understand how neglected, unwanted, and rejected children can develop an inferiority complex. Their infancy and childhood are characterized by a lack of love and security because their parents are indifferent or hostile. As a result, these children develop feelings of worthlessness, or even anger, and view others with distrust.

Whatever the source of the complex, a person may tend to overcompensate and so develop what Adler called a **superiority complex**. This involves an exaggerated opinion of one's abilities and accomplishments. Such a person may feel inwardly self-satisfied and superior and show no need to demonstrate their superiority with accomplishments. Or the person may feel

superiority complex
A condition that develops when a person overcompensates for normal inferiority feelings.

such a need and work to become extremely successful. In both cases, persons with a superiority complex are given to boasting, vanity, self-centeredness, and a tendency to denigrate others.

Inferiority feelings are the source of motivation and striving, but to what end? Do we desire simply to be rid of inferiority feelings? Adler believed that we work for something more; however, his view of our ultimate goal in life changed over the years. First he identified inferiority with a general feeling of weakness or—in recognition of the inferior standing of women in the society of his day—of femininity. He spoke of compensation for this feeling as the "masculine protest." The goal of the compensation was a will or a drive toward power in which aggression, a supposedly masculine characteristic, played a large part. Later he rejected the idea of equating inferiority feelings with femininity and developed a broader viewpoint in which we strive for superiority or perfection.

Striving for Superiority or Perfection

striving for superiority or perfection The urge toward perfection or completion that motivates each of us.

Adler described his notion of **striving for superiority** as the fundamental fact of life (Adler, 1930, pp. 398–399). Superiority is the ultimate goal toward which we strive. He did not mean superiority in the usual sense of the word, nor did the concept relate to the superiority complex. Striving for superiority is not an attempt to be better than anyone else, nor is it an arrogant or domineering tendency or an inflated opinion of our abilities and accomplishments. What Adler meant was a drive for perfection. The word *perfection* is derived from a Latin word meaning "to complete" or "to finish." Thus, Adler suggested that we strive for superiority in an effort to perfect ourselves; that is, to make ourselves complete or whole.

This innate goal—the drive toward wholeness or completion—is oriented toward the future. Whereas Freud proposed that human behavior is determined by the past (that is, by the instincts and by our childhood experiences), Adler saw human motivation in terms of expectations for the future. He argued that we cannot appeal to instincts or primal impulses as explanatory principles. Only the ultimate goal of superiority or perfection can explain personality and behavior.

Adler applied the term *finalism* to the idea that we have an ultimate goal, a final state of being, and a need to move toward it. The goals for which we strive, however, are potentialities, not actualities. In other words, we strive for ideals that exist in us subjectively. Adler believed that our goals are fictional or imagined ideals that cannot be tested against reality. We live our lives around such ideals as the belief that all people are created equal or that all people are basically good. These beliefs influence the ways we perceive and interact with other people. For example, if we believe our behaving a certain way will be rewarded in heaven, we will try to act according to that belief. Confidence in the existence of heaven is not based on reality, but it is real to the person who holds that view.

fictional finalism The idea that there is an imagined or potential goal that guides our behavior.

Adler formalized this concept as **fictional finalism**, the notion that fictional ideas guide our behavior as we strive toward a complete or whole state of being. We direct the course of our lives by many such fictions, but the most pervasive one is the ideal of perfection. He suggested that the best formulation of this ideal developed by human beings so far is the concept of God.

There are two additional points to note about striving for superiority. First, it increases rather than reduces tension. Unlike Freud, Adler did not believe that our sole motivation was to reduce tension. Striving for perfection requires great expenditures of energy and effort, a condition quite different from equilibrium or a tension-free state. Second, the striving for superiority is manifested both by each person and by society. We are very much social beings. We strive for superiority or perfection not only as individuals but also as members of a group; we try to achieve the perfection of our culture. In Adler's view, individuals and society are interrelated and interdependent. People must function constructively with others for the good of all.

Thus, to Adler, human beings perpetually strive for the fictional, ideal goal of perfection. How in our daily lives do we try to attain this goal? Adler answered this question with his concept of the style of life.

Style of Life

style of life A unique character structure or pattern of personal behaviors and characteristics by which each of us strives for perfection. Basic styles of life include the **dominant, getting, avoiding,** and **socially useful** types.

The ultimate goal for all of us may be superiority or perfection, but we try to attain that goal through many specific behaviors. Each of us expresses the striving differently. We develop a unique pattern of characteristics, behaviors, and habits, which Adler called a distinctive character or **style of life**.

To understand how the style of life develops, we return to the concepts of inferiority feelings and compensation. Infants are afflicted with inferiority feelings that motivate them to compensate for helplessness and dependency. In these attempts at compensation, children acquire a set of behaviors. For example, the sickly child may strive to increase physical prowess by running or lifting weights. These behaviors become part of the style of life, a pattern of behaviors designed to compensate for an inferiority.

Everything we do is shaped and defined by our unique style of life. It determines which aspect of our environment we attend to or ignore and what attitudes we hold. The style of life is learned from social interactions that occur in the early years of life. According to Adler, the style of life is so firmly crystallized by the age of 4 or 5 that it is difficult to change thereafter.

The style of life becomes the guiding framework for later behavior. As we stated earlier, its nature depends on social interactions, especially the person's order of birth within the family and the nature of the parent-child relationship. For example, one condition that can lead to an inferiority complex is neglect. Neglected children may feel inferior in coping with the demands of life and therefore may become distrustful and hostile toward others. Their resulting style of life may involve seeking revenge, resenting others' success, and taking whatever they feel is their due.

You may have spotted an apparent inconsistency between Adler's notion of style of life and our earlier comments that his theory was more optimistic and less deterministic than Freud's. Adler said we are in control of our fate, not victims of it. But now we find that the style of life is determined by social relationships in the early years and subject to little change after that. This seems almost as deterministic as the Freudian view, which emphasized the importance of early childhood in the formation of the adult personality. However, Adler's theory is not as deterministic as it may seem at first. He resolved the dilemma by proposing a concept he described as the **creative power of the self**.

creative power of the self The ability to create an appropriate style of life.

In his writings, Adler used several terms interchangeably: *style of life, personality, character, individuality,* and *self.* But whatever terms he used, Adler expressed his belief that the style of life is created by the individual. We create our selves, our personality; we are not passively shaped by childhood experiences. Those experiences are not as important as our conscious attitude toward them. Adler argued that neither heredity nor environment provides a complete explanation for personality development. Instead, the way we interpret these influences forms the basis for the creative construction of our attitude toward life.

Adler argued for the existence of individual free will that allows each of us to create an appropriate style of life from the abilities and experiences given us by both our genetic endowment and our social environment. Although unclear on specifics, Adler insisted that our style of life is not determined for us; we are free to choose and create it ourselves. Once created, however, the style of life remains constant throughout life.

Adler described several problems that all of us face, and he grouped them in three categories: problems involving our behavior toward others, problems of occupation, and problems of love. He proposed four basic styles of life that people can adopt for dealing with these problems:

1. the dominant type
2. the getting type
3. the avoiding type
4. the socially useful type

The first type displays a **dominant** or ruling attitude with little social awareness. Such a person behaves without regard for others. The more extreme of this type attack others and become sadists, delinquents, or sociopaths. The less virulent become alcoholics, drug addicts, or suicides; they believe they hurt others by attacking themselves.

The **getting** type, which Adler considered the most common, expects to receive satisfaction from other people and so becomes dependent on them.

The **avoiding** type makes no attempt to face life's problems. By avoiding difficulties, the person avoids any possibility of failure.

These three types are not prepared to face or cope with the problems of everyday life. They are unable to cooperate with other people, and the clash between their style of life and the real world results in abnormal behavior manifested in neuroses and psychoses. They lack what Adler called "social interest."

The **socially useful** type cooperates with others and acts in accordance with their needs. Such persons cope with problems within a well-developed framework of social interest.

Adler was generally opposed to rigidly classifying or typing people in this way, stating that he proposed these four styles of life solely for teaching purposes. He cautioned therapists to avoid the mistake of assigning people to mutually exclusive categories.

Social Interest

social interest Our innate potential to cooperate with other people to achieve personal and societal goals.

Adler believed that getting along with others is the first task we encounter in life. Our subsequent level of social adjustment, which is part of our style of life, influences our approach to all of life's problems. He proposed the concept of **social interest**, which he defined as the individual's innate potential to cooperate with other people to achieve personal and societal goals. Adler's term for this concept in the original German is best translated as "community interest" (Stepansky, 1983, p. xiii). However, *social interest* has become the accepted term in English.

Although we are influenced more strongly by social than biological forces, in Adler's view, the potential for social interest is innate. In that limited sense, Adler's approach has a biological element. However, the extent to which our innate potential for social interest is realized depends on our early social experiences.

No one is detached from other people or from obligations toward them. From earliest times, people have congregated in families, tribes, and nations. Communities are indispensable to human beings for protection and survival. Thus, it has always been necessary for people to cooperate, to express their social interest. The individual must cooperate with and contribute to society to realize personal and communal goals.

The newborn is in a situation that requires cooperation—initially from the mother, then from other family members and people at day care or school. Adler noted the importance of the mother as the first person with whom the baby comes in contact. Through her behavior toward the child, the mother can either foster social interest or thwart its development. The mother's influence also depends on how the child interprets her behavior (this relates to Adler's idea of the creative power of the self).

The mother must teach the child cooperation, companionship, and courage. Only if children feel kinship with others can they act with courage in attempting to cope with life's demands. Children—and later, adults—who look upon others with suspicion and hostility will approach life with the same attitude. Those who have no feeling of social interest may become neurotics or even criminals. Adler noted that evils ranging from war to racial hatred to public drunkenness stemmed from a lack of community feeling.

He suggested that a wide latitude exists in social feelings. Some people, such as Mother Teresa, devote all their time and energy to helping others. Other people choose a selfish existence and make no contribution to the community. Still others sacrifice excessively for a group but have no social interest at an individual level—for example, in members of their own family. Adler did not favor subordinating oneself wholly to the wants and needs of others. Rather, he urged a cooperative approach in which we strive to develop our abilities in concert with efforts to improve society.

Early in his career Adler suggested that people were driven by a lust for power and a need to dominate. During this time, he was struggling to establish his own point of view within the Freudian circle. After he broke with Freud and achieved recognition for his own work, he proposed that people are motivated more by social interest than by the needs for power and dominance. When Adler was part of Freud's group, he was considered cantankerous and ambitious, quarreling over the priority of his ideas. But years later, commented a Freud biographer, "success had brought [Adler] a certain benignity" (Jones, 1955, p. 130). As Adler changed, his system also changed—from emphasizing power and dominance as motivating forces to stressing the more benign force of social or community interest.

Birth Order

One of Adler's most enduring contributions is the idea that order of birth is a major social influence in childhood, one from which we create our style of life. Even though siblings have the same parents and live in the same house, they do not have identical social environments. Being older or younger than one's siblings and being exposed to differing parental attitudes create different childhood conditions that help determine personality. Adler liked to amaze lecture audiences and dinner guests by guessing a person's order of birth on the basis of his or her behavior. He wrote about four situations: the first-born child, the second-born child, the youngest child, and the only child.

The First-Born Child

First-born children are in a unique and enviable situation. Usually the parents are happy at the birth of the first child and devote considerable time and attention to the new baby. First-borns typically receive their parents' instant and undivided attention. As a result, first-borns have a happy, secure existence until the second-born child appears. Then, no longer the focus of attention, no longer receiving constant love and care, first-borns are, in Adler's word, "dethroned." The affection first-borns received during their reign must now be shared. They must often submit to the outrage of waiting until after the newborn's needs have been met; they are admonished to be quiet so as not to disturb the new baby.

No one could expect first-borns to suffer this drastic displacement with-

One's order of birth within the family—being older or younger than one's siblings—creates different conditions of childhood that can affect personality.

out putting up a fight. They try to recapture their former position of power and privilege. Adler believed that all first-borns feel the shock of their changed status in the family, but those who have been excessively pampered feel a greater loss. Also, the extent of the loss depends on the first-born's age at the time the rival appears. In general, the older a first-born child is when the second child arrives, the less dethronement the first-born will experience. For example, an 8-year-old will be less upset by the birth of a sibling than will a 2-year-old.

The first-born's battle to regain supremacy in the family is lost from the beginning; things will never be the same, no matter how hard the first-born tries. For a time, however, first-borns may become stubborn, ill-behaved, and destructive and may refuse to eat or go to bed. They are striking out in anger, but the parents will probably strike back—and their weapons are far more powerful. When first-borns are punished for their troublesome behavior, they may interpret the punishment as additional evidence of their fall and may grow to hate the second child, who is, after all, the cause of the problem.

Adler found that first-borns are often oriented toward the past, locked in nostalgia and pessimistic about the future. Having learned the advantages of power at one time, they remain concerned with it throughout life. They can exercise some power over younger siblings, but at the same time they are more subject to the power of their parents because more is expected of them.

First-borns take an interest in maintaining order and authority. They become good organizers, conscientious and scrupulous about detail, authoritarian and conservative in attitude. Sigmund Freud was a first-born; Adler described him as a "typical eldest son." First-borns may grow up to feel insecure and hostile toward others. Adler found that neurotics, perverts, and criminals were often first-borns.

The Second-Born Child

Second-born children, the ones who caused such upheaval in the lives of first-borns, are also in a unique situation. They never experience the powerful position once occupied by the first-borns. Even if another child is brought into the family, second-borns do not suffer the sense of dethronement felt by the first-borns. Furthermore, by this time the parents have usually changed their child-rearing attitudes and practices. A second baby is not the novelty the first was; parents may be less concerned and anxious about their own behavior and may take a more relaxed approach to the second child.

From the beginning, second-borns have a pacesetter in the older sibling. The second child is not alone but always has the example of the older child's behavior as a model, a threat, or a source of competition. Adler was a second-born child who had a competitive relationship with his older brother (whose name, incidentally, was Sigmund). Even when Adler became a famous analyst, he felt overshadowed by his brother, who was a wealthy businessman. Adler never overcame this sense of rivalry.

Competition with the first-born motivates the second-born, often stimulating a more rapid development than the first-born exhibited. Second-borns strive to catch up to and surpass the older sibling, a goal that spurs language and motor development. Second-borns usually begin to speak at an earlier age than first-borns. Not having experienced power, second-borns are not as concerned with it. They are more optimistic about the future and are likely to be competitive and ambitious, as Adler was.

Other outcomes may arise from the relationship between first-borns and second-borns. If, for example, the older sibling excels in sports or scholarship, the second-born may feel that he or she can never surpass the first-born and may give up trying. In this case, competitiveness would not become part of the second-born's style of life.

The Youngest Child

Youngest or last-born children never face the shock of dethronement by another child and often become the pet of the family, particularly if the siblings are more than a few years older. Driven by the need to surpass older siblings, youngest children often develop at a remarkably fast rate. Last-borns are often high achievers in whatever work they undertake as adults.

The opposite can occur if the youngest children are excessively pampered and come to believe they needn't learn to do anything for themselves. As they grow older, such children may retain the helplessness and dependency of childhood. Unaccustomed to striving and struggling, used to being cared for, these people find it difficult to adjust to adulthood.

The Only Child

Only children never lose the position of primacy and power they hold in the family; they remain the focus and center of attention. Spending more time in the company of adults than a child with siblings, only children often mature early and manifest adult behaviors and attitudes.

Only children are likely to experience difficulties when they find that in areas of life outside the home, such as school, they are not the center of attention. Only children have learned neither to share nor to compete. If their abilities do not bring them sufficient recognition and attention, they are likely to feel keenly disappointed.

With his ideas about order of birth, Adler was not proposing firm rules of childhood development. A child will not automatically acquire a particular kind of character based solely on his or her position in the family. What Adler was suggesting was the likelihood that certain styles of life will develop as a function of order of birth combined with one's early social interactions. Both are used by the creative self in constructing the style of life.

Adler's Image of Human Nature

Adler's system provides a hopeful, flattering picture of human nature that many consider a welcome antidote to Sigmund Freud's dreary view. Certainly it is more satisfying to our sense of self-worth to consider ourselves capable of consciously shaping our development and destiny rather than dominated by instinctual forces and childhood experiences over which we have no control.

Adler's image is an optimistic one: We are not driven by unconscious forces. We possess the free will to shape the social forces that influence us and to use them creatively to construct a unique style of life. This uniqueness is another aspect of Adler's flattering picture; Freud's system offered a depressing universality and sameness in human nature.

Although, in Adler's view, some aspects of human nature are innate— for example, the potential for social interest and striving for perfection—it is experience that determines how these inherited tendencies will be realized. Childhood influences are important (particularly order of birth and interactions with our parents), but we are not victims of childhood events. Instead, we use them to create our style of life.

Adler saw each person as striving to achieve perfection, and he viewed humanity in similar terms; he was optimistic about social progress. He was attracted to socialism and was involved in school guidance clinics and prison reform, expressing his belief in the creative power of the individual.

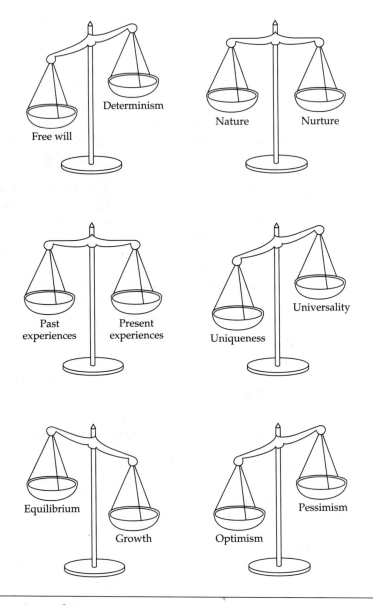

Adler

Image of Human Nature.

Assessment in Adler's Theory

Like Freud, Adler developed his theory by analyzing his patients, by evaluating their verbalizations and behavior during therapy sessions. Adler's approach was more relaxed and informal than Freud's. Whereas Freud's patients lay on a couch while he sat behind them, Adler and his patients faced each other, seated in comfortable chairs. The sessions were more like chats between friends than like the formal relationships maintained by Freud.

Adler assessed the personalities of his patients by observing everything about them—the way they walked and sat, their manner of shaking hands, even their choice of which chair to sit in. Anticipating the modern notion of body language, Adler suggested that the way we use our bodies indicates something of our style of life. Even the position in which we sleep is revealing: Those who sleep flat on their back desire to seem bigger than they are. Sleeping on one's stomach shows a stubborn and negative personality.

Adler's primary methods of assessment, which he called the "entrance gates to mental life," are order of birth (discussed earlier in this chapter), early recollections, and dream analysis. In addition, contemporary psychologists have developed psychological assessment tests based on Adler's concept of social interest. Adler's purpose in assessing personality was to discover the patient's style of life and to determine whether it was the most appropriate one for that person.

Early Recollections

early recollections A personality assessment technique in which our earliest memories, whether of real events or fantasies, are assumed to reveal our primary interest in life.

A person's **early recollections** provide an excellent guide to uncovering the style of life. According to Adler, our personality is created during our first four or five years. Our earliest memories from that period indicate the style of life that continues to characterize us as adults. Adler found that it made little difference whether his clients' early recollections were of real events or were fantasies. In either case the primary interest of the person's life revolved around the remembered incidents.

Adler asked more than 100 colleagues, all physicians, to describe their early memories. A majority of the recollections were concerned with illness or with a death in the family, which apparently led them to pursue a career in medicine, as was the case with Adler himself.

An early memory Adler recalled as an adult was that when he was 5 years old and had just started school, he was fearful because the path to school led through a cemetery (Adler, 1924/1963). He said he became terrified every time he walked to school, but he was also confused because other children seemed not to notice the cemetery. He was the only one who was afraid, and this experience heightened his sense of inferiority. One day Adler decided to put an end to his fears. He placed his schoolbag on the ground and ran through the cemetery 12 times, until he felt he had overcome his feelings. Thereafter he was able to attend school without being frightened whenever he passed the cemetery.

This recollection reveals something about Adler's personality. It suggests that from an early age he tried to overcome his fears, to compensate for them by choosing to act bravely, and to harden himself so that he would not feel inferior to others. But there is more to the story of this early recollection. Thirty years later Adler met a former schoolmate and, in the course of their conversation, asked if the old cemetery was still there. The man expressed surprise and told Adler there had never been a cemetery near the school.

Adler was shocked. His recollection had been so vivid. He sought out

Our earliest memories of childhood help reveal our style of life.

other classmates and questioned them about the cemetery. They all told him the same thing: There had been no cemetery. Adler realized that although his memory of the incident was faulty, it symbolized the fear and inferiority, and his efforts to overcome them, that characterized his style of life. He concluded that the early recollection thus revealed an important and influential aspect of his personality.

Although Adler believed that each early memory should be interpreted within the context of the patient's style of life, he found commonalities among them. He suggested that memories involving danger or punishment indicated a tendency toward hostility. Those concerning the birth of a sibling showed a continued sense of dethronement. Memories that focused on one parent showed a preference for that parent. Recollections of improper behavior warned against any attempt to repeat the behavior.

Dream Analysis

Adler agreed with Freud about the value of dreams in understanding personality but disagreed on the way in which dreams should be interpreted. Adler did not believe that dreams fulfill wishes or reveal hidden conflicts. Rather, dreams involve our feelings about a current problem and what we intend to do about it.

Adler suggested that dreams engender feelings and emotions. As proof, he pointed to the fact that often we cannot recall the specific events of a dream, but we do remember its mood. For example, we remember whether a dream was scary or comforting, even though we cannot recall its story in detail. The moods evoked by a dream can deceive us, weakening our common sense and logical thinking. In the fantasies of our dreams (both night dreams and daydreams), we believe we can surmount the most difficult obstacle or simplify the most complex problem. To Adler, that is the purpose of dreams: to help us solve present problems. Dreams are oriented toward the present and future, not toward conflicts from the past.

Dreams should never be interpreted without knowledge of the person and his or her situation. The dream is a manifestation of a person's style of life and so is unique to the individual.

From his work with patients, Adler found some common interpretations for dreams. Many people, for example, reported dreams involving falling or flying. Freud interpreted such dreams in sexual terms (see pp. 59–60). According to Adler, a dream of falling indicates that the person's emotional view involves a demotion or loss, such as the fear of losing self-esteem or prestige. The viewpoint in a flying dream indicates a sense of striving upward, an ambitious style of life in which the person desires to be above or better than others. Dreams that combine flying and falling involve a fear of being too ambitious and thus failing. A dream of being chased suggests a feeling of weakness in relation to other people. Dreaming that one is naked indicates a fear of giving oneself away.

Measures of Social Interest

Adler was not enthusiastic about the use of psychological tests to assess personality. He argued that tests create artificial situations that provide ambiguous results. Instead of relying on tests, Adler thought therapists should develop their intuition. He did, however, support tests of memory and intelligence; it was personality tests that he criticized.

Psychologists have developed tests to measure Adler's concept of social interest. The Social Interest Scale (SIS) consists of pairs of adjectives (Crandall, 1981). Subjects choose the word in each pair that best describes an attribute they would like to possess. Words such as *helpful, sympathetic,* and *considerate* are thought to indicate one's degree of social interest.

The Social Interest Index (SII) is a self-report inventory in which subjects judge the degree to which statements represent themselves or their personal characteristics (Greever, Tseng, & Friedland, 1973). The items, such as "I don't mind helping out friends," were selected to reflect Adler's ideas and to indicate a person's ability to accept and cooperate with others.

The Sulliman Scale of Social Interest has also been shown to be a promising measure of social interest (Mozdzierz, Greenblatt, & Murphy, 1988; Sulliman, 1973).

Research in Adler's Theory

Adler's primary research method was the case study. Unfortunately, little of Adler's data has survived. He did not publish case histories except for two fragments: one written by a patient, the other written by a patient's physician. Adler did not know the patients involved, but he analyzed their personalities by examining their writings.

Adler's data and research method are subject to the same criticisms we discussed for Freud and Jung. His observations cannot be repeated and duplicated, nor were they conducted in controlled and systematic fashion. Adler did not attempt to verify the accuracy of his patients' reports and did not explain the procedures he used to analyze the data.

Although most of Adler's propositions have resisted attempts at scientific validation, several topics have been the subject of research. These include dreams, early recollections, the effect of neglect in childhood, social interest, and order of birth.

Adler's belief that dreams help us solve current problems was investigated by exposing subjects to situations in which the failure to solve a puzzle was considered a threat to the personality. The subjects were then allowed to sleep. Some were permitted to dream; they were awakened only during non-rapid-eye-movement (NREM) sleep. Others were awakened during rapid-eye-movement (REM) sleep so that they could not dream.

Subjects who dreamed recalled significantly more of the uncompleted puzzle than those who did not dream. By dreaming (presumably about the puzzle), the subjects were able to reduce the impact of their failure (the threat to the ego) and had less need to repress their memory of the situation. Those who did not dream did not have the opportunity to reduce the threat to the personality and presumably repressed the memory of the situation, recalling little of it. The researchers concluded that dreaming enabled subjects to deal effectively with the current ego-threatening situation (Grieser, Greenberg, & Harrison, 1972).

In another study, the dreams of two groups of subjects were reported (Breger, Hunter, & Lane, 1971). One group consisted of college students who were anticipating a stressful psychotherapy session. The other group consisted of patients about to undergo major surgery. For both groups the recalled dreams focused on their conscious worries, fears, and hopes. Both types of subjects dreamed about the current problems they were facing.

Adler's concept of early recollection has been the subject of considerable research. For example, it has been shown that the early memories of persons diagnosed as anxiety neurotics were concerned with fear, early memories of depressed persons centered around abandonment, and early memories of persons with psychosomatic complaints involved illness (Jackson & Sechrest, 1962). Early memories of alcoholics contained threatening events, as well as situations in which they were controlled by external circumstances rather than by their own decisions. The early memories of a control group of nonalcoholics showed neither of these themes (Hafner, Fakouri, & Labrentz, 1982).

Early recollections of adult criminals dealt with disturbing or aggressive interactions with other people. They contained more unpleasant events than the early recollections of a control group (Hankoff, 1987). The early memories of adolescent delinquents involved breaking rules, having difficulty forming social relationships, perceiving parents as untrustworthy and more likely to hurt than to help, and being unable to cope with life on their own. These themes were not present in the early memories of a control group (Davidow & Bruhn, 1990).

Adler suggested that children who were neglected or rejected by their parents developed feelings of worthlessness. A study of 714 adults hospitalized for depression found that the patients rated their parents as having been hostile, detached, and rejecting (Crook, Raskin, & Eliot, 1981). Interviews with siblings, relatives, and friends of the patients confirmed that the parents had indeed behaved in hostile and neglectful ways.

In another study, parents of 8-year-old children completed a questionnaire to assess their child-rearing behaviors and their level of satisfaction with their children (Lefkowitz & Tesiny, 1984). Ten years later the children, then age 18, were given the depression scale of the MMPI. Those whose test scores showed they were more depressed had been neglected in childhood by their parents. Those whose parents had not been indifferent or unloving scored lower on the depression scale.

Research on social interest using the Social Interest Scale tested Adler's suggestion that persons higher in social interest are better adjusted emotionally than persons lower in social interest (Crandall, 1981). Correlations of SIS test scores with data from other self-report measures, peer ratings, and religious activities provided only modest support for Adler's view. The relationship between social interest test scores and the measures of adjustment were low.

Studies with the Social Interest Index showed that women who scored high in social interest were significantly higher in self-actualization, a characteristic of the healthy personality described by Abraham Maslow. Other research found that social interest was higher in women than in men and that it increased with age for both sexes (Greever, Tseng, & Friedland, 1973).

Considerable research has been conducted on the effects of order of birth. Many of these studies were undertaken not to test Adler's ideas but for other reasons. Although not all of the studies have produced supportive results, Adler deserves credit for being the first personality theorist to suggest that order of birth affects behavior and personality.

According to Adler, first-borns are concerned with power and authority. One way for first-borns to gain power and authority as adults is through achievement in their work. If Adler was correct, then first-borns should score high on measures of achievement; this idea has received much research support. In many areas, from college attendance to high-level management, first-borns have been found to be overrepresented relative to their proportion of the population. More first-borns than later-borns become eminent, and they tend to attain greater intellectual achievement in academic settings and greater power and prestige in their careers (Breland, 1974; Schachter, 1963).

First-borns consistently scored higher than later-borns on a variety of achievement tests in English, mathematics, verbal skills, and verbal reasoning (Eysenck & Cookson, 1969; Kellaghan & MacNamara, 1972; Paulhus & Shaffer, 1981). In general, evidence suggests that first-borns may be more intelligent than later-borns. The IQ scores of 400,000 European men were analyzed with respect to birth order (Belmont & Marolla, 1973). The results showed that first-borns had higher IQ scores than second-borns, second-borns had higher scores than third-borns, and so on. These findings were confirmed for men and women in several countries (Zajonc, Markus, & Markus, 1979). Vocational preferences for first-borns were found to include teaching, medicine, science, and management (Bryant, 1987).

An explanation for the apparent higher intelligence of first-borns relates not to genetic differences but to the first-born's exclusive exposure to adults. Consequently, first-borns may have a more stimulating intellectual environment than later-borns.

First-borns tend to be more dependent on other people and more suggestible. They are anxious in stressful situations and have a higher need for social relationships (Schachter, 1963, 1964). These findings could be predicted from Adler's theory. He noted that first-borns are made anxious when dethroned by a sibling, and they attempt to regain their position by eventually conforming to their parents' expectations. Other research found that first-borns scored lower than later-borns on tests of depression and anxiety but scored higher on self-esteem (Gates, Lineberger, Crockett, & Hubbard, 1988).

First-born girls were found to be more obedient and socially responsible than later-borns and tended to feel closer to their parents (Sutton-Smith & Rosenberg, 1970). Although first-borns are outgoing and enjoy socializing, research shows they are not especially popular. First-born boys were more likely than later-borns to exhibit behavior disorders and to be considered aggressive by their teachers (Lahey, Hammer, Crumrine, & Forehand, 1980).

Evidence also suggests that first-borns and only-borns exhibit some of the characteristics of the Type A personality, a pattern associated with heart disease (Ivancevich, Matteson, & Gamble, 1987).

Less research has been conducted on second-born children. There appears to be no support for Adler's contention that they are more competitive and ambitious than their siblings. One study found second-borns to be lower in self-esteem than first-borns or last-borns, particularly if the age difference between them and the other siblings was approximately two years (Kidwell, 1982).

Adler predicted that last-born children, if excessively pampered, would have adjustment problems as adults. It has been suggested that one reason people become alcoholics is that they cannot cope with the demands of everyday life. If so, then more last-borns than early-borns would be likely to become alcoholics. This prediction has been supported by many studies dealing with alcoholism and order of birth (Barry & Blane, 1977). Other research on last-borns shows that last-born children are more popular than first-borns or second-borns (Miller & Maruyama, 1976).

To Adler, only-born adults are overly concerned with being the center of attention, as they were in childhood. They are also considered more selfish than those reared with siblings. Research has not consistently supported this contention. One study found that only-borns demonstrated more cooperative behaviors than first-borns or last-borns (Falbo, 1978). Another study found that only-borns were more self-centered and less popular than children with siblings (Jiao, Ji, & Jing, 1986). An analysis of 115 studies of only-borns reported higher levels of achievement and intelligence than, and comparable social and emotional adjustment with, people who have siblings (Falbo & Polit, 1986). Later research (Mellor, 1990) confirmed those results and found that only children had higher levels of initiative, aspiration, industriousness, and self-esteem. (The senior author of this book is an only child.)

A Final Commentary

Adler's influence within psychology is substantial. In later chapters, we will see examples of his ideas in the work of several personality theorists. These contributions make Adler's personality theory one of the most enduring. He was ahead of his time, and his cognitive and social emphases are more compatible with trends in psychology today than with the psychology of his own day. "Alfred Adler becomes more and more correct year by year," wrote Abraham Maslow. "As the facts come in, they give stronger and stronger support to his image of man" (Maslow, 1970a, p. 13).

Adler's emphasis on social forces in personality can be seen in the theories of Karen Horney and Erich Fromm. His focus on the whole person and the unity of personality is reflected in the work of Gordon Allport. The creative power of the individual in shaping his or her style of life, and the insistence that future goals are more important than past events, influenced the work of Abraham Maslow. A contemporary social-learning theorist, Julian Rotter, wrote that he "was and continue[s] to be impressed by [Adler's] insights into human nature" (Rotter, 1982, pp. 1–2).

Adler's ideas also reached into Freudian psychoanalysis. It was Adler who proposed the aggressive drive—more than 12 years before Freud included aggression with sex as primary motivating forces. The neo-Freudian ego psychologists, who focus more on conscious and rational processes and less on the unconscious, follow Adler's lead.

Specific Adlerian concepts of lasting importance include the early work on organic inferiority, which has influenced the study of psychosomatic disorders; the inferiority complex; compensation; and order of birth. Adler is also considered a forerunner of social psychology and group therapy.

Although his ideas have been widely accepted, Adler's personal recognition declined after his death in 1937, and he has received relatively little subsequent praise or credit for his contributions. Many concepts have been borrowed from his theory without acknowledgment. A typical instance of this lack of recognition can be found in Sigmund Freud's obituary in the *Times* of London, which named Freud as the originator of the term *inferiority complex*. When Carl Jung died, the *New York Times* said he had coined the term. Neither newspaper mentioned Adler, the originator of the concept. However, Adler did receive one unique honor: a British composer named a string quartet for him.

As influential as Adler's work has been, it is not without its critics. Freud charged that Adler's psychology was oversimplified and would therefore appeal to many people because it eliminated the complicated nature of the unconscious, had no difficult concepts, and ignored the problems of sex. Freud remarked that it could take two years or more to learn about his psychoanalysis, but "Adler's ideas and technique can be easily learned in two weeks, because with Adler there is so little to know" (quoted in Sterba, 1982, p. 156).

It is true that Adler's theory seems simpler than Freud's or Jung's, but that was Adler's intention. He wrote that it had taken him 40 years to make his psychology simple. One point that reinforces the charge of oversimplification is that his books are easy to read because he wrote for the general public and because some of them were compiled from his popular lectures. A related charge is that Adler's concepts appear to rely heavily on common-sense observations from everyday life.

Critics allege that Adler was inconsistent and unsystematic in his thinking. His theory contains gaps and unanswered questions. Are inferiority feelings the only problem we face in life? Do all people strive primarily for perfection? Can we become reconciled to a degree of inferiority and no longer attempt to compensate for it? These and other questions that have been posed cannot all be answered adequately by Adler's system; most theorists, however, leave us with unanswered questions.

Many psychologists are concerned by the issue of determinism and free will. Early in his career, Adler did not oppose the notion of determinism. It was broadly accepted in science at the time, and it characterized Freud's position. Later Adler felt the need to grant more autonomy to the self, and his final formulation rejected determinism. His doctrine of the creative self states that, before the age of 5, we create a style of life from material provided by our heredity and environment. However, it is not clear how a child is able to make such momentous decisions. We know that Adler favored free will and opposed the idea that we are victims of innate forces and childhood events. That position is clear, but the specifics of forming the style of life are not.

Adler's followers claim that individual psychology is popular among psychologists, psychiatrists, social workers, and educators. *Individual Psychology: The Journal of Adlerian Theory, Research and Practice* is published quarterly by the North American Society of Adlerian Psychology. Adlerian training institutes have been established in New York, Chicago, and other cities. The Alfred

Adler Institute, originally under the direction of Adler's daughter Alexandra, is located in New York City.

Adlerian counseling techniques have been developed by Rudolph Dreikurs and others, and this work has influenced new generations of Adlerian clinicians in what Dreikurs calls family education centers. Dreikurs's work on child-rearing practices applies Adler's views to contemporary problems not only in child development, but also in the treatment of the family as a whole.

Summary

Alfred Adler's individual psychology differs from Freudian psychoanalysis in its focus on the uniqueness of the individual, on consciousness, and on social rather than biological forces. It minimizes the role of sex. Adler's childhood was characterized by efforts to compensate for inferiorities and by jealousy of his older brother.

Inferiority feelings are the source of all human striving, which results from our attempts to compensate for these feelings. Inferiority feelings are universal and are determined by the infant's helplessness and dependency on adults. An inferiority complex (that is, an inability to solve life's problems) results from being unable to compensate for inferiority feelings. An inferiority complex can originate in childhood through organic inferiority, spoiling, or neglect. A superiority complex (an exaggerated opinion of one's abilities and accomplishments) results from overcompensation.

Our ultimate goal is superiority or perfection; that is, making the personality whole or complete. Fictional finalism refers to fictional ideas, such as the idea of perfection, that guide our behavior. Style of life refers to unique patterns of characteristics and behaviors by which we strive for perfection. Style of life behaviors are designed to compensate for inferiorities. They are learned through childhood social interactions and are established by age 4 or 5. The creative power of the self refers to our ability to create our selves from the materials provided by our heredity and environment.

Four basic styles of life are (1) the dominant or ruling type, which has no social interest, behaves without regard for others, and may attack others; (2) the getting type, which is dependent on others and expects to receive everything from them; (3) the avoiding type, which avoids life's problems; and (4) the socially useful type, which copes with problems by cooperating with others.

Order of birth is a major social influence in childhood from which one's style of life is created. The first-born child suffers the shock of being dethroned when the second child is born. First-borns are oriented toward the past, pessimistic about the future, and concerned with maintaining order and authority. Second-borns compete with first-borns and are apt to be ambitious. Last-borns, spurred by the need to surpass older siblings, may become high achievers. Only children may mature early but are apt to face a shock in school when they are no longer the center of attention.

Adler's image of human nature is more hopeful than Freud's. In Adler's view, people are unique, and they possess free will and the ability to shape their own development. Although childhood experiences are important, we are not victims of them.

Adler's methods of assessment are order of birth, early recollections, and dream analysis. Early recollections can reveal a person's style of life, whether the recollections are of real or imagined events. Dreams reveal our feelings about a current problem and how we would like to resolve it.

Research has provided support for Adler's views on dreams, early memories, and rejection in childhood; for his belief that social interest is related to emotional well-being; for the idea that first-borns are high achievers, dependent on others, suggestible, and anxious under stress; and for the notion that last-borns are more likely to become alcoholics.

Adler's views influenced Freud and the ego psychologists through the notion of the aggressive drive and his focus on conscious, rational processes. Adler's emphasis on social factors in personality, the unity of personality, the creative power of the self, the importance of goals, and cognitive factors has influenced many personality theorists.

Critical Thinking Review

1. In Alfred Adler's theory of individual psychology, what is the difference between inferiority feelings and the inferiority complex? How does each develop?

2. According to Adler, we are motivated by a tendency to strive for superiority or perfection. How does this idea compare with Freud's views on human motivation?

3. Distinguish between the concepts of striving for superiority and the superiority complex.

4. Describe the concept of fictional finalism. How does fictional finalism relate to the concept of striving for superiority?

5. How does the self develop? Do people play an active or a passive role in the development of the self?

6. Describe the four basic styles of life.

7. Discuss some parental behaviors that may foster a child's development of social interest. Which basic style of life is identified with social interest?

8. Describe the personality characteristics that may develop in first-born, second-born, and youngest children as a result of their order of birth within the family.

9. Describe recent research on the personality of first-born children. Do the results support Adler's predictions?

10. How does Adler's image of human nature differ from Freud's?

11. What is the importance of early recollections in personality assessment?

12. What is the purpose of dreams? Does contemporary research on sleep and dreaming support Adler's views?

Suggested Reading

Adler, A. (1930). Individual psychology. In C. Murchison (Ed.), *Psychologies of 1930* (pp. 395–405). Worcester, MA: Clark University Press. Offers a clear exposition of the basic principles of Adler's individual psychology.

Ansbacher, H. L. (1990). Alfred Adler's influence on the three leading cofounders of humanistic psychology. *Journal of Humanistic Psychology, 30*(4), 45–53. Traces Adler's influence, in person and through his writings, on the development of the humanistic psychology movement in the United States, notably through his contact with Abraham Maslow, Carl Rogers, and Rollo May (see Chapters 11 and 12).

Ellenberger, H. F. (1970). *The discovery of the unconscious: The history and evolution of dynamic psychiatry.* New York: Basic Books. Traces the study of the unconscious from primitive times to Freudian psychoanalysis and its derivatives. See Chapter 8, "Alfred Adler and Individual Psychology."

Orgler, H. (1963). *Alfred Adler, the man and his work: Triumph over the inferiority complex.* New York: New American Library. Provides an overview of Adler's life and an introduction to his ideas on personality. Discusses applications of individual psychology to child counseling and education.

Stepansky, P. E. (1983). *In Freud's shadow: Adler in context.* New York: Analytic Press. Discusses Adler's early status as a Freudian disciple and shows the relationship between his ideas on psychotherapy and his training in clinical medicine.

Karen Horney

The Life of Horney (1885–1952)
The Childhood Need for Safety
Basic Anxiety: The Foundation of Neurosis
Neurotic Needs
Neurotic Trends
    The Compliant Personality
    The Aggressive Personality
    The Detached Personality
The Idealized Self-Image

Feminine Psychology: The Flight from
    Womanhood
Horney's Image of Human Nature
Assessment in Horney's Theory
Research in Horney's Theory
A Final Commentary
Summary
Critical Thinking Review
Suggested Reading

*The basic evil is invariably a lack of genuine
warmth and affection.*

—Karen Horney

Karen Danielsen Horney is another defector from the orthodox Freudian
point of view. Though not a disciple or colleague of Freud's, Horney was
trained in the official psychoanalytic doctrine. However, she did not remain
long in the Freudian camp.

Horney began her divergence from Freud's position by disputing his psychological portrayal of women. An early feminist, she argued that psychoanalysis focused more on men's development than on women's. To counter
Freud's contention that women are driven by penis envy, Horney said that in
her observation, men are envious of women for their ability to give birth. "I
know just as many men with womb envy," she said, "as women with penis
envy" (quoted in Cherry & Cherry, 1973, p. 75).

She began her career by insisting that her work was an extension of
Freud's. "I do not want to found a new school," she wrote, "but build on the
foundations Freud has laid" (letter quoted in Quinn, 1987, p. 318). By the
time Horney completed her theory, her criticisms of Freud were so broad that
she had founded a new school, a new approach to psychoanalysis, that had
little in common with Freud's views.

Horney's theory was influenced by her gender and her own personal
experiences, as well as by the social and cultural forces of the time. Working
several decades after Freud's theory was published in Vienna, she formulated
the essential lines of her theory in a radically different culture: that of the
United States. By the 1930s and 1940s, major changes had occurred in popu-

lar attitudes about sex and the roles of men and women. These changes were taking place in Europe, too, but they were more noticeable in the United States.

Horney found that her American patients were so unlike her previous German patients, both in their neuroses and in their normal personalities, that she believed only the different social forces to which they had been exposed could account for the variation. Personality, she argued, cannot depend wholly on biological forces, as Freud proposed. If it did, we would not see differences from one culture to another.

Thus, Horney, like Alfred Adler, placed a greater emphasis than Freud on social relationships as significant factors in personality formation. She argued that sex is not the governing factor in personality, as Freud had claimed, and she questioned his concepts of the Oedipus complex, the libido, and the three-part structure of personality. To Horney, people are motivated not by sexual or aggressive forces but by the need for security. Her view of human nature is flattering and optimistic: we can overcome anxiety and develop our potential to the fullest.

The Life of Horney (1885–1952)

Karen Danielsen was born in a village near Hamburg, Germany. She was the second-born child, and from an early age she envied her older brother, Berndt. He was attractive and charming—the adored first-born—but she was smarter and more vivacious. "It was always my pride," she confided to her diary, "that in school I was better than Berndt, that there were more amusing stories about me than about him" (Horney, 1980, p. 252). She also envied him because he was a boy, and girls were considered inferior. "I know that as a child I wanted for a long time to be a boy, that I envied Berndt because he could stand near a tree and pee" (Horney, 1980, p. 252).

A stronger influence was her relationship with her father. At the time she was born, he was a 50-year-old ship's captain of Norwegian background. Her mother was 33 and of a different temperament. Whereas the father was religious, domineering, imperious, morose, and silent, the mother was attractive, vivacious, and freethinking. Horney's father spent long periods away at sea, but when he was home, the opposing natures of the parents led to frequent arguments. Karen's mother made no secret of her wish to see her husband dead. She told Karen that she had married not out of love but out of fear of becoming a spinster (Sayers, 1991).

We can see roots of Horney's personality theory in her childhood experiences. For most of her childhood and adolescence, she doubted that her parents wanted her. She believed they loved her brother Berndt more than they loved her. At age 16, Horney wrote in her diary, "Why is everything beautiful on earth given to me, only not the highest thing, not love! I have a heart so needing love" (Horney, 1980, p. 30). Although Horney desired her father's love and attention, she was intimidated by him. She recalled his frightening eyes and stern, demanding manner, and she felt belittled and rejected because he made disparaging comments about her appearance and intelligence. "It must be grand to have a father one can love and esteem," she wrote (Horney, 1980, p. 21).

As a way of retaining her mother's affection, she acted the part of the adoring daughter, and until the age of 8 was a model child, clinging and compliant. Despite her efforts, however, she did not believe she was getting sufficient love and security. Her self-sacrifice and good behavior were not working, so she changed tactics and became ambitious and rebellious. Horney decided that if she could not have love and security, she would take revenge for her feelings of unattractiveness and inadequacy. "If I couldn't be beautiful," she said, "I decided I would be smart" (quoted in Rubins, 1978, p. 14). As an adult she came to realize how much hostility she had developed as a child. Her personality theory describes how a lack of love in childhood fosters anxiety and hostility, thus providing another example of a theory developed initially in personal and intuitive terms.

At 14 she developed an adolescent crush on a male teacher and filled her diary with paragraphs about him. She continued to have such infatuations, searching desperately for love, confused and unhappy as many adolescents are. At 17 she awakened to the reality of sex, established a school newspaper for "supervirgins," and roamed streets known to be frequented by prostitutes. The following year she met her first real love, but the relationship lasted only two days. Another man came into her life, prompting 76 pages of soul-searching in her diary. Horney decided that being in love eliminated, at least temporarily, her anxiety and insecurity; it offered an escape (Sayers, 1991).

Although Horney's quest for love and security was often thwarted, her search for a career was straightforward and successful. She decided at the age of 12, after being treated kindly by a physician, that she would become a doctor. Despite the medical establishment's discrimination against women and her father's strong opposition, she worked hard in high school to prepare herself for medical studies. In 1906 she entered the University of Freiburg medical school, only six years after the first woman had, reluctantly, been admitted.

She met two men, one of whom she fell in love with. The other, Oscar Horney, she married three years later. He was studying for a Ph.D. in political science and after their marriage became a successful businessman. Karen Horney excelled in her medical studies and received her degree from the University of Berlin in 1913. The early years of their marriage were a time of personal distress. She gave birth to three daughters but felt overwhelming unhappiness and oppression. She complained of crying spells, stomach pains, sexual problems, and a longing for sleep, even death. The marriage ended in 1927, after 17 years.

During and after her marriage, Horney had several affairs, including one with Erich Fromm. That relationship, begun after her divorce, lasted ten years, longer than any of her others, and she was deeply hurt when it ended.

Although Fromm was 15 years younger, she "may have looked to him as a father figure whom she admired ambivalently. To her great embarrassment, she once introduced Fromm to an American audience as 'Doctor Freud.' " It was a revealing Freudian slip, suggesting "both Fromm's loyalty to Freud and the way this differentiated his work from her own" (Burston, 1991, p. 23).

Horney underwent psychoanalysis in an attempt to deal with her depression and sexual problems. The therapist, Karl Abraham (a loyal follower of Freud's), attributed her problems to her attraction to forceful men, which he explained was a residue of her childhood Oedipal longings for her powerful father. "Her readiness to abandon herself to such patriarchal figures, said Abraham, was betrayed by her leaving her handbag [in Freud's view, a symbolic representation of the female genitals] in his office on her very first visit" (Sayers, 1991, p. 88).

From 1932 to 1952, Horney served on the faculty of psychoanalytic institutes in Chicago and New York. She was a founder of the Association for the Advancement of Psychoanalysis and the American Institute for Psychoanalysis. For many years she was a popular lecturer, writer, and therapist.

The Childhood Need for Safety

safety need A higher-level need for security and freedom from fear.

Horney agreed with Freud, in principle, about the importance of the early years of childhood in shaping the adult personality. However, they differed on the specifics of how personality is formed. Horney believed that social forces in childhood, not biological forces, influence personality development. There are neither universal developmental stages nor inevitable childhood conflicts. Instead, the social relationship between the child and his or her parents is the key factor.

Horney thought that childhood was dominated by the **need for safety**, by which she meant security and freedom from fear (Horney, 1937). Whether the infant experiences a feeling of security and an absence of fear is decisive in determining the normality of its personality development. A child's security depends entirely on how the child is treated by the parents. The major way in which parents weaken or prevent security is by displaying a lack of warmth and affection for the child; this was Horney's situation in childhood. She believed that children can withstand, without appreciable ill effect, much that is usually considered traumatic—such as abrupt weaning, occasional beatings, or premature sexual experiences—as long as they feel wanted and loved and are, therefore, secure.

Parents can act in various ways to undermine their child's security and thereby induce hostility. These parental behaviors include obvious preference for a sibling, unfair punishment, erratic behavior, unkept promises, ridicule, humiliation, and isolation of the child from peers. Horney suggested that children know whether their parents' love is genuine and are not easily fooled by false demonstrations and expressions of affection. The child may repress the hostility engendered by the parents' undermining behaviors. The

*The state of helplessness
in infancy can lead to
neurotic behavior.*

child's sense of helplessness, fear of the parents, need for genuine love, and guilt feelings may all be explanations for this repression.

Horney placed great emphasis on the helplessness of infants. Unlike Adler, she did not believe that all infants necessarily feel helpless, but when these feelings do arise, they can lead to neurotic behavior. Children's sense of helplessness depends on their parents' behavior. If children are excessively sheltered, babied, and kept in a dependent state, then helplessness will be encouraged. The more helpless children feel, the less they dare to oppose or rebel against the parents. This means that the child will repress the resulting hostility, saying, in effect, "I have to repress my hostility because I need you."

Children can easily be made to feel fearful of parents through punishment, physical abuse, or more subtle forms of intimidation. The more frightened children become, the more they will repress their hostility. In this instance the child is saying, "I must repress my hostility because I am afraid of you."

Paradoxically, love can be another reason for repressing hostility toward parents. In this case, parents tell their children how much they love them and how greatly they are sacrificing for them, but the warmth and affection the parents profess are not genuine. Children recognize that these verbalizations and behaviors are poor substitutes for real love and security, but they are all that is available. The child must repress his or her hostility for fear of losing even these unsatisfactory expressions of love.

Guilt is another reason that children repress hostility. They are often made to feel guilty about any hostility or rebelliousness. They may be made to feel unworthy, wicked, or sinful for expressing or even harboring resentments toward their parents. The more guilt the child feels, the more deeply repressed will be the hostility.

This repressed hostility, resulting from a variety of parental behaviors, undermines the childhood need for safety, and is manifested in the condition Horney called basic anxiety.

Basic Anxiety: The Foundation of Neurosis

basic anxiety A
pervasive feeling of
loneliness and
helplessness; the
foundation of neurosis.

Horney identified an "insidiously increasing, all-pervading feeling of being lonely and helpless in a hostile world" (Horney, 1937, p. 89). **Basic anxiety** is the foundation on which later neuroses develop, and it is inseparably tied to feelings of hostility.

Regardless of how we express basic anxiety, the feeling is more or less the same for all of us. We feel "small, insignificant, helpless, deserted, endangered, in a world that is out to abuse, cheat, attack, humiliate, betray" (Horney, 1937, p. 92). In childhood we try to protect ourselves against basic anxiety in four ways: gaining affection, being submissive, attaining power, or withdrawing.

By securing affection and love from other people, the person is saying, in effect, "If you love me, you will not hurt me." There are several ways by which we may gain affection, such as trying to do whatever the other person wants, trying to bribe others, or threatening others into providing the desired affection.

Submissiveness as a means of self-protection involves complying with the wishes either of one particular person or of everyone in our social environment. Submissive persons avoid doing anything that might antagonize others. They dare not criticize or give offense, must repress their personal desires, and cannot defend themselves against abuse for fear that such defensiveness will antagonize the abuser. Most people who act submissive believe they are unselfish and self-sacrificing. Such persons seem to be saying, "If I give in, I will not be hurt." This describes Horney's own childhood behavior until the age of 8 or 9.

Attaining power over others is another self-protective mechanism. In this way a person can compensate for helplessness and achieve security through success or through a sense of superiority. Such persons seem to believe that if they have power, no one will harm them. This may characterize Horney's childhood once she decided to strive for academic success.

These three self-protective devices have something in common; by engaging in any of them, the person is attempting to cope with basic anxiety by interacting with other people. The fourth way of protecting oneself against basic anxiety involves withdrawing from other people, not physically but psychologically. Such a person attempts to become independent of others, not relying on anyone else for the satisfaction of internal or external needs. For example, if someone amasses a houseful of material possessions, then he or she can rely on them to satisfy external needs. Unfortunately, that person may be too burdened by basic anxiety to enjoy the possessions; he or she must guard the possessions carefully because they are the person's only protection against anxiety.

The withdrawn person achieves independence with regard to psychological needs by becoming aloof from others, no longer seeking them out to satisfy emotional needs. The process involves a blunting, or minimizing, of emotional needs. By renouncing these needs, the withdrawn person guards against being hurt by other people.

The four self-protective mechanisms Horney proposed have a single goal: to defend against basic anxiety. They motivate the person to seek security and reassurance rather than happiness or pleasure. They are a defense against pain, not a pursuit of well-being.

Another characteristic of these self-protective mechanisms is their power and intensity. Horney believed they could be more compelling than sexual or other physiological needs. These mechanisms may reduce anxiety, but the cost to the individual is usually an impoverished personality. Often the neurotic will pursue the search for safety and security by using more than one of these mechanisms, and the incompatibility among the four mechanisms can lay the groundwork for additional problems. For example, a person may be driven by both the need to attain power and the need to gain affection. A person may want to submit to others while also desiring power over them. Such incompatibilities cannot be resolved and can lead to more severe conflicts.

Neurotic Needs

neurotic needs Ten irrational defenses against anxiety that become a permanent part of personality and affect behavior.

Horney believed that any of these self-protective mechanisms could become so permanent a part of the personality that it assumes the characteristics of a drive or need in determining the individual's behavior. She listed ten such needs, which she termed *neurotic* because they are irrational solutions to one's problems. The ten **neurotic needs** are as follows:

1. Affection and approval
2. A dominant partner
3. Power
4. Exploitation
5. Prestige
6. Admiration
7. Achievement or ambition
8. Self-sufficiency
9. Perfection
10. Narrow limits to life

These neurotic needs encompass the four ways of protecting ourselves against anxiety. Gaining affection is expressed in the neurotic need for affection and approval. Being submissive includes the neurotic need for a dominant partner. Attaining power relates to the needs for power, exploitation, prestige, admiration, and achievement or ambition. Withdrawing includes the needs for self-sufficiency, perfection, and narrow limits to life.

Horney noted that we all manifest these needs to some degree. At one time or another, everyone seeks affection or desires to achieve. None of the needs is abnormal or neurotic in an everyday, transient sense. What makes them neurotic is the person's intensive and compulsive pursuit of their satisfaction as the only way to resolve basic anxiety. Satisfying these needs will not help us feel safe and secure but will aid only in our desire to escape the discomfort caused by our anxiety. Also, when we pursue gratification of these needs solely to cope with anxiety, we tend to focus on only one need and compulsively seek its satisfaction in all situations.

In her later writings, Horney reformulated the list of needs (Horney, 1945). From her work with patients, she came to realize that the ten needs could be presented in three groups, each indicating a person's attitudes toward the self and others. Horney called these three categories of directional movement the neurotic trends (see Table 5.1).

Neurotic Trends

neurotic trends Three categories of behaviors and attitudes toward oneself and others that express a person's needs; a revision of the concept of neurotic needs.

Because the **neurotic trends** evolve from the self-protective mechanisms and are elaborations of them, we can see similarities with our earlier descriptions. The neurotic trends involve attitudes and behaviors that are compulsive; that is, neurotic persons are compelled to behave in accordance with at least one of them. They are also displayed indiscriminately. The neurotic trends are (1) movement toward other people (the compliant personality), (2) movement against other people (the aggressive personality), and (3) movement away from other people (the detached personality).

The Compliant Personality

compliant personality Behaviors and attitudes associated with the neurotic trend of **moving toward people**, such as a need for affection and approval.

The **compliant personality** displays attitudes and behaviors that reflect a desire to move toward other people—an intense and continuous need for affection and approval—an urge to be loved, wanted, and protected. Compliant personalities are self-effacing and display these needs toward all other people, although they usually have a need for one dominant person, such as a friend or spouse, who will take charge of their lives and offer protection and guidance.

Compliant personalities manipulate other people, particularly their partners, to achieve their goals. They often behave in ways that others find attractive or endearing. For example, they may seem unusually considerate, appreciative, responsive, and sensitive to the needs of others and they provide empathy and understanding. Compliant people are concerned with living up to others' ideals and expectations and act in ways that others perceive as unselfish and generous.

In dealing with other people, compliant personalities are conciliatory

Table 5.1   *Horney's neurotic needs and neurotic trends.*

Needs	Trends
Affection and approval A dominant partner	Movement toward other people (the compliant personality)
Power Exploitation Prestige Admiration Achievement or ambition	Movement against other people (the aggressive personality)
Self-sufficiency Perfection Narrow limits to life	Movement away from other people (the detached personality)

and subordinate their personal desires to those of other people. They are willing to assume blame and to defer to others, never being assertive, critical, or demanding. They do whatever the situation requires—as they interpret it—to gain affection, approval, and love. Their attitude toward themselves is consistently one of helplessness and weakness. Horney suggested that compliant people are saying, "Look at me. I am so weak and helpless that you must protect and love me."

Consequently, they regard other people as superior, and even in situations in which they are notably competent, they see themselves as inferior. Because the security of compliant personalities depends on the attitudes and behavior of other people toward them, they become excessively dependent, needing constant approval and reassurance. Any sign of rejection, whether actual or imagined, is terrifying to them, leading to increased efforts to regain the affection of the person they believe has rejected them.

The source of these behaviors is the person's repressed hostility. Horney found that compliant persons have repressed profound feelings of defiance and vindictiveness. They have a desire to control, exploit, and manipulate others and lack interest in others—the opposite of what their behaviors and attitudes express. Because their hostile impulses must be repressed, compliant personalities become subservient, always trying to please and asking nothing for themselves.

The Aggressive Personality

aggressive personality Behaviors and attitudes associated with the neurotic trend of **moving against people,** such as a domineering and controlling manner.

Aggressive personalities move or act against other people. In their world, as they see it, everyone is hostile; only the fittest and most cunning survive. Life is a jungle in which supremacy, strength, and ferocity are the paramount virtues. Although their motivation is the same as that of the compliant type—to alleviate basic anxiety—aggressive personalities never display fear of rejection. They act in a tough, domineering manner with no regard for others. To achieve the control and superiority so vital to their lives, they must consistently perform at a high level. By excelling and receiving recognition, they find satisfaction in having their superiority affirmed by others.

Because aggressive personalities are driven to surpass others, they judge everyone in terms of the benefit they will receive from the relationship. They make no effort to appease others but will argue, criticize, demand, and do whatever is necessary to achieve and retain superiority and power.

They drive themselves hard to become the best; therefore, they may actually be successful in their careers, although the work itself will not provide intrinsic satisfaction. Like everything else in life, work is a means to an end, not an end in itself.

Aggressive personalities may appear confident of their abilities and uninhibited in asserting and defending themselves. However, like compliant personalities, they are driven by insecurity, anxiety, and hostility.

The Detached Personality

detached personality
Behaviors and attitudes associated with the neurotic trend of **moving away from people,** such as an intense need for privacy.

People described as **detached personalities** are driven to move away from other people and to maintain that emotional distance. They must not love, hate, or cooperate with others or become involved in any way. To achieve this total detachment, they strive to become self-sufficient and resourceful. If they are to function as detached personalities, they must rely on their own resources, which must therefore be well developed.

Detached personalities have an almost desperate desire for privacy. They need to spend as much time as possible alone, and it disturbs them to share even such an experience as listening to music. Their need for independence makes them sensitive to any attempt to influence, coerce, or obligate them. Detached personalities must avoid constraints, including timetables and schedules, long-term commitments such as marriages or mortgages, and sometimes even the pressure of a belt or necktie.

They experience the need to feel superior, but not in the same sense that aggressive personalities do. Because detached people cannot actively compete with others for superiority, they believe that their greatness should be recognized automatically, without struggle or effort on their part. One manifestation of this sense of superiority is the feeling that one is unique—different and apart from everyone else.

Detached personalities suppress or deny all feelings toward others, particularly love and hate. Intimacy would lead to conflict, and that must be avoided. Because of this constriction of their emotions, detached personalities place great stress on reason, logic, and intelligence.

You have probably noticed the similarity between the three personality types proposed by Horney and the styles of life in Adler's personality theory (pp. 112–113). Horney's compliant personality is similar to Adler's getting type, the aggressive personality is rather like the dominant or ruling type, and the detached personality is similar to the avoiding type. This is yet another example of how Adler's ideas influenced later explanations of personality.

Horney found that in the neurotic person, one of these three trends is dominant, and the other two are present to a lesser degree; for example, the person who is predominantly aggressive also has some need for compliance and detachment. The dominant neurotic trend is the one that determines the person's behaviors and attitudes toward others. This is the mode of acting and thinking that best serves to control basic anxiety, and any deviation from it is threatening to the person. For this reason, the other two trends must actively be repressed, which can lead to additional problems. Any indication that a repressed trend is pushing for expression causes conflict within the individual.

conflict The basic incompatibility of the neurotic trends.

In Horney's system, **conflict** is defined as the basic incompatibility of the three neurotic trends; this conflict is the core of neurosis. All of us, whether neurotic or normal, suffer some conflict among these basically irreconcilable modes. The difference between the normal person and the neurotic person lies in the intensity of the conflict; it is much more intense in the neurotic. Neurotic people must battle to keep the nondominant trends from being expressed. They are rigid and inflexible, meeting all situations with the behaviors and attitudes that characterize the dominant trend, regardless of their suitability.

In the person who is not neurotic, all three trends can be expressed. As circumstances warrant, a person may sometimes be aggressive, sometimes compliant, and sometimes detached. The trends are not mutually exclusive and can be integrated harmoniously within the personality. The normal person is flexible in behaviors and attitudes and can adapt to changing situations.

The Idealized Self-Image

Horney argued that all of us, normal or neurotic, construct a picture of ourselves that may or may not be based on reality. Horney's own search for self was difficult. When she was 21, she wrote, "There's still such chaos in me. Still so little firmly outlined. Just like my face: a formless mass that only takes on shape through the expression of the moment. The searching for our selves is the most agonizing" (Horney, 1980, p. 174).

In normal persons the self-image is built on a realistic appraisal of our abilities, potentials, weaknesses, goals, and relations with other people. This image supplies a sense of unity and integration to the personality and a framework within which to approach ourselves and others. If we are to realize our full potential, our self-image must clearly reflect our true self.

idealized self-image In normal people, an idealized picture of oneself built on a flexible, realistic assessment of our abilities. In neurotics, the idealized self-image is based on an inflexible, unrealistic self-appraisal.

Neurotic persons, who experience conflict between incompatible modes of behavior, have personalities characterized by disunity and disharmony. They construct an **idealized self-image** for the same purpose as normal persons do—to unify the personality. But their attempt is doomed to failure because their self-image is not based on a realistic appraisal of personal strengths and weaknesses. Instead, it is based on an illusion, an unattainable ideal.

Although the neurotic or idealized self-image does not coincide with reality, it is real and accurate to the person who created it. Other people can easily see through this false picture, but the neurotic cannot. The neurotic person believes that the incomplete and misleading self-picture is real. The idealized self-image is a model of what the neurotic thinks he or she is, can be, or should be.

A realistic self-image is flexible and dynamic, adapting as the individual develops and changes. It reflects strengths, growth, and self-awareness. The realistic image is a goal, something to strive for, and as such it reflects and leads the person. By contrast, the neurotic self-image is static, inflexible, and unyielding. It is not a goal but a fixed idea, not an inducement to growth but a hindrance demanding rigid adherence to its proscriptions.

The neurotic's self-image is an unsatisfactory substitute for a reality-based sense of self-worth. The neurotic has little self-confidence because of insecurity and anxiety, and the idealized self-image does not allow for correction of those deficiencies. It provides only an illusory sense of worth and alienates the neurotic from the true self. Developed to reconcile incompatible modes of behavior, the idealized self-image becomes just one more element in that conflict. Far from resolving the problem, it adds to a growing sense of futility. The slightest crack in the neurotic's idealized self-picture threatens the false sense of superiority and security the whole edifice was constructed to provide, and little is needed to topple it. Horney wrote that the neurotic self-image is a "treasure house loaded with dynamite."

Feminine Psychology: The Flight from Womanhood

Horney's disagreement with Freud's views on female psychology was her initial point of departure from orthodox psychoanalysis. She was especially critical of Freud's notion of penis envy, which she believed was derived from inadequate evidence (that is, Freud's clinical interviews with neurotic women). Freud offered descriptions and interpretations of this alleged phenomenon from a male point of view in a place and time when women were second-class citizens. He suggested that women were victims of their anatomy, forever envious and resentful of men for possessing a penis. Freud also concluded that women had poorly developed superegos (a result of inadequately resolved Oedipal conflicts) and inferior body images; women saw themselves as castrated men.

womb envy The envy a male feels toward a female because she can bear children and he cannot. Womb envy was Horney's response to Freud's concept of **penis envy** in females.

Horney countered these ideas by arguing that men, both as children and as adults, envied women because of their capacity for motherhood, which gives women a physiological superiority. Her position on this issue was based on her own experience. "The pleasure and pride she had felt in childbirth . . . became the touchstone of her argument for an alternative theory of female development" (Quinn, 1987, p. 171). Paralleling her own experiences, Horney uncovered in her male patients what she called **womb envy**. "When one begins, as I did, to analyze men only after a fairly long experi-

Horney disputed Freud's views on the accepted sex stereotypes of men and women.

ence of analyzing women, one receives a most surprising impression of the intensity of this envy of pregnancy, childbirth, and motherhood" (Horney, 1967a, pp. 60–61).

In the act of creating new life, Horney noted, men have such a small part to play that they must sublimate their womb envy and overcompensate for it by seeking achievement in their work. Womb envy and the resentment that accompanies it are manifested unconsciously in behaviors designed to disparage and belittle women, to reinforce their inferior status. By denying women equal rights, minimizing their opportunities to contribute to society, and downgrading their efforts to achieve, men retain their so-called natural superiority. Underlying such typical male behavior is a sense of inferiority deriving from their womb envy.

Horney did not deny that many women believe themselves inferior to men. What she questioned was Freud's claim of a biological basis for these feelings. Although women may view themselves as inadequate compared to men, they do so for societal reasons, not because they were born female. If women feel unworthy, it is because they have been treated that way in male-dominated cultures. They have experienced generations of social, economic, and cultural discrimination, and it is understandable that many women would see themselves in this light.

These women may choose to deny their femininity and to wish, unconsciously, that they were men. Horney called this the "flight from womanhood," a condition that can lead to inhibitions and frigidity (Horney, 1926). Part of the sexual fear associated with frigidity arises from childhood fantasies about the difference in size between the adult penis and the girl child's vagina. The fantasies focus on vaginal injury and the pain of forcible penetration. This produces a conflict between the unconscious desire to have a child and the fear of intercourse. If the conflict is sufficiently strong, it can lead to emotional disturbances that manifest themselves in relations with men. These women distrust and resent men and reject their sexual advances.

Horney disagreed with Freud about the nature of the Oedipus complex. She did not deny the existence of conflicts between children and parents, but she did not believe they had a sexual origin. In de-sexing the Oedipus complex, she interpreted the situation as a conflict between dependence on one's parents and hostility toward them.

Earlier in this chapter, we discussed parental behaviors that undermine the satisfaction of the childhood need for safety and security, thus leading to the development of hostility. At the same time, the child remains dependent on the parents so that expressing this hostility is unacceptable; it could further damage the child's security. The child is saying, in effect, "I have to repress my hostility because I need you." As we noted, the hostile impulses remain and create basic anxiety. "The resulting picture," Horney wrote, "may look exactly like what Freud describes as the Oedipus complex: passionate clinging to one parent and jealousy toward the other" (Horney, 1939, p. 83). Thus, Horney's explanation for Oedipal feelings lies in neurotic conflicts that evolve from parent-child interactions. These feelings are not based on sex or other biological forces, nor are they universal. They develop only when parents act to undermine their child's security.

Freud did not respond to Horney's criticisms of his views on women, nor did he alter his theory of the Oedipus complex. Toward the end of his life, in what may have been a veiled allusion to Horney's work, Freud wrote: "We shall not be very greatly surprised if a woman analyst, who has not been sufficiently convinced of the intensity of her own wish for a penis, also fails to attach proper importance to that factor in her patients" (Freud, 1940). Of Horney herself, Freud remarked, "She is able but malicious" (quoted in Blanton, 1971, p. 65).

As an early feminist, Horney adopted several positions that have a contemporary ring. In 1934 she wrote an essay describing the psychological conflicts in defining women's roles, contrasting the traditional ideal of womanhood with a more modern view (Horney, 1967b). In the traditional scheme—promoted and endorsed by most men of the day—the woman's role was to love, admire, and serve her man. Her identity was a reflection of her husband's. Horney suggested that women should seek their own identity by developing their abilities and pursuing careers.

These traditional and modern roles create conflicts that many women have difficulty resolving. Drawing on Horney's work, a contemporary feminist wrote that

modern women are caught between wanting to make themselves desirable
to men and pursuing their own goals. The competing purposes elicit conflicting behaviors: seductive versus aggressive, deferential versus ambitious.
Modern women are torn between love and work and are consequently dissatisfied in both. [Westkott, 1986, p. 14]

It remains as troublesome for the woman of the 1990s to combine marriage,
motherhood, and career as it was for Karen Horney in the 1930s. Her decision to develop her abilities and focus on her work brought her enormous
satisfaction, but she continued throughout her life to search for security and
love.

Horney's Image of Human Nature

Like Alfred Adler's, Horney's image of human nature is considerably more
optimistic than Freud's. One reason for her optimism was her belief that we
are not doomed by biological forces to conflict, anxiety, neurosis, or a universality in personality. To Horney, each person is unique. Neurotic behavior,
when it occurs, results from social forces in childhood. Parent-child relationships will either satisfy or frustrate the child's need for safety. If that need is
frustrated, the outcome is neurotic behavior. Neuroses and conflicts are not
inevitable conditions that we are all fated to suffer. Instead, they can be
avoided if children are raised with love, acceptance, and trust.

Given the proper conditions, any child will develop an integrated, uni-
fied adult personality. Each of us has the innate potential for self-realization,
and this is our ultimate and necessary goal in life. Our intrinsic abilities and
potential will blossom as inevitably and naturally as an acorn grows into an
oak tree. The only thing that can obstruct our development is the thwarting
in childhood of our need for safety and security.

Horney also believed that we have the capacity to consciously shape and
change our personality. Because human nature is flexible, it is not formed
into immutable shapes in childhood. Each of us possesses the capacity to
grow. Therefore, adult experiences may be as important as those of childhood.

So confident was Horney of our capacity for self-growth that she emphasized self-analysis in her therapeutic work. In her book entitled *Self-Analysis*
(Horney, 1942), she argues in favor of our ability to help resolve our own
problems. On the issue of free will versus determinism, then, Horney argued
in favor of the former. We can all shape our lives and achieve self-realization.

Assessment in Horney's Theory

The methods Horney used to inquire into the functioning of the human personality were essentially those favored by Freud—free association and
dream analysis—but with some modification. The most basic difference in

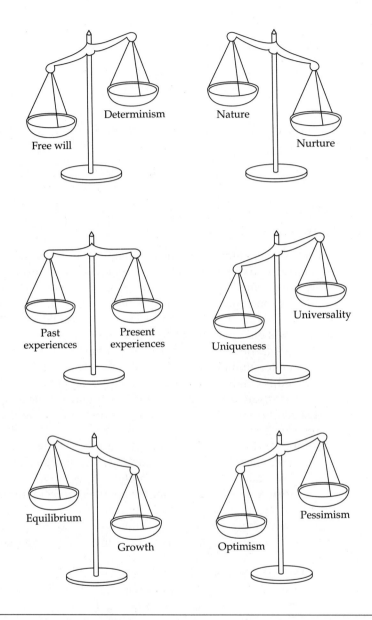

Horney

Image of Human Nature.

technique between Horney and Freud was in the relationship between analyst and patient. Horney believed that Freud played too passive a role and was too distant and intellectual. She suggested that analysis should be an "exquisitely cooperative enterprise" between patient and therapist (quoted in Cherry & Cherry, 1973, p. 84).

Although Horney kept a couch in her office, she did not believe it was necessary for analysis. "This is something one needs to try through trial and error," she said in a lecture, "asking if the patient operates better lying on the couch or sitting upright. It is particularly helpful to encourage a patient so he feels free to sit up, lie down, walk around, or whatever he wants" (Horney, 1987, p. 43). This was part of the attitude of "constructive friendliness" she adopted toward her patients.

In her use of free association, Horney did not follow Freud's lead in trying to probe the unconscious mind. She believed that patients could easily distort or hide aspects of their inner lives or falsify their feelings about events they remembered. Instead, Horney focused on her patients' visible emotional reactions toward her, believing that these could explain her patients' attitudes toward other people. She pursued these attitudes through free association. She did not delve into presumed infantile sexual fantasies at the beginning of a course of analysis but inquired about the early years only after evaluating present attitudes, defenses, and conflicts.

Horney believed that each attitude or feeling results from a deeper, pre-existing attitude, which in turn had resulted from a deeper one, and so on. Through free association, the analyst gradually uncovers the patient's early experiences. To Horney, the personality was like "an onion, with each layer being peeled off until one arrived at the deepest core emotion" (Rubins, 1978, p. 183). Sometimes Horney used free association on herself to assess a patient's personality, responding to the material the patient presented.

She also believed that dreams could reveal a person's true self and that they represented attempts to solve problems, in either a constructive or a neurotic way. Dreams can show us a set of attitudes that may differ from those of our self-image. Horney believed that the true meaning of a dream must be interpreted by the analyst, but she did not offer a list of universal symbols. She insisted that each dream be explained within the context of the patient's conflict. Focusing on the emotional content of dreams, she concluded that the "safest clue to the understanding of a dream is in the feelings of the patient as he has them in the dream" (Horney, 1987, p. 61).

Free association and dream analysis were Horney's primary assessment techniques, but she did not restrict herself to those methods. Believing that every person is unique and offers the analyst a situation never before encountered, Horney noted that the analyst should be flexible in deciding how best to proceed to uncover the patient's problems. The analyst must be adaptable enough to use whatever tools are appropriate.

Research in Horney's Theory

Horney used the case study method. Therefore, her approach, data, and interpretations are subject to the same criticisms made of Freud, Jung, and Adler. The weaknesses inherent in the case study method apply to her work no less than to theirs. Horney was opposed to taking verbatim notes of her patients' recollections. "I don't see how anybody can employ a wholehearted receptivity and productivity of attention at the same time that he is anxiously scribbling everything down," she said (Horney, 1987, p. 30). As with Freud, Jung, and Adler, we do not have complete records of her analytic sessions and the data she collected during them.

Horney tried to be rigorous and scientific in her clinical observations. She formulated hypotheses, testing them in the therapeutic situation and maintaining that her data were tested in the same way scientists in other fields test theirs. Thus, she approached her work in the spirit of science, collecting data, testing them, and revising her theory on the basis of her findings.

Contemporary researchers have studied Horney's three neurotic trends, redefining them as follows: moving against people (ill-tempered), moving away from people (shy), and moving toward people (dependent) (Caspi, Elder, & Bem, 1987, 1988). The behavior of people belonging to each of these types in late childhood was compared with their behavior 30 years later to discover whatever continuities might exist.

Ill-tempered children, both boys and girls, tended to become ill-tempered adults, prone to divorce and downward occupational mobility. Gender differences were found in the shy and dependent types. Shy boys became aloof adults who experienced marital and job instability. On the other hand, shy girls manifested no such problems later in life. Dependent boys became agreeable, socially poised, warm, and giving adults with stable marriages and careers; the opposite was found for dependent girls (Caspi, Bem, & Elder, 1989).

A study dealing with the neurotic trends of moving against people (aggressive) and moving away from people (detached) compared measures from aggressive and detached children at ages 7 to 13 with their behavior five to seven years later (Moskowitz & Schwartzman, 1989). Those high in aggressiveness were found to be low in school achievement and to have psychiatric problems. Those who were detached or withdrawn were found to have inaccurate and negative self-images. The researchers concluded that Horney's proposed personality types had predictive value for later behavior.

Some research applies indirectly to Horney's ideas on feminine psychology. In our discussion of research on the Oedipus complex (see Chapter 2), we mentioned a study on dreams that provided support for the Freudian concept of penis envy (Hall & Van de Castle, 1965); this study fails to support Horney's questioning of the concept of penis envy. However, research that refutes Freud's notion that women have inadequately developed superegos and inferior body images can be taken to support Horney's views.

A Final Commentary

Horney's contributions to psychology, although impressive, are not as well known or recognized as those of Freud, Jung, and Adler. Professionally, Horney suffered a disadvantage that limited the spread of her ideas: she never formed a group of disciples to disseminate and elaborate on her theory. Further, there is no professional journal dedicated to examining and propounding her ideas.

On the other hand, her work drew a large public following, partly because of her personal qualities. A student recalled:

> There was about her an air of wholeness, of certainty, of total dedication and commitment, of a conviction that her ideas were valuable, that they were worth sharing with colleagues and students, because knowing them would make a difference to helping those in need. [Clemmens, 1987, p. 108]

These characteristics are evident in her books, which are written in a style readily understood by people who do not have professional analytical training. Her theory has a commonsense appeal and, to many people, seems applicable to their own personality or to that of a relative or friend.

Primarily due to the women's movement that began in the 1960s, Horney's books have enjoyed renewed interest. Her writings on femininity and female sexuality may constitute the most influential of her contributions. "Had she written nothing else," a biographer stated, "these papers would have earned Horney a place of importance in the history of psychoanalysis" (Quinn, 1987, p. 211). Her adolescent diaries have recently been published, along with two new biographies.

Horney's ideas may be more relevant to problems inherent in American culture than are the ideas of Freud, Jung, or Adler. Many personality researchers see Horney's conception of the neurotic trends as a valuable way to categorize deviant behavior. Others accept Horney's emphasis on self-esteem, the need for safety and security, the role of basic anxiety, and the importance of the idealized self-image.

Although Horney was trained in orthodox Freudian theory and paid tribute to Freud for providing the foundation and tools for her work, her theory deviated from psychoanalysis in several ways. Not surprisingly, she received a great deal of criticism from those who continued to adhere to Freud's position. To the Freudians, Horney's denial of the importance of biological instincts and her reduced emphasis on sexuality and the unconscious were obvious weaknesses.

Horney's personality theory is not as completely or consistently developed as Freud's. It has been suggested that because Freud's model was constructed so elegantly and precisely, it would have been better for Horney to reject it and start anew rather than attempt to refashion it along different lines. Another criticism is that although Horney's theory notes the impact of social and cultural forces on personality, it makes little use of research data from sociology and anthropology to detail precisely how social forces shape personality. A related charge is that her observations and interpretations were too greatly influenced by middle-class American culture. In her defense, it must be said that all personality theorists are affected by the class, culture, and time in which they work.

Summary

Karen Horney differed from Freud in her views on feminine psychology and her emphasis on social rather than biological forces as shapers of personality. Horney's childhood involved a lack of parental love, which fostered basic anxiety and hostility; these ideas were reflected in her theory.

The need for safety refers to security and freedom from fear. It depends on being loved and wanted as a child. When security is undermined, hostility is induced. The child may repress this hostility out of a sense of helplessness, fear of the parents, the need to receive parental affection, and guilt about expressing hostility. Repressing hostility leads to basic anxiety, defined as a feeling of being lonely and helpless in a hostile world.

There are four ways to protect oneself against basic anxiety: gaining affection, being submissive, attaining power, and withdrawing. Any of these protective devices can become a neurotic need or drive. Horney proposed ten neurotic needs, which she later grouped as three neurotic trends: moving toward people (the compliant personality), moving against people (the aggressive personality), and moving away from people (the detached personality). Compliant types need affection and approval and will do what other people want. Aggressive types are hostile toward others and seek to achieve control and superiority. Detached types keep an emotional distance from others and have a deep need for privacy.

In the normal person, the idealized self-image is built on a realistic appraisal of one's abilities and goals. It helps the person achieve self-realization—the maximum development and use of one's potential. The idealized self-image in the neurotic person is based on an unrealistic, misleading appraisal of one's abilities.

Horney argued against Freud's contention that women have penis envy, poorly developed superegos, and inferior body images. She believed that men envied women because of their capacity for motherhood and, consequently, that men had womb envy, which they sublimated through achievement. She rejected the sexual basis for the Oedipus complex, suggesting that it involved a conflict between dependence on parents and hostility toward them.

Horney's image of human nature is more optimistic than Freud's. Each person is unique and is not doomed to conflict. Childhood influences are important, but later experiences also shape personality. The ultimate goal of life is self-realization, an innate urge to grow, which can be helped or hindered by social forces. According to Horney, we can consciously shape and change our personalities.

Horney's methods of assessment were free association and dream analysis, and her research method was the case study. Some psychologists see value in her concepts of neurotic trends, the need for safety, the role of anxiety, and the idealized self-image. The theory has been criticized for not being developed as fully as Freud's, for not using research data from sociology and anthropology, and for being heavily influenced by middle-class American culture.

Critical Thinking Review

1. Describe how Karen Horney's childhood experiences may be reflected in her theory of personality.

2. Describe the childhood need for safety. What parental behaviors are necessary for a child's security?

3. What is the origin of basic anxiety? Describe four self-protective ways in which we may express basic anxiety.

4. Discuss the three neurotic trends and the behaviors associated with each.

5. How are the neurotic trends related to the self-protective defenses against anxiety?

6. Explain the difference between normal persons and neurotic persons in terms of the neurotic trends.

7. How does the idealized self-image of the normal, realistic person differ from the idealized self-image of the neurotic person?

8. Horney rejected Freud's contention that there was a biological basis for so-called female inferiority. How did she account for women's feelings of inadequacy?

9. What was Horney's interpretation of the Oedipus complex?

10. How does Horney's image of human nature differ from Freud's?

11. How did Horney's use of the free-association technique differ from Freud's?

12. Describe the results of research conducted on the three neurotic trends.

Suggested Reading

Horney, K. (1937). *The neurotic personality of our time.* New York: Norton. Describes the development of conflict and anxiety within the personality and relates neuroses to past experiences and to the sociocultural climate.

Horney, K. (1980). *The adolescent diaries of Karen Horney.* New York: Basic Books. Reprints diary entries Horney wrote between the ages of 13 and 25; the entries are characterized by intense emotion and intellectual honesty.

Horney, K. (1987). *Final lectures.* New York: Norton. Contains lectures Horney delivered during the last year of her life. Presents refinements of her views on psychoanalytic techniques, such as free association and dream analysis.

Quinn, S. (1987). *A mind of her own: The life of Karen Horney.* New York: Summit Books. Draws on previously unpublished material to describe Horney's life, her work on feminine psychology, and her conflicts with the orthodox Freudian establishment.

Sayers, J. (1991). *Mothers of psychoanalysis: Helene Deutsch, Karen Horney, Anna Freud, Melanie Klein.* New York: Norton. Describes the work of four influential psychoanalysts in modifying psychoanalytic theory from patriarchal to matriarchal since the death of Sigmund Freud. Shows how these women's experiences as daughters and mothers (or surrogate mothers) changed the focus of psychoanalysis from sex, repression, and castration anxiety to identification, projection, and separation anxiety.

Erich Fromm

The Life of Fromm (1900–1980)
Freedom Versus Security: The Basic Human Dilemma
  Psychic Mechanisms for Regaining Security
Personality Development in Childhood
Psychological Needs
Character Types

Fromm's Image of Human Nature
Assessment in Fromm's Theory
Research in Fromm's Theory
A Final Commentary
Summary
Critical Thinking Review
Suggested Reading

The most beautiful as well as the most ugly
inclinations are not part of a fixed and biologically
given human nature but result from the social
processes which create [us].

—Erich Fromm

Erich Fromm, like Alfred Adler and Karen Horney, argued that we are not inexorably driven or inevitably shaped by instinctive biological forces, as Freud had proposed. Instead, Fromm suggested that personality is influenced by social and cultural forces—those that affect the individual within a culture and those universal forces that have influenced humanity throughout history.

Fromm's emphasis on the social determinants of personality is broader than that of Adler and Horney. We might say that Fromm takes a longer view of personality development than other theorists because of his concern with history. He suggested that we can find in historical events the roots of human loneliness, isolation, and insignificance. To find meaning in life, we need to escape these feelings of isolation and develop a sense of belonging. Paradoxically, the increasing freedom we have achieved over the centuries—both from nature and from rigid social systems—has intensified our loneliness and isolation. Too much freedom has become a trap, a negative condition from which we attempt to escape.

Fromm believed that the personal conflicts we suffer arise from the societies we construct. However, we are not doomed to suffering. Fromm was optimistic about our ability to create our own character and solve our problems—problems that we as a society have created. We do not passively accept the impact of social forces as determinants of personality or of society.

Fromm was a psychoanalyst, philosopher, historian, anthropologist, and sociologist. He assembled data from many sources beyond the psychoanalytic couch to offer a unique interpretation of the interaction between human nature and society.

The Life of Fromm (1900–1980)

Fromm was born in Frankfurt, Germany, in an Orthodox Jewish family. His father was a businessman, his grandfather a rabbi, and his mother's uncle a well-known scholar of the Talmud (writings on Jewish laws and traditions). As a child, Fromm was devoted to his religious studies; the moral fervor of the Old Testament affected him greatly. He was also influenced by the Jewish tradition of reason and intellect and by the emotional difficulties of being a member of a minority group. Fromm later severed all his connections with organized religion and referred to himself as an "atheistic mystic."

His home life was not happy. Fromm characterized his family situation as tense. His father was moody, aloof, anxious, and morose, and his mother was frequently depressed. He described himself as an "unbearable, neurotic child" (quoted in Funk, 1982, p. 1). When Fromm was 12, he was shocked by the behavior of a friend of his parents, a 25-year-old artist who chose to abandon her painting and devote her life to her widowed father. Fromm may simply have been jealous, but he could not understand why the young woman preferred the company of this unattractive old man.

Shortly after her father died, the woman killed herself. Her will stipulated that she be buried with her father in the same coffin. Troubled by the suicide, Fromm agonized over her decision and her attraction to her father. "I had never heard of an Oedipus complex," he wrote, "or of incestuous fixations between daughter and father. But I was deeply touched. How is it possible that a beautiful young woman should be so in love with her father, that she prefers to be buried with him to being alive to the pleasures of life and of painting?" (Fromm, 1962, p. 4). It is not hard to see why Fromm later found meaning in Freud's work on the Oedipus complex, which seemed to explain this puzzling and tragic experience.

When Fromm was 14, another manifestation of irrationality unnerved him: the eruption of hysterical fanaticism in the German nation during World War I. He was astonished by the hatred that swept the country as people were whipped by government propaganda into a frenzy of maniacal thought and action. Fromm noted the changes in his relatives, friends, and teachers and wondered why "decent and reasonable people suddenly go crazy" (quoted in Evans, 1966, p. 57). After the war, Fromm wrote: "I was a deeply troubled young man who was obsessed with the question of how war was possible, by the wish to understand the irrationality of human mass behavior, by a passionate desire for peace and international understanding" (Fromm, 1962, p. 9).

It was primarily from these baffling personal experiences—his home life, the suicide, and the wartime behavior of an entire nation—that Fromm developed the need to seek an understanding of the causes of irrationality. "My main interest was clearly mapped out," he wrote. "I wanted to understand the laws that govern the life of the individual man, and the laws of society" (Fromm, 1962, p. 9). He suspected that the human personality was profoundly affected by social, economic, political, and historical forces, and that a sick society produced sick people. Thus, his view of personality was shaped along intuitive lines, fashioned from his own experiences, and later refined along empirical lines.

Fromm began his search for the causes of irrational behavior at the University of Heidelberg, where he studied psychology, sociology, and philosophy. He read the works of such economic and political theorists as Karl Marx, Herbert Spencer, and Max Weber, and received his Ph.D. in sociology in 1922. Fromm underwent Freudian psychoanalytic training in Munich and at the Psychoanalytic Institute in Berlin. He married his first analyst, Frieda Reichmann, who was ten years older than Fromm.

Freud's theories did not satisfy Fromm for long. By the 1930s, Fromm was writing critical articles disputing Freud's refusal to admit the impact of socioeconomic forces on personality. Like Karen Horney, Fromm initially believed that his criticisms of Freudian psychoanalysis were intended merely to elaborate on Freud's position, not to replace it. He considered himself "like a pupil and translator of Freud who is attempting to bring out his most important discoveries in order to enrich them and to deepen them by liberating them from the somewhat narrow libido theory" (Evans, 1966, p. 59). Fromm later moved far beyond Freud's views.

In 1934, Fromm emigrated to the United States to escape the Nazi menace in Germany. He went to Chicago to work with Karen Horney and then followed her to New York. He divorced his wife and began a long affair with Horney. During those years, Horney's ideas had a great impact on Fromm's work—a debt he rarely acknowledged. After their affair ended, he married twice more; unlike Reichmann and Horney, Fromm's second and third wives were younger than he was, and neither was an analyst.

Fromm presented his theory in several books written in a popular style, intended more for the general public than for colleagues. He taught at Columbia and Yale universities and established the department of psychoanalytic training at the medical school of the National University of Mexico. He became active in the peace movement of the 1960s and 1970s and helped to found SANE, the Organization for a Sane Nuclear Policy. He opposed the Cold War, the nuclear arms race, and the Vietnam War, and he was invited to present his views to a U.S. Senate investigating committee. Fromm died at his home in Switzerland in 1980.

Freedom Versus Security: The Basic Human Dilemma

The title of Fromm's first book, *Escape from Freedom* (1941), indicates his vision of the human condition: In the history of Western civilization, as people have achieved more freedom, they have come to feel more lonely, insignificant, and alienated. Conversely, the less freedom people have had, the greater their feelings of belonging and security. Fromm contended that people in the 20th century, possessing greater freedom than in any other era, feel more lonely, alienated, and insignificant than people of ages past.

To understand this apparent paradox, we must consider the history of Western civilization, as Fromm interpreted it. He began by discussing human evolution, noting the distinction between animal nature and human nature. Humans are free of the instinctive biological mechanisms that guide animal behavior. Furthermore, humans are conscious beings, aware of themselves and their world. Through learning, we accumulate a knowledge of the past. Through imagination, we can project ourselves far beyond the present. Because we possess a conscious awareness and the ability to master nature, we are no longer at one with nature, as are the lower animals. As Fromm said, we have transcended nature. As a result, although we are subject to natural laws and cannot change them, we are divorced from nature—in a sense, homeless, isolated, and alienated.

Fromm suggested that early peoples tried to cope with feelings of alienation from nature by identifying with their tribes or clans. Sharing myths, religions, and tribal rites, they attained the security of belonging to a group. Membership in the group provided acceptance, affiliation, and a set of customs and rules. The religions that early peoples developed also helped reestablish the link with nature. Worship was focused on natural objects, such as the sun, the moon, fire, plants, and animals.

But this tenuous security could not last. Human beings are striving creatures who develop and grow, and postprimitive peoples revolted against subservience to the group. According to Fromm, each period of history has been characterized by increasing movement away from the group and toward individuality, as people have struggled to achieve independence, freedom, and the opportunity to express all their uniquely human abilities. This striving for individuality reached its peak between the Reformation in the 16th century and the present day—when, in Fromm's view, alienation has been matched by a high degree of freedom.

Fromm designated the Middle Ages (about A.D. 400 to 1400) as the last era of stability, security, and belonging. It was a time of little individual freedom because the feudal system determined everyone's place in society. People remained in the role and class status to which they were born. There was no geographic or social mobility and little choice of occupation, social customs, or habits of dress. Although people were not free, they were not alienated from others. The rigid social structure meant that a person's place in society was clear. There was no doubt or indecision about where—or to whom—one belonged.

The social upheavals of the Renaissance and the Protestant Reformation destroyed this stability and security by increasing personal freedom. People began to have more choice in and power over their lives. However, they achieved this freedom at the expense of the societal ties that had provided security and a sense of belonging. As a result, they were beset by feelings of personal insignificance and doubts about the meaning of life.

Fromm proposed two approaches to restoring meaning and belongingness in life. The first approach, achieving positive freedom, involves an attempt to become reunited with others without giving up freedom and integrity. In this optimistic, altruistic approach, Fromm suggested that we relate to others through work and love, through the sincere and open expression of our intellectual and emotional abilities. We could build an idealistic and humanistic society in which no one would feel lonely and insignificant, because all people would be brothers and sisters.

The second way to regain security is by renouncing freedom and surrendering our individuality and integrity. Although such a solution would not lead to self-expression and personal development, it would remove the anxiety of alienation. According to Fromm, this approach explains why so many people are attracted to totalitarian systems, such as the Nazi regime in Germany in the 1930s.

Psychic Mechanisms for Regaining Security

Within these two general approaches to regaining our lost security, Fromm posited three psychic mechanisms of escape: authoritarianism, destructiveness, and automaton conformity.

authoritarianism A psychic mechanism for regaining security, displayed in either masochistic or sadistic feelings.

Authoritarianism is manifested in either masochistic or sadistic strivings. People described as masochistic believe they are inferior and inadequate. They may complain of these feelings and declare they would like to be free of them, but they have a strong need for dependence on a person or a group. They willingly submit to the control of other people or of social forces, and they behave in a weak and helpless manner. They achieve security by these actions because submissiveness assuages their feelings of loneliness.

Authoritarian persons described as sadistic strive for power over others. They may try to make others dependent on them and thus achieve control. They may exploit others by taking or using anything desirable the other person possesses, whether material goods or intellectual and emotional qualities. Or they may desire to see others suffer and to be the cause of that suffering. Although the suffering may involve physical pain, it most often is emotional suffering, such as embarrassment or humiliation.

destructiveness A psychic mechanism for regaining security, displayed in a desire to eliminate threatening objects, persons, and institutions.

The authoritarian escape mechanism involves some form of continuing interaction with an object or person. By contrast, **destructiveness** aims at eliminating that object or person. A destructive person says, in effect, ''I can escape my feelings of loneliness and powerlessness in this world by destroying it.'' Fromm saw evidence of destructiveness in all societies. He believed that many human characteristics were used as a rationalization for destructiveness, including love, duty, conscience, and patriotism.

The escape mechanism Fromm described as having the greatest social

People can achieve a feeling of security by renouncing freedom and accepting a totalitarian system such as the Nazi regime.

automaton conformity A psychic mechanism for regaining security, displayed in unconditional obedience to the prevailing rules that govern behavior.

significance is **automaton conformity**. Through this mechanism, we ease our loneliness and isolation by erasing the differences between ourselves and others. We accomplish this by striving to become exactly like everyone else, by conforming to the societal rules that govern behavior. Fromm compared automaton conformity with the protective coloring of animals. Animals protect themselves by becoming indistinguishable from their surroundings. So it is with fully conforming human beings.

Although such people temporarily gain the security and sense of belonging they so desperately need, they do so at the price of the self. People who conform completely have sacrificed their personality; as Fromm said, there is no longer an "I," distinct from "them." The conforming person becomes part of "them," and a false self takes the place of the genuine self. This loss of self leaves the person with insecurity and doubt. No longer possessing a separate identity or personality, the person functions reflexively and automatically, like an automaton or robot, in response to what others expect or demand. This new identity, the false one, can be maintained only through continued conformity; there can be no relaxation. If the person were to do anything at variance with society's norms and values, then approval, recognition, and security would be lost.

Personality Development in Childhood

Fromm believed that the development of the individual in childhood paralleled the development of the human species. The history of the species is repeated in the childhood of each human being. As children grow, they achieve increasing freedom and independence from their parents. Infants know little freedom but are secure in their dependent relationship. However, the less dependent children become—especially on the primary ties with the mother—the less secure they feel.

Because the maturation process brings some degree of isolation and helplessness, children will attempt to regain the security of infancy and escape their growing freedom. They may use several mechanisms, similar to the psychic mechanisms described in the preceding section. Which mechanism the child employs is determined by the nature of the parent-child relationship. Fromm proposed three mechanisms of interpersonal relatedness: symbiotic relatedness, withdrawal-destructiveness, and love.

symbiotic relatedness A childhood mechanism for regaining security in which children remain close to and dependent on their parents.

In **symbiotic relatedness**, children never achieve independence but escape their loneliness and insecurity by becoming part of someone else, either by "swallowing" or by being swallowed by that other person. Masochistic behavior arises from being swallowed; the child remains dependent on the parents and abnegates the self. Sadism arises from swallowing; the parents surrender authority to the child by submitting to the child's will. The child regains security by manipulating and exploiting the parents. In both cases, the relationship is one of closeness and intimacy; the child needs the parents for its security.

withdrawal-destructiveness A childhood mechanism for regaining security in which children distance themselves from their parents.

The **withdrawal-destructiveness** interaction is characterized by a distance and separation from others. Fromm stated that withdrawal and destructiveness are the passive and active forms of the same type of parent-child relationship. Which form the child's behavior takes depends on the parents' behavior. For example, parents who act destructively, attempting to subordinate or subjugate their child, will cause the child to withdraw.

love A form of parent-child interaction in which parents provide respect and a balance between security and responsibility.

Love is the most desirable form of parent-child interaction. In this instance, the parents provide the greatest opportunity for the child's positive personality development by offering respect and a balance between security and responsibility. As a result, the child feels little need to escape the growing freedom and is able to love himself or herself as well as others.

Fromm agreed with Freud that the first five years of life are important, but Fromm did not believe that personality is fixed by the age of 5. Instead, he asserted that later events can also influence personality. He agreed with Freud that the family functioned as society's representative to the child; it is through family interactions that the child acquires character as well as appropriate ways of adjusting to society.

Although every family is different, most people in a given culture have a common social character, a set of beliefs and values that define the proper way of behaving. As children develop their unique character or personality from their genetic endowment and their interactions with their parents, they also develop a social character. This explains why different people react to the same environment in different ways. Overall, it is the complex of social and environmental experiences—especially how the child is treated by the parents—that largely, but not irrevocably, determines the adult personality.

If the parent–child relationship is characterized by love, the child will feel little need to escape from freedom and will develop self-esteem and be able to love others.

Psychological Needs

The drive to attain security and escape loneliness and the conflicting drive for freedom and the creation of the self are universal. All human cravings are determined by the opposition of these drives. This opposition is manifested in six needs:

1. Relatedness
2. Transcendence
3. Rootedness
4. Identity
5. Frame of orientation and an object of devotion
6. Excitation and stimulation

relatedness need The need to maintain contact with other people, ideally through productive love.

The **need for relatedness** arises from the disruption of our primary ties with nature. By virtue of our powers of reason and imagination, we are aware of our separation from nature, our relative powerlessness, and the arbitrariness of birth and death. Because we have lost our instinctive relationship with nature, we must use reason to create a new relationship with other people. The ideal way to achieve this is through productive love, which involves caring, responsibility, respect, and knowledge. By loving, we become concerned with the growth and happiness of other people. We respond to their needs and respect and know them as they really are.

Productive love can be directed toward someone of the same sex (which

Fromm described as brotherly or sisterly love), toward a person of the opposite sex (erotic love), or toward one's child (parental love). In all three forms, the person's ultimate concern is with the development and growth of the other person's self.

Failure to satisfy the need for relatedness results in narcissism. Narcissistic people cannot perceive the world in objective terms. Their only reality is the subjective world of their own thoughts, feelings, and needs. Because they focus solely on themselves, they cannot relate to others or cope with the outside world.

transcendence need
The need to rise above our animal nature by becoming either creative or destructive.

Transcendence refers to the need to rise above a passive animal state, a state with which we cannot be satisfied because of our capacity for reason and imagination. We need to become creative and productive individuals. In the act of creation, whether of life (as in rearing children), or of material objects, art, or ideas, we surpass the animal state and enter a state of freedom and purposiveness. If a person's creative need is blocked, he or she will become destructive; that is the only alternative to creativity. Destructiveness and creativity are innate tendencies that satisfy the need for transcendence. Creativity, however, is the dominant tendency.

rootedness need The need to feel an attachment or sense of belonging to family, community, and society.

The **need for rootedness** also arises from the loss of our primary ties with nature. Because we stand detached and alone, we must establish new roots in our relationships with others to replace our earlier roots in nature. Feelings of kinship are the most satisfying kind of roots we can develop. The least satisfying way of achieving rootedness is to maintain childhood ties with the mother by clinging to the security of infancy. Such ties can generalize beyond the parent-child relationship to include the community and the nation. "Nationalism is our form of incest," Fromm wrote (1955, p. 58). Nationalism restricts our feelings of solidarity to a specific group, thus isolating us from humanity in general.

identity need The need to achieve an awareness of our unique abilities and characteristics.

Fromm also suggested that people need a sense of **identity** as unique individuals. There are several ways of satisfying this need. For example, a person could develop his or her talents or could identify with a group—a religious sect, a union, or a nation—sometimes to the point of conformity. Fromm noted that conformity was an unhealthy way to satisfy the need for an identity because one's identity would then be defined only in reference to the qualities and characteristics of the group, rather than to the qualities of the self. Thus the self becomes a borrowed one, not a genuine one.

frame-of-orientation need The need for a consistent, coherent picture of our world within which to understand life events.

The **need for a frame of orientation and an object of devotion** stems from our powers of reason and imagination, which require a framework for making sense of the phenomena of the external world. We must develop a consistent and coherent view of our environment within which to perceive and understand what is going on around us. This frame of orientation can be based on rational or irrational considerations. A rational framework provides an objective perception of reality. An irrational one involves a subjective view, which eventually severs our connection with reality. In addition to a frame of orientation, we need an ultimate goal or an object to which we are devoted and through which we can find meaning and a sense of direction.

excitation need The need for a stimulating external environment so that the brain can function at a peak level of activity and alertness.

The **need for excitation and stimulation** refers to the drive for a stimulating external environment in which we can function at a peak of alertness and activity. The brain requires a certain level of stimulation to maintain optimal performance. Without such excitation, we would find it difficult to maintain our involvement with daily life.

The way in which these psychological needs are satisfied depends on our cultural and social conditions and opportunities. Therefore, the way we cope with or adjust to society is to work out a compromise between our needs and our environment. As a result of our compromise, we develop the structure of the personality—what Fromm called our character type.

Character Types

Fromm proposed character types or orientations that underlie all behavior. They are powerful forces by which we relate or orient ourselves to the real world. Pure forms of these types are rare; most personalities are a combination of traits, although one orientation is usually dominant.

Fromm distinguished between nonproductive and productive types. Nonproductive orientations are unhealthy ways of relating to the world. These include the receptive, exploitative, hoarding, and marketing orientations. The productive orientation is the ideal state of human development.

receptive orientation A character type that is highly dependent on others.

Individuals with **receptive orientations** expect to get whatever they want—love, knowledge, or pleasure, for example—from some outside source, usually another person. People of this type are receivers in their relations with others, needing to be loved rather than loving, taking rather than creating. Such people are highly dependent on others and feel paralyzed when left on their own; they feel incapable of doing the smallest thing without outside help. A similarity exists between the receptive character and Freud's oral incorporative personality type in that both find satisfaction in eating and drinking. The receptive type is also similar to Horney's compliant personality type, the one described as moving toward people. The society that fosters the receptive character type is one in which the exploitation of one group by another is practiced.

exploitative orientation A character type that takes from others by force or cunning.

In the **exploitative orientation**, the person is also directed toward others for what he or she wants. However, instead of expecting to receive from others, people of this type take, either by force or by cunning. If something is given to them, they see it as worthless. They want only what belongs to and is valued by others—whether it be a spouse, an object, or an idea. To this type of person, what has to be stolen or appropriated has greater value than what is given freely. The exploitative type is similar to Freud's oral aggressive type and Horney's aggressive type (moving against people). Examples of the exploitative orientation include domineering people, such as corporate raiders and fascist leaders.

hoarding orientation A character type that

In the **hoarding orientation**, the person derives security from what he or she can hoard and save. This miserly behavior applies not only to money derives security from amassing and preserving material possessions and personal feelings.

and material possessions, but also to emotions and thoughts. Such people build walls around themselves and sit surrounded by all they have amassed, protecting it from outside intruders and letting as little out as possible. They are characterized by a compulsive orderliness about their possessions, thoughts, and feelings. A parallel exists here with Freud's anal retentive personality and Horney's detached type (moving away from people). Fromm suggested that the hoarding orientation was common in the 18th and 19th centuries in countries that had stable middle-class economies typified by the Protestant ethic of thrift, conservatism, and sober business practices.

marketing orientation
A character type that values superficial qualities.

The **marketing orientation** is a 20th-century phenomenon identified with capitalist societies, particularly that of the United States. In a commodity-based marketplace culture, Fromm argued, our success or failure depends on how well we sell ourselves. The set of values is the same for personalities as for goods; one's personality becomes a commodity to be sold. Thus, it is not our personal qualities, skills, knowledge, or integrity that count, but rather how nice a "package" we are. Superficial qualities, such as smiling, being agreeable, and laughing at the boss's jokes, become more important than inner characteristics and abilities.

Such an orientation cannot produce security because we are left without any genuine relatedness to other people. If the game is played long enough, we no longer have a relationship with or awareness of our selves. The packaged role we are forced to play obscures our true character from ourselves as well as from others. As a result, we become alienated, with no personal core and no meaningful relationships.

productive orientation
A character type that is the ideal of self-development.

To Fromm, the **productive orientation** is the ideal and represents the ultimate goal of human development. This concept assumes our ability to use all our capacities to realize our potential and to develop the self. Productivity is not restricted to artistic creativity or to the acquisition of material things. Rather, the productive orientation is an attitude that each of us can attain. Although the productive character is the ideal both for people and for societies, it has not yet been achieved; the best we can accomplish within our present social structure is a combination of productive and nonproductive orientations. The influence of the productive orientation may transform the nonproductive types. For example, the aggressiveness of the exploitative type can be transformed into initiative, and the miserliness of the hoarding type can become sound economy. Fromm believed that through social and cultural change, the productive orientation can become dominant.

necrophilous orientation
A character type attracted to inanimate objects and to things associated with death.

In his 1964 book, *The Heart of Man,* Fromm introduced another pair of orientations: necrophilous and biophilous. The **necrophilous** character type is attracted to death—to corpses, decay, feces, and dirt. Such people seem happiest when talking about illness, death, and burials. They dwell on the past and tend to be cold and aloof. They are devoted to law and order, and to the use of force and power. Their dreams center around murder, blood, and skulls. Fromm suggested that Adolf Hitler was an example of the necrophilous type. Not all such people are savages, however. Some appear harmless, but they leave a path of emotional destruction in their wake.

Fromm offered the example of a mother who is obsessively concerned with her child's failures and makes gloomy predictions about the child's future.

> She will not respond to the child's joy; she will not notice anything new that is growing within him. . . . She does not harm the child in any obvious way, yet she may slowly strangle his joy in life, his faith in growth, and eventually she will infect him with her own necrophilous orientation. [Fromm, 1964, p. 39]

Necrophilous persons also have a passion for technology and may surround themselves with appliances such as sophisticated stereo equipment, not for the joy of the music produced but for the love of the machine. Such a person turns "away from life, persons, nature, ideas—in short from everything that is alive [and] transforms all life into things, including himself" (Fromm, 1973, p. 350).

biophilous orientation A character type congruent with the productive orientation; this type is concerned with personal growth and development.

The opposite type, the **biophilous character**, is congruent with the productive orientation. These people are in love with life and are attracted to growth, creation, and construction. They try to influence others, not by force or power, but by love, reason, and example. They are concerned with the development of the self and of others, and their view is toward the future.

Fromm viewed his formulation of the necrophilous and biophilous types as a return to the ideas of Freud. A biographer noted: "Despite Fromm's resolutely anti-instinctivist posture, his thinking in his later years, polarized as it was between life- and death-promoting forces, came to resemble Freud's in many respects" (Burston, 1991, p. 73).

Fromm's Image of Human Nature

Fromm presented an optimistic picture of human nature. In contrast to Freud, he did not consider people to be doomed to conflict and anxiety by immutable biological forces. According to Fromm, we are shaped by our society's social, political, and economic characteristics; however, these forces do not completely determine our character. We are not puppets reacting to the strings pulled by society. Instead, we have a set of psychological qualities or mechanisms by which we shape our own nature and our society.

Fromm believed that we have an innate tendency to grow, develop, and realize our potential. This is our major task in life, our ultimate and necessary goal. We also possess an innate striving for justice and truth. Failure to become what we have the potential to become—failure to attain the productive character type—results in unhappiness and mental illness. Although Fromm proposed a universality in personality—a common social character within a given culture—he also believed that each person is unique. To have an identity as a unique individual is a basic human need. He did not think that we are inherently either good or evil, but rather that we can become evil if we fail to realize our potential.

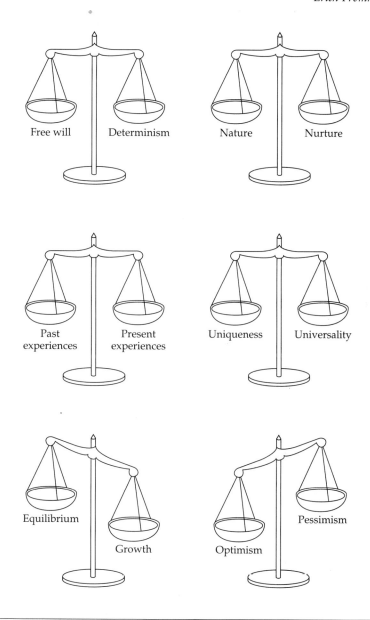

Image of Human Nature.

Fromm

---

humanistic communitarian socialism An ideal system of society typified by positive human relationships and the full expression of the productive orientation.

Fromm continued to believe that humanity would eventually reach a state of harmony and integration, and he was saddened by our failures to date. He proposed an ideal society, which he called **humanistic communitarian socialism**, and described it as one in which love, brotherhood, and solidarity characterize all human relationships. The productive orientation will become dominant, and all feelings of loneliness, insignificance, and alienation will disappear.

Assessment in Fromm's Theory

The neopsychoanalytic theorists we have already discussed based their systems on the clinical data they obtained from patients and were clear about their methods of assessing or evaluating their patients' personalities. In contrast, Fromm wrote little about his assessment techniques. He occasionally referred to "psychoanalytic observations" but did not offer specific analytical findings or case studies. Colleagues of Fromm suggest that he focused primarily on those comments from his patients that supported his theories, and that he was "inattentive, impatient, or actually dismissive of those facets of their experience . . . that did not coincide with his 'intuitive' sense of their problems and situations" (Burston, 1991, p. 82). Thus, the possibility exists that the data Fromm collected from his patients was highly selective.

Fromm did use a form of free association and considered dream analysis an important therapeutic tool. For the most part, though, Fromm based his theory on generalizations and speculations derived from his interpretation of historical, social, and cultural events. He also drew on religious, economic, political, and anthropological sources.

Although Fromm did not use self-report techniques, he developed an interpretive questionnaire to assess the necrophilous character type (Fromm, 1973). The questionnaire included items such as "What is your opinion of women who use cosmetics?" Responses such as "Cosmetics are poisonous" or "Makeup makes women look like whores" were considered to indicate the necrophilous type.

Research in Fromm's Theory

We do not know how widely Fromm used the case study method, nor can we say how comprehensive were the case histories he developed on his patients. He did collect data of a psychoanalytic nature from his patients, however, and the criticisms of case studies discussed in earlier chapters also apply to Fromm. It is impossible to duplicate and verify Fromm's clinical observations or the conditions under which he made them.

Fromm was convinced of the scientific worth and credibility of the case study as a research method. He admitted that the results could not be tested by experimental or correlational methods but insisted that they could be tested by repeated analyses. A hypothesis generated from observations of one patient could be verified by observing additional patients. Nevertheless, no matter how carefully analysts make their observations, it remains impossible for anyone else to repeat them or to establish identical conditions. Thus, the case study method fails to meet the basic requirements of the scientific method.

Late in his career, Fromm and his colleagues undertook a multidisciplinary study to test his idea of social character (Fromm & Maccoby, 1970). Over several years, psychologists, anthropologists, physicians, statisticians, and other specialists visited an isolated village in Mexico to analyze its history, its economic and social structure, and the health, attitudes, and dreams of its inhabitants. The investigators lived among the villagers and came to be accepted by them. Through a combination of techniques—including questionnaires, interviews, the Rorschach inkblot test, and the Thematic Apperception Test—the researchers found substantial support for the receptive, hoarding, and exploitative character types. No evidence was found for the marketing orientation. This is not surprising because Fromm described the marketing orientation as common to 20th-century capitalist societies, not to less developed rural villages. Some evidence was found for the productive type. The personal characteristics of the villagers described as receptive, hoarding, exploitative, and productive were found to match the descriptions in Fromm's writings.

The co-author of the Mexican village study, Michael Maccoby, an anthropologist and psychiatrist, conducted research on Fromm's character types in the world of American business. One study involved interviews with 250 male managers in 12 large corporations (Maccoby, 1976). Maccoby identified a personality type analogous to the marketing orientation and called it "the company man." "When they describe themselves," he wrote, "they seem to be trying to give the right impression, to sell themselves to the interviewers. It is as though they are constantly working on themselves in order to have the right kind of personality to fit the job" (Maccoby, 1976, p. 92).

Like Fromm's marketing type, the company man focuses more on superficial personal qualities to attain success than on actual job skills, abilities, or knowledge. The personality or packaging of this type of person is all-important, and it can be changed to fit the perceived needs of superiors as readily as clothes are changed to fit different social situations.

A later study of corporate leaders in the United States suggested a new character type, which Maccoby called "the self orientation" (Maccoby, 1981). This type is a product of the turbulent American society of the 1960s, which was marked by questioning of traditional authority, of the Protestant work ethic, and of the commitment to corporate success. This is the generation of employees now in the middle and late stages of their careers. Maccoby described the self orientation as cynical, rebellious, detached, undisciplined, self-indulgent, lacking in loyalty, and unconcerned with others' well-being. To use Fromm's term, this type is narcissistic.

Although Maccoby's research does not provide direct support for Fromm's proposed character types, it suggests types within the framework of Fromm's system that are products of historical, social, and cultural forces. Fromm believed that as these forces change, so will the character types or orientations associated with them.

There is indirect evidence to support Fromm's receptive, exploitative, and hoarding orientations. As we noted earlier, each of these types is similar to one of Freud's oral or anal personality types. To the degree that empirical research support exists for Freud's types (see Chapter 2), by extension it exists for Fromm's similar orientations.

For the marketing personality type found among American businessmen, superficial qualities are more important than knowledge or skills.

Using Fromm's interpretive questionnaire approach, Maccoby investigated a variety of subject samples and found evidence to support the existence of the necrophilous character type (Maccoby, 1972). Approximately 10 to 15 percent of those tested were judged to be necrophilous. Correlating the questionnaire responses with the subjects' political opinions revealed that persons labeled necrophilous supported military force against those they considered enemies and favored repressive measures against those who criticized the government. Necrophilous types also wanted to strengthen police forces and improve enforcement of antidrug laws.

A Final Commentary

Fromm's books have been popular with audiences in many countries. He wrote for the general public because he wanted to reach the maximum number of people with his message about the kind of society we must develop if human civilization is to survive. His books are highly readable, with a minimum of technical jargon. This does not mean that they are simple, but rather that he presented his ideas in an engaging and interesting manner.

Fromm's importance to psychology lies in his focus on social, historical, and cultural forces and their role in shaping personality. We see similarities between Fromm's productive character type and Gordon Allport's concept of the mature personality (Chapter 8), as well as Abraham Maslow's description of the self-actualizing person (Chapter 11).

Fromm's approach to personality is broad in both perspective and propositions. He was not exclusively a psychoanalyst but drew on data from many disciplines. One criticism of his theory is that it lacks supporting empirical data. Fromm has also been faulted for not keeping current with developments in psychoanalysis. His major references were the works of Freud, Jung, and Horney; more recent ideas, such as those of the humanistic psychologists, were not recognized in his system. In addition, some of Fromm's concepts are defined imprecisely and in terms that are often contradictory, thus making it difficult to test his propositions experimentally.

Scholars who are knowledgeable about the history and social conditions of the Middle Ages have challenged Fromm's suggestion that people during that period had attained security, identity, and belongingness. They charge that Fromm painted an idealized picture of the Middle Ages and omitted calamities such as religious persecutions, witch hunts, plagues, wars, and other physical and psychological hardships. These scholars argue that the Middle Ages must have been a time of great instability and insecurity.

Nevertheless, Fromm presented us with an unusual interpretation of the interaction between people and their society. He made us aware of the continuing and interrelated impact of social, economic, and psychological factors on human nature. Whether or not his proposals turn out to be valid, he has shown us that personality is not the product of a single set of factors but the result of an interplay of forces and events. He challenged us to think beyond the boundaries of any one discipline and goaded us to create a more humane society. Fromm's contributions extend beyond psychoanalysis and psychology to include the spectrum of social problems that concern us all.

Summary

Erich Fromm argued that personality is influenced by historical, economic, political, and social forces rather than solely by biological forces. He believed that as people throughout history have gained more freedom, they have come to feel more lonely and alienated. The less freedom people have, the greater their sense of belonging and security. The Middle Ages, a time of little individual freedom, was the last era of security and belonging, because everyone's place in society was fixed. The social upheaval of the Renaissance and the Protestant Reformation expanded human freedom and choice but reduced the sense of security.

People desire to escape from too much freedom and from the loneliness and insignificance that accompany it. Three psychic mechanisms of escape are (1) authoritarianism, in which people submit to others or gain power over others; (2) destructiveness; and (3) automaton conformity.

The development of an individual in childhood parallels the development of humankind throughout history. As children grow, they gain increasing independence and freedom at the expense of the security of the primary maternal ties. Children attempt to escape this freedom through (1) symbiotic relatedness (escaping loneliness and insecurity by becoming part of someone else), (2) withdrawal-destructiveness (maintaining a separation from others), or (3) love.

Six psychological needs result from the polarity between the drive for security and the drive for freedom: (1) relatedness (the need to achieve connection with others, preferably through productive love); (2) transcendence (the need to rise above the passive animal state and become creative and productive); (3) rootedness (the need to establish new roots in relationships with others, to replace previous roots in nature); (4) identity (the need to develop one's talents and abilities to the fullest); (5) a frame of orientation and an object of devotion (the need for a framework within which to organize life events and to find an overall goal or an object to provide a consistent sense of meaning); and (6) excitation and stimulation (the need for sufficient external stimulation to maintain peak levels of mental alertness and activity).

Orientations or character traits are grouped into nonproductive and productive types. Nonproductive types include the receptive, exploitative, hoarding, and marketing orientations. Receptive types depend on others for satisfaction of their needs. Exploitative types take what they need from others. Hoarding types derive security from what can be amassed and saved. Marketing types see themselves as commodities to be packaged and sold. Productive types represent the ultimate goal of human development: the achievement of self-realization. Fromm later proposed two other orientations: necrophilous and biophilous. Necrophilous types are in love with death, power, and technology; biophilous types are in love with life, growth, and development.

Fromm's image of human nature is optimistic. We have the ability to shape our personality and society. Life's ultimate, innate goal is the realization of our potentialities and capacities.

Fromm's methods of assessment included free association, dream analysis, and his unique interpretation of social and cultural data. His research method relied on psychoanalytic observations, which cannot be repeated or verified. His theory has been criticized for ignoring developments in psychoanalysis, containing vague terminology, and presenting an idealized picture of the Middle Ages. His importance lies in his focus on broad social, historical, and cultural forces in the shaping of personality.

Critical Thinking Review

1. How does Fromm's approach to personality differ from those of the other personality theorists we have discussed?

2. What experiences in Fromm's early years influenced the direction of his work?

3. According to Fromm, why have people become less secure as they have achieved greater freedom?

4. Describe the three psychic mechanisms by which we can regain security and ease our feelings of loneliness.

5. Describe the parental behaviors that can foster symbiotic relatedness, withdrawal-destructiveness, and love.

6. Define the six psychological needs in Fromm's theory and describe how the satisfaction of each contributes to the creation of the self.

7. Describe the productive and nonproductive character orientations.

8. Distinguish between the biophilous and necrophilous character types.

9. What methods of assessment did Fromm use in developing his theory?

10. Which character orientation did Fromm consider typical of American society? Which orientations were supported by the results of the Mexican village studies?

11. According to Fromm, what is the relationship between personality and society?

Suggested Reading

Burston, D. (1991). *The legacy of Erich Fromm.* Cambridge, MA: Harvard University Press. Portrays Fromm as a member of Freud's "loyal opposition" and places Fromm's work in the context of 20th-century intellectual thought.

Evans, R. I. (1966). *Dialogue with Erich Fromm.* New York: Harper & Row. Conversations with Fromm about his life and work.

Fromm, E. (1941). *Escape from freedom.* New York: Holt, Rinehart & Winston. Fromm's views on the human character and how it is affected by social and political forces.

Fromm, E. (1947). *Man for himself: An inquiry into the psychology of ethics.* New York: Holt, Rinehart & Winston. Describes the productive and nonproductive character orientations and relates them to ethical behavior for the individual and for society.

Fromm, E. (1968). *The revolution of hope: Toward a humanized technology.* New York: Harper & Row. Discusses the choice between a mechanistic and a humanistic world and argues for a psychospiritual renewal to deal with the problem.

Henry Murray

The Life of Murray (1893–1988)
The Principles of Personology
Id, Superego, and Ego: The Divisions of
    Personality
Needs: The Motivation of Behavior
    Categories of Needs
    Characteristics of Needs
Personality Development in Childhood
Murray's Image of Human Nature

Assessment in Murray's Theory
    The OSS Assessment Program
    The Thematic Apperception Test
Research in Murray's Theory
A Final Commentary
Summary
Critical Thinking Review
Suggested Reading

For me, personality is [a] jungle without boundaries.

—Henry Murray

Henry Murray designed an approach to personality that combined ideas from Freudian psychoanalysis with original concepts and methods. Murray's formulations reflect his work in biochemistry, medicine, and psychoanalytic research and practice, as well as his personal study of literature. His theory includes conscious and unconscious forces; the influence of the past, present, and future; and the impact of physiological and sociological factors.

Murray's system places great emphasis on physiological functioning as it directs the personality. His interest in physiology is also evident in his concern with tension reduction as a major motivating force. The further influence of Freudian psychoanalysis can be seen in Murray's recognition of the effect on adult behavior of childhood experiences and in his notions of the id, ego, and superego. Although Freud's imprint is clear, Murray gave unique interpretations to these phenomena. His deviations from orthodox psychoanalysis are so extensive that his system must be classified with the neo-Freudians rather than with the Freudian loyalists.

Two distinctive features of Murray's system are a sophisticated approach to human needs and the source of the data on which he based his theory. His proposed list of needs is widely used in personality research and assessment and in clinical treatment. His data, unlike those of theorists discussed in earlier chapters, come from so-called normal individuals (male undergraduate students at Harvard University) rather than from patients undergoing psychotherapy. Also, some of the data were derived from more empirically based laboratory procedures rather than from case histories.

Because of his long affiliation with a major university instead of relative isolation in a clinic or private practice, and because of his personal charisma, Murray gathered and trained a large number of psychologists, many of whom have since achieved prominence and carried on his teachings.

The Life of Murray (1893–1988)

Neither neurotic parents nor poverty marked Henry Murray's childhood. However, it contained elements of Adlerian compensation for a physical defect, a supernormal sensitivity to the sufferings of others, and a hint of maternal rejection to ensure that his childhood was not intolerably dull.

Murray was born to great wealth—a legacy from his grandfather—and grew up in New York City, in a house on what is now the site of Rockefeller Center. His summers were spent on a Long Island beach. As a child, he accompanied his parents on four long trips to Europe. For the Adlerians among you, Murray reported that some of his earliest recollections focused on his privileged background (Triplet, 1992).

Another significant early memory is more intriguing. Murray called it "the marrow-of-my-being memory." At about 4 years of age, he was looking at a picture of a sad woman sitting next to her equally sad son. (This was the same kind of gloomy picture Murray later used in his Thematic Apperception Test.) Murray's mother told him, "It is the prospect of death that has made them sad."

Murray interpreted the memory as indicating the death of his emotional ties to his mother because she had abruptly weaned him when he was 2 months old. Murray was left with what he called "a limited, third-best portion" of her affection. He believed this led to his lifelong depression, a condition that formed a central part of his personality (Murray, 1967, p. 299). Murray referred to his depression as his "marrow of misery and melancholy" and attempted to mask it in his everyday behavior by developing an ebullient, cheerful, and outgoing manner. This lack of a childhood attachment to his mother later caused Murray to question Freud's description of the Oedipus complex because it did not coincide with his childhood experience (J. W. Anderson, 1988, 1990).

At an early age, Murray became sensitized to the emotional problems and sufferings of others, largely because of his relationships with two neurotic aunts, one a depressive, the other a hysteric.

Murray was afflicted with crossed eyes, and at the age of 9 he underwent an operation that was performed in the dining room of his home. The condition was corrected, but a slip of the surgeon's blade left Murray with no stereoscopic vision. No matter how hard he tried, he was never able to succeed at games such as tennis or baseball because he could not focus both eyes on the ball. He remained unaware of his visual defect until he was in medical school, when a physician asked him if he had had trouble playing sports as a child.

Murray's ineptness at sports, together with another defect he developed in childhood—a stutter—created in him the need to compensate. When he tried to play football, he had to be quarterback; when calling plays, he never stuttered. After being bested in a schoolyard fight, Murray took up boxing and won the local featherweight championship. He later noted that "an Adlerian factor was at work" in these childhood efforts to compensate for his physical disabilities (Murray, 1967, p. 302).

After attending Groton, a preparatory school, Murray enrolled at Harvard University. He majored in history and earned mediocre grades because he devoted so much time to "rowing and romance." His career followed a devious route to the study of personality. He disliked the psychology course he took in college and by the second lecture had begun "looking for the nearest exit." He did not attend another psychology course until years later, when he taught one himself.

In 1919 Murray graduated from Columbia University Medical School at the top of his class. He earned an M.A. in biology from Columbia and taught physiology at Harvard. He served a two-year internship in surgery at a New York hospital and helped care for a future U.S. president, Franklin D. Roosevelt, in his struggle with polio. Following the internship Murray spent two years at the Rockefeller Institute conducting biomedical research in embryology. He went abroad for further study and in 1927 received his Ph.D. in biochemistry from Cambridge University.

Murray's unusual sensitivity and empathy toward others were reinforced during his internship, when he became interested in the psychological factors in his patients' lives. In 1923 he read Carl Jung's book *Psychological Types* and found it fascinating. "I found this book at the medical school bookstore on the way home one night," he said, "and I read it all night long and all the next day" (quoted in J. W. Anderson, 1988, p. 147). A few weeks after finishing the book, Murray was faced with a serious personal problem. He fell in love with Christiana Morgan, a young woman who also felt an affinity with Jung's work. Murray did not want to leave his wife of seven years—he claimed to abhor the idea of divorce—but neither did he want to give up his lover, whose spirited, artistic nature was the opposite of his wife's. Murray insisted that he needed both women.

He lived with the conflict for two years until, at Morgan's insistence, he went to Zurich to meet with Carl Jung. The two men spent a month together, and Jung was able to resolve Murray's difficulty by instruction and example. Jung was also having an affair with a younger woman, a relationship he maintained openly while living with his wife. Jung counseled Murray to do the same, and Murray did so for 40 years. Morgan and Murray also collaborated on the Thematic Apperception Test.

This experience with Jung turned Murray toward a career in psychology.

He had "brought his most wrenching problem to psychology and psychology provided an answer. Nothing would carry greater weight, for someone trying to decide whether psychology had anything to offer, than a real-life experience like this" (J. W. Anderson, 1988, p. 150). Thus, Jung did more than resolve Murray's personal and career dilemmas; he made Murray aware of the breadth and impact of unconscious forces. "The great floodgates of the wonder-world swung open," Murray wrote. "I had experienced the unconscious" (Murray, 1940, p. 153).

Murray was offered an appointment by psychologist Morton Prince at the new Harvard Psychological Clinic, established specifically to study personality. A former student described the clinic as "wisteria on the outside, hysteria on the inside" (Smith, 1990, p. 537). As part of his training, Murray underwent orthodox Freudian psychoanalysis and reported that his analyst became bored by the phlegmatic nature of his childhood and his lack of complexes. Murray recalled that the analyst had little to say. The analyst's stomach rumbled, and his office was "depressing, the color of feces." Murray described the office as a "miserable room . . . enough to send a patient into a morbid phase" (quoted in J. W. Anderson, 1988, p. 159).

In the 1930s, Murray and Morgan developed the Thematic Apperception Test (TAT), still one of the most widely used projective measures of personality in both research and assessment (Morgan & Murray, 1935). The idea for the test was Murray's; Morgan selected the cards and drew some of the pictures. The gloomier pictures were chosen by Murray and reflected his pervasive depression.

During World War II, Murray joined the U.S. Army and became director of assessment for the Office of Strategic Services (the OSS; a forerunner of the CIA), screening candidates for dangerous assignments. He maintained an interest in literature, especially the work of Herman Melville, and in 1951 published an analysis of the psychological meaning of Melville's novel *Moby Dick.*

Murray met with Carl Jung several times, and his attitude toward the man who helped him through his early crises changed dramatically. His initial acceptance of Jung's views turned to scathing dismissal. Jung would "believe anything I told him that was along the lines that he liked," Murray said, "but he would overlook what did not fit his theories" (quoted in J. W. Anderson, 1988, p. 155).

Murray remained at Harvard until his retirement in 1962, conducting research, refining his personality theory, and training new generations of psychologists. He received the American Psychological Foundation's Gold Medal Award and the American Psychological Association's Distinguished Scientific Contribution Award.

When Murray's wife died in 1962, his depression threatened to overcome him. He "turned old overnight," a student wrote. "He would cry all day, and he would leave meetings because he was overwhelmed by his grief" (J. W. Anderson, 1990, p. 329). Five years later, Christiana Morgan also died. And two years after that, at the age of 76, Murray remarried. "If you get into your late seventies," he told a friend, "and you're debating whether you should get married again—do it!" (quoted in J. W. Anderson, 1990, p. 330).

The Principles of Personology

personology Murray's system of personality.

"No brain, no personality" (Murray, 1951, p. 267). This comment sums up the first principle in Murray's **personology** (his term for the study of personality). Murray was committed to the notion that psychological processes depend on physiological processes. Personality is rooted in the brain; the individual's cerebral physiology guides and governs the personality. We have all seen a simple example of this; namely, that certain drugs can alter the functioning of the brain, and so the personality. Everything on which personality depends exists in the brain—feeling states, conscious and unconscious memories, beliefs, attitudes, fears, and values.

A second principle in Murray's system involves the idea of tension reduction. Other theorists (notably Freud) supported the importance of altering need-induced tension levels, but Murray went a step further. He agreed that we act to reduce physiological and psychological tension but that this does not mean we are striving to achieve a tension-free state. It is the process of reducing tension that is satisfying, not the attainment of a condition free of tension.

To Murray, a tension-free situation is a source of distress. We need excitement, activity, and movement, all of which involve increasing tension, not decreasing it. We generate tension in order to have the satisfaction of reducing it. Murray believed that the ideal state of human nature involves always having a certain level of tension to reduce.

A third principle of Murray's personology is that personality is longitudinal. An individual's personality continues to develop over time and is constructed of all the events that occur during the course of that person's life. Therefore, the study of one's past is of great importance.

Murray's fourth principle involves the idea that personality changes and progresses. Personality is not static or fixed. Because it is in a state of flux, it is difficult to describe precisely.

Fifth, Murray emphasized the uniqueness of each person while recognizing similarities among all people. As he saw it, an individual human being is like no other person, like some other people, and like every other person.

Id, Superego, and Ego: The Divisions of Personality

Murray divided personality into three parts, using the Freudian terms *id, superego,* and *ego,* but his concepts are not what Freud envisioned. Like Freud, Murray suggested that the **id** is the repository of all innate impulsive tendencies. As such, it provides energy and direction to behavior and is concerned with motivation. The id contains the primitive, amoral, and lustful impulses

id To Murray, the id contains the primitive, amoral, and lustful impulses described by Freud, but it also contains desirable impulses, such as empathy and love.

Freud described. However, unlike in Freud's conception, in Murray's personological system the id also encompasses innate impulses that society considers acceptable and desirable. Here we see the influence of Jung's shadow archetype, which has both good and bad aspects. The id contains the tendencies to empathy, imitation, and identification; forms of love other than lustful ones; and the tendency to master one's environment.

The strength or intensity of the id varies among individuals. For example, one person may possess more intense appetites and emotions than another. Therefore, the problem of controlling and directing the id forces is not the same for all people because some of us have greater id energy with which we must cope.

superego To Murray, the superego is shaped not only by parents and other authority figures, but also by the peer group and culture.

Murray emphasized the importance of societal influences on personality. Agreeing with Freud, he defined the **superego** as the internalization of the culture's values and norms, by which rules we come to evaluate and judge our behavior and that of others. The substance of the superego is imposed on children at an early age by their parents and other authority figures.

Other factors that shape the superego include the peer group and the literature and mythology of the culture. Thus, Murray deviated from Freudian ideas by allowing for influences beyond the parent-child interaction. According to Murray, the superego is not rigidly crystallized by age 5 but continues to develop throughout life, thus reflecting the greater complexity and sophistication of our experiences as we grow older.

Because the id contains good forces as well as bad ones, the superego is not in constant conflict with the id, as Freud had proposed. Good forces do not have to be suppressed. The superego must try to thwart the socially unacceptable impulses, but it also functions to determine when, where, and how an acceptable need can be expressed and satisfied.

ego-ideal The repository of the moral or ideal behaviors for which we should strive.

While the superego is developing, so is the **ego-ideal**, which provides us with long-range goals for which to strive. The ego-ideal represents what we could become at our best and is the sum of our ambitions and aspirations.

ego To Murray, the ego is the conscious organizer of all behavior; this is a broader conception than Freud's.

The **ego** is the rational governor of the personality; it tries to modify or delay the id's unacceptable impulses. Murray extended Freud's formulation of the ego by proposing that the ego is the central organizer of all behavior. It consciously reasons, decides, and wills the direction of behavior. Thus, the ego is more active in determining behavior than Freud believed. Not merely the servant of the id, the ego consciously plans courses of action. It functions not only to suppress id pleasure but also to foster pleasure by organizing and directing the expression of acceptable id impulses.

The ego is also the arbiter between the id and the superego and may favor one over the other. For example, if the ego favors the id, it may direct the personality toward a life of crime. The ego may also integrate these two aspects of the personality so that what we want to do (id) is in harmony with what society believes we should do (superego).

Opportunity exists in Murray's system for conflict to arise between the id and the superego. A strong ego can mediate effectively between the two, but a weak ego leaves the personality a battleground. Unlike Freud, however, Murray did not believe that this conflict was inevitable.

Needs: The Motivation of Behavior

Murray's most important contribution to theory and research in personality is his use of the concept of needs to explain the motivation and direction of behavior. His extensive work on motivation, which forms the core of his personality theory, provides one of psychology's more elaborate and extensive classifications of needs. He derived his concept of needs not from personal experience or intuition, or from case studies of emotionally disturbed patients, but from the intensive study of normal subjects.

A need is a physiologically based hypothetical construct; it involves a physicochemical force in the brain that organizes and directs intellectual and perceptual abilities. Needs may arise either from internal processes, such as hunger or thirst, or from events in the environment. Needs arouse a level of tension that the organism tries to reduce by acting to satisfy them. As stated earlier, needs energize and direct behavior—they activate behavior in the appropriate direction to satisfy the needs.

Murray's research led him to formulate a list of 20 needs. Some modifications have been offered since then, but his original work represents the major needs in his system (Murray, 1938, pp. 144–145). Not every person has all of these needs. Some people may experience all the needs over the course of a lifetime; others will never experience some of them. Some needs support other needs, and some oppose other needs.

> *Dominance (n Dom).* To control one's environment. To influence or direct the behavior of others by suggestion, seduction, persuasion, or command. To get others to cooperate. To convince another of the rightness of one's opinion.
>
> *Deference (n Def).* To admire and support a superior other. To yield eagerly to the influence of an allied other. To conform to custom.
>
> *Autonomy (n Auto).* To get free, shake off restraint, or break out of confinement. To resist coercion and restriction. To be independent and free to act according to impulse. To defy conventions.
>
> *Aggression (n Agg).* To overcome opposition forcefully. To fight, attack, injure, or kill another. To maliciously belittle, censure, or ridicule another.
>
> *Abasement (n Aba).* To submit passively to external force. To accept injury, blame, criticism, and punishment. To become resigned to fate. To admit inferiority, error, wrongdoing, or defeat. To blame, belittle, or mutilate the self. To seek and enjoy pain, punishment, illness, and misfortune.
>
> *Achievement (n Ach).* To accomplish something difficult. To master, manipulate, or organize physical objects, human beings, or ideas. To

The need for affiliation is expressed in cooperation, loyalty, and friendship.

overcome obstacles and attain a high standard. To rival and surpass others.

Sex (n Sex). To form and further an erotic relationship. To have sexual intercourse.

Sentience (n Sen). To seek and enjoy sensuous impressions.

Exhibition (n Exh). To make an impression. To be seen and heard. To excite, amaze, fascinate, entertain, shock, intrigue, amuse, or entice others.

Play (n Play). To act for fun, without further purpose.

Affiliation (n Aff). To draw near and enjoyably cooperate or reciprocate with an allied other who resembles one or who likes one. To adhere and remain loyal to a friend.

Rejection (n Rej). To exclude, abandon, expel, or remain indifferent to an inferior other. To snub or jilt another.

Succorance (n Suc). To be nursed, supported, sustained, surrounded, protected, loved, advised, guided, indulged, forgiven, or consoled. To remain close to a devoted protector.

Nurturance (n Nur). To give sympathy to and gratify the needs of a helpless other, an infant or one who is weak, disabled, tired, inexperienced, infirm, humiliated, lonely, dejected, or mentally confused.

Infavoidance (n Inf). To avoid humiliation. To quit embarrassing situations or to avoid conditions that may lead to the scorn, derision, or indifference of others. To refrain from action because of the fear of failure.

Defendance (n Dfd). To defend the self against assault, criticism, and blame. To conceal or justify a misdeed, failure, or humiliation.

Counteraction (n Cnt). To master or make up for a failure by restriving. To obliterate a humiliation by resumed action. To overcome weaknesses and to repress fear. To search for obstacles and difficulties to overcome. To maintain self-respect and pride on a high level.

Harmavoidance (n Harm). To avoid pain, physical injury, illness, and death. To escape from a dangerous situation. To take precautionary measures.

Order (n Ord). To put things in order. To achieve cleanliness, arrangement, organization, balance, neatness, and precision.

Understanding (n Und). To be inclined to analyze events and to generalize. To discuss and argue and to emphasize reason and logic. To state one's opinions precisely. To show interest in abstract formulations in science, mathematics, and philosophy.

Categories of Needs

primary and **secondary needs** Primary needs are survival and related needs arising from internal bodily processes. Secondary needs are emotional and psychological needs, such as achievement and affiliation.

Primary and secondary needs.   The first category Murray posited is the primary (or viscerogenic) and secondary (or psychogenic) distinction. **Primary needs** arise from internal bodily states and include those needs required for survival (such as food, water, air, and harmavoidance), as well as such needs as sex and sentience. **Secondary needs** arise indirectly from primary needs (in a way Murray did not make clear), but they have no specifiable origin within the body. They are called secondary not because they are less important but because they develop after the primary needs. Secondary needs are concerned with emotional satisfaction and include most of the needs on Murray's original list.

reactive and **proactive needs** Reactive needs involve a response to a specific object. Proactive needs arise spontaneously.

Reactive and proactive needs.   **Reactive needs** involve a response to something specific in the environment; that is, the need is aroused only when that object appears. For example, the harmavoidance need appears only when a threat is present. **Proactive needs** do not depend on the presence of a particular object. They are spontaneous needs that elicit appropriate behavior whenever they are aroused, independent of the environment. For example, hungry people look for food to satisfy their need; they do not wait for a stimulus, such as a television ad for a hamburger, before acting to find food.

Characteristics of Needs

Needs differ in terms of the urgency with which they impel behavior, a characteristic Murray called a need's prepotency. For example, if the needs for air and water are not satisfied, they can become insistent and dominate behavior, taking precedence over all other needs.

Some needs are complementary and can be satisfied by one behavior or a set of behaviors. Murray called this a fusion of needs. For instance, by working to acquire fame and wealth, we can satisfy the needs for achievement, dominance, and autonomy.

subsidiation
A situation in which one need is activated to aid in the satisfaction of another need.

The concept of **subsidiation** refers to a situation in which one need is activated to aid in satisfying another need. For example, to satisfy the affiliation need by being in the company of other people, it may be necessary to act deferentially toward them, thus invoking the deference need. In this case, the deference need is subsidiary to the affiliation need.

press The influence of the environment and past events on the current activation of a need.

Murray recognized that childhood events can affect the development of specific needs and, later in life, can activate those needs. He called this influence **press** because an environmental object or event presses or pressures the individual to act a certain way.

thema A combination of press (the environment) and need (the personality) that brings order to our behavior.

Because of the possibility of interaction between need and press, Murray introduced the concept of **thema** (or unity thema). The thema combines personal factors (needs) with the environmental factors that pressure or compel our behavior (presses). The thema is formed through early childhood experiences and becomes a powerful force in determining personality. Largely unconscious, the thema relates needs and presses in a pattern that gives coherence, unity, order, and uniqueness to our behavior.

Personality Development in Childhood

Drawing on Freud's work, Murray divided childhood into five stages, each characterized by a pleasurable condition that is inevitably terminated by society's demands (Murray, 1938). Each stage leaves its mark on our personality in the form of an unconscious **complex** or pattern that directs our later development. According to Murray, everyone experiences these five complexes because everyone passes through the same developmental stages. There is nothing abnormal about them except when they are manifested in the extreme, a condition that leaves the person fixated at that stage. The personality is then unable to develop spontaneity and flexibility, a situation that interferes with the formation of the ego and superego. The stages of childhood and their corresponding complexes are shown in Table 7.1.

complex A normal pattern of childhood development that influences the adult personality. Childhood stages of development include the **claustral, oral, anal, urethral,** and **genital** complexes. When manifested in the extreme, fixation occurs, thwarting the full development of the ego and superego.

The claustral stage.   In the womb, the fetus is secure, serene, and dependent, conditions we may all occasionally wish to reinstate. The simple claustral complex is experienced as a desire to be in small, warm, dark places that are safe and secluded. For example, one might long to remain under the blankets instead of getting out of bed in the morning. People with this complex tend to be dependent on others, passive, and oriented toward safe, familiar behaviors that worked in the past.

The "insupport" form of the claustral complex centers on feelings of insecurity and helplessness that cause the person to fear open spaces, falling, drowning, fires, earthquakes, or any situation of novelty and change.

Table 7.1   **The childhood stages and complexes in Murray's personology.**

Stage	Complex
The secure existence within the womb	Claustral complexes
The sensuous enjoyment of sucking nourishment while being held	Oral complexes
The pleasure resulting from defecation	Anal complexes
The pleasure accompanying urination	Urethral complex
Genital pleasures	Genital or castration complex

The anticlaustral or egression form of the claustral complex is based on a need to escape from restraining womblike conditions. It includes a fear of suffocation and confinement and manifests itself in a preference for open spaces, fresh air, travel, movement, change, and novelty.

The oral stage. The oral succorance complex features a combination of mouth activities, passive tendencies, and the need to be supported and protected. Behavioral manifestations include sucking, kissing, eating, drinking, and a hunger for affection, sympathy, protection, and love. The oral aggression complex combines oral and aggressive behaviors, including biting, spitting, shouting, and verbal aggression such as sarcasm. Behaviors characteristic of the oral rejection complex include vomiting, being picky about food, eating little, fearing oral contamination (such as from kissing), desiring seclusion, and avoiding dependence on others.

The anal stage. In the anal rejection complex, there is a preoccupation with defecation, anal humor, and feces-like material such as dirt, mud, plaster, and clay. Aggression is often part of this complex and is shown in dropping and throwing things, firing guns, and setting off explosives. Persons with this complex may be dirty and disorganized. The anal retention complex is manifested in accumulating, saving, and collecting things, and in cleanliness, neatness, and orderliness.

The urethral stage. Unique to Murray's system, the urethral complex is associated with excessive ambition, a distorted sense of self-esteem, exhibitionism, bed-wetting, and self-love. It is sometimes called the Icarus complex, after the mythical Greek figure who flew so close to the sun that the wax holding his wings melted. Like Icarus, persons with this complex aim too high, and their dreams are shattered by failure.

The genital or castration stage. Murray disagreed with Freud's contention that fear of castration is the core of anxiety in adult males. He interpreted the complex in narrower and more literal fashion as "anxiety evoked by the fantasy that the penis might be cut off" (Murray, 1938, p. 385). Murray believed that such a fear grows out of childhood masturbation and the parental punishment that may have accompanied it.

Murray's Image of Human Nature

Although Murray's personality theory is similar to Freud's in several ways, his image of human nature is quite different. Even the ultimate and necessary goal in life—which, like Freud's, is the reduction of tension—is considered from a different perspective. According to Murray, our goal is not a tension-free state but rather the satisfaction derived from acting to reduce tension.

On the free will versus determinism issue, Murray argued that personality is determined by needs and by the environment. He accorded us some free will in our capacity to change and to grow. Each person is unique, but there are also similarities in the personalities of all of us.

Murray believed that we are shaped by inherited attributes and by our environment; each is of roughly equal influence. We cannot understand the human personality unless we accept the impact of physiological forces and of stimuli in our physical, social, and cultural environments.

Murray's view of human nature was optimistic. He criticized a psychology that projected a negative and demeaning image of human beings. He argued that, with our vast powers of creativity, imagination, and reason, we are capable of solving any problem we face.

In Murray's view, our orientation is largely toward the future. Although he recognized the imprint of childhood experiences on current behavior, he did not envision us as captives of the past. The childhood complexes he proposed unconsciously affect our development, but personality is also determined by present events and aspirations for the future.

We have the ability to grow and develop, and such growth is a natural part of being human. We can change through our rational and creative abilities and therefore can reshape our society as well.

Assessment in Murray's Theory

Murray's techniques for assessing personality differ from those of Freud and the other neopsychoanalytic theorists. Murray was not working with emotionally disturbed persons, and he did not use such standard psychoanalytic techniques as free association and dream analysis.

For his intensive evaluation of the normal personality, Murray used a variety of techniques to collect data from 51 male undergraduate students at Harvard University. The subjects were interviewed and given projective tests, objective tests, and questionnaires covering childhood memories, family relations, sexual development, sensorimotor learning, ethical standards, goals, social interactions, and mechanical and artistic abilities. This assessment program was so comprehensive that it took Murray's staff of 28 investigators six months to complete. We discuss these data in the section entitled "Research in Murray's Theory."

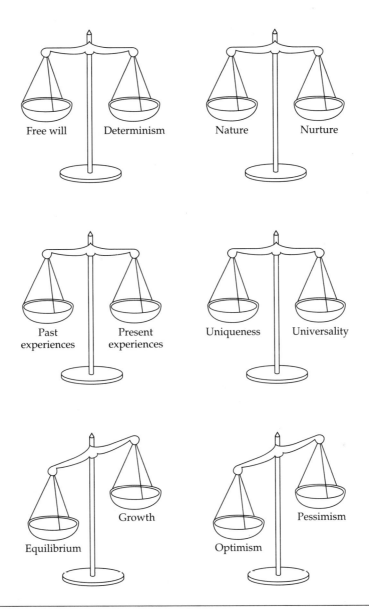

Murray

Image of Human Nature

The OSS Assessment Program

During World War II, Murray directed an assessment program for the Office of Strategic Services (OSS). His goal was to select people to serve as spies and saboteurs, operating behind enemy lines in hazardous situations. Potential candidates for OSS positions were interviewed and given the Rorschach and the TAT projective tests and questionnaires on a variety of topics.

In addition, candidates participated in situational tests—stressful situations that simulated experiences they could expect to encounter on the job. Their behavior in these tests was closely observed (OSS Assessment Staff, 1948). One such test required the candidate to build a bridge across a stream in a fixed period of time. No plans were provided, but the person was assigned a group of workers to assist him. In this way the candidate's ingenuity, ability to improvise, and leadership skills could be assessed in a realistic setting. To determine the candidate's reaction to frustration, the assistants included some "stooges," persons instructed to do everything possible to prevent the building of the bridge. Many candidates became enraged, and some were even reduced to tears, when faced with the lack of cooperation and the mounting frustration.

This pioneering attempt at employee selection through large-scale personality assessment has evolved into the successful assessment-center approach widely used in business today to select promising leaders and executives. The OSS program provides a striking example of the practical application of assessment techniques originally intended purely for research.

The Thematic Apperception Test

The assessment technique most often associated with Murray is the Thematic Apperception Test, which we described in Chapter 1. The TAT consists of 19 ambiguous pictures showing one or more persons and 1 blank card. The person taking the test is asked to compose a story that describes the scene and the characters in each picture.

Murray derived the TAT, which is a projective technique, from Freud's defense mechanism of projection. In projection, a person attributes or projects disturbing impulses onto someone else. In the TAT, the person projects those feelings onto the characters in the pictures and thereby reveals his or her troubling thoughts to the researcher or therapist. Thus, the TAT is a device for assessing unconscious thoughts, feelings, and fears. Figure 7.1 shows a sample TAT picture and some typical responses.

Interpreting the responses to the TAT pictures is a subjective process, as Murray admitted in an interview. He referred to the TAT as

> a kind of booby trap which may catch more embryo psychologists than patients. The patient reveals parts of himself when he composes a story to explain the picture. Then the psychologist may reveal parts of himself when he composes a formulation to explain the patient's story. [quoted in Hall, 1968b, p. 61]

In the hands of a trained clinician, the TAT can reveal considerable useful information. Because of its subjectivity, however, the information obtained should be used to supplement data from more objective methods rather than as the sole means of diagnosis.

The Children's Apperception Test (CAT), a modification of the TAT, is designed for use with 3- to 10-year-olds (Bellak, 1975, 1986). The pictures on

Figure 7.1

Picture contained in the Thematic Apperception Test (TAT). In describing a TAT picture, people may reveal their own feelings, needs, and values.

Typical Responses to TAT Card:

1. This is the picture of a woman who all of her life has been a very suspicious, conniving person. She's looking in the mirror and she sees reflected behind her an image of what she will be as an old woman—still a suspicious, conniving sort of person. She can't stand the thought that that's what her life will eventually lead her to and she smashes the mirror and runs out of the house screaming and goes out of her mind and lives in an institution for the rest of her life.

2. This woman has always emphasized beauty in her life. As a little girl she was praised for being pretty and as a young woman was able to attract lots of men with her beauty. While secretly feeling anxious and unworthy much of the time, her outer beauty helped to disguise these feelings from the world and, sometimes, from herself. Now that she is getting on in years and her children are leaving home, she is worried about the future. She looks in the mirror and imagines herself as an old hag—the worst possible person she could become, ugly and nasty—and wonders what the future holds for her. It is a difficult and depressing time for her [Pervin, 1984, p. 110].

SOURCE: (Reprinted by permission of the publishers from Henry A. Murray, *Thematic Apperception Test*, Cambridge, Mass.: Harvard University Press, Copyright © 1943 by the President and Fellows of Harvard College, © 1971 by Henry A. Murray.)

the cards are of animals depicted in human situations in the manner of comic strips and children's books. The scenes are designed to elicit feelings and fantasies relating to such childhood experiences as toilet training, relations with parents, sibling rivalry, and oral activities, such as sucking and feeding.

The CAT-H, for older children, uses pictures of humans (Bellak & Hurvich, 1966).

The Gerontological Apperception Test (GAT) (Wolk & Wolk, 1971) and the Senior Apperception Technique (SAT) (Bellak, 1975; Bellak & Bellak, 1973) are designed for older persons. The pictures in these tests portray elderly people in situations designed to elicit fears and fantasies appropriate to their stage of life, such as loneliness, dependence, helplessness, and problems with adult children. The pictures have been criticized, however, for perpetuating negative stereotypes about aging (Anastasi, 1988).

Another assessment device developed from Murray's personality theory is the Edwards Personal Preference Schedule (EPPS). Widely used for research and diagnostic purposes, the test assesses 15 of the needs Murray proposed. Another test, the Jackson Personality Research Form, measures 20 needs and is used almost exclusively for research. The Jackson Personality Inventory, an applied version for selection and diagnosis, measures 16 needs (Jackson, 1976, 1978). The Nonverbal Personality Questionnaire consists of line drawings of figures illustrating behaviors appropriate to satisfying various needs; test-takers indicate the likelihood of their engaging in similar behaviors (Paunonen, Jackson, & Keinonen, 1990).

Research in Murray's Theory

Murray's original research program involved intensive study of the personalities of 51 male undergraduate students. The subjects were tested, interviewed, and evaluated by a staff of psychiatrists, psychologists, and anthropologists. Each person was observed by specialists with different training and backgrounds using different techniques, in much the same way that a complex medical diagnosis is prepared.

Each observer presented a diagnosis to the Diagnostic Council, a committee of the five most experienced staff members. The council met with each subject for 45 minutes and rated the subject on several variables. As the data accumulated, the council reassessed its ratings, reviewed the information, and arrived at a final determination.

So much information was collected on each person's life that it was necessary to divide the data into time intervals. The basic temporal segment of behavior, called a **proceeding**, was defined as a period of time required for completion of an important pattern of behavior. A proceeding involves a real or fantasized interaction between the person and other people or objects in the environment. An imaginary interaction is called an internal proceeding; a real interaction is called an external proceeding.

proceeding A basic segment of behavior; a time period in which an important behavior pattern occurs from beginning to end.

Proceedings are linked in time and function. For example, on Monday a man may meet a woman (an external proceeding) and ask her for a Saturday night date. He may daydream about her throughout the week (internal proceedings) and may have his hair styled or wash his car (external proceedings) in preparation for the date. Each action is a proceeding. Taken together,

serial A succession of proceedings related to the same function or purpose.

idiographic and **nomothetic research** Idiographic research is the intensive study of a relatively small number of subjects using a variety of assessment techniques. Nomothetic research is the study of the statistical differences among large groups of subjects.

because they are related to the same function or purpose, they are called a **serial**.

Murray's approach to personality research was **idiographic**, which means that he undertook the intensive study of a relatively small number of individuals using a variety of assessment techniques. This contrasts with the **nomothetic** approach, which deals with statistical differences among groups of subjects. Murray criticized followers of the nomothetic approach for not gathering enough data on the subjects they studied. "The reason why the results of so many researches in personality have been misleading or trivial," Murray wrote, "is that experimenters have failed to obtain enough pertinent information about their subjects" (Murray, 1938, p. ix).

The controversy about whether the idiographic approach or the nomothetic approach provides the more reliable and valid information about personality continues today. In Murray's view, the best approach is the one he followed at Harvard, a multiform assessment program in which investigators study the same group of subjects and meet periodically to define each subject's personality.

Considerable research has been conducted on several of the needs Murray proposed, notably achievement and affiliation needs. We discuss the need for achievement in Chapter 17 as a limited-domain approach to personality.

The need for affiliation is strong in many people, particularly in stressful situations. In a classic experiment, subjects who knew they were going to receive an electric shock in an experiment were much more likely to prefer waiting in the company of others than were subjects who were not facing the stress of a potential electric shock (Schachter, 1959). Apparently, the presence of other people helped allay the anxiety associated with the stress of the anticipated shock.

Another study found that people who had experienced severe effects of a thunderstorm, such as property damage, were much more likely to seek the company of others than were those who had experienced no such harmful effects of the storm (Strumpfer, 1970).

A group of college students kept a daily log of their stressful experiences and social interactions for two weeks. The results showed that the students were much more likely to want to affiliate with others after stressful events than after nonstressful periods (Cohen & Wills, 1985).

Many people prefer the company of others even when not experiencing stress. Observations of college students showed that 60 percent of their activities involved at least one other person. Female students were much more likely than male students to associate with other people (Latané & Bidwell, 1977).

The need for power is not on Murray's original list of needs, but several needs, including dominance, deference, aggression, and abasement, can be subsumed under what Murray called "the response to power." The power need, defined as the motivation to be in control, to give orders, and to command obedience, has been studied through responses to the TAT pictures and has been correlated with other behaviors. Researchers have related the need for power to excessive drinking (McClelland, David, Kalin, & Wanner, 1972), to the Type A personality (McClelland, 1979), and to the possession of high-status objects, such as expensive automobiles and stereo equipment (Winter, 1973). Male college students high in the need for power tend to be officers in campus organizations, to work in media activities, to follow fashion trends, and to marry dependent women (Winter, 1973).

Although Murray's list of needs has inspired much research, little empirical support exists for other concepts in his theory, such as the divisions of personality and the complexes.

A Final Commentary

Murray has exerted an impressive and lasting influence on the study of personality. Of particular importance are his list of needs, which is of value for research, clinical diagnosis, and employee selection, and his techniques for assessing personality. In 1978, the 40th anniversary of the publication of Murray's book *Explorations in Personality* was celebrated by a symposium at the annual convention of the American Psychological Association. An award was created in his name, and the Murray Research Center at Radcliffe College was dedicated. Symposia on Murray's ideas are held every three years at Michigan State University, and the proceedings are published periodically (Rabin, Zucker, Emmons, & Frank, 1990). The fact that psychologists today are continuing work begun before many of them were born is an impressive tribute.

However, Murray's theory is not without its critics. One problem in evaluating his position is that only some portions of it have been published. His ingenuity and full range of thought were revealed only in limited amounts. Murray's influence was most keenly felt by those who worked with him and had access to his wide-ranging speculations, which he revealed in almost casual conversation. Although some of these ideas have been pursued by students and colleagues, others have been lost to public scrutiny.

Much research has been conducted on certain aspects of Murray's theory, such as the achievement and affiliation needs, the response to power, and the assessment techniques, but only limited portions of his theory have been put to experimental test. Of course, as we have seen in previous chapters, this criticism is not unique to Murray's work.

Murray's research method in the study of Harvard undergraduates has been questioned. The Diagnostic Council may have been laudably democratic, but it was hardly scientific; to reach a scientific conclusion by majority rule is not the most objective procedure. In addition, some critics have argued that proceedings and serials are defined too vaguely to be identified precisely. What constitutes an important pattern of behavior? What happens to those judged insignificant? How long is a proceeding? These questions have not been answered satisfactorily.

In Murray's classification scheme—considered by some psychologists to be overly complex—a great deal of overlap exists among the needs. It is unclear how the needs relate to other aspects of personality and how the needs develop within an individual. However, the list of needs has had considerable impact on the construction of psychological tests. Further, the concept of need and the importance Murray placed on motivation in his system have influenced the modern study of personality.

Overall, Murray's innovations in technique (such as the TAT), his methods for assessing personality, and the personal impact he made on at least two generations of personology researchers at Harvard have had a more lasting effect than the details of his theory.

Summary

Henry Murray's approach to personality, called personology, considers the unconscious as well as the conscious; the past, present, and future; and biological and social forces. The distinctive features of his system are a sophisticated approach to human needs and the collection of data from extensive investigations of normal persons. The major principle of Murray's work is the dependence of psychological processes on physiological processes. Altering the level of need-induced tension is vital to the personality. We generate tension to have the satisfaction of reducing it.

Three basic divisions of personality are the id, superego, and ego. The id contains primitive, amoral impulses as well as tendencies to empathy, imitation, and identification. The superego is shaped by parents, peer groups, and cultural factors. The ego consciously decides and wills the direction of behavior.

Needs are physiologically based hypothetical constructs that arise from internal processes or environmental events. Needs arouse a tension level that must be reduced; thus, they energize and direct behavior. Needs may be primary (viscerogenic), arising from internal bodily processes, or secondary (psychogenic), concerned with mental and emotional satisfaction. Proactive needs are spontaneous and do not depend on environmental objects; reactive needs involve a response to a specific environmental object.

A need's prepotency is its urgency or insistence. The fusion of needs refers to needs that can be satisfied by one behavior or set of behaviors. Subsidiation involves a situation in which one need is activated to aid in the satisfaction of another need.

Press refers to the pressure, caused by environmental objects or childhood events, to behave in a certain way. Thema is an amalgamation of personal factors (needs) and environmental factors (presses).

Complexes are patterns formed in the five childhood stages of development that unconsciously direct adult development. The claustral complex involves the secure existence within the womb. The oral complex involves the sensuous enjoyment of sucking nourishment. The anal complex involves the pleasure resulting from defecation. The urethral complex involves the pleasure accompanying urination. The castration complex involves genital pleasure and the fantasy that the penis might be cut off.

According to Murray, the ultimate goal in life is to reduce tension. Although we have some free will, much of personality is determined by needs and by the environment. Each person is unique yet shares similarities with other people, which are determined by inherited and environmental forces. Murray held an optimistic view of human nature, which is oriented toward the future and grants us the ability to grow and develop.

In Murray's assessment program for the OSS, he used situational tests (behavioral observations). This led to the development of assessment centers, which are popular in business today. Murray and a colleague developed the Thematic Apperception Test (TAT), based on the Freudian concept of projection. Murray's research involved the extensive analysis of 51 normal male undergraduates. Thus, his approach was idiographic (involving the intensive study of a small number of people) rather than nomothetic (involving the statistical differences found among large groups of subjects). Considerable research has been conducted on Murray's proposed needs for achievement and affiliation and the response to power. His importance lies in his list of needs and his techniques for assessing personality.

Critical Thinking Review

1. Discuss the influence of Carl Jung on Henry Murray's personal life and on his theory of personality.

2. In Murray's view, what is the relationship between physiological processes and psychological processes?

3. What is the role of tension in the development of personality? Is our ultimate goal a life free of tension? Why or why not?

4. How do Murray's views of the id, ego, and superego differ from Freud's conception of these structures of personality?

5. From what sources do needs arise? Describe ways of classifying needs, and give examples for each category.

6. Define the concepts of subsidiation, thema, and press.

7. Describe the five childhood stages of personality development and the complexes associated with each stage.

8. How does Murray's image of human nature differ from Freud's?

9. How is the Thematic Apperception Test used to assess personality? What criticisms can be made of projective techniques to assess personality?

10. Distinguish between proceedings and serials.

11. What is the difference between the idiographic and the nomothetic approaches to personality research? Which did Murray prefer?

12. What type of data did Murray collect in his study of undergraduate students at Harvard?

13. Is Murray's view of human nature optimistic or pessimistic? Why?

Suggested Reading

Anderson, J. W. (1988). Henry A. Murray's early career: A psychobiographical exploration. *Journal of Personality, 56*(1), 139–171. Presents an analysis of Murray's life through his early thirties, examining his decision to become a psychologist, his initial involvement with psychoanalysis, and the impact of his personal and academic experiences on his work in personality.

Murray, H. A. (1938). *Explorations in personality: A clinical and experimental study of fifty men of college age.* New York: Oxford University Press. Murray's classic work on his system of personology. Includes the evaluation of a typical subject by the Diagnostic Council, describes the list of human needs, and discusses the advantages of projective techniques for personality assessment.

Murray, H. A. (1967). Autobiography. In E. G. Boring & G. Lindzey (Eds.), *A history of psychology in autobiography* (vol. 5, pp. 283–310). New York: Appleton-Century-Crofts. Murray's reflections on his life and work.

Murray, H. A. (1981). *Endeavors in psychology: Selections from the personology of Henry A. Murray.* New York: Harper & Row. A collection of Murray's writings on personality theory, human creativity, and the Thematic Apperception Test. Edited by Edwin S. Schneidman.

Smith, M. B. (1990). Henry A. Murray (1893–1988): Humanistic psychologist. *Journal of Humanistic Psychology, 30*(1), 6–13. A biographical sketch relating Murray, as a founder of American personality psychology, to the humanistic psychology movement.

Triplet, R. G. (1992). Henry A. Murray: The making of a psychologist? *American Psychologist, 47,* 299–307. Assesses the impact of Murray's work at the Harvard Psychological Clinic on personality, abnormal psychology, and clinical psychology, and recounts the personal and academic disputes between the clinic and the psychology department.

The Trait Approach:
The Genetics of Personality

A college dictionary defines the word *trait* as a distinguishing characteristic or quality of a person. This represents an approach we frequently take in our daily lives when we try to describe the personality of someone we know. We tend to select outstanding characteristics or factors and use them to summarize what that person is like. For example, we may say, "Allison is self-assured," or "Ramon is outgoing." This way of categorizing someone is quick, easy, and potentially useful. However, our personal judgments can sometimes be wrong.

Grouping people by traits seems easy and has a commonsense appeal, and the trait approach to personality has been in use for a long time. Such classifications date back to the time of the Greek physician Hippocrates (460–377 B.C.), more than 2,000 years before the modern attempts to study personality described in this book.

Some personality psychologists criticize the notion that our personality consists of distinct traits. Recall the person-situation debate in Chapter 1 about the relative importance of personal variables (such as traits) and situational or environmental variables in influencing behavior. The argument was advanced that if traits exist, then people will behave consistently in all situations; this idea is not supported by research. Human behavior does, indeed, vary with different situations.

Participants in that debate overlooked the fact that the early exponents of trait theory, Gordon Allport and Raymond Cattell, never implied a cross-situational consistency in behavior. Instead both theorists took into account the effect on behavior of the specific situation. They subscribed to an interactionist approach, recognizing that behavior is a function of the interaction between personal and situational variables.

Despite the controversy, the trait approach to personality remains vital, and the enterprise begun by Allport and Cattell more than 60 years ago is central to the study of personality today. Some psychologists suggest that traits are not only "alive and well," but that "no better building blocks or units of personality have been identified" (Kreitler & Kreitler, 1990, p. 331).

The works of Allport and Cattell represent the beginnings of the trait approach. These theorists differ from others we have discussed in one respect: they studied personality by observing emotionally healthy persons in an academic laboratory setting. Their insights are not based on interviews with neurotics in a clinical setting, nor did they obtain data from the practice of psychotherapy.

Beyond that similarity, and the fact that their goal was to identify personality traits, Allport and Cattell approached their study in different ways. Allport may also be considered within the humanistic framework (see Part VI) because he focused on the total human being and the innate potential for growth and self-realization.

Allport and Cattell agreed on the importance of genetic factors in the formation of traits. Over the past two decades, evidence has grown steadily to indicate that personality traits are influenced by inherited biological factors. The results of these studies demonstrate a significant genetic component of personality. Researchers are now turning their attention to the interaction of those genetic factors with environmental factors.

After discussing the theories of Allport and Cattell in developing the trait approach to personality, we will describe more current developments, such as the five-factor model and the temperament theory.

E I G H T

Gordon Allport

The Life of Allport (1897–1967)
A Definition of Personality
Personality Traits
    Habits and Attitudes
Personality and Motivation
    The Functional Autonomy of Motives
    Principles of Propriate Functional
        Autonomy
Personality Development in Childhood:
    The Unique Self

The Adult Personality
Allport's Image of Human Nature
Assessment in Allport's Theory
    The Personal-Document Technique
    The Study of Values
Research in Allport's Theory
A Final Commentary
Summary
Critical Thinking Review
Suggested Reading

As the individual matures, the bond with the past is broken.

—Gordon Allport

During a career that spanned more than four decades, Gordon Allport became one of the most stimulating and provocative psychologists to study personality. It was Allport who made the study of personality an academically respectable part of psychology. Psychoanalysis and the theories that derived from it were not considered part of the mainstream of scientific psychology. The study of personality was not formalized and systematized in psychology until the 1930s.

In 1937, Allport published *Personality: A Psychological Interpretation.* The book was an immediate success. Today, over 50 years later, it is still considered a landmark in the study of personality.

Allport served two purposes in the study of personality: he helped bring it into the mainstream of scientific psychology, and he formulated a theory of personality development in which traits play a prominent role.

Allport disagreed with Freud on several points. First, Allport did not accept the notion that unconscious forces dominate the personality of normal, mature adults. Instead, he proposed that emotionally healthy people function in rational and conscious terms, aware and in control of many of the forces that motivate them. According to Allport, the unconscious is only of importance in neurotic or disturbed behavior.

A second point on which Allport disputed traditional psychoanalysts concerned the importance of the past in determining the present. To Allport, we are not prisoners of childhood conflicts and past experiences, as Freud had suggested. Rather, we are guided more by the present and by our view of the future. Allport wrote that people are "busy leading their lives into the future, whereas psychology, for the most part, is busy tracing them into the past" (Allport, 1955, p. 51).

Third, Allport opposed the collection of data from pathological subjects. Whereas Freud proposed a continuum between the normal and the abnormal personality, Allport saw a break between the two and suggested that the abnormal personality functions at an infantile level. He insisted that the only way to study personality is to collect data from emotionally healthy, mature adults; other populations—neurotics, children, and animals, for example—should not be compared with normal adults. No functional similarity in personality exists between child and adult, abnormal and normal, or animal and human.

A distinctive feature of Allport's theory is his emphasis on the uniqueness of personality as defined by an individual's traits. Allport opposed the traditional scientific emphasis on forming general constructs or laws to be applied universally. Personality is not general or universal, but particular and specific to each of us.

Allport and his students, many of whom became prominent in psychology, conducted empirical research on numerous aspects of personality. Allport also developed tests for assessing personality that are still used in clinics and laboratories.

The Life of Allport (1897–1967)

Born in Montezuma, Indiana, Allport was the youngest of four sons. His mother was a teacher. His father, a businessman who turned to medicine late in life, opened a private practice when Allport was born. Allport believed that his own delivery was his father's first case. As the youngest child, Allport was independent, too young to be a playmate to his brothers. He apparently was isolated from children outside the family as well: "I fashioned my own circle of activities. It was a select circle, for I never fitted the general boy assembly." He described himself as skillful with words but not at sports or games and as someone who worked hard to be the center of attention of the few friends he did have.

Although he ranked second in his high school graduating class of 100, Allport admitted to being "uninspired and uncurious" and had no idea what to do next. At the end of the summer of 1915, he applied to Harvard and was accepted. "Overnight," he wrote, "my world was remade." Allport's college years were a time of great adventure and excitement as he discovered new frontiers of intellect and culture. Shocked by the low grades he received on his first exams, he doubled his efforts and finished the year with straight As.

Allport's interest in social ethics and social service, acquired from his parents, was reinforced at Harvard, where he undertook volunteer work for a boy's club, a group of factory workers, and a contingent of foreign students.

He also acted as a volunteer probation officer. He found these activities satisfying because he genuinely liked to help people and because, he wrote, "it gave me a feeling of competence, to offset a generalized inferiority feeling." He believed that this kind of service reflected his search for an identity (Allport, 1967, pp. 4–7).

He took undergraduate courses in psychology but did not intend to pursue a career in the field. After his graduation from Harvard, he joined the faculty of Robert College in Istanbul, Turkey, to see whether he liked teaching. Allport enjoyed his year there very much. He then accepted a fellowship offered him by Harvard for graduate study in psychology.

On his way back to the United States, Allport stopped in Vienna to see one of his brothers. While there, he sent a note to Sigmund Freud and received an invitation to visit the great man. When Allport entered Freud's office, he found Freud waiting in silence, expecting the young American to explain the purpose of his visit. The silence wore on until Allport blurted out an account of an incident he had witnessed on the streetcar ride to Freud's office. He told of watching a small boy who had an obvious fear of dirt. Everything seemed dirty to the child; he changed his seat on the streetcar and told his mother not to let a dirty man sit beside him.

Freud regarded the prim and proper Allport and asked, "Was that little boy you?" By asking this question, Freud was expressing his belief that Allport's behavior betrayed his inner conflicts and fears. Allport appeared "neat, meticulous, orderly and punctual—possessing many of the characteristics associated by Freud with the compulsive personality" (Pervin, 1984, p. 267). Henry Murray commented about Allport that "Freud just hit him right on the head, right on the nose" (quoted in J. W. Anderson, 1990, p. 326).

Allport was shaken by Freud's question and quickly changed the subject, but the incident left a deep impression on him. Years later he wrote, "My single encounter with Freud was traumatic" (Allport, 1967, p. 22). He suspected that psychoanalysis explored the unconscious too deeply. Psychology, Allport thought, should pay more attention to conscious or visible motivations. This was the path he would choose for his personality theory.

He completed his Ph.D. at Harvard in 1922, after two years of graduate study. His dissertation, "An Experimental Study of the Traits of Personality," foreshadowed his lifelong work and was the first research conducted on personality traits in the United States. Awarded a traveling fellowship, Allport spent two years studying with noted psychologists in Germany and England. He returned to Harvard as an instructor in social ethics, offering a course on the psychological and social aspects of personality, probably the first formal American college course on personality. He married a clinical psychologist, whom he had met as a graduate student, and accepted an appointment at Dartmouth College, where he taught social psychology and personality and relished the more relaxed atmosphere that permitted him to take the time to read and think about traits and the structure of personality. After four years he rejoined the Harvard faculty and spent nearly four decades conducting research on personality and social psychology and instructing several generations of students.

Considered an elder statesman in psychology, Allport received many awards, including the American Psychological Foundation's Gold Medal, the American Psychological Association's Distinguished Scientific Contribution Award, and the presidencies of the American Psychological Association and the Society for the Psychological Study of Social Issues.

One of Allport's major propositions is that psychologically healthy adults are unaffected by childhood events. Perhaps reflecting this belief, Allport revealed little information about his childhood years. What he did reveal demonstrates a parallel between his early experiences and his later theory. Out of boyhood conditions of isolation and rejection, Allport developed inferiority feelings for which he attempted to compensate by trying to excel. He wrote about the "self-seeking and vanity" that resulted from his inferiority feelings with respect to his brothers and to other children. As Allport grew older, he began to identify with his oldest brother, Floyd, perhaps out of envy of his brother's accomplishments. He followed in Floyd's footsteps by enrolling at the same college and studying the same subject as Floyd, and by obtaining a Ph.D., as Floyd had also done. (Floyd Allport became a noted social psychologist.)

This attempt to emulate Floyd may have threatened Gordon's identity. In an effort to assert his individuality, perhaps, Gordon Allport may have negated his identification with his brother by declaring that adult motives and interests were autonomous or independent of their childhood origins—an idea he formalized as the concept of functional autonomy (Atwood & Tomkins, 1976).

A Definition of Personality

In his book *Pattern and Growth in Personality,* Allport reviewed some 50 definitions of personality before offering his own: "Personality is the dynamic organization within the individual of those psychophysical systems that determine . . . characteristic behavior and thought" (Allport, 1961, p. 28). Let us examine the key concepts in this definition.

By *dynamic organization,* Allport means that although personality is constantly changing and growing (dynamic), it is an organized growth. *Psychophysical* means that personality is composed of mind and body functioning together as a unit. Personality is neither all mental nor all biological but a combination of the two. By *determine,* Allport means that all facets of personality activate or direct specific behaviors and thoughts. The phrase *characteristic behavior and thought* means that everything we think and do is characteristic, or typical, of us. Thus, each person is unique.

To support his emphasis on the uniqueness of the individual personality, Allport stated that we are the product of heredity and environment. Heredity provides the personality with raw materials, which are shaped (expanded or limited) by the conditions of our environment. In this way, Allport invokes both personal and situational variables.

The biological raw materials include physique, intelligence, and temperament. Temperament involves a person's general emotional tone, susceptibility to stimulation, and fluctuation and intensity of moods.

It is our genetic background and the raw material it provides to the personality that is responsible for the major portion of our uniqueness. There is an infinite number of possible gene combinations, and the chance that one's genetic endowment will be duplicated in someone else is, except in the case of identical twins, too small to consider. Our individual combination of genes interacts with our environment, and no two people—not even siblings reared in the same house—have precisely the same environment. The inevitable result is a unique personality. Allport concluded, therefore, that to study personality, psychology must deal with the individual case—an approach we described in Chapter 7 as idiographic.

Allport considered personality to be discrete, or discontinuous. Not only is each person distinct from all others, but each person is also divorced from his or her past. There is no continuum of personality between childhood and adulthood. The infant's behavior is driven by primitive urges and reflexes; the adult operates on a different level. There are, in a sense, two personalities: one for childhood and one for adulthood. The first is more biological in nature, the second more psychological. The latter does not develop out of the former. An adult's functioning is not constrained by past experiences.

We have, then, a distinctive picture of the nature of personality: a stress on the conscious rather than the unconscious and on the present and future rather than the past, a recognition of uniqueness rather than of generalities or similarities over all people, and a focus on the normal rather than the abnormal.

Personality Traits

traits Distinguishing characteristics or qualities, measured on a continuum, that guide our behavior.

Allport looked at predispositions to respond, in the same or a similar manner, to different kinds of stimuli. **Traits** are consistent and enduring ways of reacting to the stimulus aspects of our environment. Allport summarized the characteristics of traits as follows (Allport, 1937):

1. Personality traits are real and exist within each of us. They are not theoretical constructs or labels made up to account for or explain our behavior.
2. Traits determine or cause behavior. They do not arise only in response to certain stimuli. They motivate us to seek appropriate stimuli, and they interact with the environment to produce behavior.
3. Traits can be demonstrated empirically. By observing behavior over time, we can infer evidence of the existence of traits in the coherence and consistency of a person's responses to the same or similar stimuli.
4. Traits are interrelated; they may overlap, even though they represent different characteristics. For example, aggressiveness and hostility are

distinct but related traits and are frequently observed to occur simultaneously in a person's behavior.

5. Traits vary with the situation. For instance, a person may display the trait of neatness in one situation and the trait of disorderliness in another.

Allport first proposed two categories of traits: individual traits and common traits. Individual traits are unique to a person and define his or her character. Common traits are shared by a number of people, such as the members of a culture. Common traits are likely to change over time as social standards and values change.

Because confusion could result from calling both of these phenomena traits, Allport revised his terminology. He relabeled common traits as *traits* and individual traits as **personal dispositions**.

personal dispositions
Traits that are peculiar to an individual, as opposed to traits shared by a number of people.

cardinal traits The most pervasive, general, and powerful traits.

central traits The handful of outstanding traits that describe a person's behavior.

secondary traits The least important traits, which a person displays inconspicuously and inconsistently.

Our individual traits, or personal dispositions, do not all have the same intensity or significance. Therefore, Allport proposed three types: cardinal, central, and secondary. A **cardinal trait** is so pervasive and influential that it touches almost every aspect of one's life. It is so powerful—like a "ruling passion," as Allport said—that it comes to dominate behavior. He offered sadism and chauvinism as examples. Not everyone has a ruling passion, and even those who do may not display it in every situation.

Everyone possesses a few **central traits**, five to ten themes that describe our behavior. Allport gave as examples aggressiveness, self-pity, and cynicism. These are the kinds of characteristics we would mention in discussing an acquaintance or writing a letter of recommendation.

The least influential individual traits are the **secondary traits**, which appear less conspicuously and consistently than cardinal and central traits. Secondary traits may be displayed so seldom or so weakly that only a close friend would notice. They may include, for example, a preference for a particular type of music or for certain foods.

Habits and Attitudes

Allport distinguished traits and personal dispositions from other personal characteristics, such as habits and attitudes, that are also capable of initiating and guiding behavior.

habits Specific, inflexible responses to specific stimuli; several habits may combine to form a trait.

You have only to consider your own habits to see how they influence the way you behave. **Habits** have a more limited impact than traits and personal dispositions because they are relatively inflexible and involve a specific response to a specific stimulus. Traits and personal dispositions are broader because they arise from the integration of several habits that share some adaptive function. Thus, habits may combine to form a single trait.

Children learning to brush their teeth or wash their hands before eating illustrate Allport's point. After a while, these behaviors become automatic, or habitual. Taken together, these habits are directed toward the same purpose and form the trait we can label "cleanliness."

attitudes Similar to traits, except that attitudes have specific objects of reference and involve either positive or negative evaluations.

It is more difficult to distinguish between a trait and an **attitude**. Consider patriotism: Is it a trait fostered by the traditions of a culture, or is it an attitude toward one's nation? Authoritarianism and extraversion could also be called either traits or attitudes. Allport did not resolve the question, except to note that both categories are appropriate.

It is possible, however, to distinguish between traits and attitudes in two general ways. First, attitudes have some specific object of reference. A person has an attitude toward something: red-haired people, a musical group, a brand of athletic shoe. A trait or personal disposition is not specifically directed toward a single object or category of objects. A person with the personal disposition of shyness will interact with most other people in the same way, regardless of their hair color. Traits, therefore, are broader in scope than attitudes. Second, attitudes are positive or negative, either for something or against it. They lead a person to like or hate, accept or reject, approach or avoid. Unlike a trait or personal disposition, an attitude involves a judgment or evaluation.

Personality and Motivation

Allport believed that the central problem for any personality theory is how it describes the concept of motivation. We noted that Allport stressed the impact of the present in his approach to understanding personality; this emphasis is at the core of his view of motivation. It is the individual's present state—not what occurred during toilet training or other childhood crises—that is important. Whatever happened in the past is exactly that: past. It is no longer active and does not explain present behavior, unless it exists as a current motivating force.

Allport also recognized the influence of cognitive processes—our conscious plans and intentions. He criticized approaches (such as Freud's) that focused on unconscious and irrational forces at the expense of the conscious and rational. Deliberate, conscious intentions are an essential part of personality. What we want and what we strive for are keys to understanding our present behavior. Thus, Allport attempted to explain the present in terms of the future rather than of the past.

The Functional Autonomy of Motives

functional autonomy of motives The idea that motives in the normal, mature adult are independent of the childhood experiences in which they originally appeared.

Allport's concept of **functional autonomy** proposes that the motives of mature, emotionally healthy adults are not functionally connected to the past experiences in which they initially appeared. Forces that motivated us early in life become autonomous; that is, independent of their original circumstances. Similarly, when we mature, we become independent of our parents. Although we remain related to them, we are no longer functionally dependent on them; they no longer control or guide our life. Allport offered the example of a tree. Obviously, the growth and development of a tree can be traced back to its seed. Yet when the tree is fully grown, the seed is no longer needed as a source of nourishment. The tree is now self-determining, no longer functionally related to its seed.

Consider new college graduates embarking on a career in business. They are hired for low salaries but are motivated to work hard to achieve financial success and prestige. Eventually their investment of time and energy pays off, and they become financially secure, amassing enough money to retire by the age of 50. Yet they continue to work just as hard as they did when first hired. Such behavior can no longer be for the same goal; the goal of financial security has been reached and surpassed. The motivation to work hard, once a means to a specific end (money), is now an end in itself. The motive has become independent of its original source.

We are all familiar with similar instances—the skilled craftsperson who insists on doing a meticulous job, even when the extra effort brings in no additional money, or the miser who chooses to live in poverty while hoarding vast wealth. The behavior that once satisfied a specific motive now serves only itself. The original motive has been transformed into something autonomous. Therefore, adult motives cannot be understood by exploring a person's childhood. The only way to understand the motivations of adults is to investigate why they behave as they do today.

Allport proposed two levels of functional autonomy: perseverative functional autonomy and propriate functional autonomy. **Perseverative functional autonomy**, the more elementary level, is concerned with such behaviors as addictions and repetitive physical actions—habitual ways of performing some everyday task. The behaviors continue or persevere on their own without any external reward. These behaviors once served a purpose but no longer do so and are at too low a level to be considered an integral part of personality.

Perseverative functional autonomy relates to low-level and routine behaviors.

Allport cited both animal and human examples as evidence for perseverative functional autonomy. When a rat that is well trained to run a maze for food is given more than enough food, it may still run the maze—obviously for some other purpose. At the human level is our preference for the routine and familiar behaviors that we maintain and continue without any external reinforcement.

Propriate functional autonomy relates to our values, self-image, and lifestyle.

proprium Allport's term for the ego or self.

Propriate functional autonomy is more important and is essential to the understanding of adult motivation. The word *propriate* derives from **proprium**, Allport's term for the ego or self. Propriate motives are unique to the individual. The ego determines which motives will be maintained and which will be discarded. We retain motives that enhance our self-esteem or self-image. Thus, a direct relationship exists between our interests and our abilities: we enjoy doing what we do well.

The original motivation for learning a skill, such as playing the piano, may have nothing to do with our interests. As children, we may be forced to take piano lessons and to practice. If we become proficient, however, we may become more committed to playing the piano. The original motive (fear of parental displeasure) has disappeared, and the behavior of playing the piano becomes necessary to our self-image. Therefore, the behavior will be maintained.

Our propriate functioning is an organizing process that maintains our sense of self. It determines how we perceive the world, what we remember from our experiences, and how our thoughts are directed. Our perceptual and cognitive processes are selective, choosing among the mass of stimuli available only what is relevant to our interests and values. This organizing process is governed by three principles.

Principles of Propriate Functional Autonomy

Allport proposed three principles of propriate functional autonomy: organizing the energy level, mastery and competence, and propriate patterning.

Although the first principle, organizing the energy level, does not explain how an adult motive is transformed from an earlier motive, it tries to account for our acquisition of new motives. These motives arise from necessity to help consume excess energy that we might otherwise express in destructive and harmful ways. For example, when people retire from their jobs, they find themselves with additional time and energy, which, ideally, they should direct toward new interests and motives.

Mastery and competence refers to the high level at which we choose to satisfy motives. It is not enough for us to achieve at an adequate level. Mature adults are motivated to perform better and more efficiently, to master new skills, and to increase their degree of competence.

Propriate patterning is a striving for consistency and integration of the personality. We organize or pattern our perceptual and cognitive processes around the self, keeping what enhances our self-image and rejecting the rest. Thus, our propriate motives are dependent on the structure or pattern of the self.

Allport noted that not all behaviors and motives can be explained by the principles of functional autonomy. Some—such as reflexes, fixations, some neuroses, and behaviors arising from biological drives—are not under the control of functionally autonomous motives.

Personality Development in Childhood: The Unique Self

Allport chose the term *proprium* for the self or ego. He rejected the latter terms because of the diversity of meanings ascribed to them by other theorists. The word *proprium* can best be understood by considering the adjective form *propriate,* as in the word *appropriate.* The proprium includes those aspects of personality that are distinctive and thus are appropriate to our emotional life. These aspects are unique to each of us and unite our attitudes, perceptions, and intentions.

Allport described the nature and development of the proprium over seven stages from infancy through adolescence (see Table 8.1). Before the

Table 8.1   **The development of the proprium.**

Stage	Development
1. Bodily self	Stages 1–3 emerge during the first three years. In this stage, infants become aware of their own existence and distinguish their own bodies from objects in the environment.
2. Self-identity	Children realize that their identity remains intact despite the many changes that are taking place.
3. Self-esteem	Children learn to take pride in their accomplishments.
4. Extension of self	Stages 4 and 5 emerge during the fourth through sixth year. In this stage, children come to recognize the objects and people that are part of their own world.
5. Self-image	Children develop actual and idealized images of themselves and their behavior and become aware of satisfying (or failing to satisfy) parental expectations.
6. Self as a rational coper	Stage 6 develops during ages 6–12. Children begin to apply reason and logic to the solution of everyday problems.
7. Propriate striving	Stage 7 develops during adolescence. Young people begin to formulate long-range goals and plans.
Adulthood	Normal, mature adults are functionally autonomous, independent of childhood motives. They function rationally in the present and consciously create their own lifestyle.

proprium begins to emerge, the infant experiences no self-consciousness, no awareness of self. There is not yet a separation of "me" from everything else. Infants receive sensory impressions from the external environment and react to them automatically and reflexively, with no ego to mediate between stimulation and response.

The first three stages in the gradual development of the proprium occur during the first three to four years of life. The bodily self, the initial aspect of the proprium to form, develops when infants begin to be aware of a "bodily me." For example, infants begin to distinguish between their fingers and the object they are grasping. The stage of self-identity is marked by a sense of continuity of identity; children realize that they are the same people despite changes in growth and ability. Self-identity is enhanced when a child learns his or her name and comes to see himself or herself as distinct from others.

Self-esteem develops when children discover they can accomplish things on their own. They are motivated to build, to explore, and to manipulate objects in their environment, behaviors that sometimes can be destructive. Allport viewed this stage as crucial. If parents frustrate the need to explore, the emerging self-esteem can be thwarted and replaced by feelings of humiliation and anger.

The extension-of-self stage involves the child's awareness of other objects and people in the environment and the identification of some of them

Children develop actual and idealized self-images, reflecting how they actually see and would like to see themselves.

as belonging to the child. For example, at this stage, children begin to speak of "my house," "my parents," and "my school." A self-image develops next; it incorporates how children see and would like to see themselves. These actual and ideal self-images develop from interactions with the parents, who make the child aware of their expectations and of the extent to which the child's behavior is satisfying or failing to satisfy those expectations. The self-extension and self-image stages typically occur between the ages of 4 and 6.

The self as a rational coper develops between the ages of 6 and 12, when the child realizes that rational and logical abilities can be applied to solving everyday problems. Propriate striving occurs during adolescence, when we realize the existence within ourselves of long-range goals. We begin to formulate our intentions and plan for the future. Until we do so, our sense of self—that is, our proprium—will remain incomplete.

Allport described infants as pleasure-seeking, destructive, "unsocialized horrors," selfish, impatient, and dependent on their parents. Our genetic endowment, the basis of an eventual personality, exists, but in infancy there is little of what could be called a personality. The infant is driven by reflexes to reduce tension and maximize pleasure.

As the proprium develops, our social interaction with our parents is vitally important. Of particular importance is the infant's relationship with the mother as the primary source of affection and security. If these conditions are met, the proprium will develop through the seven stages, and the

Normal, mature adults are functionally autonomous, independent of childhood motives. They function rationally in the present and consciously create their own lifestyles.

child will achieve positive psychological growth. Childhood motives will be free to be transformed into autonomous propriate strivings, the self will differentiate and grow, and a pattern of personal dispositions will form. The inevitable result is a mature, emotionally healthy adult.

The Adult Personality

Between infancy and adulthood we change from a biologically dominated organism to a psychological organism; our motivations become divorced from childhood and oriented toward the future. If the childhood needs for affection and security are met, the proprium will develop satisfactorily. The adult personality grows out of childhood but is no longer dictated to or dominated by childhood drives.

If one's childhood needs are frustrated, however, the proprium will not mature properly. The child then becomes insecure, aggressive, demanding, jealous, and self-centered. Psychological growth is stunted, and the resulting neurotic adult will function at the level of childhood drives. Adult motives will not become functionally autonomous but will remain tied to their original conditions. The proprium does not develop, nor do traits or personal dispositions, and the personality remains undifferentiated, as it was in infancy.

Allport did not explain whether the neurotic adult could counteract or overcome unfortunate childhood experiences. He was more interested in normal development and positive psychological growth. Allport offered six criteria for the mature, emotionally healthy, adult personality:

1. The mature adult extends the sense of self to persons and to activities beyond the self.

2. The mature adult relates warmly to others, exhibiting intimacy, compassion, and tolerance.
3. The mature adult shows self-acceptance and thus achieves emotional security.
4. The mature adult holds a realistic perception, develops his or her skills, and makes a commitment to some form of work.
5. The mature adult exhibits a sense of humor and has what Allport called self-objectification, that is, an understanding or insight into the self.
6. The mature adult has a unifying philosophy of life, which directs the personality toward future goals.

By meeting these criteria, we become functionally autonomous, independent of our infancy and childhood. As a result, we can cope with the present and plan for the future without being victimized or imprisoned by the experiences of our early years.

Allport's Image of Human Nature

"As the individual matures," Allport wrote, "the bond with the past is broken." We have seen this in his concepts of functional autonomy and personality development. Emotionally healthy adults are not inexorably tied to and irreversibly driven by childhood conflicts. Allport's theory presents an optimistic picture, a view of adults in conscious control of their lives, rationally attending to the present, planning for the future, and actively fashioning an identity. Always in the process of "becoming," we creatively design and implement an appropriate style of life.

The basic urge to grow and find meaning is pervasive in human nature. Within the framework of this inherent need for autonomy, individuality, and selfhood, we develop through our conscious efforts. In doing so, we are influenced more by events of the present and our view of the future than by the past.

Allport took a moderate stance on the question of free will versus determinism. He granted free choice in our deliberations about our future, but he also recognized that much of our behavior is determined by traits and personal dispositions. Once these are formed, they are difficult to change.

On the nature-nurture issue, Allport believed that both heredity and environment influence the personality. Our genetic background is responsible for a significant portion of personality. It supplies our basic physique, temperament, and intelligence. These raw materials are then shaped by experience and learning.

Allport believed in each person's uniqueness. Although common traits connote some degree of universality in behavior, individual traits or personal dispositions define and describe our nature more precisely.

According to Allport, the ultimate and necessary goal of life is not the reduction of tension, as Freud proposed, but rather increases in tension,

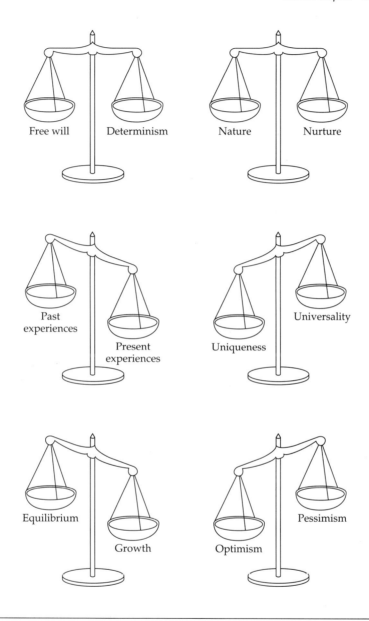

Allport

Image of Human Nature.

which impel us to seek new sensations and challenges. When we have met one challenge, we are motivated to seek another. What is rewarding to us is achieving rather than achievement, striving for the goal rather than reaching it. We always need new goals to pull us and to maintain an optimal level of tension in the personality.

Allport's optimistic image of human nature was reflected in his personal liberal stance and his interest in social reform. The humanistic attitude expressed in his work was mirrored in his own nature. His colleagues and students recall that he genuinely cared about people and that these feelings were reciprocated.

Assessment in Allport's Theory

Allport wrote more about assessment techniques for personality than most other theorists. In a popular book, *Pattern and Growth in Personality* (1961), he devoted three chapters to the topic. He noted that, despite the existence of many approaches, there is no one best technique; the human personality is so complex that to evaluate it we must employ all legitimate techniques. Of the 11 major methods for assessing personality (see Table 8.2), Allport relied heavily on the personal-document technique and the Study of Values test. He also observed expressive behavior, which we discuss in the section entitled "Research in Allport's Theory."

The Personal-Document Technique

personal-document technique A method of personality assessment that involves the study of a person's written or spoken records.

Allport used the **personal-document technique** to study personality. This technique involves examining diaries, autobiographies, letters, literary compositions, and other samples of a person's written or spoken records to determine the number and kinds of personality traits. Allport's most famous case is a collection of more than 300 letters written over a period of 12 years by a middle-aged woman identified as Jenny (Allport, 1965).

A similar analysis can be performed with third-person material, such as that found in case histories and biographies. With both autobiographical and biographical material, a group of judges reads the material and records the traits they find in it. Given a reasonable degree of agreement among the judges, the judgments can be grouped into a relatively small number of categories. Often the judges' agreement is high, which shows consistency in their assessments. In Allport's research with Jenny's letters, 36 judges listed nearly 200 traits. Because so many of the terms listed were synonymous, Allport was able to reduce them to eight categories.

Table 8.2   ***Allport's suggested methods for assessing personality.***

Constitutional and physiological diagnosis
Cultural setting, membership, role
Personal documents and case studies
Self-appraisal
Conduct analysis
Ratings
Tests and scales
Projective techniques
Depth analysis
Expressive behavior
Synoptic procedures (combining information from several sources in a synopsis)

One of Allport's students performed a computer analysis on the letters to find categories of words that might indicate the existence of a particular trait (Paige, 1966). For example, words expressing anger, rage, hostility, and aggression were coded as constituting the trait of aggression. This approach is more sophisticated and quantitative than Allport's original analysis of the letters and involves less subjective judgment. The computer analysis yielded eight prominent traits in Jenny's personality that were similar to the categories Allport identified (Allport, 1966). Because of that similarity, Allport concluded that his subjective approach to personality assessment provided as much valid information on traits as the sophisticated computer analysis.

The Study of Values

Allport and two colleagues developed an objective self-report inventory, the Study of Values, to assess the values an individual holds (Allport, Vernon, & Lindzey, 1960). Our personal values form the basis of our unifying philosophy of life, one of the six criteria for a mature, healthy personality. According to Allport, values are traits, and they represent our deepest interests and motivations.

The interests and motives assessed by the Study of Values test were drawn from an analysis of value systems undertaken by Eduard Spranger in the 1920s. Allport agreed with Spranger that everyone possesses each of the following types of values to some extent but that one or two will be dominant in an individual's personality.

1. *Theoretical values:* Concerned with the discovery of truth and characterized by an empirical, intellectual, and rational approach to life.
2. *Economic values:* Concerned with what is useful and practical.
3. *Aesthetic values:* Concerned with artistic experiences and with form, harmony, and grace.
4. *Social values:* Concerned with human relationships, altruism, and philanthropy.
5. *Political values:* Concerned with personal power, influence, and prestige in all endeavors, not just in political activities.
6. *Religious values:* Concerned with the mystical and with the understanding of the world as a whole.

The Study of Values has proven to be a useful assessment device for personality research, counseling, and employee selection.

Research in Allport's Theory

Allport criticized psychologists who said that experimental and correlational methods were the only legitimate research approaches to the study of personality. Not every aspect of personality, he argued, can be tested by these approaches. Therefore, psychologists must be more open and eclectic in their research methodology.

He also opposed applying methods used with emotionally disturbed persons, such as case studies and projective techniques, to the study of the normal personality. Because case studies focus on the past, Allport considered them of no value in understanding the normal adult, whose personality is divorced from childhood influences. Projective techniques, such as the Thematic Apperception Test and the Rorschach inkblot test, may present a distorted picture of the normal personality because they deal with the unconscious, with forces that have little effect on the normal adult personality. Allport suggested that more reliable information can be obtained by simply asking people to describe themselves. In that way, they will reveal their dominant traits.

Allport favored the idiographic approach (that is, the study of the individual case) over the nomothetic approach. He argued that the latter, in which means or averages are compared among groups of subjects, reveals nothing about the functioning of the individual. In general, idiographic research techniques, such as his analysis of the letters from Jenny, uncover more useful information about the individual personality. However, Allport did use nomothetic methods when he believed them to be appropriate. For example, his use and development of psychological tests, including the Study of Values, employed the nomothetic approach.

expressive behavior
Spontaneous and seemingly purposeless behavior, usually displayed without our conscious awareness.

coping behavior
Consciously planned behavior determined by the needs of a given situation and designed for a specific purpose, usually to bring about a change in one's environment.

Allport conducted considerable research on what he called **expressive behavior**, the behavior that expresses our personality traits. He divided behavior into two types: coping behavior and expressive behavior. **Coping behavior** is oriented toward a specific purpose and is consciously planned and formally carried out. It is determined by needs inspired by the situation and ordinarily is directed toward bringing about some change in the environment.

Expressive behavior, on the other hand, is spontaneous and reflects basic aspects of the personality. It is difficult to change, has no specific purpose, and is usually displayed without our being aware of it. Allport offered the example of public speaking. The lecturer communicates with the audience on two levels. The formal, planned level (coping behavior) includes the content of the lecture. The informal, unplanned level consists of the lecturer's movements, gestures, and vocal inflections (expressive behaviors). Perhaps the lecturer is perspiring and flushed, speaks rapidly in a shaky voice, fidgets with a tie or an earring, or paces back and forth. These spontaneous behaviors reflect elements of the lecturer's personality.

To study expressive behavior, Allport gave subjects a variety of tasks to perform and judged the consistency of their expressive movements over the different situations (Allport & Vernon, 1933). He found a high level of consistency in voice, handwriting, posture, and gestures and deduced the existence of such traits as introversion and extraversion.

Additional research on expressive behavior has shown that personality can be judged on the basis of tape recordings and films. Facial expressions, tone of voice, and idiosyncratic gestures and mannerisms tend to reveal personality traits to a trained observer (Allport & Cantril, 1934; Estes, 1938). These findings were extended and confirmed in more recent research that assessed specific traits, such as extraversion and masculinity-femininity, using videotapes, handwriting samples, speech, and still photographs (Berry, 1990, 1991; Riggio & Friedman, 1986; Riggio, Lippa, & Salinas, 1990).

A Final Commentary

Allport's theory did not grow directly out of Freudian psychoanalysis, nor was Allport psychoanalyzed. He did not provide treatment for emotionally disturbed persons, and his system does not derive from therapeutic sessions with neurotics. His work originated in an academic rather than an analytic setting and therefore has been of great interest to academic psychologists.

Although much research has been conducted on expressive behavior, Allport's theory has not stimulated a great deal of research designed to test his other concepts or the theory as a whole. Allport's emphasis on idiographic research ran against the main current of thought in contemporary psychology, which dictated that the only valid approach was to study large numbers of subjects and describe them in group terms through sophisticated statistical analyses. Allport's insistence on studying emotionally healthy adult subjects is also at variance with the prevalent position on research in clinical psychology, which emphasizes the study of the neurotic and psychotic.

It is difficult to translate Allport's concepts into specific terms and operations suitable for study by the experimental method. For example, how can we observe functional autonomy or propriate striving in the laboratory? How can we manipulate them to observe their effects or the effects of other variables upon them?

There are other criticisms of Allport's system, particularly of functional autonomy. Allport did not make clear how an original motive is transformed into an autonomous one. For example, once a person is financially secure, by what process is the motive to work hard for money changed into a motive to work hard for the sake of the work itself? If the mechanism of transformation is not known, how can we predict which childhood motives will become autonomous motives in adulthood?

Allport's emphasis on the uniqueness of personality has also been criticized because his position focuses so exclusively on the individual that it is impossible to generalize from one person to another. The traditional approach in science is to seek uniformities and generalities.

Many psychologists find it difficult to accept Allport's proposed discontinuity between child and adult, animal and human, normal and abnormal. They point out that research on childhood, animals, and abnormal behavior has yielded considerable knowledge about the functioning of the normal adult.

Despite these criticisms, Allport's theory has been well received in the academic community. His approach to personality, his emphasis on uniqueness, and his focus on the importance of goals and expectations for the future are reflected in the work of the humanistic psychologists Carl Rogers and Abraham Maslow. Allport's work on traits has assumed importance as part of the current resurgence of interest in traits. His ideas "look remarkably sound even with 53 years of hindsight, and yield a large number of implications for conceptualization and research in modern personality psychology" (Funder, 1991, p. 32). Allport's assertion that traits are real is receiving a great deal of empirical support.

Allport's books are written in a readable style, and he presents his concepts in a manner that has a commonsense appeal. His emphasis on rational and conscious determinants of behavior provides an alternative to the psychoanalytic position that we are irrationally and unconsciously driven by uncontrollable forces. His view that we are shaped more by future events than past events is congenial with those who depict human nature in hopeful and humanistic terms.

Summary

Gordon Allport focused on the conscious instead of the unconscious, believed that personality is guided more by the present and future than by the past, and studied normal rather than emotionally disturbed persons. His approach emphasizes the uniqueness of the individual personality. Allport defined personality as the dynamic organization within the individual of those psychophysical systems that determine characteristic behavior and thought. Personality is a product of heredity and environment and is divorced from childhood experiences.

Traits are consistent, enduring predispositions to respond in the same or a similar way to different stimuli. Individual traits are unique to the person; common traits are shared by many people. Allport later called individual traits "personal dispositions." Habits are narrower than traits and are relatively inflexible; they involve a specific response to a specific stimulus. Attitudes have specific objects of reference and are for or against something.

Cardinal traits are powerful and pervasive. Central traits are less pervasive. Secondary traits are displayed less conspicuously and less consistently than the other types of traits.

According to the concept of functional autonomy, a motive in the normal adult is not functionally related to the past experiences in which it originally appeared. Two levels of functional autonomy are perseverative (behaviors such as addictions and repeated physical movements) and propriate (interests, values, attitudes, intentions, lifestyle, and self-image related to the core of personality). Three principles of propriate functional autonomy are (1) organizing the energy level, (2) mastery and competence, and (3) propriate patterning.

The proprium (the self or ego) develops from infancy to adolescence in seven stages: bodily self, self-identity, self-esteem, extension of self, self-image, self as a rational coper, and propriate striving.

An infant is controlled by drives and reflexes and has little personality. The mature, healthy personality is characterized by an extension of self to other people and activities, a warm relating of self to others, emotional security, a realistic perception, the development of skills, a commitment to work, self-objectification, and a unifying philosophy of life.

Allport presented an optimistic image of human nature. We are not driven by childhood events. We are in conscious control of our lives, creatively design a lifestyle, and grow through an inherent need for autonomy, individuality, and selfhood. Our ultimate goal is to experience increases in tension that impel us to seek new sensations and challenges.

The personal-document approach to personality assessment involves the study of diaries, letters, and other personal records to uncover personality traits. The Study of Values is a psychological test to assess six types of values. Allport's research on expressive behavior revealed a consistency in expressive movements and related them to personality.

Allport's theory has been criticized for its idiographic approach and its focus on normal subjects only. In addition, it is difficult to test empirically such concepts as functional autonomy. Allport's focus on the uniqueness of personality, on the stability and consistency of traits over all situations, and on the discontinuity between childhood and adult personalities has also been questioned.

Critical Thinking Review

1. Discuss the debate about the relative importance of personal variables and situational variables as influences on personality. What was the outcome of that debate?

2. Explain Gordon Allport's definition of personality. How does his view differ from Freud's?

3. How was Allport's view of personality affected by his meeting with Freud and by his own childhood feelings of inferiority?

4. Describe four characteristics of traits. How do traits differ from attitudes?

5. According to Allport, what is the relationship between personality and motivation?

6. What is the role of the cognitive processes in personality?

7. What is the relationship between adult motives and childhood experiences? What term did Allport use to describe this situation?

8. What are the three principles of functional autonomy?

9. Define the concept of proprium and describe the seven stages in its development.

10. What parental behaviors are necessary for a child to achieve positive psychological growth?

11. How does Allport's theory account for mental illness in adulthood?

12. What are the characteristics of the mature, healthy personality?

13. What is expressive behavior? Name several behaviors that can express the personality traits of aggressiveness and possessiveness.

Suggested Reading

Allport, G. W. (1937). *Personality: A psychological interpretation.* New York: Holt. Allport's classic book that established the study of personality as an integral part of scientific academic psychology and defined the focus of personality psychology as the unique individual.

Allport, G. W. (1955). *Becoming: Basic considerations for a psychology of personality.* New Haven, CT: Yale University Press. Outlines Allport's approach to personality, emphasizing the human capacity for growth and development.

Allport, G. W. (1967). Autobiography. In E. G. Boring & G. Lindzey (Eds.), *A history of psychology in autobiography* (vol. 5, pp. 1–25). New York: Appleton-Century-Crofts. Allport's account of his life and career.

Evans, R. I. (1971). *Gordon Allport: The man and his ideas.* New York: Dutton. Interviews with Allport about his life and work.

Kreitler, S., & Kreitler, H. (1990). *The cognitive foundations of personality traits.* New York: Plenum Press. Describes the study of personality traits as "alive and well" and asserts that no better building blocks of personality have thus far been proposed.

Morey, L. C. (1987). Observations on the meeting between Allport and Freud. *Psychoanalytic Review, 74*(1), 135–139. Analyzes the 1920 encounter between Gordon Allport and Sigmund Freud, as reported by Allport, and considers the context in which the meeting took place.

Wiggins, J. S., & Pincus, A. L. (1992). Personality: Structure and assessment. *Annual Review of Psychology, 43,* 473–504. Reviews current research and issues in trait theory in the study of personality.

Raymond Cattell
and Other Trait Theorists

The Life of Cattell (1905–)
Cattell's Approach to Personality Traits
Source Traits: The Basic Factors of Personality
Dynamic Traits: The Motivating Forces
The Influences of Heredity and Environment
Personality Development
Cattell's Image of Human Nature
Assessment in Cattell's Theory
    The 16 PF Test
Research in Cattell's Theory
A Final Commentary

Other Trait Approaches
Hans Eysenck: Extraversion, Neuroticism, and
    Psychoticism
Robert McCrae and Paul Costa: The Five-Factor
    Model
Arnold Buss and Robert Plomin:
    The Temperament Theory
Summary
Critical Thinking Review
Suggested Reading

Personality is that which permits a prediction of what a person will do in a given situation.

—Raymond Cattell

Cattell's goal in his study of personality is to predict behavior—to predict what a person will do in response to a given stimulus situation. He makes no reference to changing or modifying behavior from undesirable to desirable or from abnormal to normal, something that has been the aim of many of the theorists we have discussed. The patients from whose cases more clinically oriented theories were derived sought a psychologist's services because they were unhappy or disturbed by some emotion or aspect of their behavior that they wanted to change. Cattell's subjects were normal people whose personalities he studied, not treated. Cattell believes it is impossible (or at least unwise) to attempt to change a personality before understanding in detail what is to be changed.

Cattell's theory of personality, then, did not originate in a clinical setting. Instead, his approach is a rigorously scientific one, relying on observations of behavior and collection of masses of data on each subject. In Cattell's research, it is not unusual for more than 50 kinds of measurements to be made of a subject.

factor analysis
A statistical technique based on correlations between a number of measures, which may be explained in terms of underlying factors.

The distinguishing aspect of Cattell's approach is what he does with the data thus generated. He applies the statistical procedure of **factor analysis**, which involves assessing the relationship between each possible pair of measurements taken from a group of subjects to determine common factors. For example, scores on two different psychological tests or on two subscales of the same test are analyzed to determine their correlation. If the two measures show a high correlation, Cattell is confident in suggesting that they measure similar or related aspects of personality. For example, if we assume that the guilt-proneness and introversion subscales of a personality test yield a high correlation coefficient, then we may suggest that both subscales provide information on the same factor of personality (hence the term *factor analysis*).

Cattell calls these factors "traits," which he sees as the mental elements of the personality. Only when we know someone's characteristic traits are we able to predict how that person will behave in a given situation. To fully understand a person, then, we must be able to describe in precise terms the entire pattern of traits that define that person as an individual.

The Life of Cattell (1905–   )

Cattell was born in Staffordshire, England, where he had a happy childhood and youth. His parents were exacting about the standards of performance they expected from their children but permissive about how the children spent their time. Cattell, his brothers, and his friends spent much time outdoors, sailing, swimming, exploring caves, and fighting mock battles over terrain. They "occasionally drowned or fell over cliffs," he recalled.

When Cattell was 9, England entered World War I. A mansion near his home was converted to a hospital, and Cattell saw trainloads of wounded men returning from the battlefields of France. He wrote that this experience made him unusually serious for a young boy and aware of the "brevity of life and the need to accomplish while one might." His later dedication to his work may have originated in these times. Cattell also felt a sense of competitiveness with a brother who was three years older. He wrote of the problems of trying to maintain his own freedom of development when confronted with a brother who could not be "overcome" (Cattell, 1974a, pp. 62–63).

At 16, Cattell entered the University of London to study physics and chemistry. He graduated three years later with honors, but his years in London intensified his interest in social problems. He realized that his training in the physical sciences did not equip him to deal with social ills and concluded that his only recourse was to study the human mind.

This was a courageous decision to make in 1924 because psychology in England was regarded as a discipline for eccentrics, and there were few professional opportunities; in all England there were only six psychology professorships. Against the advice of his friends, Cattell began graduate studies at the University of London, working with the eminent psychologist-statistician Charles E. Spearman, who had developed the technique of factor analysis.

Awarded his Ph.D. in 1929, Cattell found that his friends had been correct: there were few jobs for psychologists. He lectured at Exeter University, wrote a book about the English countryside, and established a psychology clinic for the school system of Leicester, all while conducting research and writing. He resolved to apply factor analysis, which Spearman had used to measure certain mental abilities, to the structure of personality.

During this period Cattell developed chronic digestive disorders as a result of overwork, poor food, and living in a cold attic apartment. His wife left him because of his poor economic prospects and his total absorption in his work. However, Cattell claimed some positive benefits from that time of hardship. "Those years made me as canny and distrustful as a squirrel who has known a long winter. It bred asceticism, and impatience with irrelevance, to the point of ruthlessness" (Cattell, 1974b, p. 90). The experience forced him to focus on practical problems rather than on theoretical or experimental issues, which he might have pursued had he been in more comfortable and secure circumstances.

Eight years after he earned his doctoral degree, Cattell finally received an opportunity to undertake full-time work in psychology. The prominent American psychologist Edward L. Thorndike invited Cattell to spend a year in Thorndike's laboratory at Columbia University in New York. The following year Cattell became professor of psychology at Clark University in Worcester, Massachusetts, and in 1941 he moved to Harvard University, where, as he said, the "sap of creativity" rose (Cattell, 1974a, p. 71). He married a mathematician who shared his research interests, and at the age of 40 moved to the University of Illinois as a research professor.

Unburdened by teaching or other academic duties, Cattell devoted himself fully to his research. He frequently stayed late at the laboratory, joking that it was easy to find his car in the parking lot at night because it was the only one left. He published more than 400 articles and 35 books, a monumental accomplishment that reflects his dedication and perseverance. In his seventies, Cattell joined the graduate faculty of the University of Hawaii, where he permitted himself the luxury of swimming in the ocean every day and worked "as hard as an assistant professor up for tenure and not sure that it will be granted" (Johnson, 1980, p. 300).

Cattell's Approach to Personality Traits

trait A reaction tendency, derived by factor analysis, that is a relatively permanent part of personality.

Cattell defined **traits** as relatively permanent reaction tendencies that are the basic structural units of the personality. He derived his descriptions of traits through factor analysis. Cattell classified traits in several ways. First, he distinguished between common traits and unique traits. A **common trait** is one that is possessed by everyone to some degree. Intelligence, extraversion, and gregariousness are examples of common traits. Everyone has these traits, but some people have them to a greater degree than others. Cattell's reason for suggesting that common traits are universal is that all people have a similar hereditary potential and are subject to similar social pressures, at least within the same culture.

common traits Traits possessed in some degree by all persons.

unique traits Traits possessed by one or a few persons.

People differ in that they possess different amounts or degrees of these common traits. They also differ because of their **unique traits,** those aspects of personality shared by few other people. Unique traits are particularly apparent in our interests and attitudes. For example, one person may have a consuming interest in butterflies, whereas another may be passionately in favor of banning bare feet from public view.

A second way to classify traits is to divide them into ability traits, temperament traits, and dynamic traits. **Ability traits** determine how efficiently a person will be able to work toward a goal. Intelligence is an ability trait; our level of intelligence will help determine how we strive for a goal, such as a college degree. **Temperament traits** describe the general style and emotional tone of our behavior—for example, how assertive, easygoing, or irritable we are. These traits affect the way we act and react to situations. **Dynamic traits** are the driving forces of our behavior and define our motivations, interests, and ambitions.

A third way of classifying traits—surface traits versus source traits—is according to their stability and permanence. **Surface traits** are personality characteristics that correlate with one another but do not constitute a personality factor because they are not determined by a single source. For example, several behavioral elements, such as anxiety, indecision, and irrational fear, form the surface trait of neuroticism. Thus, neuroticism does not derive from a single source. Because surface traits are composed of several elements, they are less stable and permanent and therefore less important in the understanding of personality.

Of greater importance are **source traits,** unitary personality factors that are much more stable and permanent. Each source trait gives rise to some aspect of behavior. Source traits are the individual factors, derived from factor analysis, that combine to account for surface traits.

According to their origin, source traits are classified as either constitutional traits or environmental-mold traits. **Constitutional traits** originate in biological conditions but are not necessarily innate. For example, alcohol intake can cause such behaviors as carelessness, talkativeness, and slurred speech. Factor analysis would indicate that these characteristics are source traits.

Environmental-mold traits derive from influences in our social and physical environments. These traits are learned characteristics and behaviors that impose a pattern on the personality. The behavior of a person reared in an inner-city ghetto is molded differently from the behavior of someone raised in upper-class luxury. A career military officer shows a different pattern of behavior from a jazz musician. Thus, we see that Cattell recognized the interaction of personal and situational variables.

ability traits Traits that describe our skills and how efficiently we will be able to work toward a goal.

temperament traits Traits that describe our general behavioral style in responding to our environment.

dynamic traits Traits that describe our motivations and interests.

surface traits Traits that show a correlation but do not constitute a factor because they are not determined by a single source.

source traits, Stable, permanent traits that are the basic factors of personality, derived by factor analysis.

constitutional traits Source traits that depend on our physiological characteristics.

environmental-mold traits Source traits that are learned from social and environmental interactions.

Source Traits: The Basic Factors of Personality

After more than two decades of intensive factor-analytic research, Cattell identified 16 source traits as the basic factors of the human personality. These factors are perhaps best known in the form in which they are most often used, in an objective test of personality called the Sixteen Personality Factor (16 PF) Questionnaire. Cattell presented the traits in bipolar form.

A person with a low score on this factor is described as:	A person with a high score on this factor is described as:
Factor A	
Reserved	Outgoing
Factor B	
Less intelligent	More intelligent
Factor C	
Affected by feelings	Emotionally stable
Factor E	
Submissive	Dominant
Factor F	
Serious	Happy-go-lucky
Factor G	
Expedient	Conscientious
Factor H	
Timid	Venturesome
Factor I	
Tough-minded	Sensitive
Factor L	
Trusting	Suspicious
Factor M	
Practical	Imaginative
Factor N	
Forthright	Shrewd
Factor O	
Self-assured	Apprehensive
Factor Q_1	
Conservative	Experimenting
Factor Q_2	
Group-dependent	Self-sufficient
Factor Q_3	
Uncontrolled	Controlled
Factor Q_4	
Relaxed	Tense

It is important to remember that in Cattell's system these source traits are the basic elements of the personality as atoms are the basic units of the physical world. Cattell argues that psychologists cannot generate laws about personality, or fully understand it, without being able to describe precisely the nature of these elements.

Dynamic Traits: The Motivating Forces

We noted that Cattell defined dynamic traits as those concerned with motivation, an important issue in many personality theories. Cattell argued that a

ergs Permanent constitutional source traits that provide energy for our goal-directed behavior. Ergs are the basic innate units of motivation.

sentiments Environmental-mold source traits that motivate behavior.

attitudes Our interests in and emotions and behaviors toward some person, object, or event. To Cattell, attitudes encompass emotions, actions, and opinions; this is a broader definition than is typically used in psychology.

subsidiation The relationships among ergs, sentiments, and attitudes, in which some elements are subordinate to others.

dynamic lattice The graphic representation of the relationships among ergs, sentiments, and attitudes.

self-sentiment The self-concept; the organizer of our attitudes and motivations.

personality theory that fails to consider dynamic or motivating forces is incomplete, like a description of an engine that omits any mention of fuel.

There are two kinds of dynamic traits: ergs and sentiments. The word *erg* derives from the Greek *ergon,* which means "work" or "energy." Cattell used **erg** to denote the concept of instinct or drive. Ergs are the innate energy source for all behavior; they are the basic units of motivation that direct our behavior toward specific goals. Cattell's factor-analytic research identified 11 ergs: curiosity, sex, gregariousness, protection, self-assertion, security, hunger, anger, disgust, appeal, and self-submission.

Whereas an erg is a constitutional source trait, a **sentiment** is an environmental-mold source trait, which means it derives from external social and physical influences. A sentiment is a pattern of learned attitudes that focus on an important aspect of a person's life, such as one's nation, spouse, occupation, religion, or hobby. Ergs and sentiments both motivate behavior, but a vital difference exists between them. Because it is a constitutional trait, an erg is a permanent structure of the personality. It may grow stronger or weaker, but it cannot disappear. A sentiment, which results from learning, can be unlearned and can disappear so that it is no longer important in a person's life.

Cattell defined **attitudes** as our interests in and emotions and behavior toward some person, object, or event. As Cattell applies the term, it does not refer exclusively to an opinion for or against something, which is the traditional use of the word *attitude* in psychology. Cattell's definition is broader, encompassing all our emotions and actions toward an object or situation.

Our dynamic traits—both ergs and sentiments—and our attitudes are related through **subsidiation,** which simply means that within the personality, some elements subsidiate or are subordinate to others. Attitudes are subsidiary to sentiments; sentiments are subsidiary to ergs. Cattell expresses these relationships in a diagram called the **dynamic lattice** (see Figure 9.1). Our motivating forces, the ergs, are listed at the right. Sentiments are indicated in the circles at the center of the diagram. Note that each sentiment is subsidiary to one or more ergs. The attitudes, at the left, show the person's feelings and behavior toward an object.

Each person's pattern of sentiments is organized by a master sentiment, which Cattell called the **self-sentiment.** This is our self-concept, which is reflected in virtually all our attitudes and behaviors. The self-sentiment provides stability, coherence, and organization to the source traits and is linked to the expression of the ergs and sentiments. It is among the last of the sentiments to reach a full level of development. The self-sentiment contributes to the satisfaction of all the dynamic traits and therefore controls all the structures in the personality.

The Influences of Heredity and Environment

Cattell has shown great interest in the relative influences of heredity and environment in shaping personality. He investigated the importance of

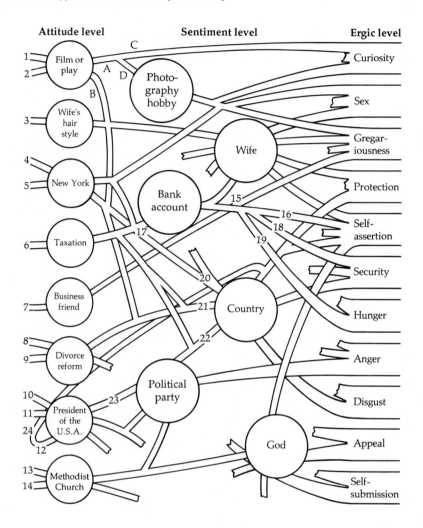

Figure 9.1

Fragment of a dynamic lattice showing attitude subsidiation, sentiment structure, and ergic goals. SOURCE: R. B. Cattell, *Personality: A Systematic Theoretical and Factual Study* (New York: McGraw-Hill, 1950), p. 158. Copyright 1950 by Raymond B. Cattell. Reprinted by permission.

hereditary and environmental or situational factors by statistically comparing similarities found between twins reared in the same family, twins reared apart, non-twin siblings reared in the same family, and non-twin siblings reared apart. Thus, he has been able to estimate the extent to which differences in traits may be attributed to genetic or to environmental influences.

For some traits, the results demonstrate that heredity plays an important role. For example, Cattell's data suggest that 80 percent of intelligence (Factor B) and 80 percent of timidity versus venturesomeness (Factor H) can be

Adolescence can be a stressful stage of development.

accounted for by genetic factors. With these and other traits, heredity was found to be the dominant influence, a finding that led Cattell to argue for selective breeding to promote a more intelligent population. In general, Cattell concluded that one-third of our personality is genetically determined, and two-thirds is determined by social and environmental influences.

Personality Development

Cattell proposed six stages in the development of the human personality. These stages cover the full range of life, from birth through old age (see Table 9.1).

Table 9.1   *Cattell's stages of personality development.*

Stage	Age	Development
Infancy	0–6	Weaning, toilet training, formation of ego, superego, and social attitudes
Childhood	6–14	Independence from parents and identification with peers
Adolescence	14–23	Conflicts about independence, self-assertion, and sex
Maturity	23–50	Satisfaction with career, marriage, and family
Late maturity	50–65	Personality changes in response to changes in physical and social circumstances
Old age	65+	Adjustment to loss of friends, career, and status

In late maturity, after one's children have left home, there is often a reexamination of the values of one's life.

Infancy, lasting from birth until the age of 6, is the major formative period in personality development. During this stage, the child is influenced by parents and siblings and by the experiences of weaning and toilet training. Social attitudes are formed along with the ego and the superego, feelings of security or insecurity, an attitude toward authority, and a possible tendency to neuroticism. Cattell was not a follower of Freud's, but he incorporated the Freudian ideas that the early years of life are crucial in the formation of personality and that oral and anal conflicts can affect personality.

Between ages 6 and 14, the childhood stage, there are few psychological problems. This stage marks the beginning of a trend toward independence from our parents and an increasing identification with our peers. This is followed by a more troublesome and stressful stage of development—adolescence, between ages 14 and 23. The incidence of emotional disorders and delinquency rises during this period. Young people manifest a great deal of conflict around the drives for independence, self-assertion, and sex.

The fourth phase of development, maturity, lasts from ages 23 to 50. In general, it is a satisfying and productive time in terms of career, marriage, and family. The personality becomes less fluid and more set, as compared with earlier stages, and emotional stability increases. Cattell found little change in interests and attitudes during this stage.

Late maturity involves personality developments in response to physical, social, and psychological changes. Health and vigor may decline after age 50, along with attractiveness, and the end of one's life is in view. During this phase, people usually reexamine their personal values and search for a new self. This is similar to Jung's view of midlife personality changes (see Chapter 3).

Old age, the final stage, involves adjustment to losses—the deaths of spouses, relatives, and friends; a career lost to retirement; loss of status in a culture that worships youth; and a pervasive sense of loneliness and insecurity.

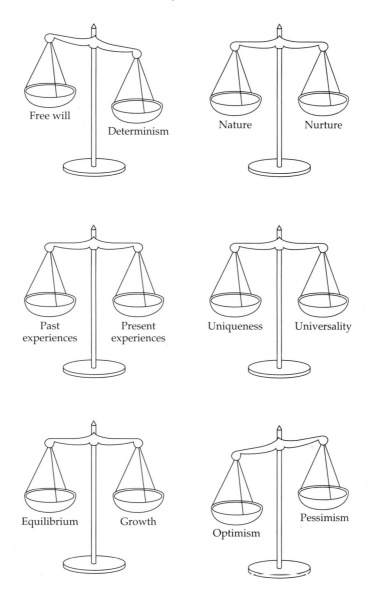

Free will — Determinism

Nature — Nurture

Past experiences — Present experiences

Uniqueness — Universality

Equilibrium — Growth

Optimism — Pessimism

Cattell

Image of Human Nature.

Cattell's Image of Human Nature

Cattell's definition of personality indicates his view of human nature. He wrote, ''Personality is that which permits a prediction of what a person will do in a given situation'' (Cattell, 1950, p. 2).

For behavior to be considered predictable, it must be lawful and orderly. Prediction would be difficult without regularity and consistency in the personality. For example, Cattell noted that one spouse can usually predict with considerable accuracy what the other spouse will do in a given situation because his or her past behavior has been consistent and orderly. Therefore, Cattell's image of human nature allows for little spontaneity because that would preclude predictability. On the free will versus determinism issue, then, Cattell's view seems to fall more on the side of determinism.

Cattell did not posit any ultimate and necessary goal that dominates behavior. There is no drive for self-actualization or some other form of ultimate fulfillment to pull us, nor are there universal or instinctual psychosexual conflicts to propel us. Although Cattell noted the determining influence of infancy and childhood, we do not receive the impression from Cattell's writings that he believes people are imprisoned by childhood forces and unable to modify the influence of those forces at a later stage of development.

Cattell accepts the influence of both nature and nurture. For example, constitutional traits may be innate (as are ergs), whereas environmental-mold traits are learned. His research has demonstrated the quantifiable impact of heredity and environment on various traits. On the uniqueness-universality issue, Cattell takes a moderate position, noting the existence of both common traits, applicable to everyone in a culture, and unique traits, characteristic of each individual.

Cattell's personal view of human nature is clearer. In his younger years, he was optimistic about our ability to solve the problems facing society. He predicted that we would gain greater knowledge of and control over our environment. He also expected to see the general level of intelligence increase, along with the development of "a more gracious community life of creatively occupied citizens" (Cattell, 1974b, p. 88). However, reality has not lived up to Cattell's expectations, and his optimism has dimmed. He has since suggested that human nature and society have regressed.

Assessment in Cattell's Theory

L-data Life-record ratings of behaviors observed in real-life situations, such as in the classroom or office.

Cattell undertook to assess personality objectively using three primary assessment techniques. He called the resulting data L-data (life records), Q-data (questionnaires), and T-data (tests). The **L-data** technique involves observers' ratings of specific behaviors exhibited by the subjects. The behaviors being observed occur in real-life situations rather than in a laboratory. For example, observers might record frequency of absence from work, grades in school, conscientiousness in performing duties, emotional stability on the baseball field, or sociability in the office. The important points about L-data are that they involve overt behaviors that can be seen by an observer and behaviors that occur in a naturalistic setting.

Q-data Self-report questionnaire ratings of our characteristics, attitudes, and interests.

The **Q-data** technique relies on questionnaires. Whereas the L-data technique calls for an observer to rate the subjects, the Q-data technique requires the subjects to rate themselves. Various questionnaires are used, including standard self-report personality inventories, such as the MMPI, and scales that measure attitudes, interests, and opinions. Even interviews can be used, as long as the subjects introspect and rate themselves on whatever aspect of behavior is being examined.

Cattell recognized that the Q-data technique had its limitations. First, some subjects may have a limited self-awareness, so their answers may not accurately reflect the true nature of their personality. Second, even if subjects do know themselves well, they may not want the researchers to know them and therefore may deliberately falsify their answers. This effect is aggravated by the fact that Q-data involves questionnaires that most subjects are able to figure out; they can easily judge what aspect of their personality is being assessed. For example, if you were asked whether you preferred to be alone or with other people, you would guess that the question related to your degree of sociability. If you were shy—and sensitive about it—you might say that you preferred to be with other people, to conceal what you consider a disturbing aspect of your personality. Because of this potential for bias, Cattell warned that Q-data reports must not be automatically accepted as accurate.

T-data Data derived from personality tests that are resistant to faking.

The **T-data** technique involves the use of what Cattell called "objective" tests, in which a person responds without knowing what aspect of behavior is being evaluated. These tests circumvent the Q-data's shortcomings by making it difficult for a subject to know what a test is measuring. If you cannot guess what the experimenter is trying to find out, then you cannot distort your responses to conceal something about yourself. For example, if you were shown an inkblot, you could not predict whether the interpretation of your response would reveal that you are sociable or shy, insecure or placid. Cattell calls such tests as the Rorschach, the Thematic Apperception Test, and the word-association test "objective" tests because they are resistant to faking. It is important to note that to most psychologists this use of the word *objective* is misleading. As we stated in Chapter 1, such tests are usually called "subjective" because of the bias that can affect scoring and interpretation.

The 16 PF Test

Cattell developed several tests to assess personality, the most notable being the 16 PF, based on his 16 major source traits. This test is intended for use with persons 16 years of age and older and yields scores on each of the 16 scales. The responses are scored objectively, and a computerized service is available for scoring and interpreting the results. The test is widely used to assess personality for research purposes, for clinical diagnosis, and for predicting occupational success.

Figure 9.2 shows a sample 16 PF test profile for a hypothetical airline pilot. By reading the high and low points of the plot of test scores, we can see that this person is emotionally stable, conscientious, venturesome, tough-minded, practical, self-assured, controlled, and relaxed. The pilot is not tense, apprehensive, or timid.

Cattell developed several variations of the 16 PF. To assess a wide range

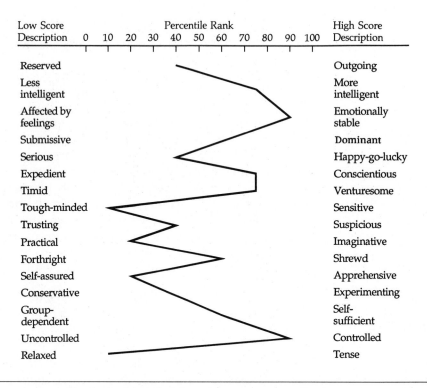

Low Score Description				Percentile Rank						High Score Description

Reserved — Outgoing
Less intelligent — More intelligent
Affected by feelings — Emotionally stable
Submissive — **Dominant**
Serious — Happy-go-lucky
Expedient — Conscientious
Timid — Venturesome
Tough-minded — Sensitive
Trusting — Suspicious
Practical — Imaginative
Forthright — Shrewd
Self-assured — Apprehensive
Conservative — Experimenting
Group-dependent — Self-sufficient
Uncontrolled — Controlled
Relaxed — Tense

Figure 9.2

16 PF profile of a hypothetical airline pilot.   SOURCE: Cattell, Eber, and Tatsuoka, 1970.

of emotional disturbances, he compiled the Clinical Analysis Questionnaire to measure 28 source traits, 16 from the 16 PF and 12 (such as anxiety, guilt, and paranoia) to assess abnormal personalities (Cattell & Kline, 1977). Tests are also available to assess personality factors in ages 12 to 18, 8 to 12, and 6 to 8. Versions have been prepared to measure specific aspects of personality, such as anxiety, depression, and neuroticism, and for designated purposes, such as marriage counseling and evaluating executives' job performance.

Research in Cattell's Theory

Cattell's research approach is nomothetic; the method of factor analysis involves the study of large groups of people and the calculation of their average performance on various assessing instruments. However, Cattell sometimes applied his data to the explanation of individual behavior. For example, if you were to take the 16 PF test, it would reveal the traits that are unique to you as an individual.

In discussing research methods, Cattell delineated three ways to study personality: bivariate, clinical, and multivariate. The bivariate, or two-variable, approach is the standard laboratory experimental method in psychology (see Chapter 1). In this approach, the psychologist manipulates the independent variable to determine its effect on the subjects' behavior (the dependent variable). The approach could also be called univariate, because only one variable is studied at a time.

Cattell agrees that this method is scientific, rigorous, and quantitative, but he argues that it can deal with only limited aspects of personality. In reality, personality is affected by many simultaneously interacting and influencing variables. Also, in the typical artificial laboratory situation, significant emotional experiences cannot be manipulated and duplicated. Thus, for Cattell, the bivariate approach is too restrictive to reveal much about the human personality.

The clinical method, which includes case studies, dream analysis, free association, and similar techniques, is, as we noted in our discussion of the psychoanalytic theorists, highly subjective. It does not yield verifiable and quantifiable data. "The clinician has his heart in the right place," Cattell wrote, "but perhaps we may say that he remains a little fuzzy in his head" (Cattell, 1959, p. 45).

The multivariate approach—Cattell's choice—involves the sophisticated statistical procedure of factor analysis and yields specific data. Cattell favors two forms of factor analysis, the R technique and the P technique. The R technique involves collecting large amounts of data from a group of subjects. Correlations among all the scores are made to determine personality factors or traits. The P technique involves collecting a large amount of data from a single subject over a long period.

Let us consider a few factor-analytic studies conducted by Cattell and his associates. We noted that Cattell was interested in the relative effects of heredity and environment on personality. From a factor analysis of data from 3,000 male subjects ages 12 to 18, Cattell concluded that three source traits were determined primarily by heredity (Cattell, 1982). These are Factor F (serious versus happy-go-lucky), Factor I (tough-minded versus sensitive), and Factor Q_3 (uncontrolled versus controlled). Three other traits were found to be determined primarily by environmental influences: Factor E (submissive versus dominant), Factor G (expedient versus conscientious), and Factor Q_4 (relaxed versus tense).

Cattell applied the 16 PF to determine the relationship between personality traits and marital stability (Cattell & Nesselroade, 1967). The subjects were married couples who were identified as having either a stable or an unstable marriage; the criterion of stability was whether a couple had taken steps toward dissolving the marriage. The results showed that the stability of a marriage could be predicted on the basis of test scores. Partners in stable marriages had similar personality traits; partners in unstable marriages showed highly different personality traits.

Using the P technique, Cattell studied a male college student for 40 days using various assessment measures (Cattell & Cross, 1952). The purpose of the study was to compare the factors derived from the factor analysis of this single subject with the factors derived from the factor analysis of a large group of subjects (the R technique). The results showed that traits may be unique to an individual, but they are also similar to traits that are common to large groups of people.

Additional research compared people who differed on the Q_1 source trait (conservative versus experimenting) (Wilson, Ausman, & Mathews, 1973). The subjects were asked for their preferences for paintings that differed in complexity and ambiguity. Some paintings were clear representations of people and objects. Others were abstract and nonrepresentational; it was not clear what these paintings were supposed to depict. As predicted, people scoring on the low, or conservative, end of Factor Q_1 preferred the straightforward, representational works. Liberal people preferred the more abstract paintings.

A Final Commentary

As a system that organizes huge volumes of research; accumulates monumental amounts of experimental data in an area often defined by subjective case histories, intuitions, and speculations; and offers new ways of assessing personality, Cattell's theory demands consideration. However, the quantity of Cattell's research and the complexity of the factor-analytic method are among the reasons for a general lack of acceptance of his point of view. Cattell wrote that he sensed "unquestionable failure" in persuading others of the wisdom of his approach, which he defends as the only method of value in the study of personality (Cattell, 1974b, p. 122). In 1990, at the age of 85, he reiterated this point, criticizing contemporary psychologists for failing to learn and apply factor analysis. He noted that his work remained isolated from the "random mainstream of personality speculation" (Cattell, 1990, p. 101).

Cattell's work has been described as much respected and seldom read. Unfortunately, this seems all too accurate. Cattell reported that sales of his undergraduate textbook, *The Scientific Analysis of Personality* (Cattell, 1970), were higher in England, Germany, Australia, and Japan than in the United States. Also, he noted that psychologists in Europe rate his theory and research as being more relevant than do psychologists in the United States.

Several specific criticisms have been directed against Cattell's approach. Despite the legitimate claim that factor analysis is an objective, precise technique, opportunity still exists for subjectivity to affect the research methodology. At several stages in Cattell's research process, decisions are required that may be influenced by personal opinions and preferences. For example, in the initial step of collecting the data, the psychologist must decide which tests to use and what aspects of behavior to measure. The researcher must determine which factor-analytic technique to apply and what level of statistical significance will be accepted as appropriate. Once the factors have been identified, the researcher must choose labels for them. If the names chosen can be ambiguously interpreted, they may not accurately express the nature of the factors. This is not to suggest that Cattell's theory is weak in this sense, but the criticisms indicate that the opportunity for subjective error exists within the factor-analytic approach.

Despite the efforts of Cattell and his associates to persuade psychologists of the utility of his methods, they have succeeded only on a small scale. His theory is one of the most firmly grounded in data and one of the most systematically constructed, and it has yielded much information about the structure of personality. Cattell remains convinced that one day his approach will enable us to predict human behavior with the same degree of accuracy with which we can predict the movement of the planets. Whatever the outcome, it is clear that the trait approach to personality, and investigations of the importance of genetic influences, are being carried on in contemporary personality research.

Other Trait Approaches

behavioral genetics
The study of the relationship between genetic or hereditary factors and personality traits.

In our introductory remarks to Part IV (the trait approach), we noted that evidence is growing to support the idea that personality traits are influenced by hereditary factors. Research supporting a connection between genes and personality is overwhelming, and the area of study devoted to this issue, **behavioral genetics,** has gained increasing acceptance and credibility. No matter how personality is assessed—whether by self-reports, ratings, or behavioral observations—a significant genetic component has been established (see Buss, 1988; Heath, 1991; Plomin, 1990).

Gordon Allport and Raymond Cattell were among the early personality researchers to suggest that inherited factors shape personality and may be as important as environmental factors. In this section, we consider more contemporary researchers who are actively pursuing this causal connection between genetic inheritance and personality.

Hans Eysenck: Extraversion, Neuroticism, and Psychoticism

Hans Eysenck (1916–), long affiliated with the Maudsley Hospital and the Institute of Psychiatry at the University of London, has conducted extensive research on the measurement of personality. Eysenck agrees with Cattell that personality is composed of traits or factors that can be derived by factor analysis. Further, Eysenck believes, based on considerable research, that all personality traits can be subsumed under three types or dimensions. These personality dimensions are combinations of traits or factors, which we might think of as "superfactors" (Eysenck, 1981, 1990a, 1990b; Eysenck & Eysenck, 1985). The three personality dimensions Eysenck proposed are as follows:

1. Extraversion versus introversion (E)
2. Neuroticism versus emotional stability (N)
3. Psychoticism versus impulse control (P)

Table 9.2   **Traits of Eysenck's personality dimensions.**

Extraversion/ Introversion	Neuroticism/ Emotional Stability	Psychoticism/ Impulse Control
sociable	anxious	aggressive
lively	depressed	cold
active	guilt feelings	egocentric
assertive	low self-esteem	impersonal
sensation seeking	tense	impulsive
carefree	irrational	antisocial
dominant	shy	creative
venturesome	moody	tough-minded

The personality traits included under each of these superfactors are shown in Table 9.2. For example, people who score high on the traits of the *E* dimension would be classified as extraverts; people who score low would be classified as introverts.

The bulk of Eysenck's research focuses on the *E* and *N* dimensions; much of this research is devoted to the biological underpinnings of these dimensions. Eysenck has found that extraverts and introverts differ in their base levels of cortical arousal, with extraverts having a lower level of arousal than introverts. Because their cortical arousal levels are low, extraverts actively seek excitement and stimulation. By contrast, introverts shy away from excitement and stimulation because their cortical arousal levels are already high (Davis & Cowles, 1988; Geen, 1984).

Other researchers showed that introverts and extraverts differed in their response to sensory stimulation, but they found less convincing evidence that the difference could be attributed to variations in base levels of cortical arousal (Stelmack, 1990). Eysenck found that subjects high in neuroticism tended to have overreactive nervous systems, which leads to instability (Eysenck & Eysenck, 1985).

Eysenck argues that people of all personality dimensions can contribute to the betterment of society, but some will adapt better than others. For example, the person high in psychoticism, which is characterized by hostile and aggressive behaviors, either may become emotionally disturbed or may channel those traits into a socially acceptable enterprise, such as coaching college football. Eysenck believes that society needs the diversity provided by all types and that all of us should be afforded opportunities to make the best use of our abilities.

To Eysenck, traits and dimensions are determined primarily by heredity. Although he does not rule out environmental influences on personality, such as family interactions during childhood, he argues that such effects are limited. He wrote that his research results "disprove the importance of family environmental influence on personality" (Eysenck, 1990a, p. 251). This research has focused largely on comparisons of identical (monozygotic) and fraternal (dizygotic) twins. The studies show that identical twins are much more alike in their personalities than are fraternal twins, even when the identical twins were reared by different parents and subjected to different environments in childhood.

Studies of adopted children demonstrate that their personalities are more like those of their biological parents than their adoptive parents, even when the children had no contact with their biological parents. This research provides additional support for Eysenck's belief that personality traits and dimensions are shaped more by inheritance than by environment (Eysenck, 1967, 1976).

Eysenck's three personality dimensions have been found consistently in various nations and cultures and at different stages throughout the individual life span. Studies in 35 countries, including the United States, England, Australia, Japan, China, Nigeria, and Sweden, support the decisive role of genetic over environmental factors in determining personality types (Bouchard, 1985; Eaves, Eysenck, & Martin, 1989; Floderus-Myrhed, Pedersen, & Rasmuson, 1980; Martin & Jardine, 1986; Tellegen et al., 1988). The existence of the same three types in such diverse countries argues in favor of the primacy of inherited factors in the shaping of personality.

The traits and dimensions Eysenck proposed have been found to remain stable throughout life, from childhood through adulthood, despite the different environmental and social influences to which each of us is exposed. Our situations may change, but the types remain consistent; for instance, the introverted child tends to remain introverted as an adult (Eysenck & Eysenck, 1985).

Over the course of a long, productive career, Eysenck has published approximately 50 books and several hundred journal articles. He has developed several widely used personality assessment devices, including the Maudsley Medical Questionnaire, the Maudsley Personality Inventory, and the Eysenck Personality Inventory. His work has been pivotal in supporting the role of inheritance in the description and determination of personality.

Robert McCrae and Paul Costa: The Five-Factor Model

Using the method of factor analysis, Raymond Cattell and Hans Eysenck derived lists of personality traits that varied in number. This does not suggest any inherent weakness in the method; rather, it reflects the way each theorist chose to measure personality. Contemporary personality researchers have expressed dissatisfaction with both theories, suggesting that Eysenck's is too simple and has too few factors, and Cattell's is too complicated and difficult to replicate. Attempts to replicate Cattell's research have typically produced no more than five factors (Goldberg, 1990). From the 1940s to the 1960s, researchers conducting independent investigations of personality reached a similar conclusion—that personality consists of five broad traits (Digman, 1990; Fiske, 1949; Norman, 1963).

In the 1980s, at the Gerontology Research Center of the National Institutes of Health in Baltimore, Maryland, Robert McCrae (1949–) and Paul

Table 9.3   ***McCrae and Costa's five robust factors of personality.***

Neuroticism	worried, insecure, nervous, highly strung
Extraversion	sociable, talkative, fun-loving, affectionate
Openness	original, independent, creative, daring
Agreeableness	good-natured, softhearted, trusting, courteous
Conscientiousness	careful, reliable, hardworking, organized

Costa (1942–) embarked on a program that identified five "robust" factors of personality (McCrae & Costa, 1985, 1987):

1. neuroticism
2. extraversion
3. openness
4. agreeableness
5. conscientiousness

These factors were confirmed with various assessment techniques—self-ratings, objective tests, and observers' reports (Piedmont, McCrae, & Costa, 1991). The researchers developed a personality test, the NEO Personality Inventory, named for the initials of the first three factors. Their consistent demonstration of the same factors from diverse assessment procedures suggests that these factors are distinguishing aspects of personality. The factors are described in Table 9.3.

The resemblance is apparent between the Neuroticism and Extraversion factors McCrae and Costa proposed and the similarly named factors in Eysenck's theory. Also, Agreeableness and Conscientiousness in the McCrae-Costa model may represent the opposite pole of Eysenck's Psychoticism dimension. Openness to experience correlates highly with intelligence, and Agreeableness is related to Adler's concept of social interest, discussed in Chapter 4 (McCrae & Costa, 1991; Zuckerman, 1991).

McCrae and Costa believe that Neuroticism and Extraversion are more strongly influenced by heredity than environment. The other three factors are thought to be determined more by environment, although they also have a genetic component. These so-called "big five" factors have been consistently observed in Eastern and Western cultures, a finding that argues for a genetic component (Buss, 1991; Digman, 1989).

These five factors have been detected both in children and in adults. Longitudinal research, in which the same subjects were tested over six years, demonstrated a high level of stability in all five traits (Costa & McCrae, 1988). Persons high in Agreeableness as children were found likely to remain so as adults. Extraversion was found to be positively related to emotional well-being, and Neuroticism negatively related to emotional well-being. Thus, the researchers concluded that persons high in Extraversion and low in Neuroticism were genetically predisposed to emotional stability. In addition, persons high in Agreeableness and Conscientiousness showed greater emotional well-being than persons low in these traits (McCrae & Costa, 1991). Other researchers found that people high in Neuroticism were prone to depression, anxiety, and self-blame (Jorm, 1987; Parkes, 1986).

Not all contemporary personality researchers accept McCrae and Costa's five factors. Some argue that no group of five factors can adequately account for the complexity of the human personality. Others agree that there may be only five major personality traits, but they disagree on what those traits are. Nevertheless, McCrae and Costa have provided an intriguing and well-supported approach to describing the composition of personality and the relative importance of heredity and environment in determining its traits.

Arnold Buss and Robert Plomin: The Temperament Theory

We noted earlier in this chapter that Raymond Cattell classified some personality factors as temperament traits—traits that describe the general style and emotional level of our behavior. Beginning in the 1970s, Arnold Buss (1924–   ) of the University of Texas at Austin, and Robert Plomin (1948–   ) of Pennsylvania State University, identified three **temperaments**—Emotionality, Activity, and Sociability—which they believe are the basic building blocks of personality. They suggest that each person's personality is composed of different amounts of each temperament. The temperaments combine to form personality patterns or ''supertraits,'' such as introversion or extraversion (Buss & Plomin, 1984, 1986).

temperaments
Inherited dispositions toward certain behaviors.

Buss and Plomin developed two tests to assess personality: the Emotionality, Activity, Sociability Infant (EASI) Temperament Survey for use with infants (the questionnaire is filled out by the child's parent or primary caregiver) and the EAS Temperament Survey for Adults (Buss & Plomin, 1975, 1986). Based on their research with identical and fraternal twins, Buss and Plomin concluded that temperaments are primarily inherited and are part of the genetic constitution with which we are equipped at birth. These inherited temperaments are broad, and they account for the range of individual differences in human behavior that allows each of us to be unique. In addition, the temperaments persist throughout the life span, indicating a relatively minor influence from environmental and social forces (Plomin, Pedersen, McClearn, Nesselroade, & Bergeman, 1988).

The theorists do recognize some environmental effects. What we inherit is not a specific amount of a temperament, but rather a range of response potential. One person may inherit a range at the high end of a scale of possible responses, another at the low end, and a third person in the middle. What determines how much or how little of the potential for a given temperament we will realize? Our social environment is the key. Thus, Buss and Plomin consider the impact of external stimulus or situational variables as well as of internal genetic variables. However, they suggest limits to how much the environment can modify a temperament. If our environment forces us to deviate from an innate temperamental tendency for a long period and to behave contrary to our nature, we will experience conflict and stress.

The inherited nature of temperaments has been demonstrated by research comparing identical and fraternal twins.

The Emotionality temperament refers to our level of arousal or excitability. It consists of three components: distress, fearfulness, and anger. When we describe people as "emotional," we mean they are easily upset and given to outbursts. At one extreme of the Emotionality continuum are people who appear unemotional; nothing seems to disturb them. At the other extreme are people who are sensitive to the slightest provocation. Both extreme responses are maladaptive because they can prevent a person from reacting appropriately to a threat or danger. An optimal degree of Emotionality arouses a person to respond quickly and alertly in emergency situations.

In Buss and Plomin's view, Emotionality refers to negative or unpleasant emotions (distress, fearfulness, and anger), not to pleasant feelings such as happiness or love. This view agrees with our common usage of the word *emotional.* In general, we do not apply that label to people who are carefree or content but only to those who are easily upset or agitated. The Emotionality components of distress, fearfulness, and anger have been observed in several animal species. In humans, Emotionality is relatively stable in childhood and persists in adulthood.

Buss and Plomin define the Activity temperament in terms of physical energy and vigor. We all know people who are more energetic and active than others, and we see them display their energy in many situations. They walk and talk fast and find it hard to sit still; they fidget with their fingers or tap their toes. Research on twins revealed an inherited component to Activity. This component was found to be moderately stable through childhood, and it persists in adulthood.

The Sociability temperament refers to the degree of preference for contact and interaction with other people. People who are highly sociable seek out other people and group activities. On the other hand, people who are not sociable choose solitary activities and tend to avoid other people. Research suggests that Sociability is a persistent trait from infancy. Approximately 10 percent of all people are born with a high degree of Sociability and 10 percent with a low degree of Sociability (Kagan, 1984). It remains stable during childhood and persists in adulthood.

Sociability is an adaptive characteristic. We must interact with others to satisfy many of our needs and to secure positive reinforcement. Many work and leisure activities are better accomplished socially than individually. In addition, the empirical evidence supporting the three temperaments is strongest for Sociability.

Interest in Buss and Plomin's temperament theory has been increasing, judging by the rate of growth in the professional literature on temperaments. It is important to note that Buss and Plomin consider their theory to be in its formative stage, and they recognize that additional research is needed. Their purpose is to stimulate personality researchers and theorists to consider the impact of inherited dispositions as well as the influence of the environment.

Much research has been conducted on temperaments. Some of it stems directly from the Buss and Plomin theory, and some focuses more generally on inherited dispositions. Let us note the results of a few representative studies. Most of them use the twin-comparison approach.

Identical twins, ages 42 to 57, were found to be more alike than fraternal twins on empathy, the ability to experience vicariously the feelings of others (Matthews, Batson, Horn, & Rosenman, 1981). If empathy is inherited, then there may be a genetic basis for altruistic behavior. Additional support for this proposition was found in a study of twins in England (Rushton, Fulker, Neale, Blizard, & Eysenck, 1984).

The results of twin studies on sociability support Buss and Plomin's position that this temperament is inherited. Identical twins during their first 12 months were found to be much more alike than fraternal twins on behaviors such as frequency of smiling at other people or displaying a fear of strangers (Freedman, 1974). When twins were compared on these behaviors at 18 and 24 months of age, researchers found the same differences in sociability between identical and fraternal twins (Matheny, 1983). Comparisons of twins between ages 6 and 10 showed that identical twins were much more similar than fraternal twins both in their desire to affiliate with other people and on ratings of friendliness and shyness (Scarr, 1968).

A study involving two sets of parental ratings, taken ten years apart, of adopted and nonadopted children measured extraversion, socialization, and stability. The results revealed that, on the average, the children tended to change in the direction of the personalities of their biological parents (Loehlin, Horn, & Willerman, 1990).

In other work, 133 subjects were rated periodically from infancy to early adulthood in an attempt to establish a temperament called "difficult." Those believed to possess this temperament were described as hard to manage as infants. "Almost anything new . . . became the occasion for noisy outbursts of crying. Sleeping and feeding schedules were irregular, and [the children] had many expressions of intense negative mood" (Thomas, 1986, p. 50). A high correlation was found between the difficult temperament and the later development of behavior disorders (Thomas, Chess, & Korn, 1982).

Twin studies on general personality attributes suggest that at least 50 percent of an individual's total personality is inherited. The research supporting this conclusion was based on 850 pairs of twins in the United States (Loehlin & Nichols, 1976), 573 pairs of twins in England (Rushton et al., 1984), and data collected by researchers in Sweden on 13,000 pairs of twins (Floderus-Myrhed et al., 1980). It is important to remember that although these results support the influence of genetic factors on personality, the evidence for the heritability of Buss and Plomin's specific Emotionality, Activity, and Sociability temperaments is even stronger than for these general personality attributes.

These studies also indicate the role of the environment in shaping personality. This point is recognized by Buss and Plomin, who do not dispute environmental or situational influences. In one study, the researchers reported a significant relationship between shyness in adopted children and the sociability of their adoptive mothers (Daniels & Plomin, 1985). Because the adopted children and adoptive mothers shared no genetic background, the researchers concluded that the subjects' similarity on the Sociability temperament was attributable to environmental influences.

Environmental factors affect the personalities of children living in the same house in different ways. Certain events and experiences are different for each child. For example, parents treat sons differently from daughters and first-borns differently from later-borns. Another source of environmental influence that differs from child to child is that provided by brothers and sisters. A dominant and assertive first-born may influence younger siblings in such a way that they develop passive, noncompetitive personalities (Rowe & Plomin, 1981).

Whatever the relative influence of heredity and environment on personality, strong evidence exists that temperaments remain stable from birth into adulthood and that the strength of that stability increases dramatically after the age of 3. Plomin also presents evidence to suggest that genetic factors influence our perception of stressful life events, such as retirement or the death of a child or spouse (Plomin, Lichtenstein, Pedersen, McClearn, & Nesselroade, 1990). Thus, our inherited temperaments may exert pervasive and long-lasting influences on our behavior throughout our lifetime.

The theories presented here, together with their supporting research, indicate that "a prime source of personality traits is inheritance," which may account for as much as 50 percent of personality (Buss, 1988, p. 20). The evidence is greatest for the factors of extraversion, neuroticism, and psychoticism, but virtually every other trait investigated by personality researchers has displayed some biological component (Plomin, DeFries, & McClearn, 1990). The research shows that a shared family environment has only a relatively minor influence, thus suggesting that "only a third of the similarities between parents and their biological children can be attributed to environmental influences; the rest comes from parental genes" (Zuckerman, 1991, p. 128).

These findings have both practical and theoretical implications for personality psychologists, who have focused over the years on the dominance of environmental influences—particularly those of our early childhood. If the research in behavioral genetics continues to indicate that our family and social situations play a minimal role in personality development, "a drastic reshaping of personality theories in the future" will be required (Eysenck, 1990a, p. 259).

However, a word of caution is necessary: we must not conclude prematurely that family and other environmental and social factors should be discounted as shapers of personality. Robert Plomin noted:

> It is good for the field of personality that it has moved away from simpleminded environmentalism. The danger now, however, is that the rush from environmentalism will carom too far—to a view that personality is almost completely biologically determined. [Plomin, Chipuer, & Loehlin, 1990, pp. 225–226]

Personality is a product of both biological and environmental forces. What is still being investigated is the relative importance of each.

Summary

Raymond Cattell studied normal subjects by using scientific methods to amass data that he evaluated by the statistical procedures of factor analysis. The resulting factors, or traits, are the basic structural units of personality. They are hypothetical constructs inferred from the objective observation of behavior. A trait is a reaction tendency that is a relatively permanent part of personality. Common traits are possessed by everyone to some degree; unique traits are possessed only by one or a few persons. Ability traits determine how efficiently a person will be able to work toward a goal. Temperament traits define one's emotional style of behavior. Dynamic traits are concerned with the motivations or driving forces of behavior.

Surface traits are personality characteristics that correlate with one another but do not constitute a factor because they are not determined by a single source. The 16 source traits Cattell identified are single factors, and each is the sole source of some aspect of behavior. Source traits may be constitutional traits, which originate in internal bodily conditions, or environmental-mold traits, which are derived from environmental influences.

Dynamic traits include ergs (the energy source for all behavior) and sentiments (learned patterns of attitudes). Ergs and sentiments are manifested in attitudes, which are a person's interests in some area, object, or other person. The interrelationship of ergs, sentiments, and attitudes can be expressed schematically in the dynamic lattice. The self-sentiment is a person's self-concept. It provides stability and organization to the source traits.

Cattell's research suggests that in general, one-third of personality is genetically determined; the rest is determined by environmental influences.

Infancy (from birth to age 6) is the major formative period of personality. Childhood (ages 6 to 14) is a time of consolidation in which there are few psychological problems. Adolescence (14 to 23) is the most stressful stage of development. Maturity (23 to 50) is a productive time in which the personality becomes more set. Late maturity involves personality adjustments to physical, social, and psychological changes. Old age involves adjustment to losses, loneliness, and insecurity.

Cattell holds a deterministic view of personality and did not suggest any ultimate life goals. Childhood influences are important in personality development, as are heredity and environment.

Cattell's three major assessment techniques are L-data (ratings made by observers), Q-data (self-ratings made through questionnaires, personality inventories, and attitude scales), and T-data (data from tests that are resistant to faking). Cattell developed several tests, including the 16 PF and the Clinical Analysis Questionnaire. He uses two forms of factor analysis: the *R* technique, in which large amounts of data are gathered from large groups of subjects, and the *P* technique, in which large amounts of data are gathered from a single subject over a long period of time.

Cattell's work is highly technical, and the amount of supporting data is massive. Factor analysis has been criticized for its potential subjectivity.

Research in behavioral genetics has revealed a significant influence of genetic factors on personality. Hans Eysenck demonstrated a genetic influence on three personality dimensions: extraversion, neuroticism, and psychoticism. McCrae and Costa propose five biologically based factors: neuroticism, extraversion, openness, agreeableness, and conscientiousness. Buss and Plomin document the innate potential for three temperaments: emotionality, activity, and sociability.

Critical Thinking Review

1. How does Cattell's concept of personality traits differ from Allport's view of traits?

2. How does Cattell use factor analysis to identify traits?

3. Describe three ways of categorizing traits.

4. Distinguish between ergs, sentiments, and attitudes. By what process are they related?

5. According to Cattell's research, which source traits are determined primarily by heredity?

6. What is the self-sentiment? What is its role in personality?

7. Describe the six stages of personality development in Cattell's theory. In which stage does the personality tend to become less flexible?

8. Identify the three types of data collected by Cattell, and give an example of each.

9. What is Cattell's position on the issue of free will versus determinism?

10. Describe the three personality types proposed by Hans Eysenck. Does Eysenck believe that personality traits are determined largely by genetic factors or by environmental factors?

11. Discuss Eysenck's research on identical and fraternal twins and on adopted children. How do the research results support his conclusion about the role of genetic factors in personality?

12. Describe McCrae and Costa's five factors of personality. What is the role of heredity and of environment in each of these factors?

13. Describe the three temperaments proposed by Buss and Plomin.

Suggested Reading

Buss, A. H. (1989). Personality as traits. *American Psychologist, 44,* 1378–1388. Discusses the trait approach to personality and notes that the goal of trait research is to understand people as combinations of traits. Describes a continuum of traits, from narrow to broad, and the variance in traits over time and situations.

Cattell, R. B. (1974). Autobiography. In G. Lindzey (Ed.), *A history of psychology in autobiography* (vol. 6, pp. 59–100). Englewood Cliffs, NJ: Prentice-Hall; Travels in psychological hyperspace. In T. S. Krawiec (Ed.), *The psychologists* (vol. 2, pp. 85–133). New York: Oxford University Press. Two essays by Cattell about his life and work.

Digman, J. M. (1990). Personality structure: Emergence of the five-factor model. *Annual Review of Psychology, 41,* 417–440. Describes the development of and research on the five-factor model. Relates the model to other work in the field, such as the personality theories of Cattell, Murray, and Eysenck.

Eysenck, H. J. (1976). H. J. Eysenck. In R. I. Evans (Ed.), *The making of psychology: Discussions with creative contributors* (pp. 255–265). New York: Knopf. Interviews with Eysenck about his work, especially his criticisms of psychoanalysis and his controversial views on the genetic basis of intelligence.

Eysenck, H. J. (1990). Genetic and environmental contributions to individual differences: The three major dimensions of personality. *Journal of Personality, 58*(1), 245–261. Describes the relative impact of heredity and environment on Eysenck's proposed dimensions of personality—extraversion, neuroticism, and psychoticism—and emphasizes the importance to psychology of the study of behavioral genetics.

Plomin, R. (1990). *Nature and nurture: An introduction to human behavioral genetics.* Pacific Grove, CA: Brooks/Cole. Reviews the research methods and empirical findings in the field of behavioral genetics. Discusses in a clear, readable style such issues as how heredity affects behavior and how these genetic influences can be detected.

Plomin, R., & Rende, R. (1991). Human behavioral genetics. *Annual Review of Psychology, 42,* 161–190. Surveys the field of behavioral genetics as it applies to personality, cognitive abilities, and psychopathology.

The Life-Span Approach

Most personality theorists devote some attention to the way in which personality develops over time. Some describe specific stages in the development of selected aspects of personality; others posit more general patterns of growth. Theorists also differ regarding the time period over which they believe personality continues to develop. Sigmund Freud proposed that personality evolves through a sequence of steps until the age of 5; Henry Murray took a similar position. Gordon Allport held a longer view, suggesting that personality growth continues to the time of adolescence. Carl Jung argued that middle age was the most important time of change in the personality, and Raymond Cattell suggested that personality evolves throughout the life span.

The life-span approach to personality, represented here by the work of Erik Erikson, focuses on the development of the personality over the entire course of life. Erikson's theory attempts to explain human behavior and growth, through eight stages, from birth to death. All aspects of personality can be explained in terms of turning points or crises that one must meet and resolve at each developmental stage.

Erik Erikson

The Life of Erikson (1902–)
Psychosocial Stages of Development: Coping
  with Conflicts
  Trust Versus Mistrust
  Autonomy Versus Doubt and Shame
  Initiative Versus Guilt
  Industriousness Versus Inferiority
  Identity Cohesion Versus Role Confusion:
    The Identity Crisis
  Intimacy Versus Isolation
  Generativity Versus Stagnation
  Ego Integrity Versus Despair

Basic Strengths
Basic Weaknesses
Erikson's Image of Human Nature
Assessment in Erikson's Theory
Research in Erikson's Theory
A Final Commentary
Summary
Critical Thinking Review
Suggested Reading

*The personality is engaged with the hazards of
existence continuously, even as the body's
metabolism copes with decay.*

—Erik Erikson

Erik Erikson is considered to be among the most influential of psychoanalysts. His books have sold hundreds of thousands of copies, and his picture has appeared on the covers of *Newsweek* and the *New York Times Magazine*—an unusual sign of recognition for a personality theorist. His book on the origins of militant nonviolence (*Gandhi's Truth*) was awarded a Pulitzer Prize. Interestingly, Erikson has achieved this prominence and influence without earning a university degree.

Trained in the Freudian tradition by Sigmund Freud's daughter Anna, Erikson developed an approach to personality that broadens the scope of Freud's work while maintaining much of its core. Although Erikson offered significant innovations, his ties to the Freudian position are strong. "Psychoanalysis is always the starting point," he once said (quoted in Keniston, 1983, p. 29).

Erikson extended Freud's theory in three ways. First, he elaborated on Freud's stages of development. Where Freud emphasized childhood and proposed that the personality is shaped by the age of 5 or so, Erikson suggested that personality continues to develop in a series of eight stages throughout the life span.

The second change Erikson made in Freud's theory was to emphasize the ego more than the id. In Erikson's view, the ego is an independent part of the personality; it is not dependent on or subservient to the id.

Third, Erikson recognized the impact of culture, society, and history on the personality. He argued that we are not ruled entirely by biological forces at work in our childhood. Although innate factors are important, they do not provide the complete explanation for the development of personality.

Because of his elaborations of basic Freudian themes, Erikson could also have been included with the neopsychoanalytic theorists in this book. Bearing in mind, then, that his is a neopsychoanalytic approach, we have chosen instead to emphasize the life-span aspect of his personality theory, in which the search for an ego identity is central.

The Life of Erikson (1902–)

It is not surprising that the theorist who gave us the concept of the identity crisis experienced several intense crises in his own early years. Erikson was born in Frankfurt, Germany, to Danish parents. His father abandoned the family before the child was born, and Erik moved with his mother to Karls-ruhe, Germany. Three years later she married Dr. Theodore Homburger, Erik's pediatrician. The boy was not told for some years that Dr. Homburger was not his biological father, and he grew up unsure of his psychological identity and his true name. He retained the surname Homburger until the age of 37, when he became a United States citizen and adopted the name Erik Homburger Erikson.

Another crisis of identity occurred when Erikson started school. Despite his Danish parentage, he considered himself German, but his German classmates rejected him because he was Jewish. At the same time, his Jewish peers rejected him because he was tall and blond and had Nordic features; he later converted to Christianity. In school Erikson achieved mediocre grades. He evidenced some talent for art, however, and when he graduated from high school he used that ability to try to establish his identity.

Erikson dropped out of conventional society and traveled through Germany and Italy, reading, recording his thoughts in a notebook, and observing life around him. He described himself as morbidly sensitive, hovering on the brink between neurosis and psychosis. He studied briefly at two art schools and had an exhibition of his work in Munich, but each time he left formal training to resume his wandering, searching for his identity. Later, when discussing his concept of the identity crisis, Erikson wrote, "No doubt, my best friends will insist that I needed to name this crisis and to see it in everybody else in order to really come to terms with it in myself" (Erikson, 1975, pp. 25–26).

In 1927, at the age of 25, Erikson received an offer to teach at a small school established in Vienna for the children of Sigmund Freud's patients and friends. (Freud was attracting patients from all over the world. Being wealthy, these patients settled in Vienna with their families for the duration of their psychoanalysis.) Erikson was drawn to Freud, he confessed, in part because of his search for a father—the father he felt he had never known. It was then that Erikson's professional career began. He received training in psychoanalysis and was analyzed by Anna Freud. Her interest was the psychoanalysis of children, and this became Erikson's specialty. When he completed his training, he became a member of the Vienna Psychoanalytic Institute.

Recognizing the growing Nazi menace, in 1933 Erikson and his Canadian-born wife emigrated to Denmark and then to the United States. He settled in Boston and established a private psychoanalytic practice, specializing in the treatment of children. The Boston years were productive. Erikson joined the staff of Henry Murray's Harvard clinic and worked in a guidance center for emotionally disturbed delinquents and at the Massachusetts General Hospital.

Erikson began graduate work at Harvard to obtain a Ph.D. in psychology but failed his first course, explaining that he found a formal academic program unsatisfying. In 1936 he was invited to the Institute of Human Relations at Yale University, where he continued his work with children and taught at the medical school. He collaborated with a Yale anthropologist on a study of child-rearing practices among the Sioux Indians of South Dakota. This work marked the beginning of his recognition of the influence of culture on childhood.

Erikson moved to San Francisco in 1939 to investigate child development at the Institute of Human Development of the University of California at Berkeley. Unlike most psychoanalysts, Erikson was concerned that his clinical experience be as broad as possible, including normal as well as emotionally disturbed children, and children of many cultures.

In his contact with Native American tribes in South Dakota and California, Erikson noticed certain psychological symptoms that could not be explained by orthodox Freudian theory. The symptoms appeared to be related to a sense of alienation from cultural traditions and resulted in the lack of a clear self-image or self-identity. This phenomenon, which Erikson initially called "identity confusion," was similar to what he had observed among emotionally disturbed veterans after World War II. Erikson believed that those men were not suffering from repressed conflicts but rather from confusion as a result of their traumatic war experiences and of being temporarily uprooted from their culture. He described this phenomenon as a confusion of identity on the part of the veterans about who and what they were.

Erikson left Berkeley in 1950 because he refused to sign the state loyalty oath, and he moved to Stockbridge, Massachusetts, to join the Austen Riggs Center, a treatment facility for emotionally disturbed adolescents. Ten years later he returned to Harvard to teach a graduate seminar and a popular undergraduate course on the human life cycle. Erikson retired from Harvard in 1970. In 1986, at the age of 84, he published a book about old age.

Psychosocial Stages of Development: Coping with Conflicts

Erikson divided the growth of the personality into eight **psychosocial stages**. The first four are similar to Freud's oral, anal, phallic, and latency stages, although Erikson emphasized psychosocial correlates, whereas Freud focused on biological ones.

psychosocial stages of development Eight successive stages encompassing the life span. At each stage, we must cope with a crisis in either an adaptive or a maladaptive way.

epigenetic principle of maturation The idea that human development is governed by a sequence of stages that depend on genetic or hereditary factors.

crisis The turning point faced at each developmental stage.

To Erikson, the developmental process is governed by the **epigenetic principle of maturation**. By this he means that the stages of development are determined by inherited factors. The prefix *epi* means "upon"; development depends upon genetic factors. The social and environmental forces to which we are exposed influence the ways in which the genetically determined stages of development are realized. In summary, then, personality development is affected by both biological and social factors—by both personal and situational variables.

Erikson suggested that human development involves a series of conflicts with which each person must cope. The potential for these conflicts exists at birth as innate predispositions that become prominent at specific developmental stages, when our environment makes certain demands on us. Each encounter or confrontation with our environment is called a **crisis**. The crisis involves a shift in perspective, thus requiring us to refocus instinctual energy in accordance with the new demands of each stage of life.

Each developmental stage has its crisis or turning point that necessitates some change in our behavior and personality. We are faced with a choice between two ways of responding to the crisis: a maladaptive or negative way, and an adaptive or positive way. Only when we have resolved each conflict can the personality continue its normal development and acquire the strength to confront the crisis associated with the next stage. When the conflict at any stage is not resolved, we are less likely to be able to adapt to later stages. However, although it will be more difficult to achieve, a successful outcome is still possible.

Erikson believes that the ego must incorporate both maladaptive and adaptive ways of coping. For example, in the first stage of psychosocial development, we can respond to the crisis by developing either a sense of trust or a sense of mistrust. Trust, the more adaptive and desirable way of coping, is obviously the healthier psychological attitude. Yet each of us must develop some degree of mistrust as a form of protection. If we are totally trusting and gullible, we will be vulnerable to others' attempts to deceive, mislead, or manipulate us. Ideally, at every stage of development the ego identity will consist primarily of the positive or adaptive attitude but will be balanced by a share of the negative attitude. Only then can the crisis be satisfactorily resolved.

The eight stages of psychosocial development, the approximate ages at which they occur, and the adaptive and maladaptive ways of coping are listed in Table 10.1.

Trust Versus Mistrust

The oral-sensory stage of psychosocial development, paralleling Freud's oral stage of psychosexual development, occurs during our first year of life, the time of our greatest helplessness. The infant is totally dependent on someone else—usually the mother—for survival, security, and affection. During this

Table 10.1   **Erikson's stages of psychosocial development.**

Stage	Approximate Ages	Adaptive vs. Maladaptive Ways of Coping	Basic Strength
Oral-sensory	Birth–1 year	Trust vs. mistrust	Hope
Muscular-anal	1–3 years	Autonomy vs. doubt, shame	Will
Locomotor-genital	3–5 years	Initiative vs. guilt	Purpose
Latency	6–11 years, to puberty	Industriousness vs. inferiority	Competence
Adolescence	12–18 years	Identity cohesion vs. role confusion	Fidelity
Young adulthood	18–35 years	Intimacy vs. isolation	Love
Adulthood	35–55 years	Generativity vs. stagnation	Care
Maturity and old age	55+ years	Ego integrity vs. despair	Wisdom

stage the mouth is of vital importance. The infant "lives through, and loves with, [the] mouth," Erikson wrote (1959, p. 57).

However, the relationship between the infant and its world is not exclusively biological. It is very much a social relationship. The interaction between infant and mother determines whether the infant will come to view the world with an attitude of trust or mistrust.

If the mother is responsive to the baby's physical needs and provides ample affection, love, and security, then the infant will begin to develop a sense of trust, an attitude that will come to characterize the child's view of himself or herself and of others. We learn to expect "consistency, continuity, and sameness" from the people and situations in our environment, and this expectation provides the beginning of our ego identity (Erikson, 1950, p. 247).

On the other hand, if the mother is rejecting, inattentive, or inconsistent in her behavior, the infant will develop an attitude of mistrust and will become suspicious, fearful, and anxious. According to Erikson, mistrust can also occur if a mother does not display an exclusive focus on the infant. For example, Erikson believed that a mother who resumes a job outside the home after her baby is born, leaving the infant in the care of relatives or in a day care center, risks engendering mistrust in the child.

Although the pattern of trust or mistrust as a dimension of personality is set in infancy, the problem may reappear at a later stage of life. For example, an ideal infant-mother relationship produces a high level of trust, but this sense of trust can be destroyed if the mother suddenly dies. In that event, mistrust may overtake the earlier attitude of trust. Childhood mistrust can be altered later in life through the companionship of a loving and patient teacher or friend.

Autonomy Versus Doubt and Shame

During the second and third years of life, Erikson's muscular-anal stage (corresponding to Freud's anal stage), children rapidly develop a variety of physical and mental abilities and are able to do many things for themselves. They begin to communicate more effectively and to walk, climb, push, pull, and hold on to an object or let it go. Children take pride in these newly develop-ing skills and want to do as much as possible for themselves.

Of all these abilities, Erikson believed the most important involved hold-ing on and letting go. He considers these behaviors to be prototypes for later conflicts in behaviors and attitudes. For example, holding on can be dis-played in either a loving or a hostile way. Letting go can become a venting of destructive rage or a relaxed passivity.

The important point is that during this stage, for the first time, children are able to exercise some degree of choice, to experience the power of their autonomous will. Although still dependent on parents, they begin to see themselves as persons or forces in their own right, and they want to exer-cise that will. At this stage the key question becomes: To what extent will society, in the form of parents, allow them to express what they are capable of doing?

The major clash of wills between parent and child at this stage typically involves toilet training, the first instance of society attempting to regulate an instinctual need. The child is taught to hold on and let go only at appropriate times and places. The parents may permit the child to proceed with toilet training at his or her own pace, or they may become annoyed and usurp the child's free will by forcing the training and showing impatience and anger when the child does not behave correctly.

When parents thwart and frustrate their child's attempt to exercise the autonomous will, the child develops a feeling of self-doubt and a sense of shame in dealing with others. The anal region is a focus of this stage because of the toilet training conflict, but the form of the crisis is not so much biologi-cal as psychosocial.

Initiative Versus Guilt

The third stage of psychosocial development, the locomotor-genital stage, occurs between ages 3 and 5 and is analogous to the phallic stage in Freud's system. Motor and mental abilities are developing, and children are able to accomplish more for themselves. They desire to take the initiative in many activities. Initiative in fantasy form also grows and is manifested in the child's desire to possess the parent of the opposite sex and in a feeling of rivalry with the parent of the same sex.

The key question is the same as at the earlier stages: How will the parents react to these self-initiated activities and fantasies? If they punish the child and otherwise inhibit these behaviors, the child will develop persistent guilt feelings that will affect all self-directed activities throughout life.

In the Oedipal relationship, the child inevitably fails, but if the parents guide this situation with love and understanding, the child will acquire a sense of what is permissible behavior and what is not. The child's initiative can then be channeled toward realistic and socially sanctioned goals, in preparation for the development of an adult sense of responsibility and morality—in Freudian terms, a superego.

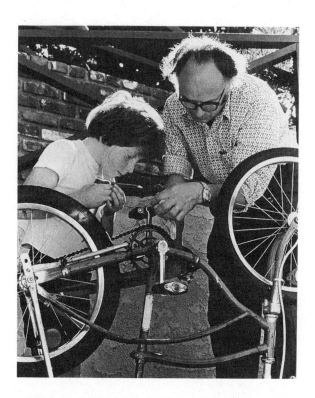

Children take pride in developing new skills and abilities.

Industriousness Versus Inferiority

Erikson's latency stage of psychosocial development, which takes place at approximately ages 6 to 11, corresponds to Freud's latency period. The child begins school and is exposed to new social influences. Both at home and at school, the child learns industriousness—that is, good work and study habits—primarily as a means of attaining praise and obtaining the pleasure derived from the successful completion of a task.

The child's growing powers of deductive reasoning and ability to play by rules lead to the deliberate refinement of skills that are often displayed in building things. Here Erikson's ideas reflect the sex stereotypes of the period in which he first presented his theory. In his view, boys at this stage build tree houses and model airplanes, whereas girls cook and sew. These are serious attempts to complete a task through the application of concentrated attention, diligence, and persistence. "The basic skills of technology are developed, as the child becomes ready to handle the utensils, the tools, and the weapons used by the big people" (Erikson, 1959, p. 83).

How well children perceive themselves to be developing their skills is determined largely by the attitudes and behaviors of their parents and teachers. If childhood efforts are scolded, ridiculed, or rejected, children are likely to develop feelings of inferiority and inadequacy. On the other hand, praise and reinforcement foster children's feelings of competence and encourage them to strive and develop.

The outcome of the crisis at each of these four childhood stages depends more on other people than on ourselves. The resolution is a function more of what is done to the child than of what the child can do. Although we experience increasing independence from birth to age 11, our psychosocial development remains greatly dependent on the behaviors and attitudes of our parents and teachers. These are significant people in our life during this period, and we have little choice or control over them.

In the last four stages of psychosocial development, we are increasingly able to control our environment. We can consciously choose our friends, our college, our career, and our spouse. However, these deliberate choices are influenced by the personality characteristics that have developed during the four psychosocial stages from birth to adolescence. Whether our ego at that point shows primarily trust, autonomy, initiative, and industriousness, or mistrust, doubt, guilt, and inferiority, will obviously affect the course of our life, no matter how independent we may later become.

Identity Cohesion Versus Role Confusion: The Identity Crisis

ego identity The self-image formed during adolescence that integrates our ideas of what we are and what we want to be.

Adolescence, between ages 12 and 18, is the stage at which we must meet and resolve the crisis of our basic **ego identity**. At this time we form our self-image, the integration of our ideas about ourselves and about what others think of us. Ideally, this process results in a consistent and congruent picture.

Shaping and accepting our identity are difficult, anxiety-filled tasks. As adolescents we must experiment with different roles and ideologies to determine the best fit. Erikson suggested that adolescence was a hiatus between childhood and adulthood, a necessary psychological moratorium that allows time and energy for role and image experimentation.

identity crisis The failure to achieve ego identity during adolescence.

Persons who emerge from this stage with a strong sense of self-identity are equipped to face adulthood with certainty and confidence. Those who fail to achieve a cohesive identity—who experience an **identity crisis**—show what Erikson called role confusion. They do not know who or what they are, where they belong, or where they want to go. They may withdraw from the normal life sequence—education, job, marriage—as Erikson did for a time, or seek a negative identity in crime or drugs. Even a negative identity (as society defines it) is preferable to no identity, although it is not as satisfactory as a positive identity.

Erikson noted the impact of peer groups on the development of ego identity in adolescence. According to Erikson, association with fanatical groups and cults or obsessive identification with icons of popular culture can restrict the developing ego.

Intimacy Versus Isolation

Young adulthood is a longer stage than the earlier ones. It extends from the end of adolescence to about age 35. During this period, we establish our

Adolescents who experience an identity crisis do not seem to know where they belong or what they want to become.

independence from parents and quasi-parental institutions, such as college, and begin to function as mature, responsible adults.

We undertake some form of productive work and establish intimate relationships with others—close friendships and sexual unions. Erikson did not restrict intimacy to sexual relationships. It also means a sense of caring and commitment, openly displayed, without resorting to self-protective devices and without fear of losing our sense of self-identity. In an intimate relationship we can merge or fuse our identity with someone else's without submerging or losing it in the process.

People who are unable to establish such intimacy in young adulthood feel isolated. They avoid social contacts and reject other people, perhaps becoming aggressive against them. They prefer to be alone because they fear intimacy and see it as a threat to their ego identity.

Generativity Versus Stagnation

Adulthood—approximately the years from 35 to 55—is a stage of maturity in which we need to be actively and directly involved in teaching and guiding the next generation. This need extends beyond our immediate family. The concern is broader and more long-range, involving future generations and the kind of society in which they will live. One need not be a parent to display generativity, nor does having children automatically satisfy this urge.

Erikson suggested that all institutions, whether business, government, or academic, provide for the expression of generativity. They seek to establish a fund of knowledge and the means to guide each new generation. Thus, in whatever organizations we are involved, we can usually find a way to become a mentor or teacher to younger people or to become involved in the betterment of society.

When middle-aged people cannot find (or choose not to find) such an outlet for generativity, they may become overwhelmed by "stagnation, boredom, and interpersonal impoverishment" (Erikson, 1968, p. 138). Erikson's depiction of these emotional difficulties in middle age is similar to Jung's description of the midlife crisis (see Chapter 3). These people regress to a stage of pseudo-intimacy, indulging themselves in childlike ways. They may become physical or psychological invalids because of their absorption with their own needs and comforts.

Ego Integrity Versus Despair

During the final stage of psychosocial development, maturity and old age, we are confronted with a choice between ego integrity or despair, attitudes that govern the way we evaluate the whole of our life. At this time our major endeavors are at or nearing completion. This is a time of reflection, of examining our life and taking its final measure. If we look back with a sense of fulfillment and satisfaction, having coped with life's victories and failures, then we are said to possess ego integrity. Simply stated, ego integrity involves accepting one's place and one's past.

If we review our life with a sense of frustration, angry about missed opportunities and regretful of mistakes that cannot be rectified, then we will feel despair. We will become disgusted with ourselves, contemptuous of others, and bitter over what might have been.

At the age of 84, Erikson published a book reporting the results of a long-term study of 29 people in their eighties on whom life-history data had been collected since 1928. The title, *Vital Involvement in Old Age,* indicates Erikson's prescription for achieving ego integrity (Erikson, Erikson, & Kivnick, 1986). Older people must do more than reflect on the past. They must remain vital and active participants in life, seeking challenge and stimulation from their environment, involving themselves in such activities as grandparenting, returning to school, and developing new skills and interests.

Basic Strengths

basic strengths
Motivating characteristics and beliefs that derive from the satisfactory resolution of the crisis at each developmental stage.

Erikson noted that each of the eight stages of psychosocial development offers a crisis to be resolved and an opportunity to develop what he called **basic strengths**. These strengths, or virtues, emerge once the crisis at each stage has been coped with satisfactorily. These basic strengths are interdependent; one cannot develop until the strength at the previous stage has been confirmed. The basic strengths Erikson proposed are hope, will, purpose, competence, fidelity, love, care, and wisdom (see Table 10.1, p. 254).

Hope grows out of the basic sense of trust that, ideally, emerges during the oral-sensory stage of development. Hope is the belief that our desires can be satisfied. It involves a persistent sense of confidence that we maintain despite temporary setbacks or reverses. Will develops from autonomy—the adaptive way of coping at the muscular-anal stage—and is a determination to exercise freedom of choice as well as self-restraint in the face of society's demands.

Purpose, arising from initiative at the locomotor-genital stage, involves the courage to envision and pursue our goals. Competence, arising from industriousness at the latency stage, involves the exertion of skill and intelligence in the pursuit and completion of tasks.

Fidelity, which grows out of the cohesive ego identity formed during adolescence, encompasses a sense of duty, sincerity, and genuineness in our relations with others. Love, arising from the intimacy of the young adulthood years, is considered by Erikson to be the greatest human virtue. He defines it as a mutual devotion in a shared identity—the finding and fusing of oneself with another.

Care, emerging from generativity at adulthood, is a broad concern for others and is manifested in the need to teach, not only for the sake of others but also to fulfill one's own identity. Wisdom, deriving from ego integrity in maturity, is expressed in a detached concern with the whole of life. It is conveyed to succeeding generations in an integration of experience best described by the word *heritage.*

Basic Weaknesses

basic weaknesses
Motivating characteristics that derive from the unsatisfactory resolution of crises.

As basic strengths develop at each stage of psychosocial development, so may **basic weaknesses** (Erikson, Erikson, & Kivnick, 1986). We noted that the adaptive and maladaptive ways of coping with the crisis at each stage of psychosocial development are incorporated in the ego identity in a kind of creative balance. Although the ego should consist primarily of the adaptive attitude, it will also contain a share of the negative attitude.

maldevelopment
occurs when the ego consists solely of a single way of coping with conflict.

In an unbalanced development the ego consists solely of one attitude, either the adaptive or the maladaptive one. Erikson called this condition **maldevelopment**, a concept he has so far developed only in general terms. When only the positive, or adaptive, tendency is present in the ego, the condition is called maladaption. When only the negative tendency is present, the condition is called malignancy. Maladaptions can lead to neuroses; malignancies can lead to psychoses.

Both conditions can be corrected through psychotherapy. Maladaptions (the less severe disturbances) can also be relieved through a process of readaption, induced by environmental changes, social relationships, or successful adaption at a later stage of development.

Table 10.2 lists for each psychosocial stage of development the alternative ways of coping and the respective maldevelopmental tendencies.

Table 10.2	*Erikson's maldevelopmental tendencies.*		
Stage	*Way of Coping*		*Maldevelopment*
Oral-sensory	Trust		Sensory maladjustment
	Mistrust		Withdrawal
Muscular-anal	Autonomy		Shameless willfulness
	Doubt, shame		Compulsion
Locomotor-genital	Initiative		Ruthlessness
	Guilt		Inhibition
Latency	Industriousness		Narrow virtuosity
	Inferiority		Inertia
Adolescence	Identity cohesion		Fanaticism
	Role confusion		Repudiation
Young adulthood	Intimacy		Promiscuity
	Isolation		Exclusivity
Adulthood	Generativity		Overextension
	Stagnation		Rejectivity
Maturity and old age	Ego integrity		Presumption
	Despair		Disdain

SOURCE: Adapted from *Vital Involvement in Old Age*, by Erik H. Erikson, Joan M. Erikson, and Helen Q. Kivnick by permission of W. W. Norton & Company, Inc. Copyright © 1986 by Joan M. Erikson, Erik H. Erikson, and Helen Kivnick.

Erikson's Image of Human Nature

A personality theorist who delineates basic strengths and writes of our "lofty moralism" must be described as presenting an optimistic view of human nature. Although not everyone is successful in attaining hope, purpose, wisdom, and the other basic strengths, we all have the potential to reach this goal. Nothing in our nature prevents us from doing so. Nor must we inevitably suffer conflict, anxiety, and neurosis because of instinctual biological forces.

Erikson's theory allows for optimism because each stage of psychosocial growth, although stressful enough to be labeled a crisis, offers the possibility of a positive outcome. We are capable of resolving each crisis in a way that is adaptive and strengthening. Even if we fail at one stage and develop a maladaptive response or a basic weakness, there is still hope for change at a later stage.

We have the potential to consciously direct our growth throughout our lives. We are not exclusively products of childhood experiences. Although we have little control during the first four developmental stages, from birth to puberty, we gain increasing independence and a growing ability to choose our ways of responding to crises and to society's demands. Childhood influences are important, but events at later stages can counteract unfortunate early experiences.

Erikson's theory is only partially deterministic. During the first four stages, the experiences to which we are exposed—through parents, teachers, peer groups, and various opportunities—are largely beyond our control. Free will can be exercised more during the last four stages, although our choices will be affected by the attitudes and strengths we form during the earlier stages.

In general, Erikson believes that personality is influenced more by learning and experience than by heredity. Psychosocial experiences, not instinctual biological forces, are the greater determinant of personality development. Our

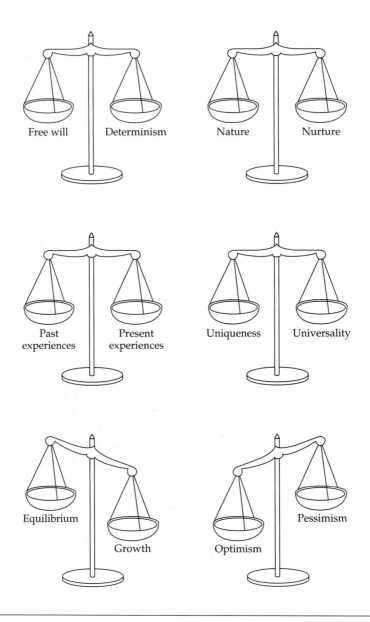

Erikson

Image of Human Nature.

ultimate, overriding goal is to develop a positive ego identity that incorporates all the basic strengths.

Assessment in Erikson's Theory

Erikson followed Freud's lead in certain theoretical formulations, but he deviated from Freud in his methods for assessing personality. Erikson questioned the usefulness and even the safety of some Freudian techniques, beginning with the psychoanalytic couch. He suggested that asking the patient to lie on a couch can lead to sadistic and faddish exploitation. It gives an illusion of objectivity, and it fosters an overemphasis on unconscious material and excessive impersonality and aloofness on the part of the therapist. To promote a more personal relationship between therapist and patient and to ensure that they view each other as equals, Erikson preferred that patients and therapists face each other and that both be seated in comfortable chairs.

Erikson relied less on formal assessment techniques than did Freud. Erikson occasionally used free association but rarely attempted to analyze dreams, a technique he called wasteful and harmful. He believed that assessment techniques should be selected and modified to fit the unique requirements of the individual patient.

In developing his personality theory, Erikson relied on data obtained primarily through three methods: play therapy, anthropological studies, and psychohistorical analysis. In working with emotionally disturbed children and in research on normal children and adolescents, Erikson used play therapy, employing a variety of toys and observing how the subjects played with them. The form and intensity of acts of play revealed to Erikson aspects of personality that might not have been manifested verbally, particularly because children have limited powers of verbal expression.

We have already mentioned Erikson's anthropological studies of Native American tribes. Living among these groups to observe them, Erikson recorded the subjects' behavior and interviewed them at length, particularly with regard to child-rearing practices.

psychohistorical analysis The application of Erikson's life-span theory, along with psychoanalytic principles, to the study of historical figures.

Erikson's most unusual assessment technique is **psychohistorical analysis**. These are biographical studies in which Erikson applied his life-span theory of personality to describe the crises and the ways of coping of significant political, religious, and literary figures, such as Mahatma Gandhi, Martin Luther, and George Bernard Shaw. Erikson's psychohistories focus on a crisis in the person's development, an episode that represents a major life theme, uniting past, present, and future activities. Using what he calls "disciplined subjectivity," Erikson adopts the subject's viewpoint as his own and assesses life events through that person's eyes.

Although Erikson did not use psychological tests for personality assessment, several instruments based on his theory have been developed. The Ego-Identity Scale is designed to measure the development of an ego identity during adolescence (Dignan, 1965). The Inventory of Psychosocial Development assesses adaptive and maladaptive development for six of the eight psychosocial stages (Constantinople, 1969). The Inventory of Psychosocial Balance covers all eight stages (Domino & Affonso, 1990), and the Children's Industry Questionnaire measures the development of industriousness in the latency stage (Kowaz & Marcia, 1991).

Research in Erikson's Theory

Erikson's primary research method was the case study. By now you are familiar with the weaknesses of this method—the difficulty of duplicating and

play constructions
A personality
assessment technique
for children in which
structures assembled
from dolls, blocks, and
other toys are
analyzed.

verifying case material—but you also know that much useful information can be obtained through this technique. Erikson argued that case histories yield many insights into personality development and can help resolve a patient's problems.

Erikson conducted research on aspects of his theory through play therapy, using what he called **play constructions** (Erikson, 1963). In one study, 300 boys and girls, ages 10 to 12, were asked to construct a scene from an imaginary movie using dolls, toy animals, automobiles, and wooden blocks. The girls tended to build static, peaceful scenes that contained low enclosed structures. Their focus was on the interior. Intruders (who were animal figures or male figures, never females) tried to force their way into the enclosures. By contrast, the boys focused on exteriors, action, and height. Their creations tended to be action-oriented, with tall towering structures and with cars and people in motion (see Figure 10.1).

Trained as a Freudian, Erikson interpreted these play constructions along orthodox psychoanalytic lines.

> Sexual differences in the organization of a play space seem to parallel the morphology of genital differentiation itself: in the male, an external organ, erectable and intrusive in character . . . in the female, internal organs, with vestibular access, leading to a statically expectant ova. [Erikson, 1968, p. 271]

In other words, based on the determining effect of biological differences, girls would build low enclosures in which people are walled in, and boys would build towers.

Erikson has been criticized for this view, one that suggests that women are victims of their anatomy and that their personalities are affected by the absence of a penis. Erikson did admit that differences in play constructions could also be the result of differential sex-role training, in which boys are more oriented toward action, aggression, and achievement than girls are.

A replication of this study used younger subjects: boys and girls between the ages of 2 and 5 (Caplan, 1979). The results failed to support Erikson's findings. No significant sex differences were reported in the building of towers and enclosures. This raises the possibility that sex-role training was more complete in Erikson's older subjects. Perhaps the younger children had not yet been sufficiently instructed in the roles society expected of them.

Other research has been concerned with testing the psychosocial developmental stages. Children aged 4, 8, and 11 were asked to make up stories based on several pictures (Ciaccio, 1971). The stories were analyzed to determine which psychosocial stage they reflected. The results supported the themes proposed in Erikson's theory. For example, the stories of the 4-year-olds concerned autonomy (the stage just completed). Similarly, the stories of the older children reflected their developmental stages.

Psychohistorical analysis of the diaries, letters, and novels of Vera Brittain, a British feminist and writer, from the age of 21 into middle age, showed an initial concern with identity, changing, over time, to a concern

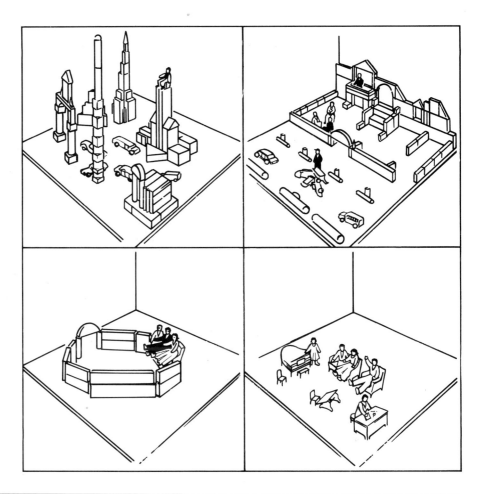

Figure 10.1

Play constructions created by boys (top) and girls (bottom)   SOURCE: Redrawn from *Childhood and Society,* 2nd ed., by Erik H. Erikson, by permission of W. W. Norton & Company, Inc. Copyright 1950, © 1963 by W. W. Norton & Company, Inc. Copyright renewed 1978, 1991 by Erik H. Erikson.

with intimacy and then generativity (Peterson & Stewart, 1990). These changes are in line with Erikson's developmental theory.

A study using the Inventory of Psychosocial Development found a significant relationship between happiness and adaptive development at each of the first six stages (Constantinople, 1969). Another study showed a high correlation between maladaptive development in the first six stages and a sense of alienation and uprootedness (Reimanis, 1974). These findings also offer support for Erikson's work.

Research conducted in South Africa on black and white adults of both sexes, ages 15 to 60, supports Erikson's theory. Childhood aspects of personality were found to be strongly interrelated in white adolescent and adult subjects, suggesting that the adaptive outcomes of each stage of childhood development had formed a cohesive personality. White female subjects resolved their identity crisis at a younger age than did the other subject groups. The correlation between ego identity and emotional well-being was high for white male and white female subjects. In general, black male subjects did not form a positive ego identity until after the age of 40—considerably later than the adolescent stage of psychosocial development. Black female subjects had difficulty resolving the crisis at every developmental stage. These findings may reflect the effects of discrimination in South African society, which limits opportunities for blacks of all ages (Ochse & Plug, 1986).

Using the Ego-Identity Scale, a researcher tested Erikson's contention that too weak or too strong an identification with the parent of the same sex can harm an adolescent's ego identity (Dignan, 1965). Scores on the Ego-Identity Scale and on a test of maternal identification were correlated for a group of female college freshmen and sophomores. The results confirmed Erikson's prediction. It was also found that female college students who had difficulty establishing an ego identity were more likely to have problems with alcohol abuse (Schnur & MacDonald, 1988).

Other research showed that secure family relations in adolescence enhanced the development of ego identity. It was found that parental warmth and autonomy were predictors of a stable family environment, which, in turn, promoted identity development (Kamptner, 1988).

Psychologists tested Erikson's belief that positive outcomes in resolving the identity crisis are related to positive outcomes in the prior developmental stages (Waterman, Buebel, & Waterman, 1970). Adolescents who developed trust, autonomy, initiative, and industriousness (adaptive ways of coping) in the first four stages of psychosocial development displayed a high level of identity cohesion rather than role confusion. Adolescents who had not resolved their identity crisis and who experienced role confusion had not developed adaptive ways of coping in the earlier stages.

An extensive research program on the adolescent stage of development identified five psychosocial types, or statuses, for that period (Marcia, 1966, 1980): identity achievement, moratorium, foreclosure, identity diffusion, and alienated achievement. Identity achievement describes adolescents who are committed to occupational and ideological choices and who have developed a strong ego identity. They are stable, concerned with realistic goals, and able to cope with changing environmental demands. They perform better on difficult tasks than adolescents who are experiencing role confusion. The stable adolescents major in more difficult fields in college, tending toward engineering and the physical sciences (Marcia & Friedman, 1970).

Moratorium, the second status of the adolescent stage of development, describes those who are still undergoing their identity crisis. Their occupational and ideological commitments are vague. They hold ambivalent views toward authority figures, alternately rebelling against them and needing guidance from them. Their behavior ranges from indecisiveness to action and creativity (Blustein, Devenis, & Kidney, 1989; Podd, Marcia, & Rubin, 1968).

Foreclosure describes adolescents who have not experienced an identity crisis but who are firmly committed to an occupation and ideology. Often, however, these commitments have been determined by their parents and accepted as their own; they do not result from the adolescents' deliberate choice. These adolescents tend to be rigid and authoritarian and have difficulty coping with changing situations (Marcia, 1967).

The identity diffusion status characterizes adolescents who have no occupational or ideological commitments and who may not have experienced an identity crisis. Their chosen lifestyle may actively reject commitments and, in the extreme, results in aimless drifting. These adolescents have distant relationships with their parents, whom they see as indifferent and rejecting (Waterman, 1982).

The fifth status, alienated achievement, describes adolescents who have experienced an identity crisis, have no occupational commitment, and cling to an ideology that is critical of the social and economic system. Their commitment to this rationale precludes any commitment to an occupation that would entangle them in the very system they oppose. As students they tend to be cerebral, philosophical, and cynical (Marcia & Friedman, 1970; Orlofsky, Marcia, & Lesser, 1973).

Four of these statuses, in the following order—identity diffusion, foreclosure, moratorium, and identity achievement—represent increasingly successful resolutions of the identity problem. Erikson predicted that people who are close to achieving or who have achieved an integrated ego identity will have greater ego strength than those who are less close to identity resolution. That prediction was supported by the results of studies of college men (Bourne, 1978a, 1978b). In cognitive and emotional terms, the identity-achievement and moratorium types functioned better than the foreclosure and identity-diffusion types. College men and women of the identity-achievement type were also found to be more confident (Berzonsky, Rice, & Neimeyer, 1990).

In other research, sex differences have been found in the resolution of the identity crisis. Men in one study showed a tendency toward separation and detachment from other people; women showed a tendency toward connection and attachment to others (Mellor, 1989).

Applying Alfred Adler's technique of early recollections, one psychologist found that college women identified as being in the moratorium status showed stronger ego development and character structure than women in the foreclosure status (Josselson, 1982). Similar results were later obtained from a study of college men (Orlofsky & Frank, 1986). Early memories were found to vary as a function of ego identity status. Identity-achievement, alienated-achievement, and foreclosure types—the more committed statuses—demonstrated greater recall for personal memories than moratorium and identity-diffusion types—the less committed statuses (Neimeyer & Rareshide, 1991).

Some personality research has focused on the question of when the identity crisis occurs. Erikson suggested that it began early in adolescence and was resolved, one way or another, by approximately the age of 18. Research suggests that for some people, the identity crisis may not occur until late in adolescence. In one study, up to 30 percent of the subjects were searching for an identity as late as age 24 (Archer, 1982).

College attendance may delay the resolution of the identity crisis and prolong the period during which young adults experiment with new roles and ideologies (Côté & Levine, 1988). When college students were compared with people in the same age group who held full-time jobs, it was found that the employed people had achieved ego identity at an earlier age than the students. The students remained longer in the moratorium status (Adams & Fitch, 1982).

Erikson emphasized the importance of our developing an early sense of trust if we are to achieve feelings of security and well-being later in life. This position has received strong research support (see Jacobson & Wille, 1986; Londerville & Main, 1981; Sroufe, Fox, & Pancake, 1983).

Studies of infants between the ages of 12 and 18 months showed that those who had a strong emotional bond with their mothers (and were therefore presumed to be high in trust) functioned, when observed three years later, at a higher social and emotional level than children of the same age whose attachment to their mothers was less secure. Children with a well-developed sense of trust were also more curious, sociable, and popular; more likely to be leaders in games; and more sensitive to the needs and feelings of others. Those low in trust were more withdrawn socially and emotionally, more reluctant to play with other children, less curious, and less forceful in pursuing their goals.

Research on the adulthood stage of psychosocial development has shown that generativity in middle-aged subjects is positively correlated with power and with intimacy motivation (McAdams, Ruetzel, & Foley, 1986). Thus, as Erikson's theory predicts, generativity evokes the needs to feel close to others and to feel strong in relation to them. Another study associated generativity with nurturance (Van DeWater & McAdams, 1989). All these are necessary characteristics for teaching and guiding the next generation.

Generativity in middle age appears to be significantly related to having had warm and affectionate parents in childhood (Franz, McClelland, & Weinberger, 1991). The researchers suggested that their findings show the importance of both parents to their child's emotional well-being.

Erikson wrote that people in the maturity and old age stage of psychosocial development spend time recalling and examining the whole of their lives, accepting or regretting their past choices. A study using 49 psychologists as subjects found that most of their memories were of their college and early adult years, the period involving the greatest number of critical decisions that affected the course of their lives (Mackavey, Malley, & Stewart, 1991).

A Final Commentary

Erikson's influence has been widely recognized in both professional and popular circles. *Time* magazine called him the "most influential living psychoanalyst" (March 17, 1975). *Psychology Today* described him as the "dean" of psychoanalysis, "an authentic intellectual hero" (Hall, 1983, p. 22). His influence has spread to the fields of education, social work, vocational and marriage counseling, and clinical work with children and adolescents. His impact on child development was recognized by the establishment of the Erikson Institute for Early Childhood Education at Chicago's Loyola University.

The field of life-span developmental psychology, which has seen a massive increase in research and theory in recent years, owes much of its impetus to Erikson's emphasis on the growth of personality throughout life. The current interest in the developmental problems of middle and old age is also an outgrowth of Erikson's work.

Erikson's method of play therapy is a standard diagnostic and therapeutic tool in work with emotionally disturbed and abused children. For example, children who cannot verbalize the details of a sexual attack can express their feelings through play with dolls that represent themselves and their abusers.

Despite these contributions to psychology, Erikson's system does not lack critics. Some point to ambiguous and poorly defined terms and concepts, to conclusions drawn in the absence of supporting data, and to an overall lack of precision (see Rosenthal, Gurney, & Moore, 1981; Waterman, 1982). Erikson accepts the validity of these charges and blames them on his artistic temperament and his lack of formal training in science. "I came to psychology from art," he wrote, "which may explain, if not justify, the fact that at times the reader will find me painting contexts and backgrounds where he would rather have me point to facts and concepts" (Erikson, 1950, p. 13).

A more specific criticism relates to the incomplete description of maturity, the final developmental stage; Erikson attempted to correct this deficiency in his latest book (Erikson, Erikson, & Kivnick, 1986). Also, some psychologists question whether personality development after age 55 is likely to be as positive as suggested by Erikson's proposed attitude of ego integrity. For many people, the period holds considerable pain, loss, and depression—even for those who develop the basic strength of wisdom.

Erikson's position on sex differences, as revealed in his interpretation of his play-constructions research, has also come under attack. What he suggested were biologically based differences in personality for boys and girls, originating in the presence or absence of a penis, are seen by others as cultural differences or differences in sex-role training. Erikson later admitted the possibility of these other explanations.

Some critics charge that Erikson's personality theory does not apply to people in reduced economic circumstances who cannot afford a period of moratorium in which to explore different roles and develop an ego identity. They suggest that this period is a luxury available only to those with the means to attend college or to take time out to travel and seek their identity through new experiences (Slugoski & Ginsburg, 1989).

Erikson has shown little interest in responding to his critics or defending his views. He recognizes that there are many ways of describing personality development, depending on one's perspective, and that no single view is adequate. His influence continues to grow through his books and through the work of succeeding generations of psychologists, psychiatrists, teachers, and counselors who see in his ideas a useful way to describe personality development from infancy through old age.

Summary

Erik Erikson built on Freud's theory by elaborating and extending the stages of development, by emphasizing the ego more than the id, and by recognizing the impact on personality of culture, society, and history. The growth of the personality is divided into eight stages. A conflict exists at each stage, in which the person is faced with adaptive and maladaptive ways of coping. Development is governed by the epigenetic principle; each stage depends on genetic factors, but the environment helps determine whether these factors are realized.

The oral-sensory stage (birth to age 1) can result in trust or mistrust. The muscular-anal stage (ages 1 to 3) leads to an autonomous will or to self-doubt. The locomotor-genital stage (3 to 5) develops initiative or guilt. The latency stage (6 to 11) results in industriousness or inferiority. Adolescence (12 to 18) is the stage in which the ego identity is formed (that is, the time of the identity crisis), leading to identity cohesion or role confusion. Young adulthood (18 to 35) results in intimacy or isolation. Adulthood (35 to 55) leads to generativity or stagnation. Maturity (over 55) is expressed in ego integrity or despair.

Each stage allows for the development of basic strengths that emerge from the adaptive ways of coping with the conflicts. The basic strengths are hope, will, purpose, competence, fidelity, love, care, and wisdom. Maldevelopment can occur if the ego consists solely of either the adaptive or the maladaptive tendency.

Erikson presents a flattering and optimistic image of human nature. He argues that we have the ability to achieve basic strengths, to resolve each conflict in an adaptive way, and to consciously direct our growth. We are not victims of biological forces or childhood experiences and are influenced more by learning and social interactions than by heredity.

Erikson's assessment methods are play therapy, anthropological studies, and psychohistory. His research relies on case studies. There is empirical research support for the first six stages of psychosocial development and for the concept of ego identity. However, the identity crisis may occur later than Erikson believes, and attending college may delay resolution of the crisis. Other research confirms Erikson's belief in the importance of developing a sense of trust early in life.

Criticisms of Erikson's theory focus on ambiguous terminology, incomplete descriptions of the psychosocial stages, and poorly supported claims of male-female personality differences based on biological factors.

Critical Thinking Review

1. In what ways does Erikson's theory extend psychoanalytic theory?

2. Discuss the identity crises that characterized Erikson's early life.

3. What is the role of conflict in the stages of psychosocial development?

4. Describe the four childhood stages of psychosocial development. Discuss the effects of various parental behaviors on the possible outcomes of each stage.

5. According to Erikson, what is the major difference between the first four developmental stages and the last four developmental stages?

6. What factors affect the development of ego identity? Why do some people fail to achieve an identity at this stage?

7. What are the positive ways of resolving the conflicts of the adult stages of psychosocial development?

8. Describe the nature and development of the basic strengths.

9. Distinguish between the two conditions of maldevelopment. How can these conditions be corrected?

10. How does Erikson's image of human nature differ from Freud's?

11. What methods of assessment did Erikson use in developing his theory?

12. Based on the results of his play-constructions research, what did Erikson conclude about sex differences in personality? On what grounds can these conclusions be criticized?

13. Describe recent research on the development of ego identity during adolescence. Do the results support Erikson's predictions?

Suggested Reading

Erikson, E. H. (1968). *Identity: Youth and crisis.* New York: Norton. Erikson's classic work on the identity crisis and the ways of coping with conflict at this stage of development.

Erikson, E. H. (1987). *A way of looking at things: Selected papers from 1930 to 1980.* New York: Norton. A collection of Erikson's writings on children's play constructions, adult dreams, cross-cultural research, and development over the life cycle. Edited by Stephen Schlein.

Erikson, E. H., Erikson, J. M., & Kivnick, H. Q. (1986). *Vital involvement in old age.* New York: Norton. A sensitive psychosocial analysis of the need for stimulation and challenge in old age and a personal perspective on Erikson as he approached the age of 90.

Evans, R. I. (1967). *Dialogue with Erik Erikson.* New York: Harper & Row. Conversations with Erikson about his life and work.

VI

The Humanistic Approach

Humanism is a system of thought in which human interests and values are of primary importance. The humanistic approach to personality is part of the humanistic movement in psychology that flourished in the 1960s and 1970s and whose proponents attempted to reform the methods and subject matter of the field. Humanistic psychologists objected to psychoanalysis and behaviorism—the two major forces in American psychology—arguing that they presented too limited and demeaning an image of human nature.

Humanistic psychologists criticized Freud and the neopsychoanalysts for studying only the emotionally disturbed side of human nature. They questioned how we could learn about positive human characteristics and qualities if we focused only on neuroses and psychoses. They proposed instead to study human strengths and virtues and to advance principles of emotional health. According to the humanistic psychologists, we need to explore what people are at their best, not just at their worst.

The humanistic psychologists saw behavioral psychologists, who disavowed conscious and unconscious forces to focus exclusively on the objective observation of overt behavior, as narrow and sterile in their outlook. A psychology based solely on conditioned responses to stimuli depicts people as robots, mechanical organisms reacting to environmental events in predetermined ways. People are not big white rats or slow computers, the humanistic psychologists argued. Human behavior is too complex to be explained by the behaviorists' methods.

The term *humanistic psychology* was first used by Gordon Allport in 1930. He and Henry Murray are considered forerunners of the humanistic approach to personality. That approach, represented in this section by the works of Abraham Maslow and Carl Rogers, emphasizes human strengths and aspirations, conscious free will, and the fulfillment of our potentialities. It presents a flattering and optimistic image of human nature and describes us as active, creative beings concerned with growth and self-actualization.

E L E V E N

Abraham Maslow

The Life of Maslow (1908–1970)
Motivation and Personality: The Hierarchy
of Needs
    Physiological Needs
    Safety Needs
    Belongingness and Love Needs
    Esteem Needs
    Self-Actualization
    Cognitive Needs
    Situational Variablcs

Characteristics of Self-Actualizers
    The Failure to Become Self-Actualizing
Maslow's Image of Human Nature
Assessment in Maslow's Theory
Research in Maslow's Theory
A Final Commentary
Summary
Critical Thinking Review
Suggested Reading

*What humans can be, they must be. They must be
true to their own nature.*

—Abraham Maslow

Abraham Maslow is considered the founder and spiritual father of psychology's humanistic movement. He criticized behaviorism and psychoanalysis, particularly Freud's approach to personality. According to Maslow, by studying only abnormal examples of humanity—the emotionally disturbed—psychologists ignore the positive human qualities, such as happiness, contentment, and peace of mind. A frequently quoted statement sums up Maslow's position: "The study of crippled, stunted, immature, and unhealthy specimens can yield only a cripple psychology" (Maslow, 1970b, p. 180).

We underestimate human nature, Maslow charged, when we fail to study the best examples of humanity, society's most creative, healthy, and mature people. This approach—assessing the best representatives of the human species—is a distinctive feature of Maslow's personality theory. When you want to determine how fast humans can run, he noted, you study not the average runner but the fastest runner you can find. Only in this way is it possible to determine the limits of human potential.

Maslow's personality theory does not derive from clinical interviews and case histories of patients but from research on the healthiest personalities he could find, studied from life and from biographical materials. He concluded that each of us is born with instinctive needs that cause us to grow, develop, and fulfill our potentialities.

Maslow proposed a hierarchy of needs, a ladder of motivations. Those needs on the bottom rung must be satisfied before the ones on the next rung assume prominence. When the second-level needs are satisfied, the third-level needs become important, and so on. His theory became extremely popular in the 1960s and 1970s and is still applied in the business world, where executives suggest that the highest motivation—the need for self-actualization—is a potential source of job satisfaction.

The Life of Maslow (1908–1970)

The oldest of seven children, Abraham Maslow was born in 1908 in Brooklyn, New York. His parents were immigrants with little education and little prospect of rising above their marginal economic circumstances. At the age of 14, Maslow's father had walked and hitchhiked from Russia across western Europe, so great was his ambition to reach the United States. This drive to succeed seems to have been instilled in his son.

Maslow's childhood was a difficult one. "With my childhood," he told an interviewer, "it's a wonder I'm not psychotic" (Hall, 1968a, p. 37). Isolated and unhappy, he grew up without close friends or loving parents. His father was emotionally cold and aloof and often absent for long periods when he fled his unhappy marriage. He "loved whiskey and women and fighting," Maslow said (quoted in Wilson, 1972, p. 131). Later in life, Maslow reconciled with his father, but as a child and adolescent he felt bitterness and animosity toward him.

Maslow's relationship with his mother was worse. A biographer reported that Maslow "grew to maturity with an unrelieved hatred toward [his mother] and he never achieved the slightest reconciliation" (Hoffman, 1988, p. 7). She was a superstitious person who punished Maslow for the slightest wrongdoing. She threatened that God would retaliate for his misbehavior, and she was unaffectionate and rejecting, openly favoring the younger siblings. One day, when Maslow brought home two stray kittens, his mother killed them, bashing their heads against a wall. Maslow never forgave her for her behavior toward him and later refused to attend her funeral.

His mother's treatment of him affected not only his emotional life but also his work in psychology. "The whole thrust of my life-philosophy," Maslow wrote, "and all my research and theorizing . . . has its roots in a hatred for and revulsion against everything she stood for" (quoted in Hoffman, 1988, p. 9).

As a child, Maslow felt that he was different from others. Embarrassed about his scrawny physique and large nose, he remembered his teenage years as "one big inferiority complex. . . . I tried to compensate for what I felt was a great [physical] lack by forcing my development in the direction of athletic achievements" (quoted in Hoffman, 1988, pp. 5, 13). Thus, the man who would later become interested in Adler's work was in many ways a living example of Adler's ideas of compensation and inferiority feelings (see Chapter 4).

When Maslow's attempts at compensation—at trying to achieve recognition, acceptance, and esteem on the athletic field—did not succeed, he turned to books for companionship. The library became the playground of his childhood and adolescence, and books and education were the road out of the ghetto of poverty and loneliness. Maslow's early memories are significant, indicating the style of life he fashioned for himself: a life of scholarship. He recalled going to the neighborhood library early in the morning and waiting on the steps until the doors opened. He typically arrived at school an hour before classes began, and his teacher would let him sit in an empty classroom, reading books she had lent him.

By the time Maslow entered high school, he was a voracious reader, yet he earned no better than mediocre grades. Still, they were sufficient to gain him acceptance at City College of New York. He failed a course during his first semester and by the end of his freshman year was on academic probation. However, he persisted, and his grades improved. He began studying law, at his father's insistence, but after two weeks he decided he did not like it. What he really wanted was to study everything.

Maslow's passion for learning was matched by a passion for his cousin Bertha. He soon left home, first for Cornell University and then for the University of Wisconsin, where Bertha joined him. They married when he was 20 and she was 19. It was a significant step for Maslow; the marriage provided him with a feeling of belonging and a sense of direction. He later said that life had little meaning for him until he got married and began his studies at Wisconsin.

Earlier, at Cornell, he had enrolled in a psychology course and pronounced it "awful and bloodless." It "had nothing to do with people, so I shuddered and turned away from it" (quoted in Hoffman, 1988, p. 26). At Wisconsin, however, he became enraptured by the behavioristic psychology of John B. Watson, the instigator of the revolution to make psychology a science of behavior. Like many people in the early 1930s, Maslow decided that behaviorism could solve all the world's problems. He received training in experimental psychology, working with Harry Harlow on his famous studies of monkeys.

It is a giant step from Maslow's graduate training and research in behaviorism to humanistic psychology and self-actualization, from monkeys to what he called the "growing tip of mankind." Several influences brought about this profound shift. He read the works of Sigmund Freud, the Gestalt psychologists, and the philosophers Alfred North Whitehead and Henri Bergson. His first child was born, an event he described as a "thunderclap." He stated, "I was stunned by the mystery and by the sense of not really being in control. I felt small and weak and feeble before all this. I'd say anyone who had a baby couldn't be a behaviorist" (quoted in Hall, 1968a, p. 56). Later, as we shall see, he was also influenced by the onset of World War II.

Maslow received his Ph.D. from the University of Wisconsin in 1934 and returned to New York, first for a postdoctoral fellowship under E. L. Thorndike at Columbia University, and later to teach at Brooklyn College, where he remained until 1951. While working with Thorndike, Maslow took a battery of intelligence and scholastic aptitude tests. Thorndike told him that his IQ was an astounding 195, well within the genius range. At first Maslow was surprised, but he quickly accepted the revelation and thereafter considered it "a mark of triumph," managing to work it into conversations at social gatherings.

Teaching in New York at a propitious time, the late 1930s and early 1940s, Maslow had the opportunity to meet the wave of emigrant intellectuals fleeing Nazi Germany—Erich Fromm, Karen Horney, and the Gestalt psychologist Max Wertheimer. He also met Alfred Adler and the American anthropologist Ruth Benedict. His admiration for Benedict and Wertheimer led to his research on self-actualization and to the personality theory he derived from it.

In 1941, when the United States entered World War II, Maslow recalled watching a local parade shortly after the attack on Pearl Harbor. "The moment changed my whole life," he told an interviewer, "and determined what I have done ever since" (Hall, 1968a, p. 54). He resolved to devote himself to the development of a psychology that would deal with the highest human ideals and capacities. He would improve the human personality and demonstrate that we can display more noble behaviors than hatred, prejudice, and war.

From 1951 to 1969, Maslow taught at Brandeis University in Waltham, Massachusetts. A foundation grant enabled him to move to California to undertake the formulation of a broad philosophy of politics, economics, and ethics, to be generated by a humanistic psychology. By the end of his life, Maslow had become an immensely popular figure both in psychology and among the general public. He received many awards and honors and was elected president of the American Psychological Association in 1967.

Motivation and Personality: The Hierarchy of Needs

hierarchy of needs
An arrangement of innate needs—from strongest to weakest—that activates and directs behavior. It includes **physiological, safety, belongingness and love, esteem,** and **self-actualization needs.**

Maslow proposed a **hierarchy of five innate needs** that activate and direct human behavior (Maslow, 1970b). These needs are instinctive; we come equipped with them at birth. However, the behaviors we use to satisfy the needs are learned and therefore are subject to variation from one person to another. The needs are arranged in a hierarchy or ladder (see Figure 11.1); those at the bottom must be at least partially satisfied before those at the upper rungs become influential. For example, hungry people will feel no urge to satisfy the need for esteem. They are obsessed with finding food, not with what others may think of them. It is only when people have adequate food, and when the rest of their lower-order needs are satisfied, that they are motivated by the higher-order needs.

We are not driven by all the needs at the same time. In general, only one need will be dominant. Which one it will be depends on which of the others have been satisfied. For example, people who are highly successful in business are no longer driven by or even aware of their physiological and safety needs. These needs have been amply taken care of. Such people may now be motivated to seek esteem or self-actualization. However, the priority of the needs can change or be reversed. If an economic recession causes business executives and managers to lose their jobs, the safety and physiological needs

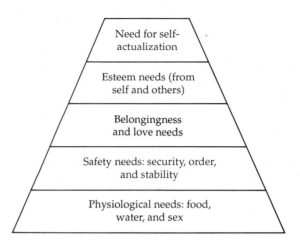

Figure 11.1

Maslow's hierarchy of needs.

may reassume priority. Being able to pay the rent might then become more prized than an award from a civic organization.

Maslow described several characteristics of needs:

1. The lower the need is in the hierarchy, the greater are its strength, potency, and priority. The higher needs are weaker needs.
2. Higher needs appear later in the human life span. Physiological and safety needs arise in infancy, belonging and esteem needs arise in adolescence, and the need for self-actualization arises in midlife.
3. Because higher needs are less necessary for survival, their gratification can be postponed. Failure to satisfy a higher need does not produce a crisis, as does failure to satisfy a lower need. For this reason, Maslow called lower needs **deficit** or **deficiency needs;** failure to satisfy them produces a deficiency in the individual.
4. Although higher needs are less necessary for survival, they do contribute to survival and growth. Satisfaction of the higher needs can lead to improved health, longer life, and an enhanced biological efficiency. For this reason, Maslow called higher needs **growth** or **being needs.**
5. Satisfaction of the higher needs is productive and beneficial, both biologically and psychologically. It can lead to contentment, happiness, and a sense of fulfillment.
6. Gratification of the higher needs requires better external circumstances (social, economic, and political) than gratification of the lower needs. For example, pursuing self-actualization depends on greater freedom of expression and opportunity than pursuing safety and security.
7. A need does not have to be satisfied fully before the next need in the hierarchy becomes important. Maslow suggested a declining percent-

deficit needs The lower needs. Failure to satisfy deficit needs produces a deficiency in the body.

growth needs The higher needs. Although growth needs are less necessary for survival, they involve the realization and fulfillment of human potential.

age of satisfaction for each need as we progress up the hierarchy. Giving a hypothetical case, he described a person who satisfied, in turn, 85 percent of the physiological needs, 70 percent of the safety needs, 50 percent of the belongingness and love needs, 40 percent of the esteem needs, and 10 percent of the self-actualization need.

Physiological Needs

If you have ever struggled for air while under water or gone too long without food, you realize how trivial the needs for love or esteem or anything else are when a physiological deficiency is not satisfied. Maslow suggested that a starving person thinks of, dreams of, and craves only food. But once that need is satisfied, the person is no longer driven by or even aware of it. The importance of the need disappears, and it ceases to direct or control behavior. This is the situation for most people in an affluent, industrialized culture. It is rare for middle-class Americans to be concerned solely with the satisfaction of the survival needs. **Physiological needs** are more important as motivating forces in cultures where basic survival remains an everyday concern. Because a need that has been gratified is no longer a need, for most of us the physiological needs play a minimal role in our lives.

Safety Needs

Maslow believed that the **needs for safety and security** are most important in infants and in neurotic adults. Emotionally healthy adults typically have satisfied the safety needs. Satisfaction requires stability, security, and freedom from fear and anxiety. In infants and children, the safety needs can be seen clearly, because youngsters react visibly and immediately to threats and fears. Adults have learned to inhibit their fear reactions to some degree.

Another visible indication of children's safety needs is their preference for a structure or routine, an orderly and predictable world. Maslow suggested that having too much freedom and permissiveness—that is, an absence of structure and order—produces anxiety and insecurity in children because it threatens their need for safety. A measure of freedom must be granted to children, but only within the limits of their capacity to cope. Freedom must be offered with guidance because children are not yet capable of directing their own behavior.

Neurotic and insecure adults also need structure and order in their environment because the safety needs have remained dominant in the personality. Neurotics compulsively avoid new, unexpected, or divergent experiences. They prefer to arrange their world to make it predictable, budgeting their time and organizing their possessions. Pencils must be kept in a certain drawer, and shirts hung in the closet all facing the same direction.

Maslow pointed out that although most normal adults have satisfied their safety needs, those needs may still influence their behavior. Many of us prefer predictability to the unknown and order to chaos. That is why we

When the basic needs for food and shelter are unsatisfied, the higher needs, such as esteem and self-actualization, are of less importance.

save for the future, buy insurance, and choose to remain in a secure job rather than to risk some new business venture. However, the need is not as compulsive and overwhelming in the normal adult as in the neurotic or the infant.

Belongingness and Love Needs

Once our physiological and safety needs have been reasonably well satisfied, we develop the **needs for belongingness and love.** These needs can be expressed in a variety of ways: through a close relationship with a friend, lover, or mate; or through social relationships formed within a chosen group.

The need to belong is more difficult to satisfy in an increasingly mobile society. Few of us live in the neighborhood where we grew up or retain the friends from our early school days. We change schools, jobs, and towns too frequently to put down roots, to develop a secure sense of belonging, and so we must attempt to satisfy this need in other ways, such as joining organizations or clubs.

The need to give and to receive love can be satisfied in an intimate relationship with another person. Maslow did not equate love with sex (which is a physiological need), but he recognized that sex is one way of expressing the love need. He suggested that the failure to satisfy the need for love is a fundamental cause of emotional maladjustment (Maslow, 1968).

Belongingness and love needs can be satisfied through a relationship with a friend.

Esteem Needs

If we feel loved and have a sense of belonging, then we develop the **need for esteem.** We require esteem and respect from ourselves, in the form of feelings of self-worth, and from others, in the form of status, recognition, or social success. Thus, there are two esteem needs: the need for self-esteem and the need for esteem granted us by other people.

Satisfaction of the need for self-esteem allows us to feel confident of our strength, worth, and adequacy. We may then become more competent and productive in all aspects of life. When we lack self-esteem, we feel inferior, helpless, and discouraged, with little confidence in our ability to cope with life's problems.

Self-Actualization

self-actualization The fullest development of the self.

The final stage of development, **self-actualization**, is the realization and fulfillment of our potentialities and capabilities. Maslow proposed that we are motivated to become all we are capable of becoming. Even though the other needs may be satisfied, the person who is not self-actualizing—that is, not using his or her talents and abilities at their fullest—will be restless, discontented, and frustrated. "A musician must make music," Maslow wrote, "an artist must paint, a poet must write . . . to be ultimately at peace" (1970b, p. 46).

Self-actualizing can take many forms. Each of us, regardless of our occupation and interests, can fulfill our potential and reach this peak of personality development. The condition is not limited to artists and poets. "A first-rate soup," Maslow wrote, "is more creative than a second-rate painting . . . cooking or parenthood or making a home could be creative, while poetry need not be" (1987, p. 159). What is important is to fulfill oneself at the highest level.

Several conditions are necessary for self-actualization. First, we must be free of constraints imposed by society and by ourselves. Second, we must not be distracted by the lower needs—by concerns for food or safety. Third, we must be secure in our self-image and with others, and love and be loved in return. Fourth, we must have a realistic knowledge of our strengths and weaknesses, virtues and vices.

Although the hierarchy of needs applies to most of us, Maslow noted several exceptions. People dedicated to an ideal have willingly sacrificed everything, including their lives, for their cause. People who fast until death for their beliefs are also obviously denying their physiological and safety needs. Religious figures who abandon worldly goods to fulfill a vow of poverty may be satisfying the need for self-actualization while frustrating their lower-order needs. Similarly, artists may endanger their health and comfort for the sake of their work. A more common reversal in the hierarchy is that some people place a greater importance on the self-esteem need than on love in the belief that the belongingness and love needs can be satisfied only if they first feel self-confident and worthy.

Cognitive Needs

Maslow proposed a second set of needs: the needs to know and to understand. These exist outside the hierarchy we described earlier. Maslow wrote that these cognitive needs were innate drives pushing for satisfaction and cited several points of evidence to support their existence (Maslow, 1970b):

1. Laboratory studies with animals show that animals actively explore and manipulate their environment for no apparent reason other than curiosity.
2. Considerable historical evidence shows that some people have sought knowledge and information at the risk of their lives, thus placing this need above the safety needs.
3. Studies suggest that many emotionally healthy adults are attracted to the unknown and mysterious, to the unorganized and unexplained.
4. In his clinical practice, Maslow saw emotionally healthy adults who complained of boredom and a lack of zest and excitement in life. He described them as "intelligent people leading stupid lives in stupid jobs" and found that they improved when they became involved in challenging activities.

Maslow believed that the needs to know and to understand appear in late infancy and early childhood and are expressed as a child's natural curiosity.

These needs do not have to be taught. However, society, in the form of schools and parents, may attempt to inhibit a child's spontaneous curiosity. Failure to satisfy the cognitive needs is harmful (as is failure to satisfy any of the needs) and can inhibit the full development and functioning of the personality.

The needs to know and to understand are also expressed as the need to analyze, to reduce things to their elemental parts; or as the need to experiment, to see what will happen if we try something different. They may also be manifested as the need to explain, to construct a system or a personal theory that makes sense of the events and conditions of our environment.

Although these needs are not part of the original hierarchy of needs, they form a separate hierarchy of their own. The need to know is more potent than the need to understand and must be at least partially satisfied before the need to understand can emerge.

The two need hierarchies overlap. Knowing and understanding, finding meaning in our environment, are basic to interacting with that environment in a mature way to obtain love, esteem, and self-fulfillment. It is impossible to become self-actualizing if the needs to know and to understand are not met.

Situational Variables

The needs Maslow postulated are innate, personal variables. He also recognized the role of situational variables. The hierarchical needs are manifested in behavior in relation to people and events in our environment. Maslow noted that we are responsible for the creation of much of the social and physical environment in which we function. The impact of the situations in which we find ourselves depends largely on how we perceive them. Our perception, however, may not reflect the objective reality of a given situation. Thus, much of the effect of any situation is a function of what we perceive it to be. In sum, then, our behavior is determined by both personal variables (the innate needs that motivate us), and situational variables (the features of our world). Maslow proposed this interactionist view a decade before the eruption of the person-situation debate described in Chapter 1.

Characteristics of Self-Actualizers

metamotivation The motivation of self-actualizing persons; it involves maximizing one's potential rather than striving for a particular goal object.

As Maslow continued his study of self-actualizing persons, he began to suspect that they differed from other people in terms of their basic motivation. He proposed a motivational theory for self-actualizing persons called **metamotivation** (sometimes referred to in his writings as "B-motivation" or "Being"). The prefix *meta-* means "after" or "beyond." Maslow used the term to indicate that metamotivation moves beyond psychology's traditional idea of motivation. To Maslow, it meant a state in which motivation played no role at all. Self-actualizing persons were not motivated to strive for something in particular; instead, they developed from within.

Maslow described the motivation of people who are not self-actualizing as "D-motivation" or "Deficiency." This type of motivation involves striving for something specific to make up for something lacking within the organism. For example, failing to eat produces a deficit in the body that is felt in discomfort and tension that the organism is then driven to reduce. A specific need (hunger) for a specific goal object (food) produces a motivation to attain something that is lacking (we search for food).

Maslow was not clear on this point, but apparently Deficiency motivation applies not only to the physiological needs but also to the needs for safety, belongingness and love, and esteem.

In contrast, people who are satisfying the need for self-actualization are concerned with fulfilling their potential and with knowing and understanding their environment. In their state of metamotivation, they are not seeking to reduce tension, satisfy a deficiency, or strive for a specific object. Rather, their goal is to enrich and enlarge their lives and to increase tension through diverse challenging experiences.

Self-actualizers function at a level beyond striving for something to satisfy a deficit need because all their deficit needs have been met. Self-actualizers are in a state of being—spontaneously, naturally, and joyfully expressing their full humanity.

Having explained that, in this sense, self-actualizers are unmotivated, Maslow proposed a list of metaneeds or Being values, which are states of growth (perhaps goals) toward which self-actualizers evolve (see Table 11.1). Metaneeds are states of being rather than specific goal objects. Failure to satisfy them is harmful—as is failure to satisfy any of the other needs—and produces a kind of metapathology, which is a diminution or thwarting of human growth and development (Maslow, 1967). Metapathology prevents self-actualizers from expressing, using, and fulfilling their potential. They may feel helpless and depressed, but they cannot point to a specific source for these feelings or strive for a specific goal that might alleviate the distress.

Maslow's research on humanity's best and healthiest examples formed the basis of his personality theory (Maslow, 1970b). Although he did not find many people he considered self-actualizing—he estimated that self-actualizers constitute 1 percent or less of the population—he studied enough of them to conclude that they shared certain characteristics.

1. An efficient perception of reality.   Self-actualizers perceive their world, including other people, clearly and objectively, unbiased by prejudgments or preconceptions.

2. An acceptance of themselves, others, and nature.   Self-actualizers accept themselves (their strengths and weaknesses) without trying to distort or falsify their self-image and without feeling guilty about their failings. They also accept the weaknesses of other people and of society in general.

3. A spontaneity, simplicity, and naturalness.   The behavior of self-actualizers is open, direct, and natural. Self-actualizers rarely hide their feelings or emo-

Table 11.1   **Maslow's metaneeds and metapathologies.**

Metaneeds	Metapathologies
Truth	Mistrust, cynicism, skepticism
Goodness	Hatred, repulsion, disgust, reliance only upon self and for self
Beauty	Vulgarity, restlessness, loss of taste, bleakness
Unity; wholeness	Disintegration
Dichotomy-transcendence	Black/white thinking, either/or thinking, simplistic view of life
Aliveness; process	Deadness, robotizing, feeling oneself to be totally determined, loss of emotion and zest in life, experiential emptiness
Uniqueness	Loss of feeling of self and individuality, feeling oneself to be interchangeable or anonymous
Perfection	Hopelessness, nothing to work for
Necessity	Chaos, unpredictability
Completion; finality	Incompleteness, hopelessness, cessation of striving and coping
Justice	Anger, cynicism, mistrust, lawlessness, total selfishness
Order	Insecurity, wariness, loss of safety and predictability, necessity for being on guard
Simplicity	Overcomplexity, confusion, bewilderment, loss of orientation
Richness, totality, comprehensiveness	Depression, uneasiness, loss of interest in the world
Effortlessness	Fatigue, strain, clumsiness, awkwardness, stiffness
Playfulness	Grimness, depression, paranoid humorlessness, loss of zest in life, cheerlessness
Self-sufficiency	Responsibility given to others
Meaningfulness	Meaninglessness, despair, senselessness of life

SOURCE: Adapted from *The Farther Reaches of Human Nature,* by A. H. Maslow. Copyright © 1971 by Bertha G. Maslow.

tions or play a role to satisfy society, although they may do so to avoid hurting another person. Self-actualizers are individualistic in their ideas and ideals but not necessarily unconventional in their behavior. They feel secure enough to be themselves without being aggressively rebellious about it.

4. A focus on problems outside themselves. Self-actualizers have a sense of mission to which they devote their energy. Dedication to some work, cause, or vocation is a requirement for self-actualization. Maslow believed it was impossible to become self-actualizing without this sense of commitment. Although self-actualizers work hard, they find great pleasure and excitement in doing so.

Through their intense dedication, self-actualizers are able to satisfy the metaneeds. For example, a writer or scientist may search for truth, an artist for beauty, an attorney for justice. Self-actualizers do not undertake their work primarily for money, fame, or power but because it satisfies the metaneeds, challenges and develops their abilities, and helps them grow and define the sense of self.

5. A sense of detachment and the need for privacy.   Self-actualizers can experience isolation without harmful effects, and they seem to need solitude more than persons who are not self-actualizing. Self-actualizers depend on themselves for their satisfactions and do not need to be dependent on others. Because of their independence, they may be perceived as aloof and unfriendly, but this is not their desire. They are simply more autonomous than most people and do not choose to cling to or demand warmth and support from others.

6. A freshness of appreciation.   Self-actualizers have the ability to continue to perceive and experience their world with freshness, wonder, and awe. An experience may grow stale for non–self-actualizing persons, but self-actualizers will enjoy a sunset, a rose, or a Mahler symphony as though it were the first one ever experienced. Even mundane events and trivial objects can be appreciated with delight. Self-actualizers continue to enjoy what they have and take little for granted.

peak experience
A moment of intense ecstasy, similar to a religious or mystical experience, during which the self is transcended.

7. Mystic or peak experiences.   Self-actualizers know moments of intense ecstasy, not unlike deeply religious experiences, that can occur in the context of virtually any activity. Maslow called these events **peak experiences**, during which the self is transcended and the person feels supremely powerful, confident, and decisive.

In later work Maslow distinguished between self-actualizers on the basis of their peak experiences. All these people are at the summit of psychological health, but they differ in terms of the quantity and quality of their peak experiences. Peakers have more peak experiences than nonpeakers, and these experiences tend to be more mystical and religious. Peakers are more saintly and poetical than nonpeakers. Peakers are found among diverse occupational groups, including artists, writers, scientists, business executives, educators, and politicians. Nonpeakers are more practical and concerned with worldly affairs. Also, it is possible for people who are not self-actualizing to have the occasional peak experience.

8. Social interest.   Maslow adopted Adler's concept of social interest to indicate the sympathy and empathy self-actualizing persons have for humanity. Although they are often irritated by the behavior of individuals, self-actualizers feel a kinship with and an understanding of others and a desire to help society.

9. Profound interpersonal relations.   Although their circle of friends is not large, self-actualizers have intense and profound friendships. They tend to select as friends those who show personal characteristics similar to their own, just as we all choose as friends people we find compatible. Self-actualizers often attract admirers or disciples. These relationships are usually one-sided; the admirer asks more of the self-actualizer than he or she is able or willing to give.

10. A democratic character structure.   Self-actualizers are tolerant and accepting and display no racial, religious, or social prejudice. They are willing to listen to and learn from anyone who is able to teach them something. They do not act superior or condescending.

11. Creativeness.   The self-actualizing people Maslow studied were highly creative, although they were not all artists or writers. They exhibited inventiveness and originality in their work and in most other facets of their life. Self-actualizers are flexible, spontaneous, and willing to make mistakes. They are open and humble, in the way children are before society teaches them to be afraid of making mistakes or doing something silly.

12. Resistance to enculturation.   Self-actualizers are autonomous, independent, and self-sufficient. They feel free to resist social and cultural pressures to think and behave in certain ways. They do not openly rebel against cultural norms or flout social codes, but they are governed by their own nature rather than that of their culture.

This is an amazing set of attributes. According to Maslow, self-actualizers seem almost perfect. He found, however, that they do have imperfections and flaws. They can be rude, even ruthless, and have moments of doubt, shame, conflict, and tension. Nevertheless, these incidents are rare and are less frequent and intense than in the average person.

The Failure to Become Self-Actualizing

If the self-actualization need is innate and therefore does not have to be learned, then why isn't everyone self-actualizing? Why has less than 1 percent of the population reached this state of being? One reason is that the higher the need in the hierarchy, the weaker it is. As the highest need, self-actualization is the least potent. Because it is not strong to begin with, it is easily interfered with or inhibited. For example, a hostile or rejecting emotional environment may make it difficult for a person to satisfy love and esteem needs, and so the self-actualization need may not emerge. At a lower level, poor economic conditions can make it difficult to satisfy the physiological and safety needs. In general, according to Maslow, the lower needs must be satisfied before the need for self-actualization becomes important.

Inadequate education and faulty child-rearing practices can also thwart self-actualization. Maslow cited contemporary sex-role training in which boys are taught to be "manly," to inhibit such qualities as tenderness and sentimentality. Thus, one aspect of their nature is not allowed to develop.

If children are overly protected and not permitted to display new behaviors, explore new ideas, or practice new skills, then they are likely to be inhibited as adults, stifled from growing and expressing themselves in activities that are vital to self-actualization. The opposite behavior, excessive parental permissiveness, can also be harmful. Maslow warned that too much freedom in childhood leads to anxiety and insecurity, thwarting the safety needs; this prevents further growth. A balance of permissiveness and regulation is required.

Maslow emphasized that sufficient love in childhood is a prerequisite for self-actualization. He also noted the importance of satisfying the physiological and safety needs within the first two years of life. If children are made to feel secure and confident in these early years, they will tend to remain so as adults. This position is similar to Erikson's emphasis on the importance of developing trust in early childhood and to Horney's ideas on the childhood need for security. Without adequate parental love, security, and esteem in childhood, it is difficult for the adult self to achieve self-actualization.

Jonah complex The fear that maximizing our potential will lead to a situation with which we will be unable to cope.

Another reason for the failure to self-actualize is what Maslow labeled the **Jonah complex**. This refers to our fears and doubts about our abilities. We are simultaneously afraid of and thrilled by our highest possibilities, but all too often the fear takes precedence.

Self-actualization also requires courage. Even when the lower needs have been satisfied, we cannot sit back and wait passively to be swept along some royal road to self-actualization and fulfillment. The process takes effort, discipline, and self-control. It may seem easier and safer to accept life as it is rather than to deliberately seek new challenges. Self-actualizers are constantly testing and challenging themselves. They abandon secure routines and give up familiar behaviors and attitudes.

Maslow's Image of Human Nature

Maslow's view of personality is a humanistic and optimistic one. His focus is on psychological health rather than illness, on growth rather than stagnation, and on human virtues and potentials rather than weaknesses and limitations. He had a strong sense of confidence, even trust, in our ability to shape our lives and our society.

Maslow also believed in free will. In his view, all of us are capable of choosing how best to satisfy our needs and actualize our potential. We can either create an actualizing self or hold back from that supreme achievement. Thus, we are responsible for the level of personality development we reach.

Although the needs in Maslow's hierarchy are innate, the behaviors by which we satisfy them are learned. Therefore, personality is determined by the interaction of nature and nurture, heredity and environment, personal and situational variables.

It is not explicit in his writings, but Maslow appeared to favor the uniqueness of the human personality. Our motivations and needs are universal, but the ways in which the needs are satisfied vary from person to person because these behaviors are learned. Although self-actualizing people share certain qualities, they are not alike in their behavior.

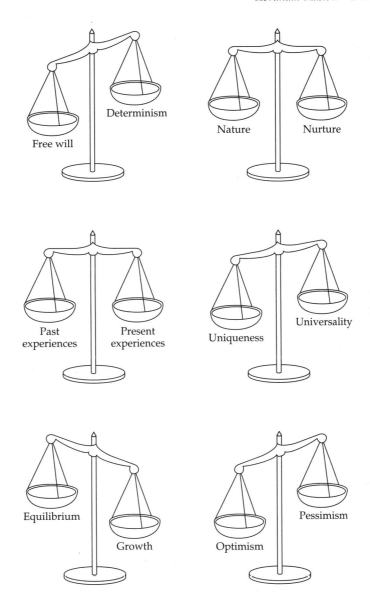

Maslow

Image of Human Nature.

Maslow recognized the importance of early childhood experiences in fostering or hampering later development, but he did not believe that we are victims of these experiences. According to Maslow, we have more potential than we realize to manage our lives and our society, and we would be happier and more productive if we would learn to do so. The notion of self-actualization as the ultimate and necessary goal in life reflects Maslow's belief that, given the proper conditions, we are capable of reaching a high level of functioning.

He argued that our innate nature is basically good, decent, and kind, but he did not deny the existence of evil. He believed that some people were evil beyond reclamation and wrote in his journal that "nothing will work ultimately [with them] but shooting" (Maslow, 1979, p. 631). Maslow thought that wickedness is not an inherent part of human nature but the result of an inappropriate environment. Maslow's compassion for humanity is clear in his writings, and his optimism is expressed in the belief that each of us can fulfill our vast human potential.

Assessment in Maslow's Theory

Maslow did not begin his work on self-actualization as a formal program of personality assessment and research. Rather, he started it out of curiosity about two people who impressed him—the anthropologist Ruth Benedict and the Gestalt psychologist Max Wertheimer. Maslow admired them, and he wanted to understand what made them so different from other people. He observed them and made notes in his journal, and concluded that they shared certain personal qualities that set them apart from the average individual.

Maslow decided to see if these characteristics could be found in other people. His first subjects were college students, but he found only 1 out of 3,000 whom he considered self-actualizing. He suggested that the characteristics involved in self-actualization—those qualities he had identified in Benedict and Wertheimer—were not allowed to develop in young people, so he turned to middle-aged and older people to continue his study. Even with

Table 11.2	**Sample items from the Personal Orientation Inventory.** **(Respondents select the item in each pair that is more descriptive of them.)**
	I do what others expect of me. I feel free to not do what others expect of me.
	I must justify my actions in the pursuit of my own interests. I need not justify my actions in the pursuit of my own interests.
	I live by the rules and standards of society. I do not always need to live by the rules and standards of society.
	Reasons are needed to justify my feelings. Reasons are not needed to justify my feelings.
	I only feel free to express warm feelings to my friends. I feel free to express both warm and hostile feelings to my friends.
	I will continue to grow only by setting my sights on a high-level, socially approved goal. I will continue to grow best by being myself.
	People should always control their anger. People should express honestly felt anger.

SOURCE: From "An Inventory for the Measurement of Self-Actualization" by E. L. Shostrom, 1964, *Educational and Psychological Measurement, 24,* pp. 207–218.

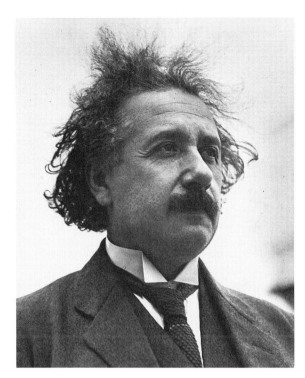 

Among the self-actualizers Maslow studied by analyzing biographies and other written records were the noted physicist Albert Einstein, and Harriet Tubman, a leader of the anti-slavery movement at the time of the American Civil War.

older subjects, however, Maslow found fewer than 1 percent of the population capable of meeting his criteria for self-actualization.

The sample of self-actualizers consisted of several dozen persons Maslow labeled sure or probable cases, partial cases, or potential cases. They included Maslow's contemporaries as well as outstanding historical figures such as Thomas Jefferson, Albert Einstein, George Washington Carver, Harriet Tubman, and Eleanor Roosevelt. To assess their personalities, Maslow used any technique that seemed appropriate to him. For the historical figures, he worked with biographical material, analyzing written records for similarities in personal characteristics. For the living subjects, he relied on interviews, free association, and projective tests. He found that many subjects became self-conscious when questioned. As a result, it became necessary to study them indirectly, but he did not explain how this was carried out.

Although Maslow did not develop any assessment techniques, the psychologist Everett Shostrom constructed a self-report questionnaire, the Personal Orientation Inventory (POI), to measure self-actualization (Shostrom, 1964, 1974). (Sample items from the POI are shown in Table 11.2.) The test consists of 150 pairs of statements; subjects indicate which of each pair is more applicable to them. The POI is scored for two major scales and ten subscales. The major scales are time competence, which measures the degree to which a person lives in the present, and inner directedness, which assesses how much a person depends on himself or herself rather than on others for judgments and values.

Research in Maslow's Theory

Maslow did not use such traditional research techniques as case studies or the experimental and correlational methods. Critics suggest that the way Maslow studied his self-actualizing subjects could not be described as rigorous and controlled research. Maslow agreed; he knew that his investigations failed to comply with the requirements of scientific research. "By ordinary standards of laboratory research," he wrote, "this simply was not research at all" (Maslow, 1971, p. 42). He also noted that, because the problem could not have been studied by accepted scientific procedures, the alternative was not to study it or to wait until appropriate techniques were developed. Maslow was too impatient for that, too committed to his conviction that he could help humanity.

Five years before his death, Maslow wrote that he did not have enough time to perform careful experiments. "They take too long in view of the years I have left and the extent of what I want to do." Although he referred to his work as "pilot studies," he was convinced that the results were valid and would be confirmed by others. He also suggested that he needed fewer data than other psychologists "to come to correct conclusions" (Maslow, 1979, p. 694).

Many psychologists have used the Personal Orientation Inventory to conduct correlational research, in which POI scores are correlated with other measures of behavior and personality. Scores indicating higher self-actualization have been shown to be positively related to emotional health, creativity, well-being following therapy, academic achievement, autonomy, and racial tolerance (Bordages, 1989; Braun & Asta, 1968; Grossack, Armstrong, & Lussieu, 1966; LeMay & Damm, 1968; Mattocks & Jew, 1974; McClain, 1970; Shostrom, 1964; Shostrom & Knapp, 1966; Stewart, 1968; Tokar & Swanson, 1991). Other studies report negative correlations between high self-actualization scores on the POI and alcoholism, institutionalization for mental disturbances, neuroticism, depression, and hypochondriasis (Eysenck & Eysenck, 1963; Fox, Knapp, & Michael, 1968; Knapp, 1965; Shostrom & Knapp, 1966; Zaccaria & Weir, 1967). These results are in the expected directions, based on Maslow's description of the characteristics of self-actualizers.

Research on 343 women, ages 19 to 55, confirmed Maslow's view that self-actualization, as measured by the POI, occurs gradually over time (Hyman, 1988).

It is important to remember that this research involves correlational studies and that there is no valid independent measure of self-actualization with which to correlate the POI scores. It does not necessarily follow that the

POI is actually measuring self-actualization, even though it correlates well with the variables believed to be associated with self-actualization.

As predicted, a study of men and women college students found that satisfaction of the needs for safety, belongingness, and esteem was negatively related to neuroticism and depression (Williams & Page, 1989). This research, using a test designed to measure those three needs, also indicated that esteem needs were stronger than belongingness needs. The subjects exhibited much less concern with safety needs, as would be expected among people of college age.

A self-report test called the Peak Scale was developed to assess the tendency to have peak experiences, which Maslow noted as a characteristic of self-actualizers (Mathes, Zevon, Roter, & Joerger, 1982). Research to measure this tendency supports Maslow's view. Subjects who scored high on the Peak Scale demonstrated, on other measures, transcendental or mystical experiences and periods of intense happiness. High scorers reported guiding their lives in terms of Maslow's Being values, ideas of beauty, truth, and justice. In other studies, people who reported peak experiences tended to show more self-awareness, a higher tolerance for ambiguity, and a greater social consciousness than those who did not have peak experiences (Thomas & Cooper, 1980; Wuthnow, 1978).

A study of college students found that 79 percent believed they had had peak experiences, but only 20 percent had ever told anyone about them. The most common reasons for not revealing the peak experiences were that (1) subjects felt peak experiences were too personal to share, (2) subjects thought other people would disparage them or fail to appreciate the value of the experiences, and (3) subjects felt unable to describe the experiences adequately (Davis, Lockwood, & Wright, 1991).

Research on self-esteem supports Maslow's position that people high in self-esteem possess a greater sense of self-worth, self-confidence, and adequacy and are more competent and productive than people low in self-esteem. People high in self-esteem seem to function better in many situations. In a study of college students seeking jobs, those with high self-esteem received more job offers and were rated more favorably by recruiters than were students with low self-esteem (Ellis & Taylor, 1983). Another study found that people with high self-esteem coped more effectively with the trauma of losing their jobs than did those with low self-esteem (Shamir, 1986).

Additional research on Maslow's theory has been conducted by industrial/organizational psychologists, especially on the concept of self-actualization. Some of this research supported Maslow's views, thus prompting him to conclude that the application and testing of his ideas required a real-life situation, such as employees on the job, rather than the artificial setting of the psychology laboratory. It was found that high-level executives were more concerned with esteem and self-actualization needs than were low-level executives (Porter, 1961, 1963). The findings suggest that high-level executives have satisfied their lower needs, thus allowing for the emergence of the higher needs. Longitudinal research has not verified this conclusion. One study showed that higher needs did not emerge once lower needs were satisfied (Hall & Nougaim, 1968).

Despite the popularity in the business community of Maslow's concept of self-actualization as a motivating force, the idea has received little research support. One psychologist examined the available evidence and concluded that the theory has a low degree of scientific validity when applied to the world of work (Miner, 1984).

An elaborate test of Maslow's needs hierarchy, using a sample representative of the general population, supported the proposed order of the five needs (Graham & Balloun, 1973). It also demonstrated that the level of concern expressed about each need increased from lowest to highest. The physiological needs, presumably well satisfied in the subjects, were of little concern to them. The self-actualization need was of the greatest interest, presumably because it was not so well satisfied.

A Final Commentary

Perhaps partly because of the optimism and compassion Maslow expressed, his theory became popular in the 1960s and 1970s. As a pioneer of humanistic psychology, Maslow attracted admirers and disciples among students and professionals who had become disenchanted with the behavioristic and psychoanalytic approaches to personality and to psychology.

There has been considerable criticism of Maslow's theory (see, for example, Daniels, 1988; Neher, 1991; Shaw & Colimore, 1988). The major targets of this criticism are his research method and the theory's supporting data. The sample from which the data were derived—fewer than half of whom were interviewed—is considered too small for generalization to the population at large. The ways Maslow amassed information about his self-actualizing subjects are inconsistent and sometimes vague. He did not describe how he interpreted test results or analyzed biographical material, nor did he indicate how free associations and interview responses led him to conclude that his subjects were self-actualizing. However, as we have noted in our discussions of other theorists, a weakness in scientific methodology is not unique to Maslow's work.

Maslow selected as subjects people he admired, according to his criteria for positive evidence of self-actualization. These criteria were not specified at the time, and he later admitted that self-actualization is "a difficult syndrome to describe accurately" (Maslow, 1970b, p. 150). His descriptions of the characteristics of self-actualizers derive from clinical interpretations of the data and may have been influenced by his personal moral values. Therefore, the descriptions may reflect Maslow's ideal of the worthy and emotionally healthy individual.

Other criticisms have been directed at Maslow's definitions of various concepts, such as metaneeds, metapathology, peak experiences, and self-actualization. His use of these terms is sometimes inconsistent and ambiguous. Critics also ask on what basis self-actualization is presumed to be innate. Why could it not be learned behavior, the result of some unique combination of childhood experiences?

Maslow's defense was that although his theory was not widely supported by laboratory research, it was successful in social, clinical, and personal terms. "It has fitted very well with the personal experience of most people, and has often given them a structured theory that has helped them to make better sense of their inner lives" (Maslow, 1970b, p. xii).

Few theories have had such a broad impact beyond the discipline of psychology. Teachers and counselors, business and government leaders, health care professionals, and people trying to cope with everyday life have all found Maslow's views compatible with their own values and needs, and useful in resolving common problems. A magazine article on the most influential people of the mid-20th century noted that Maslow had "done more to change our view of human nature and human possibilities than has any other American psychologist of the past 50 years" (Leonard, 1983, p. 326). Maslow issued a call to make psychology responsive to the problems of modern society; he argued that the survival of civilization depends on our ability to develop our full potential—to become, in his words, self-actualizing.

Summary

Abraham Maslow argued that psychologists must study the most creative and emotionally healthy persons to determine the heights of human potential. Each person is born with instinctive needs that lead to growth, development, and actualization. The hierarchy of needs includes physiological needs (for food, water, air, sleep, and sex) and the needs for safety, belongingness and love, esteem, and self-actualization. The lower needs must be satisfied before the higher needs emerge. The lower the need, the greater its strength. Lower needs are called deficit or deficiency needs because failure to satisfy them produces a deficit in the body. Higher needs (growth or being needs) are less necessary for survival but enhance physical and emotional well-being.

Safety needs (for security, stability, order, and freedom from fear and anxiety) are most important in infants and neurotic adults. Belongingness and love needs can be satisfied through association with a group or affectionate relations with one person or with people in general. Esteem needs include self-esteem and esteem from others. Self-actualization involves the realization of one's potential and requires a realistic knowledge of one's strengths and weaknesses. The needs to know and to understand form a hierarchy of cognitive needs that emerges in late infancy and early childhood.

Motivation in self-actualizers (called metamotivation) serves not to make up for deficits or to reduce tension but to enrich life and increase tension.

Metaneeds are states of growth toward which self-actualizers move. Frustration of metaneeds produces metapathology, a formless illness for which no specific cause can be identified. Self-actualizers constitute less than 1 percent of the population. They show the following characteristics: an efficient perception of reality; an acceptance of themselves, others, and nature; a spontaneity, simplicity, and naturalness; a focus on problems rather than on the self, in which metaneeds are satisfied through commitment to work; a need for privacy and independence; a freshness of appreciation; peak experiences; social interest; intense interpersonal relationships; creativeness; a democratic character structure; and a resistance to enculturation.

Not everyone is self-actualizing because self-actualization is the weakest need in the hierarchy and is easily interfered with. Too much freedom or lack of security in childhood inhibits self-actualization. Also, some people fear their own highest possibilities. Self-actualization requires courage, discipline, and hard work.

Maslow's image of human nature is optimistic, emphasizing free will, conscious choice, uniqueness, the ability to overcome childhood experiences, and innate goodness. Personality is influenced both by heredity and by environment. Our ultimate goal is self-actualization.

Maslow used interviews, free association, projective techniques, and biographical material to assess personality. The Personal Orientation Inventory is a self-report test to measure self-actualization. Some research supports the characteristics of self-actualizers, the relationship between self-esteem and competence, the order of the needs in the hierarchy, and the greater concern for higher than lower needs.

Maslow has been criticized for using too small a sample as the basis for his theory and for not making explicit his criteria for selecting self-actualizing subjects. His descriptions of self-actualizers may have been influenced by his own moral values. In addition, his research methods are scientifically weak, and definitions of key terms are inconsistent and ambiguous.

Critical Thinking Review

1. What criticisms did the humanistic psychologists make of behaviorism and psychoanalysis?

2. In what way can Maslow's childhood be considered an example of Adler's theory of personality?

3. Describe the hierarchy of needs Maslow proposed. How can each need be satisfied?

4. What are the differences between the higher needs and the lower needs?

5. At what age do we develop the needs to know and to understand? Which of these needs is the stronger?

6. What is the role of situational variables in determining the needs in the hierarchy?

7. Define metaneeds and metapathology.

8. Discuss the motivation and the characteristics of self-actualizing people.

9. What are peak experiences? Are they necessary for self-actualization?

10. List four factors that may explain why so few people satisfy the need for self-actualization.

11. How does Maslow's image of human nature differ from Freud's?

12. What does correlational research reveal about the relationship between self-actualization and certain personality characteristics?

Suggested Reading

Hall, M. H. (1968, July). A conversation with Abraham H. Maslow. *Psychology Today,* pp. 35–37, 54–57. An interview with Maslow about the scope of his work.

Hoffman, E. (1988). *The right to be human: A biography of Abraham Maslow.* Los Angeles: Tarcher. A biography based on published and unpublished material describing Maslow's difficult childhood and tracing his career from his early work with primates to his involvement with the human potential movement.

Maslow, A. H. (1968). *Toward a psychology of being* (2nd ed.). New York: Van Nostrand Reinhold. States Maslow's view that humans can be loving, noble, and creative and are capable of pursuing the highest values and aspirations.

Maslow, A. H. (1970). *Motivation and personality* (2nd ed.). New York: Harper & Row. Presents Maslow's theory of motivation and personality, emphasizing psychological health and self-actualization. A third edition of this book (Harper & Row, 1987), revised and edited by Robert Frager and James

Fadiman, includes material on Maslow's life, the historical significance of his work, and applications of self-actualization to management, medicine, and education.

Mittelman, W. (1991). Maslow's study of self-actualization: A reinterpretation. *Journal of Humanistic Psychology, 31*(1), 114–135. Suggests that Maslow's so-called self-actualizing subjects were distinguished not by some ability to actualize human potentialities but by their degree of openness. Defines *openness* as being highly receptive and responsive to information from one's own organism and from the environment, and not repressing or ignoring difficulties and problems.

Neher, A. (1991). Maslow's theory of motivation: A critique. *Journal of Humanistic Psychology, 31*(3), 89–112. Evaluates the major components of Maslow's theory—in light of internal consistency, related theories, and empirical research—and suggests significant modifications.

TWELVE

Carl Rogers

The Life of Rogers (1902–1987)
The Importance of the Self
Actualization: The Basic Human Tendency
The Experiential World
The Development of the Self in Childhood
    Positive Regard
    Conditions of Worth
    Anxiety
Characteristics of Fully Functioning Persons
Rogers's Image of Human Nature

Assessment in Rogers's Theory
    Person-Centered Therapy
    Encounter Groups
    Psychological Tests
Research in Rogers's Theory
A Final Commentary
Summary
Critical Thinking Review
Suggested Reading

The organism has one basic tendency and striving—to actualize, maintain, and enhance the experiencing organism.

—Carl Rogers

person-centered therapy Rogers's approach to therapy in which the person or client (not "patient") is assumed to be responsible for changing his or her personality.

Carl Rogers originated a popular approach to psychotherapy known initially as nondirective or client-centered therapy and more recently as **person-centered therapy**. This form of psychotherapy has generated an enormous amount of research and has found wide application in the treatment of emotional disturbances. Rogers's personality theory, like Maslow's, is rooted in the principles of humanistic psychology, which Rogers sought to apply to the patient-therapist relationship. It was developed not from experimental laboratory research but from his experiences in working with clients. Thus, his formulations on the structure and dynamics of personality are linked to his therapeutic approach.

Rogers's view of the therapeutic situation tells us much about his view of human nature. Consider the name *person-centered therapy*. It suggests that we have the ability to change and improve our personality. The person, not the therapist, directs such change; the therapist acts to assist it.

Rogers believed that we are rational beings ruled by a conscious perception of our selves and our experiential world. There is little of the Freudian position in Rogers's theory. Rogers did not ascribe a dominant influence to unconscious forces beyond our control. He also rejected the notion that past events exert a controlling influence on present behavior. Although he recognized that childhood experiences can affect the way we perceive ourselves and our environment, Rogers insisted that present feelings and emotions are of greater importance to the personality.

Because of this emphasis on the conscious and the present, Rogers believed that personality can only be understood from the person's own viewpoint, based on his or her subjective experiences. Thus, Rogers deals with reality as it is consciously perceived by each of us, and he noted that this perception may not always coincide with objective reality.

Rogers believed that we have one innate, overriding motivation—an inborn tendency to actualize, to develop our abilities and potential, from the strictly biological to the most sophisticated psychological aspects of our being. Our ultimate goal is the actualization of the self, to become what Rogers called a fully functioning person.

His approach to therapy and theory, and the optimistic and humanistic picture he painted, received enthusiastic acceptance in psychology, education, and family-life research.

The Life of Rogers (1902–1987)

The fourth child in a family of six, Carl Rogers was born in 1902 in Oak Park, Illinois, a suburb of Chicago. His parents held fundamentalist religious views and emphasized moral behavior, the suppression of any display of emotion, and the virtue of hard work. Their strict religious teachings gripped Rogers in a vise, as he described it, throughout his childhood and adolescence. These beliefs forced him to live by someone else's view of the world rather than his own and soon became a target for revolt.

His parents promoted their influence in subtle and loving ways, as Rogers later did in his nondirective approach to counseling. It was understood by all the children that they "did not dance, play cards, attend movies, smoke, drink, or show any sexual interest" (Rogers, 1967, p. 344). Rogers had little social life outside his family. He believed that his parents showed favoritism toward an older brother, and, as a result, there was considerable competitiveness as well as companionship between the brothers.

Rogers described himself as solitary, dreamy, and often lost in fantasy. He read incessantly, reading any book he could find—even the dictionary and the encyclopedia. His solitude eventually led him to rely on his own experience, his personal view of the world; this characteristic remained with him throughout his life and formed the foundation of his personality theory. In later years he realized how strongly his loneliness had influenced his personality and his work.

> As I look back, I realize that my interest in interviewing and in therapy certainly grew out of my early loneliness. Here was a socially approved way of getting really close to individuals and thus filling some of the hunger I had undoubtedly felt. [Rogers, 1980, p. 34]

When Rogers was 12, the family moved to a farm 30 miles from Chicago, an experience that awakened his interest in science. First, he became fascinated by a species of moth he discovered in the woods. He read about them and observed them, captured and bred them, and raised them over many months. Second, he became interested in methods of farming, which his father insisted on pursuing in a modern and scientific way. Rogers read books about farming and agricultural experiments and came to appreciate the scientific method, with its use of control groups, the isolation of a single variable for study, and the statistical analysis of data. It was an unusual understanding for a 15-year-old.

While Rogers was absorbing, intellectually, the scientific method, his emotional life was in turmoil, the nature of which he never fully explained. "My fantasies during this period were definitely bizarre," he wrote, "and probably would be classified as schizoid by a diagnostician, but fortunately I never came in contact with a psychologist" (Rogers, 1980, p. 30).

He chose to study agriculture at the University of Wisconsin, the college his parents, two older brothers, and a sister had attended. After his sophomore year, his goal changed. He abandoned scientific agriculture to prepare for the ministry.

In his junior year at Wisconsin, in 1922, Rogers was selected to attend an international Christian student conference in Beijing, China. During his six months of travel he wrote to his parents of his changing philosophy and goals and of the alteration of his religious views from fundamentalist to liberal. Freeing himself of his parents' way of thinking grieved them, but the shift gave Rogers an emotional and intellectual independence. He realized that he could "think my own thoughts, come to my own conclusions, and take the stands I believed in" (Rogers, 1967, p. 351). This liberation, and the confidence and direction it provided, reinforced Rogers's opinion that human beings must rely solely on their own experiences and knowledge—a belief that became the core of his approach to personality.

In 1924, Rogers graduated from the University of Wisconsin, married a childhood friend, and enrolled at the Union Theological Seminary in New York. After two years he transferred to Teachers College of Columbia University to study clinical and educational psychology. He received his Ph.D. in 1931 and joined the staff of the Child Study Department of the Society for the Prevention of Cruelty to Children in Rochester, New York. He spent most of his time diagnosing and treating delinquent and underprivileged children.

In 1940 he moved from a clinical to an academic setting with an appointment as professor of psychology at Ohio State University. There, primarily in his dealings with graduate students, Rogers began to formulate his views on ways of counseling the emotionally disturbed. He also worked to bring clinical psychology into the mainstream of contemporary psychological thought. He spent the years 1945 to 1957 at the University of Chicago, teaching and developing the Counseling Center, and taught at the University of Wisconsin from 1957 to 1963. During these years he published many articles and books that brought his personality theory and method of person-centered therapy to a wide audience.

Rogers's clinical experience while in academia was mostly with college students in the counseling centers at Ohio State and Chicago. Thus, the kind of person he treated during that time—young, intelligent, highly verbal, and facing adjustment problems rather than severe emotional disorders—was vastly different from the kind of person treated by the Freudians and by clinical psychologists in private practice.

In 1964, Rogers became a resident fellow at the Western Behavioral Sciences Institute in California, and continued his attempts to apply his person-centered philosophy to the reduction of international tensions by breaking down barriers between such groups as Protestants and Catholics in Northern Ireland, and Jews and Arabs in the Middle East. He served as president of the American Psychological Association in 1946 and received that organization's Distinguished Scientific Contribution Award and Distinguished Professional Contribution Award.

The Importance of the Self

Rogers came to recognize the importance of an autonomous self as a factor in his own development. Early in his career, the idea of the role of the self in personality was suggested and reinforced by the results of his research. In the 1930s he developed a method for determining whether a child's behavior was healthy and constructive or unhealthy and destructive. He investigated the child's background and had the child rated on factors that he believed were capable of influencing behavior. These factors included the family environment, health, intellectual development, economic circumstances, cultural influences, social interactions, and educational level. All of these are external or environmental influences. Rogers also investigated a potential internal influence: the child's self-understanding or self-insight, which Rogers described as an acceptance of self and of reality, and a responsibility for the self.

A decade later, William Kell, one of Rogers's students, used this approach in an attempt to predict the behavior of delinquent children. Rogers expected that family environment and social interactions would correlate most strongly with delinquent behavior, but he was wrong. The factor that most accurately predicted later behavior was self-insight.

Surprised to learn that family environment did not relate highly to later delinquent behavior, Rogers wrote, "At that time I was simply not prepared to accept this finding, and the study was put on the shelf" (Rogers, 1987, p. 119). (As we noted in Chapter 1, sometimes scientists reject data that do not support their views and expectations.) Two years later the study was replicated with different subjects by Helen McNeil, who obtained similar results: self-insight was the single most important predictor of later behavior.

This time, faced with an accumulation of data, Rogers accepted the findings and came to appreciate their significance. If attitudes toward the self were more important in predicting behavior than the external factors widely thought to influence us in childhood, then counselors and social workers were emphasizing the wrong things in their efforts to deal with delinquents. They traditionally focused on changing external factors, such as a poor family environment, by removing children from their homes and placing them in foster homes or reform schools. Instead, they should have been trying to modify the children's self-insight.

That realization was important to Rogers personally:

> This experience helped me decide to focus my career on the development of a psychotherapy that would bring about greater awareness of self-understanding, self-direction, and personal responsibility, rather than focusing on changes in the social environment. It led me to place greater emphasis on the study of the self and how it changes. [Rogers, 1987, p. 119]

Thus, the self became the core of Rogers's theory of personality.

Actualization: The Basic Human Tendency

Rogers believed that we are motivated by a tendency to actualize, maintain, and enhance the self. This innate tendency is our sole fundamental human need, and it encompasses all physiological and psychological needs. By attending to basic physiological needs, such as the needs for food and water, and by defending the organism against attack, the actualization tendency serves to maintain the organism, providing for sustenance and for survival.

The actualization tendency also aids and supports human growth by providing for the differentiation of the physical organs and the development of physiological functioning. It is responsible for maturation, the genetically determined development of the body's parts and processes, ranging from the growth of the fetus to the appearance of the secondary sex characteristics at puberty.

All these changes, programmed in our genetic makeup, are brought to fruition by the actualization tendency. Even though such changes are genetically determined, our progress toward full development is neither automatic nor effortless. Rogers described the process as involving struggle and pain. For example, when children take their first steps, they may fall and be hurt. It would be less painful to remain in the crawling stage, but children persist. They may fall again and cry, but they persevere despite the pain because the tendency to actualize is stronger than any urge to regress that may be brought on by the difficulties of growth.

organismic valuing process The process by which we judge experiences in terms of their value for fostering or hindering our actualization and growth.

Rogers believed that throughout life we operate in accordance with what he called the **organismic valuing process**. We evaluate all life experiences by how well they serve the actualization tendency. Those experiences that we perceive to be promoting actualization are good and desirable, and we assign them a positive value. Experiences perceived as hindering actualization are seen as undesirable and have a negative value. These perceptions influence our behavior because we tend to avoid undesirable experiences and seek to repeat desirable experiences.

The Experiential World

Rogers was concerned with the environment or situation in which we operate, the frame of reference or context that influences us. We are exposed to countless sources of stimulation every day, some trivial and some important, some threatening and some rewarding. Rogers wanted to know how we perceive and react to this multifaceted environment.

He answered the question by saying that the reality of our environment is how each of us perceives it, and our perception may not always coincide with objective reality. We may see and respond to some experiences far differently from the way someone else does. For example, you may judge the behavior of another college student in a dramatically different way than does your 70-year-old grandparent. Also, our perceptions change with time and circumstances; your own perception of acceptable college behavior will be different by the time you are 70.

The notion that perception is subjective is an old one and is not unique to Rogers. In his view, the important point is that our experiential world, our view of reality, is private and can only be known in any complete sense to the individual.

As the actualization tendency in infancy leads us to grow and develop, our experiential world broadens. Infants are exposed to more and more sources of stimulation, and they behave in reference to these stimuli as they are perceived. These events combine to make up an experiential field, a personal view of the world. Therefore, our experiences are the only basis for our judgments and behaviors. "Experience is, for me," Rogers wrote, "the highest authority. The touchstone of validity is my own experience" (Rogers, 1961, p. 23). Higher levels of development sharpen our experiential world and lead to the formation of the self.

The Development of the Self in Childhood

As infants gradually develop a more complex experiential field, stemming from ever wider social encounters, one part of their experience becomes differentiated from the rest. This new and separate part, defined by the words *I, me,* and *myself,* is the self or self-concept. Its formation involves distinguishing what is directly and immediately a part of oneself from the people, objects, and events that are external to oneself. The self-concept is our image of what we are, should be, and would like to be.

Rogers argued that, ideally, the self is a consistent pattern, an organized whole. All possible aspects of the self strive toward consistency. For example, people who deny having aggressive feelings dare not express any need for aggression—at least not in any obvious and direct manner. To do so would be to admit behavior that is inconsistent with a self-concept that includes a lack of aggressiveness.

Positive Regard

positive regard
Acceptance, love, and approval from others.

As the self emerges, infants develop a need for what Rogers called **positive regard**. This need is probably learned, although Rogers believed the source was not important. The need for positive regard is universal and persistent. Positive regard includes acceptance, love, and approval from other people, notably from the mother during infancy. Infants find it satisfying to receive positive regard and frustrating not to receive it or to have it withdrawn. Because positive regard is crucial to human development, infant behavior is guided by the amount of affection and love received.

If the mother does not bestow positive regard, then the infant's innate tendency toward actualization and the enhancement of the self will be hampered. Infants perceive parental disapproval of their behavior as disapproval of their newly developing self-concept. If this occurs frequently, infants will cease to strive for actualization and will be driven instead to secure positive regard.

unconditional positive regard
Approval granted regardless of a person's behavior. In person-centered therapy, the therapist offers unconditional positive regard.

Ideally, infants will receive sufficient acceptance, love, and approval overall (even though specific behaviors may bring punishment). This condition, called **unconditional positive regard**, implies that the mother's love for the child is not conditional on behavior but is granted freely and fully.

An important aspect of the need for positive regard is its reciprocal nature. When people perceive themselves to be satisfying someone else's need for positive regard, they will experience satisfaction of that need themselves. Therefore, it is rewarding to satisfy someone else's need for positive regard.

positive self-regard
The condition under which we grant ourselves acceptance and approval.

Because of the importance of satisfying the need for positive regard, particularly in infancy, we become sensitive to the attitudes and behaviors of other people. By interpreting the feedback or the reaction we receive from others (either approval or disapproval), we may alter or refine our self-concept. As part of the self-concept, we internalize the attitudes of others. Gradually, positive regard comes more from within ourselves than from other people—a condition Rogers called **positive self-regard**. It becomes as strong as our need for positive regard from others and may be satisfied in the same way. For example, infants who are rewarded by their mothers with affection, approval, and love when they are cheerful come to generate positive self-regard whenever they behave in a cheerful manner. Thus, they begin to reward themselves.

Conditions of Worth

Conditions of worth evolve from this developmental sequence from positive regard to positive self-regard. This is Rogers's version of the Freudian superego, and it derives from conditional positive regard. We noted that unconditional positive regard involves love and acceptance of the infant without conditions, independent of behavior; conditional positive regard is the opposite.

Ideally, a parent provides unconditional positive regard.

conditions of worth
A belief that we are worthy of approval and acceptance only when we express desirable behaviors and attitudes and refrain from expressing behaviors and attitudes that bring disapproval from others. This is similar to Freud's concept of the **superego.**

Parents do not usually react to everything their infant does with positive regard. Some behaviors annoy, frighten, or bore the parents, and for those behaviors they do not always supply affection or approval. Infants learn, then, that parental affection and approval depends on certain behaviors, and they come to see that sometimes they are prized, and sometimes they are not.

For example, if a parent expresses annoyance every time the infant drops an object out of the crib, that infant eventually learns to disapprove of itself for behaving in that way. External standards of judgment become personalized, and infants, in a sense, punish themselves as their parents did. Infants develop self-regard only in those situations that bring parental approval, and the self-concept comes to function as a parental surrogate. Thus, infants develop conditions of worth; they believe they are worthy only under certain conditions. Having internalized their parents' norms and standards in their positive self-regard, they view themselves as worthy or unworthy, good or bad, according to the terms defined by the parents.

They learn to avoid certain behaviors and attitudes, regardless of how satisfying they may otherwise be, and therefore they no longer function freely. Because they must evaluate their behaviors so carefully and refrain from certain actions, these infants are prevented from fully developing or actualizing the self. Therefore, they inhibit their own development by living within the confines of their conditions of worth.

Anxiety

Not only do we learn to inhibit certain behaviors, but we may also come to deny or distort unacceptable perceptions in our experiential world. As a result of denying ourselves an accurate perception of certain experiences, we risk becoming estranged from the self. We evaluate experiences and accept or reject them not in terms of how they contribute to the actualization tendency through the organismic valuing process, but rather in terms of whether they bring positive regard from others. Thus, what Rogers called **incongruence** develops between the self-concept and aspects of our experiential world, our environment as we perceive it.

incongruence A discrepancy between a person's self-concept and aspects of his or her experience.

Those experiences that are incongruent with our self-concept are a source of threat and are manifested as a form of anxiety. For example, if our self-concept includes the belief that we love all humanity, we will develop anxiety if we ever meet someone toward whom we feel hatred. Hating is incongruent with our image of ourselves as loving persons. To maintain our self-concept, then, we must deny the hatred. Thus, we defend against the anxiety that accompanies the threat by denying or closing off a portion of our experiential field. This results in a rigidity of our perceptions.

Our level of psychological adjustment and health is a function of the congruence or compatibility of our self-concept with our experiences. Psychologically healthy people are able to perceive themselves, other people, and the events in their environment objectively; that is, much as they really are. These people are freely open to all experience because nothing threatens their self-concept. No experience needs to be defended against by denial or distortion because they received unconditional positive regard in childhood and did not have to learn any conditions of worth. They are able to use all experience, to develop all facets of the self, and to fulfill the actualization tendency. They proceed toward the goal of becoming, in Rogers's words, fully functioning persons.

Characteristics of Fully Functioning Persons

The fully functioning person is the desired result of psychological development and social evolution. Rogers described several characteristics of fully functioning or self-actualizing persons (Rogers, 1961).

1. *Fully functioning persons exhibit an awareness of all experience.* No experience is distorted or denied; all of it filters through to the self. There is no defensiveness because there is nothing to defend against—there is nothing to threaten the self-concept. These people are open to positive feelings, such as courage and tenderness, and to negative feelings, such as fear and pain. They are more emotional in the sense that they accept a wider range of positive and negative emotions and feel them more intensely.

2. *Fully functioning persons live fully and richly in each moment.* All experiences

have the potential to be fresh and new. Experiences cannot be predicted or anticipated but are participated in fully, rather than merely observed.

3. *These emotionally healthy persons trust in their own organism.*   By this, Rogers meant that these people trust their own reactions and responses rather than being guided by the judgments of others, by a social code, or by their intellectual judgments. Rogers wrote, "I have learned that my total organism's sensing of a situation is more trustworthy than my intellect" (Rogers, 1961, p. 22). Rogers suggested that behaving in a way that feels right is a good guide to behaving in a way that is satisfying.

Rogers did not suggest that self-actualizing people ignore data from their intellect or from other people. Rather, he meant that all data are accepted and are congruent with the fully functioning person's self-concept. Nothing is threatening, and all information can be perceived, evaluated, and weighed accurately. The final decision about how to behave in a particular situation results from a consideration of all experiential data. Fully functioning persons are unaware of making such considerations, because of the congruence between the self-concept and experience, so their decisions appear to be intuitive, more emotional than intellectual.

4. *Fully functioning persons feel a sense of freedom to make choices without constraints or inhibitions.*   This brings a sense of power because they know that their future depends on their own actions and is not determined by present circumstances, past events, or other people. They do not feel compelled, either by themselves or by others, to behave in only one way.

5. *Fully functioning persons are creative and live constructively and adaptively as environmental conditions change.*   Allied with this creativity is spontaneity. Fully functioning persons are flexible and seek new experiences and challenges. They do not require predictability, security, or freedom from tension.

6. *There are difficulties involved in being a fully functioning person.*   It involves continually testing, growing, striving, and using all one's potentialities. "It involves the courage to be," Rogers wrote, and there is much complexity, trial, and challenge in that prescription (Rogers, 1961, p. 196). Rogers did not apply such words as *happy, blissful,* or *contented* to fully functioning persons, although they certainly have those feelings at times. More appropriate descriptive labels for the personality of the fully functioning person are *enriching, exciting,* and *meaningful.*

Rogers used the word *actualizing*—not *actualized*—to characterize the fully functioning person. The latter implies a finished or static personality, which was not Rogers's intent. The development of the self is always in progress. Being fully functioning is "a direction, not a destination" (Rogers, 1961, p. 186). If striving and growing ceased, the person would lose spontaneity, flexibility, and openness to new experiences. This emphasis on change

Fully functioning people feel a sense of freedom and have the ability to live richly and creatively in every moment.

and growth is neatly captured in the title of one of Rogers's books, *On Becoming a Person* (Rogers, 1961).

Rogers's Image of Human Nature

On the issue of free will versus determinism, Rogers's position is clear. Fully functioning persons have free choice in creating their selves; no aspect of personality is determined for them. On the nature–nurture issue, Rogers gave prominence to the role of the environment or situation. Although the actualization tendency is innate, the process of actualizing is influenced more by social than biological forces. Childhood experiences have some impact on personality development, but experiences later in life are more important. Our present feelings are more vital to personality than what happened to us in childhood.

Rogers recognized some universality in personality in that fully functioning persons share certain qualities. However, we may infer from his writings that there is opportunity for uniqueness in the ways these characteristics are expressed. The ultimate and necessary goal in life is to become a fully functioning person.

A personality theorist who credits us with the ability, motivation, and responsibility to understand and improve ourselves obviously views people

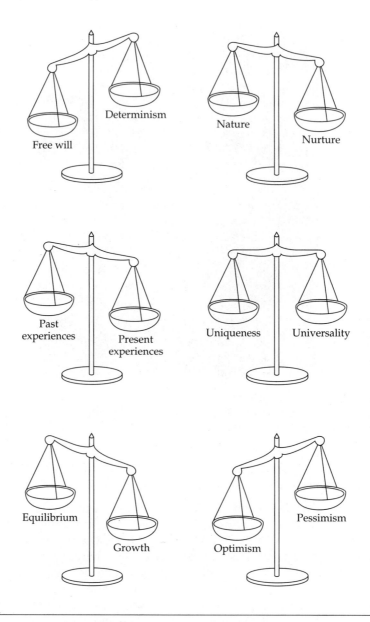

Free will — Determinism

Nature — Nurture

Past experiences — Present experiences

Uniqueness — Universality

Equilibrium — Growth

Optimism — Pessimism

Rogers

Image of Human Nature.

in an optimistic and positive light. Rogers believed that we have a basically healthy nature and an innate tendency to grow and actualize—to become all that we are capable of becoming. Throughout his life, Rogers never lost this view. In an interview at the age of 85, he said that "in working with individuals and working with groups my positive view of human nature is continually reinforced" (Rogers, 1987, p. 118).

In Rogers's opinion, we are not doomed to conflict either with our selves or with society. We are not ruled by instinctive biological forces or controlled by events that occurred in the first five years of life. Our outlook is forward, progressive rather than regressive, oriented toward growth rather than stagnation. We experience our world fully and freely, not defensively, and we seek challenge and stimulation instead of the security of the familiar.

Emotional disturbances do occur, of course, and stagnation and regression sometimes take place, but these are exceptional cases. Through Rogers's person-centered therapy, people are able to overcome these difficulties by using their inner resources, the innate urge toward actualization.

> I am quite aware that out of defensiveness and inner fear individuals can and do behave in ways which are incredibly cruel, horribly destructive, immature, regressive, antisocial, hurtful. Yet one of the most refreshing and invigorating parts of my experience is to work with such individuals and to discover the strongly positive directional tendencies which exist in them, as in all of us. [Rogers, 1961, p. 27]

Further, Rogers believed that the innate urge to become fully functioning benefits society as well. As more people in a given culture become self-actualizing, societal improvement will naturally follow.

Assessment in Rogers's Theory

Person-Centered Therapy

Rogers believed that the only way to explore and assess personality is in terms of the client's subjective experiences; that is, the events in a person's life as that person perceives them and believes them to be real. Rogers maintained that his clients possessed the ability to examine the roots of their problems and to redirect the growth and actualization that had been impeded by some incongruence between their self-concept and their experience.

In his technique of person-centered therapy, Rogers explored the client's feelings and attitudes toward the self and toward other people. He listened without preconceptions, trying to understand the client's experiential world. Although Rogers considered person-centered therapy the only worthwhile approach to personality assessment, he noted that it was not infallible.

By focusing on subjective experiences, the therapist learns about only those aspects of the experiential world that the client consciously expresses. Experience that is not represented in conscious awareness remains hidden. There is a danger in trying to infer too much about these nonconscious experiences; the inferences may represent the therapist's projections more than the client's actual experiences. Rogers also recognized that what the therapist learns about a client's internal frame of reference depends on the client's ability to communicate clearly and accurately. Because all forms of communication are imperfect, the therapist necessarily sees the client's world of experience imperfectly.

Within these limits, person-centered therapy provides a clear view of a person's experiential world that other forms of assessment and therapy cannot. One advantage Rogers claimed for his approach is that it does not rely on a predetermined theoretical structure (such as Freudian psychoanalysis) into which the patient's problem and background must be fit. The only predetermined belief of the person-centered therapist is in the client's inherent value and worth.

Clients are accepted as they are and for what they are; they are given unconditional positive regard. No judgments are made of their behavior, nor are they given advice on how to behave. Everything is centered in the client, including the responsibility for and the ability to change behavior and interpersonal relationships.

Rogers opposed assessment techniques such as free association, dream analysis, and case histories. He believed that they place clients in a position of dependency relative to the therapist, who assumes an aura of expertise and authority. These techniques remove any sense of responsibility clients would otherwise assume, by giving them the impression that the therapist knows all about them. Clients may then conclude that the therapist must also know the solution to their problem and that all they need do is sit back and follow the expert's directions.

Encounter Groups

Working with individuals, Rogers demonstrated that person-centered therapy could help people who were out of touch with their feelings and closed to life's experiences. Through the therapeutic process, people could develop or regain flexibility, spontaneity, and openness. With missionary zeal, Rogers wanted to bring this state of enhanced psychological health and functioning to greater numbers of people, so he developed a group technique in which people could learn more about themselves and how they related to, or encountered, one another. He called his approach the encounter group. During the 1960s and 1970s, millions of people in the United States enrolled in encounter groups (Rogers, 1970).

Most groups range in size from 8 to 15 people and meet from 20 to 60 hours over several sessions. The group begins with no formal structure or agenda. The group facilitator is not a leader in the usual sense of directing the group and telling the members what to do. Instead, the facilitator establishes an atmosphere in which group members can express themselves freely and focus on their experiences and how others in the group perceive them. The facilitator's job is to make it easier for members to achieve self-insight and become more fully functioning.

The evidence for the effectiveness of encounter groups is largely anecdotal. Some people reported that they felt better and were more aware of their true nature after their participation in the group experience. Rogers believed that most participants became more fully functioning, but not all psychologists agree. Rogers did note that not everyone could be helped by encounter groups.

Encounter groups are no longer as popular as they were when Rogers promoted them, but they are still conducted by a number of his followers as a way of inducing people to grow and enhance their potential.

Psychological Tests

Rogers did not use psychological tests to assess personality, nor did he develop any tests. Other psychologists, however, have devised tests to measure aspects of our experiential world. The Experience Inventory (Coan, 1972), a self-report questionnaire, attempts to assess a person's openness or receptivity to experience, which is one of the characteristics of the fully functioning person.

The Experiencing Scale (Gendlin & Tomlinson, 1967), measures another characteristic of the fully functioning person: the level of trust in our own organism. Persons being assessed by this test do not respond directly. They talk about anything they wish, and their tape-recorded comments are rated for the degree of self-trust they seem to reveal—from claiming that their feelings are an important source of information on which to base their behavior, to denying that their personal feelings have any influence over their decisions.

This test has been used with clients in person-centered therapy. Those who made the greatest improvement during therapy revealed an increase in organismic trusting from before therapy to after therapy. Those who showed little improvement during therapy revealed a small increase or no increase in organismic trusting over the period. Those with less severe emotional disorders showed greater self-trust than those with more severe disorders (Klein, Malthieu, Gendlin, & Kiesler, 1969).

Although Rogers generally opposed using tests to evaluate personality, he once agreed to take the Adjective Check List, a widely used assessment device consisting of 300 adjectives designed to measure the self-concept. The results showed that Rogers possessed the following characteristics:

> high creativity, intellectual quickness, and breadth of interests; low impulsiveness and a firm stance on ethical issues; emotional independence and effective goal-attainment; . . . gentleness and a valuing of inner feelings; tolerance of the fears and weaknesses of others, and a desire to bring people together. [Potkay & Allen, 1986, p. 254]

Research in Rogers's Theory

Rogers believed that person-centered interviews, which rely on clients' self-reports, were of greater value than the methods of the experimental laboratory. In his view, the more orthodox scientific approach yielded less information on the nature of personality than the clinical approach. "I never learned anything from research," he said. "Most of my research has been to confirm what I already felt to be true" (quoted in Bergin & Strupp, 1972,

p. 314). Although he did not use laboratory methods to collect data about personality, he did use them to attempt to verify and confirm his clinical observations.

Rogers was enthusiastic about research on the nature of the therapeutic encounter, an idea resisted by many clinicians, who accused him of "violating the sanctity of the analytic relationship" (Gendlin, 1988, p. 127). He introduced into psychotherapy what was then a radical innovation—he taped and filmed therapy sessions—to enable researchers to study the client-therapist interaction. Before that, the only data available from therapy situations were the therapist's written reconstructions. In addition to containing distortions of memory (for the therapy notes were usually made some time after the session had ended), a written record misses postural and gestural nuances. A facial expression or tone of voice can convey or reveal more than words can. With recorded therapy sessions, everything is available for study. "I [now] have a microscope," Rogers wrote, "in which I can see . . . the molecules of personality change" (1974, p. 120). Rogers always obtained the client's permission to tape or film, and he found that the equipment did not seem to impede the course of therapy.

Rogers's research focused on the self-concept and how it can change during therapy. Using both qualitative and quantitative techniques, Rogers and his associates analyzed various aspects of therapy sessions. Through the application of rating scales and content analysis of a client's verbalizations, they investigated the nature of these changes in the self-concept. Despite Rogers's claim of not being a scientist, his research to quantify the changes that occurred during therapy were within the scientific tradition.

Q sort technique A self-report technique for assessing aspects of the self-concept.

Much of his research used the **Q sort**, a procedure developed by a colleague, William Stephenson (Stephenson, 1953). In this technique, persons sort a large number of statements about the self-concept into categories that range from most descriptive to least descriptive. Typical statements are: "I enjoy being alone," "I feel helpless," and "I am emotionally mature." The *Q* sort is a way of empirically defining the client's self-image.

There are a variety of *Q* sort procedures. For example, after sorting the statements in terms of the perceived self, clients may be asked to sort the same statements in terms of an ideal self—the person they would like to be.

Applying the correlational method, Rogers used *Q* sort responses to determine how closely a client's self-image or perceived self corresponded to the ideal self and how greatly the self-concept changed from the period before therapy to the period following therapy. With one client, the data yielded an initial correlation coefficient of +.36 between perceived self and ideal self. A year after the client completed therapy, the correlation coefficient had increased to +.79, indicating to Rogers that the client's perceived self had become much more congruent with the ideal or desired self (Rogers, 1954). He concluded that this dramatic change reflected an increase in emotional health.

This client, whom Rogers identified as "Mrs. Oak," chose different *Q* sort phrases to describe herself before and after therapy. Before her sessions with

Rogers, she saw herself as dependent and passive and felt rejected by other people. Following therapy, she believed she was more like her ideal self—more secure, less fearful, and better able to relate to others (see Table 12.1).

A study by Rogers's associates measured the discrepancy between perceived self and ideal self in 25 clients (Butler & Haigh, 1954). The researchers found that the discrepancy decreased over time during and following therapy. Before therapy, the average correlation coefficient between perceived self and ideal self was −.01; following therapy, it was +.31.

Research using the *Q* sort technique has provided impressive evidence for the effectiveness of person-centered therapy, but it offers little information about the validity of Rogers's personality theory. Other studies have attempted to verify some of his concepts.

Rogers suggested that people will defend themselves against experiences that are incongruent with the self-concept. They do so by denying or distorting the inconsistent aspects of reality. This idea was tested in a study in which college students rated themselves on 100 socially desirable adjectives, indicating the degree to which each word described them (Suinn, Osborne, & Winfree, 1962). Five days later, the subjects were given a rating scale and told that it represented the ratings made of them by two other students. These ratings were fake: they contained some adjectives that were consistent with the subjects' self-ratings and some that were inconsistent.

Two days after that, the subjects were asked to complete the 100-item adjective scale again, but this time on the basis of the ratings allegedly made of them, not on the basis of their own self-perceptions. In other words, they were being asked to recall the fake ratings. Their accuracy of recall was significantly higher for those adjectives that were consistent with their self-concept than it was for the adjectives that were inconsistent with their self-concept. The researchers concluded that the subjects were defending themselves against incongruent material by being unable to recall it.

Another study was designed to test Rogers's proposition that fully functioning persons are open to all experiences, whereas psychologically unhealthy persons erect defenses to protect themselves against experiences that threaten their self-image (Chodorkoff, 1954). A group of college students used the *Q* sort statements to describe themselves. Another *Q* sort description of each subject was prepared by clinicians who based their reports on a variety of material, including responses to projective tests (the Thematic Apperception Test and the Rorschach inkblot test). Based on the clinical measurements, the subjects were divided into good- and poor-adjustment groups.

Measures of perceptual defense (defense against perceiving threatening material) were obtained from the subjects' reactions to neutral words, such as *table,* and allegedly threatening words, such as *penis.* The results showed that all subjects were slower to perceive threatening words than neutral words, but this was more marked in the defensive subjects who constituted the poor-adjustment group. Significantly less perceptual defense was displayed by the subjects in the good-adjustment group, who were presumed to be psychologi-

Table 12.1

Mrs. Oak's perceived self before and after therapy in terms of Q sort statements.

Self before Therapy	Self 12 Months after Therapy
I usually feel driven.	I express my emotions freely.
I am responsible for my troubles.	I feel emotionally mature.
I am really self-centered.	I am self-reliant.
I am disorganized.	I understand myself.
I feel insecure within myself.	I feel adequate.
I have to protect myself with excuses, with rationalizing.	I have a warm emotional relationship with others.

SOURCE: From "The Case of Mrs. Oak: A Research Analysis" by C. R. Rogers. In *Psychotherapy and Personality Change* by C. R. Rogers and R. F. Dymond, 1954, Chicago: University of Chicago Press.

cally healthier. An additional finding related to the agreement between the subjects' self-descriptions and the clinicians' descriptions. The more the descriptions agreed, the better adjusted the person was found to be.

Another study, of 56 mothers, explored the relationship between their self-acceptance and the degree to which they accepted their children as they were rather than as they wished them to be (Medinnus & Curtis, 1963). This research was based on Rogers's notion that people who accept their own nature realistically (that is, whose perceived and ideal selves are congruent) are more likely to accept others than are people whose perceived and ideal selves are inconsistent.

The results revealed significant differences between self-accepting and non–self-accepting mothers. The more self-accepting mothers were also more accepting of their children. Further, the child's degree of self-acceptance depended to some extent on the mother's degree of self-acceptance.

Other studies supported Rogers's belief that parental behavior affects a child's self-image. Parents who accepted their children unconditionally and who displayed democratic child-rearing practices had children with higher self-esteem and greater emotional security than did parents who failed to accept their children and who displayed authoritarian child-rearing practices (Baldwin, 1949). Parents of children with high self-esteem displayed more love and used rewards rather than punishments in guiding the child's behavior. Parents of children with low self-esteem were more aloof, less loving, and more likely to use punishment (Coopersmith, 1967). Adolescents whose parents provided unconditional positive regard and permission to express themselves without restraint developed greater creative potential than children whose parents did not provide those conditions (Harrington, Block, & Block, 1987).

Several studies provide support for Rogers's suggestion that incongruity between perceived self and ideal self indicates poor emotional adjustment. Researchers found that the greater the discrepancy, the higher the degree of anxiety, insecurity, self-doubt, depression, and social incompetence, and the lower the level of self-actualization (Achenbach & Zigler, 1963; Gough, Fioravanti, & Lazzari, 1983; Mahoney & Hartnett, 1973; Turner & Vanderlippe, 1958). In addition, persons with a great discrepancy between perceived self and ideal self are rated by others as awkward, confused, and unfriendly (Gough, Lazzari, & Fioravanti, 1978).

Rogers believed that if our biological potential is not realized, then the actualization tendency will be curtailed—a condition that leads to maladjustment. To test this idea, researchers studied the inherited temperaments proposed by Buss and Plomin—Emotionality, Activity, and Sociability—in a group of male and female college students (Ford, 1991). Using the EASI Temperament Survey to assess behavior, the parents of the college students were asked to recall their children's temperaments when very young. These temperament profiles were compared with the college students' current self-perceptions on the three temperaments. The results supported Rogers's views: the greater the discrepancy in temperament between childhood potential and adult realization, the greater the level of maladjustment.

A Final Commentary

Rogers's person-centered psychotherapy has been enormously popular among psychologists and has found wide application as a method of treating emotional disturbances. His personality theory, although less influential than his psychotherapy, has also received recognition and acceptance, particularly for its emphasis on the self-concept. Rogers, however, did not believe he had influenced "academic, or so-called scientific, psychology . . . in the lecture hall, the textbook, or the laboratory" (Rogers, 1980, p. 51). Nonetheless, his theory and therapy have stimulated a wealth of research on the nature of psychotherapy, the client-therapist interaction, and the self-concept. His ideas have had a significant impact on psychology's theoretical and empirical definitions of the self. If a theory is judged on the basis of its heuristic value—that is, how much research it generates—then Rogers's theory ranks high. As we have seen, much of that research supports his ideas.

Criticisms of his theory have been directed primarily at two points. First, Rogers has been faulted for failing to state precisely what constitutes the innate potentiality to actualization. Is this potential primarily physiological or psychological? Are there individual differences? Do some people have more of it than others? Rogers did not provide answers to these and related questions. He described the actualization tendency as a kind of genetic blueprint in accordance with which the organism will develop, but he did not clarify the way this mechanism operates.

Second, Rogers insisted that the only way to explore personality is through person-centered therapy to examine a person's subjective experiences. Rogers did this by listening to a client's self-reports, and thus, critics charge, he ignored those forces and factors of which the client is not consciously aware but which can influence his or her behavior. Patients may distort the reports of their subjective experiences, repressing some and elaborating on or inventing others, to conceal their true nature and to present an idealized picture of the self.

Rogers's background is a unique combination of clinic, lecture hall, and laboratory. He drew on his considerable experience in working with emotionally disturbed persons and on the intellectual stimulation provided by colleagues and students during his academic years. He attracted large numbers of followers who continue to test his ideas in the clinic and in the laboratory.

Summary

Carl Rogers's person-centered theory holds that we are conscious, rational beings who are not controlled by unconscious forces or past experiences. Personality can only be understood from an individual's viewpoint, based on his or her subjective experiences (the experiential field). Our goal is self-actualization, an innate tendency that fosters growth and development and is responsible for maturation (the genetically determined development of bodily organs and processes). The organismic valuing process evaluates life experiences in terms of how well they serve the actualizing tendency. Experiences that promote actualization will be sought out; those that hinder it will be avoided.

Positive regard is a need for acceptance, love, and approval from others, particularly from the mother during infancy. In unconditional positive regard, the mother's love and approval are granted freely and are not conditional on the child's behavior. When love and approval are conditional, a state of conditional positive regard exists. Once we internalize the attitudes of others, positive regard comes from ourselves, a situation called positive self-regard.

Conditions of worth (similar to the Freudian superego) involve seeing ourselves as worthy only under those conditions acceptable to our parents. We must avoid behaviors and perceptions that oppose our parents' conditions of worth. Incongruence will develop between the self-concept and threatening behaviors and perceptions. We must defend against the anxiety accompanying this threat by denying or distorting certain aspects of our experiential field.

The fully functioning person represents the peak of psychological development. Characteristics of the fully functioning person are an awareness of all experiences, no conditions to defend against, the ability to live fully in each moment, trust in one's self, a sense of freedom and personal power, creativity, and spontaneity.

Rogers's optimistic image of human nature encompassed a belief in free will, the prominence of environment over heredity, and some universality in personality. Individuals and societies can grow unhampered by past events.

Personality can be assessed in terms of a person's subjective experiences as revealed in self-reports. In this person-centered approach, the therapist gives the client unconditional positive regard. Rogers opposed such techniques as free association and dream analysis because they make the client dependent on the therapist. By recording therapy sessions, Rogers enabled researchers to investigate the nature of the client-therapist interaction.

The *Q* sort technique, in which clients sort statements about their self-concept into categories ranging from most to least descriptive, is a way of quantifying the self-image. *Q* sort research has revealed a greater correspondence between perceived self and ideal self after therapy. Clients defend themselves against material that is incongruent with the self-concept. The better adjusted a person is, the greater the agreement between self-descriptions and descriptions made by others. Discrepancies between perceived self and ideal self indicate poor psychological adjustment.

Rogers's work has been criticized for failing to define precisely the nature of self-actualization and for ignoring the impact of unconscious forces and the possible distortion of a client's subjective experiences in self-reports.

Critical Thinking Review

1. How did Carl Rogers's clinical experience differ from Sigmund Freud's?
2. Describe the research that influenced Rogers's view of the role of the self in personality.
3. How does the need to actualize promote biological and psychological growth?
4. What is the organismic valuing process?
5. What is the experiential field? How does our experiential field change with age?
6. What parental behaviors affect a child's development of positive self-regard?
7. Compare Rogers's concept of conditions of worth with Freud's concept of the superego.
8. Describe Rogers's concept of incongruence. How is incongruence related to anxiety?
9. Describe the characteristics of the fully functioning person.
10. How does the Rogerian clinical interview differ from the psychoanalytic clinical interview? What did Rogers call his approach? Why?
11. How does the *Q* sort technique measure a person's self-image? What has *Q* sort research shown about the self-concept before and after therapy?
12. What was Rogers's position on the importance of childhood experiences and adult experiences in personality development?
13. Discuss several criticisms of Rogers's theory.

Suggested Reading

Evans, R. I. (1975). *Carl Rogers: The man and his ideas.* New York: Dutton. Interviews with Rogers on the evolution of the self, techniques of person-centered therapy, and applications of his theory to education. Contrasts Rogers's humanistic views with B. F. Skinner's behaviorist views.

Kirschenbaum, H. (1979). *On becoming Carl Rogers.* New York: Delacorte Press. A biography of Rogers and his contributions to humanistic psychology.

Rogers, C. R. (1961). *On becoming a person: A therapist's view of psychotherapy.* Boston: Houghton Mifflin. Summarizes Rogers's views on psychotherapy, especially problems in communication and interpersonal relations. Discusses the effects of enhanced personal growth on personal and family life.

Rogers, C. R. (1967). Autobiography. In E. G. Boring & G. Lindzey (Eds.), *A history of psychology in autobiography* (vol. 5, pp. 341–384). New York: Appleton-Century-Crofts. Rogers's assessment of his work and the influence of his early experiences.

Rogers, C. R. (1974). In retrospect: Forty-six years. *American Psychologist, 29,* 115–123. Rogers evaluates the impact of his work on the fields of counseling, psychotherapy, education, leadership, and international relations and on the empirical investigation of subjective phenomena.

Rogers, C. R. (1980). *A way of being.* Boston: Houghton Mifflin. Presents the work of Rogers's later years concerning individual and group psychotherapy, the helping professions, scientific progress, and personal growth.

Rogers, C. R. (1989). *The Carl Rogers reader.* Boston: Houghton Mifflin. A selection of Rogers's writings over 60 years, edited by Howard Kirschenbaum and Valerie Henderson. Includes personal recollections, case studies, and essays on personality change, psychotherapy, education, marriage, aging, international relations, and world peace.

VII

The Cognitive Approach

If you look up the word *cognition* in a dictionary, you will find that it means the act or process of knowing. The cognitive approach to personality focuses on the ways in which people know their environment and themselves—how they perceive, evaluate, learn, think, make decisions, and solve problems. This is the most rational or truly psychological approach to personality because it focuses exclusively on conscious mental activities.

It may appear that this sole focus on the mind or mental processes neglects some of the ideas dealt with by other theorists. In the cognitive approach, we do not find needs, drives, or emotions as separate activities of the personality. Instead, they are considered to be aspects of the personality that, like all other aspects, are controlled by cognitive processes.

Other approaches to personality also recognize cognitive processes. Contemporary developments in psychoanalysis, as well as the work of Erik Erikson, which accord a greater autonomy to the ego, acknowledge the importance of cognitive functioning. So, too, does the work of the humanistic psychologists Abraham Maslow and Carl Rogers, who deal in part with how we perceive our experiences and our world. Henry Murray and Gordon Allport wrote about the concept of reasoning, and Alfred Adler proposed a creative self, which results from our perception or interpretation of experience. Social-learning theorists (see Chapters 15 and 16) also invoke cognitive processes.

The difference between the approaches of these theorists and the cognitive approach to personality, represented here by the work of George Kelly, is that Kelly attempted to describe all aspects of personality in terms of cognitive processes. The acts or processes of knowing are not merely elements of the personality—they are the entire personality.

THIRTEEN

George Kelly

The Cognitive Revolution in Psychology
The Life of Kelly (1905–1967)
Personal Construct Theory
Anticipating Life Events
Kelly's Image of Human Nature
Assessment in Kelly's Theory
    The Interview
    Self-Characterization Sketches

    The Role Construct Repertory Test
    Fixed Role Therapy
Research in Kelly's Theory
    Cognitive Styles: Complexity and Simplicity
A Final Commentary
Summary
Critical Thinking Review
Suggested Reading

*It occurred to me that what seemed true of myself
was probably no less true of others. If I initiated
my actions, so did they.*

—George Kelly

**personal construct
theory** Kelly's
approach to personality
in terms of cognitive
processes. He believed
we are capable of
interpreting behaviors
and events and using
this understanding to
guide our behavior and
to predict the behavior
of others.

Kelly's **personal construct theory** of personality shares little with the other
approaches discussed in this book. Kelly warned us that we would not find in
his system many familiar terms and concepts, such as the unconscious, the
ego, needs, drives, stimuli and responses, reinforcement—not even motivation and emotion. How can we hope to understand the human personality
without considering these ideas, especially motivation and emotion?

Kelly suggested that each of us creates "cognitive constructs" about our
environment. We interpret and organize the events and social relationships
that make up our world in a system or pattern. On the basis of this pattern,
we make predictions about other people, events, and ourselves. We use these
predictions to formulate our responses and guide our actions. To understand
personality, then, we must understand our patterns—the ways in which we
organize or construct our world. It is our interpretation of events, not the
events themselves, that is important.

The personality theory Kelly offered derived from his experience as a
clinician working with troubled individuals. For several reasons, he interpreted his clinical experience in a manner vastly different from that of Freud
and the many other theorists who treated clients and patients. The model of
human nature Kelly developed from his clinical work is unusual. He believed
that people can function in the same way scientists do.

Scientists construct theories and hypotheses and test them against a form
of reality by performing experiments in the laboratory. If the theory is sup-

ported by the results of the experiments, it is retained. If the theory is not supported by the data, it is either rejected or modified and retested.

As we have seen, this is how psychologists who study personality typically proceed. Yet, Kelly noted, these psychologists do not ascribe the same intellectual and rational facilities to their subjects that they do to themselves. It is as if psychologists have two theories about human nature—one that applies to them and their way of looking at the world, and another that applies to the rest of us, the people they study. This suggests that psychologists view their subjects as incapable of rational functioning, as motivated by all manner of drives, or as victims of unconscious forces. Human beings are believed to function largely on an emotional level, invoking few cognitive processes—quite unlike the way psychologists function.

Are psychologists superior beings? Kelly said they are not; they are really no different from the people they study. What works for one works for the other; what explains one explains the other. Both are concerned with predicting and controlling the events in their lives, and both are capable of doing so on a rational basis.

Like scientists, we construct theories—which Kelly called "personal constructs"—by which we try to predict and control the events in our lives. The way to understand the individual personality, then, is by examining a person's personal constructs.

The Cognitive Revolution in Psychology

At first glance, Kelly's cognitive theory appears compatible with the cognitive revolution in psychology that began around 1960 and that has come to dominate mainstream American experimental psychology. However, Kelly's work has not been accepted by that movement because it is not congruent with the methodology and subject matter of contemporary cognitive psychology.

Kelly's approach is that of the clinician dealing with the conscious constructs by which people order their lives. Cognitive psychologists are interested in both cognitive variables and overt behavior, which they study primarily in an experimental rather than a clinical setting. Also, cognitive psychologists attempt to account for all behavior, not just for personality. They focus their research on overt behavior—what people say and do in laboratory experiments—and on learning in social situations. They believe that cognitive processes, such as learning, will influence a person's response to a particular stimulus situation.

Although the cognitive revolution took hold after Kelly proposed his theory, the movement was little influenced by Kelly's ideas. At best, Kelly's work may be considered a precursor to contemporary cognitive psychology. The two approaches share the term *cognitive,* with its implied interest in conscious activities, but little else. In scholarly work in today's cognitive psychology, it is rare to find any mention of Kelly's ideas.

This is not a criticism of Kelly's theory—indeed, his recognition of the importance of cognitive processes is noteworthy—but we must place it in perspective with regard to modern American psychology. Kelly's cognitive approach to personality is not part of cognitive psychology, but that does not detract from its usefulness for studying personality.

The Life of Kelly (1905–1967)

Kelly was born on a farm in Kansas. An only child, he received a great deal of attention and affection from his parents, who were fundamentalists in their religious beliefs and committed to helping the sick and needy. They opposed frivolous entertainment, such as dancing and card playing. When Kelly was 4 years old, the family traveled by covered wagon to Colorado to try farming there, but they soon returned to Kansas. Kelly's early education was erratic and conducted as much by his parents as by schoolteachers. At 13 he went away to high school in Wichita and seldom lived at home again.

In 1926, Kelly earned a B.A. in physics and mathematics from Park College in Parkville, Missouri. His future was uncertain, and his interests had shifted from engineering and science to social problems. He worked briefly as an engineer, then took a teaching job at a labor college in Minneapolis. Next, he became an instructor for the American Banking Association and also taught citizenship courses to immigrants. He then enrolled in graduate school and received a master's degree in educational sociology from the University of Kansas in Lawrence.

Kelly went to a junior college in Iowa to teach and to coach students in dramatics. His career to this point indicated no interest in or inclination toward psychology. In college, he had not been impressed by his early exposure to the field.

> In the first course in psychology, I sat in the back row of a very large class, tilted my chair against the wall, made myself as comfortable as possible, and kept one ear cocked for anything interesting that might turn up. One day the professor, a very nice person who seemed to be trying hard to convince himself that psychology was something to be taken seriously, turned to the blackboard and wrote an "S," an arrow, and an "R." Thereupon I straightened up in my chair and listened, thinking to myself that now, after two or three weeks of preliminaries, we might be getting to the meat of the matter. [Kelly, 1969, p. 46]

Kelly paid attention for several more class meetings and then gave up; he could not comprehend what the arrow connecting the stimulus (*S*) and response (*R*) stood for. He later said that he never did figure it out. The traditional behaviorist, experimental approach to psychology failed to spark his interest.

He also explored the Freudian approach to psychology. "I don't remember which one of Freud's books I was trying to read," he wrote, "but I do remember the mounting feeling of incredulity that anyone could write such nonsense, much less publish it" (Kelly, 1969, p. 47).

Kelly's professional training took a different turn in 1929, when he was awarded a fellowship at the University of Edinburgh in Scotland. During his year there he earned a Bachelor of Education degree and, for reasons he never explained, developed an interest in psychology. He undertook doctoral studies at the State University of Iowa in Iowa City, receiving his Ph.D. in 1931. Kelly's academic career began at Fort Hays Kansas State College, in the midst of the economic depression of the 1930s. There was little opportunity to conduct research in physiological psychology, the area that interested him at the time, so he switched to clinical psychology, for which there was a great need.

He developed a clinical psychology service for the local public school system and for the students at his college. He established traveling clinics, going from school to school. This gave him the opportunity to deal with a variety of problems and to try out different approaches to treatment. Kelly expressed no theoretical bias; he was not committed to a particular therapeutic technique or to a firm view of the nature of personality. Instead, he felt free to experiment both with traditional methods of assessment and treatment and with those of his own design.

Kelly's clinical experiences influenced the nature of his personal construct theory. The people he treated were not severely disturbed. They were not psychotics in mental hospitals or neurotics who sought help for emotional problems. His work was with college and public school students who had been referred by their teachers for counseling.

Unlike the seriously maladjusted patients in a psychiatric ward or a psychoanalyst's office, Kelly's clients were more capable of functioning—or at least of expressing their problems—in rational and intellectual terms, the kind of functioning expected in an academic setting. In the classroom, we are taught to intellectualize, to discuss rationally the material being dealt with. This intellectual context and attitude may have carried over from the classroom to the counseling situation. Had circumstances placed Kelly during his formative professional years at work with schizophrenics in a mental institution, his theory might not have depended so heavily on cognitive abilities.

World War II interrupted Kelly's academic career. He joined the U.S. Navy and served as a psychologist in the Bureau of Medicine and Surgery in Washington, D.C. When the war ended in 1945, he taught at the University of Maryland for a year before joining the faculty at Ohio State University in Columbus. There he spent 19 years teaching, refining his personality theory, and conducting research.

During those years Kelly also lectured at universities throughout North and South America and traveled around the world, speaking on the ways in which his personal construct theory could be applied to the resolution of international problems. In 1965 he accepted an appointment to an endowed chair at Brandeis University, but he died shortly thereafter.

Kelly was a major force in the development of the clinical psychology profession during its years of rapid growth following World War II. He held several honored positions in the field, among them the presidencies of the

Clinical and Consulting divisions of the American Psychological Association and of the American Board of Examiners in Professional Psychology.

Personal Construct Theory

Kelly suggested that people look upon and organize their world in the same way scientists do, by formulating hypotheses about their environment and testing them against the reality of their experience. We observe the events in our life—the facts or data of our experience—and interpret them in our own way. This personal interpreting or construing of experience represents our unique view of these events, the pattern within which we place them. Kelly wrote that we look at the world through "transparent patterns [that] fit over the realities of which the world is composed" (Kelly, 1955, pp. 8–9).

We might compare these patterns to sunglasses that add a particular tint or coloring to everything we see. One person's glasses may have a bluish tint, another's a greenish one. Several people can look at the same scene and perceive it differently, depending on the tint of the lenses that frame their point of view. So it is with the hypotheses or patterns we construct to perceive and organize our world. This special view—the unique pattern created by each individual—is what Kelly called our construct system.

construct An intellectual hypothesis that we devise and use to interpret or explain life events. Constructs are bipolar, or dichotomous—such as tall versus short or honest versus dishonest.

A **construct** is a person's way of looking at the events in his or her world, an intellectual hypothesis devised to explain or interpret life's events. We behave in accordance with the expectation that our constructs will predict and explain the realities of our lives, and, like scientists, we test these hypotheses by basing our actions on our constructs and evaluating the effects.

Consider the student who is in danger of failing an introductory psychology course and is trying to persuade the professor to give him or her a passing grade. On the basis of observing the professor for most of the semester, the student concludes that the professor behaves in an authoritarian and superior manner in the classroom and seems to have an inflated sense of personal importance. From this observation, the student forms the hypothesis that acting in a way that reinforces the professor's exaggerated self-image will bring a favorable response. The student then proceeds to test this hypothesis or construct against reality.

The student goes to the library, reads a book the professor has written, and asks questions about it in class. If the professor is flattered and gives the student a passing grade, then the student's construct has been tested and confirmed. The construct is a useful one and can be applied the next time the student takes a course with that professor. However, if the student receives a failing grade, then the construct was probably inappropriate, and a new one must be developed for dealing with that professor or with other professors who have a similar temperament.

We develop many constructs over the course of life, one for almost every type of person or situation we encounter. We expand our inventory of constructs as we meet new people and face new situations. We may need to alter or discard constructs periodically because the people and events that affect us change over time. Thus, revising our constructs is a necessary and continuous process; we must always have alternative constructs to apply. If our constructs were inflexible and incapable of being revised—if we were victims of childhood influences or other circumstances—then we would not be able to adapt to change or cope with new situations. Kelly proposed the concept of **constructive alternativism** to express the view that we are not controlled by the constructs we have developed at any given point; we are free to revise or replace them with alternatives.

constructive alternativism The idea that we are free to revise or replace our constructs with alternatives as needed.

The personal construct theory is presented in a scientific format, organized into a fundamental postulate and 11 corollaries (Kelly, 1955).

Anticipating Life Events

The fundamental postulate in Kelly's personal construct theory states that our psychological processes are directed by the ways in which we anticipate events.

By using the word *processes,* Kelly was not suggesting the existence of any kind of inner substance, such as mental energy. Rather, he saw personality as a flowing, moving process. Our psychological processes are directed by our constructs, by the ways each of us construes our world. Another key word in the fundamental postulate is *anticipate.* Kelly's notion of constructs is anticipatory. We use constructs to predict or anticipate the future so that we have some idea of what will happen if we behave in a certain way.

1. *The construction corollary: Similarities among repeated events.* Kelly believed that no life event or experience can be reproduced exactly as it occurred the first time. An event can be repeated, but it will not be experienced in precisely the same way as before. For example, if you watch the same movie today that you saw last month, your experience will be different. Your mood today may not be the same, and during the month you were exposed to diverse people and events that may have affected your attitudes and emotions. You may have read something unpleasant about the actor in the film you are watching, or you may feel happier than you did last month because you received a good grade in one of your courses.

Although repeated events are not experienced identically, recurrent features or themes will emerge. Some aspects of an experience will be similar to those of its earlier occurrences. On the basis of these similarities, we make predictions or establish anticipations about how we will experience the event in the future. Our predictions are based on the idea that future events, although not duplicates of past events, will nevertheless be similar.

For example, some parts of the movie you are watching today are likely to affect you the same way each time you see it. If you liked the music the first time, you will probably like it again; indeed, you may base your behav-

People differ from one another in the ways they perceive and interpret the same event.

ior on your anticipations and choose to watch the movie again because you liked the music.

Themes of the past reappear in the future; we formulate our constructs on the basis of these recurring themes.

2. The individuality corollary: Individual differences in interpreting events. With this corollary, Kelly introduced the notion of individual differences. He pointed out that we differ from one another in how we perceive or interpret an event. As a result of construing events differently, people form different constructs. Our constructs do not so much reflect the objective reality of an event as they constitute the interpretation each of us places on that event.

3. The organization corollary: Relationships among constructs. We organize our individual constructs into a pattern according to our view of the relationships among them—both the similarities and the contrasts. People who have similar individual constructs may still differ from one another because they organize those constructs into divergent patterns.

We organize our constructs into a hierarchy, with some subordinate to others. One construct can include one or more subordinate constructs. For example, the construct "good" may include among its subordinates the constructs "intelligent" and "moral." Thus, if we meet someone who fits our construct of a good person, we anticipate that he or she will also have the attributes of intelligence and high moral standards.

These relationships among constructs are usually more enduring than the individual constructs themselves, but they, too, are open to change. A person who feels mistreated or belittled by someone who appears more intelligent may switch the construct "intelligent" from a subordinate place under the construct "good" to a place under the construct "bad."

The test for a construct system is its predictive efficiency. If a system no longer provides a valid prediction of events, it will be modified or discarded.

4. *The dichotomy corollary: Two mutually exclusive alternatives.* All constructs are bipolar or dichotomous. This is necessary if we are to anticipate future events correctly. Just as we must note similarities among people or events, we must also account for dissimilarities. For example, it is not enough to have a construct about a friend that describes the personal characteristic of honesty. We must also consider the opposite pole—dishonesty—to explain how the honest friend differs from people who are not honest.

If we did not make this distinction—if we held that all people are honest—then forming a construct about honesty would serve no predictive purpose. A person can be expected to be honest only in contrast to someone else who can be predicted to be dishonest.

The appropriate personal construct in this case, then, is "honest versus dishonest." Our constructs must always be in terms of a pair of qualities, two mutually exclusive alternatives.

5. *The choice corollary: Freedom of choice.* The notion that an individual has freedom of choice can be found throughout Kelly's writings. According to the dichotomy corollary, each construct has two opposing poles. For any given situation, we choose the alternative that works best for us, the one that allows us to anticipate or predict the outcome of future events.

Kelly suggested that we have some latitude in deciding between the alternatives. He described it as a choice between security and adventure. Suppose you must decide which of two courses to take next semester. One course is easy because it is not much different from a course you've already taken, and it is taught by a professor known to give high grades for little work. There is virtually no risk involved in choosing that course, but there may not be much reward or satisfaction either. You know the professor is dull, and you have already studied much of the course material. However, it is the secure choice, because you can make a highly accurate prediction about the outcome of your decision.

The other course you can take is more of a gamble. The professor is new and rumored to be tough, and you don't know much about the subject. It would expose you to a new field of study, one you've been curious about. You cannot make a very accurate prediction about the outcome of your choice. You would be taking more risk, but the potential reward and satisfaction are greater than with the first course. This is the more adventurous choice.

You must choose between the low-risk, minimal-reward secure option and the high-risk, high-reward adventurous option. The first has a high predictive efficiency; the second, a much lower one. Kelly believed that we face such choices throughout life, choices between defining or extending our system of personal constructs. The secure choice, which closely resembles past choices, further defines our construct system by repeating similar experiences and events. The more adventurous choice extends our construct system by introducing and encompassing new experiences and events.

The human tendency to take the secure, low-risk alternative may explain why some people persist in behaving in an unrewarding way. Why, for example, does someone continue to act hostile toward others, even when rebuffed for it, instead of acting friendly? Kelly's answer was that the person is simply making the low-risk choice because he or she has come to know what to expect from that behavior and thus can predict how others will react to the hostility. On the other hand, the person does not know how people will react to friendliness because he or she has so rarely tried it. The rewards might be greater for friendly rather than unfriendly behavior, but so is the uncertainty.

Our choices are made in terms of how well they allow us to anticipate or predict the future, not necessarily in terms of what is best for us. The individual, like the scientist, desires to predict the future with the highest degree of certainty.

6. The range corollary: The range of convenience.   Few personal constructs are appropriate or relevant for all situations. Consider the construct "tall versus short," which obviously has a limited **range of convenience** or applicability. It can be useful with respect to buildings, trees, or people, but it is of no value in describing a pizza or the weather.

range of convenience
The spectrum of events to which a construct is applicable. Some constructs are relevant to a limited number of people or situations; other constructs are broader.

Some constructs can be applied to many situations or people, whereas others can only be applied in a more limited way, perhaps to just one person or type of situation. What is appropriate or relevant for a construct—what is within its range of convenience—is a matter of personal choice. For example, we may believe that the construct "loyal versus disloyal" may be applicable to everyone we meet, may be relevant for only some people, or may be appropriate solely for our pet dog or cat. To understand personality, it is just as important to know what is excluded from a construct's range of convenience as it is to know what is included.

7. The experience corollary: Exposure to new experiences.   Each construct is a hypothesis generated on the basis of past experience to predict or anticipate future events. Each construct is then tested against reality by determining how well it predicted a given event. Most of us are exposed to new experiences daily, so the process of testing a construct's fit—that is, seeing how well it predicted the event—is ongoing.

If a construct is not a valid predictor of the outcome of the situation, it must be reformulated or replaced in the light of these new experiences. Thus, we will reconstrue or reinterpret our constructs as our world broadens and changes. Constructs that worked for us at age 16 may be useless, or even harmful, at age 40. In the intervening years, we will have learned much that leads us continuously to revise our construct system.

Construct systems cannot remain rigid unless life involves no change, no new experiences. In that case, constructs would not have to change because the person would have no new events to anticipate. But those of us whose lives involve meeting new people and coping with new situations must reconstrue our experiences and constructs accordingly.

8. *The modulation corollary: Adapting to new experiences.* Constructs vary in their **permeability**. To permeate means to penetrate or pass through something. A permeable construct is one that allows new elements to penetrate or be admitted to the range of convenience. Such a construct is open to new events and experiences and is capable of being defined, revised, or extended by them.

permeability The idea that constructs can be revised and extended in light of new experiences.

How much our construct system may be altered or modulated as a function of new experiences and learning depends on how permeable our individual constructs are. An impermeable or rigid construct is not capable of being changed, no matter what our new experiences tell us. For example, if a prejudiced person applies the construct "high intelligence versus low intelligence" to minority groups in an impermeable way so that he or she believes all minorities are of low intelligence, then new experiences will not alter this belief. The person will not change his or her mind, no matter how many highly intelligent minority people he or she encounters. The construct is a barrier to new ideas, and the person is closed to new learning.

9. *The fragmentation corollary: Competition among constructs.* Kelly believed that we develop and apply a variety of constructs that may be individually incompatible but that coexist within the pattern of our overall construct system. As you will recall, our construct system may change as we interpret new experiences. However, new constructs do not necessarily derive from old ones. A new construct may be compatible or consistent with an old one in a given situation, but if the situation changes, these constructs can become inconsistent.

People may accept one another as friends in one situation, such as playing a board game, but may act as adversaries in another situation, such as a political debate.

For example, a man meets a woman in a college classroom and immediately decides that he likes her. She is also a psychology major, and her interests appear similar to his. She fits the "friend" alternative of the construct "friend versus enemy"; she is someone to be liked and respected.

The man sees her again the next day at a political rally and is disappointed to find her expressing conservative opinions that are the opposite of his own liberal views. She now fits the opposite alternative of the construct, that of "enemy." This inconsistency in his construct about the woman is at a subordinate level in his construct system; in one situation she is a friend, and in another situation she is an enemy. The broader construct—liberals are friends, conservatives are enemies—remains undisturbed.

Thus, we can tolerate subordinate inconsistencies without discarding the overall construct system.

10. *The commonality corollary: Similarities among people in interpreting events.* We differ in the ways in which we construe events, and as a result, we develop unique constructs. However, we also show similarities in the ways we construe events. Kelly suggested that if people construe an experience in a similar way, then we can conclude that their cognitive processes are similar. Although they are not identical in their psychological makeup, they will have in common certain characteristics and processes.

Consider a group of people who hold common cultural norms and ideals. Their anticipations and expectations of one another will be similar, and they will construe many of their experiences in like ways. People in the same culture may behave in a typical manner even though they are exposed to different specific life events.

11. *The sociality corollary: Interpersonal relationships.* People in the same group or culture tend to construe events similarly. Although this accounts for some commonalities among people, it does not in itself bring about constructive interpersonal relationships. It is not enough for one person to construe or interpret experiences in the same way as another; the person must also construe the other person's constructs. In other words, we must understand how another person thinks if we are to anticipate how that person will predict events.

Construing others' constructs is something we often do routinely. Think about driving a car; we stake our lives on our anticipations of what other drivers on the road will do. Only when we can predict with some certainty what drivers, friends, spouses, or professors will do can we adjust our behaviors to theirs. And while we are anticipating and adjusting to others, they are doing the same to us.

Each of us assumes a role with respect to every person we encounter. We play one role with a friend, another with a child, another with our boss or the college dean. Each role is a behavior pattern that evolves from our understanding of the way that other person construes events. In a sense, then, we fit ourselves into that person's constructs.

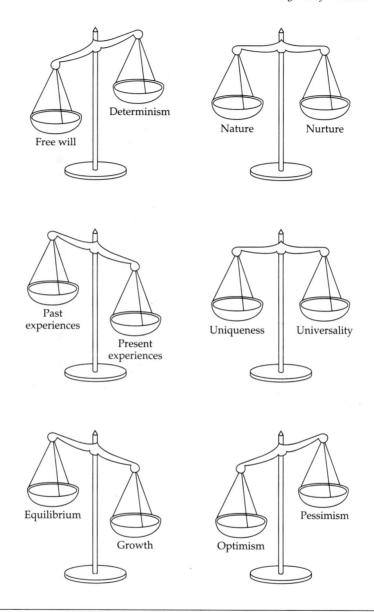

Kelly

Image of Human Nature.

Kelly's Image of Human Nature

Kelly's personality theory presents an optimistic, even flattering, image of human nature. Kelly treated people as rational beings capable of forming constructs through which to view the world, able to formulate a unique approach to reality. Kelly believed we are authors of our destiny, not victims (Kelly, 1969). His view endows us with free will—the ability to choose the path our life will take—and we are able to change that path when necessary by revising our old constructs and forming new ones. We are not bound to a path chosen in childhood or adolescence. Our direction is clearly toward the future because we formulate our constructs in terms of predictions and anticipations.

Thus, Kelly did not consider past events to be the sole determinant of present behavior. We are not prisoners of toilet training, early sex experiences, or parental rejection. Nor are we bound by biological instincts or unconscious forces. We need no push from internal drives or needs because we are motivated by the simple fact of being alive. Kelly saw no reason to invoke any other explanation.

Kelly did not state his position on the nature-nurture issue. Although he did not discuss the role of heredity in personality, he noted that we are not totally determined by environmental influences, either. We live by constructs based on our interpretation of life's events. Therefore, it is our rational functioning, and not the events themselves, that affects us. Kelly did not posit an ultimate and necessary goal, but we may infer that our goal is to establish the construct system that best enables us to predict events.

On the question of uniqueness versus universality of personality, Kelly took a moderate position. The commonality corollary states that people in the same culture develop similar constructs. The individuality corollary emphasizes the uniqueness of many of a person's constructs, and hence of the self.

Assessment in Kelly's Theory

The Interview

Kelly's primary assessment technique was the interview. "If you don't know what is going on in a person's mind," Kelly wrote, "ask him; he may tell you!" (Kelly, 1958, p. 330). Adopting what he called a credulous attitude, Kelly accepted the client's words at face value, believing that this was the best way to determine the person's constructs. He also recognized that a person may deliberately lie or distort the reported version of events. What the client says must be respected, he cautioned, even if it is not fully believed.

Self-Characterization Sketches

Another technique used to assess a client's construct system is to have the person write a self-characterization sketch. Kelly's instructions to the client were as follows:

> I want you to write a character sketch of [client's name], just as if he were the principal character in a play. Write it as it might be written by a friend who knew him very intimately and very sympathetically, perhaps better than anyone ever really could know him. [Kelly, 1955, p. 323]

Table 13.1   ***Role title list from the Role Construct Repertory Test.***

1. A teacher you liked.
2. A teacher you disliked.
3. Your wife/husband or present boyfriend/girlfriend.
4. An employer, supervisor, or officer under whom you worked or served and whom you found hard to get along with.
5. An employer, supervisor, or officer under whom you worked or served and whom you liked.
6. Your mother or the person who has played the part of a mother in your life.
7. Your father or the person who has played the part of a father in your life.
8. Your brother nearest your age or the person who has been most like a brother.
9. Your sister nearest your age or the person who has been most like a sister.
10. A person with whom you have worked who was easy to get along with.
11. A person with whom you have worked who was hard to understand.
12. A neighbor with whom you get along well.
13. A neighbor whom you find hard to understand.
14. A boy you got along well with when you were in high school.
15. A girl you got along well with when you were in high school.
16. A boy you did not like when you were in high school.
17. A girl you did not like when you were in high school.
18. A person of your own sex whom you would enjoy having as a companion on a trip.
19. A person of your own sex whom you would dislike having as a companion on a trip.
20. A person with whom you have been closely associated recently who appears to dislike you.
21. The person whom you would most like to be of help to or whom you feel most sorry for.
22. The most intelligent person whom you know personally.
23. The most successful person whom you know personally.
24. The most interesting person whom you know personally.

SOURCE: Reprinted from *The Psychology of Personal Constructs,* by George A. Kelly. Copyright © 1991 by Routledge, Chapman & Hall, Inc. Reprinted by permission.

Kelly found this technique useful for learning how clients perceived themselves in relation to others.

The Role Construct Repertory Test

Kelly devised the Role Construct Repertory (REP) Test to uncover the constructs we apply to the important people in our lives (Kelly, 1955). The client is asked to write the names of people who have played a significant role in his or her life, according to the list shown in Table 13.1. For example, clients are asked to name mother, father, spouse, closest friend, and the most intelligent or interesting person they know. The names are sorted, three at a time, and clients are then asked to select from each group of three the two people who are most alike, noting how they differ from the third person in the group. For example, a client may be given the names of his or her most threatening person, successful person, and attractive person, and the client must describe how any two of them are similar in some aspect of behavior or character and how they differ from the third.

This information is presented in a diagram called a repertory grid (see Figure 13.1). For each row, the client judges the three people indicated by the circles and formulates a construct about them, such as "happy versus sad." The client writes a word or phrase that describes two of them in the column labeled "Emergent Pole" (in our example, the word *happy*) and the opposite word (*sad*), which presumably describes the third person in the group, in the column labeled "Implicit Pole." The client then places a check mark in the squares of anyone else in the grid who shares the characteristics of those in the emergent pole column—in this case, anyone significant in the client's life who could be described as "happy."

The assumption underlying the REP Test is that people construe events in dichotomies, according to the dichotomy corollary, in terms of like versus unlike, or similar versus dissimilar. By forcing clients to make repeated judgments about their social relationships, Kelly believed he could uncover their anticipations and expectations. The dichotomies or alternatives by which we guide our life show the pattern of our personal constructs.

The REP Test has no objective scoring procedures. Its interpretation depends on the skill and training of the psychologist who administers it. Kelly did not intend the test to be a standardized, objective self-report inventory. He designed it as a way to assess constructs and as a necessary stage in therapy, to induce clients to reveal the constructs by which they view the world.

Fixed Role Therapy

fixed role therapy A psychotherapeutic technique in which the client acts out the constructs appropriate for a fictitious person. This demonstrates to the client how the new constructs are more effective than the old ones he or she has been using.

Having assessed a client's system of personal constructs, Kelly proceeded to effect a change in those constructs that were undesirable or ineffective. He offered a form of psychotherapy called **fixed role therapy**. To help clients formulate new constructs and discard old ones, he asked them to write a self-characterization sketch describing themselves, as we noted earlier, as the lead character in a play.

The therapist then prepares a fixed role sketch containing constructs that differ from the client's negative self-perceptions, as revealed in the self-characterization sketch. The client is told that the fixed role sketch is about a fictitious character and then is asked to act out that character, first in the therapist's office and later in everyday life.

In the course of this role-playing, in which the client is expected to project his or her personal needs and values onto the fictitious character, the client should discover that the new constructs offered in the fixed role sketch work better to anticipate events than the old constructs by which the client was living. Once the client realizes this, he or she works with the therapist to incorporate the new constructs into the construct system and comes to function in a more satisfying and effective way.

Constructs

Emergent Pole	Implicit Pole
1. Don't believe in God	Very religious
2. Same sort of education	Complete different education
3. Not athletic	Athletic
4. Both girls	A boy
5. Parents	Ideas different
6. Understand me better	Don't understand at all
7. Teach the right thing	Teach the wrong thing
8. Achieved a lot	Hasn't achieved a lot
9. Higher education	No education
10. Don't like other people	Like other people
11. More religious	Not religious
12. Believe in higher education	Not believing in too much education
13. More sociable	Not sociable
14. Both girls	Not girls
15. Both girls	Not girls
16. Both have high morals	Low morals
17. Think alike	Think differently
18. Same age	Different ages
19. Believe the same about me	Believe differently about me
20. Both friends	Not friends
21. More understanding	Less understanding
22. Both appreciate music	Don't understand music

Grid (Sort No. and constructs 1–22; ⊗ = circled X, ✓ = check, ○ = open circle):

Role	Sort No.	1	2	3	4	5	6	7	8	9	10	11	12	13	14	15	16	17	18	19	20	21	22
Ethical person	19	○			✓		✓	✓			⊗	✓					✓	✓	○	✓		✓	✓
Happy person	18	⊗			✓		⊗		✓			✓	✓	⊗			✓	✓	✓	✓		✓	✓
Successful person	17	⊗	✓	✓		✓			⊗	✓		✓	✓				✓		⊗	✓		✓	✓
Boss	16	○			✓			✓	⊗	✓		✓	✓						⊗	✓			
Rejected teacher	15		⊗		✓	✓	✓			⊗	○	✓	✓				✓	✓	✓	✓		⊗	✓
Accepted teacher	14		⊗	✓		✓	⊗	⊗	✓	✓		✓	✓	✓			✓	✓		✓		⊗	
Attractive person	13			⊗	✓									✓	✓	✓	⊗	✓			○		✓
Threatening person	12	✓		✓								✓	⊗	⊗				✓		○	✓		
Pitied person	11		○								○	✓	✓									✓	✓
Rejecting person	10	✓	⊗								○	⊗	✓	✓				✓				✓	
Ex-pal	9		✓				○						○				○					⊗	
Pal	8		✓		○	✓	✓				✓	✓	✓				⊗	✓			⊗	✓	⊗
Ex-boyfriend/girlfriend	7	✓		⊗						✓		✓		⊗	⊗						✓	○	✓
Spouse	6		✓	⊗	✓							✓		○	⊗	⊗		✓					○
Sister	5		✓	✓		✓	○			✓	⊗	⊗					✓	○	✓	✓			
Brother	4		✓	✓	○	✓	✓	✓	⊗			⊗	✓				✓	⊗	✓				✓
Father	3		✓	⊗		✓	○					✓	✓				○	✓		⊗			
Mother	2		✓	⊗		✓	⊗					✓	✓	✓	○		✓	✓		⊗			
Self	1		✓			✓						✓	✓				✓	⊗					⊗

Figure 13.1

A grid for the Role Construct Repertory Test. SOURCE: Reprinted from *The Psychology of Personal Constructs,* by George A. Kelly. Copyright © 1991 by Routledge, Chapman & Hall, Inc. Reprinted by permission.

Research in Kelly's Theory

Although little research has been conducted on Kelly's theory as a whole, studies using the REP Test have shown that a person's constructs, as measured by the test, are stable over time (Fjeld & Landfield, 1961; Landfield, 1971). One group of subjects took the test twice. The second time they were instructed to use different people as role figures than they had chosen the first time. Although the names of the people differed, the constructs revealed by the subjects remained the same. However, additional research has shown that the test's validity depends heavily on the skill of the psychologist who is interpreting the results (Adams-Webber, 1970; Bonarius, 1976).

One REP Test study investigated how our construct system is organized in terms of complexity, and how it changes over time. The results showed that the construct system becomes increasingly differentiated and integrated as a function of developmental level, and is able to process more information by being able to function in more abstract terms (Crockett, 1982).

Another study suggested that the formation of friendships depends on a similarity of personal constructs (Duck & Spencer, 1972). A group of students took the REP Test during their first week at college, when they were new acquaintances, and again six months later, when friendships had been established. The data showed that the similarity in constructs or attitudes among friends did not develop during the relationship but had existed before the relationship was formed. The researchers suggested that we seek as friends those whose constructs are similar to ours.

College friendships were found to be more likely to endure among persons whose constructs were similar (Duck & Allison, 1978). Analogous results were found with married subjects. Couples whose constructs were most alike reported that they were happier with their marriages than were couples whose constructs were more unlike (Neimeyer, 1984).

Other research shows a correspondence between our personal characteristics and the ways in which we construe other people. Among a group of student nurses, those who were identified as highly anxious tended to use "anxious versus non-anxious" as a construct for evaluating others. Those who were judged by their peers as friendly and pleasant tended to view others in terms of a "friendly versus unfriendly" construct (Sechrest, 1968).

The REP Test has been used to study schizophrenics, neurotics, depressives, and those suffering organic brain damage (Bannister & Fransella, 1966). Compared with normal subjects, schizophrenics were found to be unstable and inconsistent in their construing of other people. However, their construing of objects was stable and consistent, suggesting that their thought disorders applied only to interpersonal situations (Bannister & Salmon, 1966). Their thought processes were also characterized by paranoid delusions and irrational links between constructs (Bannister, Fransella, & Agnew, 1971).

REP Test research with juvenile and adult offenders revealed the following: delinquents tended to identify with action-oriented television heroes rather than with real adults, newly released prisoners showed low self-esteem and aspirations for the future, and rapists felt inadequate and immature and evidenced a preoccupation with personal failure (Needs, 1988).

Researchers have also applied the REP Test in the business world. The test has been used in market research to assess the criteria consumers use to evaluate products they are considering purchasing (Stewart & Stewart, 1982). Industrial/organizational psychologists have used the REP Test for vocational counseling, for employee selection, for evaluating how effectively employees are doing their jobs, and for developing and evaluating training programs (N. R. Anderson, 1990; Brown & Detoy, 1988; Jancowicz & Cooper, 1982; Smith, 1980; Smith & Ashton, 1975).

Cognitive Styles: Complexity and Simplicity

An outgrowth of Kelly's work on personal constructs relates to cognitive styles, the differences in how we perceive or construe the persons, objects, and situations in our environment. Research on cognitive styles was derived from the REP Test and focuses on the concept of cognitive complexity.

cognitive complexity
A cognitive style or way of construing the environment characterized by the ability to perceive differences among people.

A person's degree of **cognitive complexity** can be determined from the pattern of *X*s on the repertory grid. A highly differentiated pattern of *X*s indicates cognitive complexity, the ability to discriminate in the process of applying personal constructs to other people. People high in cognitive complexity are able to see a great deal of variety among people and can easily place a person in many categories.

cognitive simplicity
A cognitive style or way of construing the environment characterized by a relative inability to perceive differences among people.

The other extreme, **cognitive simplicity**, applies when the pattern of *X*s on the repertory grid is the same or highly similar for each construct. This indicates that the person is less capable of perceiving differences when judging other people. Persons high in cognitive simplicity are likely to place others in only one or two categories, unable to see much variety.

Research has demonstrated differences among people who possess these cognitive styles. People high in cognitive complexity are better able to make predictions about others' behavior. They more readily recognize differences between themselves and others, are more empathic, and can deal better with inconsistent information in construing others than can people high in cognitive simplicity (Bieri, 1955; Crockett, 1982; Mayo & Crockett, 1964).

Studies of politicians in the United States and England found that conservatives were high in cognitive simplicity, whereas moderates and liberals displayed higher levels of cognitive complexity (Tetlock, 1983, 1984).

In Kelly's theory, cognitive complexity is the more desirable and useful cognitive style. A goal in developing our construct system is to reduce uncertainty by being able to predict or anticipate what people will do so that we can guide our behavior accordingly. People with a more complex cognitive style will be more successful at this task than will people with a simpler cognitive style. Therefore, cognitive style is an important dimension of personality.

Studies show that cognitive complexity increases with age; adults generally possess greater cognitive complexity than children (Bigner, 1974).

However, age is not a complete explanation for the origin of cognitive complexity. Many adults still possess cognitive simplicity. Much depends on the level of complexity of our childhood experiences. Adults high in cognitive complexity were found to have been exposed in childhood to more diverse influences. Their parents were less authoritarian and more likely to have granted them autonomy than were the parents of adults high in cognitive simplicity (Sechrest & Jackson, 1961).

A Final Commentary

Kelly developed a unique personality theory that was neither a derivative of nor an elaboration on other theories. It emerged from his interpretation—his own construct system—of the data provided by his clinical practice. It is a personal view, and its originality parallels its message: that we are capable of developing our own view of life.

Although the personal construct theory has not gained wide acceptance in the United States, psychologists in Canada, Australia, England, and several European countries are carrying on Kelly's work. Many graduate programs in British universities include courses on personal construct psychology. In the mid-1980s, the Centre for Personal Construct Psychology was established in London to train clinicians in Kelly's techniques and to promote applications of the theory.

Kelly's work is not as popular in the United States for several reasons. First, many psychologists see it as too distinctive, too different from prevailing ideas. Personality psychologists tend to think in terms of familiar concepts, such as motivation and emotion, unconscious forces, drives, and needs. These concepts (the ones we learn about in our first psychology course) form no part of Kelly's system.

Second, compared with other personality theorists, Kelly published few books, articles, or case studies. He devoted most of his time to clinical work and to the training of graduate students. The writing style in his two major books is scholarly and academic, not intended for the general public or for the psychologist seeking explanations of human passions and emotions, loves and hatreds, fears and dreams. That was not the style either of the man or his theory.

Third, many psychologists take issue with a system that omits what they consider a major conceptual tool—an explanation of human motivation. And fourth, Kelly's system has been criticized for its focus on the intellectual and rational aspects of human functioning, to the exclusion of the emotional aspects. Kelly's image of a rational human being constructing the present and future, forming and testing hypotheses, and making predictions and anticipations on which to base behavior does not coincide with the everyday experiences of clinical psychologists, who see the peaks and depths of human joys and failings in their clients. Kelly's rational being seems to them an ideal that exists in the abstract and not in reality.

Although Kelly did not deal explicitly with the emotional side of life, he did so implicitly. Emotions are believed to be personal constructs, similar in their formation to other constructs.

We noted earlier that Freud's view of personality derived from his exposure to neurotic, middle-class Viennese patients, which presented him with a distorted, unrepresentative sample of human nature; other theorists face a similar criticism. Kelly's point of view was also unrepresentative, limited as it was largely to Midwestern adolescents involved in defining a construct system that would help them cope with college life.

Kelly's theory, like many others, leaves us with unanswered questions. Each of us is able to construe events and experiences in a unique way, but why does one person construe an event in one way while another person construes the identical event in a different way? What process or mechanism accounts for the difference? A person makes choices about defining or extending the construct system. What determines whether to opt for security or for adventure, for the safer or the riskier choice?

Kelly recognized the limitations of his program and made no pretense of setting forth a finished theory. Just as an individual's constructs change in light of new experiences, so Kelly expected the personal construct theory to change in the light of further research and application. His contributions have been recognized with honors from the profession and from former students, and his theory is one of the most unusual to appear in a century of theorizing about the nature of the human personality.

Summary

George Kelly explained personality in terms of the cognitive constructs we use to make predictions about ourselves and others. He viewed people as similar to scientists who construct hypotheses and test them against reality—the procedure used by psychologists to study personality.

A personal construct is a way of looking at the events in our world. Kelly's fundamental postulate states that our psychological processes are directed by the ways we anticipate events and construe our world. Kelly's theory includes the following 11 corollaries:

1. *Construction:* We anticipate events by construing them in terms of their similarities with past events.
2. *Individuality:* People differ in the ways in which they construe events.
3. *Organization:* We organize our constructs into a system or pattern according to our view of the relationships among them.
4. *Dichotomy:* All constructs are bipolar or dichotomous to take account of opposites or dissimilarities among people and events.
5. *Choice:* In a dichotomous construct, we always choose the alternative that leads to the greater possibility for defining or extending our construct system; definition refers to the secure choice, and extension refers to the adventurous choice.

6. *Range:* A construct has a limited range of convenience; it is not relevant or applicable to all situations.
7. *Experience:* Our construct system must be revised in light of new experiences.
8. *Modulation:* How thoroughly our construct system can be changed or modulated as a function of new experiences depends on how permeable, or open, our constructs are.
9. *Fragmentation:* Two constructs may be compatible or consistent in one situation, but if the situation changes, the same constructs may be inconsistent.
10. *Commonality:* If two or more persons construe an experience in a similar way, their psychological processes will be similar.
11. *Sociality:* For effective interpersonal relations, we must construe the constructs of others.

Kelly presented a flattering, optimistic image of human nature that depicts us as rational beings with free will, capable of formulating our destiny. We are not bound by constructs developed at one stage of life or by past experiences, unconscious conflicts, and biological instincts. Our ultimate goal is to define a set of constructs that enables us to predict events.

Kelly assessed personality by accepting a person's words at face value, by having the person write a self-characterization sketch, and by administering the Role Construct Repertory (REP) Test. The REP Test uncovers the dichotomies important in a person's life, revealing their pattern of personal constructs. Fixed role therapy involves having a client act out the constructs of an imaginary person to demonstrate how the new constructs can be more effective than the old ones.

Research using the REP Test has shown that constructs are stable over time. The validity of the test depends on the skill of the psychologist interpreting it. The REP Test has been used for market research, performance appraisal, and vocational counseling.

People high in cognitive complexity are better able to predict the behavior of others. They more readily recognize differences between themselves and others, are more empathic, deal better with inconsistent information in construing others, and experienced greater complexity in childhood than people high in cognitive simplicity.

Kelly's work has been criticized for omitting familiar concepts such as motivation and emotion, for focusing on the intellectual and rational aspects of human functioning to the exclusion of emotional aspects, and for relying on an unrepresentative sample of subjects.

Critical Thinking Review

1. How does Kelly's approach to personality differ from the other approaches we have discussed?

2. What is the relationship between Kelly's cognitive theory and modern cognitive psychology?

3. How might Kelly's theory have been influenced by the kinds of clients he treated?

4. What is Kelly's definition of the term *construct?* Why must constructs be dichotomous?

5. What factors influence the ways we anticipate those events that are similar to past events?

6. How do we choose between the two alternatives offered by a construct?

7. What is a construct's range of convenience? In your construct system, what is the range of convenience for the construct "cheerful versus sad"?

8. What mechanism did Kelly propose to account for changes in a construct's range of convenience?

9. How is it possible for us to hold incompatible or inconsistent constructs?

10. What is Kelly's position on the issue of free will versus determinism?

11. What is the purpose of the Role Construct Repertory Test? What does research using the REP Test show about the cognitive styles of simplicity and complexity?

12. What is fixed role therapy?

Suggested Reading

Epting, F. R. (1984). *Personal construct counseling and psychotherapy.* New York: Wiley. The first major textbook on the principles of Kelly's personality theory and their clinical applications.

Fransella, F., & Thomas, L. (Eds.). (1988). *Experimenting with personal construct psychology.* London: Routledge & Kegan Paul. Provides a survey of research worldwide on personal construct theory and on applications in clinical, educational, and industrial settings.

Jancowicz, A. D. (1987). Whatever became of George Kelly? Applications and implications. *American Psychologist, 42,* 481–487. Reviews and assesses the impact of Kelly's work; published on the 20th anniversary of his death.

Kelly, G. A. (1969). *Clinical psychology and personality: The selected papers of George Kelly.* New York: Wiley. Selections from Kelly's writings, edited by Brendan Maher. See Chapter 2, "The Autobiography of a Theory," for Kelly's description of the impact of personal experience on the development of his theory.

Thompson, G. G. (1968). George Alexander Kelly: 1905–1967. *Journal of General Psychology, 79,* 19–24. Reviews Kelly's life and work.

VIII

The Behavioral Approach

In Chapter 1 we briefly considered the behavioral approach to psychology and the work of John B. Watson, the founder of behaviorism. His behaviorist psychology focused on overt behavior—on subjects' responses to external stimuli. This natural-science approach to psychology, based on careful experimental research and precise quantification of stimulus and response variables, was popular in the psychology of the 1920s and remained a major force in the field for more than 60 years.

There was no room in Watson's behaviorism for conscious or unconscious forces because those things could not be seen, manipulated, or measured. Watson believed that whatever might be happening inside an organism—whether an animal or a person—between the presentation of a stimulus and the elicitation of a response had no value or use for science. Such internal processes could not be experimented upon.

In the behavioral approach, we find no reference to internal conditions, such as anxiety, drives, motives, needs, or defense mechanisms, the processes invoked by most other personality theorists. To the behaviorists, personality is nothing more than an accumulation of learned responses to stimuli, sets of overt behaviors, or habit systems. Personality refers only to what can be objectively observed and manipulated.

The behavioral approach to personality is represented here by the work of B. F. Skinner, whose ideas follow the Watsonian tradition. Skinner rejected as irrelevant any alleged internal forces or processes. His sole concern was with overt behavior and the external stimuli that shape it.

Skinner attempted to understand what others called personality through laboratory research rather than clinical work. His ideas have been applied in the clinical setting, however, through behavior-modification techniques.

FOURTEEN

B. F. Skinner

The Life of Skinner (1904–1990)
Reinforcement: The Basis of Behavior
   Respondent Behavior
   Operant Behavior
Schedules of Reinforcement
Successive Approximation: The Shaping of
   Behavior
Superstitious Behavior
The Self-Control of Behavior
Applications of Operant Conditioning

Skinner's Image of Human Nature
Assessment in Skinner's Theory
   Direct Observation of Behavior
   The Self-Report Technique
   Physiological Measurements
Research in Skinner's Theory
A Final Commentary
Summary
Critical Thinking Review
Suggested Reading

It is the environment which must be changed.

—B. F. Skinner

B. F. Skinner did not offer a personality theory that can be contrasted and compared with the others discussed in this book. In fact, he did not offer a personality theory at all, nor does his research deal specifically with personality.

Skinner's work is an attempt to account for all behavior—not just what some theorists call personality—and to account for it in factual and descriptive terms. "You can't get results by sitting around and theorizing about the inner world," he told an interviewer. "I want to say to those people: get down to the facts" (quoted in Hall, 1967, p. 70). Skinner argued that psychologists must restrict their investigations to what they can see, manipulate, and measure in the laboratory. That means an exclusive emphasis on the overt responses a subject makes and nothing more. His contention is that psychology is the science of behavior, the study of what an organism does.

We have noted that this approach fits the behaviorism promoted by John B. Watson. The spirit of Watson's behaviorist revolution in psychology, which influenced the young Skinner, lived on in more sophisticated and fully developed fashion in Skinner's emphasis on the study of behavior. Skinner's work, like Watson's before him, is the antithesis of the psychoanalytic, trait, life-span, cognitive, and humanistic approaches to personality, differing not only in subject matter but in methodology and aims.

In explaining the nature of personality, most other theorists look inside the person for clues. In their view, the causes, motives, and drives, the forces that direct our development and behavior, originate within each of us. Skinner, in contrast, made no reference to internal states to account for behavior. Unconscious influences, defense mechanisms, traits, and other driving forces cannot be seen and therefore have no place in a scientific psychology. He argued that such alleged internal driving forces are no more real, and have no more value to science, than the old philosophical and theological concept of the soul.

Skinner applied the same reasoning to physiological processes, which are not overtly observable and so have no relevance for science. "The inside of the organism," he claimed, "is irrelevant either as the site of physiological processes or as the locus of mentalistic activities" (quoted in Evans, 1968, p. 22). There is no need to look inside the organism for some form of inner activity. To Skinner, human beings are empty organisms; there is nothing inside us that can be invoked to explain our behavior in scientific terms. In the person-situation debate, then, Skinner was clearly and exclusively on the side of the environment or situation.

Another way Skinner diverged from other theorists is in the kind of subject he studied. Some theorists chose emotionally disturbed persons as their focus of study. Others insisted that only normal or average individuals be studied. At least one used only the best and brightest people. Skinner did not take normal, subnormal, or supernormal persons as his subjects. Although his ideas about behavior have been applied to human beings, the research that led to the development of his behavioral theory was conducted with rats and pigeons.

How can we learn about the human personality from pigeons? Remember that Skinner's interest was in responses to stimuli, not in what a patient reports about childhood experiences or adult feelings. Responding to stimuli is something animals do well, sometimes better than humans. Skinner granted that human behavior is more complex than animal behavior, but he noted that the difference is in degree, not in kind. He believed that the fundamental processes are similar. Because a science must proceed from simple to complex, the more elemental processes should be studied first. Therefore, Skinner chose to study animal behavior because it is simpler.

Skinner's work has been of monumental importance in American psychology. The American Psychological Foundation awarded Skinner its Gold Medal, and the American Psychological Association gave him the Distinguished Scientific Contribution Award. The citation read: "Few American psychologists have had so profound an impact on the development of psychology and on promising younger psychologists" ("Distinguished," 1958).

The magazine *Psychology Today* noted that "when history makes its judgment, he may well be known as the major contributor to psychology in this century" (Hall, 1967, p. 21). His first book on behaviorism, *The Behavior of Organisms: An Experimental Analysis* (Skinner, 1938), was described as "one of a handful of books that changed the face of modern psychology" (Thompson, 1988, p. 397). Skinner's controversial 1971 book, *Beyond Freedom and Dignity,* became a best-seller and prompted his appearance on television talk shows, making him a modern celebrity. He received the National Medal of Science from the U.S. government and appeared on the cover of *Time* magazine, labeled "the most famous American psychologist in the world."

Skinner's work has had wide practical applications. He invented an automatic baby-tending device and was responsible for promoting the use of teaching machines. He published a successful novel that offers a program for behavioral control of human society. His methodology is applied today in clinical settings to treat psychoses, mental retardation, and autism. His behavior-modification technique is used in a variety of settings, including schools, businesses, correctional institutions, and hospitals.

The Life of Skinner (1904–1990)

B. F. Skinner was born in Susquehanna, Pennsylvania, the older of two sons; his brother died at the age of 16. His parents were hardworking people who instilled in their children clear rules of proper behavior. "I was taught to fear God, the police, and what people will think," Skinner wrote (1967, p. 407). His mother never deviated from her strict standards. Her method of control was to say "tut-tut." Skinner's grandmother made certain that he understood the punishments of Hell by pointing out the red-hot coals in the parlor stove. Skinner's father also contributed to his son's moral education by teaching him the fate that befell criminals. He showed Skinner the county jail and took him to a lecture about life in a notorious New York state prison.

Skinner's autobiography contains many references to the influence of these childhood admonitions and instructions on his adult behavior. He told of visiting a cathedral as an adult and taking care to avoid stepping on the gravestones set in the floor. As a child he had been warned that such behavior wasn't right. These and other instances made it clear to him that many facets of his adult life were determined by the rewards and punishments—the reinforcements—he had received in childhood.

His system of psychology and his view of people as "complex system[s] behaving in lawful ways" reflected his early life experiences (Skinner, 1971, p. 202).

> I do not believe that my life shows a type of personality à la Freud, an archetypal pattern à la Jung, or a schedule of development à la Erikson. There have been a few abiding themes, but they can be traced to environmental sources. [Skinner, 1983b, p. 25]

Also prophetic of his later view of people as machines were the many hours young Skinner spent designing and constructing machines—wagons, seesaws, merry-go-rounds, slingshots, water pistols, model airplanes, a flotation system to separate ripe from unripe berries, and a steam cannon used to shoot potato and carrot plugs over neighboring houses. He also worked on a perpetual-motion machine, which perpetually failed.

Skinner's interest in animal behavior derived from childhood experiences. He caught and made pets of an assortment of animals, including turtles, snakes, toads, lizards, and chipmunks. He read about animals and once saw a flock of performing pigeons at a county fair. The pigeons raced onstage pulling a fire engine up to a burning building. They shoved a ladder against the building, and one trained pigeon fire fighter climbed to an upper-story window to rescue a stranded pigeon. Skinner later trained pigeons to perform such feats as playing Ping-Pong and guiding a missile to its target.

As a boy, Skinner liked school and was habitually the first to arrive in the morning. After graduating from high school in a class of eight, he attended Hamilton College in Clinton, New York. He felt uncomfortable with student life, was poor at sports, and objected to compulsory chapel. He was also disappointed by the lack of intellectual interest of his fellow students. By his senior year he was in open revolt. He disrupted the college community with hoaxes, including one that jammed the campus with people arriving to hear a lecture by Charlie Chaplin, the movie star, whose appearance Skinner had falsely announced with posters distributed all over town. He wrote newspaper articles critical of the college faculty and administration. His antics continued to the last possible moment, when the president warned Skinner and his friends during commencement ceremonies that they would not graduate if they did not behave.

Skinner's career plans after graduation had nothing to do with psychology. He had majored in English and was committed to becoming a novelist. Encouraged by favorable comment on his work from the eminent poet Robert Frost, Skinner built a study in the attic of his parents' home in Scranton, Pennsylvania, and sat down to write. The results were disastrous. He read, he listened to the radio, he played the piano, and he built ship models. He also considered seeing a psychiatrist. He was 22 years old and a failure at the only thing he wanted to do.

He later referred to that time as his dark year, and his dilemma soon took on the characteristics of what Erik Erikson would have called an identity crisis. Skinner's occupational identity as a writer, which he had so carefully constructed during his college years and which had been reinforced by Frost's comments, collapsed. With it went his sense of self-worth, because not only Skinner himself, but also his parents, friends, and the rest of the world, viewed him as a failure.

"The world considers me lazy because I do not earn bread," he wrote. "The world expects of me that I should measure up to its standard of strength, which means that if I 'got a job' for eight hours of office work . . . I should be a man" (Skinner, 1976, pp. 282–283). He left Scranton for New York City's Greenwich Village but found that he could not write there either. "I was floundering in a stormy sea and perilously close to drowning" (Skinner, 1976, p. 298). To make matters worse, in his view, at least half a dozen young women spurned his proclaimed love for them, leaving him so distraught that he branded the first letter of one woman's name on his arm, where it remained for years (Skinner, 1983a).

But when Skinner believed he had lost all hope, he found an identity to which he would cling for the rest of his life. He decided that writing had failed him (rather than the other way around), and he resolved to study human behavior by the methods of science rather than the methods of fiction. He read books by Ivan Pavlov and John B. Watson, and these reinforced his point of view. He became a behaviorist, and his self-image and identity were secure.

Skinner entered graduate school at Harvard University in 1928 to study psychology, having never taken a course in the field. With dedication and effort, he earned his Ph.D. in three years. His choice of behaviorism led him to reject the mental and emotional forces he had tried to draw on as a writer. One historian of psychology noted:

> [There are] essential differences between a career devoted to writing poetry and fiction and one devoted to promoting the cause of behaviorism. The former requires commitment to such intrapsychic processes as inspiration, intuition, free association, the stream of consciousness, and the participation of the unconscious, as well as considering fantasies and feelings important parts of one's being. The latter denies it all—makes fantasies and feelings, indeed the entire intrapsychic domain, recede into a background of (to use Skinner's favorite term) "pre-scientific" notions, while attention is focused on observable behavior and the operations necessary to record, predict, and control it effectively. [Mindess, 1988, p. 105]

Psychic processes appeared in Skinner's work only as objects of scorn and derision.

With postdoctoral fellowships, Skinner stayed at Harvard until 1936. He then joined the faculty of the University of Minnesota in Minneapolis, remained until 1945, spent two years at Indiana University in Bloomington, and returned to Harvard.

In 1945, at the age of 41, Skinner experienced a second period of inner turmoil—this time a midlife crisis, which he resolved by returning temporarily to his failed identity as a writer. Depressed about many aspects of his life, he poured out his personal and intellectual frustrations in a novel entitled *Walden Two,* letting his voice speak through the main character, T. E. Frazier (Skinner, 1948). "Much of the life in *Walden Two* was my own at the time," Skinner admitted. "I let Frazier say things I myself was not yet ready to say to anyone" (Skinner, 1979, pp. 297–298). In the novel, Frazier speaks openly about his emotional discontents.

The book has sold millions of copies and is still available in paperback. It describes a society in which all aspects of life are controlled by positive reinforcement, the basic principle of Skinner's system of psychology. The story inspired the establishment of several utopian communities and engendered a great deal of controversy.

Skinner continued to work into his eighties, with as much enthusiasm and dedication as when he entered the field. He regulated his work habits with precision, recording his daily work output and average time spent per published word (two minutes) and mirroring his definition of a person as a complex system behaving in lawful ways. He constructed a personal "Skinner box," a controlled environment that provided positive reinforcement, in the basement office of his home. He slept in a yellow plastic tank large enough for a mattress, some shelves, and a small television set. He went to bed each night at 10:00, slept for three hours, worked at his desk for an hour, slept three more hours, and rose at 5:00 A.M. for three more hours of work before walking a mile to his Harvard office. He administered positive reinforcement each afternoon by listening to music.

In August 1990, eight days before he died of leukemia, Skinner presented a paper at the American Psychological Association convention in Boston. "Frail and worn at 86 years of age, he spoke unhesitatingly and fluidly for fifteen minutes, without reference to notes" (Holland, 1992, p. 665). In that last speech, he denounced the cognitive psychology movement that was overtaking his behavioral approach to human behavior.

Reinforcement: The Basis of Behavior

Though based on thousands of hours of well-controlled research, Skinner's approach to behavior is simple in its essential concept, which is that all behavior can be controlled by its consequences; that is, by what follows the behavior. Skinner believed that an animal or a human could be trained to perform virtually any act by the extent and nature of the reinforcement that followed the behavior. Thus, whoever controls the reinforcers has the power to control human behavior, in the same way an experimenter can control the behavior of a laboratory rat.

Respondent Behavior

respondent behaviors
Responses made to or elicited by specific environmental stimuli.

Skinner distinguished between two kinds of behavior: respondent behavior and operant behavior. **Respondent behavior** involves a response made to or elicited by a specific stimulus. A reflex, such as a knee jerk, is an example of respondent behavior. A stimulus is applied (a tap on the knee), and the response occurs (the leg jerks). This behavior is unlearned. We do not have to be trained or conditioned to make the appropriate response; it occurs automatically and involuntarily.

At a higher level is respondent behavior that is learned. This learning, called conditioning, involves the substitution of one stimulus for another. The concept originated in the work of the Russian physiologist Ivan Pavlov in the early 1900s. (Pavlov's ideas on conditioning were adopted by the psychologist John B. Watson as the fundamental research method for his system of behaviorism.) Working with dogs, Pavlov discovered that they would salivate to neutral stimuli, such as the sound of their keeper's footsteps. Previously, the response of salivation had been elicited by only one stimulus, the sight of food.

Intrigued by this observation, Pavlov studied the phenomenon systematically. He sounded a bell shortly before feeding a dog. At first the dog salivated

Animals can be conditioned by reinforcing them with food when they exhibit desired behaviors.

only in response to the food; the bell had no meaning. After a number of pairings of the bell followed by the food, the dog began to salivate at the sound of the bell. Thus, the dog had been conditioned or trained to respond to the bell. The response had shifted from the food to a previously neutral stimulus.

The essential feature of this now-classic experiment was Pavlov's demonstration of the importance of **reinforcement**. The dogs did not learn to respond to the bell unless they were rewarded—in this case, with food. From this work, Pavlov formulated a law of learning: A conditioned response cannot be established in the absence of reinforcement.

reinforcement The act of strengthening a response by adding a reward, thus increasing the likelihood that the response will be repeated.

Nor can an established conditioned response be maintained in the absence of reinforcement. Consider a dog conditioned to respond to the sound of a bell. Every time the bell rings, the dog salivates. The experimenter suddenly stops presenting food after sounding the bell. The dog hears the bell, and nothing happens—no more food, no more reinforcement. With successive ringings of the bell, the dog's salivary response decreases in frequency and intensity until no response occurs at all. The response has been extinguished because reinforcers or rewards for it were no longer forthcoming.

Operant Behavior

operant behaviors Behaviors, emitted spontaneously or voluntarily, that operate on the environment and change it.

Respondent behavior depends on reinforcement and is made directly to a physical stimulus. Every response is elicited by a specific stimulus. Skinner believed that this respondent form of conditioning was less important than what he called **operant behavior**. We are conditioned to respond directly to many stimuli in our environment, but not all of our behavior can be accounted for in this way. Much of our behavior appears spontaneous and cannot be traced directly to specific stimuli. Such behavior is said to be emitted rather than elicited by a stimulus. It involves acting in a way that appears to be voluntary rather than reacting involuntarily to a stimulus to which we have been conditioned.

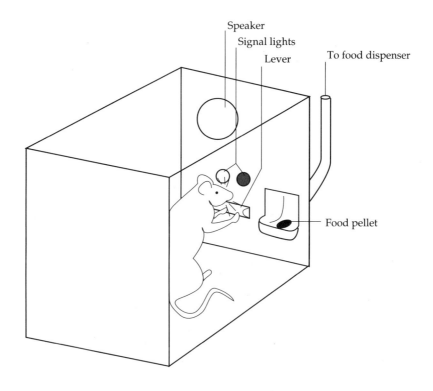

Figure 14.1

A simple operant-conditioning apparatus.

The nature and frequency of operant behavior will be determined or modified by the reinforcement that follows it. Respondent behavior has no effect on the environment: the dog's salivary response to the ringing bell does nothing to change the bell or the reinforcer (the food) that follows. In contrast, operant behavior operates on the environment and, as a result, changes it.

operant conditioning
The procedure by which a change in the consequences of a response will affect the rate at which the response occurs.

To illustrate the **operant-conditioning** process, let us follow the progress of a rat in Skinner's operant-conditioning apparatus, destined forever to be known as the "Skinner box" (see Figure 14.1). When a rat that has been deprived of food for a period of time is placed in the box, its behavior at first is spontaneous and random. The rat is active, sniffing, poking, and exploring its environment. These behaviors are emitted, not elicited; the rat is not responding to any specific stimulus in its environment.

At some time during this activity, the rat will depress a lever or bar located on one wall of the box, causing a food pellet to drop into a trough. The rat's behavior (pressing the lever) has operated on the environment and changed it. That environment now includes a food pellet. The food is a reinforcer for the behavior of depressing the bar.

The rat begins to press the bar more frequently. What happens? It receives more food (more reinforcement) and, as a result, presses the bar even more often. The rat's behavior is now under the control of the reinforcement. Its actions in the box are less random and spontaneous. It spends most of its time pressing the bar—and eating.

If we put the rat back in the box the next day, we can predict what it will do, and we can control its actions by presenting or withholding the reinforcer, or by presenting it at a different rate. Withholding the food extinguishes the operant behavior in the same way that it extinguishes respondent behavior. The unreinforced behavior no longer works—it no longer brings a reward—and so, after a while, it stops.

A classic human example of this is a baby who cries at bedtime. The crying usually brings reinforcement in the form of attention from the parents. In this way, the baby is able to influence parental behavior. The mother or father responds (provides a reward, such as a hug, a lullaby, or a bottle of warm milk) every time the infant cries. If the parents wish to stop or extinguish this crying behavior, they can do so by not reinforcing it. The behavior will be extinguished when it no longer brings the reinforcement of parental attention. Thus, the person who controls the reinforcers controls behavior.

Skinner believed that most human and animal behavior is learned in this way. An infant initially displays random, spontaneous behaviors, only some of which are reinforced by its parents. As the infant grows, the positively reinforced behaviors (those of which the parents approve) will persist, whereas those of which the parents disapprove will be discontinued. The concept is the same with the rat in the Skinner box. Those behaviors that work (such as pressing the bar to obtain food) are repeated, and those that do not work are not. The organism's behavior operates on the environment. The environment—in the form of reinforcement—operates, in turn, on the organism's behavior.

You can see how powerful reinforcement can be in determining and controlling behavior. "Operant conditioning," Skinner wrote, "shapes behavior as a sculptor shapes a lump of clay" (1953, p. 91). If the lump of clay wants or needs the reinforcer badly enough, there is virtually no limit to how it can be shaped by an experimenter with a food pellet, a puppy owner with a dog biscuit, a mother with a smile, a boss with a pat on the back, or a government with a promise.

From infancy on, we display many behaviors, and those that are reinforced grow stronger and form networks or patterns. That is all Skinner meant by personality—a pattern or collection of operant behaviors. To Skinner, what others called neurotic or abnormal behavior was nothing more mysterious than the continued performance of behaviors that have been reinforced.

Seeking to perfect a method for the modification and control of behavior, Skinner pursued a related line of research. Having demonstrated how behavior can be modified by continuous reinforcement, by presenting a reinforcer after every response, he then asked how behavior would change if he varied the rate at which it was reinforced. What led Skinner to ask this question was a practical matter, more a matter of expediency than of intellectual curiosity.

It all started with the food pellets used to reinforce the rats in the Skinner box. Today food pellets are available from commercial producers and need merely to be taken from a bag to be ready to use. In the 1930s, experimenters and their luckless graduate students spent many hours making food pellets, a tedious and laborious procedure. In Skinner's laboratory, at least 800 pellets a day were required to keep the research going.

One Saturday afternoon Skinner discovered that, unless he spent the day and evening making food pellets, the supply would be exhausted by Monday. Even for a dedicated researcher, spending the weekend slaving over the pellet machine was not an attractive prospect. Then an alternative occurred to him. Why did he have to reinforce every response? What would happen if the rat were reinforced only once a minute, regardless of how many responses it made?

As a result of this line of reasoning, Skinner and his students spent less time making food pellets, and Skinner embarked on a research program considered to be his most significant contribution—the investigation of different schedules of reinforcement.

Schedules of Reinforcement

In everyday life outside the psychology laboratory, behavior is not reinforced every time it occurs: a baby is not picked up every time it cries. The baseball player does not hit a home run every time at bat. The bagger in the supermarket does not receive a tip or a "thank you" for each bag packed. There are countless examples of behaviors that persist even though they are reinforced only intermittently.

reinforcement schedules Patterns or rates of providing or withholding reinforcers.

Seeing that his rats continued to press the bar at a fairly constant response rate even when they were not being reinforced continuously, Skinner proceeded to investigate different **reinforcement schedules** to determine which would be most effective in controlling behavior. Among the various rates of reinforcement he tested are fixed interval, fixed ratio, variable interval, and variable ratio.

A fixed-interval schedule of reinforcement means that the reinforcer is presented at fixed time intervals. It might be given every minute or every three minutes. Note that reinforcement has nothing to do with the number of responses the subject makes. Whether the rat responds once a minute or 20 times a minute, the reinforcer still arrives only after the passage of a given interval.

Many situations operate in accordance with the fixed-interval schedule of reinforcement. If your professor gives a midterm and a final examination, he or she is operating on a fixed-interval schedule. A job in which your salary is paid once a week or once a month operates on the fixed-interval schedule. You are not paid according to the number of items you produce or the number of sales you make (the number of responses) but by the number of hours, days, or weeks that elapse.

Skinner's research showed that the shorter the interval between presentations of the reinforcers, the greater the frequency of response. The response rate declined as the interval between reinforcements lengthened. How frequently the reinforcers appeared also affected how quickly the response could be extinguished. The response stopped sooner if the rat had been reinforced continuously and the reinforcement was then stopped, than if the rat had been reinforced intermittently.

In the fixed-ratio schedule of reinforcement, the reinforcer is presented only after the organism has made a specified number of responses. For example, the experimenter could reinforce after every 10th or 20th response. In this schedule, unlike the fixed-interval schedule, the presentation of reinforcement depends on how frequently the subject responds; the rat will not receive a food pellet until it emits the required number of responses. This reinforcement schedule brings about a faster response rate than the fixed-interval schedule.

The higher response rate for the fixed-ratio schedule has been found to operate in a variety of situations for rats, pigeons, and humans. In a job in which your pay is determined on a piece-rate basis, how much you earn depends on how much you produce. The more items you produce, the higher your pay. Your reward is based directly on your rate of responding. The same is true for a salesperson working on commission. Income depends on the number of units of the product sold; the more sold, the more earned. In contrast, a salesperson on a weekly salary earns the same amount each week, regardless of how much of the product he or she sells.

It often happens in everyday life that reinforcement does not follow a fixed-interval or fixed-ratio schedule but appears on a variable basis. In the variable-interval schedule of reinforcement, the reinforcer might appear after two hours in the first instance, after an hour and a half the next time, and after two hours and fifteen minutes the third time. For example, a person who spends the day fishing might be rewarded, if at all, on a variable-interval basis, the rate of reinforcement being determined by the random appearance of the fish.

A variable-ratio schedule of reinforcement is based on an average number of responses between reinforcers, but there is great variability around that average. Skinner found that the variable-ratio schedule is effective in bringing about high and stable response rates, as those who operate gambling casinos can happily attest. For example, slot machines, roulette wheels, and horse races pay off on a variable-ratio reinforcement schedule, and—as any addicted gambler can tell you—it is an extremely effective means of controlling behavior.

Skinner's research on different reinforcement schedules provides a technique for increased efficiency in controlling, modifying, and shaping behavior. If you are in charge of rats, salespersons, or assembly-line workers, or are trying to train your pet or your child, these operant-conditioning techniques can be useful in inducing the kinds of behaviors you desire. These techniques have been widely applied in clinical and business settings, as we shall see in a later section.

Successive Approximation: The Shaping of Behavior

shaping An explanation for the acquisition of complex behaviors. Behaviors, such as learning to speak, are reinforced only as they come to approximate or approach the final desired behavior. Sometimes called **successive approximation.**

In Skinner's original operant-conditioning experiment, the operant behavior (pressing the lever) is a simple behavior, one the rat would be expected to display naturally in the course of exploring its environment. Thus, the probability of its occurrence is high. It is obvious that animals and humans demonstrate more complex operant behaviors that, in the normal course of events, have a low probability of occurrence. How are these complex behaviors learned? How can an experimenter or a parent provide reinforcement and condition a pigeon or a child to perform behaviors that are not likely to occur spontaneously?

Skinner answered this question by proposing the method of **successive approximation** or **shaping**. He demonstrated its use by training a pigeon in a very short time to peck at a particular spot in its cage. The probability of the pigeon's pecking at that spot on its own was low. At first, the pigeon was reinforced with food when it turned toward the designated spot. Then reinforcement was withheld until the pigeon made some movement, however slight, toward the spot. Reinforcers were given only for movements that brought the pigeon nearer the spot. Next, the pigeon was reinforced only when it thrust its head toward the spot. In the final stage, the pigeon was reinforced only when its beak touched the spot. This sounds like a time-consuming and laborious procedure, but Skinner found that pigeons could be conditioned in fewer than three minutes.

The experimental procedure explains the term *successive approximation.* The organism is reinforced only as its behavior comes, in successive stages, to approximate the final behavior desired. This method has been used to train animals to do tricks, and Skinner contended that it is also the way in which children learn to speak.

Infants emit all sorts of meaningless sounds, which parents reinforce by smiling, laughing, and talking, Soon parents reinforce their baby's babbling differentially, providing stronger reinforcement for the sounds that approximate words. As the process continues, parental reinforcement is increasingly restricted, given only for proper usage and pronunciation. Thus, complex behavior such as the acquisition of language can be ''constructed by a continual process of differential reinforcement from undifferentiated behavior'' (Skinner, 1953, pp. 92–93).

Skinner was once responsible for shaping the behavior of the psychoanalyst Erich Fromm (Chapter 6), whose comments during a lecture annoyed him. According to Skinner, Fromm had ''something to say about almost everything, but with little enlightenment. When he began to argue that people were not pigeons, I decided that something had to be done.'' Skinner passed a note to a friend: ''Watch Fromm's left hand. I am going to shape a chopping motion.''

Fromm gestured freely with his arms and hands when he talked. Whenever Fromm raised his left hand, Skinner looked directly at him with a steady gaze. When Fromm lowered his hand, Skinner nodded and smiled. ''Within

Parents teach their children acceptable behaviors by reinforcing those activities that approximate the final desired behaviors.

five minutes," Skinner wrote, "[Fromm] was chopping the air so vigorously that his wristwatch kept slipping out over his hand" (Skinner, 1983a, pp. 150–151).

Superstitious Behavior

Life is not always as orderly or well controlled as events in the psychology laboratory. Sometimes we are reinforced accidentally after we have displayed some behavior. As a result, that behavior, which did not lead to or cause the reinforcement, may be repeated in a similar situation. Suppose an aspiring actor wears a blue shirt for an audition and gets a part. At the next audition, the actor happens to be wearing a blue shirt and again is rewarded with a part. The connection between wearing the blue shirt and receiving acting roles is coincidental, but the actor may come to believe that one event causes or depends on the other and will in future attend auditions only when wearing the "lucky" blue shirt.

superstitious behaviors Persistent behaviors that have a coincidental and not a functional relationship to the reinforcement received.

Skinner called this **superstitious behavior** and demonstrated it in the laboratory. A hungry pigeon was placed in the operant-conditioning apparatus and reinforced on a fixed-interval schedule every 15 seconds. Recall that, under such a schedule, the reinforcer is given after a specified time interval whether or not the subject has displayed the desired response.

It is likely that the pigeon will be exhibiting some behavior or activity when the reinforcer is given. It may be turning, raising its head, strutting, hopping, or standing still. Whatever behavior is being emitted at the moment of reinforcement will be reinforced. Skinner found that a single reinforcement was powerful enough for the pigeon to display the accidentally reinforced behavior more frequently for a while, increasing the probability that another food pellet would appear while the same behavior was being displayed. With short intervals between reinforcers, superstitious behaviors are learned quickly.

Like the actor and the blue shirt, the superstitious behavior offered by the pigeon has no functional relationship to the reinforcement; the connection is unintentional. Such behavior may persist throughout life, and only occasional reinforcement is required to sustain it.

The Self-Control of Behavior

The basic tenet of Skinner's approach is that behavior is controlled and modified by variables external to the organism. There is nothing inside us—no process, drive, or other internal activity—that determines our behavior. However, although external stimuli and reinforcers are the shapers of behavior, we have the power to act to change them.

self-control The ability to exert control over the variables that determine our behavior.

Skinner proposed the idea of **self-control**. He did not mean control by some mysterious force called "the self," but rather our control of the external variables that determine our behavior. For example, if the music from your neighbor's stereo annoyed you and interfered with your ability to concentrate on this book, you could leave your room and go to the library to study, thereby removing yourself from an external variable that affects and controls your behavior. By avoiding some person or situation that makes you angry, you reduce the amount of control that person or situation has over your behavior. Similarly, alcoholics can act to avoid a stimulus that controls their behavior by not allowing liquor to be kept at home.

Skinner offered other examples of self-control. Through self-administered satiation, people can cure themselves of bad habits by overdoing the behavior. Smokers who want to quit can force themselves to chain-smoke for a period of time, inhaling until they become so disgusted, uncomfortable, or ill that they quit. This technique has been successful in clinical programs designed to eliminate smoking.

Another technique of self-control involves unpleasant or aversive stimulation. For example, obese people who want to lose weight declare their intention to their friends. If they do not keep their resolution to lose weight, they face the unpleasant consequences of personal failure and embarrassment and the possibility of criticism from their friends. An additional self-control technique is self-reinforcement for displaying good or desirable behaviors. For example, a teenager who agrees to care for a younger child might reward himself or herself by buying a new pair of jeans.

The important point is that, to Skinner, external variables shape and control behavior. But we are sometimes able to modify the effects of these external forces through our own actions.

Applications of Operant Conditioning

behavior modification A form of therapy that applies the principles of reinforcement to bring about desired behavioral changes.

token economy A behavior-modification technique in which tokens, which can be exchanged for valued objects or privileges, are awarded for desirable behaviors.

In clinical, business, and educational institutions, psychologists routinely apply Skinner's ideas on operant conditioning to modify behavior. This approach, called **behavior modification**, has been successful with children and adults, with the mentally healthy and the mentally disturbed, and with individual behavior problems as well as group behavior.

The classic example of an application of Skinner's conditioning principles is the **token economy**. In the initial study, a ward of more than 40 psychotic women patients in a state mental institution was treated as a giant Skinner box (Ayllon & Azrin, 1968). The patients were considered to be beyond treatment by conventional means. They had been institutionalized for a long time, were unable to care for themselves, and spent their days aimlessly.

In this setting the patients were offered opportunities to work at jobs, usually performed by paid hospital attendants, for which they would receive tokens. These tokens could be used like money to buy privileges and possessions. With a certain number of tokens the patients could purchase candy, cigarettes, lipstick, gloves, and newspapers. By paying with tokens, they could attend a movie on the ward, take a walk around the hospital grounds, or move to a more private room. The most expensive privileges—those that required 100 tokens—were a trip into town with an escort and a private meeting with a social worker. (Incidentally, a private meeting with a psychologist cost only 20 tokens.)

Like people outside, these patients could buy items and privileges to improve the quality of their life. Their tokens functioned like money, hence the term *token economy*. What kinds of behaviors did the patients have to emit to be reinforced and receive the tokens? If they bathed at the time designated, brushed their teeth, made their beds, combed their hair, and dressed properly, they earned a token for each activity. Patients could earn up to ten tokens for each period worked in the hospital kitchen or laundry and for helping to clean the ward, run errands, or take other patients for walks. These tasks are simple, but before the program began, the patients were hopeless psychotics who could not take care of their bodily needs—not before being given reinforcement for doing so.

The behavior modification worked dramatically. Not only did the patients groom themselves and clean their surroundings, but they also busied themselves at a variety of jobs. They interacted socially with one another and with the staff and assumed some degree of responsibility for patient care. Their sense of self-worth and self-esteem improved markedly, and they became less dependent and more responsible individuals.

However, a word of caution is necessary. The token economy was found effective only within the institution in which it was implemented. In general, the modified behaviors are unlikely to carry over to life outside the institution. The reinforcement program must be continued if the desired behavior changes are to persist. When tokens are no longer given, reinforced behavior usually reverts to its original state (Kazdin & Bootzin, 1972; Repucci & Saunders, 1974). These criticisms notwithstanding, the behavior changes achieved by applying positive reinforcement make the token economy a popular technique in a variety of settings.

Skinner's operant-conditioning techniques have been successfully applied to problems in business and industry. Behavior-modification programs at major manufacturers, financial institutions, and government agencies have been shown to reduce absenteeism, tardiness, and abuse of sick-leave privileges, and to lead to improvements in job performance and safety. Some of the rewards or reinforcers used in business are pay, job security, recognition from supervisors, status, and the opportunity for personal growth. Behavior-modification techniques have also been used to teach job skills to disadvantaged workers (Luthans, Maciag, & Rosenkranz, 1983; O'Brien, Dickinson, & Rosow, 1982; Wexley & Latham, 1981).

In behavior-modification programs, no attempt is made to deal with any presumed underlying conflicts, repressed traumas, or unconscious motivating forces. Instead, the focus in the application of the behavior-modification technique is on overt behavior. There is no more concern for what might be happening in the mind of an emotionally disturbed person or a factory worker than for what might be going on inside the rat in the Skinner box. The focus is behavior, the nature of the reinforcement, and the rate of presentation of the reinforcers that will change or modify behavior.

Most applications of the operant-conditioning technique involve positive reinforcement, not punishment. The patients in the token economy study were not punished for failing to behave in desirable ways. Rather, they were reinforced only when their behavior changed in positive ways. Skinner believed that **punishment** was generally ineffective in changing behavior from undesirable to desirable or from abnormal to normal. "What's wrong with punishments is that they work immediately, but give no long-term results," Skinner told an interviewer. "The responses to punishment are either the urge to escape, to counterattack, or a stubborn apathy. These are the bad effects you get in prisons or schools, or wherever punishments are used" (quoted in Goleman, 1987). Positive reinforcement given for desirable behaviors is much more effective than punishment.

Negative reinforcement is not the same as punishment. A negative reinforcer is an aversive or noxious stimulus, the removal of which is rewarding. In the laboratory or classroom, an operant-conditioning situation can be established in which the aversive stimulus (such as a loud noise or an electric shock) will continue until the subject emits the desired response. As with positive reinforcement, the environment will change as a consequence of the behavior (that is, the noxious stimulus will disappear).

We can see examples of negative reinforcement in many situations. You

punishment The application of an aversive stimulus following a response in an effort to decrease the likelihood that the response will recur.

negative reinforcement The strengthening of a response by the removal of an aversive stimulus.

study for this course and attend most of the classes partly to avoid the aversive stimulus of a failing grade. A child behaves in a certain way to avoid or escape disapproval or loss of affection. Negative reinforcement is used in the clinical setting, where an unpleasant stimulus is continued when the undesirable behavior is displayed and discontinued when the desirable behavior is displayed.

Skinner opposed using noxious stimuli to modify behavior, suggesting that the consequences were not as predictable as with positive reinforcement. Negative reinforcement, he said, does not always work. Positive reinforcement is more consistently effective.

Skinner's Image of Human Nature

Skinner's position is clear on the nature–nurture issue. We are primarily products of learning, shaped more by external variables than by genetic factors. We may infer that our childhood experiences are more important than those that occur later in life because our basic behaviors are formed in childhood. However, this does not mean that behavior cannot change in adulthood. What has been learned in childhood can be unlearned or modified, and new behavior patterns can be acquired at any age. The success of behavior-modification techniques verifies that assertion.

It also follows from Skinner's belief that behavior is shaped by learning that each person is unique. Because we are shaped by experience—and we all have different experiences, particularly in childhood—no two people will behave in precisely the same way.

Skinner did not address the issue of an ultimate and necessary goal. There is no reference in his system to our being compelled to overcome inferiority or driven to reduce anxiety and conflict or motivated toward self-actualization. Such motives assume internal, subjective states, which were anathema to Skinner. If there is any indication of a life goal in Skinner's work, it is in societal, not individual, terms. In his novel *Walden Two* and in other writings, he discussed his notion of the ideal human society. He stated that individual behavior must be directed toward the type of society that has the greatest chance of survival.

Skinner displayed no ambiguity on the issue of free will versus determinism. To Skinner, humans function like machines, in lawful, orderly, predetermined ways. He rejected all notions of an inner being, an autonomous self, determining a course of action or choosing to act freely and spontaneously. We are operated upon by factors in the environment, not by forces within ourselves. Not since Freud have we met a theorist who is so completely deterministic in his viewpoint, who allows not the slightest hint of free will or spontaneity in behavior.

From Skinner's highly technical writings to his popular novel about a utopian society based on operant-conditioning principles, his message is the same: All aspects of behavior are controlled from without by whoever

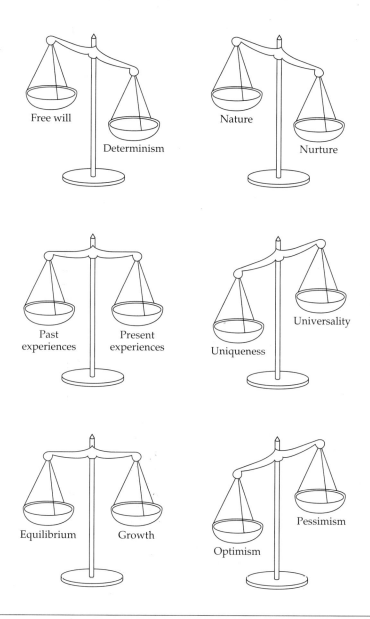

Skinner

Image of Human Nature.

controls the reinforcers. In a sense, this means it is pointless to blame or punish people for their actions. The Nazi dictator Adolf Hitler can no more be held responsible for his actions than can a driverless car that plunges down a hill. Both operate in lawful, predictable ways, controlled by external variables.

We are left, it seems, with a pessimistic view of people as helpless and passive robots, unable to play an active role in determining behavior. But this does not represent Skinner's view. Despite his belief that behavior is so thoroughly controlled, he did not see us as victims.

It is true that we are controlled by the environment, but we are responsible in the first place for designing that environment. Our buildings, vehicles, clothing, food, tools, and government institutions are the result of human fabrication. So, too, are our social system, language, customs, and recreations. We are constantly effecting change in our environment, often to our advantage. When we do, we are at once controller and controlled. We design a controlling culture and are products of that culture.

The environment may also impose limits on our freedom to bring about change. In making changes, we will be guided by those situations that provided positive reinforcement in the past. In changing our culture, we seek greater opportunities for positive reinforcement and in the process change our own behavior. We are left with a paradox, an image of person-as-machine capable of altering the environmental conditions that guide the machine's behavior.

Assessment in Skinner's Theory

Skinner did not use any of the typical assessment techniques used by other theorists. There was no place in his work for free association, dream analysis, or projective techniques. Because his system did not deal directly with personality and derived its data from laboratory studies of rats and pigeons, Skinner had no interest in assessing personality. He did, however, assess behavior. To apply behavior-modification techniques, specific behaviors, both desirable and undesirable, must be assessed, along with the features of the environment that serve as reinforcers and that can be manipulated to change behavior. No behavior can be modified properly without such assessment.

functional analysis
An approach to the study of behavior that involves an assessment of the frequency of a behavior, the situation in which it occurs, and the reinforcers associated with it.

Skinner called his approach to the assessment of behavior **functional analysis**. In general, it involves three aspects of behavior: (1) the frequency of the behavior, (2) the situation in which the behavior occurs, and (3) the reinforcement associated with the behavior. Unless these factors have been evaluated, it is not possible to plan and implement an appropriate course of behavior modification.

Consider a functional analysis for cigarette smokers who want to break the smoking habit. The smokers would be asked to keep an accurate record of the number of cigarettes they smoked per day and the situations in which the cigarettes were smoked. Does smoking occur in a particular place or at a certain time? In the presence of others or alone? After meals or while driving? What are the reinforcers? Most smokers smoke more frequently in the presence of certain stimuli; identifying these stimuli is necessary because modifying them should lead to a modification of the smoking behavior.

Behavior-modification programs use three approaches to assess behavior: direct observation, self-reports, and physiological measurements.

Direct Observation of Behavior

Many behaviors are assessed through direct observation. Usually, two or more people conduct the observation to assure accuracy and reliability. For example, in one behavior-modification situation, a woman sought treatment for her 4-year-old son whose behavior was considered unruly (Hawkins, Peterson, Schweid, & Bijou, 1966). Two psychologists observed the mother and child in their home to assess the nature and frequency of the child's undesirable behaviors, the times and places at which they occurred, and the reinforcers the child received for the behaviors.

Nine undesirable behaviors were identified, such as kicking, throwing things, biting, and pushing a sibling. The psychologists observed that the mother reinforced the child by giving him toys or food whenever he behaved badly. Her intention was to get him to stop misbehaving, but she was, instead, rewarding him for it. The direct observation assessment took 16 hours to complete, but without it the psychologists would not have known what specific undesirable behaviors to try to eliminate or what reinforcement the child expected.

Following a comprehensive direct-observation program, it is not difficult to plan a course of behavior modification. In this case, the psychologists instructed the mother to give the boy the reinforcers of attention and approval only when he behaved in positive ways, never when he displayed one of the nine observed undesirable behaviors. The frequency of the undesirable behaviors, as determined in the direct observation, provided a baseline against which to compare behavior during and after treatment.

The Self-Report Technique

Another approach to assessing behavior is the self-report technique, which can be carried out through interviews and questionnaires. The person observes his or her behavior and reports on it to the examiner. A number of self-report questionnaires are available; one of these is the Fear Survey Schedule (Geer, 1965), which assesses how much fear a person experiences in situations such as driving a car, going to the dentist, or speaking in public.

Questionnaires for assessing behavior do not differ in format from other self-report inventories. The distinction lies in the way they are interpreted. This difference is described as the sign-versus-sample approach to assessment. In the sign approach, which is used to assess personality, the psychologist infers the existence of character types, traits, or unconscious conflicts from the individual's responses. For example, if a person indicates that he or she is afraid of being in an elevator, it can be interpreted as a sign or an indirect symptom of some underlying fear, motive, or conflict.

In the sample approach, which is used to assess behavior, the questionnaire responses are interpreted as directly indicative of a sample of behavior. No attempt is made to draw inferences or conclusions about the person's character or traits; the behavior itself (such as fear) and the stimulus associated with it (such as the elevator) are the important things. There is no concern with subjective motives, childhood experiences, or anything else going on inside the person's head.

Although Skinner did not use self-report personality inventories, he did take personality tests. In 1933 he completed several paper-and-pencil tests administered at a scientific meeting to people interested in learning about their personalities. He reported that he had better judgment than 95 percent of his colleagues who were tested, was more extraverted than 57 percent, and was more easily annoyed than 65 percent. Years later he took two projective tests, the Rorschach inkblot test and the Thematic Apperception Test. He gave his responses to the Rorschach cards so fast that the examiner could not keep up with him, and he had nothing to say in response to the TAT pictures (Skinner, 1979, p. 139).

Physiological Measurements

Physiological assessment of behavior involves measuring bodily processes, such as heart rate, muscle tension, and brain waves. In this way, it is possible to evaluate the physiological effects of various stimuli. The measures can also be used to confirm the accuracy of information obtained by other assessment methods. For example, a person who is too embarrassed to reveal directly in an interview or on a questionnaire a fear of being in an elevator might show a change in heart rate or muscle tension when asked about elevators.

Whatever assessment technique is chosen, its purpose is to assess behavior in different stimulus situations. The focus is on what the person does, not on what might have motivated the person to do it. The ultimate goal is to modify behavior, not to change personality.

Research in Skinner's Theory

Skinner's methods of assessment are radically different from those used by most other theorists. His research methods also differ from mainstream experimental psychology. The usual procedure is to study large groups of animal and human subjects and to statistically compare their average responses. In contrast, Skinner chose to study a single subject intensively. He argued that knowledge of average performance is of little value in dealing with a particular case. A science that deals with averages provides little information in understanding the unique individual.

Skinner believed that valid, replicable results could be obtained without the use of statistical analysis, as long as sufficient data were collected from a single subject under well-controlled experimental conditions. He argued that the use of a large group of subjects forced the experimenter to attend to average behavior. As a result, the data do not reflect individual response behavior and individual differences in behavior. Thus, Skinner favored the idiographic rather than the nomothetic approach.

His single-subject experiments follow the reversal experimental design. The first stage involves establishing a baseline. The subject's behavior (the dependent variable) is observed to determine the normal rate of response before experimental treatment is attempted. The second stage is the conditioning or experimental stage, when the independent variable is introduced. If this variable affects behavior, it will produce a marked change from the subject's baseline response rate.

The purpose of the third stage, the reversal stage, is to determine whether some factor other than the independent variable is responsible for the observed change in behavior. During this stage, the independent variable is no longer applied. If the behavior under study returns to its baseline rate, then the researcher can conclude that the independent variable was responsible for the difference observed in the conditioning stage. On the other hand, if the behavior does not return to the baseline rate, then some factor other than the independent variable influenced the behavior.

These stages—baseline, conditioning, and reversal—are sufficient for most laboratory experiments. When the procedure is applied to behavior modification, a fourth stage, reconditioning, is added. The independent variable is reintroduced, assuming it was shown to be effective in changing behavior. Without the fourth stage, the subject in the behavior-modification program would remain in the reversal stage, with behavior at the baseline level, unchanged by the treatment that had been shown to be effective. It would be unethical not to reintroduce the effective treatment.

Skinner and his followers conducted thousands of operant-conditioning experiments on various reinforcement schedules, language acquisition, behavior shaping, superstitious behavior, and behavior modification. The work has been highly supportive of Skinner's views.

A Final Commentary

Skinner's approach has been criticized on several points. Those who oppose a deterministic view of human nature must oppose Skinner. Vocal attacks have come from theorists, such as the humanistic psychologists, who believe that people are more complex than machines or overgrown white rats directed by external forces. These critics object to Skinner's image of human nature and argue that the exclusive emphasis on overt behavior ignores the human qualities that set us apart from rats and pigeons—notably our conscious free will.

Critics also express concern about Skinner's belief that we can be directed and manipulated by whoever controls our reinforcement, arguing that this viewpoint lends support to fascist thinking, the idea that a demagogue could mold and shape a culture in any desired direction. They charge that if Skinner's view of humanity achieved widespread acceptance, it would pave the way for a government to institute control of every aspect of behavior, from birth to death.

At a more specific level, there has been criticism of the type of subject and the simplicity of the situations studied in Skinner's research. Skinner made many assertions and predictions about human behavior and society, ranging from social and economic to religious and cultural speculations, all promoted with great confidence. But how can one extrapolate from a pigeon pecking at a disc in a Skinner box to a person functioning in the real world? The gap between human and pigeon, critics argue, and between the type of stimuli impinging on each, is too vast to permit broad generalizations. Many aspects of human behavior cannot be reduced meaningfully to the level at which Skinner conducted his investigations.

Criticism has also been directed against his research methodology for ignoring behaviors other than response rate. Skinner's belief that all behavior is learned has been challenged by a former student, who conditioned more than 6,000 animals of 38 species to perform an assortment of behaviors for television commercials and tourist attractions. The animals included pigs, chickens, hamsters, porpoises, whales, and cows. All these animals displayed a tendency toward instinctive drift. In time, they substituted instinctive behaviors for those that had been reinforced, even when the instinctive behaviors interfered with receiving food (Breland & Breland, 1961).

Skinner ignored most of his critics. "I read a bit of it," he said once, referring to a negative review of one of his books, "and saw that he missed the point. . . . There are better things to do with my time than clear up their misunderstandings" (quoted in Rice, 1968).

Skinner was a potent force in 20th-century American psychology who shaped and influenced the field perhaps more than any other individual. In a survey dealing with the relative importance of more than 150 events in psychology, Skinner's contributions, and behavior modification, are ranked, respectively, in first and second place (Gilgen, 1982).

The *Journal of the Experimental Analysis of Behavior,* which has flourished since 1958, publishes research on the behavior of individual organisms. In 1968, the *Journal of Applied Behavior Analysis* was established as an outlet for the growing body of research on behavior modification methods. Behavior modification as a technique for changing behavior has gained increasing popularity, which provides additional empirical validation for Skinner's ideas.

Although Skinner's radical behaviorist position continues to be applied in laboratory, clinical, and organizational settings, it has been challenged within the behaviorist framework by the more cognitive-oriented positions of Albert Bandura and Julian Rotter (see Chapters 15 and 16). In the 1960s, the study of consciousness returned to psychology, leading to a decline in the dominance of Skinner's position. This decline was hastened by his death in 1990.

Skinner conceded that his form of psychology was losing ground to the cognitive approach. Other psychologists agreed, noting that Skinnerian behaviorism has "fallen from favor among the majority of active workers in the field [and is] often referred to in the past tense" (Baars, 1986, pp. viii, 1). Despite the inroads of cognitive psychology, however, Skinner's position remains influential in many areas, from classrooms to assembly lines, from Skinner boxes to mental institutions. Skinner believed that with operant conditioning he had presented and refined a technique to improve human nature and the societies humans design.

Summary

B. F. Skinner attempted to account for all behavior, not just personality, in factual and descriptive terms. He contended that psychology must restrict itself to overt responses if it is to be a science of behavior, of what the organism does. Skinner's approach is different because he denied the existence of an entity called personality and did not seek the causes of behavior within the organism. Neither mental or physiological processes are overtly observable, so they have no relevance for science. The causes of behavior are external to the organism. All behavior can be controlled by its consequences, by the reinforcement that follows the behavior.

Respondent behavior involves a response elicited by specific environmental stimuli. Conditioning (respondent behavior that is learned) involves the substitution of one stimulus for another. The essential feature of Pavlov's work was the demonstration of the importance of reinforcement. Conditioning will not take place without reinforcement.

Operant behavior is emitted and is determined and modified by the reinforcer that follows it. Operant behavior cannot be traced to a specific stimulus; it operates on the environment and changes it. According to Skinner, personality is nothing more than a pattern or collection of operant behaviors.

Four of the reinforcement schedules Skinner investigated are fixed interval, fixed ratio, variable interval, and variable ratio. Shaping (or successive approximation) involves reinforcing the organism only as its behavior comes to approximate the behavior desired. Superstitious behavior results when reinforcement is presented on a fixed- or variable-interval schedule. Whatever behavior is occurring at the moment of reinforcement will thus be reinforced and will come to be displayed more frequently. Self-control of behavior refers to changing or avoiding certain external stimuli and reinforcers. Other self-control techniques are satiation, aversive stimulation, and self-reinforcement for displaying desirable behaviors.

Behavior modification applies operant-conditioning techniques to real-world problems. Desirable behaviors are positively reinforced, while undesirable behaviors are ignored. The token economy involves rewarding desirable behaviors with tokens that can be used to acquire objects and experiences of value. Behavior modification deals only with overt behavior and uses positive reinforcement, not punishment.

Negative reinforcement involves the removal of an aversive or noxious stimulus. It is less effective than positive reinforcement in changing behavior.

Skinner's image of human nature emphasized determinism, uniqueness, the importance of the environment, and the goal of designing a society that maximizes the opportunity for survival. Although we are controlled by the environment, we can control our future by designing that environment properly.

Skinner assessed behavior (not personality) using functional analyses to determine the frequency of the behavior, the situation in which the behavior occurred, and the reinforcers associated with the behavior. Three ways to assess behavior are direct observation, self-reports, and physiological measurements. Skinner's research was idiographic, focusing on the intensive study of a single subject. His reversal experimental design consists of four stages: baseline, conditioning, reversal, and reconditioning.

Skinner's system has considerable empirical support but has been criticized for its deterministic view of human nature and the belief that people can be manipulated and controlled. Other criticisms relate to the simplicity of the experimental situations, the lack of interest in aspects of behavior other than response rate, and the failure to consider the human qualities that set us apart from the rats and pigeons Skinner studied.

Critical Thinking Review

1. How does Skinner's approach to personality differ from the other approaches we have discussed?

2. Describe Pavlov's classical-conditioning experiment with dogs. How were the conditioned responses extinguished?

3. What is the difference between respondent behavior and operant behavior?

4. What is the role of reinforcement in modifying and controlling behavior? How does reinforcement relate to superstitious behavior?

5. Define positive reinforcement, negative reinforcement, and punishment. According to Skinner, how effective is each technique in modifying behavior?

6. Describe four schedules of reinforcement. Which schedule applies to the person who sells computer software on commission? Which schedule applies to the child who is permitted to have an ice-cream cone only occasionally?

7. Explain how a complex behavior, such as learning to speak, is acquired through the method of successive approximation.

8. Describe Skinner's techniques for the self-control of behavior.

9. Describe the token-economy approach to behavior modification.

10. How did Skinner explain his preference for studying individuals rather than groups of subjects? Describe the stages in a typical Skinnerian experiment with a human subject. Describe a typical Skinnerian experiment using a pigeon as the subject.

11. What was Skinner's position on the issue of nature versus nurture? On the issue of free will versus determinism?

12. What techniques do Skinnerians use to assess human behavior?

13. Discuss the impact of the cognitive psychology movement on Skinnerian behaviorism.

Suggested Reading

Elms, A. C. (1981). Skinner's dark year and *Walden Two*. *American Psychologist, 36,* 470–479. Suggests that Skinner experienced an identity crisis in his youth when he failed as a writer and that writing his novel was a form of therapy when identity issues became important to him again in midlife.

Nye, R. D. (1992). *The legacy of B. F. Skinner: Concepts and perspectives, controversies and misunderstandings.* Pacific Grove, CA: Brooks/Cole. A primer on Skinner's basic concepts and their relevance for behavior in today's world. Examines controversies and misunderstandings surrounding Skinner's views and compares his system with those of Sigmund Freud and Carl Rogers.

Skinner, B. F. (1948). *Walden Two.* New York: Macmillan. Skinner's novel about human values and conduct in a utopian society based on behaviorist principles.

Skinner, B. F. (1953). *Science and human behavior.* New York: Free Press. Describes the scientific analysis of human behavior and discusses implications of behaviorist principles for governmental, religious, and educational institutions.

Skinner, B. F. (1971). *Beyond freedom and dignity.* New York: Knopf. Suggests that we must work to mod-ify our physical and social environments and cultural norms if we are ever to achieve full human freedom and dignity.

Skinner, B. F. (1976). *Particulars of my life;* (1979). *The shaping of a behaviorist;* (1983). *A matter of consequences.* New York: Knopf. Skinner's lengthy and detailed three-volume autobiography.

Skinner, B. F. (1987). *Upon further reflection.* Englewood Cliffs, NJ: Prentice-Hall. Essays on cognitive psychology, verbal behavior, the American educational system, and self-management in old age.

Skinner, B. F. (1987). Whatever happened to psychology as the science of behavior? *American Psychologist, 42,* 780–786. Charges that humanistic psychology, psychotherapy, and cognitive psychology are obstacles in the path of psychology's acceptance of his program for the experimental analysis of behavior.

Smith, L. D. (1992). On prediction and control: B. F. Skinner and the technological ideal of science. *American Psychologist, 47,* 216–223. Assesses recent challenges to Skinner's operant psychology and to his goals for social reform.

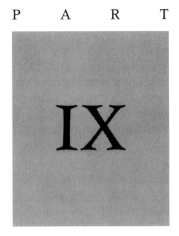

IX

The Social-Learning Approach

The social-learning approach to personality, represented here by the works of Albert Bandura and Julian Rotter, is an outgrowth of B. F. Skinner's behaviorist approach. Like Skinner, Bandura and Rotter focus on overt behavior rather than on needs, traits, drives, or defense mechanisms. However, unlike Skinner, Bandura and Rotter also consider internal cognitive variables that mediate between stimulus and response. Such cognitive variables have no place in Skinner's system.

Bandura and Rotter have investigated cognitive variables with a high degree of experimental sophistication and rigor, drawing inferences from careful observations of behavior in the laboratory. They deal with human subjects, observing their behavior in social settings, whereas Skinner dealt with animal subjects in individual settings. Bandura and Rotter agree with Skinner that behavior is learned and that reinforcement is vital to that learning, but they differ from Skinner in their interpretation of the nature of reinforcement.

Bandura, Rotter, and Skinner have all attempted to understand personality through laboratory rather than clinical work, but their principles have been applied in the clinical setting through behavior-modification techniques.

Because Bandura and Rotter use cognitive variables, their work reflects and reinforces the cognitive movement in psychology. Their approach has been called ''cognitive behavioral,'' in recognition of this emphasis.

FIFTEEN

Albert Bandura

The Life of Bandura (1925–)
Modeling: The Basis of Observational Learning
    Disinhibition
    Characteristics of Models and Observers
Processes of Observational Learning
The Self
    Self-Reinforcement
    Self-Efficacy
Developmental Stages of Modeling and
    Self-Efficacy
Behavior Modification
    Fears and Phobias

    Enhancing Self-Efficacy
    Anxiety
    Ethical Issues
Bandura's Image of Human Nature
Assessment in Bandura's Theory
Research in Bandura's Theory
    Studies on Self-Efficacy
    Television and Aggressive Behavior
A Final Commentary
Summary
Critical Thinking Review
Suggested Reading

Virtually every phenomenon that occurs by direct experience can occur vicariously as well—by observing other people and the consequences for them.

—Albert Bandura

Albert Bandura agrees with B. F. Skinner that behavior is learned. With that point, however, the similarity ends. Bandura criticized Skinner's emphasis on studying individual animal subjects rather than human subjects in interaction with others. Bandura's approach is a social kind of learning theory that investigates behavior as it is formed and modified in a social context. He argues that we cannot expect data from experiments that involve no social interaction to be relevant to the everyday world; few people function in social isolation.

Although Bandura recognizes that much learning takes place as a result of reinforcement, he also stresses that virtually all forms of behavior can be learned in the absence of directly experienced reinforcement.

His approach is also called **observational learning**. This term indicates the role in learning of observing other people's behavior. Rather than experiencing reinforcement ourselves for each of our actions, we can learn through **vicarious reinforcement** by observing the behavior of others and the consequences of that behavior. This focus on learning by observation or example, rather than always by direct reinforcement, is the most distinctive feature of Bandura's theory.

Another feature of Bandura's observational-learning approach is its treatment of internal processes. Unlike Skinner, Bandura does not rule out the existence of internal influencing variables. He believes that cognitive or thought processes can influence observational learning. We do not automati-

observational learning Learning new responses by observing the behavior of other people.

vicarious reinforcement Learning or strengthening a behavior by observing the behavior of others and its consequences rather than experiencing the reinforcement or consequences directly.

cally copy or reproduce the behaviors we see other people displaying. Rather, we make a deliberate, conscious decision whether or not to behave in the same way.

To learn through example and vicarious reinforcement, we must be capable of anticipating and appreciating the consequences of the behavior we observe in others. Bandura assumes we can regulate and guide our behavior by visualizing or imagining the consequences, even though we have not yet experienced them directly. No direct link exists between stimulus and response or between behavior and reinforcer, as Skinner proposed. Instead, there is a mediating mechanism between the two—that mechanism is our cognitive processes.

Bandura presents a less extreme form of behaviorism than Skinner. He emphasizes the role of one's observation of others as a means of learning, and he considers learning to be mediated by our cognitive processes. His theory is based on rigorous laboratory research with normal human subjects in social interactions rather than with rats in individual cages or with neurotics on couches.

The Life of Bandura (1925–)

Bandura is from the province of Alberta, Canada. He was 1 of 20 students in a high school that had only two teachers. During the summer following his graduation, he took a construction job in the wilderness of the Yukon Territory, filling holes in the Alaska Highway. It was a fascinating experience for a bright, inquisitive young man. "Finding himself in the midst of a curious collection of characters, most of whom had fled creditors, alimony, and probation officers, [Bandura] quickly developed a keen appreciation for the psychopathology of everyday life, which seemed to blossom in the austere tundra" ("Distinguished," 1981, p. 28).

Bandura attended the University of British Columbia in Vancouver as an undergraduate and earned his Ph.D. from the University of Iowa in 1952. After a year at the Wichita, Kansas, Guidance Center, he joined the faculty of Stanford University, where he has remained. Bandura has compiled an extensive record of publications and in 1973 was elected president of the American Psychological Association.

Bandura is noted for his humor, which is often directed at himself. Asked if he walked to his office or drove his car, he replied, "Both, sometimes in the same day." He has been known to drive to the university and "absorbed in his thoughts . . . walk home leaving the car behind." He also enjoys good food and once led a group of psychologists to New Orleans to consider the city as a site for the APA annual convention. "For a week," one psychologist recalled, "all we did was follow Al around and eat shrimp jambalaya" (Kiester & Cudhea, 1974, p. 27). No doubt the psychologists received both direct and vicarious reinforcement for modeling their behavior after Bandura's.

In the Bobo doll studies, children exhibited aggressive behavior after observing an aggressive model.

Modeling: The Basis of Observational Learning

Bandura's fundamental idea is that learning can occur through observation or example rather than solely by direct reinforcement. Bandura does not deny the importance of direct reinforcement as a way of influencing behavior, but he does deny the proposition that behavior can be learned or changed only through direct reinforcement.

He argues that operant conditioning, in which trial-and-error behavior continues until the person finds the correct response, is an inefficient and potentially dangerous way of learning skills such as swimming or driving; a person could drown or crash before finding the sequence of behaviors that leads to positive reinforcement. Bandura believes that most human behavior is learned through example, either intentionally or accidentally. We learn by observing other people and patterning our behavior after theirs.

modeling A behavior-modification technique that involves observing the behavior of others (called "models") and participating with them in performing the desired behavior.

Through **modeling**—observing the behavior of a model and repeating the behavior ourselves—it is possible to acquire responses never before performed or displayed and to strengthen or weaken existing responses. Bandura's now-classic demonstration of modeling involves the Bobo doll, an inflated plastic figure three to four feet tall (Bandura, Ross, & Ross, 1963). The subjects, preschool children, watched an adult hit and kick Bobo. While attacking the doll, the adult model shouted, "Sock him in the nose!" and "Throw him in the air!" Later, when the children were left alone with the doll, they modeled their behavior after the example they had just witnessed.

When their behavior was compared with that of a control group of children who had not seen the model attack the Bobo doll, it was shown to be twice as aggressive.

The intensity of the aggressive behavior was the same whether the model was seen live, on television, or as a filmed cartoon character. The effect of the model in all three media was to elicit the same kind of behavior, behavior that was not displayed at the same intensity by children of the same age who had not observed the models.

In another example of the impact of modeling on learning, Bandura compared the behavior of parents of two groups of children (Bandura & Walters, 1963). One group consisted of highly aggressive children, the other of more inhibited children. According to Bandura's theory of modeling, the children's behavior should imitate their parents' behavior. The research showed that the parents of the inhibited children were inhibited, and the parents of the aggressive children were aggressive.

Verbal modeling can also induce certain behaviors, as long as the acts involved are fully and adequately explained (Bandura & Mischel, 1965). Simply stated, verbal modeling means providing instructions, a technique often used to teach people to acquire such skills as the basics of driving a car. These verbal instructions are usually supplemented by behavioral demonstrations, such as a driving instructor serving as a model by performing the behaviors involved in driving.

Disinhibition

disinhibition The weakening of inhibitions or constraints by observing the behavior of a model.

Research has shown that an existing behavior that is usually suppressed or inhibited may be performed more readily under the influence of a model (Bandura, 1973, 1986; Bandura & Walters, 1963). This phenomenon, called **disinhibition**, refers to the weakening of an inhibition through exposure to a model. For example, people in a crowd, such as a protest demonstration, often perform physical and verbal actions that they might never perform if they were alone. They are more likely to violate or discard their inhibitions against aggressive behavior if they see others doing so.

The disinhibition phenomenon also influences sexual behavior. One experiment demonstrated that sexual responses could be disinhibited by models (Walters, Bowen, & Parke, 1963). A group of male undergraduate students was shown a film that contained erotic pictures of nude males and females. They were told that a spot of light would move over the film, indicating the eye movements of a previous subject, to show what parts of the pictures that subject had looked at; this represented the model. For half the subjects, the spot of light concentrated on breasts and genitals; for the other group, the light stayed in the background, as though the model had avoided looking at the naked bodies.

After watching the film, the subjects were shown slides made from the movie sequence, and their eye movements were recorded. Those subjects whose model was uninhibited (that is, who had looked directly at the erotic parts of the bodies) behaved similarly. Those subjects whose model had avoided looking at the bodies spent significantly more time examining the background of the pictures than the figures. The researchers concluded that modeling affected the subjects' perceptual responses to the stimuli. In other words, modeling determined not only what the subjects did, but also what they looked at and perceived.

On the basis of extensive research, Bandura was persuaded that much of our behavior—good and bad, normal and abnormal—is learned by imitating the behavior of others. From infancy on, we develop our behavioral repertoire in response to the models society offers us. Beginning with parents as models, we learn a language and become socialized in line with the customs and acceptable behaviors of our culture.

Persons who deviate from cultural norms—neurotics, drug addicts, criminals, or psychopaths, for example—have learned their behavior in the same way as everyone else. The difference is that deviant persons have followed different models, those considered undesirable by the rest of society. Bandura has been an outspoken critic of a society that provides the wrong models for its children, particularly the models of violent behavior that are regular fare on television. His research has clearly shown how effective these models are in affecting behavior. If what we see is what we become, the distance between watching a cartoon figure being attacked on television and committing a violent act ourselves is not very great.

Children can acquire many new behaviors through modeling, including nonrational fears. A child who sees parents becoming fearful during thunderstorms or acting nervous around strangers will easily adopt these fears and anxieties and carry them into adult life with little awareness of their origin. Strength and courage in the face of difficulties, and optimism in the face of novel experiences, can be learned just as easily. In Skinner's system, the person who controls the reinforcers controls behavior. In Bandura's system, the person who controls the models controls behavior.

Characteristics of Models and Observers

Bandura and his associates investigated three factors that influence modeling: the characteristics of the models, the characteristics of the observers, and the reward consequences associated with the behaviors (Bandura, 1977, 1986).

The characteristics of the models affect our tendency to imitate them. In real life, we may be more prone to be influenced by someone who appears to be like us than by someone who differs from us in obvious and significant ways. So Bandura found in the laboratory: Although children imitated the behavior of a child model in the same room, a child in a film, and a filmed cartoon character, the extent of the modeling decreased as the similarity between the model and the subject decreased. There was greater imitation of a live model than of a cartoon character, although even in the latter instance the modeled behavior was significantly greater than that of the control group.

Children tend to imitate the behavior of an adult model of the same sex who is considered high in status.

Other characteristics of the model that affected imitation were the model's age and sex. We are more likely to model our behavior after a person of the same sex than a person of the opposite sex. Also, we are more likely to be influenced by models our own age. Peers who seem to have solved problems similar to those we face are highly influential models.

Status and prestige are also important. It was found that pedestrians were much more likely to cross a street against a red light if they saw a well-dressed person crossing than if they saw a poorly dressed person crossing. Television advertising makes effective use of high-status, high-prestige models by showing athletes, musicians, or movie stars who claim to use a particular product and expecting us, as consumers, to imitate their behavior.

The kind of behavior the model performs also affects the extent of imitation. Highly complex behaviors are not imitated as quickly and readily as simpler behaviors. Hostile and aggressive behaviors tend to be strongly imitated, especially by children.

The attributes of the observers also determine the effectiveness of observational learning. People who are low in self-confidence and self-esteem are much more likely to imitate a model's behavior than those who are high in self-confidence and self-esteem. People who have been rewarded or reinforced for imitating behavior—for example, a child rewarded for behaving like an older sibling—are more likely to be susceptible to the influence of models.

The reward consequences associated with a particular behavior can affect the extent of the modeling and can override the impact of the models' and observers' characteristics. A high-status model can lead us to imitate the behavior being displayed, but if the reward consequences are insufficient, we will discontinue the behavior and be less likely to be influenced by that model in the future.

Processes of Observational Learning

Bandura analyzed the nature of observational learning and found it to be governed by four interrelated mechanisms: attentional processes, retention processes, production processes, and incentive and motivational processes.

Attentional processes.   Attentional processes affect observational learning because learning or modeling will not occur unless the subject attends to (that is, pays attention to) the model. Merely exposing the subject to the model does not guarantee that the subject will be attentive to the relevant cues and stimulus events, or even perceive the stimulus situation accurately. The subject must pay attention to the model with enough perceptual accuracy to acquire the information necessary to imitate the model's behavior.

Several variables influence how closely the subject attends to the model's behavior. In the real world, as in the laboratory, we are more attentive and responsive to some people and situations than to others. The more closely we attend to a model's behavior, the more likely we are to imitate it.

We have mentioned such characteristics as age, status, and sex of the model and the degree of similarity between model and subject. These factors help determine how closely a subject attends to the model. It has also been found that models who appear competent, who are alleged to be experts, or who are celebrities command greater attention than models who lack these attributes. Any set of characteristics that causes a model to be perceived as more attractive increases the probability that the subject will pay careful attention to the model and, consequently, will be likely to imitate the behavior displayed.

Some of the most effective models in American culture today are those who appear on television. So powerful are televised models that viewers often attend to them in the absence of reinforcement. Whether viewers imitate these models' behavior depends partly on the reward consequences.

Attention to modeled behavior also varies as a function of the observers' cognitive and perceptual skills and of the value of the behavior being modeled. The more highly developed our cognitive abilities and the more knowledge we have of the behavior being modeled, the more we will attend to the model and the more fully we will perceive the behavior.

When observers watch a model perform a behavior that they expect to perform themselves, they pay greater attention than when the modeled behavior has no personal relevance. Observers also pay closer attention to modeled behavior that produces positive or negative outcomes. Observed punishment is also effective in promoting observational learning.

Retention processes. A second mechanism in observational learning involves retention processes. Unless subjects imitate a model's behavior either as the behavior is being performed or shortly thereafter, they must retain or remember the significant aspects of the behavior to be able to imitate or repeat it later. To retain what has been attended to, we must somehow encode and represent symbolically what we have observed. This internal process of symbolic representation or image formation recognizes the operation of internal cognitive processes in developing and modifying behavior. Thus, Bandura's focus is not exclusively on overt behavior, as was Skinner's.

Bandura proposed two internal representational systems—the imaginal and the verbal—by which we retain information on a model's behavior. In the imaginal system, while observing the model we form vivid, easily retrievable images of what we are seeing. This common phenomenon accounts for your being able to summon up a picture of the person you dated last week or the place you visited last summer. In modeling, we form a mental picture of the model's behavior and use it as a basis for imitation some time after we have observed it.

The verbal representational system operates similarly and involves a verbal coding of something we have observed. For example, during observation we might describe to ourselves what the model is doing. These descriptions or codes can be rehearsed silently, without overtly displaying the behavior. We might talk ourselves through the steps in a complicated skill, mentally rehearsing the sequence of behaviors, which we will perform later. When we wish to perform the action, the verbal code will provide hints, reminders, and cues. Together, these images and verbal symbols offer the means by which we store or retain observed situations and rehearse them for later performance.

Production processes. Translating imaginal and verbal symbolic representations into overt behavior is the province of the production processes. Although we may have attended to, retained, and rehearsed symbolic representations of a model's behavior, we may not be able to perform the behavior correctly. This is likely with highly skilled actions that require many component behaviors for their successful performance.

Again, consider learning to drive a car. We can learn the fundamental motions from a lecture and from watching a model drive, and we may think about the symbolic representations of the model's behavior many times, but at first our translation of these representations into actual driving behavior will be rough and clumsy. In this case, observation is not sufficient to ensure the immediate skilled performance of the act. Practice in the proper physical movements, and feedback on their accuracy, is needed to produce the smooth performance of the behavior.

Incentive and motivational processes. No matter how well we attend to and retain the behavior we observe or how much ability we have to perform it, we will not do so without sufficient incentive or motivation. When incentives are available, observation is quickly translated into action. Incentives not only bring about the desired behavior but also influence the attentional and retention processes. We do not pay as much attention without an incentive to do so, and when little attention is paid, there is little to retain.

Our incentive to learn is influenced by our anticipation of the reinforcement or punishment for doing so. Seeing that a model's behavior produces a reward or avoids a punishment can be a strong incentive for us to pay attention to, remember, and perform a behavior. The reinforcement is experienced vicariously during our observation of the model, after which we expect that our performance of the same behavior will lead to the consequences we have seen.

Bandura pointed out that although reinforcement can facilitate learning, reinforcement is not necessary for learning to occur. Many factors other than the reward consequences of the behavior can determine what we will attend to and retain. For example, loud sounds, bright lights, and exciting videos may capture our interest even though we may not receive any reinforcement for paying attention to them.

Bandura's research has shown that children watching a model on television imitate the model's behavior regardless of whether they have been told that the imitation will lead to a reward. Reinforcement, therefore, can assist in modeling but is not vital to it. When reinforcement occurs, it can be given by another person, experienced vicariously, or administered by the self.

The Self

In Bandura's approach to personality, the self is not some psychic agent that determines or causes behavior. Rather, the self is a set of cognitive processes and structures concerned with thought and perception. Two particularly important aspects of the self are self-reinforcement and self-efficacy.

Self-Reinforcement

self-reinforcement
Administering rewards or punishments to oneself for meeting, exceeding, or falling short of one's own expectations and standards.

Self-reinforcement is at least as important as reinforcement administered by others, particularly for older children and adults. We often set personal standards of behavior and achievement and reward or punish ourselves for meeting, exceeding, or falling short of these expectations. Self-administered reinforcement can be something tangible, such as an ice-cream cone or a new car, or it can consist of feelings, such as pride or satisfaction. Self-administered punishment can be expressed in shame, guilt, or depression about not behaving the way we wanted to. Self-reinforcement appears conceptually similar to what other theorists have called the conscience or superego, although Bandura denies that it is the same.

Much of our behavior is regulated by a continuing process of self-reinforcement. It requires internal standards of performance, subjective criteria or reference points against which we evaluate our behavior. Often our past behavior becomes a reference point for evaluating present behavior and serves as an incentive for better performance in the future. When we reach a certain level of achievement, it may no longer challenge, motivate, or satisfy us, and so we may raise the standard and require more of ourselves. Failure to achieve may result in our lowering the standard to a more realistic level.

We learn our initial set of internal standards from the behavior of models—typically our parents and other significant people in our life. Once we adopt a model's standard or style of behavior, we begin a continuous and lifelong process of comparing our behavior with that standard.

Self-Efficacy

self-efficacy Our feeling of adequacy, efficiency, and competence in coping with life.

How well we meet our standards of behavior determines our sense of **self-efficacy**. In Bandura's system, self-efficacy refers to our feelings of adequacy, efficiency, and competence in coping with life. Bandura described it as our perception of our ability "to produce and to regulate" the events in our lives (Bandura, 1982, p. 122). Meeting and maintaining our performance standards enhances self-efficacy; failure to meet and maintain those standards reduces it.

People who set unrealistically high performance standards—who have observed and learned behavioral expectations from extraordinarily talented, successful models and who try to meet those excessively high expectations despite repeated failures—punish themselves with feelings of worthlessness and depression. These self-produced feelings may lead to self-destructive behaviors, such as alcohol and drug abuse or a retreat into a fantasy world.

People low in self-efficacy feel helpless, unable to exercise any influence over life's events. They believe that any effort they make is futile, and they are likely to become increasingly despondent, apathetic, and anxious. When they encounter obstacles, they quickly give up if their initial attempts to deal with problems are ineffective. People who are extremely low in self-efficacy will not even attempt to cope because they are convinced that nothing they do will make a difference.

People high in self-efficacy believe they can deal effectively with the events and situations they face. Because they expect to succeed in overcoming obstacles, they persevere at tasks and often perform at a high level. These people have greater confidence in their abilities than persons low in self-efficacy, and they express little self-doubt. They view difficulties as challenges instead of threats and will actively seek new situations.

A person's judgment about his or her level of self-efficacy is based on four sources of information: performance attainment, vicarious experiences, verbal persuasion, and physiological arousal.

The most influential source of efficacy judgments is performance, or enactive, attainment. Previous success experiences provide direct indications of our level of mastery and competence. Prior achievements or attainments demonstrate our capabilities and strengthen our feelings of self-efficacy. Prior failures, particularly repeated failures, lower our sense of efficacy.

Vicarious experiences—seeing other people perform successfully—

strengthen feelings of self-efficacy, particularly if the people we observe are judged to be similar in abilities. In effect, we are saying, "If they can do it, so can I." Seeing others fail can lower our self-efficacy. Therefore, effective models are important in influencing our feelings of adequacy and competence. These models also show us appropriate strategies and techniques for dealing with difficult situations.

Verbal persuasion—telling people they possess the ability to achieve what they want to achieve—can enhance self-efficacy. This may be the most common of the four informational sources, and the one regularly practiced by parents, teachers, spouses, friends, and therapists. To be effective, verbal persuasion must be realistic. For example, it is pointless to tell someone who is five feet tall that he or she has the ability to play professional basketball.

A fourth source of information about self-efficacy is physiological arousal, such as our level of fear or calmness in a stressful situation. We often use this type of information as a basis for judging our ability to cope. "People are more inclined to expect success," Bandura wrote, "when they are not beset by aversive arousal than if they are tense and viscerally agitated" (Bandura, 1982, p. 127).

Bandura concluded that it is possible to arrange certain conditions to increase a person's self-efficacy:

1. Exposing people to success experiences by arranging reachable goals increases performance attainment.
2. Exposing people to appropriate models who perform successfully enhances vicarious success experiences.
3. Providing verbal persuasion encourages people to believe they have the ability to perform successfully.
4. Strengthening physiological arousal through proper diet, stress reduction, and exercise programs increases strength, stamina, and the ability to cope.

Bandura applied these techniques to enhance self-efficacy in a variety of situations. For example, he has helped subjects learn to play a musical instrument, relate better to the opposite sex, master computer skills, give up cigarette smoking, and conquer phobias and physical pain.

Developmental Stages of Modeling and Self-Efficacy

Our capacity for observational learning develops over time as a function of age and level of maturation. In infancy, modeling is limited to immediate imitation. Infants have not developed the cognitive capacities, the imaginal and verbal representational systems, needed to imitate a model's behavior some time after observing it. In infancy it is necessary for the modeled behavior to be repeated several times, once the infant attempts to duplicate it. The modeled behavior must be within the infant's range of sensorimotor development, within its restricted repertoire of behaviors. At about age 2, children have developed sufficient attentional, retention, and production processes to begin imitating behavior at some time after it has been observed, rather than immediately.

The behaviors we find reinforcing, and thus choose to imitate, change with age. Infants and children are reinforced primarily by physical stimuli, such as food, affection, or punishment. Later in life we come to associate positive physical reinforcers with signs of approval from significant models—usually parents—and unpleasant or punishing experiences with signs of disapproval. In time, these rewards or punishments become self-administered.

Self-efficacy—our feeling of adequacy, efficiency, and competence in coping with life—also develops gradually. Infants begin to develop self-efficacy as they attempt to exercise influence over their physical and social environments. They come to learn about their own abilities: their physical prowess, social skills, and language competence. These abilities are in almost constant use, acting on the environment, primarily through their effects on parents. Ideally, the parents are responsive to their child's activities and attempts to communicate, and they provide stimulating surroundings and allow the child the freedom to grow and explore.

These early efficacy-building experiences are centered on the parents. That changes as the child's world expands and admits influences from siblings, peers, and other adults. Bandura agreed with Adler on a related influence, that of order of birth. He noted that first-born children and only children have different bases for judging their abilities than do later-born children. Also, siblings of the same sex are likely to be more competitive than siblings of the opposite sex, a factor that also affects the assessment of one's competence.

With playmates, children who are the most experienced and successful at tasks and games serve as high-efficacy models for other children. Peers provide comparative reference points for appraising one's own level of achievement.

Teachers influence self-efficacy judgments through their impact on the development of cognitive capabilities and problem-solving skills, which are vital to efficient adult functioning. Bandura suggested that schools that use ability groupings undermine self-efficacy in low-achieving students, thus decreasing the self-confidence of students assigned to the lower groups. Competitive practices, such as grading on a curve, also doom poor achievers to average or low grades.

The transitional experiences of adolescence involve coping with new demands and pressures, from an awareness of sex to the choice of a college and career. In each situation that requires adjustment, adolescents must establish new competencies, new appraisals of their abilities. Bandura noted that the success of this transitional phase between childhood and adulthood depends on the level of self-efficacy established during the childhood years.

Bandura divides adulthood into young adulthood and the middle years. Young adulthood involves additional adjustments, such as marriage, parenthood, and advancement in one's career. High self-efficacy is necessary to successful performance of these tasks. People who are low in self-efficacy will not be able to deal adequately with these social situations and are likely to fail to adjust.

The middle years of adulthood are also stressful, as people reevaluate their lives, confront their limitations, and redefine their sense of self-efficacy. Middle-aged people must reassess their abilities, skills, and goals and find new opportunities for development and self-expression.

Self-efficacy assessments in old age are difficult. Declining mental and physical abilities, retirement from active work, and withdrawal from social life force a new round of self-appraisal. A lowering of self-efficacy can further affect physical and mental functioning in a kind of self-fulfilling prophecy. For example, a reduced sense of self-efficacy about sex can lead to a reduction in sexual activity. Lower physical efficacy can lead to fatigue and a curtailing of physical activities. If we no longer believe we can do something, then we may not even try. To Bandura, our sense of self-efficacy is the crucial factor in determining our success or failure throughout the life span.

Behavior Modification

Bandura had a practical goal in developing his social-cognitive theory: to modify or change learned behavior that society considers undesirable or abnormal. Like Skinner's approach to therapy, Bandura's focuses on external aspects—inappropriate or destructive behaviors—in the belief that these, like all other behaviors, are learned. He does not refer to underlying unconscious conflicts that the therapist must uncover and relieve. It is the behavior or symptom, rather than any presumed inner cause for neurosis, that is the target of the social-learning approach. Bandura believes that treating the symptom is treating the disorder; they are one and the same.

Fears and Phobias

If modeling is the way we learn our behaviors originally, then it should also be an effective way for us to relearn or change our behaviors. Bandura applied modeling techniques to eliminate fears and other intense emotional reactions. In one instance, children who were afraid of dogs observed a child of the same age playing with a dog (Bandura, Grusec, & Menlove, 1967). While the subjects watched from a safe distance, the model made progressively bolder movements toward the dog. The model petted the dog through the bars of a playpen in which the dog had been placed. Eventually the child model went inside the pen and played cheerfully with the dog. The observers' fear of dogs was considerably reduced as a result of this observational learning situation.

In a now-famous study of snake phobia, Bandura and his associates eliminated an intense fear of snakes in adult subjects (Bandura, Blanchard, &

Ritter, 1969). The subjects watched a film in which children, adolescents, and adults displayed progressively closer contact with a snake. At first the models in the film handled plastic snakes, then touched live snakes, and finally let a large snake crawl over their bodies. Subjects were allowed to stop the film whenever the scenes became too threatening and to reverse the film to less threatening scenes. Gradually, their fear of snakes was overcome.

Another effective modeling procedure involves watching a live model and then participating with the model—a technique called guided participation. For example, to treat a snake phobia, subjects watch through an observation window while a live model handles a snake. Then the subjects enter the room with the model and observe the handling of the snake at close range. Wearing gloves, subjects are coaxed into touching the middle of the snake while the model holds the head and tail. Subjects eventually come to touch the snake without gloves.

Modeling has been shown to be effective even in the absence of an observable model. In covert modeling, subjects imagine a model coping with a feared or threatening situation; they do not actually see a model. Covert modeling has been used to treat snake phobias and social inhibitions (Kazdin, 1975, 1979).

You might think a fear of snakes is not so terrible, but overcoming this fear brought about significant changes in the subjects' behavior and ability to cope with life, even for those who lived in places that were free of snakes. In addition to bolstering self-esteem and self-efficacy, getting rid of a snake phobia changed personal and work habits. One subject was able to wear a necklace for the first time; previously she had not been able to do so because necklaces reminded her of snakes. A real-estate agent was able to increase his income because he was no longer afraid to visit homes in rural areas. Almost all the people treated by modeling therapy were freed from nightmares about snakes.

There are many other phobias that can restrict our lives. For example, people who fear spiders or other insects may react with rapid heartbeat, shortness of breath, or vomiting when they see a spider—or even a picture of a spider. Phobics come to doubt their self-efficacy in these fear-provoking situations and have little confidence in their ability to cope with the source of the phobia. To relieve phobics of these fears is to expand their lives and increase their self-efficacy.

Modeling therapy, particularly with films, offers several practical advantages. Complex behaviors can be seen as a whole, and extraneous behaviors can be edited out so that the subject's time is spent viewing only what is relevant to the behavior to be learned. Once a film is made, it can be repeated with several patients and used by many therapists simultaneously. Modeling techniques can also be used with groups, circumventing the expensive and time-consuming practice of treating individually people with the same problem. Bandura's approach has been successful with phobias, obsessive-compulsive disorders, and sexual dysfunctions, and the effects have been reported to last for years.

Enhancing Self-Efficacy

Although Bandura's approach to behavior modification focuses on overt behavior, Bandura has become increasingly interested in the effect of his approach on cognitive variables, particularly self-efficacy. For example, in the treatment of snake phobia, modeling therapy changed not only overt behavior with regard to snakes but also feelings and attitudes. Successfully treated people learned to handle snakes and no longer feared touching them. In addition, they came to have an enhanced feeling of competence or efficacy in that situation.

Considerable research has been conducted on behavior and self-efficacy during and after behavior-modification therapy. The results have shown that as subjects' self-efficacy improved during treatment, they were increasingly able to deal with the object that was the source of the fear. It was the therapeutic procedure itself that enhanced self-efficacy.

In another study of snake phobia, subjects in the modeling and guided participation groups showed significant increases in their ratings of self-efficacy and in their ability to approach the snakes, as compared with a control group (Bandura, Adams, & Beyer, 1977). Self-efficacy ratings correlated highly with actual behavior.

An experiment with spider phobia confirmed these findings (Bandura, Reese, & Adams, 1982). The higher the level of the subjects' perceived self-efficacy, the more successful their performance on tasks involving contact with spiders. The higher the efficacy, the lower the fear, both in anticipation of contact with spiders and in actual contact. The researchers also found that the lower the subjects' self-efficacy, the stronger their fear.

Anxiety

Many kinds of behaviors can be modified through the modeling approach. We will briefly consider two instances: fear of medical treatment, and test anxiety. Some people have such an intense fear of medical situations that they are unable to seek necessary treatment. Modeling, primarily through films, has been successful in eliminating these fears. In one study, children who were scheduled for surgery and had never been in a hospital were divided into two groups: an experimental group that watched a film about a boy's experience in the hospital, and a control group that saw a film about a boy taking a trip in the country (Melamed & Siegel, 1975). The boy in the hospital film was an exemplary model. Despite some initial anxiety, he coped well with the doctors and the medical procedures.

The subjects' anxiety was assessed by the techniques discussed in Chapter 14: direct observation of behavior, responses on self-report inventories, and physiological measurements. These assessments were carried out the night before surgery and were repeated three to four weeks later. The results showed that the modeling film had been effective in reducing anxiety. Subjects who had seen the film demonstrated fewer behavior problems after hospitalization than did subjects in the control group.

Similar procedures have been used to reduce fear of hospitalization in adults as well as fear of dental treatment in children and in adults. One study involved a medical procedure considered so stressful that more than 80 percent of patients refused to undergo it or terminated it prematurely (Allen, Danforth, & Drabman, 1989). Subjects who watched a videotape of a model undergoing the procedure and later describing how he coped with his distress were able to complete significantly more treatments with less anxiety and fewer days in the hospital.

Test anxiety among college students has also been treated successfully with modeling techniques. For some students, this is such a serious problem that their examination performance does not accurately reflect their knowledge of the material being tested. Based on performance on a personality test, a sample of college students was divided into two groups: those high in test anxiety and those low in test anxiety (Sarason, 1975b). Some of the students viewed a film in which a model talked about her anxiety when taking tests and her ways of coping with it. Other students saw a film of the same model, who talked about her test anxiety but not about coping mechanisms. Under a third condition, students watched the person on film talking about her college activities; she did not mention tests or test anxiety.

The subjects were given a list of nonsense syllables to memorize and were tested on their ability to recall them. The results showed that subjects high in test anxiety were most strongly affected by the coping model they had observed. They performed significantly better on the recall test than did high-anxiety subjects who had been exposed to the other two conditions.

Other types of anxiety have been reduced or eliminated by modeling therapy. For example, shyness in both children and adults has been treated by modeling. Clients have learned to overcome their inhibitions and relate better to others. Adults suffering from anxiety about sex have learned to reduce that anxiety and to engage in sex with fewer constraints.

Ethical Issues

Although the results of using behavior-modification techniques are impressive, these techniques have drawn criticism because they are alleged to be based on an exploitative view of human nature. Behavior modification aroused passionate attacks from educators, government officials, and psychologists; they charged that it has the potential to manipulate individuals without their awareness.

Bandura disputed this contention. Behavior modification is not inhumane. Rather, he argued, other, ineffective therapeutic techniques deserve that label. What is inhumane is to refuse to use the most effective technique available. To fail to help a troubled person, or to string a client along for years in a doubtful program of therapy, is unfair to the patient and to society.

Bandura believes that the accusation of manipulation and control in his approach to behavior modification is false and misleading. Behavior modification does not take place without the client's awareness. Bandura proposed that self-awareness and self-regulation are important in changing or relearning behavior. Modification does not occur unless the person is able to understand what behaviors are being reinforced. Further, it is wrong to talk about control by others because it is the clients who decide what it is about themselves they want to change. People come to the therapist to eliminate a fear of snakes, anxiety about taking tests, or an inability to function in crowded places.

The situation is analogous to going to a dentist; the patient has a toothache that must be relieved. Bandura emphasizes that the client-therapist relationship is a contract between two consenting individuals, not a relationship between some sinister master-controller and a slave.

Bandura noted that, far from manipulating or enslaving an individual, modeling techniques increase a person's freedom. People who are afraid to leave the house or who must wash their hands a dozen times an hour are not free. They are living within the constraints imposed by their phobic or compulsive behavior. Those constraints allow little choice about behavior. Removing the constraining symptoms through behavior modification increases freedom and opportunities for personal growth.

Many behavior modification techniques have derived from Bandura's work. Since the 1960s, hundreds of journal articles have been published about the effectiveness of these techniques in various situations. They have become increasingly popular alternatives to psychoanalysis and other psychotherapeutic approaches.

Bandura's Image of Human Nature

reciprocal determinism The idea that behavior is controlled or determined by the individual, through cognitive processes, and by the environment, through external social stimulus events.

Bandura's position is clear on the issue of free will versus determinism. Behavior is controlled by the person, through the operation of the cognitive processes, and by the environment, through external social stimulus events. He calls this view **reciprocal determinism** and notes that people are neither "powerless objects controlled by environmental forces nor free agents who can become whatever they choose. Both people and their environments are reciprocal determinants of each other" (Bandura, 1977, p. vii). Bandura later introduced the notion of triadic reciprocality, in which behavior, cognitive factors, and environmental or situational variables interact (Bandura, 1986).

Although our behavior is influenced by environmental forces, we are not helpless with respect to these external stimulus events. Our reactions to stimuli are self-activated in accordance with our learned anticipations and expectations. We observe and interpret the possible effects of our actions and determine which behaviors are appropriate for a given situation. We encode and represent these external events symbolically and expect that a certain

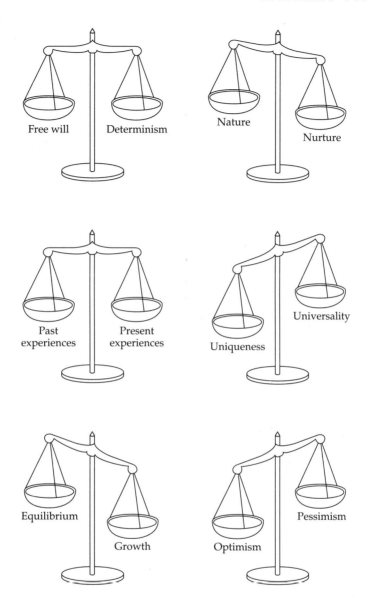

Bandura

Image of Human Nature.

behavior will bring a certain response. Thus, we choose and shape our behavior to gain reinforcement and avoid punishment.

Implicit in this view are self-awareness, self-reinforcement, and other forms of internal regulation of behavior. Reinforcement does not automatically change human behavior. When it effects a change, it does so because the individual is aware of what is being reinforced and anticipates the same reward for behaving that way again. Some degree of self-direction interacts with past and present social stimulus events. Thus, we are influenced by external forces and, in turn, are able to guide the extent and direction of such influences.

The notion of self-direction of behavior represents an optimistic view of human nature. Bandura believes that individuals can create their own environments and that abnormal behaviors, which are little more than bad habits, can be changed by behavior-modification techniques.

On the nature–nurture issue, Bandura suggests that most behaviors (except for basic reflexes) are learned. Genetic factors play a minor role. Bandura recognizes, however, that hereditary factors, such as body type, rate of physical maturation, and appearance can influence the reinforcers people receive, particularly in childhood. Children who are clumsy and unattractive will receive different reinforcement from that of children who are graceful and attractive. Bandura noted the importance of childhood experiences and suggested that childhood learning may be more influential than learning in adulthood. Our internal performance standards, which affect our sense of self-efficacy, are established in childhood, along with a set of good or ideal behaviors. However, childhood experiences can be unlearned later in life, and new performance standards and ideal behaviors may be substituted for them. Thus, we are not captives of the reinforcement we received in our early years.

Because at least some behavior results from experience, it may be inferred that Bandura accepts the uniqueness of personality. It may also be assumed that our ultimate and necessary goal in life is to set realistic performance standards so that we can maintain our sense of self-efficacy at a sufficient level.

Assessment in Bandura's Theory

Like Skinner, Bandura focuses on behavior rather than on any internal motivating variables that might constitute personality. He does not use assessment techniques such as free association, dream analysis, or projective techniques. Unlike Skinner, however, Bandura admits the operation of cognitive variables, and these, as well as behavior, can be assessed.

In the modeling study involving children about to undergo surgery, the subjects were assessed by direct observation, self-report inventories, and physiological measurements. In studies relating behavior to self-efficacy, behavioral and cognitive variables were assessed quantitatively. Self-efficacy relating to snake phobia was assessed by the subjects' self-ratings of the number of tasks on a behavioral-avoidance test that they expected to be able to complete. College students' test anxiety was assessed by a personality test.

Thus, the assessment of behavioral and cognitive variables is important in the social-learning approach to personality, and self-report techniques are widely used to evaluate cognitive variables. The purpose of these assessments is the functional analysis of behavior and of the relevant cognitive variables.

Research in Bandura's Theory

Bandura favors well-controlled laboratory investigations in the rigorous tradition of experimental psychology. We noted examples of his use of experimental and control groups and his precise measurement of independent and dependent variables. Bandura studies large groups of subjects and compares their average performance by statistical analysis. His subjects exhibit diverse behavioral disorders, such as phobias, alcoholism, fetishism, and sexual dysfunctions. The ages of his subjects range from preschool through adult. Thus, his social-learning theory is based on a broad range of human subjects; this increases the generalizability and applicability of his research findings.

We have already noted examples of some of the hundreds of studies conducted on the modeling process. To illustrate further the kind of research that has proceeded from Bandura's theory, we will consider here studies dealing with the effects of one's level of self-efficacy and with the effects of televised models on aggressive behavior.

Studies on Self-Efficacy

Self-efficacy appears to differ as a function of gender and age. Research with children and adults shows that on the average, men are higher in self-efficacy than women. These gender differences peak during the twenties and lessen in later years (Bengston, Reedy, & Gordon, 1985; Block, 1983; Lachman, 1985). For both sexes, self-efficacy increases through childhood and early adulthood, peaks in middle age, and declines after the age of 60 (Gecas, 1989; Woodward & Wallston, 1987).

Bandura has proposed that self-efficacy determines our ability to cope with life. For example, gender differences in self-efficacy play an important role in our choice of career. Research has shown that men perceive themselves to be high in self-efficacy for both so-called traditional male and traditional female occupations. Women perceive themselves as high in self-efficacy for so-called female occupations but low in self-efficacy for traditional male occupations. The male and female subjects in this research performed at comparable levels on standardized tests of verbal and quantitative skills. They possessed similar measurable abilities but perceived these abilities differently; that is, their feelings about their adequacy in dealing with career problems differed (Betz & Hackett, 1981).

Researchers have found that the higher the level of self-efficacy, the wider the range of career possibilities considered and the stronger the interest in them. Low self-efficacy may restrict the range of career options a person considers and may contribute to indecisiveness about the few options believed to be viable (Bores-Rangel, Church, Szendre, & Reeves, 1990; Taylor & Betz, 1983). Women in their first year of college were found to be lower in self-efficacy than men with regard to their perceived ability to perform well in mathematics courses (Lapan, Boggs, & Morrill,

1989). This can affect the choice of college major and can lead women to avoid such programs as engineering and science, which, in turn, limits their career possibilities.

Studies demonstrate a significant positive relationship between self-efficacy and academic performance (Multon, Brown, & Lent, 1991). Once a person is out of school, self-efficacy can influence the amount of time spent searching for a job, as well as later success on the job (Hackett, Betz, & Doty, 1985; Kanfer & Hulin, 1985; Lent & Hackett, 1987). Employees high in self-efficacy were reported to set higher goals and to be more committed to these goals than those low in self-efficacy (Locke & Latham, 1990; Wood & Bandura, 1989). Those high in self-efficacy focused on analyzing and solving problems, whereas those low in self-efficacy focused on personal deficiencies and fear of failure, which could undermine their productivity and the full use of their cognitive abilities on the job (Lazarus & Folkman, 1984; Sarason, 1975a).

Self-efficacy has also been shown to affect physical health. In some cases, people who believed they could alleviate their pain were able to do so. In one study, pregnant women who had been taught relaxation and breathing exercises to reduce pain during childbirth differed in the amount of control they believed they had over the pain (Manning & Wright, 1983). The higher their perceived self-efficacy and feelings of control, the longer they were able to tolerate pain during delivery before requesting pain medication. The higher the self-efficacy, the less pain medication required.

Other research has also shown a strong positive relationship between perceived self-efficacy and pain tolerance; the higher the self-efficacy, the higher the tolerance. It has also been found that coping techniques that increase self-efficacy can produce substantial increases in endorphins, the body's natural painkillers (Bandura, O'Leary, Taylor, Gauthier, & Gossard, 1987).

Self-efficacy is involved in how we maintain certain healthy behaviors. People high in self-efficacy were found to be more likely to stop smoking cigarettes because they believed in their ability to do so. People low in self-efficacy were found to be unlikely to try (Becona, Frojan, & Lista, 1988; DiClemente, Prochaska, & Gilbertini, 1985). Self-efficacy measured before subjects attempted to quit smoking was significantly related to smoking behavior a month after quitting (Garcia, Schmitz, & Doerfler, 1990). The higher the self-efficacy, the fewer cigarettes smoked during the month. Those who resisted smoking during that period displayed greater self-efficacy than those who resumed smoking.

Those higher in self-efficacy responded better to cognitive and behavioral treatments for pulmonary disease than did those lower in self-efficacy (Kaplan, Atkins, & Reinsch, 1984). Men who suffered heart attacks showed a higher rate of return to normal activities, and less fear and depression, when they and their spouses believed in their cardiac capabilities (McLeod, 1986). The higher their self-efficacy, the more likely they were to follow prescribed exercise programs and the more they improved.

Television and Aggressive Behavior

Bandura and other researchers have demonstrated convincingly that in laboratory situations, seeing violence begets violence. Other studies have shown the same phenomenon in the everyday world. A group of delinquent boys displayed significantly more violence toward their peers after watching violent films than did a control group of delinquent boys who saw nonviolent films (Leyens, Camino, Parke, & Berkowitz, 1975). In addition, the kinds of aggressive acts the boys displayed frequently duplicated those depicted in the films. In another study, 9-year-old children who watched numerous violent television programs were found to be more aggressive ten years later. A followup study of the same subjects showed that they were still more aggressive 20 years later. Other studies report similar relationships between watching televised violence and behaving aggressively. These results were obtained in many countries, including the United States, England, Belgium, Finland, Poland, and Australia (Eron, 1987; Eron & Huesmann, 1984; Eron, Huesmann, Lefkowitz, & Walder, 1972; Huesmann, Eron, Dubow, & Seebauer, 1987).

In a different approach to studying the relationship between observed violence and aggressive behavior, researchers investigated the incidence of aggressive acts shortly after people viewed televised violence. One analysis found a brief but sharp rise in violent acts peaking three to four days following highly publicized incidences of riots or other violence (Phillips, 1985). Murder rates in the United States were found to increase by more than 12 percent over the expected rate for the three days following televised championship boxing matches—a phenomenon studied over a 15-year period (Phillips, 1983). The largest increases in murders occurred after the most heavily publicized and widely seen matches.

Self-directed violence also appears to increase following exposure to such violence reported in the news media. The incidence of suicide was found to increase markedly following the suicide of a movie star or other celebrity (Phillips, 1974).

A Final Commentary

Many researchers and clinicians see Bandura's social-learning theory as an exciting and productive approach. The great number of books, articles, and research studies deriving from it attests to its popularity as a means of studying behavior in the laboratory and as a way of changing behavior in the real world. In 1980 the American Psychological Association awarded Bandura the Distinguished Scientific Contribution Award, citing his "masterful modeling as a researcher, teacher, and theoretician" ("Distinguished," 1981, p. 27).

The social-learning approach has several advantages. First, it is highly objective and directly amenable to precise laboratory methods of investigation, making it congruent with the emphasis on experimental research that characterizes mainstream American psychology. Most experimental psychologists reject theoretical work in personality that posits unconscious or other internal driving forces that cannot be manipulated or measured under laboratory conditions. Bandura's approach to personality boasts a great amount of empirical support.

Second, observational learning and behavior modification are compatible with the functional and pragmatic spirit of American psychology. More readily than other approaches, observational-learning techniques can be taken from the laboratory and applied to practical, everyday problems. There is more immediate reinforcement for the practitioner than with other approaches. For example, in clinical situations, dramatic changes can be seen in client behavior within weeks or even days.

Critics argue that social learning, like Skinner's more extreme form of behaviorism, deals only with peripheral aspects of personality—a person's overt behavior. This emphasis on overt behavior ignores distinctly human aspects of personality—the conscious and unconscious motivating forces, the roles of emotion and conflict. Critics draw an analogy with a physician treating a patient who complains of stomach pains by dealing only with what the patient says and does, by trying to get the patient to stop doubling over in pain and saying, "It hurts." However, what is necessary is medication or surgery; the physician must find the afflicted internal organ, the underlying cause of the pain. A related charge is that if just the symptom is treated and not the cause, substitute symptoms will appear. This has not been supported by research.

Summary

Albert Bandura believes that behavior can be learned through vicarious reinforcement, by observing the behavior of others and anticipating the reward consequences of behaving in the same way. The mediating mechanisms between stimulus and response are our cognitive processes, which bring about control of behavior through self-regulation and self-reinforcement. Directly experienced reinforcement is an inefficient, time-consuming, and potentially dangerous way to change behavior.

In the Bobo doll study, children patterned their behavior on the aggressive behavior of the model, whether the model was observed live, on television, or in a cartoon. Disinhibition involves weakening an inhibition through exposure to a model. Behavior that is usually suppressed or inhibited may be performed more readily under the influence of a model. Three factors that influence modeling are the model's characteristics, the observer's characteristics, and the reward consequences of the behavior.

Observational learning is governed by four processes: attentional, retention, production, and incentive and motivational. The self is a set of cognitive processes concerned with thought and perception. Self-reinforcement requires some internal performance standard against which behavior is evaluated. Self-efficacy refers to the ability to control the events in one's life. People low in self-efficacy feel helpless and worthless and will give up quickly when they encounter obstacles. People high in self-efficacy will persevere at tasks and perform at a high level. Judgments of self-efficacy are based on performance attainment, vicarious experiences, verbal persuasion, and physiological arousal. Using these four sources of information, it is possible to increase one's self-efficacy.

In infancy, modeling is limited to immediate imitation. By age 2, children begin to imitate behavior some time after they have observed it. Infants and children are reinforced primarily by physical stimuli. Older people are reinforced more by others' approval or disapproval; this becomes internalized so that reinforcement is then self-administered.

In behavior therapy, models are used to demonstrate ways of coping with threatening situations. Behavior can be modified through observation and guided participation. In covert modeling, subjects imagine how a model copes with a feared situation. Bandura's approach to behavior modification deals with overt behavior and with cognitive variables, particularly self-efficacy. As self-efficacy improves during treatment, the client is increasingly able to deal with threatening objects or situations. Behavior modification has been criticized for manipulating and controlling people against their will, but Bandura argues that with self-awareness and self-regulation, people undergoing behavior modification understand what is being reinforced.

Behavior is controlled both by internal cognitive processes and by external stimuli, a position Bandura calls reciprocal determinism. Most behavior is learned; genetic factors play a minor role. Learning in childhood may be more influential than learning in adulthood, but adults are not victims of childhood experiences. Our ultimate goal is to set realistic performance standards to maintain an optimal level of self-efficacy. Research shows that self-efficacy varies with age and gender and can influence our choice of career, our school performance, our job performance, and our physical health.

Bandura assesses behavior and cognitive variables through direct observation, self-report inventories, and physiological measurements. He favors controlled laboratory investigations using large groups of subjects and statistical analysis of the data. Criticisms of Bandura's theory relate to his focus on overt behavior to the exclusion of emotions and conflicts, his treatment of symptoms rather than possible internal causes, and his failure to state precisely how cognitive variables affect behavior.

Critical Thinking Review

1. How does the observational-learning approach to personality differ from the other approaches we have discussed?

2. What is Bandura's position on the role of reinforcement?

3. Describe a typical modeling experiment. How does modeling vary as a

function of the characteristics of the models, the characteristics of the observers, and the reward consequences of the behavior?

4. Describe how modeling procedures can be used to change behavior. Give two specific examples.

5. What are the four processes of observational learning? How are they related?

6. How do the types of behaviors we acquire through modeling change with age?

7. According to Bandura, what is the role of self-reinforcement?

8. How do people high in self-efficacy differ from people low in self-efficacy in terms of their ability to cope with life? On what sources of information do we base our judgment about our own level of efficacy?

9. Describe the developmental changes that occur in self-efficacy from infancy to old age. How can self-efficacy be increased?

10. Give an example of how modeling can be applied to the reduction of anxiety.

11. What is the relationship between self-efficacy and physical health?

12. What is Bandura's position on the issue of free will versus determinism? On the relative influences of heredity and environment?

13. How does self-efficacy differ as a function of gender and of age? In what ways can self-efficacy influence academic performance and career choice?

Suggested Reading

Bandura, A. (1976). Albert Bandura. In R. I. Evans (Ed.), *The making of psychology: Discussions with creative contributors* (pp. 242–254). New York: Knopf. Interviews with Bandura about his life and work.

Bandura, A. (1986). *Social foundations of thought and action: A social cognitive theory.* Englewood Cliffs, NJ: Prentice-Hall. Presents Bandura's theory of human nature emphasizing the self-regulation of behavior.

Gecas, V. (1989). The social psychology of self-efficacy. *Annual Review of Sociology, 15,* 291–316.

Evaluates the research literature on Bandura's concept of self-efficacy and discusses how social structure and group processes affect the development of self-efficacy over the life span.

Rosenthal, T. L., & Bandura, A. (1978). Psychological modeling: Theory and practice. In S. L. Garfield & A. E. Bergin (Eds.), *Handbook of psychotherapy and behavior change: An empirical analysis* (2nd ed.). New York: Wiley. Discusses the nature and processes of observational learning and its application to the elimination of fears and inhibitions.

SIXTEEN

Julian Rotter

The Life of Rotter (1916–)
Social-Learning Theory
    Behavior Potential
    Expectancy
    Reinforcement Value
    The Psychological Situation
    Freedom of Movement
    The Minimal Goal Level
Psychological Needs

Locus of Control
Interpersonal Trust
Rotter's Image of Human Nature
Assessment in Rotter's Theory
Research in Rotter's Theory
A Final Commentary
Summary
Critical Thinking Review
Suggested Reading

Behavior does not occur in a vacuum. A person is continuously reacting to aspects of [the] external and internal environments.

—Julian Rotter

Like Albert Bandura, Julian Rotter looks to both the outside and the inside of the organism, to external reinforcement and internal cognitive processes, to explain behavior. He refers to his work as a social-learning theory of personality; this indicates his belief that we learn our behavior primarily through our social experiences. Rotter was apparently the first person to use the term *social-learning theory*. He began writing about it in 1947 and published *Social Learning and Clinical Psychology* in 1954. (Bandura did not use the term in print until several years later.)

Rotter is critical of Skinner's preference for studying single subjects who are isolated from social experiences and argues that Skinner's approach does not reflect learning as it occurs in the real world, the social milieu in which we function by interacting with others. Rotter also questions Skinner's study of the responses of animal subjects to simple stimuli. He believes that such research provides little more than a starting point for understanding more complex human behavior.

In the research from which he developed his social-learning theory, Rotter and his followers studied human subjects, focusing on normal persons, mostly children and college students. His theory is grounded in rigorous, well-controlled experiments and derives directly from the laboratory, not the clinic.

Rotter deals with cognitive processes more extensively than does Bandura; some psychologists say that Rotter has "cognitivized" behaviorism

(Cantor & Zirkel, 1990, p. 137). He suggests that we perceive ourselves as conscious beings, able to influence our experiences and to make decisions that regulate our lives. External reinforcement is important in Rotter's system, but the effectiveness of the reinforcement depends on our cognitive abilities. Rotter has described personality as the "interaction of the individual and his or her meaningful environment" (Rotter, 1982, p. 5).

Our behavior, then, is influenced by several factors. We have a subjective expectation of the outcome of our behavior in terms of the reinforcement that will follow it. We estimate the likelihood that behaving a certain way will lead to a particular reinforcer, and we guide our behavior accordingly. We place different values on different reinforcers and judge their relative worth in various situations. Because each of us functions in a unique psychological context or environment, a given reinforcer may not have the same value or importance for all of us. Thus, our internal cognitive processes are vital in determining the impact of our external social-psychological experiences.

External situations also give direction to our behavior because we are motivated to strive for the maximum degree of positive reinforcement and for the avoidance of punishment. Thus, Rotter's approach to personality attempts to integrate two trends in personality research: reinforcement theories and cognitive theories.

The Life of Rotter (1916–)

Rotter has written little about his childhood. In a brief biographical sketch published in 1982, he paid homage to the local library in Brooklyn, New York, where he developed into a voracious reader while still in elementary school. During his junior year in high school he discovered the writings of Freud and Adler. By the following year he was so enamored of their work that he was interpreting his friends' dreams and planning a career in psychology. Adler's views helped him understand himself and others. Rotter wrote that Adler had been "a strong early influence on my thinking. I was and continue to be impressed by his insights into human nature" (Rotter, 1982, p. 1).

There could be no serious thought of a career in psychology for an impoverished young man in 1933, during the Great Depression. Like many people at that time, Rotter had to be pragmatic and choose a field where he could earn a living. Because job prospects for psychologists at that time were poor, when Rotter entered Brooklyn College he decided to major in chemistry. By the time he graduated, however, he had accumulated more credits in psychology than in chemistry. He had also attended monthly meetings at Adler's home for discussions of Adler's system of individual psychology.

Two of Rotter's professors urged him to undertake graduate work in psychology at the State University of Iowa. He arrived in Iowa City with only enough money to stay a few weeks, but fortunately he obtained a research assistantship and was able to remain. After receiving his M.A. in 1938, he accepted an internship in clinical psychology at Worcester State Hospital in Massachusetts, a major training and research center in clinical psychology. The following year he went to Indiana University in Bloomington to work on his Ph.D., which he received in 1941.

Rotter wanted an academic job, but the prejudices of the time were against him. "At Brooklyn College and again in graduate school, I had been warned that Jews simply could not get academic jobs, regardless of their credentials. The warnings seemed justified" (Rotter, 1982, p. 346). Instead, he found work as a clinical psychologist at Norwich State Hospital in Connecticut.

Following service as a psychologist with the U.S. Army during World War II, Rotter joined the faculty of Ohio State University, where George Kelly was director of the clinical psychology program. It is interesting that two personality theories that emphasize cognition should have developed at the same institution, although Kelly's work was well under way by the time Rotter arrived. At Ohio State, Rotter formulated his social-learning approach to personality and conducted considerable research. His work attracted many outstanding graduate students who went on to productive careers. One described the time as the "glory days" at Ohio State, with "Rotter and Kelly right in the midst of refining their theoretical positions and writing their magnum opuses" (Sechrest, 1984, p. 228).

In 1963, Rotter left Ohio State to work at the University of Connecticut in Storrs. In 1988, he received the Distinguished Scientific Contribution Award from the American Psychological Association.

Social-Learning Theory

Rotter's social-learning theory is based on four primary concepts: behavior potential, expectancy, reinforcement value, and the psychological situation. He also proposed two broader concepts: freedom of movement and the minimal goal level.

Behavior Potential

behavior potential
The likelihood that a particular behavior will occur in a given situation.

Behavior potential refers to the likelihood that of all the behaviors we could choose to display in a given situation, one particular behavior will occur. Our selection of one behavior over another is based on our subjective impression of the situation. Thus, behavior potential is affected not only by the stimulus situation but also by our conscious selection from among the behavioral alternatives available to us, given our subjective perception of the situation.

Rotter's view of behavior differs from Skinner's. Whereas Skinner dealt with objectively observable events, Rotter's definition encompasses both overt actions and those that cannot be directly observed, namely, our internal cognitive processes. For Rotter, cognitive processes include rationaliza-

People have different expectations about the rewards they will receive for their behavior. Your expectation of a good test grade depends in part on the rewards you received in past test-taking situations.

tion, repression, consideration of alternatives, and planning—variables that more radical behaviorists do not consider to be behavior.

Rotter insists that cognitive processes can be objectively observed and measured through indirect means, such as inferring them from overt behavior. Consider, for example, the way we solve problems. Problem-solving behavior can be inferred by observing the behavior of subjects who are trying to complete an assigned task. If the subjects take more time to solve one problem than they needed to solve an earlier one, Rotter takes this as evidence that they are considering alternative solutions.

The objective investigation of cognitive activities is difficult, but the principles that regulate the occurrence of these implicit behaviors are no different from those that regulate directly observable overt behaviors. Both are important in determining behavior potential.

Expectancy

expectancy Our belief that if we behave a certain way in a given situation, a predictable reinforcement will follow.

Expectancy refers to our belief that if we behave a certain way in a given situation, then we can predict the reward that will follow. We hold this belief or expectation in terms of a probability or a likelihood that the reinforcer will occur. This degree of expectancy is determined largely by two factors.

The first factor is the nature of prior reinforcement for behaving in a particular way in that situation. Did the reinforcement occur once or many times? Did it happen yesterday or a year ago? Were you reinforced every time for that behavior or only occasionally? In this way, our past reinforcement influences our expectancy about future reinforcement.

generalization The idea that responses made in one situation will also be made in similar situations.

Second, the degree of expectancy depends on the extent of **generalization** from similar, but not identical, situations. We must ask ourselves if past sequences of behavior and reinforcement apply to other situations in our lives. Generalized expectancies are particularly important when we face new situations because we cannot predict whether our behavior will lead to a given reinforcer if we have never been in that situation before. We must base our expectation of the outcome on our past responses to similar events.

A person running the 100-yard dash for the first time cannot base his or her expectancy of winning on past experience. But expectancy can be based on a generalization from participation in other athletic events, such as performance in other races. When one has run the 100-yard dash several times, the expectancy of winning can be based on past experience in that event. Then it is no longer necessary to generalize expectancy from similar situations.

Reinforcement Value

reinforcement value
The basis for preferring one reinforcer over another.

Reinforcement value refers to the degree of preference for one reinforcer over another. If you are in a situation in which it is equally likely that one of several reinforcers will occur, how much will you prefer one over the others? People differ in terms of what they find reinforcing. For example, on a quiet Sunday afternoon, some people would select a movie; others, a chamber music concert. Some would watch a football game, and others would go out to play soccer. We find reinforcement of different values in different activities.

These preferences derive from our experience in associating past reinforcers with current ones. From these associations, we develop expectancies for future reinforcement. In this way, Rotter relates the concepts of expectancy and reinforcement value, and under certain conditions, either can serve as a cue for the other.

Consider the person buying a raffle ticket for which the prize is a new car. Considering the low cost of the ticket, the reinforcement value is great. Because of this unusually high reinforcement value, most people have a low expectancy of winning because few of us have had the experience of winning a prize of such value. Many people, however, have won items of lower value. Therefore, our expectancy of winning something in a raffle, a game, or a lottery is greater when the reinforcement value of the prize is lower. Our expectancy is partially determined by the reinforcement value of the reward.

The Psychological Situation

psychological situation The combination of internal and external factors that influences our perception of and response to a stimulus.

Rotter believes we are in a continuous state of reacting to our internal and external environments. Further, these environments are themselves continually interacting. Rotter terms this the **psychological situation** because we respond according to our psychological perception of the external stimulus situation.

Behavior can be predicted only from a knowledge of the psychological situation, not from what some personality theorists call a core of personality. In the core approach, prediction of behavior is based on the assumption of constant elements of personality, such as motives and traits. A person pos-

All situations contain cues that tell us what reinforcement—such as praise from the teacher or expulsion from the classroom—will follow if we behave in a particular way.

sessing a particular trait or motive is expected always to behave in a certain way, regardless of the external situation.

Rotter contends that all situations contain cues that, based on our past experience, indicate to us an expectancy of reinforcement for behaving in a particular way. Consider the person whom a Freudian theorist would label an anal aggressive personality. In a core approach, that person would be expected to behave aggressively under all circumstances. Rotter suggests that the person's behavior will vary with the perception of the situation. The person will probably not behave aggressively if the situational cues indicate that severe punishment will follow the aggressive behavior. Thus, Rotter takes the interactionist viewpoint regarding the mutual influence of personal and situational variables.

He criticized not only the core theorists who focused solely on internal variables but also radical behaviorists who focused only on external variables. By ignoring the mediating effect of expectancies and other cognitive processes, radical behaviorists (such as Skinner) overlook the possibility that the same stimulus can have different effects on behavior in different situations.

For example, imagine a gun collector examining a valuable weapon at home and staring at the same weapon held by a robber in a dark alley. The physical stimulus (the gun) is the same in both instances, but the psychological situation (the perception of the stimulus) differs sharply. As a result, behavioral responses to the stimulus will differ.

Freedom of Movement

freedom of movement The degree of expectancy that a certain behavior will bring a given reinforcement.

Freedom of movement refers to the degree of expectancy we have that we will attain a given reinforcer as a result of certain behavior. A high expectancy leads to high freedom of movement; a low expectancy leads to low freedom of movement. A person with high freedom of movement anticipates success in achieving goals, but a person with low freedom of movement anticipates failure or punishment.

Low freedom of movement is related to several factors. One is a lack of knowledge about how to achieve a particular goal. For example, people with a low measurable level of intelligence may have a low expectancy of achieving certain goals in school because they do not have the ability to develop the necessary skills or learn the required behaviors. People with sufficient ability may develop low freedom of movement because they have misinterpreted past situations. As children they may have been punished for their behavior and may generalize from those experiences to their present situation. As a result, they anticipate disapproval in all life situations. They interpret this disapproval as failure and have a low expectancy of success.

When freedom of movement is low with regard to a goal or need that has a high value, conflict results. The person may develop various avoidance behaviors and try to achieve the goal or meet the need in a symbolic way, retreating into a fantasy world in which there is no risk of punishment or failure. Rotter suggested that most deviant or psychopathological behavior is designed to avoid the conflict between important goals and low freedom of movement.

The Minimal Goal Level

minimal goal level The lowest level of potential reinforcement in a given situation that is perceived as satisfactory.

The **minimal goal level** is the lowest level of potential reinforcement in a particular situation that we perceive as satisfactory. Reinforcers exist on a continuum, ranging from those that are highly desirable to those that are highly undesirable. The point at which desirable reinforcers become undesirable represents our minimal goal level. For example, when you apply for a job, the salary you are offered could range from unusually high to disappointingly low. Somewhere within that range is the lowest level you would find satisfying. Working for a lower salary than that would not be reinforcing.

You set minimal goal levels in many situations, from the grade you would find acceptable in this course to the kind of car, career, or mate you expect to have. Different people may have different minimal goal levels in the same situation. You might be satisfied with nothing less than a grade of A in this course, whereas your roommate might happily settle for a C. Each of you would find attaining your goal to be reinforcing. Suppose, however, that you receive a B. You may feel that you have failed; this feeling contributes to low freedom of movement—a lowered expectancy of success in future courses of this type. Your roommate would find your despondency hard to understand; he or she had expected only a C and would be delighted with the

B because for your roommate, receiving a B would lead to higher freedom of movement and expectancy of success.

Our emotional health is affected by the point at which we set our minimal goal levels. The person with high minimal goal levels who does not obtain reinforcement at or above these levels develops low freedom of movement. Thus, setting unrealistic minimal goal levels may be harmful.

Minimal goal levels that are too low in terms of our ability and reinforcement history may leave us with high freedom of movement, but we would not be living up to our capacities. For example, students who are considered underachievers, who do not perform at levels consistent with their abilities, have set minimal goal levels that are too low.

We can raise or lower our minimal goal levels by changing our reinforcement values. We achieve this by pairing present values with higher or lower values. For example, a student may believe that a grade of B on an examination has a negative value. However, if that grade is paired with the positive reinforcement of praise from the professor for classroom discussion or a term paper, then the grade of B can come to assume a positive value as a reinforcer.

Psychological Needs

Our major motivation in life is to maximize positive reinforcement and minimize punishment in all situations. Here again Rotter focuses on the interaction between internal and external determinants of behavior. When we describe external conditions, we are dealing with reinforcers. When we speak of internal cognitive conditions, we are referring to needs.

According to Rotter, our psychological needs are learned. In infancy and early childhood, these needs arise from experiences associated with the satisfaction of physiological needs, such as hunger, thirst, sensory stimulation, and freedom from pain. As children grow and develop language and cognitive skills, their psychological needs arise less from association with physiological needs and more from their relation to other acquired or learned psychological needs. Cues from the social environment become more important than internal physiological states.

Learned needs are social in origin because they depend on other people. It is obvious that infants and children depend on others, particularly parents, for need satisfaction and reinforcement. Later, reinforcement becomes dependent on a broader range of people, including teachers and friends. As adults we depend on other people for satisfaction of such needs as love, affection, and recognition.

need potential The possibility that related behaviors leading to the same or similar reinforcers will occur at the same time.

Our behaviors, needs, and goals operate within functionally related systems. Rotter proposed the concept of **need potential** to indicate the possibility that within these systems, related behaviors leading to the same or similar reinforcement can occur at the same time.

The types of behaviors that can be grouped into functional systems range from overt actions to covert cognitions. These systems are arranged in hierarchies; the needs high on the scale can include lower ones. For example, the need potential for recognition is a broad category and includes lower need potentials, such as the potential for recognition in psychology or in intercollegiate sports.

Rotter proposed six categories of needs (Rotter, Chance, & Phares, 1972):

1. *Recognition/status needs.* The need to be considered competent in a professional, social, occupational, or recreational activity; the need to gain social or vocational position, to be seen as more skilled or "better" than other people.
2. *Protection/dependency needs.* The need to have another person or group act on our behalf to prevent frustration or punishment or to provide for the satisfaction of our other needs.
3. *Dominance needs.* The need to direct and control the actions of other people, including family members and friends; the need to have any action taken by others be the one that we suggest.
4. *Independence needs.* The need to make our own decisions and to rely on ourselves; the need to develop skills for obtaining satisfaction directly, without the mediation of other people.
5. *Love and affection needs.* The need for acceptance and liking by others.
6. *Physical comfort needs.* The need for physical satisfaction that becomes associated with achieving security.

Rotter's concept of need is not based on physiological or psychological conditions of deprivation or arousal—the way in which other theorists have defined needs. Rotter's formulation refers to the direction of behavior, which is inferred from the effects of reinforcement on behavior.

Locus of Control

locus of control Our belief about the source of control of reinforcement.
Internal locus of control indicates a belief that reinforcement is brought about by our own behavior.
External locus of control indicates a belief that reinforcement is under the control of other people, fate, or luck.

Rotter proposed the concept of **locus of control** to explain personality differences in our beliefs about the source of our reinforcement. We noted earlier that people differ in their perception of whether a particular event is reinforcing. Rotter's research has shown that some people believe that reinforcement depends on their own behavior; others think reinforcement is controlled by outside forces.

People identified with the personality variable called **internal locus of control** believe that the reinforcement they receive is a function of their behaviors and attributes. Those who have **external locus of control** think reinforcement is controlled by other people, fate, or luck. They are convinced that they are powerless with respect to these outside forces.

Our locus of control has a great influence on our behavior. External locus-of-control people, who believe that their behaviors and abilities make no difference in the reinforcers they receive, see little value in putting forth any effort to improve their situation. They have little belief in the possibility of controlling their life either in the present or in the future.

In contrast, internal locus-of-control people believe that they have a firm control over life, and they behave accordingly. Research has shown that they perform at a higher level on laboratory tasks, are less susceptible to attempts to influence them, place a higher value on their skills and achievements, and are more alert to environmental cues that they use to guide behavior. They report lower anxiety and higher self-esteem, are more ready to take responsibility for their actions, and enjoy greater mental health (Phares, 1976).

Interpersonal Trust

interpersonal trust
The degree of expectancy that a given person is trustworthy.

Internal versus external locus of control is a form of generalized expectancy and a relatively stable part of personality. Rotter identified another form of generalized expectancy, called **interpersonal trust**, which is the expectation that the "word, promise, oral or written statement of another individual or group can be relied on" (Rotter, 1980, p. 1).

Rotter's research shows that people high in interpersonal trust are less likely to lie, cheat, or steal. They also are more likely to respect the rights of others and to give them a second chance than are persons low in interpersonal trust. However, highly trusting people are no more likely to be gullible or easily fooled.

High interpersonal trust can have beneficial consequences. People high in interpersonal trust have been found to be more popular and less likely to be unhappy, maladjusted, or bothered by conflicts than those who are low in interpersonal trust.

Rotter's Image of Human Nature

On the free will versus determinism issue, Rotter appears to favor free choice and action, especially for people with internal locus of control. It is clear from his emphasis on cognitive variables that Rotter believes we can regulate and direct our experiences and choose our behaviors. We may be influenced by external variables, but we can shape the nature and extent of that influence. People with external locus of control do not feel a sense of control. The possibility of free will is available to them, but they believe they are controlled by outside forces.

To Rotter, most human behavior is learned. He paid little attention to genetic factors. It is primarily nurture, not nature—our experience, not our inheritance—that guides us. Our learning experiences in childhood are important, but they do not determine our behavior throughout the life span. Personality changes and grows; it is not fixed in the pattern established in childhood. Early learning experiences affect our perception of later events,

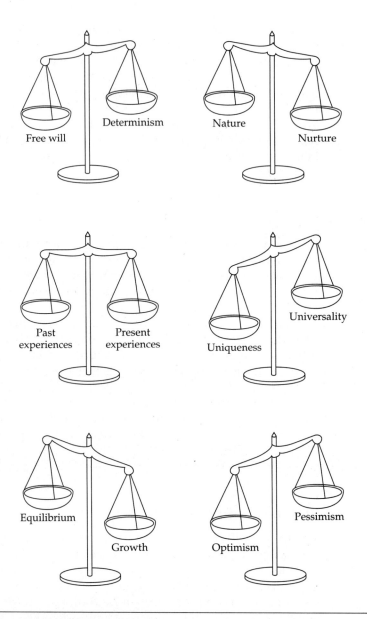

Rotter

Image of Human Nature.

but we are not victims of our past. We react continuously to our internal and external environments, and as these change, so does our perception of them.

Rotter's position on the issue of uniqueness versus universality is reflected in his concept of the psychological situation. Each of us develops a personal view of the world, and we interpret and react to external stimuli according to our perception of them. It follows, then, that each of us lives and functions in a unique psychological situation.

Rotter did not propose an ultimate and necessary life goal, such as self-actualization, but he stated that all behavior is goal-directed. Rather than being pulled by some ideal state to be attained or pushed to escape anxiety or inferiority feelings, we act to achieve personal goals. We are motivated to maximize positive reinforcement and minimize punishment, and we are capable of making conscious decisions about how to achieve this state.

Rotter's social-learning system offers an optimistic image of human nature. We are not passive victims of external events, inheritance, or childhood experiences; instead, we are free to shape our present behavior and our future.

Assessment in Rotter's Theory

Rotter has used a variety of assessment techniques, including interviews, projective tests, direct observations of behavior, and self-report inventories. He has also designed specific techniques to evaluate various concepts in his system. To measure reinforcement value, Rotter uses the ranking method and the behavioral choice method. In research with the ranking method, subjects are given verbal descriptions of reinforcers, such as praise from one's teacher, and are asked to rank the statements from most reinforcing to least reinforcing. In the behavioral choice method, subjects are asked to select behaviors they expect will be followed by a reinforcer of high rather than low value.

The behavioral choice technique has also been used to measure expectancy. When subjects choose one behavioral alternative over another, they are indicating a belief that the behavior they select has a higher expectancy of producing the desired reinforcement.

Another way to assess expectancy involves verbal techniques. For example, subjects are asked to predict the likelihood of receiving reinforcement in terms of alternatives on a scale of expectancy values. In another instance, subjects are graded on their performance of a laboratory task. Before receiving the grade, they are asked for their expectancies for the tasks. The hypothesis is that the anticipated grades represent the level of expectancy the subjects are most confident of receiving.

To measure need potential, it is necessary to have an indication of how frequently certain behaviors occur. This is accomplished by observing subjects' behaviors over time. Need potential is also assessed through questionnaires, verbal choice techniques, and ranking methods and by asking subjects what they believe they would do in a given situation.

Rotter developed self-report inventories to assess the two forms of generalized expectancy: internal versus external locus of control, and interpersonal trust. The Internal-External (I-E) Scale (Rotter, 1966) consists of 23 forced-choice alternatives. From each pair of items, subjects must pick the one that best describes their beliefs. Sample items from the I-E Scale are shown in Table 16.1. It is not difficult to determine which of each pair of alternatives represents an internal or an external locus of control.

Table 16.1   ***Sample items from the I-E Scale.***

1. a. Many of the unhappy things in people's lives are partly due to bad luck.
   b. People's misfortunes result from the mistakes they make.

2. a. One of the major reasons why we have wars is because people don't take enough interest in politics.
   b. There will always be wars, no matter how hard people try to prevent them.

3. a. In the long run people get the respect they deserve in this world.
   b. Unfortunately, an individual's worth often passes unrecognized no matter how hard he or she tries.

4. a. The idea that teachers are unfair to students is nonsense.
   b. Most students don't realize the extent to which their grades are influenced by accidental happenings.

5. a. Without the right breaks one cannot be an effective leader.
   b. Capable people who fail to become leaders have not taken advantage of their opportunities.

6. a. No matter how hard you try some people just don't like you.
   b. People who can't get others to like them don't understand how to get along with others.

SOURCE: J. B. Rotter, "Generalized Expectancies for Internal versus External Control of Reinforcement," *Psychological Monographs, 80* (1966):11.

Other scales have been developed to assess locus of control. The Children's Nowicki-Strickland Internal-External Scale is a 40-item test that has been used in more than 700 studies and translated into two dozen languages (Nowicki & Strickland, 1973; Strickland, 1989). An adult form of the scale has also been prepared, as well as a version with cartoons for preschool children (Nowicki & Duke, 1983). In addition, variations of the I-E Scale have been developed to measure specific behaviors. For example, the Dieting Beliefs Scale is designed to assess the relationship between locus of control and factors relating to weight loss (Stotland & Zuroff, 1990).

Rotter's Interpersonal Trust Scale (Rotter, 1967) consists of 25 items to measure trust and 15 items to disguise the purpose of the test. Subjects indicate their degree of agreement or disagreement with each item (see Table 16.2).

Research in Rotter's Theory

Rotter has primarily used the experimental and correlational research methods to formulate and test his theory. Much of his research focuses on the I-E Scale and how it correlates with measures of behavior and personality.

Earlier in this chapter, we noted some of the characteristics of people whose orientations are either internal or external. Additional research has been directed toward the developmental aspects of this variable. Studies have shown that people become more internally oriented as they grow older, reaching a peak in middle age (Milgram, 1971; Ryckman & Malikiosi, 1975).

More college students have been found to exhibit an internal than an

Table 16.2 ***Sample items from the Interpersonal Trust Scale.***

1. In dealing with strangers one is better off to be cautious until they have provided evidence that they are trustworthy.
2. Parents usually can be relied upon to keep their promises.
3. Parents and teachers are likely to say what they believe themselves and not just what they think is good for the child to hear.
4. Most elected public officials are really sincere in their campaign promises.

SOURCE: J. B. Rotter, "A New Scale for the Measurement of Interpersonal Trust," *Journal of Personality,* 35 (1967):654.

external orientation (Rotter, 1966). In terms of overall scores, no significant differences have been shown between men and women on the I-E Scale (DeBrabander & Boone, 1990). There is some indication, however, that men and women respond differently on certain items. In one study, men displayed greater internal locus of control than did women on items relating to academic achievement (Strickland & Haley, 1980). External locus of control appears to increase in women after divorce, followed by a return to internal locus of control (Doherty, 1983). Women who have been physically abused tend to show an external locus of control (Baron & Byrne, 1984).

Several studies reported a shift among women to a more external locus of control during the 1970s. This change was attributed to the increasing number of women entering the work force and encountering discrimination and prejudicial attitudes that thwarted their advancement. Later research showed that these earlier studies contained errors in encoding the data and that there had been no such shift in locus of control among women during that time (Smith & Dechter, 1991). (This instance demonstrates that not all research is carefully designed, controlled, and executed. We must sometimes be skeptical and consider the possible effect of other, untested influencing variables.)

Significant racial and socioeconomic differences were found in performance on the I-E Scale. In general, lower social classes and minorities, except for Asian Americans, held an external locus of control, believing they had little control over life's events (Coleman et al., 1966). This was confirmed in a study in which lower-class black children were shown to be more externally oriented than lower- and middle-class white children or middle-class black children (Battle & Rotter, 1963).

These findings were duplicated in research conducted in the African nation of Botswana. There, male and female adolescents scored higher in external locus of control than white adolescents in the United States. Those higher in socioeconomic status scored higher in internal control than those lower in socioeconomic status (Maqsud & Rouhani, 1991).

In a study of American high school students, it was found that Hispanic-American and Native-American adolescents were more likely to be externally oriented than were white adolescents (Graves, 1961). Research conducted with Chinese undergraduates in Hong Kong found evidence suggesting the existence of three factors on the I-E Scale, one involving luck or fate and the other two relating to achievement and interpersonal relations (Chan, 1989). The Hong Kong Chinese students tended to be externally oriented in luck or fate and internally oriented in achievement and interpersonal relations.

The behavior of internally oriented people has been shown to differ from that of externally oriented people. Internally oriented people are more likely to engage in significantly more daydreams about achievement and fewer daydreams about failure, to acquire and process more information in different situations, to experience a greater sense of personal choice, to be popular with peers, to be attracted to people they can manipulate, to have higher self-esteem, and to act in more socially skillful ways (Abdallah, 1989; Brannigan, Hauk, & Guay, 1991; Harvey & Barnes, 1974; Lefcourt, Martin, Fick, & Saleh, 1985; Nowicki & Roundtree, 1974; Silverman & Shrauger, 1970; Sims & Baumann, 1972; Wolk & DuCette, 1974).

Also, people high in internal locus of control are less likely to have emotional problems or become alcoholics. They experience less anxiety, fewer psychiatric symptoms, and less depression, and they are better able to cope with psychological distress (Benassi, Sweeney, & Dufour, 1988; Lefcourt, 1982; Naditch, 1975; Petrosky & Birkhimer, 1991; Strassberg, 1973). Internals tend to earn higher grades in school and score higher on standardized tests of academic achievement. They are more resistant to attempts at persuasion and coercion, more perceptive, and more inquisitive (Findley & Cooper, 1983; Lefcourt, 1982).

Internally oriented people may be physically healthier than those who are externally oriented. Research showed that they tended to have lower blood pressure and fewer heart attacks. When they did develop cardiac problems, they cooperated better with the hospital staff and were released earlier than patients who were externally oriented. They tend to be more cautious about their health and more likely to wear auto seatbelts, to engage in exercise, and to quit smoking (Seeman, Seeman, & Sayles, 1985; Strickland, 1978, 1979).

In one study, internal locus of control as it related to physical health was found to consist of four factors: self-mastery, illness prevention, illness management, and self-blame. The factor most closely associated with physical health and well-being was self-mastery, the belief in one's ability to overcome illness (Marshall, 1991).

In a variety of ways, then, it appears more desirable to have an internal rather than an external locus of control. Evidence suggests that locus of control is learned in childhood and is directly related to parental behavior (Chandler, Wolf, Cook, & Dugovics, 1980). Parents of children who possessed an internal locus of control were found to be highly supportive, to offer praise (that is, positive reinforcement) for achievements, and to be consistent in their discipline. They were not authoritarian in their attitudes. As their children grew older, these parents continued to foster an internal locus of control by encouraging independence (Loeb, 1975; Wichern & Nowicki, 1976).

Research on interpersonal trust shows that last-born children are less trusting than other children. College students who express religious beliefs tend to be more trusting than those who express no such beliefs. In addition, the higher one's socioeconomic status, the higher the degree of interpersonal trust (Rotter, 1967). In laboratory experiments, subjects low in interpersonal trust were more likely to cheat when competing for a monetary prize. They also worked less hard on an experimental task when they believed that they were not being watched (Rotter, 1980). A study of high school girls showed that those low in interpersonal trust were more likely to shoplift than were those high in interpersonal trust. Those low in trust were also more likely to believe that adults distrusted them (Wright & Kirmani, 1977).

A Final Commentary

Rotter's social-learning theory, with its emphasis on cognitive factors, has attracted enthusiastic followers. It appeals primarily to experimentally oriented researchers interested in the impact of cognitive variables. Rotter's emphasis on these variables is stronger than Bandura's, and his position represents a significant departure from Skinner's radical behaviorism.

Rotter offers concepts—defined in precise and unambiguous terms—that are amenable to testing by experimental and correlational methods. He establishes a working relationship between cognitive variables and reinforcement and gives social-learning theory a strong motivational component.

Although some psychologists consider the focus on internal variables a source of the theory's strength, others see it as a weakness. Critics have suggested that Rotter has gone too far, that his position deviates so greatly from orthodox behaviorism that it cannot be considered a behavioral approach. Because of the extent of Rotter's use of cognitive variables, some of his methods, such as interviews and projective tests, are seen as subjective.

Rotter's research, however, has been as rigorous and well controlled as the subject matter allows, and he uses objective measures wherever possible. Studies of various aspects of the theory have provided considerable empirical support. The I-E Scale has generated a wealth of research and has been applied in clinical and educational settings. Rotter has noted that his locus of control concept has become "one of the most studied variables in psychology and the other social sciences" (Rotter, 1990, p. 489).

Summary

Julian Rotter calls his theory a social-learning theory to indicate his belief that we learn behavior primarily through social experiences. He studies normal subjects and deals more extensively with conscious processes than Bandura. Rotter's system integrates reinforcement and cognitive theories and deals with the interaction of the person and his or her unique environment.

Behavior potential refers to the likelihood that a specific behavior will occur, relative to other behaviors that could be displayed in a given situation. Behavior includes directly observable acts, as well as cognitive processes that cannot be observed but can be inferred from overt behavior. Expectancy refers to the belief that if we behave in a certain way in a given situation, a predictable reinforcer will follow. Reinforcement value refers to the degree of preference for one reinforcer over another. The psychological situation is a coalition of internal and external environments—that is, of cognitive variables and external stimuli.

Freedom of movement refers to the degree of expectancy that we will attain a given reinforcer as a result of certain behavior. A high expectancy leads to high freedom of movement; a low expectancy leads to low freedom of movement. Causes of low freedom of movement include a lack of knowledge about how to achieve a particular goal and a faulty interpretation of past situations. The minimal goal level refers to the lowest level of potential reinforcement in a given situation that we perceive as satisfactory. Setting unrealistic minimal goal levels may be harmful to emotional health.

Rotter believes that behavior is directed toward maximizing positive reinforcement. Psychological needs are learned and are social in origin in that they depend on other people. Need potential refers to related behaviors that can lead to the same or similar reinforcement. Categories of needs are recognition-status, protection-dependency, dominance, independence, love and affection, and physical comfort.

People who believe that reinforcement depends on their own behavior have an internal locus of control. People who believe that reinforcement is controlled by outside forces have an external locus of control. Internals perform at higher levels, are less susceptible to outside influences, place a higher value on their skills and achievements, and take more responsibility for their actions.

People high in interpersonal trust are less likely to lie, cheat, and steal; more likely to respect the rights of others; less likely to be unhappy and maladjusted; and are more liked than people low in interpersonal trust.

Rotter's image of human nature emphasizes free will, the importance of learning, the possibility that personality will change and grow, uniqueness, and the goal of maximizing reinforcement and minimizing punishment.

To assess personality, Rotter uses interviews, projective tests, direct observation of behavior, and self-report inventories. He developed the Internal-External (I-E) Scale and the Interpersonal Trust Scale. Research has shown that people become more internally oriented as they grow older. People in lower social classes and in many minority groups tend to be externally oriented. Internals have been shown to feel a stronger sense of personal choice, to experience fewer psychiatric symptoms and less anxiety, and to earn higher grades in school than externals. Parents of internally oriented children are highly supportive and consistent in their discipline; they encourage their children's growing independence.

In terms of interpersonal trust, last-born children have been found to be less trusting than their older siblings. College students with deep religious beliefs are more trusting than those with no professed religious beliefs. The higher the social class, the greater the interpersonal trust.

Rotter's theory has been criticized as too subjective because of its emphasis on cognitive variables.

Critical Thinking Review

1. How does Rotter's personality theory differ from Skinner's approach to personality? What does Rotter's theory have in common with Bandura's theory?

2. According to Rotter, what is the role of cognitive factors in personality?

3. What factors influence our belief or expectancy that, if we behave in a certain way in a given situation, a predictable reinforcement will follow?

4. What is the relationship between minimal goal levels and reinforcement values? How are we likely to respond to a minimal goal level that is set too low for our abilities?

5. What is the difference between needs and goals? List the six categories of needs in Rotter's theory.

6. If external locus-of-control people heard that a tornado was approaching, would they be more likely to think that there was nothing they could do about it, or would they be more likely to take immediate action to protect their family and property? Why?

7. What parental behaviors can foster an internal locus of control in a child?

8. Describe the differences in behavior between people high in interpersonal trust and people low in interpersonal trust.

9. What is Rotter's position on the issue of free will versus determinism? On the uniqueness of human behavior?

10. How does Rotter measure reinforcement value and expectancy?

11. Discuss the racial and social-class differences found in research on internal versus external locus of control.

Suggested Reading

Rotter, J. B. (1980). Interpersonal trust, trustworthiness, and gullibility. *American Psychologist, 35,* 1–7. Reviews the consequences for one's social life of being high or low in interpersonal trust.

Rotter, J. B. (1982). *The development and applications of social learning theory: Selected papers.* New York: Praeger. Covers the development of Rotter's theory and its applications to clinical, personality, and social psychology. Includes a biographical sketch.

Strickland, B. R. (1989). Internal-external control expectancies: From contingency to creativity. *American Psychologist, 44,* 1–12. Reviews the research literature on internal versus external locus of control beliefs and relates the findings to measures of physical and psychological health.

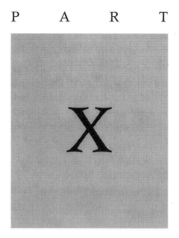

X

The Limited-Domain Approach

Personality theorists have usually considered that comprehensiveness or completeness was a major theoretical goal. Some theories come closer to achieving this than others. Today, however, more and more personality psychologists are concluding that no existing theory can be a truly comprehensive explanation for all aspects of personality and behavior, regardless of the theorist's stated aims. Indeed, such a goal may be unrealistic.

As a result, some psychologists suggested the need to develop a number of separate theories, each having a narrow range of application. These so-called limited-domain theories focus on a restricted aspect of personality. Limiting the focus of investigation allows the domain selected to be investigated more thoroughly than is possible with a global theory that deals with the total personality.

This kind of fragmentation in the study of personality has been taking place for some time. It follows the example of other areas of psychol-

ogy that have replaced attempts to develop large-scale, all-encompassing theories with "miniature" theories. For example, in the study of learning, we find theoretical formulations that focus on specific types of learning—verbal learning, conditioning, maze learning—that represent narrow, circumscribed areas of behavior. In the study of personality we find researchers focusing on variables such as altruism, cognitive dissonance, and psychological differentiation.

It is easy to see why the global approach to personality theory characterized the field for so long. The early personality theorists, such as Freud, Jung, and Adler, treated individual patients in a clinical setting. They tried to alter or cure abnormalities and emotional disturbances and therefore were forced to deal with whole human beings who were trying to function in the real world. Thus, these theorists attempted to treat the whole person, not just an aspect or two of their personality.

The focus shifted from the whole person

when the study of personality was brought out of the clinic and into the research laboratory. Experimental psychologists typically study one variable at a time, controlling or holding constant all other variables. In this way they concentrate on a limited domain. They collect large amounts of empirical data derived from their investigation of how the experimental variable relates to its antecedents and to its behavioral consequences. Limited-domain theories, then, are characterized by a type of supporting data that is different from the data generated by the clinical approach.

Limited-domain theorists place less emphasis on the therapeutic value of their theoretical formulations. They usually are not clinicians, but researchers, and they are more interested in investigating personality than in changing it. This does not mean that limited-domain theories have no therapeutic utility. Rather, it indicates that the theories were not developed specifically for use with patients, as was the case with many of the early personality theories.

Because the study of personality and the proposal of theories are becoming more experimentally oriented, it follows that the limited-domain approach will continue to grow in importance. We have chosen to discuss three limited-domain approaches: the need for achievement, sensation seeking, and learned helplessness. These formulations represent three major orientations discussed in this text: the neopsychoanalytic,

trait, and social-learning or social-cognitive approaches. Thus, each of these positions encompasses not only different aspects of personality but different approaches to the ultimate explanation of personality.

Achievement is one of the needs proposed by Henry Murray. It invokes the idea of tension reduction and reflects the influence of Freud's work. The need or motivation to achieve, as a limited-domain theory of personality, is measured by a projective test, the Thematic Apperception Test, which is also based on Freudian concepts.

Sensation seeking is one of the traits in Hans Eysenck's personality dimension E (extraversion versus introversion). It is primarily an inherited attribute and reflects the impact of behavioral genetics on personality.

Learned helplessness is, by definition, a learned behavior. It has a strong cognitive component, reflecting the influence of the behaviorist, social learning, and cognitive movements on the study of personality.

The three conceptions we have chosen to discuss in this chapter are presented as examples of the limited-domain approach. They are not comprehensive systems of personality, nor are they the only examples of miniature theories being considered by contemporary psychologists. Our intention is to give you the flavor of each theory and to acquaint you with the idea of studying personality in this limited-domain fashion.

SEVENTEEN

David McClelland

Marvin Zuckerman

Martin E. P. Seligman

Limited-Domain Theories of Personality

David McClelland: The Need for Achievement
  Assessing the Need for Achievement
  Behavioral Studies
  Behavior on the Job
  The Influence of Cultural Factors
  Developing the Need for Achievement in
    Adults
  Developing the Need for Achievement in
    Children
  Age and Gender Differences
  Work Orientation, Mastery, and
    Competitiveness
  Comment
Marvin Zuckerman: Sensation Seeking
  Assessing Sensation Seeking
  Characteristics of Sensation Seekers
  Behavioral Differences
  Personality Differences

  Cognitive Processes
  Occupational Preferences
  Attitudes
  Physiological Differences
  Heredity Versus Environment
  Comment
Martin E. P. Seligman: Learned Helplessness
  Early Research
  Learned Helplessness in Elderly Persons
  Physical Health and Explanatory Style
  Depression
  The Attribution Model
  The Development of Learned Helplessness
    in Childhood
  Comment
Summary
Critical Thinking Review
Suggested Reading

In recent years there has been a trend away from grand, comprehensive theories toward theories that are limited to conceptualizations about types of personality or about ways of personality functioning.

—Donald Fiske

David McClelland: The Need for Achievement

One of the needs posited by Henry Murray is the need for achievement, which he described as the need to overcome obstacles, to excel, and to live up to a high standard. The psychologist David McClelland (1917–), affiliated with Harvard University, has conducted a broad and intensive research program to investigate this need. He views the **need for achievement** (or **achievement motivation**) as a drive that can energize and direct behavior in virtually all situations (Koestner & McClelland, 1990).

McClelland's work provides an excellent example of how much we can learn when the domain of research is restricted to a well-defined aspect of the human personality. It also provides an example of the importance of the limited-domain approach in understanding the total personality. The focus of study is narrow, but the ramifications are far-reaching.

McClelland and his associates developed a technique to measure an individual's need for achievement and have shown how behavior varies in different situations as a function of our level of this need. Also, they have identified sources responsible for the development of achievement motivation in childhood.

Applying his theory to broader social concerns, McClelland offered an

achievement motivation The need to achieve, overcome obstacles, excel, and live up to a high standard. Also called the **need for achievement.**

empirical account of the economic growth and decline of several cultures, ancient and contemporary, in terms of each society's level of the need for achievement. He suggests that we can predict a nation's potential for economic growth or decline by measuring its level of achievement motivation.

The importance of McClelland's work was recognized in 1987 with the presentation of the American Psychological Association's Distinguished Scientific Contribution Award, honoring his pioneering studies, his bold vision, and "the productivity he inspired in his students" ("Distinguished," 1988, p. 225).

Assessing the Need for Achievement

To measure the need for achievement, McClelland was guided by certain of Freud's insights and by the methodological requirements of experimental psychology. From Freud he borrowed the approach of uncovering and measuring a motive by analyzing patients' reported fantasies. However, where Freud searched for fantasies in dreams and free associations, McClelland used the Thematic Apperception Test (TAT), developed by Henry Murray and Christiana Morgan. Thus, McClelland probed fantasies by having his subjects interpret the TAT pictures and project their needs, fears, and values onto these ambiguous stimuli.

In his initial research, McClelland and his associates asked groups of male college students to write brief stories about the TAT pictures (McClelland, Atkinson, Clark, & Lowell, 1953). To vary the experimental conditions, the researchers gave different test-taking instructions to different groups, exhorting a high achievement need in one condition and a low achievement need in the other. The content of the stories was compared to see if the groups differed significantly in the amount of achievement-oriented material they produced.

The results showed that the stories written under the high-achievement condition contained many more references to attaining standards of excellence, wanting to achieve, and performing well. For example, one of the pictures showed a young man sitting at a desk with a book open in front of him. Stories from the high need-achievement subjects involved references to excelling, striving, and doing one's best. Stories from the low need-achievement group dealt with sedentary activities, such as daydreaming, thinking, and recalling past events, rather than with working.

McClelland concluded that TAT-induced stories can be used as a valid measure of the need to achieve, and the test became the basic tool for selecting subjects for his extensive research program.

Behavioral Studies

McClelland's research attempted to discover behavioral differences between high and low need-achievement people (McClelland, 1961; McClelland, Atkinson, Clark, & Lowell, 1953). These early studies used only male subjects; later work included female subjects.

Subjects testing high in the need for achievement were found more often in middle and upper socioeconomic classes than in lower socioeconomic groups. They demonstrated a better memory for uncompleted tasks and were more likely to volunteer to serve as subjects for psychological research. They were more resistant to social pressures and less conforming than subjects testing low in the need for achievement. Later research showed that young people high in the need to achieve were more likely to attend college, to earn higher grades, and to be involved in more college and community activities (Atkinson et al., 1976; Raynor, 1970). High need-achievement people were also shown to be more likely to cheat on examinations in certain situations (Johnson, 1981). They were found to get along better with others and to enjoy greater physical health (Veroff, 1982).

Many studies have compared the performance of high and low need-achievers in experimentally designed work situations. In one experiment, subjects were assigned the task of unscrambling the letters of a large number of scrambled words. Although both groups began the task at the same measured level of performance, the high achievers showed progressive improvement (Lowell, 1952). McClelland concluded that the high achievers were so strongly motivated to achieve that they learned to perform the task better and better as they persevered.

Additional experiments revealed that high need-achievement subjects tended to estimate tasks as being easier to perform than did low need-achievement subjects (McClelland, 1985). With cognitive tasks, experimentally induced anxiety facilitated the performance of the high need achievers and impaired the performance of the low need achievers (Piedmont, 1988).

Do people high in achievement motivation perform better in every situation? To answer that question, McClelland and his colleagues tested various kinds of tasks. In one experiment the task was repetitive and routine—crossing out *E*s and *O*s in a long series of random letters. In this type of task there is little room for improvement; there is no way to learn to do the job better, only faster. The results showed that high and low need-achievement subjects performed at the same level.

In another study, subjects high in the need for achievement were given instructions before the task that eliminated all achievement significance. As a result, they performed no better than subjects low in the need for achievement. Other research investigated the effect on performance of extrinsic rewards (rewards other than the personal sense of achievement). In one case, subjects were told that those who performed at a high level could leave the research laboratory immediately on completion of the task. This kind of reward held no motivation for high achievers, and they performed slightly worse than low achievers.

These experiments suggest that subjects high in the need for achievement do not perform better than subjects low in the need for achievement unless the achievement motive is activated. Only when high need-achievement persons are challenged to excel will they do so (McClelland, Koestner, & Weinberger, 1989). From these findings, McClelland predicted that in their careers and everyday activities, people with a high need to achieve will seek situations that will allow them to satisfy this need. They will set achievement standards for themselves and work hard to meet them.

Behavior on the Job

People high in the need for achievement more frequently held high-status jobs than did people low in the need for achievement. They were found to work harder on the job, to have a greater expectation of success, and to report higher job satisfaction (Reuman, Alwin, & Veroff, 1984). They chose jobs that would provide a high level of personal responsibility, in which success depended primarily on their own efforts. They were discontent with jobs in which success depended on other people or on factors beyond their control.

Because high need-achievement people prefer jobs that provide responsibility, McClelland suggested that they would probably prefer to be entrepreneurs—to operate their own businesses and be their own bosses. This kind of work situation would seem to provide an optimal level of challenge and personal responsibility. In a followup study of college students 14 years after their achievement-motivation scores had been determined, it was found that 83 percent of those who had become successful entrepreneurs had scored high in the need to achieve. Only 21 percent of those who had become successful in non-entrepreneurial jobs had scored high in the need to achieve (McClelland, 1965a). Studies conducted in several countries support the finding that high need-achievement people are more attracted to entrepreneurial jobs (McClelland, 1987).

This does not mean that those of us who work for other people in large and small businesses and organizations are generally low in the need to achieve. For example, successful managers were found to have higher need-achievement scores than unsuccessful managers. Also, McClelland found a high positive correlation between the need-achievement scores of a company's executives and that company's level of economic success (McClelland, 1961).

The Influence of Cultural Factors

In a lengthy and ingenious research program, McClelland investigated the link between the individual need for achievement and a nation's economic health (McClelland, 1961). Some of the theorists we have discussed noted the ways in which societal forces influence personality development. Other theorists asserted that people are capable of acting deliberately to change their society. McClelland set out to discover whether a limited-domain personality variable—the need for achievement—has operated on its own to influence and shape society.

The theoretical rationale for considering the possibility of a connection between the need for achievement of a particular group and that culture's economic growth grew out of the work of the German sociologist Max

Weber. Writing early in the 20th century, Weber suggested that the Protestant Reformation had produced a new character orientation in Protestant countries, which gave impetus to the Industrial Revolution and the spirit of capitalism (Weber, 1930). This orientation emphasized a continuing focus on self-improvement and the strengthening of the need to progress, strive, and achieve. McClelland suggested that these cultural values of hard work and striving for excellence became the norm in Protestant cultures and were taught to succeeding generations. The stress on individual achievement was manifested in ways that advanced the culture's economic growth.

To test this proposed relationship between the need for achievement and economic growth, McClelland compared the average per capita consumption of electric power (taken as a measure of economic development) for 12 Protestant and 13 Catholic countries. The data showed that the Protestant countries were the more economically advanced.

The relationship between achievement motivation and economic growth was also examined for three periods of ancient Greek civilization—times of growth, climax, and decline. If a causal relationship exists between a citizenry's need to achieve and its nation's economic prosperity, then achievement motivation should be higher during the period of growth and lower during the period that precedes the decline. To assess the need for achievement in an ancient culture, the researchers obviously could not ask people to write stories projecting their achievement-related fantasies onto pictures. Instead, the methodology involved analyzing stories written at the time for evidence of need-achievement themes, on the assumption that the writers were reflecting the values of their society. When McClelland compared these empirical measures of the need for achievement with measures of economic success during the three time periods, the results were as predicted. There was a high level of need achievement during the period of growth. During the climax period, the level of individual need achievement fell, which, McClelland suggested, contributed to the economic decline that followed.

Because the measures were indirect, McClelland sought to confirm them in other cultures. Studies of Spain during the Middle Ages and of England from 1400 to the onset of the Industrial Revolution (around 1830) showed a high level of need achievement preceding a period of economic growth and a declining level of need achievement preceding economic decline. These studies support the notion that an individual personality characteristic, widely manifested in a given culture, affects the nature of that culture.

McClelland applied this idea to more contemporary times, investigating more than 20 countries to compare economic and achievement-need levels in 1925 and 1950. As a measure of the need for achievement, he analyzed the content of children's stories in second- to fourth-grade schoolbooks. He chose children's stories because they reflect the motives the prevailing society wants its children to learn. In other words, the stories represent the moral values the culture desires to teach to the next generation.

The results showed that the higher a nation's level of achievement motivation in 1925, the greater its rate of economic growth between 1925 and

1950. It is important to note that the high achievement motivation came first; it was not an increased level of economic development that led to the higher need for achievement. Thus, by determining a country's 1925 achievement-need level, McClelland could predict that country's economic situation 25 years later.

Having provided impressive evidence for the impact of the need for achievement on society, McClelland turned to the issue of how the need for achievement could be developed or increased. If enough people could become highly motivated to achieve, the consequences for them—and for society—could be significant.

Developing the Need for Achievement in Adults

Drawing on information about the learning process obtained from human and animal research studies, on the results of attitude-change research, and on principles of psychotherapy, McClelland developed formal courses to teach achievement motivation to adult men (McClelland, 1965b; McClelland & Winter, 1969). These training sessions, offered in the United States, Mexico, and India, lasted up to 14 days, 12 to 18 hours a day. From the initial classes, McClelland derived and refined guidelines to induce changes in the level of the need for achievement in adults.

The first objective of the training program was to instill confidence in the participants that the program would work—an effort to increase the trainees' self-efficacy. (Research has shown that training techniques are more likely to be effective if the trainees believe they can develop the required skills and if they are made aware of how these skills relate to real-world problems.)

Next, trainees were given information about achievement motivation and taught how to apply it; that is, how to translate theory into action. They examined personal and cultural values with respect to the need to achieve and learned how an enhanced need for achievement could better themselves and their society. They agreed to commit themselves to a specific course of action designed to achieve definite personal and career goals and to record the extent of their progress in attaining those goals.

The results showed significant increases in activities related to a high need for achievement for many of the trainees—behaviors that persisted up to two years following the training programs. Behaviors indicative of greater achievement motivation were those that led to pay raises, promotions, increased corporate profits, and greater sales.

Developing the Need for Achievement in Children

Having demonstrated that adults could be taught to increase their need for achievement, McClelland turned his attention to the family environment, focusing on child-rearing practices that could account for the development of achievement motivation in childhood.

A child's desire to achieve can be enhanced by parents who set high but attainable standards and who express pleasure in the child's accomplishments.

One study detected differences in need-achievement levels in children as young as 5, differences traced to attitudes held by their mothers. Another study found that a rigid feeding schedule and intensive toilet training in the early childhood years could be used as predictors of a high need for achievement in adulthood (McClelland & Pilon, 1983).

When 8- to 10-year-old boys were divided into high and low need-achievement groups, and their mothers were interviewed about the demands they made on their children, it was found that mothers of high need-achievement boys expected more self-reliant mastery than did mothers of boys with a low need for achievement (Winterbottom, 1958). (Self-reliant mastery was defined as doing things on their own, taking responsibility, trying hard, and performing well.) Mothers of the high need-achievement boys also placed fewer restrictions on their sons, but the restrictions they did impose were expected to be followed at an earlier age. The boys found to be high in the need to achieve were encouraged to become independent at a younger age than were boys found to be low in the need to achieve.

In another set of experiments, parents of high and low need-achievement boys observed their children performing such tasks as building towers out of blocks, playing ring-toss, and copying patterns with blocks. The parents were allowed to talk to their children, and some interesting parent-child interactions were observed. Parents of high need-achievement boys set higher standards than other parents, expecting the boys to build higher towers and to stand farther from the peg in the ring-toss game. McClelland concluded that to develop the need for achievement, one should have parents who expect a high level of performance and set challenging standards.

Another difference between the sets of parents was in the warmth of their comments to their sons during the experimental tasks. While encouraging their sons to do well, the parents of high achievement-oriented boys were pleasant, calm, and given to good-natured bantering, more so than the parents of low achievement-oriented boys. The mothers of high need-achievement boys tended to be more authoritarian than mothers of low need-achievement boys, whereas the fathers of high need-achievement children were less authoritarian than the fathers of low need-achievement children. These findings, and similar results from other studies, led McClelland to suggest that rigidity or authoritarianism, particularly in the father, can lower a son's need for achievement.

What emerges from this research is a picture of parental behaviors likely to produce a high need for achievement in boys: setting realistically high and challenging standards of performance at an age when such standards can be reached, not overprotecting or indulging, not interfering with the child's efforts to achieve, and demonstrating genuine pleasure in the child's achievements.

Age and Gender Differences

Evidence suggests that the need to achieve declines after middle age, when most people have passed the peak of their career (Maehr & Kleiber, 1981; Smith, 1970). Older people tend to redefine success in different terms. No longer motivated to strive for the same goals they pursued in their twenties and thirties, they may still desire to strive for achievement, satisfaction, and challenge. If an older person has gained security, status, and sufficient income on the job, then goals relating to personal growth may replace the earlier career goals. The new goals do not require the same kind of competitive behavior, but their attainment is nonetheless a kind of success. Thus, the quality of achievement motivation changes with age.

McClelland and his associates tested for gender differences in the need for achievement by comparing the performance of men and women subjects under experimental conditions designed to enhance achievement motivation (Veroff, Wilcox, & Atkinson, 1953). This research showed significant differences in the achievement need for men but not for women, leading McClelland to conclude that the TAT-based measure of need achievement was not valid for women. Consequently, for many years research on the need for achievement was conducted almost exclusively with male subjects.

It is important to note that the initial study of gender differences in achievement motivation was published in 1953. It was widely believed in American culture that women were not—or should not be—ambitious or desirous of achievement. Fifteen years later, psychologist Matina Horner proposed that women are motivated to achieve success but that they also fear success. To succeed in a competitive world, Horner wrote, is something many women avoid because it reflects characteristics traditionally considered unfeminine (Horner, 1973).

To test her hypothesis, Horner conducted a study in which both male and female college students were given the beginning of a story and asked to complete it (Horner, 1978). One of the story openings for female subjects was "After her first term finals, Anne finds herself at the top of her medical school class. . . . " For male subjects the statement was "After his first term finals, John finds himself at the top of his medical school class. . . . "

Approximately two-thirds of the female subjects wrote stories that reflected a fear of success. Achieving at too high a level was seen to have negative consequences. Anne would be judged unfeminine and would be rejected socially because of her high grades. She would feel guilty about her success and worry that her desire for achievement was abnormal.

The women offered various solutions in their stories. One suggested that because Anne did not really want to be at the top of her class, her grades would fall and she would marry the man who was best in the class. Another subject wrote that because of Anne's guilt, she would have a nervous break-down, drop out of medical school, and marry a doctor. Anne's future success was defined not by her own achievements, but by the achievements of the man she would marry.

By contrast, the stories of the male subjects showed positive feelings about success. Fewer than 10 percent indicated any fear of success or of the consequences of achieving at a high level.

To determine how fear of success might influence behavior in an achievement situation, four days after writing their stories the subjects were asked to participate in competitive and noncompetitive games. Men and women who measured high in fear of success performed better in noncompetitive than in competitive games. Those who scored low in fear of success performed better at competitive games.

Other research did not consistently support these findings on sex differences in the need to achieve. One study found that 65 percent of female subjects were high in fear of success—approximately the same as in the Horner study—but 77 percent of the male subjects were also judged high in fear of success. Some 30 percent of the men's stories questioned the value of success and achievement; only 15 percent of the women's stories did so. Stories for both groups contained fewer achievement images than had been advanced by Horner's subjects (Hoffman, 1974). In addition, psychologists questioned whether Horner's research measured fear of success or fear of failure in achievement-related activities (Gelbort & Winer, 1985).

Although some women may be motivated to avoid success and achievement, so are some men, and the differences between them on this variable may not be as great today as in the past. Psychologist Janet Spence suggested that "with greater social acceptance of women's educational and vocational aspirations, sex differences in fear of success appear to be evaporating" (Spence, 1983, p. 37). Additional data indicate that the need for achievement was increasing among women college students and that their level of achievement could be used to predict job choice (Jenkins, 1987; Veroff, Depner, Kulka, & Douvan, 1980).

The achievement need in women may be manifested in different ways, depending on their goal orientation. Research has shown that among college women who are oriented toward both career and family, those with high need achievement earned better grades, were more likely to finish college, and married and started a family at a later age than those with low need achievement. Among women oriented toward family rather than career goals, those with high need achievement manifested that need in activities related to dating, courtship, and marriage and placed greater emphasis on physical appearance than did career-oriented women with high need achievement (Elder & MacInnis, 1983).

Work Orientation, Mastery, and Competitiveness

Additional research on the need for achievement has identified three components of the need: work orientation, mastery, and competitiveness (Spence & Helmreich, 1983). Instead of measuring the need for achievement with the TAT approach used by McClelland, these researchers developed an objective test called the Work and Family Orientation Questionnaire (WOFO) to measure attitudes toward achievement-related activities. The work orientation factor involves the desire to work hard and to do a good job at whatever task is undertaken. The mastery factor involves a preference for difficult and challenging tasks and for meeting personal standards of excellence. The competitiveness factor relates to the enjoyment of competition and the desire to win.

Initial research with the WOFO, using high school and college student subjects, showed that men scored significantly higher than women on the mastery and competitiveness components. Women scored significantly higher on the work orientation component.

The WOFO was then administered to groups of men and women to whom achievement was believed to be important: college varsity athletes, M.B.A. graduates, and academic psychologists. A comparison of their WOFO scores with those of the college students in the earlier study showed that college students scored lower than the other three groups on work orientation and mastery. For all groups, men scored higher than women on competitiveness. For both sexes, college varsity athletes scored highest on competitiveness, followed in turn by M.B.A. graduates, college students, and academic psychologists.

Another study compared the WOFO scores of more than 1,300 college students with their later grade point averages. For both sexes, those with low grades had scored low on all three components of the need for achievement—a finding that was not unexpected. What was surprising was that those with the highest grade point averages had scored high in work orientation and mastery but low in competitiveness. Those who scored high on all three factors did not perform well academically. Correlations between WOFO scores and scores on the Scholastic Aptitude Test (SAT) were near zero, indicating virtually no relationship between achievement motivation and scholastic aptitude as measured by these tests.

Comment

McClelland's work demonstrates that it is possible for a limited-domain approach to personality to have a wide domain of influence and application. Some psychologists suggest that McClelland's investigation of this single facet of personality is more useful than broader theories that attempt to account for all aspects of personality. The need-achievement theory has a solid foundation of empirical support, and the data derive exclusively from experimental research. Whereas other theorists have speculated on the relationship between personality and environmental factors, McClelland has empirically investigated that relationship. His work has generated considerable additional research by a large network of followers.

Marvin Zuckerman: Sensation Seeking

sensation seeking
The need for varied, novel, and complex sensations and experiences.

Since the early 1970s, psychologist Marvin Zuckerman (1928–), at the University of Delaware, has conducted research on a limited-domain aspect of personality that he calls **sensation seeking**, a trait with a large hereditary component initially described by Hans Eysenck. Zuckerman defines sensation seeking as the need for "varied, novel, and complex sensations and experiences and the willingness to take physical and social risks for the sake of such experiences" (Zuckerman, 1979, p. 10).

Assessing Sensation Seeking

Zuckerman constructed a 40-item paper-and-pencil questionnaire called the Sensation Seeking Scale (SSS). In developing this test, he administered it to many people whose behavior corresponded to his definition of sensation seeking. These included people who volunteered for psychological experiments that exposed them to novel experiences, people whose jobs involved physical danger (police officers and race-car drivers), and people who admitted to experimenting with drugs or to having varied sexual experiences. Their SSS scores were compared with the scores of people who chose to avoid novel or risky activities. Those who deliberately sought unusual activities scored high on the SSS, and those who preferred less venturesome activities scored low. Sample items from the test are shown in Table 17.1.

Zuckerman (1983) identified four components of sensation seeking:

1. *Thrill and adventure seeking:* a desire to engage in physical activities involving speed, danger, novelty, and defiance of gravity (for example, parachuting, scuba diving, or bungee jumping).
2. *Experience seeking:* the search for novel experiences through travel, music, art, or a nonconformist life-style with similarly inclined persons.
3. *Disinhibition:* the need to seek release in uninhibited social activities.

Table 17.1

Sample items from the Sensation Seeking Scale.
(Respondents choose the statement in each pair that they prefer.)

1. a. I like wild uninhibited parties.
   b. I prefer quiet parties with good conversation.

2. a. I get bored seeing the same old faces.
   b. I like the comfortable familiarity of everyday friends.

3. a. A sensible person avoids activities that are dangerous.
   b. I sometimes like to do things that are a little frightening.

4. a. I would like to take off on a trip with no preplanned or definite routes or timetables.
   b. When I go on a trip I like to plan my route and timetable fairly carefully.

5. a. I would like to try parachute jumping.
   b. I would never want to try jumping out of a plane with or without a parachute.

6. a. There is altogether too much portrayal of sex in movies.
   b. I enjoy watching many of the sexy scenes in movies.

SOURCE: From *Sensation Seeking: Beyond the Optimal Level of Arousal* (pp. 397–399) by M. Zuckerman, 1979, Hillsdale, NJ: Erlbaum.

4. *Boredom susceptibility:* an aversion to repetitive experiences, routine work, and predictable people, and a reaction of restless discontent when exposed to such situations.

Characteristics of Sensation Seekers

Zuckerman and his associates found that sensation seeking varies as a function of age; younger people are more inclined to seek adventure, risk, and novel experiences than are older people. Test scores on subjects ranging in age from adolescence to 60 showed that sensation seeking decreased with advancing age, beginning in the twenties (Zuckerman, Eysenck, & Eysenck, 1978).

Significant sex differences were found in the four components of sensation seeking. Men scored higher on thrill and adventure seeking, disinhibition, and boredom susceptibility. Women scored higher on experience seeking. Similar results were obtained from subjects in the United States, England, Scotland, Japan, and Thailand.

Researchers also found significant racial and cultural differences in sensation seeking. Asians scored lower on the SSS than did people in Western countries. White subjects scored higher than non-whites. No significant differences were reported as a function of educational level. Those who attended college did not score significantly higher or lower on the SSS than those who did not attend college.

Behavioral Differences

People who scored high on the SSS tended to behave differently from those who scored low. Zuckerman found that although some people high in sensation seeking enjoy activities such as mountain climbing and parasailing and

The need for sensation seeking manifests itself in the desire for varied, novel, and sometimes dangerous experiences.

those low in sensation seeking generally do not, the behavioral differences are not always so dramatic.

Some high sensation seekers preferred new and varied experiences rather than dangerous ones. They chose to participate in encounter groups, meditation training, and novel psychological experiments. In one study, SSS scores were significantly higher among volunteers than among non-volunteers for a psychological experiment considered to be exciting. There were no test score differences for an experiment rated as unexciting (Thomas, 1989). Once the initial excitement of these experiences has subsided, high sensation seekers usually discontinue the activities because they no longer provide the desired level of stimulation.

High sensation seekers were found to be more likely than low sensation seekers to use illicit drugs, smoke cigarettes, drink alcohol, drive fast, and have frequent sex. In addition, 16 percent of high sensation seekers in Zuckerman's research reported engaging in homosexual activities, as compared with 7 percent of low sensation seekers.

Gambling is another form of sensation seeking. In one study, college students who volunteered for a project that involved betting scored higher than a control group on the experience seeking and disinhibition scales of the SSS. Those high in sensation seeking preferred to bet on riskier ventures.

Physical risk-taking behavior was found to be related to sensation seeking. Skydivers, fire fighters, riot-control police officers, and race-car drivers scored higher on the SSS than groups not engaged in these kinds of activities.

In addition, research on male college undergraduate students in Israel found that high sensation seekers were more likely than low sensation seekers to participate in risky sports and to volunteer for special army combat units (Hobfoll, Rom, & Segal, 1989).

Other findings point to different types of risk takers. Those identified as antisocial risk takers (residents in a long-term drug treatment facility) or as adventurous risk takers (mountain climbers) showed significantly higher SSS scores than those identified as prosocial risk takers (police officers and fire fighters). The researcher suggested that the motives of the last group are more likely to be based on factors other than thrill and adventure seeking (Levenson, 1990).

The apparent fearlessness of some high sensation seekers may induce them to be more adventurous in fear-producing situations, which low sensation seekers would prefer to avoid. A study compared high and low sensation seekers in three situations: approaching and picking up a snake, looking down from an open landing 16 stories high, and being confined in a completely dark room. The thrill and adventure seeking scale of the SSS was better at predicting behavior in these situations than were other measures of anxiety (Mellstrom, Cicala, & Zuckerman, 1976).

High sensation seekers appeared more willing than low sensation seekers to move from familiar to new surroundings and to travel to exotic places, even when the journey involved physical hazards.

Women high in sensation seeking were found to be more domineering and less obliging in situations involving conflict with other people than were women low in sensation seeking. No such differences were found between high and low sensation seeking men (Pilkington, Richardson, & Utley, 1988).

Personality Differences

Zuckerman and his colleagues conducted much research correlating SSS scores with measures of other aspects of personality. One study showed that SSS scores, particularly on the component of disinhibition, were related to the factor of extraversion and to the asocial tendencies associated with psychoticism, as defined by Eysenck. Zuckerman concluded that high sensation seekers are egocentrically extraverted, which means that they are concerned with other people only as an audience or as a source of stimulation. They do not relate to other people in a dependent or a nurturing way.

Evidence also suggests that high sensation seeking scores correlate positively with extraversion as described by Jung and measured by the Myers-Briggs Type Indicator (Morehouse, Farley, & Youngquist, 1990).

High scores on the SSS were found to correlate with a high degree of autonomy. Further, high scorers openly expressed their emotions, were assertive in their relations with others, were nonconforming, and were confirmed to be risk takers. They acted independently of social conventions and of other people's needs and attitudes. Governed primarily by their own needs, they ordered their lives to maximize opportunities for self-fulfillment and acted in a hedonistic manner in the company of others who behaved similarly.

Investigations of sensation seeking and neuroticism, as determined by psychological test scores, showed no correlation. Zuckerman suggested that SSS scores did not indicate neurotic behavior but that neuroses, such as phobias and obsessive-compulsive behaviors, may be related to low sensation seeking. Overall, however, little evidence exists to link sensation seeking with abnormal behavior. "Being a very high or very low sensation seeker," Zuckerman noted, "is not abnormal in itself" (1979, p. 313).

Cognitive Processes

Additional research related sensation seeking to cognitive processes, such as thought, perception, and intelligence. Some differences were reported in the way in which people perceive external stimuli. High sensation seekers were found to recognize symbols and figures more quickly than low sensation seekers, which suggests that high sensation seekers process information more rapidly. They were also better able to incorporate new information into their view of the world. High sensation seekers preferred greater complexity in visual stimulation, whereas low sensation seekers preferred stability, simplicity, and symmetry.

Correlations between SSS scores and scores on general intelligence tests were positive but not high. High sensation seekers did not earn better grades in school than low sensation seekers. Zuckerman suggested that because high sensation seekers were more involved in recreational pursuits, they used less time for study. Tests of creativity and originality of thought revealed that high sensation seekers possessed a greater capacity for original thinking than did low sensation seekers, although they did not necessarily manifest it in their academic work.

Persons who scored high on the SSS appeared to be attracted to speculative, even bizarre, pseudoscientific ideas and were inclined to accept those ideas uncritically. They tended to engage in what Freud called primary-process thought—that is, imagery, dreams, and daydreams so vivid that the distinction between these internal stimuli and the real world sometimes became vague. Zuckerman suggested that because high sensation seekers continually search for novel experiences, if they cannot find them in external events, they may look inward, creating their own fantasy world.

Occupational Preferences

Because high sensation seekers have a greater need for stimulating and varied experiences, the kinds of jobs they prefer differ from those chosen by low sensation seekers. On tests of vocational interests, such as the Kuder Preference Record, high and low sensation seekers showed significant differences. For example, high SSS scores correlated positively with scientific interests and negatively with clerical interests.

Men with high SSS scores also scored high on the Strong Vocational Interest Blank scales that indicated an interest in helping professions involving social interaction, such as psychologist, physician, psychiatrist, social worker, and minister. Their scores correlated negatively with jobs in the business world, such as accountant, purchasing agent, and banker. Women with high SSS scores had high interest test scores for the profession of lawyer and low interest test scores for traditionally female occupations, such as elementary school teacher, home economics teacher, and dietician. High sensation seekers of both sexes who were interested in the helping professions expressed a preference for exciting and dangerous jobs, such as crisis-intervention work or paramedic duty on emergency response teams.

Attitudes

High sensation seekers were shown to be more liberal in their religious and political attitudes than were low sensation seekers. Low sensation seekers scored high on measures of authoritarianism, a personality style characterized by rigid opinions and prejudiced attitudes. Low sensation seekers also showed a low tolerance for ambiguity; they viewed ambiguous ideas and situations as threats rather than challenges.

High scorers on the SSS expressed more permissive attitudes regarding their sexual behaviors and those of their peers. They did not require "socially defined relationships, such as engagement or marriage, or the romantic equivalent of deep emotional commitment to legitimate sexual activities. They tend to accept sex as a basically sensual-pleasurable activity" (Zuckerman, 1979, p. 267). Today, these attitudes are likely to have changed because of the AIDS epidemic and because of changing societal views of acceptable behavior.

Physiological Differences

Zuckerman and his associates found that high and low sensation seekers showed different physiological responses to new stimuli and to changes in stimulation. High sensation seekers demonstrated stronger or more highly aroused physiological responses and higher tolerance thresholds for pain and loud noise (Zuckerman, 1990). In studies of high sensation seekers exposed to novel stimuli, researchers detected increases in the electrical activity of the brain and the level of sex hormones. The level of monoamine oxidase (an enzyme that controls the neurotransmitters, which produces rapid emotional swings) showed a decrease, which heightened feelings of excitement and euphoria (Zuckerman, Buchsbaum, & Murphy, 1980).

Heredity Versus Environment

Using the twin-comparison approach, research has shown a strong hereditary basis for sensation seeking. A study by Eysenck suggested that 58 percent of the sensation-seeking trait could be accounted for by genetic factors (Eysenck, 1983). Although Zuckerman believes that sensation seeking is primarily an inherited trait, he also recognizes the influence of situational or environmental factors.

One such factor is our parents' level of sensation seeking. Low sensation-seeking parents may be overly fearful, protective, and inhibiting of their children, forbidding them to engage in adventurous or potentially risky behaviors. High sensation-seeking parents may encourage and reinforce their children for engaging in novel activities, thus promoting additional sensation-seeking behaviors.

Relatively little research has been conducted on the situational factors that may affect the development of sensation seeking, but one study compared the behaviors of parents of high and low adult sensation seekers. High sensation seekers described their fathers as more active and forceful than did low sensation seekers. High sensation seekers also reported that as children they had been more disobedient and unafraid of their fathers than were low sensation seekers. Another study found that first-borns and only-borns of both sexes scored higher on the SSS than later-borns. Zuckerman suggested that first-borns and only-borns received more stimulation and attention from their parents at an early age, which set a "higher optimal level of stimulation for future years" (Zuckerman, 1979, p. 378).

Comment

Zuckerman's focus on the sensation-seeking personality trait has stimulated a great deal of research. Sensation seeking has been related to a wide range of behavioral, cognitive, personality, and physiological variables. Zuckerman's emphasis on the heritability of sensation seeking places his work in a different category from the behavioral and social-learning approaches to personality, which focus on the influences of situational factors and of learning.

The theory has a commonsense feel and appeal. It is easy to accept the idea that we differ in our need for excitement and risk, change and adventure. We can subjectively describe our own level of sensation seeking and make fairly accurate assessments of the levels of our friends and relatives by considering the activities they enjoy and those they avoid. Zuckerman asked high and low sensation seekers to choose from a list of adjectives those that best described themselves. You can compare your own characteristics with the results shown in Table 17.2.

Martin E. P. Seligman: Learned Helplessness

Since the mid-1960s, psychologist Martin Seligman (1943–), at the University of Pennsylvania, has been conducting research on a limited-domain aspect of personality he calls **learned helplessness**. He observed this phenomenon in a laboratory experiment on dogs on his first day as a graduate

Table 17.2	*Self-descriptions of high and low sensation seekers.*

High Sensation Seekers	Low Sensation Seekers
Enthusiastic	Frightened
Playful	Panicky
Adventurous	Tense
Elated	Nervous
Imaginative	Shaky
Daring	Fearful
Zany	Worried
Mischievous	Upset

SOURCE: From "Sensation Seeking" by M. Zuckerman. In *Dimensions of Personality* by H. London and J. E. Exner, Jr. (Eds.), 1978, New York: Wiley.

learned helplessness
A condition resulting from the perception that we have no control over our environment.

student. The dogs were subjects in a two-part conditioning experiment. In the first part they were being conditioned to associate a high-pitched sound with an electric shock. This was a simple Pavlovian classical conditioning situation involving what B. F. Skinner referred to as respondent behavior—the pairing of the tone with the shock.

In the second part of the experiment, the dogs were placed individually in a large box that contained two compartments divided by a low wall. A shock was delivered through the floor of the compartment in which the dogs had been placed. To escape the shock, the dogs had to emit the appropriate operant behavior—that is, to jump over the low barrier into the other compartment where there was no electric shock. Once the dogs learned to jump over the wall—something dogs were expected to do very quickly—they would be tested to see if the high-pitched tone without the electric shock would bring about the same reaction. The goal of the experiment was to determine whether learning in the first situation carried over to the second situation.

As Seligman observed, the research did not work out the way it was supposed to. The dogs did not cross the barrier to escape the shock. Instead, when the shock was administered through the floor of their compartment, they lay down, whimpered, and made no effort to escape. The experimenters were baffled, but Seligman thought he had a clue. Perhaps, during the first part of the experiment, the dogs had learned that they were helpless. When the tone was sounded, there was nothing they could do to avoid the paired shock, so why should they try? That learning apparently generalized to the second part of the experiment, even though a means of escape was available for the dogs.

Seligman wrote:

> I was stunned by the implications. If dogs could learn something as complex as the futility of their actions, here was an analogy to human helplessness, one that could be studied in the laboratory. Helplessness was all around us—from the urban poor to the newborn child to the despondent patient with his face to the wall. . . . Was this a laboratory model of human helplessness, one that could be used to understand how it comes about, how

to cure it, how to prevent it, what drugs worked on it, and who was particularly vulnerable to it? [1990, p. 20]

Determined to find the answers to these questions, Seligman launched an intensive research program into learned helplessness, a condition he described as resulting from our perception that we have no control over our environment, that nothing we do can alter our situation.

Early Research

In Seligman's early experiments, dogs were harnessed and exposed to painful, though not physically harmful, electric shock. There was no action the dogs could take to escape or avoid the shock. After a series of shocks, the dogs were placed in a two-compartment shuttlebox. As in the first research Seligman had observed, a shock was administered through the floor of the compartment in which the dogs had been placed. The dogs' behavior was then compared with that of a control group of dogs that had not been exposed to the initial series of electric shocks.

When the dogs in the control group were placed in the box and received the shock through the floor, they raced about the compartment aimlessly until they accidentally leaped the barrier into the other compartment. On succeeding trials, they jumped over the barrier more quickly each time as they learned that this was the way to escape the shock.

The dogs in the experimental group, who had received the series of electric shocks before being placed in the shuttlebox, behaved differently. After feeling the shock through the compartment floor, they ran about frantically for approximately 30 seconds before giving up, dropping to the floor, and whimpering. They never learned to escape the shock, not even when experimenters enticed them with food. These dogs had become passive and helpless, and they made no attempt to alter their situation (Overmier & Seligman, 1967; Seligman & Maier, 1967).

Similar results were obtained with humans. Subjects in the experimental group were exposed to a loud noise and told they could turn it off if they pressed a series of buttons in the correct sequence. The conditions were arranged so that there was no correct sequence; the noise continued no matter what the subjects did. In the control group, the subjects could turn off the noise by pressing buttons in a sequence that was relatively easy to learn.

In the next step, the subjects were placed in a situation in which all they had to do to turn off the unpleasant sound was move their hand from one side of a box to the other in response to a light signal. The control-group subjects quickly learned this series of behaviors, but the subjects in the experimental group did not. They sat passively, making no effort to attempt to turn off the irritating noise (Hiroto, 1974).

Other studies using human subjects confirmed and extended these findings. Learned helplessness was found to occur after the subjects observed helpless models, especially when the subjects recognized similarities between themselves and the models. The experimenters suggested that the subjects were saying to themselves, in effect, "If the models can't do anything about this, then neither can I." Learned helplessness was also found to occur simply when subjects were told that they could do nothing to change their situation (Brown & Inouye, 1978; Maier & Seligman, 1976). Additional research showed that subjects experiencing experimentally produced learned helplessness were slower to solve cognitive problems, were less competitive in games, showed a disrupted ability to learn, and manifested symptoms of emotional disturbances, such as frustration and anxiety (Seligman, 1975).

As we discuss this phenomenon, it is important to keep in mind that approximately one-third of the animal and human subjects in Seligman's early research did not succumb to learned helplessness (Seligman, 1990).

Learned Helplessness in Elderly Persons

Applying the concept of learned helplessness to a real-world situation, two psychologists investigated whether elderly residents of nursing homes, living in a situation over which they had little control, might have learned to be helpless, as subjects in the laboratory had (Langer & Rodin, 1976). The researchers designed an experiment to determine whether giving nursing home residents greater control would affect their feelings of lethargy and their lack of motivation and activity. Perhaps their listlessness stemmed from ceding control to the nursing home staff and from learning that their desires and behaviors did little to change their living conditions.

The residents of one floor in a nursing home were given the opportunity to make decisions regarding their daily lives, from choosing what they wanted for breakfast, to caring for their plants, to arranging the furniture in their rooms. They were told that they would assume responsibility for caring for themselves in many ways and would make many of the decisions formerly made by the staff.

Residents of the other floor remained under the control of the staff. Their quarters, food, and recreational activities were identical, but they had no responsibility for them. For example, each resident had a plant in his or her room, but it was chosen and cared for by the staff.

Behavioral differences became apparent within a few weeks. Residents given control and responsibility became happier and more physically active. They spent more time engaging in social activities and less time alone in their rooms. The nursing staff reported that 93 percent of these residents showed greater social and personal adjustment. Of the residents living under the old system, with no increase in personal control, only 21 percent showed positive changes. A followup visit 18 months later showed that the differences had persisted. Also, of the residents given personal control, only 15 percent had died since the beginning of the study; in the other group, 30 percent had died. Later research confirmed the positive effects of permitting elderly people to maintain control over their lives (Baltes & Bates, 1986).

Physical Health and Explanatory Style

The results of the nursing home study raised the possibility that learned help-lessness could affect physical health. To test this hypothesis, Seligman and his associates designed a study in which rats were injected with cells from a malignant tumor and exposed to one of three conditions: an electric shock from which they could escape, a shock from which they could not escape, and no shock (Visintainer, Volpicelli, & Seligman, 1982). Under normal cir-cumstances, based on the number of cells injected, half the rats would be expected to reject the cells and survive.

In the control group—the rats that received no electric shock—50 per-cent rejected the tumor as expected. Among the rats that received a shock but could escape it—thus giving them some degree of control over their situa-tion—70 percent rejected the tumor and survived. But in the group that could not escape the shock—the learned helplessness group—only 27 per-cent of the rats rejected the malignant cells and survived.

These results received support from a study in which young rats were exposed to similar experimental conditions: escapable shock, inescapable shock, or no shock. When the rats reached adulthood, malignant cells were injected, and the rats were reexposed to the experimental conditions. The majority of the rats who had learned to be helpless when young failed as adults to reject the tumor. In contrast, the majority of the rats who had learned control when young rejected the tumor as adults (Seligman & Visintainer, 1985). Seligman noted: "Childhood experiences proved to be crucial in tumor rejection by adults. Childhood mastery [being able to control the shocks] immunized, and early helplessness put adult rats at risk for can-cer" (Seligman, 1990, p. 170).

Learned helplessness was also shown to weaken the immune system in rats (Maier, Laudenslager, & Ryan, 1985). The immune system forms a major part of the body's defense against illness. It contains several kinds of cells, including T-cells and NK (natural killer) cells, both of which kill viruses, bacteria, and tumor cells. In rats subjected to inescapable shock, T-cells no longer multiplied rapidly in response to specific invaders, and NK cells lost their ability to destroy other infections. This may provide a physiological explanation for the finding that the helpless rats were unable to reject their tumors.

explanatory style
A way of explaining to ourselves our relative lack of control over our environment. An **optimistic explanatory style** prevents helplessness. A **pessimistic explanatory style** spreads helplessness to all facets of life.

Seligman believes that these findings can be applied to humans. He argues, however, that it is not only the lack of control under conditions of learned helplessness that affects human health. Also important is how we explain this lack of control to ourselves. He proposed the concept of **explan-atory style**, of which there are two broad types. An **optimistic explana-tory style** prevents helplessness; a **pessimistic explanatory style** spreads helplessness to all facets of life.

People with an optimistic explanatory style tend to be healthier than people with a pessimistic explanatory style. Because pessimists believe that their actions are of little consequence, they are unlikely to try to prevent

Table 17.3   **Similarity of symptoms of learned helplessness and depression.**

Learned Helplessness	Depression
Passivity	Passivity
Difficulty learning that responses produce relief	Difficulty learning that responses produce outcomes
Lack of aggression	Introjected hostility
Weight loss and anorexia	Loss of libido
Norepinephrine depletion*	Norepinephrine depletion
Ulcers and stress	Ulcers and stress; feelings of helplessness

* The norepinephrine hormone acts as a neurotransmitter; severe depression is associated with norepinephrine deficiency.
SOURCE: Adapted from *Learned Helplessness and Depression in Animals and Men,* by M. E. P. Seligman. Copyright © 1976 by General Learning Press, Morristown, NJ.

illness by changing their behavior—for example, by taking responsibility for quitting smoking, exercising, losing weight, or seeking medical help.

In an investigation of the impact of explanatory style on physical health, researchers found that among a group of college undergraduates, pessimists had twice as many infectious illnesses over a one-year period than did optimists (Peterson & Seligman, 1987). Among a group of breast cancer patients who were having a recurrence of the disease, the optimists lived longer, over a five-year period, independent of the severity of their illness (Levy, Morrow, Bagley, & Lippman, 1989).

The health of a group of 200 men was monitored from age 25 to their late sixties (Peterson, Seligman, & Vaillant, 1988). At the beginning of the study they wrote personal essays, which were analyzed for themes that indicated either an optimistic or a pessimistic explanatory style. The subjects were interviewed periodically and responded to questionnaires about various life events. They also received physical examinations every five years. No differences in health were reported up to age 45. By the age of 60, however, it was clear to the researchers that the optimists were in far better health. They had fewer and less severe symptoms of the diseases of middle age than did the pessimists.

Depression

Seligman's research program found a link between learned helplessness and emotional health, especially depression. A major symptom of depression is the feeling of being unable to control the events in one's life. Seligman referred to depression as the "ultimate pessimism" (Seligman, 1990, p. 54). People who are severely depressed believe they are helpless: there is little point in trying to do anything, because they do not expect that anything will work out well for them. Seligman observed several similarities between the symptoms of depression and the characteristics of learned helplessness, which we have summarized in Table 17.3.

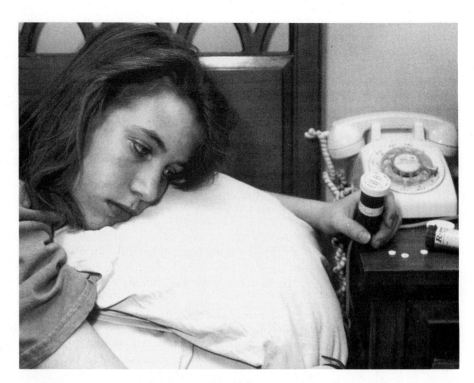

People who are severely depressed believe they are helpless. They generalize their failure in one situation, such as a poor grade in one course, to all other aspects of life.

All of us experience occasional feelings of helplessness when we fail at something or when outside events seem overwhelming. No matter how unhappy or angry we may feel, most of us tend to recover after a period of time. Some people, however, do not recover so easily, and their depression can last for months. They may generalize their failure in one activity—such as getting a poor grade or losing a job—to other aspects of life and they feel helpless, worthless, and depressed in all situations. They may lose all impetus to strive.

According to Seligman, the difference between people who recover from a temporary depression and those who do not is related to their explanatory style. "A pessimistic explanatory style changes learned helplessness from brief and local to long-lasting and general. Learned helplessness becomes full-blown depression when the person who fails is a pessimist. In optimists, a failure produces only brief demoralization" (Seligman, 1990, p. 76). Further, pessimists formulate explanations about negative situations in personal and pervasive terms: "It's all my fault," "It's always going to be this way," and "It's going to undermine every aspect of my life."

Research conducted with his undergraduate students supports Seligman's hypothesis that learned helplessness can lead to depression in people with a pessimistic explanatory style (Seligman, 1990). At the beginning of the semester, the students were tested to determine their explanatory style. They were asked to state the course grade they believed would represent a personal failure. After the midterm examination, the students took a personality test that measured their level of depression. The results showed that 30 percent of those with an optimistic explanatory style and who received grades they consider a personal failure showed signs of depression. Among those with a pessimistic explanatory style who received disappointing grades, 70 percent became depressed. Similar results were found in other research with college students and in studies of third-grade elementary school students. In both cases, explanatory style predicted the incidence of depression (Nolen-Hoeksema, Girgus, & Seligman, 1987; Zullow & Seligman, 1985).

The Attribution Model

The concept of explanatory style describes how people differ in the way they explain to themselves their feeling of learned helplessness or lack of control. Some people are devastated by learned helplessness. They seem to give up, to become depressed, and to experience health problems. Others, facing similar situations, recover after a period of time. Seligman proposed a cognitive explanation for these differences, which he called the revised learned helplessness model, or the **attribution model** (Abramson, Seligman, & Teasdale, 1978). The key word is *attribution.* When we fail at something, we attribute that failure to some cause. This is how we explain to ourselves the cause of our failure and our lack of control.

attribution model
The idea that we attribute our lack of control or failure to some cause.

Seligman contended that pessimists attribute their failures to internal, stable, and global causes; optimists attribute failures to external, unstable, and specific causes. For example, if you fail a course and make an internal attribution, you are saying there is something wrong with you—maybe you are not smart enough to pass. If you make an external attribution, you are saying that the cause lies elsewhere—the professor does not like you or your job doesn't leave you enough time to study.

If the cause of your failure cannot be changed, it is considered stable. If it can be modified—such as reducing your hours on the job so you will have more time to study—it is considered unstable. If you make a global attribution, you are saying that whatever caused you to fail that course will cause you to fail all others. By making a specific attribution you are limiting your failure to one course; the failure does not transfer to other courses or areas of life.

Seligman and his colleagues developed a questionnaire to measure explanatory or attributional style (Peterson et al., 1982). The Attributional Style Questionnaire (ASQ) presents 12 hypothetical situations. Six are positive events, such as becoming wealthy, and six are negative events, such as a disappointing social experience. Some events deal with achievement in school or on the job; others involve getting along with people. When you take the test, you are asked to suggest a cause for each event and to rate that cause on a scale relevant to the dimensions of internal versus external, stable versus unstable, and global versus specific causes (see Table 17.4).

In one study, first-year college students who had experienced negative events were given the ASQ. Those who made internal, stable, and global attributions for their situations (the more pessimistic style) received lower

Table 17.4   **Sample item from the Attributional Style Questionnaire.**

You have been looking for a job unsuccessfully for some time.
1. Write down the *one* major cause _____ .

2. Is your unsuccessful job search due to something about you or to something about other people or circumstances? Circle one number.
   Totally due to other   1 2 3 4 5 6 7   Totally due to me.
   people or circumstances.

3. When looking for a job in the future, will this cause again be present? Circle one number.
   Will never again be   1 2 3 4 5 6 7   Will always be present.
   present.

4. Is the cause something that influences looking for a job only, or does it also influence other areas of your life? Circle one number.
   Influences just this   1 2 3 4 5 6 7   Influences all situations
   particular situation.   in my life.

5. How important would this situation be if it happened to you? Circle one number.
   Not at all important.   1 2 3 4 5 6 7   Extremely important.

SOURCE: From "The Attributional Style Questionnaire," by C. Peterson, A. Semmel, C. von Baeyer, L. Y. Abramson, G. I. Metalsky, and M. E. P. Seligman, 1982, *Cognitive Therapy and Research,* 6, 287–300. Copyright © 1982 by Plenum Publishing Corporation. Reprinted by permission.

grades than those who made external, unstable, and specific attributions (the more optimistic style) (Peterson & Barrett, 1987). Both groups were of similar intelligence, so that was not a factor in explaining the difference in their grades. The pessimists responded to negative events and problems passively and made few attempts to alter their situations.

Other research suggested that the global-versus-specific dimension is the most important in learned helplessness and depression. Subjects who failed in one situation and attributed that failure to a global cause also failed in other situations (Mikulincer, 1986). In another study, subjects who made global attributions reported the intrusion of irrelevant thoughts that interfered with their performance on cognitive tasks (Mikulincer & Nizan, 1988). The researchers concluded that persons who think poorly of themselves perform poorly, in ways that continue to confirm their attributions and lower their self-esteem and confidence about dealing with future situations.

The Development of Learned Helplessness in Childhood

Although learned helplessness can occur at any time throughout the life span, Seligman believes we are particularly vulnerable to it in infancy and early childhood. It is during these formative years that the experience of learned helplessness may dispose us to the pessimistic explanatory style (Seligman, 1975).

Infants begin life in a state of total helplessness, having no control over their environment. As they mature, they become increasingly able to exercise control. They cry, and parents come to tend to their needs. They crawl, walk, and speak, and the mastery of each skill brings greater possibilities for control—and for failure. Through these early interactions with the environment, then, our sense of helplessness—or of mastery and control—is determined.

When infants make a response, that action may bring about some change in the environment (such as food, a toy, or a hug), or it may have no effect whatever. At a primitive level, infants come to make associations between responses and outcomes. If there is no correlation between them— if the responses do not lead to successful outcomes—the result is learned helplessness. Infants learn that these particular responses don't work, and they may generalize to other responses, believing that none of them will work. This results in a generalized learned helplessness and a sense of having no control over life. In contrast, a high correlation provides feedback about what works, about the correspondence between a particular response and its outcome. This leads to a sense of mastery and control.

Learned helplessness can develop in later childhood in response to brutality from peers, a harsh school environment, or other negative experiences. Race and poverty are also factors in the development of learned helplessness. For example, students who are treated as though they have less intelligence or ability than others may come to develop learned helplessness.

Comment

Learned helplessness has become a popular and influential concept in the field of personality, generating hundreds of research studies. Seligman and his associates have applied the idea to sports, politics, religion, child-rearing, and job performance.

Critics charge that there is little difference between learned helplessness and Julian Rotter's concept of external locus of control. Both express the idea that some people believe there is little they can do to influence their own lives and therefore give up trying.

The learned helplessness theory leaves several questions unanswered. For example, does a person's explanatory style cause depression, or does depression cause a particular explanatory style? Is the effect of prolonged failure on self-esteem more important than its relationship to learned helplessness? Critics also question the validity of the Attributional Style Questionnaire.

Overall, however, a large and impressive body of data supports the learned helplessness concept. More recently, Seligman has turned his attention to a related idea, learned optimism (Seligman, 1990). He is developing a program of exercises to teach optimism to adults and to children, applying his findings beyond the laboratory to the home and the workplace.

Summary

The need for achievement has been studied by David McClelland using the Thematic Apperception Test. Research has shown that men high in the need for achievement are more often middle-class, have a better memory for uncompleted tasks, are more active in college and community activities, and are more resistant to social pressures. People high in the need for achievement are more likely to attend college and do well, to take high-status jobs with a great deal of personal responsibility, and to expect to achieve success. They are often successful entrepreneurs or managers.

McClelland found a high positive correlation between a nation's need-achievement level and its economic prosperity. Studies of past cultures also revealed a strong positive relationship between need achievement and economic success. When the need for achievement declined among the population, the economy declined.

Parental behaviors likely to produce high need achievement in children include setting realistically high performance standards, not overprotecting or indulging, not interfering with the child's efforts to achieve, and showing pleasure in the child's achievements. Authoritarianism, particularly in fathers, tends to lower a child's need for achievement. The need to achieve declines after middle age, perhaps as a result of the tendency to redefine success at this stage of life.

Men and women are motivated to achieve success, but some women may fear success because it reflects so-called unfeminine characteristics. Three components of achievement motivation are work orientation, mastery, and competitiveness. Research has shown that men score higher in mastery and competitiveness; women score higher in work orientation.

According to Marvin Zuckerman, sensation seeking is an inherited trait concerned with the need for novel and complex sensations and experiences. The Sensation Seeking Scale is designed to assess this aspect of personality. Four components of sensation seeking are thrill and adventure seeking, experience seeking, disinhibition, and boredom susceptibility.

Research has shown higher levels of sensation seeking among white subjects, males, people from Western cultures, and young people from adolescence to their early twenties. High sensation seekers are more likely to use drugs, smoke cigarettes, drink alcohol, drive fast, engage in frequent sex, gamble, take physical risks, and travel to exotic places, even when the trip involves danger. In terms of personality, high sensation seekers tend to be egocentrically extraverted, autonomous, assertive, nonconforming, and uninhibited in expressing emotions. In cognitive functioning, high sensation seekers recognize symbols and figures more quickly than low sensation seekers and prefer complexity in visual stimulation. They are attracted to speculative and pseudoscientific ideas and engage in primary-process thought.

Vocational interests of high sensation-seeking males are oriented toward science and the helping professions. Low sensation-seeking males are more oriented toward clerical and business concerns. High sensation seekers also tend to hold more liberal religious and political attitudes. They are higher in tolerance for ambiguity, more permissive in sexual attitudes, and lower in authoritarianism. In addition, they display stronger physiological responses to novel stimuli.

Zuckerman concluded that sensation seeking is primarily inherited but can be influenced by environmental factors, such as order of birth and parental levels of sensation seeking.

Learned helplessness, investigated by Martin Seligman, results from our perception that we have no control over our environment. An optimistic explanatory style can prevent learned helplessness; a pessimistic style spreads helplessness to all facets of life and can lead to physical illness and depression. Pessimists make personal, permanent, and pervasive explanations to themselves about negative events. Thus, helplessness changes character from brief and localized to long-lasting and generalized.

The attribution model of learned helplessness involves attributing a failure to some cause. Pessimists attribute their failures to internal, stable, and global causes. Optimists attribute their failures to external, unstable, and specific causes. The Attributional Style Questionnaire measures these causal dimensions. The global-versus-specific dimension may be the most important in learned helplessness and the depression that results from it.

Although learned helplessness can occur at any age, infants and young children are particularly vulnerable. Infants learn that a correspondence exists between their responses and outcomes when responses bring changes in their environment; they learn helplessness when these responses do not work to bring about desired changes. Major causes of learned helplessness are maternal deprivation and being reared in an environment that provides a low level of stimulation and feedback.

Critical Thinking Review

1. How does McClelland's research on the need for achievement relate to the work of Freud and Murray?

2. Describe McClelland's technique for measuring the need for achievement.

3. Describe the differences between high and low achievers in terms of their college and career performance.

4. What differences have been reported between men and women in the need for achievement?

5. What parental behaviors can influence the development of a child's need for achievement?

6. Describe three components of the need for achievement.

7. Define the concept of sensation seeking proposed by Zuckerman, and describe its four components.

8. What does research show about differences in sensation seeking as a function of age, gender, culture, and race?

9. How do people high in sensation seeking appear to differ from people

low in sensation seeking in terms of personality and cognitive functioning?

10. Describe the occupational interests and political attitudes identified among high sensation seekers.

11. Discuss the relative importance of heredity and environment in determining one's level of sensation seeking.

12. Define learned helplessness and describe the early research by Seligman on this concept.

13. In the research study on elderly residents of nursing homes, how did having greater control over their own lives affect the residents' behavior and attitudes?

14. How can learned helplessness affect physical health? How does it appear to relate to depression?

15. Distinguish between optimistic and pessimistic explanatory styles. How can they affect health?

16. How does the attribution model of learned helplessness differ from Seligman's earlier version of learned helplessness?

17. Six questions about human nature were posed in Chapter 1. Now that you have studied the diverse approaches to personality presented in this book, reconsider your answers to these questions to see how your views might have changed.

Suggested Reading

The Need for Achievement

McClelland, D. C. (1961). *The achieving society.* New York: Free Press. Applies the methods of psychology to the evaluation of economic, historical, and social forces that explain the rise and fall of civilizations.

McClelland, D. C., & Winter, D. G. (1969). *Motivating economic achievement.* New York: Free Press. Describes programs of psychological training to increase the need for achievement among business leaders in the hope of accelerating a nation's economic development.

Sensation Seeking

Zuckerman, M. (1990). The psychophysiology of sensation seeking. *Journal of Personality, 58*(1), 313–345. Summarizes research showing the differences in psychophysiological response of high and low sensation seekers to novel or intense stimuli.

Zuckerman, M. (1991). *Psychobiology of personality.* New York: Cambridge University Press. Outlines a behavioral genetics approach to personality and summarizes relevant research from neuropsychology, psychopharmacology, psychophysiology, and abnormal psychology.

Learned Helplessness

Seligman, M. E. P. (1975). *Helplessness: On depression, development, and death.* San Francisco: W. H. Freeman. Describes the early research on learned helplessness, its development in childhood, and its impact on depression and physical health.

Seligman, M. E. P. (1990). *Learned optimism.* New York: Knopf. Describes differences in explanatory style between optimists and pessimists and relates these styles to physical and mental health. Offers techniques for changing pessimism to optimism.

REFERENCES

Abdallah, T. M. (1989). Self-esteem and locus of control of college men in Saudi Arabia. *Psychological Reports, 65*(3, Pt. 2), 1323–1326.

Abramson, L. Y., Seligman, M. E. P., & Teasdale, J. D. (1978). Learned helplessness in humans: Critique and reformulation. *Journal of Abnormal Psychology, 87,* 49–74.

Achenbach, T., & Zigler, E. (1963). Social competence and self-image disparity in psychiatric and non-psychiatric patients. *Journal of Abnormal and Social Psychology, 67,* 197–205.

Adams, D. (1954). *The anatomy of personality.* Garden City, NY: Doubleday.

Adams, G. R., & Fitch, S. A. (1982). Ego stage and identity status development: A cross-sequential analysis. *Journal of Personality and Social Psychology, 43,* 574–583.

Adams-Webber, J. R. (1970). An analysis of the discriminant validity of several repertory grid indices. *British Journal of Psychology, 60,* 83–90.

Adler, A. (1930). Individual psychology. In C. Murchison (Ed.), *Psychologies of 1930* (pp. 395–405). Worcester, MA: Clark University Press.

Adler, A. (1939). *Social interest: A challenge to mankind.* J. Linton & R. Vaughan (Trans.). New York: Putnam. (Original work published 1933)

Adler, A. (1963). *The practice and theory of individual psychology.* P. Radin (Trans.). Paterson, NJ: Littlefield, Adams. (Original work published 1924)

Alderfer, C. P. (1972). *Existence, relatedness and growth: Human needs in organizational settings.* New York: Free Press.

Alderfer, C. P. (1989). Theories reflecting my personal experience and life development. *Journal of Applied Behavioral Science, 25,* 351–365.

Alexander, I. E. (1991). C. G. Jung: The man and his work, then and now. In G. A. Kimble, M. Wertheimer, & C. White (Eds.), *Portraits of pioneers in psychology* (pp. 153–169). Washington, DC: American Psychological Association; Hillsdale, NJ: Erlbaum.

Allen, K. D., Danforth, J. S., & Drabman, R. C. (1989). Videotaped modeling and film distraction for fear reduction in adults undergoing hyperbaric oxygen therapy. *Journal of Consulting and Clinical Psychology, 57,* 554–558.

Allport, G. W. (1937). *Personality: A psychological interpretation.* New York: Holt.

Allport, G. W. (1942). *The use of personal documents in psychological science.* New York: Social Science Research Council.

Allport, G. W. (1955). *Becoming: Basic considerations for a*

459

psychology of personality. New Haven, CT: Yale University Press.

Allport, G. W. (1961). *Pattern and growth in personality.* New York: Holt.

Allport, G. W. (Eds.). (1965). *Letters from Jenny.* New York: Harcourt, Brace & World.

Allport, G. W. (1966). Traits revisited. *American Psychologist, 21,* 1–10.

Allport, G. W. (1967). Autobiography. In E. G. Boring & G. Lindzey (Eds.), *A history of psychology in autobiography* (Vol. 5, pp. 1–25). New York: Appleton-Century-Crofts.

Allport, G. W., & Cantril, H. (1934). Judging personality from voice. *Journal of Social Psychology, 5,* 37–55.

Allport, G. W., & Vernon, P. (1933). *Studies in expressive movement.* New York: Macmillan.

Allport, G. W., Vernon, P., & Lindzey, G. (1960). *A study of values* (3rd ed.). Boston: Houghton Mifflin.

Anastasi, A. (1988). *Psychological testing* (6th ed.). New York: Macmillan.

Anderson, J. W. (1988). Henry A. Murray's early career: A psychobiographical exploration. *Journal of Personality, 56*(1), 139–171.

Anderson, J. W. (1990). The life of Henry A. Murray: 1893–1988. In A. I. Rabin, R. A. Zucker, R. A. Emmons, & S. Frank (Eds.), *Studying persons and lives* (pp. 304–334). New York: Springer.

Anderson, N. R. (1990). Repertory grid technique in employee selection. *Personnel Review, 19*(3), 9–15.

Ansbacher, H. L. (1990). Alfred Adler's influence on the three leading cofounders of humanistic psychology. *Journal of Humanistic Psychology, 30*(4), 45–53.

Archer, R. P., Maruish, M., Imhof, E. A., & Piotrowski, C. (1991). Psychological test usage with adolescent clients: 1990 survey findings. *Professional Psychology: Research and Practice, 22,* 247–252.

Archer, S. L. (1982). The lower age boundaries of identity development. *Child Development, 53,* 1551–1556.

Ardrey, R. (1966). *The territorial imperative: A personal inquiry into the animal origins of property and nations.* New York: Atheneum.

Atkinson, J. W., Lens, W., & O'Malley, P. M. (1976). Motivation and ability: Interactive psychological determinants of intellectual performance, educational achievement, and each other. In W. H. Sewell, R. H. Hanser, & D. L. Featherman (Eds.), *Schooling and achievement in American society.* New York: Academic Press.

Atwood, G. E., & Tomkins, S. S. (1976). On the subjectivity of personality theory. *Journal of the History of the Behavioral Sciences, 12,* 166–177.

Ayllon, T., & Azrin, N. (1968). *The token economy.* New York: Appleton-Century-Crofts.

Baars, B. J. (1986). *The cognitive revolution in psychology.* New York: Guilford Press.

Balay, J., & Shevrin, H. (1988). The subliminal psychodynamic activation method: A critical review. *American Psychologist, 43,* 161–174.

Baldwin, A. L. (1949). The effect of home environment on nursery school behavior. *Child Development, 20,* 49–61.

Baltes, M. M., & Bates, P. B. (1986). *Psychology of control and aging.* Hillsdale, NJ: Erlbaum.

Bandura, A. (1973). *Aggression: A social learning analysis.* Englewood Cliffs, NJ: Prentice-Hall.

Bandura, A. (1977). *Social learning theory.* Englewood Cliffs, NJ: Prentice-Hall.

Bandura, A. (1978). The self system in reciprocal determinism. *American Psychologist, 33,* 334–358.

Bandura, A. (1982). Self-efficacy mechanism in human agency. *American Psychologist, 37,* 122–147.

Bandura, A. (1986). *Social foundations of thought and action: A social cognitive theory.* Englewood Cliffs, NJ: Prentice-Hall.

Bandura, A. (1989). Human agency in social cognitive theory. *American Psychologist, 44,* 1175–1184.

Bandura, A., Adams, N. E., & Beyer, J. (1977). Cognitive processes in mediating behavioral change. *Journal of Personality and Social Psychology, 35,* 125–139.

Bandura, A., Blanchard, E. B., & Ritter, B. (1969). The relative efficacy of desensitization and modeling approaches for inducing behavioral, affective, and attitudinal changes. *Journal of Personality and Social Psychology, 13,* 173–199.

Bandura, A., Grusec, J. E., & Menlove, F. L. (1967). Vicarious extinction of avoidance behavior through symbolic modeling. *Journal of Personality and Social Psychology, 5,* 16–22.

Bandura, A., & Mischel, W. (1965). The influence of models in modifying delay of gratification patterns. *Journal of Personality and Social Psychology, 2,* 698–705.

Bandura, A., O'Leary, A., Taylor, C. B., Gauthier, J., & Gossard, D. (1987). Perceived self-efficacy and pain control: Opioid and nonopioid mechanisms. *Journal of Personality and Social Psychology, 53,* 563–571.

Bandura, A., Reese, L., & Adams, N. E. (1982). Microanalysis of action and fear arousal as a function of differential levels of perceived self-efficacy. *Journal of Personality and Social Psychology, 43,* 5–21.

Bandura, A., Ross, D., & Ross, S. A. (1963). Imitation of film-mediated aggressive models. *Journal of Abnormal and Social Psychology, 66,* 3–11.

Bandura, A., & Walters, R. (1963). *Social learning and personality development.* New York: Holt, Rinehart & Winston.

Bannister, D., & Fransella, F. (1966). A grid test of schizophrenic thought disorder. *British Journal of Social and Clinical Psychology, 5,* 95–102.

Bannister, D., Fransella, F., & Agnew, J. (1971). Characteristerics and validity of the grid test on thought disorder. *British Journal of Social and Clinical Psychology, 10,* 144–151.

Bannister, D., & Salmon, P. (1966). Schizophrenic thought disorder: Specific or diffuse? *British Journal of Medical Psychology, 39,* 215–219.

Baron, R., & Byrne, D. (1984). *Social psychology: Understanding human interaction* (4th ed.). Newton, MA: Allyn & Bacon.

Barry, H., & Blane, H. T. (1977). Birth order of alcoholics. *Journal of Individual Psychology, 62,* 62–79.

Battle, E., & Rotter, J. B. (1963). Children's feelings of personal control as related to social class and ethnic group. *Journal of Personality, 31,* 482–490.

Becona, E., Frojan, M. J., & Lista, M. J. (1988). Comparison between two self-efficacy scales in maintenance of smoking cessation. *Psychological Reports, 62,* 359–362.

Bellak, L. (1975). *The TAT, CAT, and SAT in clinical use* (3rd ed.). New York: Grune & Stratton.

Bellak, L. (1986). *The Thematic Apperception Test, the Children's Apperception Test, and the Senior Apperception Technique in clinical use* (4th ed.). Orlando, FL: Academic Press.

Bellak, L., & Bellak, S. S. (1973). *Manual: Senior Apperception Technique.* Larchmont, NY: CPS.

Bellak, L., & Hurvich, M. S. (1966). A human modification of the Children's Apperception Test (CAT-H). *Journal of Projective Techniques and Personality Assessment, 30,* 228–242.

Belmont, L., & Marolla, F. A. (1973). Birth order, family size and intelligence. *Science, 182,* 1096–1101.

Benassi, V. A., Sweeney, P. D., & Dufour, C. L. (1988). Is there a relationship between locus of control orientation and depression? *Journal of Abnormal Psychology, 97,* 357–367.

Benesch, K. F., & Page, M. M. (1989). Self-construct systems and interpersonal congruence. *Journal of Personality, 57,* 139–173.

Bengston, V. L., Reedy, M. N., & Gordon, C. (1985). Aging and self-conceptions: Personality processes and social contexts. In J. E. Birren & K. W. Schaie (Eds.), *Handbook of the psychology of aging* (2nd ed., pp. 544–593). New York: Van Nostrand Reinhold.

Ben-Porath, Y. S., & Butcher, J. N. (1989). Psychometric stability of rewritten MMPI items. *Journal of Personality Assessment, 53,* 645–653.

Bergin, A. E., & Strupp, H. H. (1972). *Changing frontiers in the science of psychotherapy.* New York: Aldine-Atherton.

Berry, D. S. (1990). Taking people at face value: Evidence for the kernel of truth hypothesis. *Social Cognition, 8,* 343–361.

Berry, D. S. (1991). Accuracy in social perception: Contributions of facial and vocal information. *Journal of Personality and Social Psychology, 61,* 298–307.

Berzonsky, M. D., Rice, K. G., & Neimeyer, G. J. (1990). Identity status and self-construct systems: Process × structure interactions. *Journal of Adolescence, 13,* 251–263.

Bettelheim, B. (1984). *Freud and man's soul.* New York: Vintage.

Betz, N. E., & Hackett, G. (1981). The relationships of career-related self-efficacy expectations to perceived career options in college women and men. *Journal of Counseling Psychology, 28,* 399–410.

Bieri, J. (1955). Cognitive complexity-simplicity and predictive behavior. *Journal of Abnormal and Social Psychology, 51,* 263–268.

Biernat, M. (1989). Motives and values to achieve: Different constructs with different effects. *Journal of Personality, 57,* 69–95.

Bigner, J. J. (1974). A Wernerian developmental analysis of children's descriptions of siblings. *Child Development, 45,* 317–323.

Blanton, S. (1971). *Diary of my analysis with Sigmund Freud.* New York: Hawthorn Books.

Block, J. H. (1983). Differential premises arising from differential socialization of the sexes: Some conjectures. *Child Development, 54,* 1335–1354.

Blustein, D. L., Devenis, L. E., & Kidney, B. A. (1989). Relationship between the identity formation process and career development. *Journal of Counseling Psychology, 36,* 196–202.

Bonarius, J. (1976). The interaction model of communication: Through experimental research towards existential relevance. In A. W. Landfield (Ed.), *Nebraska symposium on motivation.* Lincoln: University of Nebraska Press.

Bordages, J. W., Jr. (1989). Self-actualization and personal autonomy. *Psychological Reports, 64*(3, Pt. 2), 1263–1266.

Bores-Rangel, E., Church, A. T., Szendre, D., & Reeves, C. (1990). Self-efficacy in relation to occupational consideration and academic performance in high school equivalency students. *Journal of Counseling Psychology, 37,* 407–418.

Bottome, P. (1939). *Alfred Adler: A biography.* New York: Putnam.

Bouchard, T. J. (1985). Twins reared together and apart: What they tell us about human diversity. In S. W. Fox (Ed.), *Individuality and determinism: Chemical and biological bases* (pp. 147–184). New York: Plenum Press.

Bouchard, T. J., & McGue, M. (1990). Genetic and rearing environmental influences on adult personality: An analysis of adopted twins reared apart. *Journal of Personality, 58,* 263–292.

Bourne, E. (1978a). The state of research on ego identity: A review and appraisal. Part I. *Journal of Youth and Adolescence, 7,* 223–257.

Bourne, E. (1978b). The state of research on ego identity: A review and appraisal. Part II. *Journal of Youth and Adolescence, 7,* 371–392.

Brannigan, G. G., Hauk, P. A., & Guay, J. A. (1991). Locus of control and daydreaming. *Journal of Genetic Psychology, 152,* 29–33.

Braun, J., & Asta, P. (1968). Intercorrelations between the Personal Orientation Inventory and the Gordon Personal Inventory scores. *Psychological Reports, 23,* 1197–1198.

Breger, L., Hunter, I., & Lane, R. W. (1971). *The effect of stress on dreams.* New York: International Universities Press.

Breland, H. M. (1974). Birth order, family configuration and verbal achievement. *Child Development, 45,* 1011–1019.

Breland, K., & Breland, M. (1961). The misbehavior of organisms. *American Psychologist, 16,* 681–684.

Breuer, J., & Freud, S. (1895). Studies on hysteria. In *Standard edition* (Vol. 2). London: Hogarth Press.

Briggs, K. C., & Myers, I. B. (1943, 1976). *Myers-Briggs Type Indicator.* Palo Alto, CA: Consulting Psychologists Press.

Brody, L. R., Rozek, M. K., & Muten, E. O. (1985). Age, sex, and individual differences in children's defensive styles. *Journal of Clinical Child Psychology, 14,* 132–138.

Brody, N. (1987). Introduction: Some thoughts on the unconscious. *Personality and Social Psychology Bulletin, 13,* 293–298.

Brome, V. (1981). *Jung: Man and myth.* New York: Atheneum.

Brown, C. A., & Detoy, C. J. (1988). A comparison of the personal constructs of management in new and experienced managers. In F. Fransella & L. Thomas (Eds.), *Experimenting with personal construct psychology* (pp. 426–434). London: Routledge & Kegan Paul.

Brown, J. B., Jr., & Inouye, D. K. (1978). Learned helplessness through modeling: The role of perceived similarity in competence. *Journal of Personality and Social Psychology, 36,* 900–908.

Brown, S. R., & Hendrick, C. (1971). Introversion, extraversion and social perception. *British Journal of Social and Clinical Psychology, 10,* 313–319.

Bryant, B. L. (1987). Birth order as a factor in the development of vocational preferences. *Individual Psychology, 43,* 36–41.

Buie, J. (1989, December). MMPI-2 earns praise as improved instrument. *APA Monitor,* p. 22.

Burston, D. (1991). *The legacy of Erich Fromm.* Cambridge, MA: Harvard University Press.

Buss, A. H. (1988). *Personality: Evolutionary heritage and human distinctiveness.* Hillsdale, NJ: Erlbaum.

Buss, A. H. (1989). Personality as traits. *American Psychologist, 44,* 1378–1388.

Buss, A. H., & Plomin, R. (1975). *A temperament theory of personality development.* New York: Wiley.

Buss, A. H., & Plomin, R. (1984). *Temperament: Early developing personality traits.* Hillsdale, NJ: Erlbaum.

Buss, A. H., & Plomin, R. (1986). The EAS approach to temperament. In R. Plomin & J. Dunn (Eds.), *The study of temperament: Changes, continuities and challenges* (pp. 67–79). Hillsdale, NJ: Erlbaum.

Buss, D. M. (1991). Evolutionary personality psychology. *Annual Review of Psychology, 42,* 459–491.

Butler, J. M., & Haigh, G. V. (1954). Changes in the relationship between self-concepts and ideal concepts consequent upon client-centered counseling. In C. R. Rogers & R. F. Dymond (Eds.), *Psychotherapy and personality change.* Chicago: University of Chicago Press.

Campagna, A. F., & Harter, S. (1975). Moral judgment in sociopathic and normal children. *Journal of Personality and Social Psychology, 31,* 199–205.

Cann, D. R., & Donderi, D. C. (1986). Jungian personality typology and the recall of everyday and archetypal dreams. *Journal of Personality and Social Psychology, 50,* 1021–1030.

Cantor, N., & Zirkel, S. (1990). Personality, cognition, and purposive behavior. In L. A. Pervin (Ed.), *Handbook of personality: Theory and research* (pp. 135–164). New York: Guilford Press.

Caplan, P. J. (1979). Erikson's concept of inner space: A data-based reevaluation. *American Journal of Orthopsychiatry, 49,* 100–108.

Carlson, R. (1980). Studies of Jungian typology: II. Representations of the personal world. *Journal of Personality and Social Psychology, 38,* 801–810.

Carlson, R., & Levy, N. (1973). Studies of Jungian typology: I. Memory, social perception, and social action. *Journal of Personality, 41,* 559–576.

Carskadon, T. G. (1978). Use of the Myers-Briggs Type Indicator in psychology courses and discussion groups. *Teaching of Psychology, 5,* 140–142.

Carson, R. C. (1989). Personality. *Annual Review of Psychology, 40,* 227–248.

Carson, R. C. (1990). Assessment: What role the assessor? *Journal of Personality Assessment, 54,* 435–445.

Caspi, A., Bem, D. J., & Elder, G. H. (1989). Continuities and consequences of interactional styles across the life course. *Journal of Personality, 57,* 375–406.

Caspi, A., Elder, G. H., & Bem, D. J. (1987). Moving against the world: Life course patterns of explosive children. *Developmental Psychology, 23,* 308–313.

Caspi, A., Elder, G. H., & Bem, D. J. (1988). Moving away from the world: Life course patterns of shy children. *Developmental Psychology, 24,* 824–831.

Cattell, R. B. (1950). *Personality: A systematic theoretical and factual study.* New York: McGraw-Hill.

Cattell, R. B. (1957). *Personality and motivation: Structure and measurement.* New York: World.

Cattell, R. B. (1959). Foundations of personality measurement theory in multivariate expression. In B. M. Bass & I. A. Berg (Eds.), *Objective approaches to personality assessment* (pp. 42–65). Princeton, NJ: Van Nostrand.

Cattell, R. B. (1970). *The scientific analysis of personality.* Baltimore, MD: Penguin Books.

Cattell, R. B. (1974a). Autobiography. In G. Lindzey (Ed.), *A history of psychology in autobiography* (Vol. 6, pp. 59–100). Englewood Cliffs, NJ: Prentice-Hall.

Cattell, R. B. (1974b). Travels in psychological hyperspace. In T. S. Krawiec (Ed.), *The psychologists* (Vol. 2, pp. 85–133). New York: Oxford University Press.

Cattell, R. B. (1982). *The inheritance of personality and ability: Research methods.* New York: Academic Press.

Cattell, R. B. (1990). Advances in Cattellian personality theory. In L. A. Pervin (Ed.), *Handbook of personality: Theory and research* (pp. 101–110). New York: Guilford Press.

Cattell, R. B., & Cross, K. P. (1952). Comparison of the ergic and self-sentiment structure found in dynamic traits by R- and P-techniques. *Journal of Personality, 21,* 250–271.

Cattell, R. B., Eber, H. W., & Tatsuoka, M. M. (1970). *Handbook for the Sixteen Personality Factor Questionnaire.* Champaign, IL: Institute for Personality and Ability Testing.

Cattell, R. B., & Kline, P. (1977). *The scientific analysis of personality and motivation.* New York: Academic Press.

Cattell, R. B., & Nesselroade, J. R. (1967). Likeness and completeness theories examined by Sixteen Personality Factor measures by stably and unstably married couples. *Journal of Personality and Social Psychology, 7,* 351–361.

Chan, D. W. (1989). Dimensionality and adjustment correlates of locus of control among Hong Kong Chinese. *Journal of Personality Assessment, 53,* 145–160.

Chandler, T. A., Wolf, R. M., Cook, B., & Dugovics,

D. A. (1980). Parental correlates of locus of control in fifth graders: An attempt at experimentation in the home. *Merrill-Palmer Quarterly, 26,* 183–195.

Cherry, R., & Cherry, L. (1973, August 26). The Horney heresy. *New York Times Magazine,* pp. 12ff.

Chodorkoff, B. (1954). Self-perception, perceptual defense, and adjustment. *Journal of Abnormal and Social Psychology, 49,* 508–512.

Ciaccio, N. (1971). A test of Erikson's theory of ego epigenesis. *Developmental Psychology, 4,* 306–311.

Clemmens, E. R. (1987). Karen Horney, a reminiscence. In K. Horney, *Final lectures* (pp. 107–115). New York: Norton.

Coan, R. W. (1972). Measurable components of openness to experience. *Journal of Consulting and Clinical Psychology, 39,* 346.

Cohen, S., & Wills, T. A. (1985). Stress, social support, and the buffering hypothesis. *Psychological Bulletin, 98,* 310–357.

Coleman, J. S., Campbell, E. Q., Hobson, C. J., McPartland, J., Mood, A. M., Weinfeld, F. D., & York, R. L. (1966). *Equality of educational opportunity.* Washington, DC: U.S. Office of Education.

Coles, R. (1992). *Anna Freud: The dream of psychoanalysis.* Reading, MA: Addison-Wesley.

Constantinople, A. (1969). An Eriksonian measure of personality development in college students. *Developmental Psychology, 1,* 357–372.

Coopersmith, S. (1967). *The antecedents of self-esteem.* New York: W. H. Freeman.

Costa, P. T., Jr., & McCrae, R. R. (1985). *The NEO Personality Inventory manual.* Odessa, FL: Psychological Assessment Resources.

Costa, P. T., Jr., & McCrae, R. R. (1988). Personality in adulthood: A six-year longitudinal study of self-reports and spouse ratings on the NEO Personality Inventory. *Journal of Personality and Social Psychology, 54,* 853–863.

Côté, J. E., & Levine, C. (1988). The relationship between ego identity status and Erikson's notions of institutionalized moratoria, value orientation stage, and ego dominance. *Journal of Youth and Adolescence, 17,* 81–99.

Cowan, D. A. (1989). An alternative to the dichotomous interpretation of Jung's psychological functions: Developing more sensitive measurement technology. *Journal of Personality Assessment, 53,* 459–471.

Cox, R. (1987). The rich harvest of Abraham Maslow. In A. H. Maslow, *Motivation and personality* (3rd ed.) (pp. 245–263). New York: Harper & Row.

Cramer, P. (1987). The development of defense mechanisms. *Journal of Personality, 54,* 597–614.

Cramer, P. (1990). *The development of defense mechanisms:*

Theory, research and assessment. New York: Springer-Verlag.

Cramer, P. (1991). Anger and the use of defense mechanisms in college students. *Journal of Personality, 59,* 39–55.

Crandall, J. E. (1981). *Theory and measurement of social interest: Empirical tests of Alfred Adler's concept.* New York: Columbia University Press.

Crewsdon, J. (1988). *By silence betrayed: Sexual abuse of children in America.* Boston: Little, Brown.

Crockett, W. H. (1982). The organization of construct systems: The organization corollary. In J. C. Mancuso & J. R. Adams-Webber (Eds.), *The construing person.* New York: Praeger.

Crook, T., Raskin, A., & Eliot, J. (1981). Parent-child relationships and adult depression. *Child Development, 52,* 950–957.

Csikszentmihalyi, M., & Larson, R. (1984). *Being adolescent.* New York: Basic Books.

Daniels, D., & Plomin, R. (1985). Origins of individual differences in infant shyness. *Developmental Psychology, 21,* 118–121.

Daniels, M. (1988). The myth of self-actualization. *Journal of Humanistic Psychology, 28,* 7–38.

Davidow, S., & Bruhn, A. R. (1990). Earliest memories and the dynamics of delinquency: A replication study. *Journal of Personality Assessment, 54,* 601–616.

Davis, C., & Cowles, M. (1988). A laboratory study of temperament and arousal: A test of Gale's hypothesis. *Journal of Research in Personality, 22,* 101–116.

Davis, J., Lockwood, L., & Wright, C. (1991). Reasons for not reporting peak experiences. *Journal of Humanistic Psychology, 31,* 86–94.

Davis, P. J. (1987). Repression and the inaccessibility of affective memories. *Journal of Personality and Social Psychology, 53,* 585–593.

DeBrabander, B., & Boone, C. (1990). Sex differences in perceived locus of control. *Journal of Social Psychology, 130,* 271–272.

DeCarvalho, R. J. (1991). Gordon Allport and humanistic psychology. *Journal of Humanistic Psychology, 31,* 8–13.

Dement, W. C., & Wolpert, E. A. (1958). The relationship of eye movements, body motility, and external stimuli to dream content. *Journal of Experimental Psychology, 55,* 543–553.

DeVito, A. J. (1985). Review of Myers-Briggs Type Indicator. In J. V. Mitchell, Jr. (Ed.), *Ninth mental measurements yearbook* (Vol. 2, pp. 1030–1032). Lincoln: University of Nebraska Press.

DiClemente, C. C., Prochaska, J. O., & Gilbertini, M. (1985). Self-efficacy and the stages of self-change of smoking. *Cognitive Therapy and Research.*

Digman, J. M. (1989). Five robust trait dimensions: Development, stability, and utility. *Journal of Personality, 57,* 195–214.

Digman, J. M. (1990). Personality structure: Emergence of the five-factor model. *Annual Review of Psychology, 41,* 417–440.

Dignan, M. (1965). Ego identity and maternal identification. *Journal of Personality and Social Psychology, 1,* 476–483.

Distinguished Scientific Contribution Award. (1958). *American Psychologist, 13,* 729–738. [B. F. Skinner]

Distinguished Scientific Contribution Award. (1981). *American Psychologist, 36,* 27–42. [A. Bandura]

Distinguished Scientific Contribution Award. (1988). *American Psychologist, 43,* 225–226. [D. McClelland]

Doherty, W. (1983). Impact of divorce on locus of control orientation in adult women: A longitudinal study. *Journal of Personality and Social Psychology, 44,* 834–840.

Dollard, J., Doob, L. W., Miller, N. E., Mowrer, O. H., & Sears, R. R. (1939). *Frustration and aggression.* New Haven, CT: Yale University Press.

Domino, G., & Affonso, D. D. (1990). A personality measure of Erikson's life stages: The Inventory of Psychosocial Balance. *Journal of Personality Assessment, 54,* 576–588.

Duck, S. W., & Allison, D. (1978). I liked you but I can't live with you: A study of lapsed friendships. *Social Behavior and Personality, 6,* 43–47.

Duck, S. W., & Spencer, C. (1972). Personal constructs and friendship formation. *Journal of Personality and Social Psychology, 23,* 40–45.

Eagle, M. N. (1988). How accurate were Freud's case histories? [Review of *Freud and the Rat Man*]. *Contemporary Psychology, 33,* 205–206.

Eaves, L. J., Eysenck, H. J., & Martin, N. G. (1989). *Genes, culture, and personality: An empirical approach.* New York: Academic Press.

Edwards, A. L. (1953). *Manual for Edwards Personal Preference Schedule.* New York: Psychological Corporation.

Eissler, K. R. (1971). *Talent and genius: The fictitious case of Tausk contra Freud.* New York: Quadrangle Books.

Elder, G. H., & MacInnis, D. J. (1983). Achievement imagery in women's lives from adolescence to adulthood. *Journal of Personality and Social Psychology, 45,* 394–404.

Ellenberger, H. F. (1970). *The discovery of the unconscious: The history and evolution of dynamic psychiatry.* New York: Basic Books.

Ellis, R. A., & Taylor, M. S. (1983). Role of self-esteem within the job search process. *Journal of Applied Psychology, 68,* 632–640.

Elms, A. C. (1981). Skinner's dark year and *Walden Two*. *American Psychologist, 36,* 470–479.

Enns, C. Z. (1989). Toward teaching inclusive personality theories. *Teaching of Psychology, 16*(3), 111–117.

Epstein, S. (1979). Explorations in personality today and tomorrow: A tribute to Henry A. Murray. *American Psychologist, 34,* 649–653.

Erikson, E. H. (1950). *Childhood and society.* New York: Norton.

Erikson, E. H. (1959). Identity and the life cycle: Selected papers. *Psychological Issues, 1* (Monograph 1).

Erikson, E. H. (1963). *Childhood and society* (2nd ed.). New York: Norton.

Erikson, E. H. (1968). *Identity: Youth and crisis.* New York: Norton.

Erikson, E. H. (1975). *Life history and the historical moment.* New York: Norton.

Erikson, E. H., Erikson, J. M., & Kivnick, H. Q. (1986). *Vital involvement in old age.* New York: Norton.

Eron, L. (1987). The development of aggressive behavior from the perspective of a developing behaviorism. *American Psychologist, 42,* 435–442.

Eron, L., & Huesmann, L. (1984). The control of aggressive behavior by changes in attitudes, values, and the conditions of learning. In R. J. Blanchard & D. C. Blanchard (Eds.), *Advances in the study of aggression* (Vol. 1, pp. 130–171). New York: Academic Press.

Eron, L., Huesmann, L., Lefkowitz, M., & Walder, L. (1972). Does television violence cause aggression? *American Psychologist, 27,* 253–263.

Estes, S. G. (1938). Judging personality from expressive behavior. *Journal of Abnormal and Social Psychology, 33,* 217–236.

Evans, R. I. (1966). *Dialogue with Erich Fromm.* New York: Harper & Row.

Evans, R. I. (1968). *B. F. Skinner: The man and his ideas.* New York: Dutton.

Exner, J. E., Jr. (1986). *The Rorschach: A comprehensive system: Vol. 1. Basic foundations* (2nd ed.). New York: Wiley.

Eysenck, H. J. (1947). *Dimensions of personality.* London: Routledge & Kegan Paul.

Eysenck, H. J. (1967). *The biological basis of personality.* Springfield, IL: Charles C Thomas.

Eysenck, H. J. (Ed.). (1976). *The measurement of personality.* Baltimore, MD: University Park Press.

Eysenck, H. J. (Ed.). (1981). *A model for personality.* New York: Springer-Verlag.

Eysenck, H. J. (1983). A biometrical-genetical analysis of impulsive and sensation seeking behavior. In M. Zuckerman (Ed.), *Biological bases of sensation seeking, impulsivity, and anxiety* (pp. 1–27). Hillsdale, NJ: Erlbaum.

Eysenck, H. J. (1990a). Genetic and environmental contributions to individual differences: The three major dimensions of personality. *Journal of Personality, 58*(1), 245–261.

Eysenck, H. J. (1990b). Biological dimensions of personality. In L. A. Pervin (Ed.), *Handbook of personality: Theory and research* (pp. 244–276). New York: Guilford Press.

Eysenck, H. J., & Cookson, D. (1969). Personality in primary school children: 3. Family background. *British Journal of Educational Psychology, 40,* 117–131.

Eysenck, H. J., & Eysenck, M. W. (1985). *Personality and individual differences.* New York: Plenum Press.

Eysenck, H. J., & Eysenck, S. (1963). *Eysenck Personality Inventory.* San Diego, CA: Educational and Industrial Testing Service.

Falbo, T. (1978). Only children and interpersonal behavior: An experimental and survey study. *Journal of Applied Social Psychology, 8,* 244–253.

Falbo, T., & Polit, D. F. (1986). Quantitative review of the only child literature: Research evidence and theory development. *Psychological Bulletin, 100,* 176–189.

Findley, M. J., & Cooper, H. M. (1983). Locus of control and academic achievement: A literature review. *Journal of Personality and Social Psychology, 44,* 419–427.

Fisher, S., & Greenberg, R. P. (1977). *The scientific credibility of Freud's theories and therapy.* New York: Basic Books.

Fiske, D. W. (1949). Consistency of the factorial structures of personality ratings from different sources. *Journal of Abnormal and Social Psychology, 44,* 329–344.

Fjeld, S. P., & Landfield, A. W. (1961). Personal construct consistency. *Psychological Reports, 8,* 127–129.

Floderus-Myrhed, B., Pedersen, N., & Rasmuson, I. (1980). Assessment of heritability for personality, based on a short form of the Eysenck Personality Inventory: A study of 12,898 twin pairs. *Behavior Genetics, 10,* 153–162.

Ford, J. G. (1991). Inherent potentialities of actualization: An initial exploration. *Journal of Humanistic Psychology, 31*(3), 65–88.

Fowler, R. D. (1990). In memoriam: Burrhus Frederick Skinner, 1904–1990. *American Psychologist, 45,* 1203.

Fox, J., Knapp, R., & Michael, W. (1968). Assessment of self-actualization of psychiatric patients: Validity of the Personal Orientation Inventory. *Educational and Psychological Measurement, 28,* 565–569.

Fransella, F. (1988). PCT: Still radical thirty years on? In F. Fransella & L. Thomas (Eds.), *Experimenting with personal construct psychology* (pp. 26–35). London: Routledge & Kegan Paul.

Franz, C. E., McClelland, D. C., & Weinberger, J. (1991). Childhood antecedents of conventional social accomplishment in midlife adults: A 36-year prospective study. *Journal of Personality and Social Psychology, 60,* 586–595.

Freedman, D. G. (1974). *Human infancy: An evolutionary perspective.* Hillsdale, NJ: Erlbaum.

Freud, A. (1936). *The ego and the mechanisms of defense.* London: Hogarth Press.

Freud, S. (1901). The psychopathology of everyday life. In *The standard edition of the complete psychological works of Sigmund Freud* (Vol. 6). J. Strachey (Ed. & Trans.). London: Hogarth Press.

Freud, S. (1925). An autobiographical study. In *Standard edition* (Vol. 20). London: Hogarth Press.

Freud, S. (1940). An outline of psychoanalysis. In *Standard edition* (Vol. 23, pp. 141–207). London: Hogarth Press.

Freud, S. (1954). *The origins of psychoanalysis: Letters to Wilhelm Fliess, drafts and notes: 1887–1902.* M. Bonaparte, A. Freud, & E. Kris (Eds.). New York: Basic Books.

Freud, S. (1963). *Psychoanalysis and faith: The letters of Sigmund Freud and Oskar Pfister.* H. Meng & E. Freud (Eds.). New York: Basic Books.

Freud, S. (1985). *The complete letters of Sigmund Freud to Wilhelm Fliess, 1887–1904.* J. M. Masson (Ed.). Cambridge, MA: Belknap Press of Harvard University.

Freud, S., & Jung, C. G. (1974). *The Freud/Jung letters.* W. McGuire (Ed.). Princeton, NJ: Princeton University Press.

Friedman, A. F., Webb, J. T., & Lewak, R. (1989). *Psychological assessment with the MMPI.* Hillsdale, NJ: Erlbaum.

Fromm, E. (1941). *Escape from freedom.* New York: Holt, Rinehart & Winston.

Fromm, E. (1955). *The sane society.* New York: Holt, Rinehart & Winston.

Fromm, E. (1962). *Beyond the chains of illusion: My encounter with Marx and Freud.* New York: Simon & Schuster.

Fromm, E. (1964). *The heart of man: Its genius for good or evil.* New York: Harper & Row.

Fromm, E. (1973). *The anatomy of human destructiveness.* New York: Holt, Rinehart & Winston.

Fromm, E., & Maccoby, M. (1970). *Social character in a Mexican village.* Englewood Cliffs, NJ: Prentice-Hall.

Funder, D. C. (1991). Global traits: A neo-Allportian approach to personality. *Psychological Science, 2,* 31–39.

Funk, R. (1982). *Erich Fromm: The courage to be human.* New York: Continuum.

Garcia, M. E., Schmitz, J. M., & Doerfler, L. A. (1990). A fine-grained analysis of the role of self-efficacy in self-initiated attempts to quit smoking. *Journal of Consulting and Clinical Psychology, 58,* 317–322.

Gates, L., Lineberger, M. R., Crockett, J., & Hubbard, J. (1988). Birth order and its relationship to depression, anxiety, and self-concept test scores in children. *Journal of Genetic Psychology, 149,* 29–34.

Gay, P. (1988). *Freud: A life for our time.* New York: Norton.

Gecas, V. (1989). The social psychology of self-efficacy. *Annual Review of Sociology, 15,* 291–316.

Geen, R. G. (1984). Preferred stimulation levels in introverts and extroverts: Effects on arousal and performance. *Journal of Personality and Social Psychology, 46,* 1303–1312.

Geer, J. H. (1965). The development of a scale to measure fear. *Behavior Research and Therapy, 3,* 45–53.

Gelbort, K. R., & Winer, J. L. (1985). Fear of success and fear of failure: A multitrait multi-method validation study. *Journal of Personality and Social Psychology, 48,* 1009–1014.

Gendlin, E. T. (1988). Carl Rogers (1902–1987) [Obituary]. *American Psychologist, 43,* 127–128.

Gendlin, E. T., & Tomlinson, T. M. (1967). The process conception and its measurement. In C. R. Rogers, E. T. Gendlin, D. J. Kiesler, & C. B. Truax (Eds.), *The therapeutic relationship and its impact: A study of psychotherapy with schizophrenics.* Madison: University of Wisconsin Press.

Gilgen, A. R. (1982). *American psychology since World War II: A profile of the discipline.* Westport, CT: Greenwood.

Glucksberg, S., & King, L. J. (1967). Motivated forgetting mediated by implicit verbal chaining: A laboratory analog of repression. *Science, 158,* 517–519.

Goldberg, L. R. (1990). An alternative "description of personality": The big-five factor structure. *Journal of Personality and Social Psychology, 59,* 1216–1229.

Goleman, D. (1987, August 31). B. F. Skinner: On his best behavior. *New York Times.*

Gorer, G. (1968). Man has no "killer" instinct. In M. F. A. Montague (Ed.), *Man and aggression.* New York: Oxford University Press.

Gough, H. G. (1987). *California Psychological Inventory: Administrator's guide.* Palo Alto, CA: Consulting Psychologists Press.

Gough, H. G., Fioravanti, M., & Lazzari, R. (1983). Some implications of self versus idealized self-congruence on the Revised Adjective Check List. *Journal of Personality and Social Psychology, 44,* 1214–1220.

Gough, H. G., & Heilbrun, A. B., Jr. (1983). *The Adjective Check List Manual* (rev. ed.). Palo Alto, CA: Consulting Psychologists Press.

Gough, H. G., Lazzari, R., & Fioravanti, M. (1978). Self versus ideal self: A comparison of five Adjective Check List indices. *Journal of Consulting and Clinical Psychology, 35,* 1085–1091.

Graham, W., & Balloun, J. (1973). An empirical test of Maslow's need hierarchy theory. *Journal of Humanistic Psychology, 13,* 97–108.

Graves, T. D. (1961). *Time perspective and the deferred gratification pattern in a tri-ethnic community.* Boulder: University of Colorado Institute of Behavioral Science.

Greever, K., Tseng, M., & Friedland, B. (1973). Development of the Social Interest Index. *Journal of Consulting and Clinical Psychology, 41,* 454–458.

Grieser, C., Greenberg, R., & Harrison, R. H. (1972). The adaptive function of sleep: The differential effects of sleep and dreaming on recall. *Journal of Abnormal Psychology, 80,* 280–286.

Grossack, M., Armstrong, T., & Lussieu, G. (1966). Correlates of self-actualization. *Journal of Humanistic Psychology, 37.*

Hackett, G., Betz, N. E., & Doty, M. S. (1985). The development of a taxonomy of career competencies for professional women. *Sex Roles, 12,* 393–409.

Hafner, J. L., Fakouri, M. E., & Labrentz, H. L. (1982). First memories of "normal" and alcoholic individuals. *Individual Psychology, 38,* 238–244.

Hall, C., & Van de Castle, R. (1965). An empirical investigation of the castration complex in dreams. *Journal of Personality, 33,* 20–29.

Hall, D. T., & Nougaim, K. E. (1968). An examination of Maslow's need hierarchy in an organizational setting. *Organizational Behavior and Human Performance, 3,* 12–35.

Hall, E. (1970, February). Alfred Adler, a sketch. *Psychology Today,* pp. 45, 67.

Hall, E. (1983, June). A conversation with Erik Erikson. *Psychology Today,* pp. 22–30.

Hall, M. H. (1967, September). An interview with "Mr. Behaviorist" B. F. Skinner. *Psychology Today,* pp. 21–23, 68–71.

Hall, M. H. (1968a, July). A conversation with Abraham H. Maslow. *Psychology Today,* pp. 35–37, 54–57.

Hall, M. H. (1968b, September). A conversation with Henry A. Murray. *Psychology Today,* pp. 56–63.

Hanewitz, W. B. (1978). Police personality: A Jungian perspective. *Crime and Delinquency, 24,* 152–172.

Hankoff, L. D. (1987). The earliest memories of criminals. *International Journal of Offender Therapy and Comparative Criminology, 31,* 195–201.

Harrington, D. M., Block, J. H., & Block, J. (1987). Testing aspects of Carl Rogers' theory of creative environments: Child-rearing antecedents of creative potential in young adolescents. *Journal of Personality and Social Psychology, 52,* 851–856.

Harvey, J. H., & Barnes, R. (1974). Perceived choice as a function of internal-external locus of control. *Journal of Personality, 42,* 437–452.

Hausdorff, D. (1972). *Erich Fromm.* Boston: Twayne.

Hawkins, R. P., Peterson, R. F., Schweid, E., & Bijou, S. W. (1966). Behavior therapy in the home: Amelioration of problem parent-child relations with the parent in a therapeutic role. *Journal of Experimental Child Psychology, 4,* 99–107.

Heath, A. C. (1991). The genetics of personality [Review of *Nature's thumbprint: The new genetics of personality*]. *Contemporary Psychology, 36,* 1063–1064.

Hetherington, E. M., & Frankie, G. (1967). Effect of parental dominance, warmth, and conflict on imitation in children. *Journal of Personality and Social Psychology, 6,* 119–125.

Hiroto, D. S. (1974). Locus of control and learned helplessness. *Journal of Experimental Psychology, 102,* 187–193.

Hobfoll, S. E., Rom, T., & Segal, B. (1989). Sensation seeking, anxiety, and risk taking in the Israeli context. In S. Einstein (Ed.), *Drug and alcohol use: Issues and factors* (pp. 53–59). New York: Plenum Press.

Hoffman, E. (1988). *The right to be human: A biography of Abraham Maslow.* Los Angeles: Tarcher.

Hoffman, L. W. (1974). Fear of success in males and females. *Journal of Consulting and Clinical Psychology, 42,* 353–358.

Holener, D. (1986). Semantic activation without conscious identification in dichotic listening, parifocal vision, and visual masking: A survey and appraisal. *Behavioral and Brain Sciences, 9,* 1–66.

Holland, J. G. (1992). B. F. Skinner (1904–1990) [Obituary]. *American Psychologist, 47,* 665–667.

Holmes, D. S., & McCaul, K. D. (1989). Laboratory research on defense mechanisms. In R. W. J. Neufeld (Ed.), *Advances in the investigation of psychological stress* (pp. 161–192). New York: Wiley.

Holtzman, W. H. (1988). Beyond the Rorschach. *Journal of Personality Assessment, 52,* 578–609.

Horner, M. S. (1973). A psychological barrier to achievement in women: The motive to avoid success. In D. C. McClelland & R. S. Steele (Eds.), *Human motivation.* Morristown, NJ: General Learning Press.

Horner, M. S. (1978). The measurement and behavioral implication of fear of success in women. In J. W. Atkinson & J. O. Raynor (Eds.), *Personality, motivation, and achievement.* Washington, DC: Hemisphere.

Horney, K. (1926). The flight from womanhood. *International Journal of Psychoanalysis, 7.*

Horney, K. (1937). *The neurotic personality of our time.* New York: Norton.

Horney, K. (1939). *New ways in psychoanalysis.* New York: Norton.

Horney, K. (1942). *Self-analysis.* New York: Norton.

Horney, K. (1945). *Our inner conflicts.* New York: Norton.

Horney, K. (1967a). The flight from womanhood: The masculinity-complex in women as viewed by men and by women. In H. Kelman (Ed.), *Feminine psychology.* New York: Norton.

Horney, K. (1967b). The overvaluation of love. In H. Kelman (Ed.), *Feminine psychology* (pp. 182–213). New York: Norton. (Original work published 1934.)

Horney, K. (1980). *The adolescent diaries of Karen Horney.* New York: Basic Books. [Diaries written 1899–1911]

Horney, K. (1987). *Final lectures.* D. H. Ingram (Ed.). New York: Norton. [Lectures delivered 1952]

Hornstein, G. A. (1992). The return of the repressed: Psychology's problematic relations with psychoanalysis, 1909–1960. *American Psychologist, 47,* 254–263.

Huesmann, L., Eron, L., Dubow, E., & Seebauer, E. (1987). Television viewing habits in childhood and adult aggression. *Child Development, 58,* 357–367.

Hyman, R. B. (1988). Four stages of adulthood: An exploratory study of growth patterns of inner-direction and time-competence in women. *Journal of Research in Personality, 22,* 117–127.

Ivancevich, J. M., Matteson, M. T., & Gamble, G. O. (1987). Birth order and the Type A coronary behavior pattern. *Individual Psychology, 43,* 42–49.

Jackson, D. N. (1976). *Jackson Personality Inventory: Manual.* Port Huron, MI: Research Psychologists Press.

Jackson, D. N. (1978). Interpreter's guide to the Jackson Personality Inventory. In P. McReynolds (Ed.), *Advances in psychological assessment* (Vol. 4, pp. 56–102). San Francisco: Jossey-Bass.

Jackson, M., & Sechrest, L. (1962). Early recollections in four neurotic diagnostic categories. *Journal of Individual Psychology, 18,* 52–56.

Jacobson, J. L., & Wille, D. E. (1986). The influence of attachment patterns on developmental changes in peer interaction from the toddler to the preschool period. *Child Development, 57,* 338–347.

Jacoby, L. L., & Kelley, C. M. (1987). Unconscious influences of memory for a prior event. *Personality and Social Psychology Bulletin, 13,* 314–336.

Jaffé, A. (1971). *The myth of meaning: Jung and the expansion of consciousness.* New York: Putnam.

Jahoda, M. (1988). The range of convenience of personal construct psychology—an outsider's view. In F. Fransella & L. Thomas (Eds.), *Experimenting with personal construct psychology* (pp. 1–14). London: Routledge & Kegan Paul.

Jancowicz, A. D. (1987). Whatever became of George Kelly? Applications and implications. *American Psychologist, 42,* 481–487.

Jancowicz, A. D., & Cooper, K. (1982). The use of focussed repertory grids in counselling. *British Journal of Guidance and Counselling, 10,* 136–150.

Jenkins, S. R. (1987). Need for achievement and women's careers over 14 years: Evidence for occupational structure effects. *Journal of Personality and Social Psychology, 53,* 922–932.

Jiao, S., Ji, G., & Jing, Q. (1986). Comparative study of behavioral qualities of only children and sibling children. *Child Development, 57,* 357–361.

John, O. P. (1989). Towards a taxonomy of personality descriptors. In D. M. Buss & N. Cantor (Eds.), *Personality psychology: Recent trends and emerging directions* (pp. 261–271). New York: Springer-Verlag.

John, O. P. (1990). The "big five" factor taxonomy: Dimensions of personality in the natural language and in questionnaires. In L. A. Pervin (Ed.), *Handbook of personality: Theory and research* (pp. 66–100). New York: Guilford Press.

Johnson, P. B. (1981). Achievement motivation and success: Does the end justify the means? *Journal of Personality and Social Psychology, 40,* 374–375.

Johnson, R. C. (1980). Summing up [Review of *Personality and learning theory, Vol. 1: The structure of personality in its environment*]. *Contemporary Psychology, 25,* 299–300.

Jones, E. (1953, 1955, 1957). *The life and work of Sigmund Freud* (3 vols.). New York: Basic Books.

Jorm, A. F. (1987). Sex differences in neuroticism: A quantitative synthesis of published research. *Australian and New Zealand Journal of Psychiatry, 21,* 501–506.

Josselson, R. L. (1982). Personality structure and identity status in women as viewed through early memories. *Journal of Youth and Adolescence, 11,* 293–299.

Jung, C. G. (1919). Instinct and the unconscious. In *The collected works of C. G. Jung* (Vol. 8, pp. 129–138). H. Read, M. Fordham, & G. Adler (Eds.). Princeton, NJ: Princeton University Press.

Jung, C. G. (1927). The structure of the psyche. In *Collected works* (Vol. 8, pp. 139–158). Princeton, NJ: Princeton University Press.

Jung, C. G. (1928). On psychic energy. In *Collected*

works (Vol. 8, pp. 3–66). Princeton, NJ: Princeton University Press.

Jung, C. G. (1930). The stages of life. In *Collected works* (Vol. 8, pp. 387–403). Princeton, NJ: Princeton University Press.

Jung, C. G. (1947). On the nature of the psyche. In *Collected works* (Vol. 8, pp. 159–234). Princeton, NJ: Princeton University Press.

Jung, C. G. (1952). Synchronicity. In *Collected works* (Vol. 8, pp. 417–531). Princeton, NJ: Princeton University Press.

Jung, C. G. (1953). *Two essays on analytical psychology.* New York: Pantheon.

Jung, C. G. (1961). *Memories, dreams, reflections.* New York: Vintage Books.

Kagan, J. (1984). *The nature of the child.* New York: Basic Books.

Kagan, J., Kearsley, R., & Zelazo, P. (1978). *Infancy.* Cambridge, MA: Harvard University Press.

Kamptner, N. L. (1988). Identity development in late adolescence: Causal modeling of social and familial influences. *Journal of Youth and Adolescence, 17,* 493–514.

Kanfer, R., & Hulin, C. L. (1985). Individual differences in successful job searches following layoff. *Journal of Vocational Behavior.*

Kaplan, R. M., Atkins, C. J., & Reinsch, S. (1984). Specific efficacy expectations mediate exercise compliance in patients with COPD. *Health Psychology, 3,* 223–242.

Katcher, A. (1955). The discrimination of sex differences by young children. *Journal of Genetic Psychology, 87,* 131–143.

Kazdin, A. E. (1975). Covert modeling, imagery assessment, and assertive behavior. *Journal of Consulting and Clinical Psychology, 43,* 716–724.

Kazdin, A. E. (1979). Covert modeling and the reduction of avoidance behavior. In D. Upper & J. R. Cautela (Eds.), *Covert conditioning.* Elmsford, NY: Pergamon Press.

Kazdin, A. E., & Bootzin, R. (1972). The token economy: An evaluative review. *Journal of Applied Behavioral Analysis, 5,* 343–372.

Keiser, R. E., & Prather, E. N. (1990). What is the TAT? A review of ten years of research. *Journal of Personality Assessment, 55,* 800–803.

Kellaghan, T., & MacNamara, J. (1972). Family correlates of verbal reasoning ability. *Developmental Psychology, 7,* 49–53.

Kelly, G. A. (1955). *The psychology of personal constructs.* New York: Norton.

Kelly, G. A. (1958). The theory and technique of assessment. *Annual Review of Psychology, 9,* 323–352.

Kelly, G. A. (1969). *Clinical psychology and personality:*

The selected papers of George Kelly. B. Maher (Ed.). New York: Wiley.

Keniston, K. (1983, June). Remembering Erikson at Harvard. *Psychology Today,* p. 29.

Kenrick, D. T., & Funder, D. C. (1988). Profiting from controversy: Lessons from the person-situation debate. *American Psychologist, 43,* 23–34.

Kidwell, J. (1982). The neglected birth order: Middleborns. *Journal of Marriage and the Family, 44,* 225–235.

Kiester, E., Jr., & Cudhea, D. (1974). Albert Bandura: A very modern model. *Human Behavior,* 27–31.

Klein, M. H., Malthieu, P. L., Gendlin, E. T., & Kiesler, D. J. (1969). *The Experiencing Scale: A research and training manual.* Madison: Wisconsin Psychiatric Institute.

Kline, P. (1972). *Fact and fantasy in Freudian theory.* London: Methuen.

Kline, P. (1987). The experimental study of the psychoanalytic unconscious. *Personality and Social Psychology Bulletin, 13,* 363–378.

Knapp, R. J. (1965). Relationship of a measure of self-actualization to neuroticism and extraversion. *Journal of Consulting Psychology, 29,* 168–172.

Koestner, R., & McClelland, D. C. (1990). Perspectives on competence motivation. In L. A. Pervin (Ed.), *Handbook of personality: Theory and research* (pp. 527–548). New York: Guilford Press.

Kowaz, A. M., & Marcia, J. E. (1991). Development and validation of a measure of Eriksonian industry. *Journal of Personality and Social Psychology, 60,* 390–397.

Kreitler, S., & Kreitler, H. (1990). *The cognitive foundations of personality traits.* New York: Plenum Press.

Krug, S. E. (1980). *Clinical Analysis Questionnaire manual.* Champaign, IL: Institute for Personality and Ability Testing.

Krüll, M. (1986). *Freud and his father.* New York: Norton.

Lachman, M. E. (1985). Personal efficacy in middle and old age: Differential and normative patterns of change. In G. H. Elder, Jr. (Ed.), *Life course dynamics* (pp. 188–216). Ithaca, NY: Cornell University Press.

Lahey, B. B., Hammer, D., Crumrine, P. L., & Forehand, R. L. (1980). Birth order × sex interactions in child behavior problems. *Developmental Psychology, 16,* 608–615.

Landfield, A. W. (1971). *Personal construct systems in psychotherapy.* Chicago: Rand McNally.

Langer, E. J., & Rodin, J. (1976). The effects of choice and enhanced personal responsibility for the aged: A field experiment in an institutional setting. *Journal of Personality and Social Psychology, 34,* 191–198.

Lapan, R. T., Boggs, K. R., & Morrill, W. H. (1989).

Self-efficacy as a mediator of investigative and realistic general occupational themes on the Strong-Campbell Interest Inventory. *Journal of Counseling Psychology, 36,* 176–182.

Latané, B., & Bidwell, L. D. (1977). Sex and affiliation in college cafeterias. *Personality and Social Psychology Bulletin, 3,* 571–574.

Lazarus, R. S., & Folkman, S. (1984). *Stress, appraisal, and coping.* New York: Springer.

Lefcourt, H. M. (1982). *Locus of control: Current trends in theory and research* (2nd ed.). Hillsdale, NJ: Erlbaum.

Lefcourt, H. M., Martin, R. A., Fick, C. M., & Saleh, W. E. (1985). Locus of control for affiliation in social interactions. *Journal of Personality and Social Psychology, 48,* 755–759.

Lefkowitz, M. M., & Tesiny, E. P. (1984). Rejection and depression: Prospective and contemporaneous analysis. *Developmental Psychology, 20,* 776–785.

LeMay, M., & Damm, V. (1968). The Personal Orientation Inventory as a measure of self-actualization of underachievers. *Measurement and Evaluation in Guidance,* 110–114.

Lent, R. W., & Hackett, G. (1987). Career self-efficacy: Empirical status and future directions. *Journal of Vocational Behavior, 30,* 347–382.

Leonard, G. (1983, December). Abraham Maslow and the new self. *Esquire,* pp. 326–336.

Lerman, H. (1986). *A mote in Freud's eye: From psychoanalysis to the psychology of women.* New York: Springer-Verlag.

Levenson, M. R. (1990). Risk taking and personality. *Journal of Personality and Social Psychology, 58,* 1073–1080.

Levy, S., Morrow, L., Bagley, C., & Lippman, M. (1989). Survival hazards analysis in first recurrent breast cancer patients: Seven-year follow-up. *Psychosomatic Medicine.*

Lewis, P. H. (1991, July 21). For face-to-face talks, ask your machine first. *New York Times,* p. 7.

Leyens, J., Camino, L., Parke, R., & Berkowitz, L. (1975). Effects of movie violence on aggression in a field setting as a function of group dominance and cohesion. *Journal of Personality and Social Psychology, 32,* 346–360.

Liebert, R. M., Sprafkin, J. N., & Davidson, E. S. (1982). *The early window: Effects of television on children and youth* (2nd ed.). Elmsford, NY: Pergamon Press.

Locke, E. A., & Latham, G. P. (1990). *A theory of goal setting and task performance.* Englewood Cliffs, NJ: Prentice-Hall.

Loeb, R. C. (1975). Concomitants of boys' locus of control examined in parent-child interactions. *Developmental Psychology, 11,* 353–358.

Loehlin, J. C., Horn, J. M., & Willerman, L. (1990). Heredity, environment, and personality change: Evidence from the Texas adoption project. *Journal of Personality, 58,* 221–243.

Loehlin, J. C., & Nichols, R. C. (1976). *Heredity, environment, and personality: A study of 850 sets of twins.* Austin: University of Texas Press.

Londerville, S., & Main, M. (1981). Security of attachment, compliance, and maternal training methods in the second year of life. *Developmental Psychology, 17,* 289–299.

Lorenz, K. (1966). *On aggression.* San Diego: Harcourt Brace Jovanovich.

Lowell, E. L. (1952). The effect of need for achievement on learning and speed of performance. *Journal of Psychology, 33,* 31–40.

Lubin, B., Larsen, R. M., Matarazzo, J. D., & Seever, M. (1985). Psychological test usage patterns in five professional settings. *American Psychologist, 40,* 857–861.

Luthans, F., Maciag, W. S., & Rosenkranz, S. A. (1983). O.B.Mod.: Meeting the productivity challenge with human resources management. *Personnel, 60*(2), 28–36.

Maccoby, M. (1972, Winter). Emotional attitudes and political choices. *Politics and Society,* pp. 209–239.

Maccoby, M. (1976). *The gamesman.* New York: Simon & Schuster.

Maccoby, M. (1981). *The leader.* New York: Simon & Schuster.

Mackavey, W. R., Malley, J. E., & Stewart, A. J. (1991). Remembering autobiographically consequential experiences: Content analysis of psychologists' accounts of their lives. *Psychology and Aging, 6,* 50–59.

Maehr, M. L., & Kleiber, D. A. (1981). The graying of achievement motivation. *American Psychologist, 36,* 787–793.

Magnusson, D. (1990). Personality development from an interactional perspective. In L. A. Pervin (Ed.), *Handbook of personality: Theory and research* (pp. 193–222). New York: Guilford Press.

Mahoney, J., & Hartnett, J. (1973). Self-actualization and self-ideal discrepancy. *Journal of Psychology, 85,* 37–42.

Mahoney, P. J. (1986). *Freud and the Rat Man.* New Haven: Yale University Press.

Maier, S. F., Laudenslager, M., & Ryan, S. M. (1985). Stressor controllability, immune function, and endogenous opiates. In F. R. Brush and J. B. Overmier (Eds.), *Affect, conditioning, and cognition: Essays on the determinants of behavior* (pp. 203–210). Hillsdale, NJ: Erlbaum.

Maier, S. J., & Seligman, M. E. P. (1976). Learned helplessness: Theory and evidence. *Journal of Experimental Psychology, 105,* 3–46.

Malcolm, J. (1984). *In the Freud archives.* New York: Knopf.

Manning, M. M., & Wright, T. L. (1983). Self-efficacy expectancies, outcome expectancies, and the persistence of pain control in childbirth. *Journal of Personality and Social Psychology, 45,* 421–431.

Maqsud, M., & Rouhani, S. (1991). Relationships between socioeconomic status, locus of control, self-concept, and academic achievement of Botswana adolescents. *Journal of Youth and Adolescence, 20,* 107–114.

Marcia, J. E. (1966). Development and validation of ego-identity status. *Journal of Personality and Social Psychology, 3,* 551–558.

Marcia, J. E. (1967). Ego identity status: Relationship to change in self-esteem, "general maladjustment" and authoritarianism. *Journal of Personality, 35,* 118–133.

Marcia, J. E. (1980). Identity in adolescence. In J. Adelson (Ed.), *Handbook of adolescent psychology* (pp. 159–187). New York: Wiley.

Marcia, J. E., & Friedman, M. L. (1970). Ego identity status in college women. *Journal of Personality, 38,* 249–263.

Mariotto, M. J., & Paul, G. L. (1974). A multimethod validation of the Inpatient Multidimensional Psychiatric Scale with chronically institutionalized patients. *Journal of Consulting and Clinical Psychology, 42,* 497–509.

Marshall, G. N. (1991). A multidimensional analysis of internal health locus of control beliefs: Separating the wheat from the chaff? *Journal of Personality and Social Psychology, 61,* 483–491.

Martin, N., & Jardine, R. (1986). Eysenck's contributions to behaviour genetics. In S. Modgill & L. Modgill (Eds.), *Hans Eysenck: Consensus and controversy* (pp. 13–47). London: Falmer.

Masling, J. M., Rabie, L., & Blondheim, S. H. (1967). Obesity, level of aspiration, and Rorschach and TAT measures of oral dependence. *Journal of Consulting Psychology, 31,* 233–239.

Maslow, A. H. (1957). A philosophy of psychology: The need for a mature science of human nature. *Main Currents in Modern Thought, 13,* 27–32.

Maslow, A. H. (1967). Self-actualization and beyond. In J. F. T. Bugental (Ed.), *Challenges of humanistic psychology* (pp. 279–286). New York: McGraw-Hill.

Maslow, A. H. (1968). *Toward a psychology of being* (2nd ed.). New York: Van Nostrand Reinhold.

Maslow, A. H. (1970a). Tribute to Alfred Adler. *Journal of Individual Psychology, 26,* 13.

Maslow, A. H. (1970b). *Motivation and personality* (2nd ed.). New York: Harper & Row.

Maslow, A. H. (1971). *The farther reaches of human nature.* New York: Viking Press.

Maslow, A. H. (1979). *The journals of A. H. Maslow.* R. J. Lowry (Ed.). Pacific Grove, CA: Brooks/Cole.

Maslow, A. H. (1987). *Motivation and personality* (3rd ed.). New York: Harper & Row.

Masson, J. M. (1984). *The assault on truth: Freud's suppression of the seduction theory.* New York: Farrar, Straus & Giroux.

Matheny, A. P. (1983). A longitudinal twin study of the stability of components from Bayley's Infant Behavior Record. *Child Development, 54,* 356–360.

Mathes, E. W., Zevon, M. A., Roter, P. M., & Joerger, S. M. (1982). Peak experience tendencies: Scale development and theory testing. *Journal of Humanistic Psychology, 22,* 92–108.

Matthews, K. A., Batson, C. D., Horn, J., & Rosenman, R. H. (1981). "Principles in his nature which interest him in the fortune of others . . .": The heritability of empathic concern for others. *Journal of Personality, 49,* 237–247.

Mattocks, A. L., & Jew, C. (1974). Comparison of self-actualization levels and adjustment scores of incarcerated male felons. *Journal of Educational and Psychological Measurement, 34,* 69–74.

Mayo, C. W., & Crockett, W. H. (1964). Cognitive complexity and primacy-recency effects in impression formation. *Journal of Abnormal and Social Psychology, 68,* 335–338.

McAdams, D. P., Ruetzel, K., & Foley, J. M. (1986). Complexity and generativity at midlife: Relations among social motives, ego development, and adults' plans for the future. *Journal of Personality and Social Psychology, 50,* 800–807.

McCaulley, M. H. (1990). The Myers-Briggs Type Indicator: A measure for individuals and groups. *Measurement and Evaluation in Counseling and Development, 22,* 181–195.

McClain, E. (1970). Further validation of the Personal Orientation Inventory: Assessment of self-actualization of school counselors. *Journal of Consulting and Clinical Psychology, 35,* 21–22.

McClelland, D. C. (1961). *The achieving society.* New York: Free Press.

McClelland, D. C. (1965a). N achievement and entrepreneurship: A longitudinal study. *Journal of Personality and Social Psychology, 1,* 389–392.

McClelland, D. C. (1965b). Toward a theory of motive acquisition. *American Psychologist, 20,* 321–333.

McClelland, D. C. (1979). *The need for power and sympathetic nervous system arousal.* Paper presented at the meeting of the Society for Psychophysiological Research, Cincinnati, OH.

McClelland, D. C. (1985). *Human motivation.* Glenview, IL: Scott, Foresman.

McClelland, D. C. (1987). Characteristics of successful

entrepreneurs. *Journal of Creative Behavior, 3,* 219–233.

McClelland, D. C., Atkinson, J. W., Clark, R. A., & Lowell, E. L. (1953). *The achievement motive.* New York: Appleton-Century-Crofts.

McClelland, D. C., David, W. N., Kalin, R., & Wanner, E. (1972). *The drinking man.* New York: Free Press.

McClelland, D. C., Koestner, R., & Weinberger, J. (1989). How do self-attributed and implicit motives differ? *Psychological Review, 96,* 690–702.

McClelland, D. C., & Pilon, D. A. (1983). Sources of adult motives in patterns of parent behavior in early childhood. *Journal of Personality and Social Psychology, 44,* 564–574.

McClelland, D. C., & Winter, D. G. (1969). *Motivating economic achievement.* New York: Free Press.

McCrae, R. R., & Costa, P. T., Jr. (1985). Updating Norman's "adequate taxonomy": Intelligence and personality dimensions in natural language and questionnaires. *Journal of Personality and Social Psychology, 49,* 710–721.

McCrae, R. R., & Costa, P. T., Jr. (1986). Clinical assessment can benefit from recent advances in personality psychology. *American Psychologist, 41,* 1001–1003.

McCrae, R. R., & Costa, P. T., Jr. (1987). Validation of the five-factor model of personality across instruments and observers. *Journal of Personality and Social Psychology, 52,* 81–90.

McCrae, R. R., & Costa, P. T., Jr. (1989). Reinterpreting the Myers-Briggs Type Indicator from the perspective of the five-factor model of personality. *Journal of Personality, 57,* 17–40.

McCrae, R. R., & Costa, P. T., Jr. (1991). Adding *Liebe und Arbeit*: The full five-factor model and well-being. *Personality and Social Psychology Bulletin, 17,* 227–232.

McGonaghy, M. J. (1979). Gender permanence and the genital basis of gender: Stages in the development of constancy of gender identity. *Child Development, 50,* 1223–1226.

McLeod, B. (1986, October). Rx for health: A dose of self-confidence. *Psychology Today,* pp. 46–50.

McReynolds, P. (1989). Diagnosis and clinical assessment: Current status and major issues. *Annual Review of Psychology, 40,* 83–108.

Medinnus, G., & Curtis, F. (1963). The relation between maternal self-acceptance and child acceptance. *Journal of Counseling Psychology, 27,* 542–544.

Meichenbaum, D., & Gilmore, J. B. (1984). The nature of unconscious processes: A cognitive-behavioral perspective. In K. Bowers & D. Meichenbaum (Eds.), *The unconscious reconsidered.* New York: Wiley.

Melamed, B. G., & Siegel, L. J. (1975). Reduction of anxiety in children facing hospitalization and surgery by use of filmed modeling. *Journal of Consulting and Clinical Psychology, 43,* 511–521.

Mellor, S. (1989). Gender differences in identity formation as a function of self-other relationships. *Journal of Youth and Adolescence, 18,* 361–375.

Mellor, S. (1990). How do only children differ from other children? *Journal of Genetic Psychology, 151,* 221–230.

Mellstrom, M., Jr., Cicala, G. A., & Zuckerman, M. (1976). General versus specific trait anxiety measures in the prediction of fear of snakes, heights and darkness. *Journal of Consulting and Clinical Psychology, 44,* 83–91.

Messer, S. B. (1986). Behavioral and psychoanalytic perspectives at therapeutic choice points. *American Psychologist, 41,* 1261–1272.

Messer, S. B., & Warren, S. (1990). Personality change and psychotherapy. In L. A. Pervin (Ed.), *Handbook of personality: Theory and research* (pp. 371–398). New York: Guilford Press.

Mikulincer, M. (1986). Attributional processes in the learned helplessness paradigm: Behavioral effects of global attributions. *Journal of Personality and Social Psychology, 51,* 1248–1256.

Mikulincer, M., & Nizan, B. (1988). Causal attribution, cognitive interference, and the generalization of learned helplessness. *Journal of Personality and Social Psychology, 55,* 470–478.

Milgram, N. A. (1971). Locus of control in Negro and white children at four age levels. *Psychological Reports, 29,* 459–465.

Miller, N., & Maruyama, G. (1976). Ordinal position and peer popularity. *Journal of Personality and Social Psychology, 33,* 123–131.

Mindess, H. (1988). *Makers of psychology: The personal factor.* New York: Human Sciences Press.

Miner, J. B. (1984). The validity and usefulness of theories in an emerging organizational science. *Academy of Management Review, 9,* 296–306.

Mischel, W. (1968). *Personality and assessment.* New York: Wiley.

Mischel, W. (1973). Toward a cognitive social-learning reconceptualization of personality. *Psychological Review, 80,* 252–283.

Mittelman, W. (1991). Maslow's study of self-actualization: A reinterpretation. *Journal of Humanistic Psychology, 31*(1), 114–135.

Moraglia, G. (1991). The unconscious in information processing and analytical psychology. *Journal of Analytical Psychology, 36,* 27–36.

Morehouse, R. E., Farley, F., & Youngquist, J. V. (1990). Type T personality and the Jungian classification system. *Journal of Personality Assessment, 54,* 231–235.

Moreland, K. L. (1990). Some observations on computer-assisted psychological testing. *Journal of Personality Assessment, 55,* 820–823.

Morey, L. C. (1987). Observations on the meeting between Allport and Freud. *Psychoanalytic Review, 74*(1), 135–139.

Morgan, C. D., & Murray, H. A. (1935). A method for investigating fantasies. *Archives of Neurology and Psychiatry, 34,* 289–306.

Moskowitz, D. S., & Schwartzman, A. E. (1989). Life paths of aggressive and withdrawn children. In D. M. Buss & N. Cantor (Eds.), *Personality psychology: Recent trends and emerging directions* (pp. 99–114). New York: Springer-Verlag.

Motley, M. T. (1985). Slips of the tongue. *Scientific American, 253,* 116–127.

Motley, M. T. (1987, February). What I meant to say. *Psychology Today,* pp. 24–28.

Motley, M. T., Camden, C. T., & Baars, B. J. (1979). Personality and situational influences upon verbal slips: A laboratory test of Freudian and prearticulatory editing hypotheses. *Human Communication Research, 5,* 195–202.

Mozdzierz, G. J., Greenblatt, R. L., & Murphy, T. J. (1988). Further validation of the Sulliman Scale of Social Interest and the Social Interest Scale. *Individual Psychology, 44,* 30–34.

Mueller, P., & Major, B. (1989). Self-blame, self-efficacy, and adjustment to abortion. *Journal of Personality and Social Psychology, 57,* 1059–1068.

Multon, K. D., Brown, S. D., & Lent, R. W. (1991). Relation of self-efficacy beliefs to academic outcomes: A meta-analytic investigation. *Journal of Counseling Psychology, 38,* 30–38.

Murray, H. A. (1938). *Explorations in personality: A clinical and experimental study of fifty men of college age.* New York: Oxford University Press.

Murray, H. A. (1940). What should psychologists do about psychoanalysis? *Journal of Abnormal and Social Psychology, 35,* 150–175.

Murray, H. A. (1951). Some basic psychological assumptions and conceptions. *Dialectica, 5,* 266–292.

Murray, H. A. (1967). Autobiography. In E. G. Boring & G. Lindzey (Eds.), *A history of psychology in autobiography* (Vol. 5, pp. 283–310). New York: Appleton-Century-Crofts.

Naditch, M. P. (1975). Locus of control and drinking behavior in a sample of men in army basic training. *Journal of Consulting and Clinical Psychology, 43,* 96.

Needs, A. (1988). Psychological investigations of offending behaviour. In F. Fransella & L. Thomas (Eds.), *Experimenting with personal construct psychology* (pp. 493–506). London: Routledge & Kegan Paul.

Neher, A. (1991). Maslow's theory of motivation: A critique. *Journal of Humanistic Psychology, 31*(3), 89–112.

Neimeyer, G. J. (1984). Cognitive complexity and marital satisfaction. *Journal of Social and Clinical Psychology, 2,* 258–263.

Neimeyer, G. J., & Rareshide, M. B. (1991). Personal memories and personal identity: The impact of ego identity development on autobiographical memory recall. *Journal of Personality and Social Psychology, 60,* 562–569.

Neubauer, P. B., & Neubauer, A. (1990). *Nature's blueprint: The new genetics of personality.* Reading, MA: Addison-Wesley.

Nolen-Hoeksema, S., Girgus, J., & Seligman, M. E. P. (1987). Learned helplessness in children: A longitudinal study of depression, achievement, and explanatory style. *Journal of Personality and Social Psychology, 51,* 435.

Norman, W. T. (1963). Toward an adequate taxonomy of personality attributes: Replicated factor structure in peer nomination personality ratings. *Journal of Abnormal and Social Psychology, 66,* 574–583.

Nowicki, S., & Duke, M. P. (1983). The Nowicki-Strickland life-span locus of control scales: Construct validation. In H. M. Lefcourt (Ed.), *Research with the locus of control construct* (Vol. 2, pp. 13–51). Orlando, FL: Academic Press.

Nowicki, S., & Roundtree, J. (1974). Correlates of locus of control in secondary age students. *Developmental Psychology, 10,* 33–37.

Nowicki, S., & Strickland, B. R. (1973). A locus of control scale for children. *Journal of Consulting Psychology, 40,* 148–154.

O'Brien, R. M., Dickinson, A. M., & Rosow, M. P. (Eds.). (1982). *Industrial behavior modification: A management handbook.* Elmsford, NY: Pergamon Press.

Ochse, R., & Plug, C. (1986). Cross-cultural investigation of the validity of Erikson's theory of personality development. *Journal of Personality and Social Psychology, 50,* 1240–1252.

Olweus, D. (1979). The stability of aggressive reaction patterns in human males: A review. *Psychological Bulletin, 86,* 852–875.

O'Neill, R. M., & Bornstein, R. F. (1990). Oral-dependence and gender: Factors in help-seeking response set and self-reported pathology in psychiatric inpatients. *Journal of Personality Assessment, 55,* 28–40.

Orgler, H. (1963). *Alfred Adler, the man and his work:*

Triumph over the inferiority complex. New York: New American Library.

Orlofsky, J. L., & Frank, M. (1986). Personality structure as viewed through early memories and identity status in college men and women. *Journal of Personality and Social Psychology, 50,* 580–586.

Orlofsky, J. L., Marcia, J. E., & Lesser, I. M. (1973). Ego identity status and the intimacy versus isolation crisis of young adulthood. *Journal of Personality and Social Psychology, 27,* 211–219.

OSS Assessment Staff. (1948). *Assessment of men: Selection of personnel for the U.S. Office of Strategic Services.* New York: Rinehart.

Overmier, J. B., & Seligman, M. E. P. (1967). Effects of inescapable shock upon subsequent escape and avoidance learning. *Journal of Comparative and Physiological Psychology, 63,* 28–33.

Paige, J. M. (1966). Letters from Jenny: An approach to the clinical analysis of personality structure by computer. In P. J. Stone (Ed.), *The general inquirer: A computer approach to content analysis.* Cambridge, MA: MIT Press.

Parkes, K. R. (1986). Coping in stressful episodes: The role of individual differences, environmental factors, and situational characteristics. *Journal of Personality and Social Psychology, 51,* 1277–1292.

Parkinson, B., & Lea, M. (1991). Investigating personal constructs of emotions. *British Journal of Psychology, 82,* 73–86.

Paulhus, D., & Shaffer, D. R. (1981). Sex differences in the impact of number of younger and number of older siblings on scholastic aptitude. *Social Psychology Quarterly, 44,* 363–368.

Paunonen, S. V., Jackson, D. N., & Keinonen, M. (1990). The structured nonverbal assessment of personality. *Journal of Personality, 58,* 481–502.

Pervin, L. A. (1984). *Current controversies and issues in personality* (2nd ed.). New York: Wiley.

Pervin, L. A. (1990). A brief history of modern personality theory. In L. A. Pervin (Ed.), *Handbook of personality: Theory and research* (pp. 3–18). New York: Guilford Press.

Peterson, B. E., & Stewart, A. J. (1990). Using personal and fictional documents to assess psychosocial development: A case study of Vera Brittain's generativity. *Psychology and Aging, 5,* 400–411.

Peterson, C., & Barrett, L. C. (1987). Explanatory style and academic performance among college freshmen. *Journal of Personality and Social Psychology, 53,* 603–607.

Peterson, C., & Seligman, M. E. P. (1987). Explanatory style and illness. Special issue: Personality and physical health. *Journal of Personality, 55,* 237–265.

Peterson, C., Seligman, M. E. P., & Vaillant, G. (1988).

Pessimistic explanatory style as a risk factor for physical illness: A 35-year longitudinal study. *Journal of Personality and Social Psychology, 55,* 23–27.

Peterson, C., Semmel, A., von Baeyer, C., Abramson, L. Y., Metalsky, G. I., & Seligman, M. E. P. (1982). The Attributional Style Questionnaire. *Cognitive Therapy and Research, 6,* 287–300.

Petrosky, M. J., & Birkhimer, J. C. (1991). The relationship among locus of control coping styles and psychological symptom reporting. *Journal of Clinical Psychology, 47,* 336–345.

Pettigrew, T. F. (1990). A bold stroke for personality a half century ago [Review of *Personality: A psychological interpretation*]. *Contemporary Psychology, 35,* 533–536.

Phares, E. J. (1976). *Locus of control in personality.* Morristown, NJ: General Learning Press.

Phillips, D. P. (1974). The influence of suggestion on suicide: Substantive and theoretical implications of the Werther effect. *American Sociological Review, 39,* 340–354.

Phillips, D. P. (1983). The impact of mass media violence on U.S. homicides. *American Sociological Review, 48,* 560–568.

Phillips, D. P. (1985). The found experiment: A new technique for assessing impact of mass media violence on real-world aggressive behavior. In G. Comstock (Ed.), *Public communication and behavior* (Vol. 1). New York: Academic Press.

Piedmont, R. L. (1988). The relationship between achievement motivation, anxiety, and situational characteristics on performance on a cognitive task. *Journal of Research in Personality, 22,* 177–187.

Piedmont, R. L., McCrae, R. R., & Costa, P. T., Jr. (1991). Adjective Check List Scales and the five-factor model. *Journal of Personality and Social Psychology, 60,* 630–637.

Pilkington, C. J., Richardson, D. R., & Utley, M. E. (1988). Is conflict stimulating? Sensation seekers' responses to interpersonal conflict. *Personality and Social Psychology Bulletin, 14,* 596–603.

Plomin, R. (1990). *Nature and nurture: An introduction to human behavioral genetics.* Pacific Grove, CA: Brooks/Cole.

Plomin, R., Chipuer, H. M., & Loehlin, J. C. (1990). Behavioral genetics and personality. In L. A. Pervin (Ed.), *Handbook of personality: Theory and research* (pp. 225–243). New York: Guilford Press.

Plomin, R., DeFries, J. C., & McClearn, G. E. (1990). *Behavioral genetics: A primer* (2nd ed.). New York: W. H. Freeman.

Plomin, R., Lichtenstein, P., Pedersen, N. L., McClearn, G. E., & Nesselroade, J. R. (1990). Genetic influence on life events during the last half of the life span. *Psychology and Aging, 5,* 25–30.

Plomin, R., Pedersen, N. L., McClearn, G. E., Nesselroade, J. R., & Bergeman, C. S. (1988). EAS temperaments during the last half of the life span: Twins reared apart and twins reared together. *Psychology and Aging, 3,* 43–50.

Podd, M. H., Marcia, J. E., & Rubin, R. (1968). The effects of ego identity status and partner perception on a prisoner's dilemma game. *Journal of Social Psychology, 82,* 117–126.

Porter, L. A. (1961). A study of perceived need satisfactions in bottom and middle management jobs. *Journal of Applied Psychology, 45,* 1–10.

Porter, L. A. (1963). Job attitudes in management: II. Perceived importance of needs as a function of job level. *Journal of Applied Psychology, 47,* 141–148.

Potkay, C. R., & Allen, B. P. (1986). *Personality: Theory, research, and applications.* Pacific Grove, CA: Brooks/Cole.

Quinn, S. (1987). *A mind of her own: The life of Karen Horney.* New York: Summit Books.

Rabin, A. I., Aronoff, J., Barclay, A. M., & Zucker, R. A. (Eds.). (1981). *Further explorations in personality.* New York: Wiley.

Rabin, A. I., Zucker, R. A., Emmons, R. A., & Frank, S. (Eds.). (1990). *Studying persons and lives.* New York: Springer.

Raynor, J. O. (1970). Relationships between achievement-related motives, future orientation, and academic performance. *Journal of Personality and Social Psychology, 15,* 28–33.

Reimanis, G. (1974). Personality development, anomie, and mood. *Journal of Personality and Social Psychology, 29,* 355–357.

Repucci, N. D., & Saunders, J. T. (1974). Social psychology of behavior modification: Problems of implementation in natural settings. *American Psychologist, 29,* 649–660.

Reuman, D. A., Alwin, D. F., & Veroff, J. (1984). Assessing the validity of the achievement motive in the presence of random measurement error. *Journal of Personality and Social Psychology, 47,* 1347–1362.

Rice, B. (1968, March 17). Skinner agrees he is the most important influence in psychology. *New York Times Magazine,* pp. 27ff.

Riggio, R. E., & Friedman, H. S. (1986). Impression formation: The role of expressive behavior. *Journal of Personality and Social Psychology, 50,* 421–427.

Riggio, R. E., Lippa, R., & Salinas, C. (1990). The display of personality in expressive movement. *Journal of Research in Personality, 24,* 16–31.

Roazen, P. (1975). *Freud and his followers.* New York: Knopf.

Robbins, P. R., Tanck, R. H., & Houshi, F. (1985). Anxiety and dream symbolism. *Journal of Personality, 53,* 17–22.

Rogers, C. R. (1954). The case of Mrs. Oak: A research analysis. In C. R. Rogers & R. F. Dymond (Eds.), *Psychotherapy and personality change.* Chicago: University of Chicago Press.

Rogers, C. R. (1961). *On becoming a person: A therapist's view of psychotherapy.* Boston: Houghton Mifflin.

Rogers, C. R. (1967). Autobiography. In E. G. Boring & G. Lindzey (Eds.), *A history of psychology in autobiography* (Vol. 5, pp. 341–384). New York: Appleton-Century-Crofts.

Rogers, C. R. (1970). *Carl Rogers on encounter groups.* New York: Harper & Row.

Rogers, C. R. (1974). In retrospect: Forty-six years. *American Psychologist, 29,* 115–123.

Rogers, C. R. (1980). *A way of being.* Boston: Houghton Mifflin.

Rogers, C. R. (1987). An interview with Carl Rogers. In A. O. Ross, *Personality: The scientific study of complex human behavior* (pp. 118–119). New York: Holt, Rinehart & Winston.

Rosenthal, D. R., Gurney, M. R., & Moore, S. M. (1981). From trust to intimacy: A new inventory for examining Erikson's stages of psychosocial development. *Journal of Youth and Adolescence, 10,* 525–536.

Rosenzweig, S. (1985). Freud and experimental psychology: The emergence of idiodynamics. In S. Koch & D. Leary (Eds.), *A century of psychology as science* (pp. 135–207). New York: McGraw-Hill.

Ross, M. (1989). Relation of implicit theories to the construction of personal histories. *Psychological Review, 96,* 341–357.

Rotter, J. B. (1954). *Social learning and clinical psychology.* Englewood Cliffs, NJ: Prentice-Hall.

Rotter, J. B. (1966). Generalized expectancies for internal versus external control of reinforcement. *Psychological Monographs, 80* (Whole No. 609).

Rotter, J. B. (1967). A new scale for the measurement of interpersonal trust. *Journal of Personality, 35,* 651–665.

Rotter, J. B. (1975). Some problems and misconceptions related to the construct of internal versus external control of reinforcement. *Journal of Consulting and Clinical Psychology, 43,* 56–57.

Rotter, J. B. (1980). Interpersonal trust, trustworthiness, and gullibility. *American Psychologist, 35,* 1–7.

Rotter, J. B. (1982). *The development and applications of social learning theory: Selected papers.* New York: Praeger.

Rotter, J. B. (1990). Internal versus external control of reinforcement: A case history of a variable. *American Psychologist, 45,* 489–493.

Rotter, J. B., Chance, J. E., & Phares, E. J. (1972). *Applications of a social learning theory of personality.* New York: Holt, Rinehart & Winston.

Rotter, J. B., & Rafferty, J. E. (1950). *Manual: The Rotter Incomplete Sentences Blank.* San Antonio, TX: Psychological Corporation.

Rowe, D. C. (1987). Resolving the person-situation debate: Invitation to an interdisciplinary dialogue. *American Psychologist, 42,* 218–227.

Rowe, D. C., & Plomin, R. (1981). The importance of nonshared (E₁) environmental influences in behavioral development. *Developmental Psychology, 17,* 517–531.

Rubins, J. L. (1978). *Karen Horney: Gentle rebel of psychoanalysis.* New York: Dial Press.

Rushton, J. P., Fulker, D. W., Neale, M. C., Blizard, R. A., & Eysenck, H. J. (1984). Altruism and genetics. *Acta Geneticae et Gemellologiae, 33,* 265–271.

Ryckman, R. M., & Malikiosi, M. X. (1975). Relationship between locus of control and chronological age. *Psychological Reports, 36,* 655–658.

Sappington, H. A. (1990). Recent psychological approaches to the free will versus determinism issue. *Psychological Bulletin, 108,* 19–29.

Sarason, I. G. (1975a). Anxiety and self-preoccupation. In I. G. Sarason & C. D. Spielberger (Eds.), *Stress and anxiety* (Vol. 2, pp. 27–44). Washington, DC: Hemisphere.

Sarason, I. G. (1975b). Test anxiety and the self-disclosing coping model. *Journal of Consulting and Clinical Psychology, 43,* 148–153.

Saunders, F. (1991). *Mother's light, daughter's journey: Katharine and Isabel.* Palo Alto, CA: Consulting Psychologists Press.

Sayers, J. (1991). *Mothers of psychoanalysis: Helene Deutsch, Karen Horney, Anna Freud, Melanie Klein.* New York: Norton.

Scarr, S. (1968). Environmental bias in twin studies. *Eugenics Quarterly, 15,* 34–40.

Schachter, S. (1959). *The psychology of affiliation.* Stanford, CA: Stanford University Press.

Schachter, S. (1963). Birth order, eminence, and higher education. *American Sociological Review, 28,* 757–767.

Schachter, S. (1964). Birth order and sociometric choice. *Journal of Abnormal and Social Psychology, 68,* 453–456.

Schnur, R. E., & MacDonald, M. L. (1988). Stages of identity development and problem drinking in college women. *Journal of Youth and Adolescence, 17,* 349–369.

Schuerger, J. M., Zarrella, K. L., & Hotz, A. S. (1989). Factors that influence the temporal stability of personality by questionnaire. *Journal of Personality and Social Psychology, 56,* 777–783.

Schultz, D. P. (1990). *Intimate friends, dangerous rivals: The turbulent relationship between Freud and Jung.* Los Angeles: Tarcher.

Schur, M. (1972). *Freud: Living and dying.* New York: International Universities Press.

Sechrest, L. (1968). Personal constructs and personal characteristics. *Journal of Individual Psychology, 24,* 162–166.

Sechrest, L. (1984). Review of J. B. Rotter's *The development and applications of social learning theory: Selected papers. Journal of the History of the Behavioral Sciences, 20,* 228–230.

Sechrest, L., & Jackson, D. N. (1961). Social intelligence and accuracy of interpersonal predictions. *Journal of Personality, 29,* 169–182.

Seeman, M., Seeman, T., & Sayles, M. (1985). Social networks and health status: A longitudinal analysis. *Social Psychology Quarterly, 48,* 237–248.

Seligman, M. E. P. (1975). *Helplessness: On depression, development, and death.* San Francisco: W. H. Freeman.

Seligman, M. E. P. (1976). *Learned helplessness and depression in animals and men.* Morristown, NJ: General Learning Press.

Seligman, M. E. P. (1990). *Learned optimism.* New York: Knopf.

Seligman, M. E. P., & Maier, S. F. (1967). Failure to escape traumatic shock. *Journal of Experimental Psychology, 74,* 1–9.

Seligman, M. E. P., & Visintainer, M. (1985). Tumor rejection and early experience of uncontrollable shock in the rat. In F. R. Brush & J. B. Overmier (Eds.), *Affect, conditioning, and cognition: Essays on the determinants of behavior* (pp. 203–210). Hillsdale, NJ: Erlbaum.

Shamir, B. (1986). Self-esteem and the psychological impact of unemployment. *Social Psychology Quarterly, 49,* 61–72.

Shaw, R., & Colimore, K. (1988). Humanistic psychology as ideology: An analysis of Maslow's contradictions. *Journal of Humanistic Psychology, 28*(3), 51–74.

Shevrin, H. (1977). Some assumptions of psychoanalytic communication: Implications of subliminal research for psychoanalytic method and technique. In N. Freedman & S. Grand (Eds.), *Communicative structures and psychic structures.* New York: Plenum.

Shostrom, E. L. (1964). An inventory for the measurement of self-actualization. *Educational and Psychological Measurement, 24,* 207–218.

Shostrom, E. L. (1974). *Manual for the Personal Orientation Inventory.* San Diego, CA: Educational and Industrial Testing Service.

Shostrom, E. L. (1975). *Personal orientation dimensions.*

San Diego, CA: Educational and Industrial Testing Service.

Shostrom, E. L., & Knapp, R. R. (1966). The relationship of a measure of self-actualization (POI) to a measure of pathology (MMPI) and to therapeutic growth. *American Journal of Psychotherapy, 20,* 193–202.

Siegelman, M. (1988). "Origins" of extroversion-introversion. *Journal of Psychology, 69,* 85–91.

Silverman, L. H. (1976). Psychoanalytic theory: "The reports of my death are greatly exaggerated." *American Psychologist, 31,* 621–637.

Silverman, L. H. (1983). The subliminal psychodynamic activation method: Overview and comprehensive listing of studies. In J. Masling (Ed.), *Empirical studies in psychoanalysis* (Vol. 1). Hillsdale, NJ: Erlbaum.

Silverman, R. E., & Shrauger, J. S. (1970). *Locus of control and correlates of attraction toward others.* Paper presented at the meeting of the Eastern Psychological Association, Atlantic City, NJ.

Sims, J. H., & Baumann, D. D. (1972). The tornado threat: Coping styles of the north and south. *Science, 176,* 1386–1392.

Skinner, B. F. (1938). *The behavior of organisms: An experimental analysis.* New York: Appleton-Century.

Skinner, B. F. (1948). *Walden Two.* New York: Macmillan.

Skinner, B. F. (1953). *Science and human behavior.* New York: Free Press.

Skinner, B. F. (1967). Autobiography. In E. G. Boring & G. Lindzey (Eds.), *A history of psychology in autobiography* (Vol. 5, pp. 385–413). New York: Appleton-Century-Crofts.

Skinner, B. F. (1971). *Beyond freedom and dignity.* New York: Knopf.

Skinner, B. F. (1974). *About behaviorism.* New York: Knopf.

Skinner, B. F. (1976). *Particulars of my life.* New York: Knopf.

Skinner, B. F. (1979). *The shaping of a behaviorist.* New York: Knopf.

Skinner, B. F. (1983a). *A matter of consequences.* New York: Knopf.

Skinner, B. F. (1983b, September). Origins of a behaviorist. *Psychology Today,* pp. 22–33.

Skinner, B. F. (1987). *Upon further reflection.* Englewood Cliffs, NJ: Prentice-Hall.

Slugoski, B. F., & Ginsburg, G. P. (1989). Ego identity and explanatory speech. In J. Shotter & K. F. Gergen (Eds.), *Texts of identity* (pp. 36–55). London: Sage.

Smith, D. (1986, March 31). What would Freud think? The uproar in the shrine of psychoanalysis. *New York,* pp. 38–45.

Smith, H. L., & Dechter, A. (1991). No shift in locus of control among women during the 1970s. *Journal of Personality and Social Psychology, 60,* 638–640.

Smith J. (1970). Age differences in achievement motivation. *British Journal of Social and Clinical Psychology, 9,* 175–176.

Smith, M. (1980). An analysis of three managerial jobs using repertory grids. *Journal of Management Studies, 17,* 205–213.

Smith, M., & Ashton, D. (1975). Using repertory grid technique to evaluate management training. *Personnel Review, 4*(4), 15–21.

Smith, M. B. (1990). Henry A. Murray (1893–1988): Humanistic psychologist. *Journal of Humanistic Psychology, 30*(1), 6–13.

Smith, R. E. (1989). Effects of coping skills training on generalized self-efficacy and locus of control. *Journal of Personality and Social Psychology, 56,* 228–233.

Spence, J. T. (Ed.). (1983). *Achievement and achievement motives: Psychological and sociological approaches.* New York: W. H. Freeman.

Spence, J. T., & Helmreich, R. L. (1983). Achievement-related motives and behavior. In J. T. Spence (Ed.), *Achievement and achievement motives: Psychological and sociological approaches* (pp. 7–74). New York: W. H. Freeman.

Spranger, E. (1928). *Types of men.* P. J. W. Pigors (Trans.). Halle, Germany: Niemeyer.

Sroufe, L. A., Fox, N. E., & Pancake, V. R. (1983). Attachment and dependency in developmental perspective. *Child Development, 54,* 1615–1627.

Steele, R. S. (1982). *Freud and Jung: Conflicts of interpretation.* London: Routledge & Kegan Paul.

Stelmack, R. M. (1990). Biological bases of extraversion: Psychophysiological evidence. *Journal of Personality, 58,* 293–311.

Stepansky, P. E. (1983). *In Freud's shadow: Adler in context.* New York: Analytic Press.

Stephenson, W. (1953). *The study of behavior: Q-technique and its methodology.* Chicago: University of Chicago Press.

Sterba, R. F. (1982). *Reminiscences of a Viennese psychoanalyst.* Detroit, MI: Wayne State University Press.

Stevens, A. (1990). *On Jung.* London: Routledge.

Stewart, R. A. C. (1968). Academic performance and components of self-actualization. *Perceptual and Motor Skills, 26,* 918.

Stewart, V., & Stewart, A. (1982). *Business applications of repertory grid.* New York: McGraw-Hill.

Stotland, S., & Zuroff, D. C. (1990). A new measure of weight locus of control: The Dieting Beliefs Scale. *Journal of Personality Assessment, 54,* 191–203.

Strassberg, D. S. (1973). Relationships among locus of control, anxiety and valued goal expectations. *Journal of Consulting and Clinical Psychology, 2,* 319.

Stricker, L. J., & Ross, J. (1962). *A description and evaluation of the Myers-Briggs Type Indicator.* Princeton, NJ: Educational Testing Service.

Strickland, B. R. (1978). Internal-external expectancies and health-related behaviors. *Journal of Consulting and Clinical Psychology, 46,* 1192–1211.

Strickland, B. R. (1979). Internal-external expectancies and cardiovascular functioning. In L. C. Perlmutter & R. A. Monty (Eds.), *Choice and perceived control.* Hillsdale, NJ: Erlbaum.

Strickland, B. R. (1989). Internal-external control expectancies: From contingency to creativity. *American Psychologist, 44,* 1–12.

Strickland, B. R., & Haley, W. E. (1980). Sex differences on the Rotter I-E Scale. *Journal of Personality and Social Psychology, 39,* 930–939.

Strumpfer, D. (1970). Fear and affiliation during a disaster. *Journal of Social Psychology, 82,* 263–268.

Styles, I. (1991). Clinical assessment and computerized testing. *International Journal of Man-Machine Studies, 35*(2), 133–150.

Suinn, R., Osborne, D., & Winfree, P. (1962). The self-concept and accuracy of recall of inconsistent self-related information. *Journal of Clinical Psychology, 18,* 473–474.

Sulliman, J. R. (1973). The development of a scale for the measurement of social interest. *Dissertation Abstracts International, 34.* (University Microfilms No. 73–31, 567).

Sulloway, F. J. (1979). *Freud, biologist of the mind: Beyond the psychoanalytic legend.* New York: Basic Books.

Sutton-Smith, B., & Rosenberg, B. C. (1970). *The sibling.* New York: Holt, Rinehart & Winston.

Sweeney, J. A., Clarkin, J. F., & Fitzgibbon, M. L. (1987). Current practice of psychological assessment. *Professional Psychology, 18,* 377–380.

Taylor, K. M., & Betz, N. E. (1983). Applications of self-efficacy theory to the understanding and treatment of career indecision. *Journal of Vocational Behavior, 22,* 63–81.

Tellegen, A., Lykken, D. T., Bouchard, T. J., Wilcox, K., Segal, N., & Rich, S. (1988). Personality similarity in twins reared apart and together. *Journal of Personality and Social Psychology, 54,* 1031–1039.

Tetlock, P. E. (1983). Cognitive style and political ideology. *Journal of Personality and Social Psychology, 45,* 118–126.

Tetlock, P. E. (1984). Cognitive style and political belief systems in the British House of Commons. *Journal of Personality and Social Psychology, 46,* 365–375.

Thomas, A. (1986). The New York Longitudinal Study: From infancy to early adult life. In R. Plomin & J. Dunn (Eds.), *The study of temperament: Changes, continuities and challenges* (pp. 39–52). Hillsdale, NJ: Erlbaum.

Thomas, A., Chess, S., & Korn, S. (1982). The reality of difficult temperament. *Merrill-Palmer Quarterly, 28,* 1–20.

Thomas, D. A. (1989). Measuring volunteers for exciting psychology experiments with the Sensation Seeking Scale. *Journal of Personality Assessment, 53,* 790–801.

Thomas, L., & Cooper, P. (1980). Incidence and psychological correlates of intense spiritual experiences. *Journal of Transpersonal Psychology, 12,* 75–85.

Thompson, T. (1988). Benedictus behavior analysis: B. F. Skinner's magnum opus at fifty [Review of *The behavior of organisms: An experimental analysis*]. *Contemporary Psychology, 33,* 397–402.

Tilander, A. (1991). Why did C. G. Jung write his autobiography? *Journal of Analytical Psychology, 36*(1) 111–124.

Tokar, D. M., & Swanson, J. L. (1991). An investigation of the validity of Helms's (1984) model of white racial identity development. *Journal of Counseling Psychology, 38,* 296–301.

Tribich, D., & Messer, S. (1974). Psychoanalytic character type and states of authority as determiners of suggestibility. *Journal of Consulting and Clinical Psychology, 42,* 842–848.

Trierweiller, S. J. (1990). Flirting with George Kelly [Review of *Experimenting with personal construct psychology*]. *Contemporary Psychology, 35,* 127–128.

Triplet, R. G. (1992). Henry A. Murray: The making of a psychologist? *American Psychologist, 47,* 299–307.

Turner, R. H., & Vanderlippe, R. (1958). Self-ideal consequence as an index of adjustment. *Journal of Abnormal and Social Psychology, 57,* 202–206.

Van DeWater, D., & McAdams, D. P. (1989). Generativity and Erikson's "belief in the species." *Journal of Research in Personality, 23,* 435–449.

Vane, J. R., & Guarnaccia, V. J. (1989). Personality theory and personality assessment measures: How helpful to the clinician? *Journal of Clinical Psychology, 45,* 5–19.

Veroff, J. (1982). Assertive motivation: Achievement versus power. In A. J. Stewart (Ed.), *Motivation and society: A volume in honor of David C. McClelland* (pp. 99–132). San Francisco: Jossey-Bass.

Veroff, J., Depner, C., Kulka, R., & Douvan, E. (1980). Comparison of American motives: 1957 versus 1976. *Journal of Personality and Social Psychology, 39,* 1249–1273.

Veroff, J., Wilcox, S., & Atkinson, J. W. (1953). The achievement motive in high school and college-age women. *Journal of Abnormal and Social Psychology, 48,* 108–119.

Visintainer, M., Volpicelli, J., & Seligman, M. E. P. (1982). Tumor rejection in rats after inescapable or escapable shock. *Science, 216,* 437–439.

Walters, R. H., Bowen, N. V., & Parke, R. D. (1963). Experimentally induced disinhibition of sexual responses. [Cited in A. Bandura & R. H. Walters, *Social learning and personality development.* New York: Holt, Rinehart & Winston]

Waterman, A. S. (1982). Identity development from adolescence to adulthood: An extension of theory and a review of research. *Developmental Psychology, 18,* 341–358.

Waterman, C. K., Buebel, M. E., & Waterman, A. S. (1970). Relationship between resolution of the identity crisis and outcomes of previous psychosocial crises. *Proceedings of the 78th Annual Convention of the American Psychological Association, 5,* 467–468.

Weber, M. (1930). *The Protestant ethic and the spirit of capitalism.* New York: Scribner.

Wehr, G. (1987). *Jung: A biography.* Boston: Shambhala.

Westen, D. (1990). Psychoanalytic approaches to personality. In L. A. Pervin (Ed.), *Handbook of personality: Theory and research* (pp. 21–65). New York: Guilford Press.

Westkott, M. (1986). *The feminist legacy of Karen Horney.* New Haven, CT: Yale University Press.

Wexley, K. N., & Latham, G. P. (1981). *Developing and training human resources in organizations.* Glenview, IL: Scott, Foresman.

Wichern, F., & Nowicki, S. (1976). Independence training practices and locus of control orientation in children and adolescents. *Developmental Psychology, 12,* 77.

Wiedenfeld, S. A., Bandura, A., Levine, S., O'Leary, A., Brown, S., & Raska, K. (1990). Impact of perceived self-efficacy in coping with stressors on components of the immune system. *Journal of Personality and Social Psychology, 59,* 1082–1094.

Wiggins, J. S., & Pincus, A. L. (1992). Personality: Structure and assessment. *Annual Review of Psychology, 43,* 473–504.

Williams, D. E., & Page, M. M. (1989). A multidimensional measure of Maslow's hierarchy of needs. *Journal of Research in Personality, 23,* 192–213.

Wilson, C. (1972). *New pathways in psychology.* New York: Taplinger.

Wilson, G. (1977). Introversion-extroversion. In T. Blass (Ed.), *Personality variables in social behavior.* Hillsdale, NJ: Erlbaum.

Wilson, G. (1978). Introversion/extroversion. In H. London & J. E. Exner, Jr. (Eds.), *Dimensions of personality.* New York: Wiley

Wilson, G. D., Ausman, J., & Mathews, T. R. (1973). Conservatism and art preferences. *Journal of Personality and Social Psychology, 25,* 286–288.

Winter, D. G. (1973). *The power motive.* New York: Free Press.

Winterbottom, M. R. (1958). The relation of need for achievement to learning experiences in independence and mastery. In J. W. Atkinson (Ed.), *Motives in fantasy, action, and society.* Princeton, NJ: Van Nostrand.

Wittels, F. (1924). *Sigmund Freud: His personality, his teaching, and his school.* London: Allen & Unwin.

Wolk, R. L., & Wolk, R. B. (1971). *Manual: Gerontological Apperception Test.* New York: Human Sciences Press.

Wolk, S., & DuCette, J. (1974). Intentional performance and incidental learning as a function of personality and task dimensions. *Journal of Personality and Social Psychology, 29,* 91–101.

Wood, R. E., & Bandura, A. (1989). Social cognitive theory of organizational management. *Academy of Management Review, 14,* 361–384.

Woodward, N. J., & Wallston, B. S. (1987). Age and health care beliefs: Self-efficacy as a mediator of low desire for control. *Psychology and Aging, 2,* 3–8.

Wright, T. L., & Kirmani, A. (1977). Interpersonal trust, trustworthiness, and shoplifting in high school. *Psychological Reports, 41,* 1165–1166.

Wuthnow, R. (1978). Peak experiences: Some empirical tests. *Journal of Humanistic Psychology, 18,* 59–75.

Young-Bruehl, E. (1988). *Anna Freud: A biography.* New York: Summit Books.

Zaccaria, J. S., & Weir, R. W. (1967). A comparison of alcoholics and selected samples of non-alcoholics in terms of a positive concept of mental health. *Journal of Social Psychology, 71,* 151–157.

Zajonc, R. B., Markus, H., & Markus, G. B. (1979). The birth order puzzle. *Journal of Personality and Social Psychology, 37,* 1325–1341.

Zucker, R. A. (1990). Henry Murray's legacy: An epilogue. In A. I. Rabin, R. A. Zucker, R. A. Emmons, & S. Frank (Eds.), *Studying persons and lives* (pp. 335–340). New York: Springer.

Zuckerman, M. (1978). Sensation seeking. In H. London & J. E. Exner, Jr. (Eds.), *Dimensions of personality.* New York: Wiley.

Zuckerman, M. (1979). *Sensation seeking: Beyond the optimal level of arousal.* Hillsdale, NJ: Erlbaum.

Zuckerman, M. (1983). *Biological bases of sensation seeking, impulsivity, and anxiety.* Hillsdale, NJ: Erlbaum.

Zuckerman, M. (1990). The psychophysiology of sensation seeking. *Journal of Personality, 58*(1), 313–345.

Zuckerman, M. (1991). *Psychobiology of personality.* New York: Cambridge University Press.

Zuckerman, M., Buchsbaum, M. S., & Murphy, D. L. (1980). Sensation seeking and its biological correlates. *Psychological Bulletin, 88,* 187–214.

Zuckerman, M., Eysenck, S., & Eysenck, H. J. (1978). Sensation seeking in England and America: Cross-cultural, age and sex comparisons. *Journal of Consulting and Clinical Psychology, 46,* 139–149.

Zullow, H., & Seligman, M. E. P. (1985). Pessimistic ruminations predict increase in depressive symptoms. Unpublished manuscript. [Cited in D. L. Rosenhan & M. E. P. Seligman, *Abnormal psychology* (2nd ed.). New York: Norton]

Zuroff, D. C. (1980). Learned helplessness in humans: An analysis of learning processes and the roles of individual and situational differences. *Journal of Personality and Social Psychology, 39,* 130–146.

Zuroff, D. C. (1986). Was Gordon Allport a trait theorist? *Journal of Personality and Social Psychology, 51,* 993–1000.

Abdallah, T. M., 422
Ability traits, 223
Abraham, K., 134
Abramson, L. Y., 453
Achenbach, T., 318
Achievement motivation, 430–440
Activity temperament, 239–243
Adams, D., 8
Adams, G. R., 268
Adams, N. E., 396
Adams-Webber, J. R., 342
Adjective Check List, 315
Adler, A., 99, 104–129, 135, 140, 277, 279, 409
Adolescence, personality development in, 56, 89, 208, 228, 257, 263, 266–267, 393
Adulthood, personality development in, 89–92, 209–210, 228, 257–259, 268, 393–394, 435
Affiliation need, 189
Affonso, D. D., 263
Age differences, 343–344, 437, 441, 449
Aggressive behavior, 384–386, 403
Aggressive drive, 42, 65
Aggressive personality type, 139–140, 162
Agnew, J., 342
Agreeableness trait, 238–239
Alcoholism, 124–125, 190, 422, 442
Alexander, I. E., 78
Allen, B. P., 315
Allen, K. D., 397

Allison, D. 342
Allport, F., 201
Allport, G., 8, 125, 169, 197–218, 235
Alwin, D. F., 433
Anal complexes, 183
Anal personality types, 52–53, 65, 163
Anal stage of psychosexual development, 52–53
Analytical psychology, 76
Anastasi, A., 188
Anderson, J. W., 174–177, 193, 200
Anderson, N. R., 343
Anima/animus archetypes, 86–87, 91
Animal subjects, 353
Ansbacher, H. L., 129
Anxiety, 46–50, 136–137, 309, 396–397
Archer, R. P., 13
Archer, S. L., 268
Archetypes, 86–88
Ardrey, R., 65
Armstrong, T., 294
Ashton, D., 343
Asian subjects, 421, 441
Asta, P. 294
Atkins, C. J., 402
Atkinson, J. W., 23, 431, 432, 437
Attentional processes, 388
Attitudes, 203–204, 225, 445
Attribution theory, 453–454
Attributional Style Questionnaire, 453–455

Atwood, G. E., 32, 201
Ausman, J., 234
Authoritarianism, 157, 445
Automaton conformity, 158
Ayllon, T., 366
Azrin, N., 366

Baars, B. J., 374
Bagley, C., 451
Balay, J., 63
Baldwin, A. L., 318
Balloun, J., 296
Baltes, M. M., 449
Bandura, A., 21–22, 65, 374, 381–406, 408, 423
Bannister, D., 342
Barnes, R., 422
Baron, R., 421
Barrett, L. C., 454
Barry, H., 125
Basic anxiety, 136–137
Basic strengths, 259–260
Basic weaknesses, 260–261
Bates, P. B., 449
Batson, C. D., 241
Battle, E., 421
Baumann, D. D., 422
Becona, E., 402
Behavior modeling, 384–388, 392–398, 448–449
Behavior modification, 366–368, 370–372, 394–398
Behavior potential, 410–411
Behavioral choice method, 419
Behavioral genetics, 235
Behavioral observations, 17–18, 371
Behaviorism, 6–7, 352, 357
Being needs, 280
Bellak, L., 186, 188
Bellak, S. S., 188
Belmont, L., 124
Belongingness needs, 282
Bem, D. J., 148
Benassi, V. A., 422
Benedict, R., 279, 292
Bengston, V. L., 401
Ben-Porath, Y. S., 13
Bergeman, C. S., 239
Bergin, A. E., 315
Berkowitz, L., 403
Berry, D. S., 215
Berzonsky, M. D., 267
Bettelheim, B., 41
Betz, N. E., 401, 402
Beyer, J., 396
Bidwell, L. D., 189
Bieri, J., 343
Bigner, J. J., 343
Bijou, S. W., 371
Biophilous character type, 164
Birkhimer, J. C., 422
Birth trauma, 46
Black subjects, 441
Blanchard, E. B., 394

Blane, H. T., 125
Blanton, S., 144
Bleuler, E., 78
Blizard, R. A., 241
Block, J., 318, 401
Blondheim, S. H., 65
Blustein, D. L., 266
Bobo doll research, 384–385
Boggs, K. R., 401
Bonarius, J., 342
Boone, C., 421
Bootzin, R., 367
Bordages, J. W., Jr., 294
Bores-Rangel, E., 401
Bornstein, R. F., 65
Bottome, P., 106
Bouchard, T. J., 237
Bourne, E., 267
Bowen, N. V., 385
Brannigan, G. G., 422
Braun, J., 294
Breger, L., 64, 122
Breland, H. M., 124
Breland, K., 374
Breland, M., 274
Breuer, J., 38, 58
Briggs, K. C., 95
Brittain, V., 264
Brody, L. R., 64
Brody, N., 62
Brome, V., 94
Brown, C. A., 343
Brown, J. B., Jr., 449
Brown, S. D., 402
Brown, S. R., 98
Bruhn, A. R., 123
Bryant, B. L., 124
Buchsbaum, M. S., 445
Buebel, M. E., 266
Buie, J., 13
Burston, D., 134, 164, 166, 171
Buss, A. H., 17, 235, 239–243, 245, 319
Buss, D. M., 32, 238
Butcher, J. N., 13
Butler, J. M., 317
Byrne, D., 421

California Psychological Inventory, 13–14
Camino, L., 403
Cann, D. R., 98
Cantor, N., 409
Cantril, H., 215
Caplan, P. J., 264
Cardinal traits, 203
Carlson, R., 97, 98
Carskadon, T. G., 98
Case study method, 19, 60–62, 96–97, 122, 147–148, 166, 233
Caspi, A., 148
Castration anxiety, 54
Castration complex, 183

Catharsis, 59
Cathexis, 42
Cattell, R. B., 98, 99, 219–235, 237, 245
Central traits, 203
Chan, D. W., 421
Chance, J. E., 416
Chandler, T. A., 422
Character types, 162–168
Charcot, J. M., 38
Cherry, L., 131, 146
Cherry, R., 131, 146
Chess, S., 242
Childhood, personality development in, 28–29, 50–56, 65,
    88–89, 114–117, 134–136, 158–159, 182–183, 206–
    209, 227–228, 253–257, 306–309, 392–393, 417,
    434–437, 446, 454–455
Childhood sexual abuse, 38–39
Children's Apperception Test, 186–188
Children's Industry Questionnaire, 263
Children's Nowicki-Strickland Internal-External Scale, 420
Chipuer, H. M., 243
Chodorkoff, B., 317
Church, A. T., 401
Ciaccio, N., 264
Cicala, G. A., 443
Clark, R. A., 431
Classical conditioning, 447–448
Claustral complex, 182–183
Clemmens, E. R., 149
Client-centered therapy, 301, 313–317
Clinical Analysis Questionnaire, 232
Clinical interviews, 17, 338
Clinical research methods, 19–20, 233
Coan, R. W., 315
Cognitive complexity, 343–344
Cognitive needs, 284–285
Cognitive processes, 204, 326–328, 343–344, 382–383,
    408–413, 444, 454
Cognitive psychology, 327–328
Cognitive simplicity, 343–344
Cohen, S., 189
Coleman, J. S., 421
Colimore, K., 296
Collective unconscious, 85–88
College success, and need achievement, 439–440
Common traits, 222
Compensation, 108
Complexes, 84, 108–110, 182–183
Compliant personality type, 138–139
Computerized test scoring, 14
Conditional positive regard, 307
Conditioned responses, 357–358
Conditioning, 357–358, 447–448
Conditions of worth, 307–308
Conscience, 45, 390
Conscientiousness trait, 238–239
Constantinople, A., 263, 265
Constitutional traits, 223
Construct theory, 330
Construct validity, 12
Constructive alternativism, 331

Content validity, 12
Control group, 21
Cook, B., 422
Cookson, D., 124
Cooper, H. M., 422
Cooper, K., 343
Cooper, P., 295
Coopersmith, S., 318
Coping behavior, 214
Core approach, 412–413
Correlation coefficient, 23
Correlational method, 22–24
Costa, P. T., Jr., 97, 237–239
Côté, J. E., 268
Cowan, D. A., 97
Cowles, M., 236
Cramer, P., 64
Crandall, J. E., 123
Creative self, 112
Crewsdon, J., 39
Crockett, J., 124
Crockett, W. H., 342, 343
Crook, T., 123
Cross, K. P., 233
Crumrine, P. L., 124
Cudhea, D., 383
Curtis, F., 318

Damm, V., 294
Danforth, J. S., 397
Daniels, D., 242
Daniels, M., 296
David, W. N., 190
Davidow, S., 123
Davis, C., 236
Davis, J., 295
Davis, P. J., 64
Death instincts, 42–43
DeBrabander, B., 421
Dechter, A., 421
Defense mechanisms, 47–50, 64
Deficit needs, 280
DeFries, J. C., 242
Dement, W. C., 64
Denial, 48
Dependent variable, 20
Depner, C., 439
Depression, 451–453
Destructiveness, 157
Detached personality type, 140–141, 163
Determinism, 28
Detoy, C. J., 343
Devenis, L. E., 266
DeVito, A. J., 97
Dickinson, A. M., 367
DiClemente, C. C., 402
Dieting Beliefs Scale, 420
Digman, J. M., 237, 248, 245
Dignan, M., 263, 266
Disinhibition, 385–386
Displacement, 49

Doerfler, L. A., 402
Doherty, W., 421
Dollard, J., 65
Domino, G., 263
Donderi, D. C., 98
Doob, L. W., 65
Doty, M. S., 402
Douvan, E., 439
Drabman, R. C., 397
Dream analysis, 59–60, 94–95, 120–121, 147
Dream research, 64, 98–99, 122
Dreikurs, R., 127
Dubow, E., 403
DuCette, J., 422
Duck, S. W., 342
Dufour, C. L., 422
Dugovics, D. A., 422
Duke, M. P., 420
Dynamic lattice, 225
Dynamic traits, 223–225

Eagle, M. N., 61
Early recollections, 119–120, 122–123, 267
EAS Temperament Survey for Adults, 239
EASI Temperament Survey, 18, 239, 319
Eaves, L. J., 237
Edwards Personal Preference Schedule, 188
Ego, 43–46, 81–84, 178–179
Ego-ideal, 45, 178
Ego identity, 257, 263, 266–267
Ego-Identity Scale, 263, 266
Eissler, K. R., 43
Elder, G. H., 439
Electra complex, 54–55
Eliot, J., 123
Ellenberger, H. F., 70, 97, 102, 129
Ellis, R. A., 295
Elms, A. C., 377
Emmons, R. A., 190
Emotionality temperament, 239–243
Empty-organism concept, 353, 365
Encounter groups, 314–315
Enns, C. Z., 32
Entropy principle, 80–81
Environmental-mold traits, 223
Epigenetic principle of maturation, 253
Epting, F. R., 347
Equilibrium/growth issue, 29
Equivalence principle, 80
Equivalent-forms reliability, 11–12
Ergs, 225
Erikson, E. H., 99, 249–271
Erikson, J. M., 259, 260, 269, 271
Eron, L., 403
Esteem needs, 283
Estes, S. G., 215
Ethics, and behavior modification, 397–398
Evans, R. I., 154, 155, 171, 218, 271, 322, 353
Excitation need, 162
Exner, J. E., Jr., 15
Expectancy, 411–414, 419

Experience Inventory, 315
Experiencing Scale, 315
Experiential world, 306, 309, 313, 315
Experimental group, 21
Experimental method, 20–22
Explanatory style, 450–454
Exploitative character type, 162
Expressive behavior, 214–215
External locus of control, 416–417, 419–423
Extraversion, 81–84, 97–98, 235–239, 443
Eysenck, H. J., 96, 124, 235–238, 241, 243, 245, 294, 440, 441, 443, 446
Eysenck, M. W., 235–237
Eysenck, S., 96, 294, 441
Eysenck Personality Inventory, 96, 98, 237

Factor-analytic research, 220–221, 233–234, 237
Fakouri, M. E., 122
Falbo, T., 125
Farley, F., 443
Fear-of-success theory, 437–439
Fear Survey Schedule, 371
Feeling personality type, 82–84
Feminine psychology, 131, 142–145
Fick, C. M., 422
Fictional finalism, 111
Finalism, 110–111
Findley, M. J., 422
Fioravanti, M., 318, 319
First-borns, 114–116, 123–124, 242
Fisher, S., 62
Fiske, D. W., 237, 430
Fitch, S. A., 268
Five-factor theory, 237–239
Fixation, 51
Fixed role therapy, 340
Fjeld, S. P., 342
Floderus-Myrhed, B., 237, 242
Foley, J. M., 268
Folkman, S., 402
Ford, J. G., 319
Forehand, R. L., 124
Fox, J., 294
Fox, N. E., 268
Frame-of-orientation need, 161
Frank, M., 267
Frank, S., 190
Frankie, G., 65
Fransella, F., 342, 347
Franz, C. E., 268
Free association, 58–59, 147
Free will/determinism issue, 28
Freedman, D. G., 241
Freedom of movement, 414–415
Freud, A., 41, 67–68, 250, 251
Freud, S., 7, 15, 19, 35–71, 76–79, 88, 92, 94–97, 99, 102, 105, 107, 111–122, 126, 131–134, 142–149, 159, 162–164, 169, 177–179, 198–200, 431
Freudian slips, 65–66, 134
Friedland, B., 121, 123
Friedman, H. S., 215

Friedman, M. L., 266, 267
Frojan, M. J., 402
Fromm, E., 99, 125, 133, 152–171, 363–364
Fromm-Reichmann, F., 155
Frustration-aggression hypothesis, 65
Fulker, D. W., 241
Fully functioning persons, 309–311, 317
Functional analysis, 370
Functional autonomy of motives, 204–206, 209–210
Funder, D. C., 216

Gamble, G. O., 124
Garcia, M. E., 402
Gates, L., 124
Gauthier, J., 402
Gay, P., 39, 70
Gecas, V., 401, 406
Geen, R. G., 236
Geer, J. H., 371
Gelbort, K. R., 438
Gender differences, 264, 421, 437–439, 441
Gendlin, E. T., 315, 316
Generalized expectancy, 411–412, 419
Generativity, 258–259
Genital complex, 183
Genital stage of psychosexual development, 56
Gerontological Apperception Test, 188
Gestalt psychology, 6
Gilbertini, M., 402
Gilgen, A. R., 374
Gilmore, J. B., 63
Ginsburg, G. P., 269
Girgus, J., 453
Glucksberg, S., 63
Goldberg, L. R., 237
Goleman, D., 64, 367
Gordon, C., 401
Gorer, G., 65
Gossard, D., 402
Gough, H. G., 14, 318, 319
Graham, W., 296
Graves, T. D., 421
Greenberg, R., 62, 122
Greenblatt, R. L., 121
Greever, K., 121, 123
Grieser, C., 122
Grossack, M., 294
Growth needs, 280
Grusec, J. E., 394
Guay, J. A., 422
Guided participation, 395
Gurney, M. R., 269

Habits, 203–204
Hackett, G., 401, 402
Hafner, J. L., 122
Haigh, G. V., 317
Haley, W. E., 421
Hall, C., 64, 148
Hall, D. T., 296
Hall, E., 269

Hall, M. H., 186, 277–279, 299, 352, 353
Hammer, D., 124
Hanewitz, W. B., 97
Hankoff, L. D., 123
Hannah, B., 102
Harrington, D. M., 318
Harrison, R. H., 122
Hartnett, J., 318
Harvey, J. H., 422
Hauk, P. A., 422
Hawkins, R. P., 371
Heath, A. C., 235
Helmreich, R. L., 439
Hendrick, C., 98
Heredity/environment issue, 28
Hetherington, E. M., 65
Hiroto, D. S., 448
Hispanic subjects, 421
Hoarding character type, 162–163
Hobfoll, S. E., 443
Hoffmann, E., 277, 278, 299
Hoffmann, L. W., 438
Holener, D., 63
Holland, J. G., 357
Holmes, D. S., 63
Holtzman, W., 15
Holtzman Inkblot Technique, 15
Horn, J., 241
Horner, M., 437–438
Horney, K., 125, 130–151, 155, 162, 163, 169
Hornstein, G. A., 70
Hostility, 134–136
Houshi, F., 64
Hubbard, J., 124
Huesmann, L., 403
Hulin, C. L., 402
Humanistic psychology, 273
Humanistic socialism, 165
Hunter, I., 64, 122
Hurvich, M. S., 188
Hyman, R. B., 294
Hypnosis, 38

Icarus complex, 183
Id, 43–46, 177–178
Ideal self, 316–318
Idealized self-image, 141–142
Identity crisis, 257, 266–268
Identity need, 161
Idiographic research, 189, 214, 372
Imhof, E. A., 13
Incentive processes, 389–390
Incongruence, 309, 313, 316–318
Independent variable, 20
Individual differences (in constructs), 332
Individual psychology, 105
Individuation, 90
Infancy. See Childhood, personality development in
Inferiority complex, 108
Inferiority feelings, 107–110
Inouye, D. K., 449

Instincts, 41–43
Insupport complex, 182
Internal-External (I-E) Scale, 419–423
Internal locus of control, 416–417, 419–423
Interpersonal trust, 417, 420, 422–423
Interpersonal Trust Scale, 420–421
Introversion, 81–84, 97–98, 235–237
Intuiting personality type, 82–84
Inventory of Psychosocial Balance, 263
Inventory of Psychosocial Development, 263, 265
Irrational functions, 81–82
Ivancevich, J. M., 124

Jackson, D. N., 188, 344
Jackson, M., 122
Jackson Personality Inventory, 188
Jackson Personality Research Form, 188
Jacobson, J. L., 268
Jacoby, L. L., 63
Jaffé, A., 99
Jancowicz, A. D., 343, 347
Jardine, R., 237
Jenkins, S. R., 439
Jenny case study, 212–213
Jew, C., 294
Ji, G., 125
Jiao, S., 125
Jing, Q., 125
Joerger, S. M., 295
Johnson, P. B., 432
Johnson, R. C., 222
Jonah complex, 290
Jones, E., 37, 40, 114
Jorm, A. F., 239
Josselson, R. L., 267
Jung, C., 75–103, 107, 126, 169, 175–176, 228, 443

Kagan, J., 65, 241
Kalin, R., 190
Kamptner, N. L., 266
Kanfer, R., 402
Kaplan, R. M., 402
Katcher, A., 64
Katharina case study, 19
Kazdin, A. E., 367, 395
Kearsley, R., 65
Keinonen, M., 188
Kell, W., 304
Kellaghan, T., 124
Kelley, C. M., 63
Kelly, G., 325–347, 410
Keniston, K., 250
Kidney, B. A., 266
Kidwell, J., 124
Kiesler, D. J., 315
Kiester, E., Jr., 383
King, L. J., 63
Kirmani, A., 423
Kirschenbaum, H., 322
Kivnick, H. Q., 259, 260, 269, 271
Kleiber, D. A., 437

Klein, M. H., 315
Kline, P., 63, 65, 232
Knapp, R., 294
Koestner, R., 430, 432
Korn, S., 242
Kowaz, A. M., 263
Kreitler, H., 196, 218
Kreitler, S., 196, 218
Krüll, M., 39, 54, 70
Kuder Preference Record, 444
Kulka, R., 439

L (life record) data, 230
Labrentz, H. L., 122
Lachman, M. E., 401
Lahey, B. B., 124
Landfield, A. W., 342
Lane, R. W., 64, 122
Langer, E. J., 449
Lapan, R. T., 401
Larsen, R. M., 13
Latané, B., 189
Latency period, 56
Latham, G. P., 367, 402
Laudenslager, M., 450
Lazarus, R. S., 402
Lazzari, R., 318, 319
Learned helplessness, 446–455
Learned optimism, 450–454
Lefcourt, H. M., 422
Lefkowitz, M., 123, 403
LeMay, M., 294
Lens, W., 23
Lent, R. W., 402
Leonard, G., 297
Lerman, H., 70
Lesser, I. M., 267
Levenson, M. R., 443
Levine, C., 268
Levy, N., 97
Levy, S., 451
Lewis, P. H., 96
Leyens, J., 403
Libido, 42, 79–81
Lichtenstein, P., 242
Life-history reconstruction, 96–97
Life instincts, 42
Lifestyles, 111–113
Lindzey, G., 213
Lineberger, M. R., 124
Lippa, R., 215
Lippman, M., 451
Lista, M. J., 402
Locke, E. A., 402
Lockwood, L., 295
Locus of control, 416–417, 419–423
Loeb, R. C., 422
Loehlin, J. C., 241–243
Londerville, S., 268
Lorenz, K., 65
Lowell, E. L., 431, 432

Lubin, B., 13
Lucy case study, 19
Lussieu, G., 294
Luthans, F., 367

Maccoby, M., 166–168
MacDonald, M. L., 266
Maciag, W. S., 367
MacInnis, D. J., 439
Mackavey, W. R., 268
MacNamara, J., 124
Maehr, M. L., 437
Magnusson, D., 9
Mahoney, J., 318
Mahoney, P. J., 61
Maier, S., 448–450
Main, M., 268
Malcolm, J., 39, 40
Maldevelopment, 260
Malikiosi, M. X., 420
Malley, J. E., 268
Malthieu, P. L., 315
Manning, M. M., 402
Maqsud, M., 421
Marcia, J. E., 263, 266–267
Marketing character type, 163, 167
Marshall, G. N., 422
Mariotto, M. J., 18
Markus, G. B., 124
Markus, H., 124
Marolla, F. A., 124
Martin, N. G., 237
Martin, R. A., 422
Maruish, M., 13
Maruyama, G., 125
Masling, J. M., 65
Maslow, A. H., 99, 123, 125, 169, 216, 275–299
Masson, J. M., 39
Matarazzo, J. D., 13
Matheny, A. P., 241
Mathes, E. W., 295
Mathews, T. R., 234
Matteson, M. T., 124
Matthews, K. A., 241
Mattocks, A. L., 294
Maudsley Medical Questionnaire, 237
Maudsley Personality Inventory, 96, 98, 237
Mayo, C. W., 343
McAdams, D. P., 268
McCaul, K. D., 63
McCaulley, M. H., 95, 96
McClain, E., 294
McClearn, G. E., 239, 242
McClelland, D. C., 23, 190, 268, 430–440, 458
McCrae, R. R., 97, 237–239
McGonaghy, M. J., 64
McLeod, B., 402
McNeil, H., 304
Medinnus, G., 318
Meichenbaum, D., 63
Melamed, B. G., 396

Mellor, S., 125, 267
Mellstrom, M., Jr., 443
Menlove, F. L., 394
Messer, S. B., 63, 65
Metamotivation, 285–286
Metaneeds, 286
Metapathology, 286
Mexican village study, 167
Michael, W., 294
Midlife crisis, 89–92, 228, 259
Mikulincer, M., 454
Milgram, N. A., 420
Miller, N., 65, 125
Mindess, H., 4, 32, 356
Miner, J. B., 296
Minimal goal level, 414–415
Minnesota Multiphasic Personality Inventory (MMPI), 13–14
Mischel, W., 9, 385
Mittelman, W., 299
Modeling, 384–388, 392–398, 448–449
Moore, S. M., 269
Moraglia, G., 63
Moral anxiety, 47
Morehouse, R. E., 443
Morey, L. C., 218
Morgan, C. D., 15, 175, 176, 431
Morrill, W. H., 401
Morrow, L., 451
Moskowitz, D. S., 148
Motivation, 204–206, 224–225, 279–286, 388–390
Motley, M. T., 66
Mowrer, O. H., 65
Mozdzierz, G. J., 121
Mrs. Oak case study, 316–318
Multiform assessment program, 184, 188, 189
Multivariate research method, 233
Multon, K. D., 402
Murphy, D. L., 445
Murphy, T. J., 121
Murray, H. A., 8, 15, 23, 99, 172–193, 200, 252, 430, 431
Muten, E. O., 64
Myers, I. B., 95, 96
Myers-Briggs Type Indicator (MBTI), 94–98, 443

Naditch, M. P., 422
Native-American subjects, 421
Nature/nurture issue, 28
Nazi regime, 40, 41, 78, 157, 252, 279
Neale, M. C., 241
Necrophilous character type, 163–164, 168
Need achievement, 430–440
Need potential, 415, 419
Needs, 41–43, 134–138, 160–162, 179–182, 279–285, 415–416 See also Motivation
Needs, A., 343
Needs-hierarchy theory, 279–285
Negative reinforcement, 367–368
Neher, A., 296, 299
Neimeyer, G. J., 267, 342
NEO Personality Inventory, 238

Nesselroade, J. R., 233, 239, 242
Neurotic anxiety, 47
Neurotic needs, 137–138
Neurotic self-image, 141–142
Neurotic trends, 138–141, 148
Neuroticism, 235–239, 444
Neurotransmitters, 445
Nichols, R. C., 242
Nizan, B., 454
Nolen-Hoeksema, S., 453
Nomothetic research, 189, 214, 372
Nonproductive orientations, 162
Nonverbal Personality Questionnaire, 188
Norman, W. T., 237
Nougaim, K. E., 296
Nowicki, S., 420, 422
Nye, R. D., 377

O'Brien, R. M., 367
Object of devotion need, 161
Objective anxiety, 46
Objective tests, 14, 231
Observational learning, 382, 384–390
Ochse, R., 266
Oedipus complex, 53–55, 64, 78, 106, 132, 144, 154, 255
Old age, personality development in, 92, 228, 259, 268, 394
O'Leary, A., 402
Olweus, D., 65
O'Malley, P. M., 23
O'Neill, R. M., 65
Only-born children, 117, 124–125
Openness trait, 238–239
Operant behavior, 358–361
Operant conditioning, 358–361, 366–368, 373
Operant conditioning apparatus (Skinner box), 359–361
Opposition principle, 80
Optimism/pessimism isue, 29–30
Oral complexes, 183
Oral personality types, 52, 65, 162
Oral stage of psychosexual development, 51–52
Organismic valuing process, 305
Organismic trusting, 315
Orgler, H., 106, 129
Orlofsky, J. L., 267
Osborne, D., 317
OSS assessment program, 176, 185–186
Overmier, J. B., 448

Page, M. M., 295
Paige, J. M., 213
Pancake, V. R., 268
Parent-child interaction, 45, 50–56, 123, 134–136, 178, 268, 281–282, 289–290, 306–309, 318, 344, 393, 422, 435–437, 446, 454–455
Parke, R., 385, 403
Parkes, K. R., 239
Past/present issue, 28–29
Paul, G. L., 18
Paulhus, D., 124
Paunonen, S. V., 188

Pavlov, I. P., 356–358
Peak experiences, 288, 295
Peak Scale, 295
Pedersen, N., 237, 239, 242
Penis envy, 54–55, 142–143, 148
Perceptual defense, 317
Perera, S. B., 103
Perfection, 110
Permeability, 335
Perseverative functional autonomy, 205
Person-centered therapy, 301, 313–317
Persona, 7, 86, 90
Personal constructs, 326–347
Personal dispositions, 203
Personal-document technique, 212–213
Personal Orientation Inventory, 293–295
Personal unconscious, 84
Personality assessment, 10–18
Personality definitions, 8–10, 201–202
Personality research methods, 18–24
Personality tests, 9–16
Personality theories, characteristics of, 24–27
Personology, 177
Pervin, L. A., 27, 32, 98, 200
Peterson, B. E., 265
Peterson, C., 451, 453, 454
Peterson, R. F., 371
Petrosky, M. J., 422
Phallic personality types, 55
Phallic stage of psychosexual development, 53–55
Phares, E. J., 416, 417
Phillips, D. P., 403
Phobias, 394–395
Physical health, 402, 422, 450–451
Physiological measurements, 372, 445
Physiological needs, 281
Piedmont, R. L., 238, 432
Pilkington, C. J., 443
Pilon, D. A., 436
Pincus, A. L., 218
Piotrowski, C., 13
Play constructions, 264
Pleasure principle, 44
Plomin, R., 17, 235, 239–243, 245, 319
Plug, C., 266
Podd, M. H., 266
Polit, D. F., 125
Porter, L. A., 295
Positive regard, 307
Positive reinforcement. See Reinforcement
Positive self-regard, 307
Potkay, C. R., 315
Power need, 189–190
Preconscious, 43
Predictive validity, 12
Press (of childhood events), 182
Primary needs, 181
Primary-process thought, 44, 444
Prince, M., 176
Proactive needs, 181
Proceedings, 188

Prochaska, J. O., 402
Production processes, 389
Productive character type, 163
Productive love, 160
Projection, 48
Projective techniques, 14–17
Propriate functional autonomy, 205–206
Proprium, 206–210
Psyche, 80
Psychic birth, 89
Psychic energy, 79–81
Psychoanalysis, 7, 36
Psychohistorical analysis, 263, 264
Psychological situation, 412–413
Psychological types, 82–84, 95–98
Psychosexual development, 50–56
Psychosocial development, 252–259
Psychoticism trait, 235–237
Punishment, 367

Q (questionnaire) data, 230–231
Q sort technique, 316–317
Quinn, S., 131, 142, 149, 151

Rabie, L., 65
Rabin, A. I., 190
Radical behaviorism, 374, 413
Range of convenience, 334
Rank, O., 46
Ranking method, 419
Rareshide, M. B., 267
Raskin, A., 123
Rasmuson, I., 237
Rational functions, 81–82
Rationalization, 49
Raynor, J. O., 432
Reaction formation, 48
Reactive needs, 181
Reality anxiety, 46
Reality principle, 44
Receptive character type, 162
Reciprocal determinism, 398
Reedy, M. N., 401
Reese, L., 396
Reeves, C., 401
Regression, 49
Reichmann, F., 155
Reimanis, G., 265
Reinforcement, 357–365, 387–388, 412
Reinforcement schedules, 361–362
Reinforcement values, 412–415, 419
Reinsch, S., 402
Relatedness need, 160–161
Reliability, 11–12
Rende, R., 245
Repertory grid, 340
Repression, 48
Repucci, N. D., 367
Resistances, 59
Respondent behavior, 357–358, 447
Retention processes, 389

Reuman, D. A., 433
Reversal experimental design, 373
Rewards, 358, 387–388, 412
Rice, B., 374
Rice, K. G., 267
Richardson, D. R., 443
Riggio, R. E., 215
Risk-taking behavior, 440–446
Ritter, B., 395
Roazen, P., 71, 102, 107
Robbins, P. R., 64
Robust personality traits, 238
Rodin, J., 449
Rogers, C. R., 216, 300–322
Role Construct Repertory (REP) Test, 339–343
Rom, T., 443
Rootedness need, 161
Rorschach, H., 15
Rorschach inkblot test, 15–16, 65, 99
Rosenberg, B. C., 124
Rosenkranz, S. A., 367
Rosenman, R. H., 241
Rosenthal, D. R., 269
Rosenthal, T. L., 406
Rosenzweig, S., 62
Rosow, M. P., 367
Ross, D., 384
Ross, J., 97
Ross, M., 32
Ross, S. A., 384
Roter, P. M., 295
Rotter, J. B., 125, 374, 407–425
Rouhani, S., 421
Roundtree, J., 422
Rowe, D. C., 242
Rozek, M. K., 64
Rubin, R., 266
Rubins, J. L., 133, 147
Ruetzel, K., 268
Rushton, J. P., 241, 242
Ryan, S. M., 450
Ryckman, R. M., 420

Safety need, 134–136, 281–282
Saleh, W. E., 422
Salinas, C., 215
Salmon, P., 342
Sarason, I. G., 397, 402
Saunders, F., 95
Saunders, J. T., 367
Sayers, J., 132, 133, 151
Sayles, M., 422
Scarr, S., 241
Schachter, S., 124, 189
Schmitz, J. M., 402
Schnur, R. E., 266
Scholastic Aptitude Test (SAT), 439
Schultz, D. P., 79, 103
Schur, M., 41
Schwartzman, A. E., 148
Schweid, E., 371

Sears, R. R., 65
Sechrest, L., 122, 342, 344, 410
Second-borns, 116
Secondary needs, 181
Secondary-process thought, 44
Secondary traits, 203
Security need, 155–158
Seduction theory, 38–39
Seebauer, E., 403
Seeman, M., 422
Seeman, T., 422
Seever, M., 13
Segal, B., 443
Self, 88, 206–210, 304–309
Self-actualization, 283–290, 292–294, 305, 306, 309–311, 317
Self-characterization sketches, 338, 340
Self-concept, 309, 315–319
Self-control of behavior, 365–366
Self-efficacy, 391–394, 396, 401–402
Self-esteem need, 283
Self-image, 141–142
Self-insight, 304–305
Self-reinforcement, 390–391
Self-report technique, 315, 371–372
Self-report tests, 13–14
Self-sentiment, 225
Self-worth, 307–308
Seligman, M. E. P., 446–455, 458
Senior Apperception Technique, 188
Sensation seeking, 440–446
Sensation Seeking Scale, 440–446
Sensing personality type, 82–84
Sentence-completion technique, 17
Sentiments, 225
Serials, 189
Sex differences, 264, 421, 437–439, 441
Sex drive, 41–42
Shadow archetype, 87–88, 90–91
Shaffer, D. R., 124
Shamir, B., 295
Shaping method, 363–364
Shaw, R., 296
Shevrin, H., 63
Shostrom, E. L., 293, 294
Shrauger, J. S., 422
Siegel, L. J., 396
Siegelman, M., 98
Sign-versus-sample approach, 371
Silverman, L. H., 63
Silverman, R. E., 422
Sims, J. H., 422
Situational variables, 8, 195, 223, 285, 327, 353, 412–413, 446
Sixteen Personality Factor (16PF) Questionnaire, 98, 223–224, 231–233
Skinner, B. F., 7, 351–377, 382, 383, 386, 400, 408, 410, 423
Skinner box, 359–361
Slugoski, B. F., 269
Smith, H. L., 421
Smith, J., 437

Smith, L. D., 377
Smith, M., 343
Smith, M. B., 176, 193
Snake phobia, 394–395
Sociability temperament, 239–243
Social character, 159
Social interest, 113–114, 121, 123, 238, 288
Social Interest Index, 121, 123
Social Interest Scale, 121, 123
Social learning, 382, 408
Source traits, 223–224, 231
Spearman, C. E., 221
Spence, J. T., 438, 439
Spencer, C., 342
Split-halves reliability, 11–12
Spranger, E., 213
Sroufe, L. A., 268
Standardization, 10–11
Steele, R. S., 27
Stelmack, R. M., 236
Stepansky, P. E., 113, 129
Stephenson, W., 316
Sterba, R. F., 126
Stern, P. J., 102
Stewart, A., 265, 268, 343
Stewart, R. A. C., 294
Stewart, V., 343
Stimulus variable, 20
Stotland, S., 420
Strassberg, D. S., 422
Stricker, L. J., 97
Strickland, B. R., 420–422, 425
Strong Vocational Interest Blank, 445
Strumpfer, D., 189
Strupp, H. H., 315
Study of Values, 212–214
Style of life, 111–113
Styles, I., 32
Subjective tests, 13–16, 231
Sublimation, 49
Subliminal perception, 63–64
Subsidiation, 182, 225
Successive approximation, 363–364
Suinn, R., 317
Sulliman, J. R., 121
Sulliman Scale of Social Interest, 121
Sulloway, F. J., 43, 71
Superego, 45–46, 178, 390
Superiority complex, 109–110
Superiority drive, 110–111
Superstitious behavior, 364–365
Surface traits, 223
Sutton-Smith, B., 124
Swanson, J. L., 294
Sweeney, P. D., 422
Symbiotic relatedness, 159
Symptom analysis, 94
Szendre, D., 401

T (test) data, 231
Tanck, R. H., 64
Taylor, C. B., 402

Taylor, K. M., 401
Taylor, M. S., 295
Teasdale, J. D., 453
Television viewing, and behavior, 386, 388, 390, 403
Tellegen, A., 237
Temperament traits, 223
Temperaments, 239–243, 319
Tension reduction, 41–42
Tesiny, E. P., 123
Test anxiety, 397
Test-retest reliability, 11
Tetlock, P. E., 343
Thema, 182
Thematic Apperception Test (TAT), 15–17, 175, 176, 186–189, 431
Thinking personality type, 82–84
Thomas, A., 242
Thomas, D. A., 442
Thomas, L., 295, 347
Thompson, G. G., 347
Thompson, T., 353
Thorndike, E. L., 222, 278
Thought processes. See Cognitive processes
Thought sampling, 18
Tilander, A., 103
Toilet training, 52–53
Tokar, D. M., 294
Token economy, 366–367
Tomkins, S. S., 32, 201
Tomlinson, T. M., 315
Trait-situation debate, 8
Traits, 202–204, 222–225, 235–243
Transcendence, 91–92
Transcendence need, 161
Transpersonal unconscious, 85
Tribich, D., 65
Triplet, R. G., 193
Tseng, M., 121, 123
Turner, R. H., 318
Twin research, 240–243, 445–446
Type A personality, 124, 190

Unconditional positive regard, 307, 314
Unconscious, 43, 63, 84–86
Unique traits, 222
Uniqueness/universality issue, 29
Unity thema, 182
Urethral complex, 183
Utley, M. E., 443

Vaillant, G., 451
Validity, 12–13
Van de Castle, R., 64, 148
Van DeWater, D., 268
Vanderlippe, R., 318
Verbal modeling, 385
Vernon, P., 213, 214
Veroff, J., 432, 433, 437, 439
Vicarious reinforcement, 382
Visintainer, M., 450
Volpicelli, J., 450

Walden Two, 356, 368
Walder, L., 403
Wallston, B. S., 401
Walters, R., 385
Wanner, E., 190
Waterman, A. S., 266, 267, 269
Waterman, C. K., 266
Watson, J. B., 6–7, 278, 352, 356, 357
Weber, M., 434
Wehr, G., 77
Weinberger, J., 268, 432
Weir, R. W., 294
Wertheimer, M., 279, 292
Westen, D., 62
Westkott, M., 145
Wexley, K. N., 367
Whitmont, E. C., 103
Wichern, F., 422
Wiggins, J. S., 218
Wilcox, S., 437
Wille, D. E., 268
Willerman, L., 241
Williams, D. E., 295
Wills, T. A., 189
Wilson, C., 277
Wilson, G., 78
Wilson, G. D., 234
Winer, J. L., 438
Winfree, P., 317
Winter, D. G., 190, 435, 458
Winterbottom, M. R., 436
Withdrawal/destructiveness, 159
Wittels, F., 107
Wolf, R. M., 422
Wolk, R. B., 188
Wolk, R. L., 188
Wolk, S., 422
Wolpert, E. A., 64
Womb envy, 142–143
Women subjects, 55, 123, 131, 142–145, 401–402, 421, 431, 437–439
Wood, R. E., 402
Woodward, N. J., 401
Word-association technique, 17, 94
Work and Family Orientation Questionnaire, 439
Wright, C., 295
Wright, T. L., 402, 423
Wundt, W., 6–7
Wuthnow, R., 295

Young-Bruehl, E., 71
Youngquist, J. V., 443

Zaccaria, J. S., 294
Zajonc, R. B., 124
Zelazo, P., 65
Zevon, M. A., 295
Zigler, E., 318
Zirkel, S., 409
Zucker, R. A., 190
Zuckerman, M., 238, 243, 440–446, 458
Zullow, H., 453
Zuroff, D. C., 420

TO THE OWNER OF THIS BOOK:

We hope that you have found *Theories of Personality, Fifth Edition,* useful. So that this book can be improved in a future edition, would you take the time to complete this sheet and return it? Thank you.

School and address: _____

Department: _____

Instructor's name: _____

_____

1. What I like most about this book is: _____

_____

2. What I like least about this book is: _____

_____

_____

3. My general reaction to this book is: _____

_____

4. The name of the course in which I used this book is: _____

_____

5. Were all of the chapters of the book assigned for you to read? _____

    If not, which ones weren't? _____

6. In the space below, or on a separate sheet of paper, please write specific suggestions for improving this book and anything else you'd care to share about your experience in using the book.

_____

_____

_____

_____

_____

_____

Optional:

Your name: _____ Date: _____

May Brooks/Cole quote you, either in promotion for *Theories of Personality, Fifth Edition,* _
or in future publishing ventures?

      Yes: _____ No: _____

      Sincerely,

      Duane Schultz
      Sydney Ellen Schultz

FOLD HERE

BUSINESS REPLY MAIL
FIRST CLASS   PERMIT NO. 358   PACIFIC GROVE, CA

POSTAGE WILL BE PAID BY ADDRESSEE

ATT: *Duane Schultz & Sydney Ellen Schultz*

Brooks/Cole Publishing Company
511 Forest Lodge Road
Pacific Grove, California 93950-9968

FOLD HERE